# Index to the 1800 Massachusetts Federal Census
## for the Counties of
### Barnstable, Dukes & Nantucket

Rebecca M. Sullivan
Deborah Lee Larsson

Index to the 1800 Massachusetts Federal Census
for the Counties of
Barnstable, Dukes & Nantucket

August 2014

Published by CreateSpace.com

ISBN-13: 978-1501017568

# FOREWARD:

This is the first volume of several containing the heads of household that were enumerated in the 1800 United States Federal Census in Massachusetts. Our first volume consists of the Counties of Barnstable, Dukes & Nantucket. In order to make it easy for the researcher, towns are alphabetized within their respective county, followed by an alphabetical index of that county.

We have made every attempt at correctly transcribing each town. However, many of these documents are torn, covered with ink, tape marks, rips and poor handwriting. Spelling errors have been left as they were originally written. Any names & enumerations illegible are denoted with an asterisk.

This book should be used as a guide and research aid. When possible the actual image should be obtained for proper verification and citation.

In order to get all of the information on one page to make for easy reading we had to reduce the size of the font.

Drop us a line, we'd love to hear what you're researching:
rsulli1219@aol.com

Becky & Deb
August 2014

# INDEX

Barnstable County Stats

Microfilm Reel Number: M32-13

| Town: | Page Numbers: | Enumerated By: |
|---|---|---|
| Barnstable | 83-101 | Eben Bacon |
| Chatham | 15-21 | Unknown |
| Dennis | 26-32 | Unknown |
| Eastham | 76-80 | Unknown |
| Falmouth | 43-51 | Unknown |
| Harwich | 3-15 | John D. Bangs |
| Mashpee | 51-52 | Unknown |
| Orleans | 21-25 | Unknown |
| Provincetown | 59-61 | Lewis Hamlen |
| Sandwich | 34-42 | Jona Leonard |
| Truro | 62-69 | Unknown |
| Wellfleet | 69-75 | Unknown |
| Yarmouth | 96-100 | Unknown |

Dukes County Stats

Microfilm Reel Number: M32-19

| Town: | Page Numbers: | Enumerated By: |
|---|---|---|
| Chilmark | 448-450 | Unknown |
| Edgartown | 441-447 | Benjamin Bassett |
| Tisbury | 451-454 | Unknown |

Nantucket County Stats

Microfilm Reel Number: M32-18

| Town: | Page Numbers: | Enumerated By: |
|-------|---------------|----------------|
| Nantucket | 2-20 | Abner Coffin |

# 1800 Barnstable, Barnstable County, Massachusetts

| TOWN | PG# | LN# | LAST NAME | FIRST NAME | FREE WHITE MALES | | | | | FREE WHITE FEMALES | | | | | TOTAL ALL OTHER | TOTAL SLAVES | TOTALS | DISTRICT/ TOWNSHIP | NOTES |
|---|---|---|---|---|---|---|---|---|---|---|---|---|---|---|---|---|---|---|---|
| | | | | | under 10 | 10 to 16 | 16 to 26 | 26 to 45 | 45 and over | under 10 | 10 to 16 | 16 to 26 | 26 to 45 | 45 and over | | | | | |
| Barnstable | 83 | 1 | Gorham | Job | 1 | | | | 1 | 2 | | | 1 | | | | 5 | | |
| Barnstable | 83 | 2 | Hallet | Thomas | | | | 1 | | 1 | | 1 | | | | | 3 | | |
| Barnstable | 83 | 3 | Hallet | Isaac | 2 | | | 1 | | 2 | | 1 | | | | | 6 | | |
| Barnstable | 83 | 4 | Harston | John | | | 1 | 1 | 1 | | | 1 | | 1 | | | 5 | | |
| Barnstable | 83 | 5 | Harston | Ebenzr | 1 | | | 1 | | 3 | | | 1 | | | | 6 | | |
| Barnstable | 83 | 6 | Davis Esq | John | | 1 | 4 | | 1 | 1 | 2 | 1 | | 1 | | | 11 | | |
| Barnstable | 83 | 7 | Gorham | Hannah | | | | | | | | | | 1 | | | 1 | | |
| Barnstable | 83 | 8 | Thacher | Peleg | | | | 1 | | 1 | | | 1 | | | | 3 | | |
| Barnstable | 83 | 9 | Gray | Thomas | 2 | | | 1 | | 1 | | | 1 | | | | 5 | | |
| Barnstable | 83 | 10 | Cobb | Martha | 1 | | | | | 1 | 1 | | 1 | | | | 4 | | |
| Barnstable | 83 | 11 | Gorham | Prince | | | 2 | | | | | | 1 | | | | 4 | | |
| Barnstable | 83 | 12 | Gorham | Silvanus | 1 | 2 | 1 | 2 | 1 | 1 | 1 | 1 | | 1 | | | 11 | | |
| Barnstable | 83 | 13 | Gorham | James | | | | | 1 | | | | 1 | | | | 2 | | |
| Barnstable | 83 | 14 | Gorham | Jonathan | 3 | | | | 1 | 1 | 1 | | 1 | | | | 7 | | |
| Barnstable | 83 | 15 | Easterbrook | Gorham | 1 | 1 | | | 1 | 1 | 2 | 1 | | 1 | | | 8 | | |
| Barnstable | 83 | 16 | Hall | Gorham | | | | 1 | | 3 | | 1 | | | | | 5 | | |
| Barnstable | 83 | 17 | Baker | Mary | | | 1 | | | | | 1 | 1 | | | | 3 | | |
| Barnstable | 83 | 18 | Easterbrook | Joseph | 1 | | | 1 | | 2 | | | 1 | | | | 5 | | |
| Barnstable | 83 | 19 | Thacher | Anthony | | | | 1 | | | | 1 | | 1 | | | 3 | | |
| Barnstable | 83 | 20 | Davis | Elisha T | 2 | 1 | 1 | 1 | | 2 | | | 1 | | | | 8 | | |
| Barnstable | 83 | 21 | Davis | Joseph | | 1 | | | 1 | | | | 1 | | | | 3 | | |
| Barnstable | 83 | 22 | Davis | John 3d | | | 1 | | | | | 1 | | | | | 2 | | |
| Barnstable | 83 | 23 | Davis | Edward | | | | | 1 | | | | 1 | | | | 2 | | |
| Barnstable | 83 | 24 | Davis | Josiah | 1 | | | 1 | | 1 | 1 | | 1 | | | | 5 | | |
| Barnstable | 84 | 1 | Davis | Isaac | 1 | | | 1 | | 4 | | | 1 | | | | 7 | | |
| Barnstable | 84 | 2 | Easterbrook | John | | | | 1 | | | | | | | | | 1 | | |
| Barnstable | 84 | 3 | Easterbrook | John Jn | 1 | | | 1 | | 3 | 1 | | 1 | | | | 7 | | |
| Barnstable | 84 | 4 | Easterbrook | Saml | 4 | 1 | | 1 | | | | | | | | | 7 | | |
| Barnstable | 84 | 5 | Cobb | Nathaniel | | | 1 | | 1 | | | | 2 | | | | 4 | | |
| Barnstable | 84 | 6 | Cobb | Orris | 1 | 1 | | | 1 | | | 2 | | 1 | | | 6 | | |
| Barnstable | 84 | 7 | Lothrop | Nathl | | | | | 1 | | | | 1 | | | | 2 | | |
| Barnstable | 84 | 8 | Cobb | Benjamin | | | | | 1 | | | | | | | | 1 | | |
| Barnstable | 84 | 9 | Cobb | Eleazer | 1 | | | | 1 | | | 2 | | 1 | | | 5 | | |
| Barnstable | 84 | 10 | Lothrop | John | | | 2 | | 1 | | 2 | 2 | | 1 | | | 8 | | |
| Barnstable | 84 | 11 | Lothrop | Mary | | | | | | | | | | 1 | | | 1 | | |
| Barnstable | 84 | 12 | Lothrop | Benjamin | | | | 1 | | 1 | | | 1 | | | | 3 | | |
| Barnstable | 84 | 13 | Davis | Job C | 1 | | | 1 | | 4 | | | 1 | | | | 7 | | |
| Barnstable | 84 | 14 | Davis | James | | | 1 | | 1 | | 1 | 2 | | 1 | | | 6 | | |
| Barnstable | 84 | 15 | Gorham | George | 1 | 1 | | 1 | | 2 | 1 | | 1 | | | | 7 | | |
| Barnstable | 84 | 16 | Cobb | Joseph Jn | 1 | 1 | | 1 | | 1 | 1 | | 1 | | | | 6 | | |
| Barnstable | 84 | 17 | Cobb | Samuel | 1 | | | 1 | | 3 | | | 1 | | | | 6 | | |
| Barnstable | 84 | 18 | Cobb | Benjamin Jn | 1 | | | 1 | | 1 | 1 | | 1 | | | | 5 | | |
| Barnstable | 84 | 19 | Wood | Matthew | | | | | 1 | | | | 1 | | | | 2 | | |
| Barnstable | 84 | 20 | Taylor | William | | | 1 | | 1 | | | | 1 | | | | 3 | | |
| Barnstable | 84 | 21 | Cobb | Hary | | | | | | | 1 | 1 | | 1 | | | 3 | | |
| Barnstable | 84 | 22 | Cobb | Daniel | 3 | 1 | | | 1 | 1 | 2 | 1 | 1 | | | | 10 | | |
| Barnstable | 84 | 23 | Cobb | David | | 1 | 2 | | 1 | 1 | 1 | | | | | | 7 | | |
| Barnstable | 84 | 24 | Crocker | Thankful | | | | | | | | | 2 | | | | 2 | | |
| Barnstable | 84 | 25 | Downs | Barnabas | | | | | 1 | | 1 | 1 | 1 | | | | 4 | | |
| Barnstable | 84 | 26 | Downs | Barna Jn | 1 | 1 | | 1 | | 3 | 1 | | 1 | 2 | | | 10 | | |
| Barnstable | 84 | 27 | Downs | James | | | | | 1 | 2 | 2 | | 1 | | | | 6 | | |
| Barnstable | 84 | 28 | Downs | Mary | 1 | 2 | | | | 1 | | | 1 | | | | 5 | | |
| Barnstable | 84 | 29 | Blachford | Uriah | | | 1 | 2 | | 1 | | | 1 | | | | 5 | | |
| Barnstable | 84 | 30 | Blachford | William | | | | | 1 | | | | 1 | 1 | 1 | | 3 | | |
| Barnstable | 84 | 31 | Swinerton | Timothy | 2 | | | 1 | | 2 | | | 1 | 1 | | | 7 | | |
| Barnstable | 84 | 32 | Thacher | John | | 1 | 2 | | 1 | 1 | | | 1 | 1 | | | 7 | | |
| Barnstable | 84 | 33 | Thacher | Jethro | | 1 | | | 1 | 2 | 1 | 1 | 1 | 3 | | | 10 | | |
| Barnstable | 84 | 34 | Gorham | Desire | | 1 | | | | | | | 1 | | | | 2 | | |
| Barnstable | 84 | 35 | Lovell | Christopher | 1 | | | 1 | | 2 | | | 1 | | | | 5 | | |
| Barnstable | 84 | 36 | Dimock | Thomas | | | | | 1 | | | | 1 | 1 | | | 3 | | |
| Barnstable | 84 | 37 | Dimock | Charles | 1 | | | 1 | | 3 | 3 | 1 | 1 | | | | 10 | | |
| Barnstable | 84 | 38 | Young | Moses | | 1 | 1 | | 1 | 1 | | | | 1 | | | 5 | | |
| Barnstable | 84 | 39 | Sturgis | Ebenezer | 2 | 1 | | 1 | | 2 | 1 | 2 | 1 | | | | 10 | | |
| Barnstable | 84 | 40 | Savage | John | | | | 1 | | | | | | | | | 1 | | |
| Barnstable | 84 | 41 | Young | Thomas | | | | | 1 | | | | | | | | 1 | | |
| Barnstable | 84 | 42 | Young | Bangs | 1 | 1 | 3 | 1 | | 3 | 2 | 1 | 1 | | | | 13 | | |
| Barnstable | 84 | 43 | Downs | David | 2 | | | 1 | | 1 | | | 1 | | | | 5 | | |
| Barnstable | 84 | 44 | Collio | Lydia | | | | | | | | | 2 | | | | 2 | | |
| Barnstable | 84 | 45 | Bacon | Orris | | | 2 | 1 | | | | 2 | 1 | | | | 6 | | |
| Barnstable | 84 | 46 | Bacon | Orris Jr | | 1 | | | | 1 | | 1 | | | | | 3 | | |
| Barnstable | 84 | 47 | Davis | Jonathan | | 1 | | 1 | | | | 1 | 1 | | | | 4 | | |
| Barnstable | 84 | 48 | Otis | Amos | 1 | | | 1 | | | | 1 | 1 | | | | 4 | | |
| Barnstable | 84 | 49 | Case | Ebenezer | 1 | | 1 | | 1 | 1 | 1 | | 1 | | | | 6 | | |
| Barnstable | 84 | 50 | Cobb | Henry | 1 | | | 1 | | 1 | | | 1 | | | | 4 | | |
| Barnstable | 84 | 51 | Bacon | Issac Jr | 2 | | | 1 | | 3 | | | 1 | | | | 7 | | |
| Barnstable | 84 | 52 | Ewer | Abigail | | 1 | 1 | | | | | 1 | | 1 | | | 4 | | |
| Barnstable | 85 | 1 | Hinckley | Adino | 3 | | | 1 | 1 | | | | 1 | | | | 7 | | |
| Barnstable | 85 | 2 | Childs | Josiah | | | 2 | | 1 | | 2 | 1 | | 1 | | | 7 | | |
| Barnstable | 85 | 3 | Childs | Edward | 1 | | | | 1 | | | 2 | | 1 | | | 5 | | |
| Barnstable | 85 | 4 | Cobb | Joseph | 2 | 2 | 1 | 1 | | 3 | 1 | | 1 | | | | 11 | | |

11

| TOWN | PG# | LN# | LAST NAME | FIRST NAME | FREE WHITE MALES | | | | | FREE WHITE FEMALES | | | | | TOTAL ALL OTHER | TOTAL SLAVES | TOTALS | DISTRICT/ TOWNSHIP | NOTES |
|---|---|---|---|---|---|---|---|---|---|---|---|---|---|---|---|---|---|---|---|
| | | | | | under 10 | 10 to 16 | 16 to 26 | 26 to 45 | 45 and over | under 10 | 10 to 16 | 16 to 26 | 26 to 45 | 45 and over | | | | | |
| Barnstable | 85 | 5 | Cobb | Desire | 1 | | | | | | | | | 1 | | | 2 | | |
| Barnstable | 85 | 6 | Thacher | Martha | 1 | | | | | | | | 1 | 1 | | | 3 | | |
| Barnstable | 85 | 7 | Smith | Samuel | | | | 1 | | 1 | 1 | | | | | | 3 | | |
| Barnstable | 85 | 8 | Otis | Solomon | 1 | | | 1 | | | | | 1 | | | | 3 | | |
| Barnstable | 85 | 9 | Bacon | Isaac | | | | 1 | | | | 2 | 2 | | 1 | | 6 | | |
| Barnstable | 85 | 10 | Stetson | Thomas | 2 | | | 1 | | 1 | 1 | | 1 | | | | 6 | | |
| Barnstable | 85 | 11 | Hallet | Abner | 1 | | 1 | 1 | | | | | 1 | | | | 4 | | |
| Barnstable | 85 | 12 | Tupper | Lothrop | 2 | 1 | | | | 2 | 2 | | 1 | | | | 9 | | |
| Barnstable | 85 | 13 | Tupper | Abigail | | | | | | | | | | 1 | | | 1 | | |
| Barnstable | 85 | 14 | Samson | William | | | | 1 | | 1 | | | 1 | | | | 3 | | |
| Barnstable | 85 | 15 | Lothrop | Rachel | | | | | | | | | | 1 | | | 1 | | |
| Barnstable | 85 | 16 | Green | Isaiah L | | | | 1 | | | | 2 | 1 | | | | 4 | | |
| Barnstable | 85 | 17 | Lewis | Hannah | | 1 | | | | | | | 1 | 1 | | | 3 | | |
| Barnstable | 85 | 18 | Lewis | Joseph G | 2 | | | 1 | | | | | 1 | | | | 4 | | |
| Barnstable | 85 | 19 | Phinney | Timothy | | 2 | | | 1 | 1 | 1 | 1 | | 1 | | | 7 | | |
| Barnstable | 85 | 20 | Freeman | James | | | | 1 | | 1 | 1 | 1 | | | | | 4 | | |
| Barnstable | 85 | 21 | Lewis | David | | 1 | 1 | 1 | | | | | 1 | 1 | | | 5 | | |
| Barnstable | 85 | 22 | Alten | Thomas | | 1 | | | | | | | | | | | 1 | | |
| Barnstable | 85 | 23 | Lawrence | Sarah | | 1 | | | | | | | 1 | 1 | | | 3 | | |
| Barnstable | 85 | 24 | Sturgis | Thomas | 1 | 1 | | 1 | | 2 | 1 | 1 | 1 | | | | 8 | | |
| Barnstable | 85 | 25 | Swift | Ebenezer | | 1 | 1 | | | | | 1 | | | | | 3 | | |
| Barnstable | 85 | 26 | Mellen | John Rev | 1 | | | 1 | | 2 | | 1 | | | | | 5 | | |
| Barnstable | 85 | 27 | Childs | David | | | 2 | 1 | | 1 | | 1 | | 1 | | | 5 | | |
| Barnstable | 85 | 28 | Carsley | Hannah | | | | | | | | | 2 | | | | 2 | | |
| Barnstable | 85 | 29 | Lewis | Seth | | 1 | | | | | | | 1 | | | | 2 | | |
| Barnstable | 85 | 30 | Baker | Ebenezer | | | 1 | | | | 1 | 1 | | | | | 3 | | |
| Barnstable | 85 | 31 | Baker | Lydia | | | | | | 1 | | | 1 | | | | 2 | | |
| Barnstable | 85 | 32 | Scudder | Sarah | | | | | | | | | 1 | 1 | | | 2 | | |
| Barnstable | 85 | 33 | Lawson | Southworth | | | | 1 | | | | | 3 | 1 | | | 5 | | |
| Barnstable | 85 | 34 | Doane | Hezekiah | 1 | | | 1 | | 1 | | | 1 | | | | 4 | | |
| Barnstable | 85 | 35 | Davis | Mary | | | | | | 2 | 1 | | 2 | | | | 5 | | |
| Barnstable | 85 | 36 | Lewis | Nathl | 1 | 2 | 1 | | | | | 1 | | 1 | | | 7 | | |
| Barnstable | 85 | 37 | Lothrop | Robert | | 1 | | 1 | | 3 | | 1 | 1 | | | | 7 | | |
| Barnstable | 85 | 38 | Green | John | | | 1 | 1 | | | | | | 1 | | | 3 | | |
| Barnstable | 85 | 39 | Lothrop | Ebenezer | 1 | 1 | 2 | | | | | 2 | | | | | 6 | | |
| Barnstable | 85 | 40 | Crocker | Thomas | | 1 | 1 | | 1 | 1 | 1 | 2 | | | | | 7 | | |
| Barnstable | 85 | 41 | Young | Thomas | | | | 1 | | 3 | | | 1 | | | | 5 | | |
| Barnstable | 85 | 42 | Holmes | Nelson | 2 | | | 1 | | | | | 1 | | | | 4 | | |
| Barnstable | 85 | 43 | Crowell | James | 1 | | | 1 | | 1 | | | | | | | 3 | | |
| Barnstable | 85 | 44 | Eldredge | Gideon | 2 | | | 1 | | 1 | | | | 1 | | | 5 | | |
| Barnstable | 85 | 45 | Hinckley | Freeman | | 1 | | 1 | | | | | 1 | | | | 3 | | |
| Barnstable | 85 | 46 | Phinney | Edward | 1 | | | 1 | | 1 | | 1 | | | | | 4 | | |
| Barnstable | 85 | 47 | Lothrop | John | | | | 1 | | 2 | | | 1 | | 2 | | 6 | | |
| Barnstable | 85 | 48 | Daniel | Daniel | 2 | | | 2 | | 2 | 2 | | 1 | 2 | | | 11 | | |
| Barnstable | 85 | 49 | Bacon | Edward | | 1 | | 1 | | | | | | | | | 2 | | |
| Barnstable | 85 | 50 | Bacon | Ebenz | 2 | 1 | | 1 | | 2 | 3 | 2 | 1 | 1 | 1 | | 14 | | |
| Barnstable | 86 | 1 | Jackson | Richard | | 2 | | 1 | | | | | 1 | | | | 4 | | |
| Barnstable | 86 | 2 | Sturgis | Hannah | | 1 | | | | 1 | | | 1 | | | | 3 | | |
| Barnstable | 86 | 3 | Davis | Mehitable | | | | | | | 1 | | 1 | | | | 2 | | |
| Barnstable | 86 | 4 | Crocker | Ezekiel | 2 | | | 1 | | 1 | | | 1 | | | | 5 | | |
| Barnstable | 86 | 5 | Baker | Benjamin | 3 | | | 1 | | | | | 1 | | | | 5 | | |
| Barnstable | 86 | 6 | Loring | David | 1 | | | 1 | | 1 | | | 1 | | | | 4 | | |
| Barnstable | 86 | 7 | Hinckley | James | 4 | | | 1 | | | | | 1 | | | | 6 | | |
| Barnstable | 86 | 8 | Loring | Edward | | 1 | | | | | 1 | | 1 | | | | 3 | | |
| Barnstable | 86 | 9 | Bacon | Sarah | | | | | | | | | 1 | | | | 1 | | |
| Barnstable | 86 | 10 | Crocker | Abiah | | 2 | 1 | | 1 | | | | 1 | | | | 5 | | |
| Barnstable | 86 | 11 | Lothrop | Isaac | 1 | 1 | 2 | 1 | | 3 | 1 | | 1 | | | | 10 | | |
| Barnstable | 86 | 12 | Lothrop | Benja Jr | 2 | | | 1 | | 1 | | | 1 | | | | 5 | | |
| Barnstable | 86 | 13 | Crocker | Samuel | | | 1 | 1 | | | | | 1 | 1 | | | 4 | | |
| Barnstable | 86 | 14 | Savage | Saml Esq | | 2 | | 1 | 1 | | | | 1 | | | | 5 | | |
| Barnstable | 86 | 15 | Crowell | Ezra | 2 | | | 1 | 1 | 2 | | 1 | 1 | | | | 8 | | |
| Barnstable | 86 | 16 | Gorham | Deborah | | | | | | | 1 | | 1 | | | | 2 | | |
| Barnstable | 86 | 17 | Lothrop | Eunice | | | | | | | | | 1 | | | | 1 | | |
| Barnstable | 86 | 18 | Hinckley | Jabez | | 1 | | 1 | | 1 | 1 | | 1 | | | | 5 | | |
| Barnstable | 86 | 19 | Berry | Joseph | | 1 | | 1 | | 1 | 1 | | | | | | 4 | | |
| Barnstable | 86 | 20 | Lothrop | Ebenezer | 1 | 1 | 2 | | 1 | | | | 1 | 1 | | | 7 | | |
| Barnstable | 86 | 21 | Howes | Martha | | | | | | | | | 1 | | | | 1 | | |
| Barnstable | 86 | 22 | Berry | Ephraim | | | | 1 | | | 1 | 2 | 1 | | | | 5 | | |
| Barnstable | 86 | 23 | Annable | Joseph | 2 | 1 | | 1 | | 1 | 3 | | 1 | | | | 9 | | |
| Barnstable | 86 | 24 | Bacon | Richard | | | | 1 | | | 1 | 1 | 1 | | | | 4 | | |
| Barnstable | 86 | 25 | Annable | Samuel | 1 | | 1 | | | 1 | | | 1 | | | | 4 | | |
| Barnstable | 86 | 26 | Lewis | William | | 1 | | 1 | | 1 | 1 | | | | | | 3 | | |
| Barnstable | 86 | 27 | Hinckley | Ebenezer | 1 | | 1 | | 1 | 2 | | | 1 | | | | 6 | | |
| Barnstable | 86 | 28 | Hinckley | Samuel | | | | 1 | | 1 | | | 1 | 2 | | | 5 | | |
| Barnstable | 86 | 29 | Hinckley | William | | 1 | | 1 | | 2 | 1 | | | | | | 5 | | |
| Barnstable | 86 | 30 | Allyn | Benjamin | 1 | | 1 | | 1 | 1 | 2 | | 1 | | | | 7 | | |
| Barnstable | 86 | 31 | Allyn | Lydia | | | | | | | | | 2 | | | | 2 | | |
| Barnstable | 86 | 32 | Allyn | Thomas | | 1 | | 1 | | 2 | | | 1 | | | | 5 | | |
| Barnstable | 86 | 33 | Allyn | Samuel | | | 1 | | 1 | | | | 1 | 1 | | | 4 | | |

# 1800 Barnstable, Barnstable County, Massachusetts

| Town | PG# | LN# | Last Name | First Name | FWM under 10 | FWM 10 to 16 | FWM 16 to 26 | FWM 26 to 45 | FWM 45 and over | FWF under 10 | FWF 10 to 16 | FWF 16 to 26 | FWF 26 to 45 | FWF 45 and over | Total All Other | Total Slaves | Totals | District/Township | Notes |
|---|---|---|---|---|---|---|---|---|---|---|---|---|---|---|---|---|---|---|---|
| Barnstable | 86 | 34 | Gorham | Josiah | 2 | | | 1 | | 2 | 1 | | 1 | 1 | | | 8 | | |
| Barnstable | 86 | 35 | Gorham | Edward | 2 | 2 | | 1 | | 3 | 2 | | 1 | 1 | | | 12 | | |
| Barnstable | 86 | 36 | Allyn | James | 1 | | | | 1 | 2 | 2 | 2 | | 1 | | | 9 | | |
| Barnstable | 86 | 37 | Smith | Desire | | | | | | | | | 1 | | | | 1 | | |
| Barnstable | 86 | 38 | Taylor | Mary | | | | | | | | 1 | | 1 | 2 | | 4 | | |
| Barnstable | 86 | 39 | Hinckley | Robinson | 1 | | | 1 | | 1 | | | 1 | 1 | | | 5 | | |
| Barnstable | 86 | 40 | Hatch | Gorham | | | 1 | | | | | | 1 | | | | 2 | | |
| Barnstable | 86 | 41 | Loring | Abner | | 1 | 1 | | 1 | | | | 1 | | | | 5 | | |
| Barnstable | 86 | 42 | Smith | Elijah | 1 | | 1 | 1 | 1 | | | | 1 | | | | 5 | | |
| Barnstable | 86 | 43 | Smith | Solomon | 3 | | | 1 | | | | 1 | | | | | 5 | | |
| Barnstable | 86 | 44 | Smith | James | | | | 1 | | | | 1 | | | | | 2 | | |
| Barnstable | 86 | 45 | Carsley | Lemuel | | | | | 1 | | | | | 2 | | | 3 | | |
| Barnstable | 86 | 46 | Hinckley | John | 1 | 2 | | | 1 | | 1 | | 2 | 1 | | | 8 | | |
| Barnstable | 86 | 47 | Childs | Elijah | 1 | | | 2 | | 2 | 1 | 1 | | | | | 7 | | |
| Barnstable | 86 | 48 | Hinckley | John 3d | | 1 | | | | | | 1 | | | | | 2 | | |
| Barnstable | 86 | 49 | Hinckley | John | 1 | 2 | | | 1 | | | 2 | 1 | 1 | | | 8 | | |
| Barnstable | 86 | 50 | Huckins | James | | | | | 1 | | | | | 1 | 1 | | 3 | | |
| Barnstable | 86 | 51 | Huckins | Samuel | 1 | 2 | | 1 | | 3 | 2 | 1 | 1 | | 1 | | 12 | | |
| Barnstable | 87 | 1 | Dexter | John | | | 1 | 1 | 1 | | | 1 | 1 | 1 | | | 6 | | |
| Barnstable | 87 | 2 | Crocker | Ebenezr Jr | | | 2 | 1 | | 1 | | 1 | | | | | 5 | | |
| Barnstable | 87 | 3 | Jenkins | Sarah | 2 | | | | | | | 1 | | 2 | | | 5 | | |
| Barnstable | 87 | 4 | Jenkins | Joseph Jr | 1 | | | 1 | | 1 | | 1 | | | | | 4 | | |
| Barnstable | 87 | 5 | Crocker | William | | | | | 1 | | | | 1 | | | | 2 | | |
| Barnstable | 87 | 6 | Crocker | William Jr | 1 | | | 1 | | 2 | | | 1 | | | | 5 | | |
| Barnstable | 87 | 7 | Crocker | Bathsheba | | | 1 | | | | | 1 | 1 | | | | 3 | | |
| Barnstable | 87 | 8 | Crocker | John 3d | | 1 | 1 | | | | | | 1 | | | | 3 | | |
| Barnstable | 87 | 9 | Crocker | Walley | | | 1 | | | | | | | | | | 1 | | |
| Barnstable | 87 | 10 | Crocker | Thomas Jr | | | 1 | | | 1 | | 1 | | | | | 3 | | |
| Barnstable | 87 | 11 | Killey | Remember | 1 | | | | | | | 2 | | 1 | | | 4 | | |
| Barnstable | 87 | 12 | Weeks | Nathan | 1 | | 1 | | | 2 | | | 1 | | | | 5 | | |
| Barnstable | 87 | 13 | Howes | Peter | | | 3 | 1 | | | | 1 | | 1 | | | 6 | | |
| Barnstable | 87 | 14 | Cotelle | Peter | | 2 | 1 | 1 | | | 1 | | | 2 | | | 7 | | |
| Barnstable | 87 | 15 | Whelden | Thomas | | | | 1 | | | | 1 | | 1 | | | 3 | | |
| Barnstable | 87 | 16 | Whelden | Peter | 1 | | | 1 | | 1 | | | 1 | | | | 4 | | |
| Barnstable | 87 | 17 | Ewer | Ebenezer | | 1 | | 1 | | 1 | 1 | | 1 | | | | 5 | | |
| Barnstable | 87 | 18 | Crocker | Winslow | 3 | 1 | | 1 | | | | 2 | 1 | 1 | | | 9 | | |
| Barnstable | 87 | 19 | Garret | Andrew | 1 | | | 1 | | | | 2 | 1 | | | | 5 | | |
| Barnstable | 87 | 20 | Crocker | Joseph 3d | 1 | 1 | | 1 | | 2 | | | 1 | | | | 6 | | |
| Barnstable | 87 | 21 | Parker | Isaiah | 2 | 2 | | | 1 | | | 2 | 1 | 1 | | | 9 | | |
| Barnstable | 87 | 22 | Parker | Desire | | | 2 | | | 1 | | | | 2 | | | 5 | | |
| Barnstable | 87 | 23 | Shaw | Rev Oakes | | | 1 | | 1 | | | 1 | | 1 | 6 | | 10 | | |
| Barnstable | 87 | 24 | Jenkins | Alvin | 1 | | | 1 | | 1 | | | 1 | | 1 | | 5 | | |
| Barnstable | 87 | 25 | Jenkins | Joseph W. | | | 1 | | 1 | | | | | 1 | 1 | | 4 | | |
| Barnstable | 87 | 26 | Jenkins | Simeon Jr | 1 | 1 | | 1 | | 2 | 1 | | 1 | | | | 7 | | |
| Barnstable | 87 | 27 | Smith | Benjamin | 1 | | | 1 | | 1 | | | 1 | | | | 4 | | |
| Barnstable | 87 | 28 | Whelden | Eben | 2 | | | | 1 | 3 | | | 1 | 1 | | | 8 | | |
| Barnstable | 87 | 29 | Jenkins | Nathl | 2 | 1 | 1 | | | 1 | 1 | | 1 | 1 | | | 9 | | |
| Barnstable | 87 | 30 | Jenkins | Simeon | | | | | | | | 1 | 1 | 1 | | | 3 | | |
| Barnstable | 87 | 31 | Jenkins | Prince | 1 | | 1 | | | | | | 1 | | | | 3 | | |
| Barnstable | 87 | 32 | Jenkins | Braley | | 1 | | | | 1 | | | 1 | | | | 3 | | |
| Barnstable | 87 | 33 | Nye | Lemuel | | 1 | | 1 | | | | 1 | | 1 | | | 4 | | |
| Barnstable | 87 | 34 | Nye | Lemuel Jr | | 1 | | | | | | | 1 | | | | 2 | | |
| Barnstable | 87 | 35 | Jenkins | Zaccheus | 1 | 1 | 1 | | 1 | | | | 1 | 1 | | | 6 | | |
| Barnstable | 87 | 36 | Nye | Jonathan | 1 | 1 | | 1 | | 2 | | | 1 | 1 | | | 7 | | |
| Barnstable | 87 | 37 | Smith | Patrick | | | | 1 | | 3 | | | 1 | | | | 5 | | |
| Barnstable | 87 | 38 | Blish | Silas | 2 | | | 1 | | 3 | 1 | | 1 | | | | 8 | | |
| Barnstable | 87 | 39 | Crocker | Joseph | | 1 | 1 | 1 | | | | | | 2 | 1 | | 6 | | |
| Barnstable | 87 | 40 | Crocker | Moody | 3 | | 1 | 1 | | | | | 1 | | | | 6 | | |
| Barnstable | 87 | 41 | Crocker | Nathl | 1 | 1 | 1 | | 1 | 1 | | 1 | | 1 | | | 7 | | |
| Barnstable | 87 | 42 | Crocker | Edmund | | 1 | 1 | | 1 | 1 | 1 | 3 | | 1 | | | 9 | | |
| Barnstable | 87 | 43 | Howland | Ansel | | | | | 1 | | | | | 1 | | | 2 | | |
| Barnstable | 87 | 44 | Howland | Jabez | 1 | | 1 | | | 1 | | 1 | | | 1 | | 5 | | |
| Barnstable | 87 | 45 | Howland | Ansel Jr | 2 | | | 1 | | 1 | | | | 1 | | | 5 | | |
| Barnstable | 87 | 46 | Jenkins | Lot | 1 | | | 1 | | 1 | 1 | | 1 | | | | 5 | | |
| Barnstable | 87 | 47 | Chipman | John | | 1 | | 1 | | 3 | 1 | | 1 | | | | 7 | | |
| Barnstable | 87 | 48 | Chipman | Timothy | | | | 1 | | | | | 1 | 1 | | | 3 | | |
| Barnstable | 87 | 49 | Bassett | Samuel | 1 | 2 | | 1 | | 1 | | | 1 | | | | 6 | | |
| Barnstable | 87 | 50 | Howland | John | | | 1 | | | 1 | | | 1 | | | | 3 | | |
| Barnstable | 87 | 51 | Woods | Ansel | 2 | | | 1 | | 3 | | | 1 | | | | 7 | | |
| Barnstable | 87 | 52 | Smith | Levi | | | 1 | | | | | | 1 | | | | 2 | | |
| Barnstable | 87 | 53 | Ohr | Joseph Esq | | 2 | | 1 | | | | 1 | 1 | 1 | | | 6 | | |
| Barnstable | 87 | 54 | Hinckley | Isaac Esq | | | | 1 | | | | 1 | 1 | 1 | | | 4 | | |
| Barnstable | 88 | 1 | Blish | Ebenezer | | | | 1 | | | | | | 1 | | | 2 | | |
| Barnstable | 88 | 2 | Blish | Joseph | | | | | 2 | | | 2 | | 1 | | | 5 | | |
| Barnstable | 88 | 3 | Blish | Joseph Jr | 4 | 1 | | 1 | | 1 | | 1 | 1 | | | | 9 | | |
| Barnstable | 88 | 4 | Carver | Lemuel | 1 | | | 1 | | 3 | 2 | | 1 | | | | 8 | | |
| Barnstable | 88 | 5 | Hathaway | Benja | | 1 | | | | 1 | 1 | | 1 | | | | 5 | | |
| Barnstable | 88 | 6 | Lewis | Benjamin | 3 | | | | 1 | | | | | 1 | | | 5 | | |
| Barnstable | 88 | 7 | Hathaway | James | | | 2 | 1 | 1 | | | | | 1 | | | 5 | | |

# 1800 Barnstable, Barnstable County, Massachusetts

| TOWN | PG# | LN# | LAST NAME | FIRST NAME | FREE WHITE MALES | | | | | FREE WHITE FEMALES | | | | | TOTAL ALL OTHER | TOTAL SLAVES | TOTALS | DISTRICT/ TOWNSHIP | NOTES |
|---|---|---|---|---|---|---|---|---|---|---|---|---|---|---|---|---|---|---|---|
| | | | | | under 10 | 10 to 16 | 16 to 26 | 26 to 45 | 45 and over | under 10 | 10 to 16 | 16 to 26 | 26 to 45 | 45 and over | | | | | |
| Barnstable | 88 | 8 | Nye | Benjamin | | 1 | 1 | | 2 | | | 4 | 2 | 1 | | | 11 | | |
| Barnstable | 88 | 9 | Hinckley | Prince | 3 | 1 | | | 2 | | | | 1 | | | | 8 | | |
| Barnstable | 88 | 10 | Hinckley | Timothy | | | 4 | 1 | 1 | | | 1 | | 1 | | | 8 | | |
| Barnstable | 88 | 11 | Baker | Isaiah | 1 | 1 | 1 | | 1 | | | 1 | | 1 | | | 6 | | |
| Barnstable | 88 | 12 | Howland | Isaac | 1 | 1 | 1 | | 1 | | | 1 | | 1 | | | 6 | | |
| Barnstable | 88 | 13 | Howland | Samuel | | | 2 | | 1 | | | 2 | | 1 | | | 6 | | |
| Barnstable | 88 | 14 | Crocker | Isaac | | | 2 | | 1 | | | 2 | | 1 | | | 6 | | |
| Barnstable | 88 | 15 | Crocker | Isaac Jr | | | 1 | | | | | 1 | | | | | 2 | | |
| Barnstable | 88 | 16 | Crocker | Reuben | | 1 | | | | 1 | | 1 | | | | | 3 | | |
| Barnstable | 88 | 17 | Hennlen | Ruth | | | | | | | | | 2 | 1 | | | 3 | | |
| Barnstable | 88 | 18 | Hamlen | Shubael | 3 | 1 | | 1 | | | 1 | | | | | | 6 | | |
| Barnstable | 88 | 19 | Adams | Ansel | 5 | 3 | | 1 | | | | | 1 | 1 | | | 11 | | |
| Barnstable | 88 | 20 | Goodspeed | Cornelius | 2 | | 1 | | | 2 | | | 1 | | | | 6 | | |
| Barnstable | 88 | 21 | Adams | Benjamin | 2 | | 1 | | | | | 1 | | | | | 4 | | |
| Barnstable | 88 | 22 | Goodspeeed | Joseph | | | | 1 | | | | | | 1 | | | 2 | | |
| Barnstable | 88 | 23 | Hinckley | Joseph | | | | 1 | | | | | | 1 | | | 2 | | |
| Barnstable | 88 | 24 | Sudder | Ebenezer | 4 | | | 1 | | | | | 1 | | | | 6 | | |
| Barnstable | 88 | 25 | Russell | Jonathan | 1 | | | 1 | | 4 | 1 | | 1 | | | | 8 | | |
| Barnstable | 88 | 26 | Jones | Goodspeed | | | | 1 | | 2 | | | 1 | | | | 4 | | |
| Barnstable | 88 | 27 | Goodspeeed | Timothy | | | | 1 | | | | | | 1 | | | 2 | | |
| Barnstable | 88 | 28 | Thomas | Ansel | 4 | | | 1 | | 2 | | | 1 | | | | 8 | | |
| Barnstable | 88 | 29 | Fuller | Josiah Jr | 2 | 1 | | 1 | | | | | 1 | | | | 5 | | |
| Barnstable | 88 | 30 | Marston | Isaiah | 2 | | 3 | 1 | | 1 | 2 | | 1 | | | | 10 | | |
| Barnstable | 88 | 31 | Corsley | Seth | | 1 | | 1 | | | | | | 1 | | | 3 | | |
| Barnstable | 88 | 32 | Crocker | Benjamin | 1 | 2 | 2 | | 1 | | 1 | 1 | | 1 | | | 9 | | |
| Barnstable | 88 | 33 | Chipman | Joseph | 3 | | | 1 | | 1 | 1 | | | 1 | | | 7 | | |
| Barnstable | 88 | 34 | Hinckley | Nathaniel | | | 1 | 1 | 1 | 1 | 1 | | | | | | 4 | | |
| Barnstable | 88 | 35 | Goodspeed | Asa | 1 | | | 1 | | | | | 1 | | | | 5 | | |
| Barnstable | 88 | 36 | Adams | Edward | | | | 1 | | | 1 | 1 | | 1 | | | 3 | | |
| Barnstable | 88 | 37 | Bates | Sarah | | 1 | | | | 3 | | | 1 | | | | 5 | | |
| Barnstable | 88 | 38 | Bates | Hannah | | | | | | 2 | | | 1 | | | | 3 | | |
| Barnstable | 88 | 39 | Stevens | Richard | | | | 1 | | | | | | 1 | | | 2 | | |
| Barnstable | 88 | 40 | Marston | Benjamin | 1 | | | 1 | | 1 | 1 | | 1 | | | | 5 | | |
| Barnstable | 88 | 41 | Marston | Allen | 1 | | 1 | | | 1 | | 1 | | | | | 4 | | |
| Barnstable | 88 | 42 | Marston | Prince | | | 1 | | | | | 1 | | | | | 2 | | |
| Barnstable | 88 | 43 | Smith | Benjmain | | 2 | | 1 | | | 2 | | 1 | | | | 6 | | |
| Barnstable | 88 | 44 | Thomas | Eliza | | 2 | | | | | 1 | | 1 | | | | 4 | | |
| Barnstable | 88 | 45 | Goodspeed | Rufus | | 1 | 1 | | 1 | 1 | | | 1 | | | | 5 | | |
| Barnstable | 88 | 46 | Marston | Nymphas | 2 | | | 1 | | 2 | | | 1 | | | | 6 | | |
| Barnstable | 88 | 47 | Fuller | Zacheus | 1 | 1 | | 1 | | 2 | 1 | | 1 | | | | 7 | | |
| Barnstable | 88 | 48 | Holmes | Bartlet | | | | 1 | | 2 | 1 | | 1 | | | | 5 | | |
| Barnstable | 88 | 49 | Martin | Winslow | 2 | 1 | | 1 | | 1 | 1 | 1 | 1 | 1 | 1 | | 10 | | |
| Barnstable | 88 | 50 | Crocker | Ebenz Esq | | 2 | | 1 | | 1 | | | 1 | | | | 5 | | |
| Barnstable | 88 | 51 | Childs | James | 2 | | | 1 | | 1 | | 1 | | | | | 5 | | |
| Barnstable | 88 | 52 | Bassett | William | | | 1 | | | 1 | | 1 | | | | | 3 | | |
| Barnstable | 89 | 1 | Bassett | Luther | | 1 | | | | 1 | | | | | | | 2 | | |
| Barnstable | 89 | 2 | Bassett | William Jr | 2 | | 1 | | 2 | 1 | | | | | | | 6 | | |
| Barnstable | 89 | 3 | Lavell | Andrew | | 2 | 2 | 1 | | | 2 | | 1 | | | | 8 | | |
| Barnstable | 89 | 4 | Samson | Josiah | | 2 | 1 | 1 | 1 | 1 | 2 | | 1 | | | | 10 | | |
| Barnstable | 89 | 5 | Crocker | Alvin | 1 | | 2 | 1 | 1 | | 2 | | 1 | 2 | | | 10 | | |
| Barnstable | 89 | 6 | Crocker | Zenas | 2 | | | 1 | | 2 | | | 1 | 1 | 2 | | 9 | | |
| Barnstable | 89 | 7 | Crocker | Elizabeth | | 1 | | | | 1 | | 1 | | | | | 3 | | |
| Barnstable | 89 | 8 | Fuller | Samuel | | | | 1 | 1 | | | | 1 | | | | 3 | | |
| Barnstable | 89 | 9 | Fish | David | 1 | | | 1 | | 1 | | 1 | | | | | 4 | | |
| Barnstable | 89 | 10 | Wright | Martin | | 1 | | | | | | | 1 | | | | 2 | | |
| Barnstable | 89 | 11 | Carsley | Isaac | 1 | | 1 | | 1 | 1 | 1 | | 2 | | | | 8 | | |
| Barnstable | 89 | 12 | Hilliard | George | 1 | 1 | | 1 | | 2 | 1 | 1 | 1 | | | | 8 | | |
| Barnstable | 89 | 13 | Backus | Thomas | | 1 | 5 | | 1 | 1 | 1 | | 1 | | | | 11 | | |
| Barnstable | 89 | 14 | Backus | Simeon | 1 | | 1 | | | | | | 1 | | | | 3 | | |
| Barnstable | 89 | 15 | Backus | Clark | 2 | 1 | 1 | 2 | 1 | | 1 | | 1 | | | | 9 | | |
| Barnstable | 89 | 16 | Lothrop | Prince | | 1 | | 1 | | | | | 1 | | | | 3 | | |
| Barnstable | 89 | 17 | Jones | Lemuel | 4 | | | 1 | | | 1 | 1 | | | | | 7 | | |
| Barnstable | 89 | 18 | Meiggs | Reubeh | | | | 1 | | | | | 1 | | | | 2 | | |
| Barnstable | 89 | 19 | Crocker | Ansel | 1 | 1 | | 1 | | 2 | | | 1 | | | | 6 | | |
| Barnstable | 89 | 20 | Jones | Nye | | 1 | | 1 | | | | | 1 | | | | 3 | | |
| Barnstable | 89 | 21 | Jones | Stephen | | | 1 | | | | | | 1 | | | | 2 | | |
| Barnstable | 89 | 22 | Crocker | Eleazer | 2 | 1 | 3 | | 1 | 1 | 1 | | 1 | | | | 10 | | |
| Barnstable | 89 | 23 | Jones | Hannah Jr | | 1 | 1 | | 1 | 2 | 1 | 1 | | | | | 7 | | |
| Barnstable | 89 | 24 | Hamblin | John Jr | 1 | | | 1 | | | 1 | | | | | | 3 | | |
| Barnstable | 89 | 25 | Hamblin | John | | | | 1 | | | | | 3 | | | | 4 | | |
| Barnstable | 89 | 26 | Jones | Lot | 2 | | | 1 | 1 | | | 1 | | | | | 5 | | |
| Barnstable | 89 | 27 | Jones | Abner | 2 | 1 | | 2 | | 1 | | 1 | 1 | | | | 8 | | |
| Barnstable | 89 | 28 | Jones | Jedidiah | 2 | 1 | | 1 | | 1 | | 1 | 1 | | | | 7 | | |
| Barnstable | 89 | 29 | Wright | Benjamin | | | 1 | | 1 | 1 | | | | | | | 3 | | |
| Barnstable | 89 | 30 | Crocker | Calvin | 1 | 1 | 2 | | 3 | | | 1 | | | | | 8 | | |
| Barnstable | 89 | 31 | Crocker | Joseph Jr | | 2 | 2 | | 1 | 1 | | 1 | 2 | | | | 9 | | |
| Barnstable | 89 | 32 | Fuller | Joseph | 2 | | 1 | 1 | | 2 | | | 1 | 1 | | | 8 | | |
| Barnstable | 89 | 33 | Hamblin | Lewis | 2 | | | 1 | | 2 | | | 1 | 1 | | | 7 | | |
| Barnstable | 89 | 34 | Goodspeed | Thankful | 2 | 2 | 1 | | 1 | 1 | 1 | | 1 | 1 | | | 10 | | |

# 1800 Barnstable, Barnstable County, Massachusetts

| TOWN | PG# | LN# | LAST NAME | FIRST NAME | FREE WHITE MALES | | | | | FREE WHITE FEMALES | | | | | TOTAL ALL OTHER | TOTAL SLAVES | TOTALS | DISTRICT/ TOWNSHIP | NOTES |
|---|---|---|---|---|---|---|---|---|---|---|---|---|---|---|---|---|---|---|---|
| | | | HEADS OF HOUSEHOLD | | under 10 | 10 to 16 | 16 to 26 | 26 to 45 | 45 and over | under 10 | 10 to 16 | 16 to 26 | 26 to 45 | 45 and over | | | | | |
| Barnstable | 89 | 35 | Goodspeed | Philemon | 1 | 1 | 1 | | 1 | 2 | 1 | 2 | 2 | 1 | | | 12 | | |
| Barnstable | 89 | 36 | Hinckley | Timo Jr | 1 | 1 | | 1 | | 1 | | | 1 | | | | 5 | | |
| Barnstable | 89 | 37 | Hinckley | Asa | 1 | | | 1 | | 1 | | | 1 | | | | 4 | | |
| Barnstable | 89 | 38 | Lovell | Enoch | 2 | 1 | | | 1 | | 1 | 1 | 1 | | | | 7 | | |
| Barnstable | 89 | 39 | Jenkins | Asa | 2 | | | 1 | | | 1 | | 1 | | 1 | | 6 | | |
| Barnstable | 89 | 40 | Hamlen | Micah | | 4 | | 1 | | | 1 | | | 2 | 1 | | 9 | | |
| Barnstable | 89 | 41 | Hamblin | Joseph | 1 | | | 1 | | | | 1 | | | | | 3 | | |
| Barnstable | 89 | 42 | Crocker | Benjamin Jr | 2 | 3 | 1 | 1 | | | | 1 | | 1 | | | 9 | | |
| Barnstable | 89 | 43 | Hinckley | Warren | 1 | | 2 | 1 | | | | 1 | | 1 | | | 6 | | |
| Barnstable | 89 | 44 | Blist | Achiah | 1 | | | | | | | | 1 | | | | 2 | | |
| Barnstable | 89 | 45 | Parker | Daniel | | 1 | | 1 | | | | 2 | | 1 | | | 5 | | |
| Barnstable | 89 | 46 | Parker | Daniel Jr | 1 | | | 1 | | | | 1 | | | | | 3 | | |
| Barnstable | 90 | 1 | Parker | Joseph | 1 | | | 1 | | | | 1 | | | 1 | | 4 | | |
| Barnstable | 90 | 2 | Snow | Samuel | 2 | 1 | | 1 | | 2 | 2 | | 1 | | | | 9 | | |
| Barnstable | 90 | 3 | Howland | Mary | | 2 | | | | 1 | | 2 | 1 | 1 | | | 7 | | |
| Barnstable | 90 | 4 | Howland | Zacheus | 2 | | | 1 | | | 1 | | | 1 | | | 5 | | |
| Barnstable | 90 | 5 | Nye | Asa | 2 | | | 1 | | 1 | | 1 | | 1 | 1 | | 7 | | |
| Barnstable | 90 | 6 | Parker | David | 2 | 1 | 1 | | 1 | | 1 | | | 1 | 1 | | 8 | | |
| Barnstable | 90 | 7 | Gallison | John | 2 | | 1 | | 1 | 2 | 2 | | | 1 | | | 9 | | |
| Barnstable | 90 | 8 | Lewis | Edward Jr | | | 1 | | | 1 | | 1 | | | | | 3 | | |
| Barnstable | 90 | 9 | Phinney | Joseph | | | 1 | | 1 | | | 1 | | | | | 3 | | |
| Barnstable | 90 | 10 | Phinney | William | 1 | | 1 | | | 1 | 1 | 1 | | | | | 5 | | |
| Barnstable | 90 | 11 | Phinney | Solomon | 3 | 1 | | 1 | | 1 | 1 | | 1 | | | | 8 | | |
| Barnstable | 90 | 12 | Hadaway | Benjamin | 1 | 1 | 1 | 1 | | 2 | | | 1 | | | | 7 | | |
| Barnstable | 90 | 13 | Phinney | Paul | 2 | | | 1 | | 1 | 2 | | 1 | | | | 7 | | |
| Barnstable | 90 | 14 | Phinney | Levi | 2 | | 1 | 1 | | 1 | 1 | | 1 | | | | 7 | | |
| Barnstable | 90 | 15 | Lumberd | Sarah | | | | | | | | 1 | 1 | 1 | | | 3 | | |
| Barnstable | 90 | 16 | Hinckley | Silvanus | 3 | | 1 | | 1 | 2 | 2 | | 1 | | | | 10 | | |
| Barnstable | 90 | 17 | Hinckley | Levi | 1 | 1 | | 1 | | 3 | | | 2 | 1 | | | 9 | | |
| Barnstable | 90 | 18 | Lumberd | Joseph | | | | 1 | | | | | | 1 | | | 2 | | |
| Barnstable | 90 | 19 | Hodges | Hex* | | | | 1 | | | | | | 1 | | | 2 | | |
| Barnstable | 90 | 20 | Hodges | Isaac | 2 | | 1 | | | 1 | | | 1 | | | | 5 | | |
| Barnstable | 90 | 21 | Lumberd | Samuel | | 1 | 1 | | | | | | 1 | | | | 3 | | |
| Barnstable | 90 | 22 | Lumberd | Prince | 1 | | | 1 | | 3 | | | 1 | | | | 6 | | |
| Barnstable | 90 | 23 | Lumberd | Joshua | 1 | | | 1 | | 2 | | 1 | | | | | 5 | | |
| Barnstable | 90 | 24 | Linnell | David | 1 | | 1 | | | | | | 1 | | | | 2 | | |
| Barnstable | 90 | 25 | Linnell | James | | | 2 | | | | | 1 | 1 | | | | 4 | | |
| Barnstable | 90 | 26 | Crosby | Lewis | | | 1 | | | | | 1 | | | | | 2 | | |
| Barnstable | 90 | 27 | Killey | Levi | 3 | 2 | 2 | 1 | | | 1 | | | 1 | | | 10 | | |
| Barnstable | 90 | 28 | Bearse | Isaac | | | 2 | | | | | 1 | | | | | 3 | | |
| Barnstable | 90 | 29 | Bearse | James | 3 | | 1 | | | 1 | | | 1 | | | | 6 | | |
| Barnstable | 90 | 30 | Cole | Mary | | 1 | | | | | | | | 1 | | | 2 | | |
| Barnstable | 90 | 31 | Coleman | Ebenezer | | 1 | | 1 | | | | | | 1 | | | 3 | | |
| Barnstable | 90 | 32 | Lewis | Timothy | 2 | | | 1 | | 3 | 3 | | 1 | | | | 10 | | |
| Barnstable | 90 | 33 | Childs | Job | 2 | 2 | 1 | | | 1 | 1 | | 1 | 1 | | | 9 | | |
| Barnstable | 90 | 34 | Crosby | Jesse | | 1 | | 1 | | | 1 | | | 1 | | | 4 | | |
| Barnstable | 90 | 35 | Lewis | Asenath | | 1 | | | | | | | | 3 | | | 4 | | |
| Barnstable | 90 | 36 | Parker | Jehiel | 1 | | | | | 1 | | 1 | | | | | 4 | | |
| Barnstable | 90 | 37 | Richardson | John | | | | 1 | | | | 1 | | | | | 2 | | |
| Barnstable | 90 | 38 | Crosby | James | 1 | | | 1 | | | | | 1 | | | | 3 | | |
| Barnstable | 90 | 39 | Davis | John | | | | 1 | | | | 1 | | 1 | | | 3 | | |
| Barnstable | 90 | 40 | Lewis | Bethiah | | | | | | | | 1 | | 2 | | | 3 | | |
| Barnstable | 90 | 41 | Sturgis | John | 4 | | 3 | | 1 | 1 | 1 | 1 | | 1 | | | 12 | | |
| Barnstable | 90 | 42 | Lewis | Isaac | | | | | 1 | | | | 1 | | | | 2 | | |
| Barnstable | 90 | 43 | Lewis | Lothrop | | | 1 | | | | | | 1 | | | | 2 | | |
| Barnstable | 90 | 44 | Hathaway | James Jr | | 1 | | 1 | | | 1 | 1 | 1 | | | | 5 | | |
| Barnstable | 90 | 45 | Lewis | Bethiah 2d | 2 | 1 | 1 | | | 1 | 1 | 1 | 1 | | | | 8 | | |
| Barnstable | 90 | 46 | Linnell | John | 2 | | 1 | | | 2 | | | | | | | 6 | | |
| Barnstable | 90 | 47 | Ludden | Ebenezer | | | 2 | 1 | | | | | | 1 | | | 4 | | |
| Barnstable | 90 | 48 | Ludden | Asa | | | 1 | | | | | | | | | | 1 | | |
| Barnstable | 90 | 49 | Ludden | Isaiah | 1 | | | 1 | | 2 | | 1 | | | | | 5 | | |
| Barnstable | 91 | 1 | Ludden | Josiah | | | 1 | | | | | 1 | | | | | 2 | | |
| Barnstable | 91 | 2 | Hinckley | Abner | 1 | 1 | 2 | | 1 | | 1 | 2 | 1 | | 1 | | 10 | | |
| Barnstable | 91 | 3 | Ishand | Samuel | | | | | 1 | | | | 1 | | | | 2 | | |
| Barnstable | 91 | 4 | Ishand | Herman | | 1 | | 1 | | 3 | 1 | | 1 | 1 | | | 8 | | |
| Barnstable | 91 | 5 | Ames | Enos | 2 | 2 | 1 | 1 | | 3 | | | 1 | | | | 10 | | |
| Barnstable | 91 | 6 | Hinckley | Enoch | 1 | 1 | 1 | | 1 | | 1 | 1 | | 2 | | | 8 | | |
| Barnstable | 91 | 7 | Goodspeed | Seth | | 1 | | 1 | | | | | 1 | 1 | | | 4 | | |
| Barnstable | 91 | 8 | Goodspeed | Allen | 1 | | | 1 | | 1 | | 1 | | | | | 4 | | |
| Barnstable | 91 | 9 | Killey | Freeman | 1 | | | 1 | | | | 1 | | | | | 3 | | |
| Barnstable | 91 | 10 | Crosley | Samuel | | 1 | | | | | | 1 | | | | | 2 | | |
| Barnstable | 91 | 11 | Lumberd | Joshua | | | | 1 | | | | | 1 | | | | 2 | | |
| Barnstable | 91 | 12 | Lumberd | Simeon | 3 | | | 1 | | | | | 1 | | | | 5 | | |
| Barnstable | 91 | 13 | Hallet | Benj | 1 | 1 | | 1 | | 4 | 3 | 1 | 1 | | | | 12 | | |
| Barnstable | 91 | 14 | Crosby | Daniel | 3 | | | 1 | | 1 | | | 1 | | | | 6 | | |
| Barnstable | 91 | 15 | Hinckley | Nymphar | 2 | 2 | | | 1 | 2 | | 1 | 1 | | | | 9 | | |
| Barnstable | 91 | 16 | Cammett | Peter | 2 | 1 | | 1 | | 1 | | 3 | 1 | | | | 9 | | |
| Barnstable | 91 | 17 | Cammett | Eliza | | 1 | 1 | | | | | 1 | | 1 | 1 | | 4 | | |
| Barnstable | 91 | 18 | Hallet | Samuel | 1 | | | 2 | 1 | | | 1 | 1 | 1 | | | 10 | | |

15

# 1800 Barnstable, Barnstable County, Massachusetts

| TOWN | PG# | LN# | LAST NAME | FIRST NAME | FREE WHITE MALES | | | | | FREE WHITE FEMALES | | | | | TOTAL ALL OTHER | TOTAL SLAVES | TOTALS | DISTRICT/ TOWNSHIP | NOTES |
|---|---|---|---|---|---|---|---|---|---|---|---|---|---|---|---|---|---|---|---|
| | | | | | under 10 | 10 to 16 | 16 to 26 | 26 to 45 | 45 and over | under 10 | 10 to 16 | 16 to 26 | 26 to 45 | 45 and over | | | | | |
| Barnstable | 91 | 19 | Holmes | Elisha Jr | 3 | | | 1 | | 2 | | | 1 | | | | 7 | | |
| Barnstable | 91 | 20 | Crosby | Jesse Jr | | | 1 | 1 | | 2 | | 1 | | | | | 5 | | |
| Barnstable | 91 | 21 | Parker | James | 2 | 1 | 2 | | 1 | 1 | 1 | 2 | | 1 | 2 | | 13 | | |
| Barnstable | 91 | 22 | Holmes | Elisha | | | | 1 | | | | | 2 | 1 | | | 4 | | |
| Barnstable | 91 | 23 | Holmes | Lazarus | 3 | | | 1 | | 1 | | | | 1 | | | 6 | | |
| Barnstable | 91 | 24 | Holmes | Samuel | 1 | | | 1 | | 2 | | 1 | | | | | 5 | | |
| Barnstable | 91 | 25 | Lovell | Simeon | 1 | | 2 | 1 | | 2 | 1 | 1 | 1 | | | | 9 | | |
| Barnstable | 91 | 26 | Lovell | James | 1 | 1 | 1 | | 1 | | | 1 | 1 | | | | 7 | | |
| Barnstable | 91 | 27 | Lovell | James Jr | | | 1 | | | | | 1 | | | | | 2 | | |
| Barnstable | 91 | 28 | Bayman | John | | 1 | | | | | | 1 | | | | | 2 | | |
| Barnstable | 91 | 29 | Thomas | Samuel | 1 | | | 1 | | | | 1 | | | | | 3 | | |
| Barnstable | 91 | 30 | Lovell | Cornelius | 2 | 3 | | 1 | | 3 | | | 1 | 1 | | | 11 | | |
| Barnstable | 91 | 31 | Lovell | Sarah | | | | | | | | | | 3 | | | 3 | | |
| Barnstable | 91 | 32 | Black | Thomas | 2 | 1 | | | 1 | 3 | 1 | 2 | | 1 | | | 11 | | |
| Barnstable | 91 | 33 | Lovell | Daniel | | 1 | | | 1 | 2 | | 1 | | | | | 5 | | |
| Barnstable | 91 | 34 | Lovell | Asa | 1 | | | 1 | | 1 | | 1 | | | | | 4 | | |
| Barnstable | 91 | 35 | Allen | Andrew | | | | 1 | | | | | 1 | | | | 2 | | |
| Barnstable | 91 | 36 | Allen | David | 1 | | 1 | | | 1 | | 1 | | | | | 4 | | |
| Barnstable | 91 | 37 | Allen | Nathl | | | | 1 | | | | | 1 | | | | 2 | | |
| Barnstable | 91 | 38 | Crosby | Nathan | 2 | | 1 | 1 | | 3 | | | 1 | | | | 8 | | |
| Barnstable | 91 | 39 | Lovell | Elizabeth | | | | | | | | | 2 | | | | 2 | | |
| Barnstable | 91 | 40 | Claghorn | Jabez | | 1 | | | | 1 | | | 1 | 1 | | | 4 | | |
| Barnstable | 91 | 41 | Tobey | James | | | | 1 | | 2 | | | 3 | 1 | | | 7 | | |
| Barnstable | 91 | 42 | Jones | Statson | | | 1 | | | 2 | | | 1 | | | | 4 | | |
| Barnstable | 91 | 43 | Lavell | Jacob | | | | 1 | | | | | 1 | | | | 2 | | |
| Barnstable | 91 | 44 | Lavell | Joshua | 1 | 2 | 1 | | 1 | | | | 1 | | | | 6 | | |
| Barnstable | 91 | 45 | Crocker | Morton | 2 | | | 1 | | 1 | | 1 | | | | | 5 | | |
| Barnstable | 91 | 46 | Lewis | Jesse | 1 | | | 1 | | 1 | | 1 | | | | | 4 | | |
| Barnstable | 91 | 47 | Lewis | Thomas | 2 | 2 | 2 | 1 | 1 | 1 | | 2 | | | | | 11 | | |
| Barnstable | 91 | 48 | Marchant | James | 1 | 1 | 1 | | 1 | 4 | 2 | 3 | 1 | 1 | | | 15 | | |
| Barnstable | 92 | 1 | Marchant | Barney | | 1 | | | | | | | 1 | | | | 2 | | |
| Barnstable | 92 | 2 | Lumberd | Hezekiah | | | | 1 | | | | 1 | 1 | | | | 3 | | |
| Barnstable | 92 | 3 | Wood | Wilson | 1 | | 1 | 1 | | 1 | | | 1 | | | | 5 | | |
| Barnstable | 92 | 4 | Wood | Zenas | | | 1 | | | 1 | | | | | | | 2 | | |
| Barnstable | 92 | 5 | Blossom | Churchil | 1 | 1 | | 1 | | 1 | | 1 | | 1 | | | 6 | | |
| Barnstable | 92 | 6 | Foster | Nathan | | | | 1 | | 1 | | 1 | | 1 | | | 4 | | |
| Barnstable | 92 | 7 | Sturgis | Lucretia | | | | | | | | | 1 | | | | 1 | | |
| Barnstable | 92 | 8 | Killey | David | | | 1 | 1 | | 2 | 2 | | 1 | | | | 7 | | |
| Barnstable | 92 | 9 | Jones | Rosanna | | 1 | | | | 2 | 3 | | 1 | | | | 7 | | |
| Barnstable | 92 | 10 | Fish | Josiah | | 3 | | 1 | 1 | 3 | 1 | | 1 | | | | 10 | | |
| Barnstable | 92 | 11 | Fish | Reuben | | | | 1 | 1 | 1 | | | 2 | | | | 5 | | |
| Barnstable | 92 | 12 | Fish | Herman | | | | 1 | | | | | 1 | | | | 2 | | |
| Barnstable | 92 | 13 | Wood | Francis | | | 1 | 1 | 1 | | | | 1 | 1 | | | 5 | | |
| Barnstable | 92 | 14 | Crocker | Barna | | | 2 | | 2 | | | 2 | 1 | | | | 7 | | |
| Barnstable | 92 | 15 | Crocker | Bursley | 2 | | | 1 | | 2 | 1 | | 1 | | | | 7 | | |
| Barnstable | 92 | 16 | Adams | Obed | | 1 | | 1 | | 1 | | | 1 | | | | 4 | | |
| Barnstable | 92 | 17 | Crocker | Abner | | 1 | 1 | 1 | | | | | 1 | | | | 4 | | |
| Barnstable | 92 | 18 | Bursley | John | 1 | | 1 | 1 | | | | | 1 | 1 | 1 | | 6 | | |
| Barnstable | 92 | 19 | Bursley | Lemuel | 1 | | | 1 | | 1 | | | 1 | | | | 4 | | |
| Barnstable | 92 | 20 | Bursley | John Jr | 3 | | | 1 | | | | | 1 | | | | 5 | | |
| Barnstable | 92 | 21 | Crocker | Abram | 2 | 1 | | 1 | | | | 1 | 1 | | | | 6 | | |
| Barnstable | 92 | 22 | Crocker | Francis | | | | 1 | | | | | | | | | 1 | | |
| Barnstable | 92 | 23 | Goodspeed | Benjamin | | | | 1 | | | 1 | | 2 | 1 | 1 | | 6 | | |
| Barnstable | 92 | 24 | Goodspeed | Joseph Jr | | 1 | | | | | | | 1 | | | | 2 | | |
| Barnstable | 92 | 25 | Bodfish | Ebenz | 2 | 2 | 1 | | 1 | 2 | | 1 | 1 | | | | 10 | | |
| Barnstable | 92 | 26 | Smith | Mathias | | 2 | | 1 | | | | | 1 | | | | 4 | | |
| Barnstable | 92 | 27 | Smith | Nathaniel | 1 | | | 1 | | | | | 1 | 1 | | | 4 | | |
| Barnstable | 92 | 28 | Bodfish | Patience | 1 | | 1 | | | | | 1 | | 1 | | | 4 | | |
| Barnstable | 92 | 29 | Smith | Hannah | | | | | | | | | 1 | 1 | | | 2 | | |
| Barnstable | 92 | 30 | Conant | Charles | | | | 1 | | | | | | 1 | | | 2 | | |
| Barnstable | 92 | 31 | Conant | Asa | 2 | | | 1 | 1 | | | | 1 | | | | 5 | | |
| Barnstable | 92 | 32 | Whitman | Jonas | 3 | 1 | 1 | | 1 | 1 | 1 | | 1 | 1 | | | 10 | | |
| Barnstable | 92 | 33 | Goodspeed | Timo Jr | 1 | 1 | 2 | | 1 | 2 | | 1 | 1 | | | | 9 | | |
| Barnstable | 92 | 34 | Smith | Nathan | 2 | | | 1 | | 1 | | | 1 | | | | 5 | | |
| Barnstable | 92 | 35 | Smith | Joseph | | | 1 | 1 | | 1 | | | 1 | | | | 4 | | |
| Barnstable | 92 | 36 | Bodfish | Jona | | | 3 | 1 | | | | 1 | | 1 | | | 6 | | |
| Barnstable | 92 | 37 | Bodfish | John | 3 | | | 1 | | | | 1 | | 1 | | | 6 | | |
| Barnstable | 92 | 38 | Fuller | Mathias | | | 1 | 1 | 1 | | | | 1 | | | | 4 | | |
| Barnstable | 92 | 39 | Fuller | Mathias Jr | 1 | | | 1 | | | | 1 | | | | | 3 | | |
| Barnstable | 92 | 40 | Atkins | Asa | 4 | | | 1 | | 1 | 1 | | 1 | | | | 8 | | |
| Barnstable | 92 | 41 | Jones | Hannah | | | | | | | | | 1 | | | | 1 | | |
| Barnstable | 92 | 42 | Jones | Asa | 4 | 1 | | 1 | | 1 | | | 1 | | | | 8 | | |
| Barnstable | 92 | 43 | Jones | Simon | 3 | 1 | | 1 | | 2 | 1 | 1 | | | | | 9 | | |
| Barnstable | 92 | 44 | Thomas | Joseph | | | | 1 | | | | 1 | 1 | | | | 3 | | |
| Barnstable | 92 | 45 | Hayes | Hannah | | 1 | | | | | | | | 1 | | | 2 | | |
| Barnstable | 92 | 46 | Crocker | John | 3 | 1 | | 1 | 3 | | | | 1 | 1 | | | 10 | | |
| Barnstable | 92 | 47 | Fuller | James | 1 | 1 | | 2 | | 1 | 3 | 1 | | | | | 9 | | |
| Barnstable | 92 | 48 | Weeks | Barzilla | | 2 | | 1 | | | 2 | | 1 | | | | 6 | | |
| Barnstable | 92 | 49 | Fuller | Benjamin | | 1 | 1 | | | 1 | | | | | | | 3 | | |

# 1800 Barnstable, Barnstable County, Massachusetts

| TOWN | PG# | LN# | LAST NAME | FIRST NAME | M under 10 | M 10 to 16 | M 16 to 26 | M 26 to 45 | M 45 and over | F under 10 | F 10 to 16 | F 16 to 26 | F 26 to 45 | F 45 and over | TOTAL ALL OTHER | TOTAL SLAVES | TOTALS | DISTRICT/ TOWNSHIP | NOTES |
|---|---|---|---|---|---|---|---|---|---|---|---|---|---|---|---|---|---|---|---|
| Barnstable | 92 | 50 | Weeks | Barzilla Jr | 2 | | 1 | | | | | 1 | | | | | 4 | | |
| Barnstable | 92 | 51 | Bassett | Sarah | | | | | | | 1 | | 1 | | | | 2 | | |
| Barnstable | 92 | 52 | Balsom | Nathaniel B | | | | 1 | | | | | 1 | | 1 | | 3 | | |
| Barnstable | 92 | 53 | Fuller | Jonathan | 2 | | 1 | | | | | | 1 | | | | 4 | | |
| Barnstable | 93 | 1 | Bodfish | Robert | | | 1 | | | 1 | | | 1 | | | | 3 | | |
| Barnstable | 93 | 2 | Linnell | Josiah | | | 1 | | | 1 | | | 1 | | | | 3 | | |
| Barnstable | 93 | 3 | Bassett | Seth | 2 | | 1 | | | | | | 1 | 1 | | | 5 | | |
| Barnstable | 93 | 4 | Bassett | Daniel | 1 | | 1 | | | 3 | | | 1 | | | | 6 | | |
| Barnstable | 93 | 5 | Hamblin | Martha | | | | | | | | | | 2 | | | 2 | | |
| Barnstable | 93 | 6 | Ray | Sarah | | 1 | 1 | | | 1 | | | 2 | | | | 5 | | |
| Barnstable | 93 | 7 | Simmons | Silvanus | 3 | 1 | | 1 | | 1 | | | 1 | | | | 7 | | |
| Barnstable | 93 | 8 | Bacon | Deborah | | | | | | | | | | 2 | | | 2 | | |
| Barnstable | 93 | 9 | Gage | Nathl | 1 | | | 1 | | 1 | 1 | | 1 | | | | 5 | | |
| Barnstable | 93 | 10 | Gage | Joseph | | 1 | 1 | | | | | 1 | | | | | 3 | | |
| Barnstable | 93 | 11 | Scudder | David | 3 | 1 | | 1 | | 2 | | | 1 | 1 | 1 | | 10 | | |
| Barnstable | 93 | 12 | Lavell | Shubael | | | | | 1 | | 1 | | 1 | | | | 3 | | |
| Barnstable | 93 | 13 | Scudder | Eleazer | | | | | 1 | | | 1 | 1 | | 1 | | 4 | | |
| Barnstable | 93 | 14 | Scudder | William | 2 | | 1 | | | 1 | | | 1 | | 1 | | 6 | | |
| Barnstable | 93 | 15 | Scudder | Eleazer Jr | 1 | | 1 | | | 1 | | | 1 | | | | 4 | | |
| Barnstable | 93 | 16 | Lawrence | Abigail | 2 | | | | | 1 | | | 1 | | 1 | | 5 | | |
| Barnstable | 93 | 17 | Bearse | Josiah | | | 1 | | | 1 | 1 | | | | | | 3 | | |
| Barnstable | 93 | 18 | Berry | Enoch | | 1 | 1 | | | 3 | | 2 | 1 | | | | 8 | | |
| Barnstable | 93 | 19 | Shaw | Samuel | 1 | | 1 | | | 1 | | | 1 | | | | 4 | | |
| Barnstable | 93 | 20 | Bearse | Gershom | | 1 | 1 | 1 | | 1 | 1 | 1 | 1 | | | | 7 | | |
| Barnstable | 93 | 21 | Lumberd | Ichabod | | | | 2 | | | 1 | | 1 | | | | 4 | | |
| Barnstable | 93 | 22 | Lumberd | Solomon | | | 1 | | | | 2 | | | | | | 3 | | |
| Barnstable | 93 | 23 | Blish | Elisha | | | 1 | | | | | | 1 | | | | 2 | | |
| Barnstable | 93 | 24 | Hamblin | David | 2 | | 1 | | | 2 | | | 1 | | | | 6 | | |
| Barnstable | 93 | 25 | Eldredge | Ezra | 1 | | 1 | | | 3 | | | 1 | 1 | | | 7 | | |
| Barnstable | 93 | 26 | Scudder | Lot | 2 | | 1 | | | | | | 1 | | | | 4 | | |
| Barnstable | 93 | 27 | Scudder | Samuel | | | 1 | 1 | | | | | | 1 | | | 3 | | |
| Barnstable | 93 | 28 | Sands | William | 1 | | | 1 | | 3 | 1 | 2 | | | | | 8 | | |
| Barnstable | 93 | 29 | Stewart | James | 1 | | 1 | | | 1 | | | 1 | 2 | | | 6 | | |
| Barnstable | 93 | 30 | Coleman | Nathaniel | 1 | 1 | 1 | 1 | | 2 | | 2 | | 1 | | | 10 | | |
| Barnstable | 93 | 31 | Ritcher | Jonathan | | 2 | 3 | 1 | 1 | 1 | | 1 | | 1 | | | 10 | | |
| Barnstable | 93 | 32 | Bearse | Levi | | 1 | 2 | 1 | | 1 | | | | 1 | | | 6 | | |
| Barnstable | 93 | 33 | Norris | Peter | 1 | 1 | 1 | | 1 | 1 | 1 | | | 1 | | | 7 | | |
| Barnstable | 93 | 34 | Norris | Peter Jr | | | 1 | | | | | 1 | | | | | 2 | | |
| Barnstable | 93 | 35 | Stuart | Solomon | 2 | | 1 | | | 1 | | | 1 | | | | 5 | | |
| Barnstable | 93 | 36 | Bassett | Joseph | 4 | 1 | | 1 | | 2 | 1 | | 1 | | | | 10 | | |
| Barnstable | 93 | 37 | Bacon | Jabez | | 1 | 2 | | 1 | 1 | 2 | 2 | 1 | | | | 10 | | |
| Barnstable | 93 | 38 | Bacon | Onan | | | 1 | | | | | | 1 | | | | 2 | | |
| Barnstable | 93 | 39 | Lewis | Sarah | | | | | | | | 2 | | 1 | | | 3 | | |
| Barnstable | 93 | 40 | Lewis | Lot | 2 | | 1 | | | | | | 1 | | | | 4 | | |
| Barnstable | 93 | 41 | Bearse | David | 1 | | 1 | 1 | 1 | 1 | 1 | | 2 | 1 | | | 9 | | |
| Barnstable | 93 | 42 | Hope | Timothy | 2 | | 1 | | | | | | 1 | 1 | | | 5 | | |
| Barnstable | 93 | 43 | Cobb | Thomas | 1 | | 1 | | | 2 | | 1 | | | | | 5 | | |
| Barnstable | 93 | 44 | Snow | Nathaniel | | 1 | 2 | 1 | 1 | 3 | | 2 | | 1 | | | 11 | | |
| Barnstable | 93 | 45 | Bearse | Edward | | 2 | | 1 | | | 1 | | | 1 | | | 5 | | |
| Barnstable | 93 | 46 | Bearse | Edward Jr | | | 1 | | | | | | 1 | | | | 2 | | |
| Barnstable | 93 | 47 | Bearse | Samuel | 1 | | 1 | | | | | | 1 | | | | 3 | | |
| Barnstable | 93 | 48 | Hallet | Rebecca | | | 1 | | | | | | 1 | 1 | | | 3 | | |
| Barnstable | 93 | 49 | Hallet | Daniel | | | | 1 | | 1 | | | 1 | | | | 3 | | |
| Barnstable | 93 | 50 | Hallet | Edward | 4 | 1 | | 1 | | | 1 | | 1 | | | | 8 | | |
| Barnstable | 93 | 51 | Hallet | Jonathan | | | | 1 | | | | | | 1 | | | 2 | | |
| Barnstable | 93 | 52 | Hallet | Jonathan | | | 1 | | | | | | 1 | | | | 2 | | |
| Barnstable | 94 | 1 | Cathcart | John | | | 1 | | | 1 | | | 1 | | | | 3 | | |
| Barnstable | 94 | 2 | Lewis | Lemuel | 2 | | 1 | | | 2 | 1 | | 1 | | | | 7 | | |
| Barnstable | 94 | 3 | Loring | Elpalet | 2 | 1 | 1 | | | | | | 1 | | | | 5 | | |
| Barnstable | 94 | 4 | Hallet | John | 1 | 2 | 1 | | 2 | 1 | | 1 | | 1 | | | 9 | | |
| Barnstable | 94 | 5 | Hallet | Nathaniel | 2 | 1 | 1 | | 1 | 2 | 1 | 1 | | 1 | | | 10 | | |
| Barnstable | 94 | 6 | Lewis | George | | 1 | | | 1 | 3 | 1 | 3 | 1 | | | | 10 | | |
| Barnstable | 94 | 7 | Eldredge | Revd Enoch | | 2 | | 1 | | 3 | 1 | | 1 | | | | 8 | | |
| Barnstable | 94 | 8 | Gage | Jane | 1 | | | | | 1 | | | 1 | | | | 3 | | |
| Barnstable | 94 | 9 | Lewis | Richard | | | 1 | | 1 | | | 1 | 1 | | | | 4 | | |
| Barnstable | 94 | 10 | Hallet | Joseph | | | 3 | | 1 | | | 2 | 1 | 1 | | | 8 | | |
| Barnstable | 94 | 11 | Hallet | Rowland | 1 | 2 | 3 | | 1 | | | 2 | 2 | | | | 11 | | |
| Barnstable | 94 | 12 | Crocker | John | | | | | 1 | | | | | 1 | | | 2 | | |
| Barnstable | 94 | 13 | Hallet | Rowland Jr | 1 | | 1 | | | 2 | | 1 | | | | | 5 | | |
| Barnstable | 94 | 14 | Hawes | Joshua | 2 | | | 1 | | 3 | 2 | | 1 | 1 | | | 10 | | |
| Barnstable | 94 | 15 | Lovell | Abner W | | | 1 | | | 1 | | | 1 | 1 | | | 4 | | |
| Barnstable | 94 | 16 | Gage | Zenas | 1 | 1 | | 1 | | 1 | | 1 | 1 | | | | 6 | | |
| Barnstable | 94 | 17 | Hallet | Bethiah | 1 | | | | | | | | 1 | | | | 2 | | |
| Barnstable | 94 | 18 | Bearse | Prince | | | | | 1 | | 1 | | | | | | 2 | | |
| Barnstable | 94 | 19 | Bearse | Judah | 1 | 2 | 1 | | 1 | 1 | 1 | 1 | 1 | | | | 9 | | |
| Barnstable | 94 | 20 | Bearse | Prince Jr | 3 | | 2 | | 1 | 3 | 1 | | 1 | | | | 11 | | |
| Barnstable | 94 | 21 | Bearse | Obed | 3 | 1 | | | 1 | 2 | | | 1 | | | | 8 | | |
| Barnstable | 94 | 22 | Hallet | David | 1 | | | 1 | | 3 | | | 1 | | 10 | | 16 | | |
| Barnstable | 94 | 23 | Hamblin | Joshua | 1 | 2 | | 1 | | 1 | 1 | 2 | | 1 | | | 10 | | |

17

# 1800 Barnstable, Barnstable County, Massachusetts

| TOWN | PG# | LN# | LAST NAME | FIRST NAME | under 10 | 10 to 16 | 16 to 26 | 26 to 45 | 45 and over | under 10 | 10 to 16 | 16 to 26 | 26 to 45 | 45 and over | TOTAL ALL OTHER | TOTAL SLAVES | TOTALS | DISTRICT/ TOWNSHIP | NOTES |
|---|---|---|---|---|---|---|---|---|---|---|---|---|---|---|---|---|---|---|---|
| Barnstable | 94 | 24 | Ames | Thomas | | 1 | 2 | | 1 | 1 | 1 | 1 | | 1 | | | 8 | | |
| Barnstable | 94 | 25 | Bearse | Enoch | | 2 | 2 | | 1 | 1 | | 1 | | 1 | | | 8 | | |
| Barnstable | 94 | 26 | Lewis | Thankful | | | 1 | | | | | 1 | | 2 | | | 4 | | |
| Barnstable | 94 | 27 | Hoskins | Seth | 1 | 1 | 1 | | | 1 | | 1 | | | | | 5 | | |
| Barnstable | 94 | 28 | Crowell | Isaac Jr | 1 | | | 1 | | | | | 1 | | | | 3 | | |
| Barnstable | 94 | 29 | Crowell | Gorham | 2 | 2 | | | 1 | 1 | | 1 | | 1 | | | 8 | | |
| Barnstable | 94 | 30 | Crowell | Edmind | 2 | | 1 | | | 2 | 2 | 1 | | | | | 9 | | |
| Barnstable | 94 | 31 | Crowell | Isaac | 1 | 1 | | | 1 | 1 | 1 | | | 2 | | | 7 | | |
| Barnstable | 94 | 32 | Crowell | Abner Jr | | | | 1 | | 1 | | 1 | | | | | 3 | | |
| Barnstable | 94 | 33 | Crowell | Zira | 1 | | | 1 | | | | 1 | | | | | 3 | | |
| Barnstable | 94 | 34 | Killey | David | | 1 | | | 1 | | 1 | | | 1 | | | 4 | | |
| Barnstable | 94 | 35 | Crowell | Silva Jr | 2 | 1 | 1 | 1 | | 3 | 1 | | 1 | | | | 10 | | |
| Barnstable | 94 | 36 | Shiverick | Thomas | 2 | 2 | 2 | 1 | | 1 | 2 | | 1 | | | | 11 | | |
| Barnstable | 94 | 37 | Crowell | Sarah | | 1 | 1 | | 1 | | | 2 | | 1 | | | 6 | | |
| Barnstable | 94 | 38 | Crowell | Thomas | 1 | | | 1 | | 1 | | 1 | | | | | 4 | | |
| Barnstable | 94 | 39 | Crowell | Barnabas | | | | 1 | | 1 | | 1 | | | | | 3 | | |
| Barnstable | 94 | 40 | Brown | Thaddeus | 1 | 3 | 1 | | 1 | | | | 1 | | | | 7 | | |
| Barnstable | 94 | 41 | Furnald | Benjamin | 2 | | | | 1 | 1 | 1 | | 1 | 1 | | | 7 | | |
| Barnstable | 94 | 42 | Lavell | Gorham | | 1 | | 1 | | 2 | | 1 | 1 | | | | 6 | | |
| Barnstable | 94 | 43 | Baker | Seth | 1 | | 1 | | 1 | 2 | 3 | | | 1 | | | 9 | | |
| Barnstable | 94 | 44 | Baxter | Isaac | 1 | 2 | | | 1 | 1 | | | | 1 | | | 6 | | |
| Barnstable | 94 | 45 | Baxter | Sarah | 4 | 1 | 1 | | | | 1 | 1 | 1 | | | | 9 | | |
| Barnstable | 94 | 46 | Baxter | David | 2 | 2 | 3 | | 1 | 1 | 1 | | | 1 | | | 11 | | |
| Barnstable | 94 | 47 | Linnell | Heman | | | | 1 | | 2 | | | 1 | 2 | | | 6 | | |
| Barnstable | 94 | 48 | Buck | John | 1 | | | 1 | | 1 | | | | 1 | | | 4 | | |
| Barnstable | 94 | 49 | Lothrop | David | 1 | | | 1 | | 3 | | | 1 | | | | 6 | | |
| Barnstable | 94 | 50 | Baxter | Barna | 2 | | | 1 | | 1 | | | 1 | | | | 5 | | |
| Barnstable | 101 | 1 | Baxter | Shubael | 2 | | | 1 | | 2 | | | 1 | | | | 6 | | |
| Barnstable | 101 | 2 | Linnell | Levi | | | | 1 | | | 1 | 1 | 1 | | | | 4 | | |
| Barnstable | 101 | 3 | Baxter | Daniel | | | | 1 | | | | 1 | 1 | | | | 3 | | |
| Barnstable | 101 | 4 | Baxter | Alexr | 3 | | | 1 | | 1 | | 1 | | | | | 6 | | |
| Barnstable | 101 | 5 | Baxter | Obed | | | | 1 | | | | 1 | | | | | 2 | | |
| Barnstable | 101 | 6 | Baker | Timothy | 2 | 2 | | | | 1 | | | 1 | | | | 6 | | |
| Barnstable | 101 | 7 | Buck | Thomas | | | | 2 | | | | 1 | | 1 | | | 4 | | |
| Barnstable | 101 | 8 | Robbins | James | | 2 | | | 1 | 1 | 1 | | 1 | | | | 6 | | |
| Barnstable | 101 | 9 | Bragg | Jane | | | 2 | | | | | | | 1 | | | 3 | | |
| Barnstable | 101 | 10 | Bearse | Stephen | 3 | | | 1 | | 2 | | | 1 | | | | 9 | | |
| Barnstable | 101 | 11 | Chase | Anthony | 4 | 1 | 1 | 1 | | | 1 | 1 | 1 | | | | 10 | | |
| Barnstable | 101 | 12 | Baxter | Prince | 2 | 2 | 1 | | 1 | 1 | 1 | 1 | | 1 | | | 10 | | |
| Barnstable | 101 | 13 | Bradley | Abind | | | | 1 | | | | 1 | | | | | 2 | | |
| Barnstable | 101 | 14 | Crowell | Daniel | | 1 | 2 | | 1 | | 1 | 1 | 1 | 1 | | | 8 | | |

# 1800 Chatham, Barnstable County, Massachusetts

| TOWN | PG# | LN# | LAST NAME | FIRST NAME | M under 10 | M 10 to 16 | M 16 to 26 | M 26 to 45 | M 45 and over | F under 10 | F 10 to 16 | F 16 to 26 | F 26 to 45 | F 45 and over | TOTAL ALL OTHER | TOTAL SLAVES | TOTALS | DISTRICT/TOWNSHIP | NOTES |
|---|---|---|---|---|---|---|---|---|---|---|---|---|---|---|---|---|---|---|---|
| Chatham | 15 | 2 | Bradshell | William | | | 2 | | 1 | 1 | | | | 1 | | | 5 | | |
| Chatham | 15 | 3 | Atwood | Sears | 1 | 3 | 1 | 1 | | | | | | 1 | 1 | | 8 | | |
| Chatham | 15 | 4 | Buck | David | | 1 | 1 | | 1 | | 1 | | | 1 | | | 5 | | |
| Chatham | 15 | 5 | Berse | George | 1 | | | | 1 | | 1 | | | 1 | | | 4 | | |
| Chatham | 15 | 6 | Baker | William | | | | 2 | | 3 | | | 1 | | | | 6 | | |
| Chatham | 15 | 7 | Baker | Gideon | | | 1 | | | 1 | | 1 | | | | | 3 | | |
| Chatham | 15 | 8 | Butler | Nathaniel | 2 | | | 1 | | 1 | | | 1 | | | | 5 | | |
| Chatham | 15 | 9 | Buck | Mary Wid | 1 | 1 | | 1 | | 1 | | | 1 | 1 | | | 6 | | |
| Chatham | 15 | 10 | Briggs | Ephraim | 1 | | | 1 | | | | 1 | 1 | | | | 4 | | |
| Chatham | 15 | 11 | Buck | Joshua | 1 | | | 1 | | 2 | | | 1 | | | | 5 | | |
| Chatham | 15 | 12 | Berse | Simeon | 2 | 1 | | | 1 | | | 2 | | 1 | | | 7 | | |
| Chatham | 15 | 13 | Berse | Ebenezer | 2 | 1 | | 1 | | 2 | 1 | | 1 | | | | 8 | | |
| Chatham | 15 | 14 | Bassett | Nathan Jr | 1 | | 2 | | 2 | 1 | | 1 | 1 | | | | 8 | | |
| Chatham | 15 | 15 | Bassett | Samuel | 1 | | 2 | | 1 | 2 | | | | 1 | | | 7 | | |
| Chatham | 15 | 16 | Bassett | Sarah Wd | | | | | | | | 1 | | 1 | | | 2 | | |
| Chatham | 15 | 17 | Buck | Elizabeth Wd | | | | | | 1 | 1 | | 1 | 1 | | | 4 | | |
| Chatham | 15 | 18 | Badshell | William Jun | 1 | | | 1 | | 2 | 1 | | 1 | | | | 6 | | |
| Chatham | 15 | 19 | Badshell | Caty | | | | | | 1 | | | 1 | | | | 2 | | |
| Chatham | 15 | 20 | Bea | Thomas | | 1 | | | 1 | | | | | 2 | | | 4 | | |
| Chatham | 15 | 21 | Buck | Benjm | 2 | | | 1 | | 2 | | | 1 | | | | 6 | | |
| Chatham | 15 | 22 | Berse | Betsy | | | | | | 1 | | | 1 | | | | 2 | | |
| Chatham | 15 | 23 | Bea | Isaac | | | 1 | | | 1 | | 1 | | | | | 3 | | |
| Chatham | 15 | 24 | Berry | Willis | 1 | | 1 | | | 1 | | 1 | | | | | 4 | | |
| Chatham | 15 | 25 | Crowell | John | | | 1 | | | | | 1 | | | | | 2 | | |
| Chatham | 15 | 26 | Collins | Samuel | 1 | | | 1 | | 2 | | | 1 | | 1 | | 6 | | |
| Chatham | 16 | 1 | Cyk | Reuben | | | 1 | 1 | | | | | | 1 | | | 3 | | |
| Chatham | 16 | 2 | Coleman | John | | | | 1 | | | | 1 | | | | | 2 | | |
| Chatham | 16 | 3 | Chase | Bassett | | | 1 | | | 1 | | 1 | | | | | 3 | | |
| Chatham | 16 | 4 | Crowell | David | | | 1 | | 1 | | | 1 | | 1 | | | 4 | | |
| Chatham | 16 | 5 | Crowell | Paul | | | | 1 | | | | | | 1 | | | 2 | | |
| Chatham | 16 | 6 | Crowell | Hallet | | | 1 | | | 2 | | | 1 | | | | 4 | | |
| Chatham | 16 | 7 | Crowell | Zenus | 1 | 2 | 1 | | 1 | 2 | | 1 | 1 | 1 | | | 10 | | |
| Chatham | 16 | 8 | Crowell | Ezra | 1 | | | 1 | | 3 | | | 1 | | | | 6 | | |
| Chatham | 16 | 9 | Clark | Thomas | | 1 | | | 1 | 1 | | | | 2 | | | 5 | | |
| Chatham | 16 | 10 | Cobb | Elezar | | 1 | 1 | | | | | 1 | | | | | 3 | | |
| Chatham | 16 | 11 | Crowell | Stetson | | 1 | 1 | | | | | 1 | | | | | 3 | | |
| Chatham | 16 | 12 | Doane | Samuel | 2 | | | | 2 | 2 | 1 | | | 1 | | | 8 | | |
| Chatham | 16 | 13 | Doane | Joseph | | 3 | 2 | | 1 | 1 | | | | 1 | | | 8 | | |
| Chatham | 16 | 14 | Dexter | Joseph | 2 | | | 1 | | 2 | 1 | 2 | | 1 | | | 9 | | |
| Chatham | 16 | 15 | Davis | Benjm | | | | 1 | | 3 | | | 1 | | | | 5 | | |
| Chatham | 16 | 16 | Doane | Hezekiah | | 2 | 2 | | 1 | 1 | 1 | | | 1 | | | 8 | | |
| Chatham | 16 | 17 | Doane | John | 1 | | | 1 | | 1 | | | 1 | | | | 4 | | |
| Chatham | 16 | 18 | Deland | Ebenezer | | | 1 | | | | | 1 | | | | | 2 | | |
| Chatham | 16 | 19 | Eldrege | Seth | | 1 | 1 | | 1 | 1 | | | | 2 | | | 6 | | |
| Chatham | 16 | 20 | Eldrege | Caleb | 1 | 1 | 1 | | | 2 | | 1 | 1 | 1 | | | 8 | | |
| Chatham | 16 | 21 | Eldrege | Zephaniah | | 1 | | 1 | | | | | 1 | 1 | | | 4 | | |
| Chatham | 16 | 22 | Emory | John | 1 | 2 | 1 | | 1 | 2 | 1 | | 1 | 1 | | | 10 | | |
| Chatham | 16 | 23 | Eldrege | Anthony | 1 | | | 1 | | 1 | 1 | 2 | | 1 | | | 7 | | |
| Chatham | 16 | 24 | Eldrege | Isaac | 3 | | 1 | | 1 | 1 | 1 | 2 | | 1 | | | 10 | | |
| Chatham | 16 | 25 | Eldrege | John | 2 | 1 | 1 | 1 | | 2 | | | | 1 | | | 8 | | |
| Chatham | 16 | 26 | Eldrege | James | 1 | | | 1 | 2 | | 1 | 1 | | 1 | | | 7 | | |
| Chatham | 16 | 27 | Eldrege | Daniel | 2 | 1 | | 1 | | 1 | | | 1 | | | | 6 | | |
| Chatham | 16 | 28 | Eldrege | Nathaniel | 1 | 3 | | 1 | | 2 | | | 2 | 1 | | | 11 | | |
| Chatham | 16 | 29 | Eldrege | Stephen | | | 2 | | 1 | | 2 | | | 1 | | | 6 | | |
| Chatham | 16 | 30 | Eldrege | Jonathan | | 1 | 1 | | | | 1 | | 1 | | | | 4 | | |
| Chatham | 16 | 31 | Eldrege | William | 1 | | | 1 | | | 2 | | 1 | | | | 5 | | |
| Chatham | 16 | 32 | Eldrege | Josiah | 4 | | | | 1 | 1 | 2 | 1 | | 1 | | | 10 | | |
| Chatham | 16 | 33 | Eldrege | Thomas | | 1 | | | 1 | 2 | | 1 | | 1 | | | 6 | | |
| Chatham | 16 | 34 | Eldrege | Hannah Wid | | | 3 | | | 1 | 1 | | 1 | | | | 6 | | |
| Chatham | 16 | 35 | Eldrege | Elisha | 4 | 2 | 1 | 1 | 1 | 1 | 1 | | | 1 | | | 12 | | |
| Chatham | 16 | 36 | Eldrege | Nathaniel Jr | 2 | | 1 | | 1 | 2 | | | | 1 | | | 7 | | |
| Chatham | 16 | 37 | Eldrege | Thankfull Wid | 3 | | | | | 1 | | | 1 | | | | 5 | | |
| Chatham | 16 | 38 | Eldrege | Edward | 1 | | 1 | | | 1 | | 1 | | | | | 4 | | |
| Chatham | 16 | 39 | Godfrey | Rachel Wid | | | | | | | | | 1 | 1 | | | 2 | | |
| Chatham | 16 | 40 | Godfrey | Lewvi | 1 | | 1 | | | 1 | | | 1 | | | | 4 | | |
| Chatham | 16 | 41 | Godfrey | Benjm | | 1 | | 1 | | | | | | 1 | | | 3 | | |
| Chatham | 16 | 42 | Godfrey | David | 2 | | | 1 | | 1 | | | 1 | | | | 5 | | |
| Chatham | 16 | 43 | Gould | Nathaniel | 2 | | 1 | | | 1 | | 1 | | | | | 5 | | |
| Chatham | 16 | 44 | Gould | Joshua Junr | | 1 | | | 1 | 2 | 2 | | 1 | | | | 7 | | |
| Chatham | 16 | 45 | Gould | Josiah | 1 | 2 | | 1 | | 2 | | | 1 | | | | 7 | | |
| Chatham | 16 | 46 | Gage | Reuben | 1 | | | 1 | | | | 1 | | 1 | 1 | | 5 | | |
| Chatham | 17 | 1 | House | Thomas Jun | | | 1 | | | 1 | | | 1 | | | | 3 | | |
| Chatham | 17 | 2 | House | David Jun | 1 | | 1 | | | 1 | | | 1 | | | | 4 | | |
| Chatham | 17 | 3 | House | Richard | | | 1 | | 1 | | | 1 | | 1 | | | 4 | | |
| Chatham | 17 | 4 | Hamilton | Jeptha | | 1 | 1 | 1 | | 2 | 1 | | 1 | | | | 7 | | |
| Chatham | 17 | 5 | Hamilton | Nathaniel | | | 2 | | 1 | | 1 | | | 1 | | | 5 | | |
| Chatham | 17 | 6 | Hamilton | Elizabeth | | | 1 | | | | | | | 1 | | | 2 | | |
| Chatham | 17 | 7 | House | Enoch | 2 | 1 | | 1 | | 2 | | | 1 | | | | 7 | | |
| Chatham | 17 | 8 | Harding | John | | 2 | | | 1 | | 1 | | | 1 | | | 5 | | |
| Chatham | 17 | 9 | House | Mulford | 1 | 1 | 1 | 1 | | | | | 1 | | | | 5 | | |
| Chatham | 17 | 10 | House | Joseph | | 1 | 1 | | 1 | | | 2 | | 1 | | | 6 | | |
| Chatham | 17 | 11 | Harding | Josiah | 4 | 1 | | 1 | | | | | 1 | | | | 7 | | |
| Chatham | 17 | 12 | House | David | | | | 1 | | | | | 1 | | | | 2 | | |
| Chatham | 17 | 13 | Hunt | Lemuel | 1 | | | 1 | | 2 | | | 1 | | | | 5 | | |
| Chatham | 17 | 14 | House | James | 1 | 1 | | | 1 | | 1 | 2 | | 1 | | | 7 | | |
| Chatham | 17 | 15 | House | Stephen | 1 | | | 1 | | 3 | | | 1 | | | | 6 | | |
| Chatham | 17 | 16 | House | Joshua | | | 1 | | | 1 | | | 1 | | | | 3 | | |
| Chatham | 17 | 17 | House | Joshua Jun | | 1 | | | | | | | 1 | | | | 3 | | |
| Chatham | 17 | 18 | House | Joshua 3d | 1 | | 1 | | | | | | 1 | | | | 3 | | |
| Chatham | 17 | 19 | House | Abraham | | | 1 | | | | | 1 | | 1 | | | 3 | | |

| TOWN | PG# | LN# | LAST NAME | FIRST NAME | FREE WHITE MALES | | | | | FREE WHITE FEMALES | | | | | TOTAL ALL OTHER | TOTAL SLAVES | TOTALS | DISTRICT/ TOWNSHIP | NOTES |
|---|---|---|---|---|---|---|---|---|---|---|---|---|---|---|---|---|---|---|---|
| | | | | | under 10 | 10 to 16 | 16 to 26 | 26 to 45 | 45 and over | under 10 | 10 to 16 | 16 to 26 | 26 to 45 | 45 and over | | | | | |
| Chatham | 17 | 20 | House | Daniel | | | 1 | | 1 | 1 | | 1 | | 1 | | | 5 | | |
| Chatham | 17 | 21 | Hamilton | Benja | 4 | | | 1 | | | | | 2 | 1 | | | 8 | | |
| Chatham | 17 | 22 | Hawes | John | 2 | 1 | 3 | | 1 | 1 | 1 | | 1 | 1 | | | 11 | | |
| Chatham | 17 | 23 | Harding | Amos | 1 | 1 | | | 1 | | 1 | | | 2 | | | 6 | | |
| Chatham | 17 | 24 | Harding | Prenie | | | 1 | | 1 | 1 | | | 1 | | | | 4 | | |
| Chatham | 17 | 25 | Hammond | John | 3 | 1 | | 1 | | | 1 | | 1 | 1 | | | 8 | | |
| Chatham | 17 | 26 | Hinkley | Shubal | | 1 | | | 1 | 2 | 2 | | 1 | | | | 7 | | |
| Chatham | 17 | 27 | Hopkins | James | 1 | 1 | 1 | | 1 | 5 | | 2 | | 1 | | | 12 | | |
| Chatham | 17 | 28 | Harding | Silvanus | 1 | 2 | 1 | | 1 | 2 | | 1 | | 1 | | | 9 | | |
| Chatham | 17 | 29 | Harding | Seth Junr | 2 | 2 | 3 | | 1 | 1 | | | | 1 | | | 10 | | |
| Chatham | 17 | 30 | Hamilton | Nehemiah | 2 | | | 1 | | | | | 1 | | | | 4 | | |
| Chatham | 17 | 31 | Hamilton | Meltiah | 1 | 2 | | 1 | | 2 | | | 1 | | | | 7 | | |
| Chatham | 17 | 32 | Hamilton | Elizabeth | | 1 | | 1 | | | | 1 | | 1 | | | 4 | | |
| Chatham | 17 | 33 | Hamilton | Seth | 1 | | | 1 | | | | | 1 | | | | 3 | | |
| Chatham | 17 | 34 | Hamilton | Richard | 1 | | 1 | | 1 | 5 | 2 | | | 1 | | | 11 | | |
| Chatham | 17 | 35 | Hamilton | Jonathan | 3 | | | 1 | | | | | 1 | | | | 5 | | |
| Chatham | 17 | 36 | House | Benjm | 1 | | | 1 | | 1 | | | 1 | | | | 4 | | |
| Chatham | 17 | 37 | Harding | Content Wid | | 1 | 1 | | | | 1 | 1 | | 1 | | | 5 | | |
| Chatham | 17 | 38 | Harding | Prince Junr | 1 | | | 1 | | 1 | | | 1 | | | | 4 | | |
| Chatham | 17 | 39 | House | Solomon | 1 | | 1 | | 1 | | 1 | | 1 | | | | 5 | | |
| Chatham | 17 | 40 | Jackson | Barbara Wid | | | | | | | | | 1 | | | | 1 | | |
| Chatham | 17 | 41 | Hunt | Edward | 1 | 2 | | 1 | | 1 | | | 1 | | | | 6 | | |
| Chatham | 17 | 42 | Knowles | Hannah Wid | | | | | | | 1 | | 1 | | | | 2 | | |
| Chatham | 17 | 43 | Lewis | Calvin | 1 | | 1 | | | 1 | | 1 | | | | | 4 | | |
| Chatham | 17 | 44 | Loveland | Timothy | 2 | | | 1 | | 1 | | | 1 | | | | 5 | | |
| Chatham | 17 | 45 | Morris | Lidia | | | | | | | | | 1 | | | | 1 | | |
| Chatham | 17 | 46 | Mayo | Paul | | | 1 | | 1 | | 3 | 1 | | 1 | | | 7 | | |
| Chatham | 17 | 47 | Morse | Seth | | 2 | | | 1 | 1 | 1 | | | 1 | | | 6 | | |
| Chatham | 18 | 1 | Nickerson | Simeon | | | | 1 | | | | | | | | | 1 | | |
| Chatham | 18 | 2 | Nickerson | Caleb | 1 | 1 | | | 1 | | 1 | | | 1 | | | 5 | | |
| Chatham | 18 | 3 | Nickerson | Minich | | | 1 | | 2 | | | 1 | | | | | 4 | | |
| Chatham | 18 | 4 | Nickerson | Tabitha Wid | 1 | | | | 1 | | 2 | 1 | | | | | 6 | | |
| Chatham | 18 | 5 | Nickerson | Jonathan | | | 1 | | 1 | | 2 | 1 | | 1 | | | 6 | | |
| Chatham | 18 | 6 | Nickerson | Jememiah | | 2 | 1 | | 1 | 1 | | 1 | | 1 | | | 7 | | |
| Chatham | 18 | 7 | Nickerson | Constant | | 1 | | | 2 | | 1 | | | 1 | | | 5 | | |
| Chatham | 18 | 8 | Nickerson | Moses Junr | 1 | | | 1 | | 2 | 1 | 1 | 1 | | | | 7 | | |
| Chatham | 18 | 9 | Nickerson | Ezra | 2 | | 1 | | | 1 | | 1 | | | | | 5 | | |
| Chatham | 18 | 10 | Nickerson | Moses | | 1 | 1 | | 1 | | 2 | | 1 | | | | 6 | | |
| Chatham | 18 | 11 | Nickerson | Zaheth | 1 | | | 1 | | 3 | 1 | 1 | | | | | 7 | | |
| Chatham | 18 | 12 | Nickerson | Flathiel | | 2 | | 1 | | 5 | 2 | 1 | 1 | | | | 12 | | |
| Chatham | 18 | 13 | Nickerson | Ensign | 4 | 2 | | | 1 | 1 | 1 | | 1 | | | | 10 | | |
| Chatham | 18 | 14 | Nickerson | Lumberd | | | | 1 | | | | | 2 | | | | 3 | | |
| Chatham | 18 | 15 | Nickerson | Caleb Jun | 1 | | 1 | | | | 1 | | | | | | 3 | | |
| Chatham | 18 | 16 | Nickerson | Leonard | 1 | | | 1 | | 1 | 1 | 1 | | | | | 5 | | |
| Chatham | 18 | 17 | Nickerson | David | 2 | | 1 | | | | 1 | | | | | | 4 | | |
| Chatham | 18 | 18 | Rider | Joseph | 1 | 1 | 2 | | 1 | | 2 | | 1 | | | | 8 | | |
| Chatham | 18 | 19 | Rider | Thacker | 1 | | | 1 | | 2 | | | 1 | | 1 | | 6 | | |
| Chatham | 18 | 20 | Rider | Moses | 1 | | | 1 | | | 1 | | 1 | | | | 4 | | |
| Chatham | 18 | 21 | Rider | Josiah | | 1 | 1 | | 1 | | 1 | 2 | | 1 | | | 7 | | |
| Chatham | 18 | 22 | Rider | Stephen | 3 | | | 1 | | 1 | | | 1 | | | | 6 | | |
| Chatham | 18 | 23 | Rider | Harding | | 1 | 1 | | 1 | | | 1 | | 1 | | | 5 | | |
| Chatham | 18 | 24 | Rider | Reuben | 3 | 1 | | | 1 | 1 | 1 | 2 | 1 | | | | 10 | | |
| Chatham | 18 | 25 | Rider | Kimbal | | 1 | 1 | | 1 | | 1 | 2 | | 1 | | | 6 | | |
| Chatham | 18 | 26 | Rider | Simeon | 2 | | 2 | | 1 | 2 | | 1 | 1 | | | | 9 | | |
| Chatham | 18 | 27 | Rider | Zenus | | | 1 | | 1 | | | 1 | | | | | 3 | | |
| Chatham | 18 | 28 | Rider | James | | | 1 | | 2 | | 1 | | | | | | 4 | | |
| Chatham | 18 | 29 | Snow | Nathaniel | 4 | | 1 | | | 1 | | 1 | | | | | 7 | | |
| Chatham | 18 | 30 | Sears | Richard | 1 | 1 | 2 | 1 | 1 | 1 | 2 | 1 | | 1 | | | 11 | | |
| Chatham | 18 | 31 | Smith | Dean | | | 1 | | 3 | | | 1 | | | | | 5 | | |
| Chatham | 18 | 32 | Smith | Jane Wd | | 1 | 1 | | | 1 | | | 1 | | | | 4 | | |
| Chatham | 18 | 33 | Smith | Nathaniel | 2 | | 1 | | | 1 | 1 | | | | | | 5 | | |
| Chatham | 18 | 34 | Snow | *uinyton | | | 1 | | 3 | | | 1 | | | | | 5 | | |
| Chatham | 18 | 35 | Stewart | William | | 1 | | 1 | | 1 | | | 1 | | | | 4 | | |
| Chatham | 18 | 36 | Smith | Thankful Wid | | | | | | | | 1 | | | | | 1 | | |
| Chatham | 18 | 37 | Snow | Aaron | | | 1 | | 3 | 2 | | 1 | | | | | 7 | | |
| Chatham | 18 | 38 | Smith | Gorge | | | 1 | | | | | 1 | | | | | 2 | | |
| Chatham | 18 | 39 | Smith | Gorge Jun | 2 | 2 | 1 | | 3 | 2 | | 1 | | | | | 11 | | |
| Chatham | 18 | 40 | Smith | Obadiah | 1 | | 1 | | | | | 1 | | | | | 3 | | |
| Chatham | 18 | 41 | Smith | Issac | 1 | 1 | 1 | | 2 | 2 | | 1 | | | | | 8 | | |
| Chatham | 18 | 42 | Smith | Stephen | 3 | | 1 | | 3 | | | 1 | | | | | 8 | | |
| Chatham | 18 | 43 | Smith | Richard | 4 | | 1 | | | | | 1 | | | | | 6 | | |
| Chatham | 18 | 44 | Smith | John | 2 | 1 | 1 | | | 1 | | 1 | | | | | 6 | | |
| Chatham | 18 | 45 | Smith | Benjm | 2 | | 1 | | | | | 1 | | | | | 4 | | |
| Chatham | 19 | 1 | Smith | Knowles | 2 | | 1 | | | | | 1 | | | | | 4 | | |
| Chatham | 19 | 2 | Trip | Jeptha | 2 | 2 | 1 | 1 | | 1 | | 1 | | | | | 8 | | |
| Chatham | 19 | 3 | Tailor | Janye | | | 1 | | 4 | | | 1 | | | | | 6 | | |
| Chatham | 19 | 4 | Tailor | Reuben | 3 | | 1 | | 3 | | | 1 | | | | | 8 | | |
| Chatham | 19 | 5 | Tailor | Thomas | 1 | | 2 | | 1 | 2 | | | 1 | | | | 7 | | |
| Chatham | 19 | 6 | Tailor | Zenas | 1 | | 1 | | 2 | | | 1 | | | | | 5 | | |
| Chatham | 19 | 7 | Tailor | John | 1 | | 1 | | 1 | | | 1 | | | | | 4 | | |
| Chatham | 19 | 8 | Tailor | James | 1 | | 1 | | 1 | | | 1 | | | | | 4 | | |
| Chatham | 19 | 9 | House | Elijah | | 1 | | | 1 | | | | | | | | 2 | | |
| Chatham | 19 | 10 | House | Seth | 2 | | 1 | | | | | 1 | | | | | 4 | | |
| Chatham | 19 | 11 | Smith | Araph | | 1 | | | 2 | | 1 | | | | | | 4 | | |
| Chatham | 19 | 12 | Hopkins | William | | 1 | | 2 | 1 | | 1 | | | | | | 5 | | |
| Chatham | 19 | 13 | Eldrege | Elnathan | | | 1 | 2 | 1 | | 1 | | | | | | 5 | | |
| Chatham | 19 | 14 | Higgins | Joseph | | | 1 | | 1 | | | | | | | | 3 | | |
| Chatham | 19 | 15 | Doane | Elisha | | 1 | | | 1 | | | | | | | | 2 | | |
| Chatham | 19 | 16 | Stetson | John | 1 | | 1 | | 2 | | | 1 | | | | | 5 | | |
| Chatham | 19 | 17 | Share | James | | | 1 | | 2 | | | | | | | | 4 | | |

# 1800 Chatham, Barnstable County, Massachusetts

| TOWN | PG# | LN# | LAST NAME | FIRST NAME | FREE WHITE MALES | | | | | FREE WHITE FEMALES | | | | | TOTAL ALL OTHER | TOTAL SLAVES | TOTALS | DISTRICT/ TOWNSHIP | NOTES |
|---|---|---|---|---|---|---|---|---|---|---|---|---|---|---|---|---|---|---|---|
| | | | | | under 10 | 10 to 16 | 16 to 26 | 26 to 45 | 45 and over | under 10 | 10 to 16 | 16 to 26 | 26 to 45 | 45 and over | | | | | |
| Chatham | 19 | 18 | Berre | David Jun | 1 | | 1 | | | | | 1 | | | | | 3 | | |
| Chatham | 19 | 19 | Tailor | Barnabas | | | 1 | | | 1 | | 1 | | | | | 3 | | |
| Chatham | 19 | 20 | Young | *yat | | 2 | | | 1 | 1 | | | 1 | | | | 5 | | |
| Chatham | 19 | 21 | Brussels | Phillip | 1 | | | 1 | | 1 | | | 1 | | | | 4 | | |
| Chatham | 19 | 22 | Harding | John Jun Widow | 1 | | 1 | | | 2 | 1 | | | | | | 5 | | |
| Chatham | 19 | 23 | Phips | Samuel | | | | 1 | | 2 | 1 | 1 | | | | | 5 | | |
| Chatham | 19 | 24 | Abelthough | William | | | | 1 | | 2 | | | 1 | | | | 4 | | |
| Chatham | 19 | 25 | Crowell | John | | | | 1 | | | | | 1 | | | | 2 | | |
| Chatham | 19 | 26 | Eldrege | Caleb | 1 | 1 | | 1 | | 2 | | | 1 | | | | 6 | | |
| Chatham | 19 | 27 | Eldrege | Jeremiah | | | 1 | 1 | 1 | | 1 | | 1 | | | | 5 | | |
| Chatham | 19 | 28 | Eldrege | Isaac Jun | 1 | | 1 | | | | | 1 | | | | | 3 | | |
| Chatham | 19 | 29 | Eldrege | Daniel Jun | 1 | | 1 | | | 1 | | | 1 | | | | 4 | | |
| Chatham | 19 | 30 | Harding | Thomas | 2 | | | 1 | | 1 | | 1 | | | | | 5 | | |
| Chatham | 19 | 31 | Stetson | John | 1 | | 1 | | | 2 | | 1 | | | | | 5 | | |
| Chatham | 19 | 32 | Smith | Asaph | | | 1 | | | 2 | | 1 | | | | | 4 | | |
| Chatham | 19 | 33 | Mouse | Seth | 2 | | | 1 | | | 1 | | 1 | | | | 5 | | |
| Chatham | 19 | 34 | Gould | David | | | 1 | | | 1 | | 1 | | | | | 3 | | |
| Chatham | 19 | 35 | Eldrege | Thankful Wid | 2 | 1 | | | | 2 | | | 1 | | | | 6 | | |
| Chatham | 19 | 36 | Crowell | David Jun | | | 1 | | | 1 | | 1 | | | | | 3 | | |
| Chatham | 19 | 37 | Rider | John | 2 | | | 1 | | 3 | | | 1 | | | | 7 | | |
| Chatham | 19 | 38 | Harding | Seth Junr | 1 | 1 | | | 1 | 3 | | 1 | 1 | | | | 8 | | |
| Chatham | 19 | 39 | Friday | Doane | 2 | | 1 | | | | | | 1 | | | | 4 | | |
| Chatham | 19 | 40 | Tailor | Seth | 1 | 1 | 1 | | | | 1 | 1 | | 1 | | | 6 | | |
| Chatham | 19 | 41 | Tailor | Mathew | | | | 1 | | | | | | 1 | | | 2 | | |
| Chatham | 19 | 42 | Tailor | Mathew Jun | 2 | | 1 | | | 2 | 2 | | 1 | | | | 8 | | |
| Chatham | 19 | 43 | Wing | Joseph | | | | 1 | | | | | | 1 | | | 2 | | |
| Chatham | 19 | 44 | Wing | Levi | | | 1 | | | 1 | 1 | | 1 | | | | 4 | | |
| Chatham | 19 | 45 | Young | Prince | 1 | 1 | | | 1 | 1 | | 1 | 1 | 1 | | | 7 | | |
| Chatham | 19 | 46 | Young | John | 2 | 1 | 1 | | | | | | 1 | | | | 5 | | |
| Chatham | 19 | 47 | Young | Simeon | 2 | | 1 | | 1 | 2 | 2 | 1 | 1 | 1 | | | 11 | | |
| Chatham | 19 | 48 | Young | Samuel | 2 | | 1 | | | 2 | | 1 | 1 | | | | 7 | | |
| Chatham | 20 | 1 | Young | Joseph | 1 | 1 | 1 | | | 3 | 1 | | 1 | | | | 8 | | |
| Chatham | 20 | 2 | Young | Ezekel | | 1 | | | | | | | 1 | | | | 2 | | |
| Chatham | 20 | 3 | Phillips | John | 1 | | | 1 | | | | | 1 | | | | 3 | | |
| Chatham | 20 | 4 | Higgins | Joseph 3rd | | | 1 | | | 1 | | | | 1 | | | 3 | | |
| Chatham | 20 | 5 | Harding | Theodore | | | 1 | | | | | | 1 | | | | 2 | | |
| Chatham | 20 | 6 | Woodson | Wid | | 1 | | | | 1 | | | 1 | | | | 3 | | |
| Chatham | 20 | 7 | Harding | Seth | 1 | 1 | | | 1 | 2 | 1 | 1 | | 1 | | | 8 | | |
| Chatham | 20 | 8 | Godfrey | Richard | 4 | 1 | | 1 | | 1 | | 1 | | | | | 8 | | |
| Chatham | 20 | 9 | Rider | William | | | 1 | | | 1 | | 1 | | | | | 3 | | |
| Chatham | 20 | 10 | Eldrege | Martha Wid | | | 1 | | | | 2 | | | 1 | | | 4 | | |
| Chatham | 20 | 11 | Gould | Richard | 1 | | 1 | | | 1 | | 1 | | | | | 4 | | |
| Chatham | 20 | 12 | Crowell | Stetson | 3 | | 1 | | | | | 1 | 1 | | | | 6 | | |
| Chatham | 20 | 13 | Harding | Thomas | 1 | | 1 | 1 | | 1 | | 1 | | | | | 5 | | |
| Chatham | 20 | 14 | Eldrege | Berse | 4 | | 1 | | | 1 | | 1 | | | | | 7 | | |
| Chatham | 20 | 15 | Berse | Ezra | | | 1 | | | 3 | | 1 | | | | | 5 | | |
| Chatham | 20 | 16 | Jackson | Bassett | 2 | | | 1 | | 3 | | | | | | | 6 | | |
| Chatham | 20 | 17 | Crowell | David Jun | | | 1 | | | 2 | | 1 | | | | | 4 | | |
| Chatham | 20 | 18 | Smith | John | 2 | 1 | | 1 | | 2 | 1 | 1 | | | | | 8 | | |
| Chatham | 20 | 19 | Snow | Nathaniel | 4 | | | 1 | | 1 | | | | 1 | | | 7 | | |
| Chatham | 20 | 20 | Atkins | Joshua | | 1 | | | | | | | 1 | | | | 2 | | |
| Chatham | 20 | 21 | Nickerson | Richard | 1 | 1 | | 1 | | | 1 | | 1 | | | | 5 | | |
| Chatham | 20 | 22 | Eldrege | Enos | 1 | | 1 | | | | | | 1 | | | | 3 | | |
| Chatham | 20 | 23 | Harding | Mulford | | | 1 | | | 1 | | | 1 | | | | 3 | | |
| Chatham | 20 | 24 | Rider | Thacher | 1 | | | 1 | | 2 | | | 1 | | | | 5 | | |
| Chatham | 20 | 25 | Hopkins | William | | | | 1 | | 3 | | | | 1 | | | 5 | | |
| Chatham | 20 | 26 | Nickerson | David | 2 | | 1 | | | | | | 1 | | | | 4 | | |
| Chatham | 20 | 27 | Bodshell | Mulford | | | 1 | | | | | | 1 | | | | 2 | | |
| Chatham | 20 | 28 | Buck | David | | 1 | | | 1 | 1 | | | | 1 | | | 4 | | |
| Chatham | 20 | 29 | Higgins | Joseph Jr | 2 | 1 | 1 | | 1 | 1 | 1 | | | 1 | | | 8 | | |
| Chatham | 20 | 30 | Godfrey | Joshua Jun | | 1 | | | 1 | 2 | 2 | | | 1 | | | 7 | | |
| Chatham | 20 | 31 | Young | Hemon | 1 | | 2 | 1 | | | | 1 | 1 | | | | 6 | | |
| Chatham | 20 | 32 | Godfrey | Bethiah Wd | | | | | | | | | 1 | | | | 1 | | |
| Chatham | 20 | 33 | Nickerson | Simeon | 1 | | 1 | | | | | | 1 | | | | 3 | | |
| Chatham | 20 | 34 | Rider | James | | | 1 | | | 3 | | | 1 | | | | 5 | | |
| Chatham | 20 | 35 | Hamilton | Samuel | | | 1 | | | 3 | | | 1 | | | | 5 | | |
| Chatham | 20 | 36 | Rider | Zenus | | | 1 | | | 1 | | 1 | | | | | 3 | | |
| Chatham | 20 | 37 | House | Salomon | 1 | 1 | | | | 1 | | 2 | | | | | 5 | | |
| Chatham | 20 | 38 | Crowell | John | | 1 | | | | | | 1 | | | | | 2 | | |
| Chatham | 20 | 39 | Smith | Isaac | 1 | 1 | | 1 | | 2 | 2 | | 1 | | | | 8 | | |
| Chatham | 20 | 40 | Kent | Edward | 1 | 2 | | 1 | | 1 | | | 1 | | | | 6 | | |
| Chatham | 20 | 41 | Nickerson | Ezra | 1 | | | 1 | | 2 | | | 1 | | | | 5 | | |
| Chatham | 20 | 42 | House | Mary Wd | 1 | | | | | 1 | | 1 | | | | | 3 | | |
| Chatham | 21 | 1 | Rider | Harding | | 1 | 1 | | 1 | | | 1 | 1 | | | | 5 | | |

## 1800 Dennis, Barnstable County, Massachusetts

| TOWN | PG# | LN# | LAST NAME | FIRST NAME | FREE WHITE MALES under 10 | 10 to 16 | 16 to 26 | 26 to 45 | 45 and over | FREE WHITE FEMALES under 10 | 10 to 16 | 16 to 26 | 26 to 45 | 45 and over | TOTAL ALL OTHER | TOTAL SLAVES | TOTALS | DISTRICT/ TOWNSHIP | NOTES |
|---|---|---|---|---|---|---|---|---|---|---|---|---|---|---|---|---|---|---|---|
| Dennis | 26 | 1 | Sears | Elisha | 1 | | | | 1 | 1 | 1 | | 1 | | | | 5 | | |
| Dennis | 26 | 2 | Sears | John | | | | | 1 | | | | | | | | 1 | | |
| Dennis | 26 | 3 | Sears | Seth | 1 | | | 1 | | 3 | | | 2 | 1 | | | 8 | | |
| Dennis | 26 | 4 | Sears | Joseph | 2 | 2 | 1 | 1 | | 1 | 1 | | 1 | | | | 9 | | |
| Dennis | 26 | 5 | Sears | Ekkanah | 2 | | | 1 | | 3 | 1 | | 1 | | | | 8 | | |
| Dennis | 26 | 6 | Sears | Hannah Wid | | | | | | | | | 1 | 1 | | | 2 | | |
| Dennis | 26 | 7 | Sears | Joshua | 1 | 2 | 1 | | 1 | 3 | | | 1 | 1 | | | 10 | | |
| Dennis | 26 | 8 | Sears | Micajah | 1 | | 1 | | 1 | | | | 1 | 1 | | | 5 | | |
| Dennis | 26 | 9 | Sears | John Jun | | 1 | 2 | | 1 | 1 | | | 3 | 1 | | | 9 | | |
| Dennis | 26 | 10 | Sears | Edmond | 1 | | 1 | | 1 | 2 | 1 | 2 | | 1 | | | 9 | | |
| Dennis | 26 | 11 | Sears | Jacob | 1 | | | 1 | | | | | 1 | | | | 3 | | |
| Dennis | 26 | 12 | Sears | Judah | | | | 1 | | 1 | | | 1 | | | | 3 | | |
| Dennis | 26 | 13 | Sears | Nathaniel | | | | 1 | | | | | | 1 | | | 2 | | |
| Dennis | 26 | 14 | Sears | Nathaniel Jun | 2 | 1 | 1 | 1 | | 1 | 1 | | 1 | | | | 8 | | |
| Dennis | 26 | 15 | Sears | Isaac | | 2 | | 1 | | | 1 | | 1 | | | | 5 | | |
| Dennis | 26 | 16 | Sears | Leonard | 2 | 1 | | 1 | | 3 | | | 1 | | | | 8 | | |
| Dennis | 26 | 17 | Sears | Stephen | | | | | 1 | 1 | | | 1 | | | | 3 | | |
| Dennis | 26 | 18 | Sears | Stephen Jun | 3 | 1 | 1 | 1 | | 1 | 2 | | 1 | | | | 10 | | |
| Dennis | 26 | 19 | Sears | Christopher | 1 | 1 | | 1 | | 3 | | | 1 | | | | 7 | | |
| Dennis | 26 | 20 | House | Seth | | | | 1 | | | | | | 1 | | | 2 | | |
| Dennis | 26 | 21 | Crowell | John | 1 | 2 | 1 | | 1 | 2 | | 1 | 1 | | | | 9 | | |
| Dennis | 26 | 22 | Crowell | Christopher | | 2 | 2 | | 1 | | | | 1 | 1 | | | 7 | | |
| Dennis | 26 | 23 | Hall | Thomas | 1 | | 1 | | | | | 1 | | | | | 3 | | |
| Dennis | 26 | 24 | Crowell | William | | | | 1 | | 1 | | | | 1 | | | 3 | | |
| Dennis | 26 | 25 | Crowell | Paul | | 1 | | | | 2 | | 1 | | | | | 4 | | |
| Dennis | 26 | 26 | Horton | Zabina | 2 | | | 1 | | | | | 1 | | | | 4 | | |
| Dennis | 26 | 27 | Homer | Stephen | 2 | | | | | | | 1 | | 1 | 1 | | 6 | | |
| Dennis | 26 | 28 | Chapman | David | | | | 1 | | | | 1 | | 1 | | | 3 | | |
| Dennis | 26 | 29 | Chapman | Paul | 2 | | | 1 | | | | 1 | 1 | 1 | | | 6 | | |
| Dennis | 26 | 30 | Chapman | John | | | | 1 | | | | | | 1 | | | 2 | | |
| Dennis | 26 | 31 | Chapman | John Jun | 1 | 1 | 1 | 1 | | 1 | 1 | | 1 | | | | 7 | | |
| Dennis | 26 | 32 | Wing | David | 1 | | | 1 | | 3 | | | 1 | | | | 6 | | |
| Dennis | 26 | 33 | House | Barnabas | | 1 | | 1 | | | | 2 | | 1 | | | 5 | | |
| Dennis | 26 | 34 | House | Sturges | | 1 | | 1 | | 1 | 1 | | 1 | | | | 5 | | |
| Dennis | 26 | 35 | Crowell | William Jun | 1 | | 1 | | | | | | 1 | | | | 3 | | |
| Dennis | 26 | 36 | Paddack | Judah | | 1 | 2 | | 1 | 3 | | 2 | | 1 | | | 10 | | |
| Dennis | 26 | 37 | House | Rebeccah Wid | | 2 | | | | | | 1 | 1 | | | | 4 | | |
| Dennis | 26 | 38 | Hall | Daniel | | 1 | | | | | | 1 | | 1 | | | 3 | | |
| Dennis | 26 | 39 | Hall | Enoch | 1 | 2 | | 1 | | 2 | 1 | | 1 | | | | 8 | | |
| Dennis | 26 | 40 | Paddack | Samuel | | 1 | | 1 | | | | 1 | | | | | 3 | | |
| Dennis | 26 | 41 | Burger | William | | 1 | 2 | | 1 | | 1 | | 1 | | | | 6 | | |
| Dennis | 26 | 42 | Hall | Edmond | 1 | | 1 | | | | | 1 | | | | | 3 | | |
| Dennis | 26 | 43 | Crosby | Barnabas | 2 | 1 | | 1 | | 1 | 2 | 1 | 1 | | | | 9 | | |
| Dennis | 26 | 44 | Aspendelow | Amanuel | 1 | | 1 | | | | | 1 | | | | | 3 | | |
| Dennis | 26 | 45 | House | Jonathan | | | | 1 | | | | | 1 | | | | 2 | | |
| Dennis | 26 | 46 | House | Levi | | 1 | | 1 | | | | | 1 | | | | 3 | | |
| Dennis | 26 | 47 | House | David 3d | | 1 | | | | | | 1 | | | | | 2 | | |
| Dennis | 27 | 1 | Crowell | Nathan | 2 | | 1 | | 2 | | | | 1 | | | | 6 | | |
| Dennis | 27 | 2 | Seabury | David | | 1 | 1 | | 2 | 1 | 1 | 1 | | | | | 7 | | |
| Dennis | 27 | 3 | House | Stephen | 1 | | 1 | | 1 | 2 | 2 | | 1 | | | | 8 | | |
| Dennis | 27 | 4 | Capp | John | | | | 1 | | | | 1 | | 1 | | | 3 | | |
| Dennis | 27 | 5 | House | Paul | | 1 | 1 | | 2 | 2 | 1 | | 1 | | | | 8 | | |
| Dennis | 27 | 6 | House | Ezra | 1 | | 1 | | 1 | 2 | 1 | 1 | | 1 | | | 8 | | |
| Dennis | 27 | 7 | House | Seth | | 1 | 1 | | 1 | 1 | | 2 | | 1 | | | 7 | | |
| Dennis | 27 | 8 | House | Joseph | 1 | 2 | 1 | | 1 | 2 | 2 | | | | | | 9 | | |
| Dennis | 27 | 9 | Crowell | Josiah | | 1 | 1 | | 1 | 2 | 1 | | 1 | | | | 7 | | |
| Dennis | 27 | 10 | Hall | Anna Wid | | | | | | | | 1 | | 1 | | | 2 | | |
| Dennis | 27 | 11 | Hall | Donwell | | | 1 | | | | | | 1 | | | | 2 | | |
| Dennis | 27 | 12 | Hall | Benjm | 1 | | 1 | | 1 | | | 1 | | 1 | | | 5 | | |
| Dennis | 27 | 13 | Crowell | Aaron | | 2 | 2 | | 1 | | 1 | 1 | 2 | | | | 9 | | |
| Dennis | 27 | 14 | Hall | Josiah | | 3 | | 1 | | | 1 | | 1 | | | | 6 | | |
| Dennis | 27 | 15 | Hall | Nathan | 1 | 1 | 1 | 1 | | 3 | 1 | 1 | 2 | | | | 11 | | |
| Dennis | 27 | 16 | Hall | Joshua | 1 | | 1 | | | 1 | | 1 | | | | | 4 | | |
| Dennis | 27 | 17 | Hall | Barnabas | | 1 | 1 | | 1 | | | 2 | | 1 | | | 6 | | |
| Dennis | 27 | 18 | Hall | Nathaniel | | 1 | | 1 | | | | 1 | | 1 | | | 4 | | |
| Dennis | 27 | 19 | Hall | Jesse | 1 | | 1 | | | 1 | | 1 | | | | | 4 | | |
| Dennis | 27 | 20 | Hall | Josiah Junr | | 1 | | | | | | 1 | | | | | 2 | | |
| Dennis | 27 | 21 | House | Thankfull Wid | | | | | | | | 1 | 1 | | | | 2 | | |
| Dennis | 27 | 22 | Stone | Nathan Jun | 2 | | 1 | | 1 | | | 1 | | | | | 5 | | |
| Dennis | 27 | 23 | Hall | Henry | | 2 | | 1 | | 3 | 1 | | 1 | | | | 8 | | |
| Dennis | 27 | 24 | Tailor | Reuben | 2 | | | 1 | | 1 | | | 1 | | | | 5 | | |
| Dennis | 27 | 25 | House | Elijah | 1 | | 1 | | | | | 1 | | | | | 3 | | |
| Dennis | 27 | 26 | Vincent | Isaac | 1 | 1 | 2 | | 1 | | 1 | | 1 | | | | 7 | | |
| Dennis | 27 | 27 | Hall | Josiah | | 2 | 2 | | 1 | | | 1 | | 1 | | | 7 | | |
| Dennis | 27 | 28 | Vincent | David | | | | 1 | | | | | 1 | | | | 2 | | |
| Dennis | 27 | 29 | Hall | Stephen | | | | 1 | | | | | 1 | | | | 2 | | |
| Dennis | 27 | 30 | House | Nehemiah | 1 | 1 | 3 | | 1 | | | 2 | 1 | | | | 9 | | |
| Dennis | 27 | 31 | House | Elisha | | | | 1 | | | | | 1 | | | | 2 | | |
| Dennis | 27 | 32 | House | Elisha 3d | 1 | | 1 | | 1 | 2 | 1 | | 1 | | | | 8 | | |

# 1800 Dennis, Barnstable County, Massachusetts

| TOWN | PG# | LN# | LAST NAME | FIRST NAME | FREE WHITE MALES | | | | | FREE WHITE FEMALES | | | | | TOTAL ALL OTHER | TOTAL SLAVES | TOTALS | DISTRICT/ TOWNSHIP | NOTES |
|------|-----|-----|-----------|------------|---|---|---|---|---|---|---|---|---|---|---|---|---|---|---|
| | | | | | under 10 | 10 to 16 | 16 to 26 | 26 to 45 | 45 and over | under 10 | 10 to 16 | 16 to 26 | 26 to 45 | 45 and over | | | | | |
| Dennis | 27 | 33 | House | Elkanah | 1 | 1 | 2 | | 1 | | 1 | | | 1 | | | 7 | | |
| Dennis | 27 | 34 | House | Thankfull Jun Wid | | | | | | | 1 | | | 1 | | | 2 | | |
| Dennis | 27 | 35 | House | Nathan Rev | | | 1 | 1 | | | | 2 | | 1 | | | 5 | | |
| Dennis | 27 | 36 | House | John | | 1 | 1 | 1 | | | | 1 | | 1 | | | 5 | | |
| Dennis | 27 | 37 | House | Obed | 2 | | | 1 | | 2 | 1 | | 1 | 1 | | | 8 | | |
| Dennis | 27 | 38 | House | Abraham | | | | 1 | | | | | | 2 | | | 3 | | |
| Dennis | 27 | 39 | House | Micah | | 1 | | | | | | 1 | | | | | 2 | | |
| Dennis | 27 | 40 | House | Judah | | 1 | | | | 1 | | 1 | | | | | 3 | | |
| Dennis | 27 | 41 | House | William | | | 1 | | | | | | 1 | | | | 2 | | |
| Dennis | 27 | 42 | House | Jonah | | 1 | | 1 | | 1 | 1 | 1 | 1 | | | | 6 | | |
| Dennis | 27 | 43 | House | Jabez | | | 1 | | | 1 | 1 | | | | | | 3 | | |
| Dennis | 28 | 1 | Hedge | Daniel | 1 | | 1 | | | 1 | | 2 | | | | | 5 | | |
| Dennis | 28 | 2 | Eldrege | Daniel | 1 | | | 1 | | 2 | | 2 | 1 | | | | 7 | | |
| Dennis | 28 | 3 | House | Jerusha Wd | 1 | 1 | 1 | | | | 1 | 1 | | 1 | | | 6 | | |
| Dennis | 28 | 4 | House | Joshua | | | 1 | | | | | 1 | | | | | 2 | | |
| Dennis | 28 | 5 | House | Phillip | | | 1 | | | 2 | | | 1 | | | | 4 | | |
| Dennis | 28 | 6 | Gerom | Lot | 2 | 1 | | 1 | | 2 | | | 1 | | | | 7 | | |
| Dennis | 28 | 7 | House | Nathaniel Jun | | | 1 | | | | | | 1 | | | | 2 | | |
| Dennis | 28 | 8 | House | Jeremiah | 1 | | 2 | | 1 | | | 1 | 1 | 1 | | | 7 | | |
| Dennis | 28 | 9 | House | Jonathan Jun | 2 | 1 | 1 | 1 | | | | 2 | 1 | | | | 8 | | |
| Dennis | 28 | 10 | House | Ira | | 1 | | | | | | 2 | | | | | 3 | | |
| Dennis | 28 | 11 | House | Noah | | | 1 | | | 2 | 1 | | 1 | | | | 5 | | |
| Dennis | 28 | 12 | House | Nehemiah | 1 | | 1 | | | 2 | | | 1 | | | | 5 | | |
| Dennis | 28 | 13 | House | Elisha Jun | 1 | | 2 | | 1 | 2 | 1 | 2 | | 1 | | | 10 | | |
| Dennis | 28 | 14 | House | James | | 3 | | 1 | | | | 2 | | 1 | | | 7 | | |
| Dennis | 28 | 15 | House | Reuben | 2 | | 1 | | | 2 | | 1 | | | | | 6 | | |
| Dennis | 28 | 16 | House | Josiah | | 1 | | 1 | | 1 | 1 | | 1 | | | | 5 | | |
| Dennis | 28 | 17 | House | David Jun | 2 | | 1 | | | 1 | | | | 1 | | | 5 | | |
| Dennis | 28 | 18 | House | Samuel | | | | 1 | | | | 1 | | 1 | | | 4 | | |
| Dennis | 28 | 19 | Toby | Stephen | | | | 2 | | | 1 | 1 | | | | | 4 | | |
| Dennis | 28 | 20 | Toby | Seth | | | | 1 | | | | | | 1 | | | 2 | | |
| Dennis | 28 | 21 | Toby | Seth Jun | 2 | | | 1 | | 1 | 1 | | 1 | | | | 6 | | |
| Dennis | 28 | 22 | Tailor | Simeon | | | 2 | 1 | 1 | | | | 1 | 1 | | | 6 | | |
| Dennis | 28 | 23 | Tailor | Simeon | | | 1 | | | | | | 1 | | | | 2 | | |
| Dennis | 28 | 24 | House | Edmand | | | | 1 | | | | | 1 | | | | 2 | | |
| Dennis | 28 | 25 | House | Gamiel | | 1 | | | | | | 1 | | | | | 2 | | |
| Dennis | 28 | 26 | Bourn | Richard | | 1 | | | | 1 | | 1 | | | | | 3 | | |
| Dennis | 28 | 27 | Wexsom | Joshua | | 2 | 1 | 1 | | 4 | | 1 | 1 | | | | 10 | | |
| Dennis | 28 | 28 | Wexsom | Daniel | 2 | 1 | 1 | | 1 | | 1 | | | 1 | | | 7 | | |
| Dennis | 28 | 29 | Whitamore | Edward | 1 | 1 | | | 1 | 3 | 1 | | | | | | 7 | | |
| Dennis | 28 | 30 | Witamore | Edward Jun | 1 | 1 | | | | | | | 1 | | | | 3 | | |
| Dennis | 28 | 31 | Covil | Jonathan | 1 | | | 1 | | 1 | | | 1 | | | | 4 | | |
| Dennis | 28 | 32 | Covil | Nathaniel | | | 1 | 1 | 1 | | | | 1 | 1 | | | 5 | | |
| Dennis | 28 | 33 | Covil | John | 1 | | 1 | | | | | | 1 | | | | 3 | | |
| Dennis | 28 | 34 | Bangs | Seth | | | 1 | | | | | | 1 | | | | 2 | | |
| Dennis | 28 | 35 | Covil | Samuel | 2 | 1 | | 1 | | 2 | | | 1 | | | | 7 | | |
| Dennis | 28 | 36 | Baker | Seth | | 2 | 3 | 1 | 1 | | | 1 | 2 | 1 | | | 11 | | |
| Dennis | 28 | 37 | Baker | Goram | 1 | 1 | | 1 | | | | 1 | 1 | | | | 5 | | |
| Dennis | 28 | 38 | Baker | Judah | | 1 | | | | | | 1 | 1 | | | | 4 | | |
| Dennis | 28 | 39 | Baker | Nathaniel | | | 1 | | | | | | 1 | 1 | | | 3 | | |
| Dennis | 28 | 40 | Whelding | Abahail Wd | | 1 | | | | | 1 | 1 | | 1 | | | 4 | | |
| Dennis | 28 | 41 | Collins | David | | | 2 | | 1 | 1 | 2 | | | 1 | | | 7 | | |
| Dennis | 28 | 42 | Shearman | Abraham | 1 | | 2 | | | | 1 | | | | | | 4 | | |
| Dennis | 28 | 43 | Killey | Sy* | 1 | | | 1 | | 2 | | | 1 | | | | 5 | | |
| Dennis | 28 | 44 | Killey | Hettel | | | 1 | | | | | | | 1 | | | 2 | | |
| Dennis | 29 | 1 | Killey | Hettel Jun | 2 | | 3 | 1 | | 2 | | 1 | | | | | 9 | | |
| Dennis | 29 | 2 | Nickerson | Josiah | 2 | | 2 | | 1 | 1 | 1 | | | 1 | | | 8 | | |
| Dennis | 29 | 3 | Ellis | Levi | 2 | | | 1 | | | | 1 | 1 | | | | 5 | | |
| Dennis | 29 | 4 | Hording | Gidion | 3 | | | 1 | | | 1 | 1 | 1 | 1 | | | 8 | | |
| Dennis | 29 | 5 | Bangs | Jonathan | | 1 | | 1 | | | 1 | | 1 | | | | 4 | | |
| Dennis | 29 | 6 | Bangs | Allen | 2 | | | 1 | | 2 | | | 1 | | | | 6 | | |
| Dennis | 29 | 7 | Rider | William | 1 | 1 | 2 | | 1 | | | | | 1 | | | 6 | | |
| Dennis | 29 | 8 | Baker | David | | | 1 | | | 2 | | | 1 | | | | 4 | | |
| Dennis | 29 | 9 | Nickerson | James | 1 | 1 | | 1 | | | | | | 1 | | | 4 | | |
| Dennis | 29 | 10 | Nickerson | James Jun | 1 | | 1 | | | 1 | | | 1 | | | | 4 | | |
| Dennis | 29 | 11 | Warner | Gilbert | | 1 | | | | 1 | | 1 | | | | | 3 | | |
| Dennis | 29 | 12 | Nick | Jeptha | | | 1 | | | 1 | | 1 | | | | | 3 | | |
| Dennis | 29 | 13 | Chase | Nathan | 1 | 2 | | | 1 | 3 | | 1 | 1 | | | | 9 | | |
| Dennis | 29 | 14 | Ellis | Stephen | 2 | | | 1 | | 1 | | | 1 | | | | 5 | | |
| Dennis | 29 | 15 | Baxter | Benjm | | 1 | | 1 | | | | 1 | 1 | 1 | | | 5 | | |
| Dennis | 29 | 16 | Baxter | David | 1 | | 1 | | | | | | 1 | | | | 3 | | |
| Dennis | 29 | 17 | Nickerson | Silvanus | 2 | | 1 | | | | 1 | | 1 | | | | 5 | | |
| Dennis | 29 | 18 | Nickerson | Thankfull Wid | 1 | | 3 | | | 1 | | 1 | 1 | 1 | | | 8 | | |
| Dennis | 29 | 19 | Nickerson | John Jun | 1 | 1 | | 1 | | 2 | | | 1 | | | | 6 | | |
| Dennis | 29 | 20 | Nickerson | David | | | 1 | | | 3 | | | 1 | | | | 5 | | |
| Dennis | 29 | 21 | Nickerson | Heman | | | 1 | | | 1 | | 1 | | | | | 3 | | |
| Dennis | 29 | 22 | Killey | Verna | | 2 | | 1 | | 1 | 1 | 1 | | 1 | | | 7 | | |
| Dennis | 29 | 23 | Killey | Hiram | 1 | | 1 | | | | | 1 | | | | | 3 | | |
| Dennis | 29 | 24 | Nickerson | Eleazor | | | | 1 | | | | | | 2 | | | 3 | | |

# 1800 Dennis, Barnstable County, Massachusetts

| TOWN | PG# | LN# | LAST NAME | FIRST NAME | FREE WHITE MALES | | | | | FREE WHITE FEMALES | | | | | TOTAL ALL OTHER | TOTAL SLAVES | TOTALS | DISTRICT/ TOWNSHIP | NOTES |
|---|---|---|---|---|---|---|---|---|---|---|---|---|---|---|---|---|---|---|---|
| | | | | | under 10 | 10 to 16 | 16 to 26 | 26 to 45 | 45 and over | under 10 | 10 to 16 | 16 to 26 | 26 to 45 | 45 and over | | | | | |
| Dennis | 29 | 25 | Nickerson | John | | 1 | 2 | | 1 | | 1 | | | 1 | | | 6 | | |
| Dennis | 29 | 26 | Baker | Simeon | | | 1 | | 1 | | 1 | | | 1 | | | 4 | | |
| Dennis | 29 | 27 | Rabens | Henry | 2 | | | 1 | | 1 | 1 | 1 | 1 | | | | 7 | | |
| Dennis | 29 | 28 | Trip | Jonathan | 1 | | 2 | 1 | | 3 | | 1 | 1 | | | | 9 | | |
| Dennis | 29 | 29 | Ellis | Cornelus | 1 | | | 1 | | 2 | | | 1 | | | | 5 | | |
| Dennis | 29 | 30 | Ellis | William | | 1 | | 1 | | | | 2 | | 1 | | | 5 | | |
| Dennis | 29 | 31 | Robinson | James | 1 | | | 1 | | 1 | | 1 | | | | | 4 | | |
| Dennis | 29 | 32 | Rabens | Eli | | 1 | | | | 1 | | 1 | | | | | 3 | | |
| Dennis | 29 | 33 | Studley | Samuel | 2 | | 1 | | | 1 | | | 1 | | | | 5 | | |
| Dennis | 29 | 34 | Studley | Abner | 1 | | 1 | | | | | 1 | | | | | 3 | | |
| Dennis | 29 | 35 | Studley | Anthony | | 1 | | 1 | | 2 | 1 | | 1 | | | | 6 | | |
| Dennis | 29 | 36 | Studley | Edward | | 1 | | | | | | 1 | | | | | 2 | | |
| Dennis | 29 | 37 | Tailor | John | 1 | | 1 | | | 1 | | 1 | | | | | 4 | | |
| Dennis | 29 | 38 | Bassett | Jonathan | 1 | | 2 | | 1 | | | 3 | | 1 | | | 8 | | |
| Dennis | 29 | 39 | Rogers | Smith | 2 | 1 | 1 | | 1 | 2 | | 1 | | 1 | | | 9 | | |
| Dennis | 29 | 40 | Rogers | Smith Jun | 1 | | | 1 | | | | 1 | | | | | 3 | | |
| Dennis | 29 | 41 | Chase | Thomas | | | | 1 | | | | | | 1 | | | 2 | | |
| Dennis | 30 | 1 | Baker | Henry | 2 | | 1 | | | | | 1 | | | | | 4 | | |
| Dennis | 30 | 2 | Crowell | Ephraim | | 1 | 1 | 1 | | | | | | 2 | | | 5 | | |
| Dennis | 30 | 3 | Wener | Caleb | | 2 | | 1 | | 2 | 1 | | 1 | | | | 7 | | |
| Dennis | 30 | 4 | Baxter | Ebenezer | | | 1 | | | 2 | 2 | | 1 | | | | 6 | | |
| Dennis | 30 | 5 | Baker | Paul | 2 | 1 | 1 | | 1 | 3 | 1 | 1 | 1 | | | | 11 | | |
| Dennis | 30 | 6 | Baker | Jeremiah | | 1 | 1 | 1 | | 1 | 1 | 1 | 1 | 1 | | | 7 | | |
| Dennis | 30 | 7 | Baker | Edward | | 1 | | | | 2 | | 2 | | | | | 5 | | |
| Dennis | 30 | 8 | Baker | John | 2 | | 2 | | 1 | 2 | 2 | | 2 | | | | 11 | | |
| Dennis | 30 | 9 | Baker | John Jun | | 1 | | | | | | 1 | 1 | | | | 3 | | |
| Dennis | 30 | 10 | Baker | Cornelus | | 1 | | | | | | | 1 | | | | 2 | | |
| Dennis | 30 | 11 | Chase | Thomas Jun | 2 | | | 1 | | 2 | | | 1 | | | | 6 | | |
| Dennis | 30 | 12 | Chase | Abner | | 1 | | 1 | 1 | | | | | 1 | | | 4 | | |
| Dennis | 30 | 13 | Chase | Owen | 2 | 1 | | 1 | | 3 | | | 1 | | | | 8 | | |
| Dennis | 30 | 14 | Chase | Lot | 2 | | | 1 | | | 2 | 2 | 1 | | | | 8 | | |
| Dennis | 30 | 15 | Chase | Joseph | | | | 1 | | | | | | 2 | | | 3 | | |
| Dennis | 30 | 16 | Chase | Freeman | | 1 | | | | | | 1 | | | | | 2 | | |
| Dennis | 30 | 17 | Chase | Lot Jun | 2 | | | 1 | | 1 | | 1 | | | | | 5 | | |
| Dennis | 30 | 18 | Killey | Jeremiah | 1 | 3 | 1 | 1 | | | | 1 | | 1 | | | 8 | | |
| Dennis | 30 | 19 | Killey | Richard | 1 | | 1 | | | | | | 1 | | | | 3 | | |
| Dennis | 30 | 20 | Baker | Archelus | 4 | | 1 | | | 1 | 1 | | 1 | | | | 8 | | |
| Dennis | 30 | 21 | Crowell | Abner | 1 | | 1 | | | 3 | | | 1 | | | | 6 | | |
| Dennis | 30 | 22 | Howland | Elisha | 1 | | 1 | | | 2 | | 1 | | | | | 5 | | |
| Dennis | 30 | 23 | Howland | Benjamin | | 1 | 1 | | 1 | | | 1 | | 1 | | | 5 | | |
| Dennis | 30 | 24 | Howland | Joshua | 2 | | | 1 | | 1 | | | 1 | | | | 5 | | |
| Dennis | 30 | 25 | House | David | 3 | | | 1 | | 1 | | | 1 | | | | 6 | | |
| Dennis | 30 | 26 | Crowell | Edward Jun | 2 | 1 | | 1 | | 1 | | | | 1 | | | 6 | | |
| Dennis | 30 | 27 | Bangs | Jediah | | 1 | 2 | | 1 | 1 | | | | 1 | | | 6 | | |
| Dennis | 30 | 28 | Swain | Desire | | | | | | | | | 1 | | | | 1 | | |
| Dennis | 30 | 29 | Baker | Samuel | 1 | | | 1 | | 1 | 1 | | 1 | | | | 6 | | |
| Dennis | 30 | 30 | Killey | Abner | 2 | | 1 | | | 1 | | 1 | | | | | 5 | | |
| Dennis | 30 | 31 | Killey | Silvanus | 2 | 1 | | 1 | | 1 | 1 | | 1 | | | | 7 | | |
| Dennis | 30 | 32 | Crowell | Solomon | | | | 1 | | 1 | 1 | | 1 | | | | 4 | | |
| Dennis | 30 | 33 | Killey | Joseph Jun | 2 | 1 | | 1 | | 2 | | | 1 | | | | 7 | | |
| Dennis | 30 | 34 | Killey | Reuben | 1 | 1 | | 1 | | 3 | | 1 | | | | | 7 | | |
| Dennis | 30 | 35 | Killey | Joseph | | | | 1 | | | | | | 2 | | | 3 | | |
| Dennis | 30 | 36 | Chase | Gaurel | 1 | | | 1 | | 2 | | | 1 | | | | 5 | | |
| Dennis | 30 | 37 | Wexsom | Solomon | 1 | 1 | | 1 | | 1 | | | 1 | | | | 5 | | |
| Dennis | 30 | 38 | Chase | Joseph Jun | 2 | | | 1 | | | | 2 | 1 | | | | 6 | | |
| Dennis | 30 | 39 | Baker | Richard | 2 | | 1 | | | | | | 1 | | | | 4 | | |
| Dennis | 30 | 40 | Killey | Daniel | 2 | | 2 | 1 | | 1 | 1 | 3 | | 1 | | | 11 | | |
| Dennis | 30 | 41 | Wexsom | Barnabas | 2 | 1 | | 1 | | | | | 1 | | | | 5 | | |
| Dennis | 31 | 1 | Wexsom | Darcey Wid | 1 | | | | | | 2 | | 1 | 1 | | | 5 | | |
| Dennis | 31 | 2 | Chase | Obed | 2 | | 1 | | | 1 | | 1 | | | | | 5 | | |
| Dennis | 31 | 3 | Baker | Silvanus | 2 | | | 1 | | 2 | 1 | 1 | 1 | 1 | | | 9 | | |
| Dennis | 31 | 4 | Crowell | Reuben | | | 1 | | | | 1 | 1 | | 3 | | | 6 | | |
| Dennis | 31 | 5 | Baker | Timothy | | | 1 | | | | | | 1 | | | | 2 | | |
| Dennis | 31 | 6 | Baker | Davis | | 1 | | 1 | | 3 | | | 1 | | | | 6 | | |
| Dennis | 31 | 7 | Eldrege | Prince | 1 | | 1 | | | | | 1 | | | | | 3 | | |
| Dennis | 31 | 8 | Baker | Allen | 3 | | | 1 | | | | 1 | 1 | | | | 6 | | |
| Dennis | 31 | 9 | Baxter | Reuben | | 1 | | | | | | 1 | 1 | | | | 3 | | |
| Dennis | 31 | 10 | Baxter | John | 1 | | 1 | | | | | 1 | 1 | | | | 4 | | |
| Dennis | 31 | 11 | Chase | Samuel | 1 | 2 | | 1 | | 3 | 1 | | 1 | | | | 9 | | |
| Dennis | 31 | 12 | Chase | Benjm | | 1 | | | | | | 1 | | | | | 2 | | |
| Dennis | 31 | 13 | Baker | Barnabas | | 1 | | | | 1 | | 1 | | | | | 3 | | |
| Dennis | 31 | 14 | Baker | Hemon | | 1 | | | | 1 | | 1 | | | | | 3 | | |
| Dennis | 31 | 15 | Baker | Judah Jun | | 1 | 1 | | | 1 | | 1 | 1 | | | | 5 | | |
| Dennis | 31 | 16 | Baker | Judah 3d | | | 1 | | | 1 | | 1 | | | | | 3 | | |
| Dennis | 31 | 17 | Baker | Frances | | 1 | | | | 1 | | 1 | | | | | 3 | | |
| Dennis | 31 | 18 | Nickerson | Jonathan | | | 1 | | | | | 1 | | 1 | | | 3 | | |
| Dennis | 31 | 19 | Nickerson | Betsey Wid | | 1 | 1 | | | 1 | 1 | | 1 | | | | 5 | | |
| Dennis | 31 | 20 | Nickerson | Ezrael | 2 | | | 1 | | | | | 1 | | | | 5 | | |
| Dennis | 31 | 21 | Nickerson | John | | 2 | 2 | | 1 | | 1 | | | 1 | | | 7 | | |

# 1800 Dennis, Barnstable County, Massachusetts

| TOWN | PG# | LN# | LAST NAME | FIRST NAME | FREE WHITE MALES | | | | | FREE WHITE FEMALES | | | | | TOTAL ALL OTHER | TOTAL SLAVES | TOTALS | DISTRICT/ TOWNSHIP | NOTES |
|---|---|---|---|---|---|---|---|---|---|---|---|---|---|---|---|---|---|---|---|
| | | | | | under 10 | 10 to 16 | 16 to 26 | 26 to 45 | 45 and over | under 10 | 10 to 16 | 16 to 26 | 26 to 45 | 45 and over | | | | | |
| Dennis | 31 | 22 | Nickerson | Josiah | 1 | | 1 | | | | | 1 | | | | | 3 | | |
| Dennis | 31 | 23 | Baker | Theofelus | 1 | | 1 | | | | | 1 | | | | | 3 | | |
| Dennis | 31 | 24 | Baker | Ebenezer | | | 1 | | | | | 1 | | | | | 2 | | |
| Dennis | 31 | 25 | Baker | Crowell | | | 1 | | | | | 1 | | | | | 2 | | |
| Dennis | 31 | 26 | Baker | Experience Wd | | | 1 | | | | | 1 | | 2 | | | 4 | | |
| Dennis | 31 | 27 | Baker | Zenus | 2 | 1 | | 1 | | | | | 1 | | | | 5 | | |
| Dennis | 31 | 28 | Baker | Seth 3d | 1 | | 1 | | | | | 1 | 1 | | | | 4 | | |
| Dennis | 31 | 29 | Baker | Eliphalet | | | 1 | | | 2 | | | 1 | | | | 4 | | |
| Dennis | 31 | 30 | Baker | Isaac | | 1 | | | | | | 1 | | | | | 2 | | |
| Dennis | 31 | 31 | Baker | Seth Jun | | 1 | | 1 | | | | 1 | | 1 | | | 4 | | |
| Dennis | 31 | 32 | Howland | Benjamin Jun | | | 1 | | | 1 | | 1 | | | | | 3 | | |
| Dennis | 31 | 33 | Baker | Freeman | 1 | | 1 | | | | | 1 | | | | | 3 | | |
| Dennis | 31 | 34 | Baker | Josiah | 2 | | 1 | 1 | | | | 1 | | | | | 5 | | |
| Dennis | 31 | 35 | Baker | John 3d | | | 1 | | | 2 | | 1 | | | | | 4 | | |
| Dennis | 31 | 36 | Studley | Silvanus | 1 | | | 1 | | 2 | | | 1 | | | | 5 | | |
| Dennis | 31 | 37 | Killey | Amos | | 1 | | | | | | 1 | | | | | 2 | | |
| Dennis | 31 | 38 | Nickerson | Daniel | | 1 | | | | | | 1 | | | | | 2 | | |
| Dennis | 31 | 39 | Crowell | Edward | | 1 | | | 1 | 1 | | | | 1 | | | 4 | | |
| Dennis | 31 | 40 | Crowell | Thomas | 3 | | | 1 | | 1 | 2 | | 1 | | | | 8 | | |
| Dennis | 31 | 41 | Crowell | Elisha | 1 | 1 | | 1 | 1 | | 2 | 1 | 1 | | | | 8 | | |
| Dennis | 31 | 42 | Crowell | Heman | 3 | | 2 | | 2 | 1 | 1 | | 1 | | | | 10 | | |
| Dennis | 32 | 1 | Crowell | Freeman | 1 | | 1 | | | | | 1 | | | | | 3 | | |
| Dennis | 32 | 2 | Crowell | Isaac | 2 | | 1 | | | | | 1 | | | | | 4 | | |
| Dennis | 32 | 3 | Crowell | Anthony | 3 | | | 1 | | 1 | | | 1 | 1 | | | 7 | | |
| Dennis | 32 | 4 | Gage | James | 1 | 1 | 1 | | | 1 | 2 | | 1 | 1 | | | 8 | | |
| Dennis | 32 | 5 | Crowell | Venna | 2 | | | 1 | | | | | 1 | | | | 4 | | |
| Dennis | 32 | 6 | Baxter | Obed | 2 | 1 | | | | | | | 1 | | | | 4 | | |
| Dennis | 32 | 7 | Crowell | Judah | 3 | 1 | 1 | | | 1 | | | 1 | | | | 7 | | |
| Dennis | 32 | 8 | Killey | Eleazar | 1 | 1 | 1 | | 1 | 1 | | 1 | | 2 | | | 8 | | |
| Dennis | 32 | 9 | Killey | Brownen | 1 | | 2 | 1 | | 1 | 2 | | 1 | | | | 8 | | |
| Dennis | 32 | 10 | Nickerson | Simeon | 1 | | 1 | | | 3 | | 1 | | | | | 6 | | |
| Dennis | 32 | 11 | Crowell | Jonathan | | 1 | 2 | 1 | | 2 | 1 | | 1 | | | | 8 | | |
| Dennis | 32 | 12 | Crowell | David | 1 | 2 | 1 | 1 | | 3 | | | 1 | | | | 9 | | |
| Dennis | 32 | 13 | Crowell | Sarah Wid | | 2 | | | | 2 | 1 | 3 | | 1 | | | 9 | | |
| Dennis | 32 | 14 | Crowell | Ebenezer | 1 | | 1 | | | 1 | 1 | 1 | 1 | | | | 6 | | |

# 1800 Eastham, Barnstable County, Massachusetts

| TOWN | PG# | LN# | LAST NAME | FIRST NAME | M under 10 | M 10 to 16 | M 16 to 26 | M 26 to 45 | M 45 and over | F under 10 | F 10 to 16 | F 16 to 26 | F 26 to 45 | F 45 and over | TOTAL ALL OTHER | TOTAL SLAVES | TOTALS | DISTRICT/ TOWNSHIP | NOTES |
|---|---|---|---|---|---|---|---|---|---|---|---|---|---|---|---|---|---|---|---|
| Eastham | 76 | 1 | Atwood | James | | | | | 1 | | | | | 1 | | | 2 | | |
| Eastham | 76 | 2 | Atwood | Richard | | 1 | 2 | | 1 | | | | 1 | 1 | | | 6 | | |
| Eastham | 76 | 3 | Atwood | Hezekiah | | | | 1 | | | | | | 1 | | | 2 | | |
| Eastham | 76 | 4 | Atwood | Barnabas | | 1 | | | 1 | 1 | 1 | | | 1 | | | 6 | | |
| Eastham | 76 | 5 | Anderson | William | 3 | 1 | 2 | | 1 | | 1 | 1 | | 1 | | | 10 | | |
| Eastham | 76 | 6 | Brown | David | | 2 | 2 | | 1 | | 1 | 1 | 1 | | | | 8 | | |
| Eastham | 76 | 7 | Brown | Higgins | | | | 1 | | | | | | 1 | | | 2 | | |
| Eastham | 76 | 8 | Cobb | Elkanah | 1 | | 2 | 1 | | 3 | 2 | | 1 | | | | 10 | | |
| Eastham | 76 | 9 | Cook | Caleb | | | | 1 | | | 2 | 2 | | 1 | | | 6 | | |
| Eastham | 76 | 10 | Cole | James | | 1 | | 1 | | | | | | 1 | | | 3 | | |
| Eastham | 76 | 11 | Cheven | Dorcas | | | | | | | | | 1 | 1 | | | 2 | | |
| Eastham | 76 | 12 | Cook | John | 2 | | | 1 | | 2 | | | | 1 | | | 6 | | |
| Eastham | 76 | 13 | Collins | Joseph | 1 | 2 | 2 | 1 | 1 | | 3 | 1 | | 1 | | | 12 | | |
| Eastham | 76 | 14 | Cook | Samuel | 1 | 1 | | 1 | | | 1 | | | 1 | | | 5 | | |
| Eastham | 76 | 15 | Cobb | Elisha | | 1 | | 1 | | | | | | 1 | | | 3 | | |
| Eastham | 76 | 16 | Clerk | Benjamin | | 1 | 2 | | 1 | 2 | | 2 | | 1 | | | 9 | | |
| Eastham | 77 | 1 | Collins | Michael | 2 | 2 | | 1 | | 1 | 2 | | 1 | | | | 9 | | |
| Eastham | 77 | 2 | Cole | Jesse | 2 | | | 1 | | 2 | | | 1 | | | | 6 | | |
| Eastham | 77 | 3 | Doane | Lydia | | 1 | | | | | | 2 | | 1 | | | 4 | | |
| Eastham | 77 | 4 | Doane | Herman | 3 | 2 | | 1 | | 2 | | | 1 | | | | 9 | | |
| Eastham | 77 | 5 | Doane | Isaiah | 1 | 1 | | 1 | | | | 1 | | 1 | | | 5 | | |
| Eastham | 77 | 6 | Doane | Jesse | | 1 | | 1 | | | | | | 1 | | | 4 | | |
| Eastham | 77 | 7 | Doane | Freeman | | | | 1 | | 2 | | | | 1 | | | 4 | | |
| Eastham | 77 | 8 | Doane | Zenas | 3 | 3 | | 1 | | | | | | 1 | | | 8 | | |
| Eastham | 77 | 9 | Doane | Elkanah | | 1 | | 1 | | | | | | 1 | | | 3 | | |
| Eastham | 77 | 10 | Doane | Solomon | | | 3 | | 1 | | | | | 1 | | | 5 | | |
| Eastham | 77 | 11 | Doane | Silvanus | | | | 1 | | | 1 | | | 1 | | | 3 | | |
| Eastham | 77 | 12 | Doane | Obadiah | 1 | | | 1 | | 2 | | | 1 | | | | 5 | | |
| Eastham | 77 | 13 | Doane | Prince | 1 | | | 1 | | 1 | 1 | | 1 | | | | 5 | | |
| Eastham | 77 | 14 | Doane | Betty | | 1 | | | | | | | | 1 | | | 2 | | |
| Eastham | 77 | 15 | Doane | Joshua | | | 3 | 1 | 1 | 1 | 2 | 1 | | 1 | | | 10 | | |
| Eastham | 77 | 16 | Dill | Thomas | 3 | 4 | | 1 | | 1 | | | | 1 | | | 10 | | |
| Eastham | 77 | 17 | Doanes | John | 2 | 1 | | | | | | | 1 | | | | 4 | | |
| Eastham | 77 | 18 | Freeman | Samuel | 2 | | | 1 | | 1 | 2 | 1 | 1 | 1 | | | 9 | | |
| Eastham | 77 | 19 | Gill | William | 2 | | | 1 | | 1 | | | 1 | | | | 5 | | |
| Eastham | 77 | 20 | Gill | Anna | | 1 | | | | | 3 | 1 | | | | | 6 | | |
| Eastham | 77 | 21 | Gill | Scarlet | | 1 | | 1 | | | | | 1 | 1 | | | 4 | | |
| Eastham | 77 | 22 | Gould | John | 2 | | | 1 | | 2 | | | 1 | | | | 6 | | |
| Eastham | 77 | 23 | Hopkins | John | 3 | 1 | | 1 | | 3 | | | | 1 | | | 9 | | |
| Eastham | 77 | 24 | Hickman | James | | 1 | 2 | | 2 | | 2 | 3 | | 1 | | | 11 | | |
| Eastham | 77 | 25 | Hatch | Henry | 2 | | | 1 | | | | | 1 | | | | 4 | | |
| Eastham | 77 | 26 | Higgins | Elkanah | | 1 | 1 | | 1 | 1 | | | 1 | 1 | | | 6 | | |
| Eastham | 77 | 27 | Higgins | Elkanah Junr | 2 | | | 1 | | 1 | 1 | | 1 | | | | 6 | | |
| Eastham | 77 | 28 | Harding | Ephraim | 1 | | | 1 | | 1 | | | 1 | | | | 4 | | |
| Eastham | 77 | 29 | Horton | Cushing | 2 | 2 | 2 | 1 | | | 1 | | 1 | | | | 9 | | |
| Eastham | 77 | 30 | Knowles | Obadiah | | | | 1 | | | | 1 | 1 | | | | 3 | | |
| Eastham | 77 | 31 | Knowles | Robert | | | 1 | | | 3 | | | 1 | | | | 5 | | |
| Eastham | 77 | 32 | Knowles | Rebecah | | | | | | | | 1 | | 1 | | | 2 | | |
| Eastham | 77 | 33 | Knowles | Benjamin | | 1 | 3 | | 1 | | | 1 | 1 | 1 | | | 8 | | |
| Eastham | 77 | 34 | Knowles | Henry | | | | | | 2 | 3 | | 1 | | | | 6 | | |
| Eastham | 78 | 1 | Knowles | Seth | 2 | 1 | | 1 | 1 | 1 | 2 | | | 1 | | | 9 | | |
| Eastham | 78 | 2 | Knowles | John | | 1 | 4 | | 1 | | 1 | 2 | 1 | 1 | | | 11 | | |
| Eastham | 78 | 3 | Knowles | David | 1 | | 1 | | 1 | | | 3 | | 1 | | | 7 | | |
| Eastham | 78 | 4 | Knowles | Theophilus | 2 | | 1 | 1 | | 1 | 1 | | 1 | | | | 7 | | |
| Eastham | 78 | 5 | Knowles | Joseph | | 1 | | | 1 | | | | 1 | 1 | | | 4 | | |
| Eastham | 78 | 6 | Lombard | Caleb | 2 | 1 | | 1 | | | | | | 1 | | | 5 | | |
| Eastham | 78 | 7 | Linkhornew | Joseph | 2 | 1 | | 1 | | | 1 | 2 | | 1 | | | 8 | | |
| Eastham | 78 | 8 | Myrick | William | | 1 | | 1 | | | | 2 | 1 | | | | 5 | | |
| Eastham | 78 | 9 | Mayo | James | 1 | | | 1 | 2 | 1 | 1 | | | 1 | | | 7 | | |
| Eastham | 78 | 10 | Mayo | John | 3 | 1 | | 1 | 3 | 2 | 3 | | | 1 | | | 14 | | |
| Eastham | 78 | 11 | Mayo | Abijah | | | 1 | | | | | | 1 | | | | 2 | | |
| Eastham | 78 | 12 | Mayo | Elisha | 1 | | | 1 | | | 2 | | | 1 | | | 5 | | |
| Eastham | 78 | 13 | Myrick | Isaac | 3 | 1 | 2 | 1 | | 1 | 1 | | | 1 | | | 10 | | |
| Eastham | 78 | 14 | Mayo | Henry | 1 | 1 | | | | | | | 1 | | | | 3 | | |
| Eastham | 78 | 15 | Mayo | James Junr | | | 1 | | | | | | 1 | 1 | | | 3 | | |
| Eastham | 78 | 16 | Nickerson | Uriah | 4 | | | 1 | 1 | 1 | | | 1 | | | | 8 | | |
| Eastham | 78 | 17 | Peeks | William | 4 | 1 | | 1 | | 1 | 1 | | 1 | | | | 9 | | |
| Eastham | 78 | 18 | Pepper | Joseph | | 1 | 1 | 1 | | 2 | 3 | 1 | 1 | | | | 10 | | |
| Eastham | 78 | 19 | Paine | Isaac | | 1 | | 1 | 1 | | | | 2 | 1 | | | 6 | | |
| Eastham | 78 | 20 | Paine | Ebenezer | 2 | | | 1 | | 1 | 1 | | 1 | | | | 6 | | |
| Eastham | 78 | 21 | Smith | Nehemiah | 3 | 2 | 1 | | 1 | 2 | 1 | | | 1 | | | 11 | | |
| Eastham | 78 | 22 | Smith | Herman Junr | | 1 | | 1 | | | | | 1 | | | | 3 | | |
| Eastham | 78 | 23 | Smith | Joseph | 3 | | | 1 | | | | | | 1 | | | 5 | | |
| Eastham | 78 | 24 | Smith | Nathaniel | 3 | | | 1 | | | | | 1 | | | | 5 | | |
| Eastham | 78 | 25 | Smith | Elkanah | | 1 | | 1 | | | 2 | 1 | 1 | | | | 6 | | |
| Eastham | 78 | 26 | Smith | Isaac | | | | 1 | | | 1 | | 1 | | | | 3 | | |
| Eastham | 78 | 27 | Smith | Joshua | | 1 | | 1 | | | 1 | | 1 | | | | 4 | | |
| Eastham | 78 | 28 | Smith | Samuel | 1 | | 1 | | 2 | | | | 1 | | | | 5 | | |
| Eastham | 78 | 29 | Smith | Phillip | | 2 | | 1 | | | 2 | | 1 | | | | 6 | | |
| Eastham | 78 | 30 | Snow | Joseph | 3 | 1 | | 1 | | 2 | | | 1 | | | | 8 | | |
| Eastham | 78 | 31 | Smith | John | 1 | 1 | 3 | 1 | | 1 | 1 | | 1 | | | | 9 | | |
| Eastham | 78 | 32 | Smith | Bathsheba | | | | | | | | | 2 | | | | 2 | | |
| Eastham | 78 | 33 | Smith | Seth | | 1 | | 1 | | | | | 1 | 1 | | | 4 | | |
| Eastham | 78 | 34 | Snow | James | | | | 1 | | | | 1 | | 1 | | | 3 | | |
| Eastham | 78 | 35 | Smith | Silvanus | 1 | 1 | | 2 | | 2 | | | 1 | | | | 7 | | |
| Eastham | 79 | 1 | Walker | William | | 1 | | 1 | | | | | 1 | 1 | | | 6 | | |
| Eastham | 79 | 2 | Walker | Andrew | | | | 1 | | | | | 2 | 1 | | | 4 | | |
| Eastham | 79 | 3 | Walker | Peter | | | 1 | | 3 | | | | 1 | | | | 5 | | |
| Eastham | 79 | 4 | Wiley | Moses | | | 1 | 1 | | | | | 1 | | | | 3 | | |
| Eastham | 79 | 5 | Anderson | William Junr | 2 | | 1 | | | | | 1 | | | | | 4 | | |

# 1800 Eastham, Barnstable County, Massachusetts

| TOWN | PG# | LN# | LAST NAME | FIRST NAME | FREE WHITE MALES | | | | | FREE WHITE FEMALES | | | | | TOTAL ALL OTHER | TOTAL SLAVES | TOTALS | DISTRICT/ TOWNSHIP | NOTES |
|---|---|---|---|---|---|---|---|---|---|---|---|---|---|---|---|---|---|---|---|
| | | | | | under 10 | 10 to 16 | 16 to 26 | 26 to 45 | 45 and over | under 10 | 10 to 16 | 16 to 26 | 26 to 45 | 45 and over | | | | | |
| Eastham | 79 | 6 | Cole | Daniel | 2 | 2 | 2 | | 1 | 2 | | 1 | 1 | 1 | | | 12 | | |
| Eastham | 79 | 7 | Doane | Betty | | 1 | 1 | | | | 1 | | | 1 | | | 4 | | |
| Eastham | 79 | 8 | Doane | Jesse Junr | 1 | | | 1 | | 2 | | | 1 | | | | 5 | | |
| Eastham | 79 | 9 | Mayo | Hannah | 1 | | | | | | | | 1 | 1 | | | 3 | | |
| Eastham | 79 | 10 | Mayo | Samuel | | | 1 | | | | | 1 | | | | | 2 | | |
| Eastham | 79 | 11 | Doane | Rebecca | 1 | | | | | | | 1 | | | | | 2 | | |
| Eastham | 79 | 12 | Doane | Myrick | | | 1 | | | 1 | | 1 | | | | | 3 | | |
| Eastham | 79 | 13 | Lombard | Oliver C. | 1 | | 1 | | | | | | | | | | 2 | | |
| Eastham | 79 | 14 | Mayo | Timothy | | 1 | | | | | | 1 | | | | | 2 | | |
| Eastham | 79 | 15 | Cook | Nathaniel | | 1 | | | | | | 1 | | | | | 4 | | |
| Eastham | 79 | 16 | Doane | Samuel | 2 | | 1 | | | | | 1 | | | | | 4 | | |
| Eastham | 79 | 17 | Atwood | Barnabas Junr | | | 1 | | | | | 1 | | | | | 2 | | |
| Eastham | 79 | 18 | Cobb | Thomas | | 1 | 1 | | | 1 | | 1 | | | | | 4 | | |
| Eastham | 79 | 19 | Mores | Susannah | | | | | | | | | | 2 | | | 2 | | |
| Eastham | 79 | 20 | Mayo | Samuel | | | 1 | | | | | 1 | | | | | 2 | | |
| Eastham | 79 | 21 | Shaw | Philander Revd | | | 1 | | | | | | 1 | | | | 2 | | |
| Eastham | 79 | 22 | Smith | Timothy | 1 | | 1 | | | | | 1 | | | | | 3 | | |
| Eastham | 79 | 23 | Knowles | William | 1 | 1 | 1 | 1 | | 3 | 3 | 1 | | | | | 11 | | |
| Eastham | 79 | 24 | Cole | Timothy | | 1 | | | | 1 | | 1 | 1 | 1 | | | 5 | | |
| Eastham | 79 | 25 | Townson | Obadiah | 3 | | | 1 | | 2 | | | 1 | 1 | | | 7 | | |
| Eastham | 79 | 26 | Cook | Rebeccah | | | | | | | | | 2 | | | | 2 | | |
| Eastham | 79 | 27 | Smith | Heman | | | 1 | | | | | 1 | | | | | 2 | | |
| Eastham | 79 | 28 | Gill | David | 1 | | 1 | | | | | | 1 | | | | 3 | | |
| Eastham | 79 | 29 | Fararo | John | 1 | | 1 | | | 1 | 2 | 1 | | | | | 6 | | |
| Eastham | 79 | 30 | Higgins | Benjamin | 2 | | 1 | | | 1 | | 1 | | | | | 5 | | |
| Eastham | 79 | 31 | Paine | Thomas | | | 1 | | | 3 | | 1 | | | | | 5 | | |
| Eastham | 79 | 32 | Walker | David | 2 | | 1 | | | 2 | | 1 | | | | | 6 | | |
| Eastham | 79 | 33 | Higgins | Phebe | | | | | | 1 | | 1 | | 2 | | | 4 | | |
| Eastham | 79 | 34 | Linkhornew | Joseph Junr | 1 | | 1 | | | 1 | | 1 | | | | | 4 | | |
| Eastham | 80 | 1 | Dill | Benjamin | 3 | | 1 | | | 2 | | 1 | | | | | 7 | | |

# 1800 Falmouth, Barnstable County, Massachusetts

| TOWN | PG# | LN# | LAST NAME | FIRST NAME | FREE WHITE MALES under 10 | 10 to 16 | 16 to 26 | 26 to 45 | 45 and over | FREE WHITE FEMALES under 10 | 10 to 16 | 16 to 26 | 26 to 45 | 45 and over | TOTAL ALL OTHER | TOTAL SLAVES | TOTALS | DISTRICT/ TOWNSHIP | NOTES |
|---|---|---|---|---|---|---|---|---|---|---|---|---|---|---|---|---|---|---|---|
| Falmouth | 43 | 1 | Allen | Nathaniel | 2 | 1 | | | 1 | 1 | 1 | | | 1 | | | 7 | | |
| Falmouth | 43 | 2 | Allen | David | | 1 | 1 | | 1 | | | 1 | | 1 | | | 5 | | |
| Falmouth | 43 | 3 | Bassett | Berachiah | 2 | | | 1 | 1 | | 1 | | 1 | 1 | | | 7 | | |
| Falmouth | 43 | 4 | Bourne | Timothy | | | | | 1 | 3 | | | 1 | 1 | | | 6 | | |
| Falmouth | 43 | 5 | Bourne | Samuel | | 1 | 2 | 1 | 1 | 1 | | | | 1 | | | 7 | | |
| Falmouth | 43 | 6 | Bourne | Joseph | 1 | 3 | | 1 | | 3 | | | 1 | 1 | | | 8 | | |
| Falmouth | 43 | 7 | Bourne | Elijah | 2 | 1 | | 1 | | 1 | | | 1 | 1 | | | 7 | | |
| Falmouth | 43 | 8 | Bourne | John | 1 | 1 | 1 | | 1 | 1 | 1 | 2 | 1 | | | | 9 | | |
| Falmouth | 43 | 9 | Butler | Parnel | 1 | 1 | 1 | | | 1 | 1 | | 1 | | | | 6 | | |
| Falmouth | 43 | 10 | Bowerman | Paul | | | 1 | | | 2 | | | 1 | | | | 4 | | |
| Falmouth | 43 | 11 | Bowerman | Abraham | | | 2 | | | | | 1 | 2 | | | | 5 | | |
| Falmouth | 43 | 12 | Butler | Obedl | | 1 | | 1 | | 2 | 1 | | 1 | | | | 6 | | |
| Falmouth | 43 | 13 | Butler | David | | 1 | 1 | 1 | | 1 | | 1 | 1 | | | | 6 | | |
| Falmouth | 43 | 14 | Bowerman | Stephen | 2 | | | 1 | | 1 | 1 | | 1 | | | | 6 | | |
| Falmouth | 43 | 15 | Bowerman | Daniel | | 1 | | 1 | | 3 | | | 2 | 1 | | | 8 | | |
| Falmouth | 43 | 16 | Butler | Easten | 1 | | | 1 | | | | 1 | 3 | 1 | | | 7 | | |
| Falmouth | 43 | 17 | Bowerman | Ichabod | 3 | 1 | | 1 | | | | | 1 | | | | 6 | | |
| Falmouth | 43 | 18 | Bowerman | Curtis | 1 | | | 1 | | | | | 1 | 2 | | | 5 | | |
| Falmouth | 43 | 19 | Bowerman | Joseph | 2 | | 1 | | 1 | 2 | | 1 | 2 | 2 | | | 11 | | |
| Falmouth | 43 | 20 | Bowerman | Seth | 3 | | 1 | | 1 | | 2 | | | | | | 7 | | |
| Falmouth | 43 | 21 | Baley | Zacheus | 2 | | 2 | | 1 | 2 | | 1 | 1 | | | | 9 | | |
| Falmouth | 43 | 22 | Bowerman | Stephen | 3 | 2 | | 1 | | 2 | | | 1 | | | | 9 | | |
| Falmouth | 43 | 23 | Baker | Barnabas | 4 | | 1 | | | | 1 | | 1 | | | | 7 | | |
| Falmouth | 44 | 24 | Baker | Job | 2 | 1 | | 1 | | 2 | 4 | 1 | | | | | 11 | | |
| Falmouth | 44 | 25 | Baker | Obediah | 3 | 2 | 1 | 1 | | 3 | 1 | 2 | 1 | | | | 14 | | |
| Falmouth | 44 | 26 | Bourne | Nathaniel | | 2 | | 1 | | 4 | 1 | 2 | 1 | | | | 11 | | |
| Falmouth | 44 | 27 | Baker | Henry | | | 1 | | | 1 | 1 | | | | | | 3 | | |
| Falmouth | 44 | 28 | Bradford | Susannah | | | | | | | | | 2 | | | | 2 | | |
| Falmouth | 44 | 29 | Bourne | Thomas | 1 | | | 1 | | 3 | 2 | 1 | | | | | 8 | | |
| Falmouth | 44 | 30 | Bunker | Richard | | | 1 | | | | 1 | 1 | | | | | 3 | | |
| Falmouth | 44 | 31 | Bowerman | Clifton | 1 | | | 1 | | | | | 1 | 1 | | | 4 | | |
| Falmouth | 44 | 32 | Butler | Benjamin | 3 | | | 1 | | 1 | | | 1 | | | | 6 | | |
| Falmouth | 44 | 33 | Bourne | Hannah | | 1 | | | | | | | 2 | | | | 3 | | |
| Falmouth | 44 | 34 | Crocker | Timothy | | 1 | 2 | 1 | 1 | | | 1 | | 1 | | | 7 | | |
| Falmouth | 44 | 35 | Chadwick | Elizabeth | | | | | | | | | 3 | | | | 3 | | |
| Falmouth | 44 | 36 | Childs | Nathaniel | | 2 | 2 | | 1 | 1 | | 3 | | | | | 9 | | |
| Falmouth | 44 | 37 | Chadwick | Isaiah | | 1 | 1 | | 1 | 1 | 2 | | 1 | | | | 7 | | |
| Falmouth | 44 | 38 | Crowel | David Senr | | 1 | | 1 | | | 1 | | 1 | 1 | | | 5 | | |
| Falmouth | 44 | 39 | Crosswell | Sarah | 1 | | | | 2 | 2 | 1 | | 1 | | | | 7 | | |
| Falmouth | 44 | 40 | Crocker | Joseph | | 1 | | 1 | | 3 | 1 | | 1 | | 1 | | 8 | | |
| Falmouth | 44 | 41 | Parker | Seth | 1 | | | 1 | | 1 | | | 1 | | | | 4 | | |
| Falmouth | 44 | 42 | Crowel | Lot | | | 1 | 1 | 1 | 2 | 1 | 2 | | 1 | | | 9 | | |
| Falmouth | 44 | 43 | Chadwick | Micajah | 2 | | | 1 | | 4 | | | 1 | | | | 8 | | |
| Falmouth | 44 | 44 | Crowel | Benjamin | | 1 | 1 | | 1 | | | | 1 | | | | 4 | | |
| Falmouth | 44 | 45 | Crowel | Barnabas | | 1 | | 1 | | 1 | | | 1 | | | | 4 | | |
| Falmouth | 44 | 46 | Crowel | Joshua | | | 1 | | | 2 | | | 1 | | | | 4 | | |
| Falmouth | 44 | 47 | Crowel | Stephen | 3 | | | 1 | | 2 | 1 | | 1 | 1 | | | 9 | | |
| Falmouth | 44 | 48 | Crowel | Joseph | | 3 | 1 | 1 | | 1 | | | 1 | | | | 7 | | |
| Falmouth | 44 | 49 | Chadwick | Barnabas | 2 | | | 1 | | 1 | | | 1 | | | | 5 | | |
| Falmouth | 44 | 50 | Chadwick | Reuben | | | 1 | | | 1 | | | 1 | | | | 3 | | |
| Falmouth | 44 | 51 | Cohoon | Smalley | | 1 | | | | | | | 1 | | | | 2 | | |
| Falmouth | 44 | 52 | Childs | Joseph | 2 | 2 | 1 | | 1 | 1 | | 1 | 1 | 1 | | | 10 | | |
| Falmouth | 44 | 53 | Chadwick | Thomas | 1 | | 1 | | | | | | 1 | | | | 3 | | |
| Falmouth | 44 | 54 | Crocker | Timothy Junr | 1 | | 1 | | | | | | 1 | | | | 3 | | |
| Falmouth | 44 | 55 | Coleman | Thomas | 2 | 1 | | 1 | | 2 | | 1 | | | | | 7 | | |
| Falmouth | 44 | 56 | Chadwick | Lydia | | 1 | | 1 | | | | | 1 | | | | 3 | | |
| Falmouth | 44 | 57 | Dimmick | Lot | 1 | 1 | | 1 | | | | | 1 | | | | 4 | | |
| Falmouth | 44 | 58 | Dimmick | Robinson | 1 | | | 1 | | 1 | | 1 | 1 | | | | 5 | | |
| Falmouth | 44 | 59 | Davis | Solomon Junr | 2 | 1 | 1 | 1 | | 1 | | 1 | | | | | 7 | | |
| Falmouth | 44 | 60 | Davis | Francis | 2 | 2 | | 1 | | 2 | 1 | 2 | 1 | | | | 11 | | |
| Falmouth | 44 | 61 | Davis | Thomas | 1 | 2 | 1 | 1 | | | | | 1 | | | | 6 | | |
| Falmouth | 44 | 62 | Davis | Abner | 2 | 1 | | 1 | | 1 | 1 | | 1 | | | | 7 | | |
| Falmouth | 44 | 63 | Davis | John | 2 | 1 | | 1 | 1 | 1 | | 2 | 1 | | | | 10 | | |
| Falmouth | 44 | 64 | Davis | Jabez | 1 | | 1 | | | | | | 1 | | | | 3 | | |
| Falmouth | 44 | 65 | Dillingham | Ignatius | | | | 1 | | | | | 2 | | | | 3 | | |
| Falmouth | 44 | 66 | Dimmick | Joseph | | 1 | | 1 | | | | 1 | | | | | 4 | | |
| Falmouth | 44 | 67 | Dimmick | Jabez | | 1 | | | | | | 1 | 1 | | | | 3 | | |
| Falmouth | 44 | 68 | Davis | Joseph | 2 | 1 | | 1 | 1 | | 1 | 1 | 1 | | | | 10 | | |
| Falmouth | 44 | 69 | Dimmick | Anselm | | 1 | | 1 | | 1 | | | | | | | 3 | | |
| Falmouth | 44 | 70 | Davis | Ichabod | | | 1 | 2 | | 1 | | | 1 | | | | 5 | | |
| Falmouth | 44 | 71 | Davis | Malachai | | 2 | | 1 | | | | 1 | 1 | | | | 5 | | |
| Falmouth | 45 | 72 | Davis | Crocker | 3 | | 1 | | 2 | | 1 | 1 | 1 | | | | 9 | | |
| Falmouth | 45 | 73 | Davis | Joanna | | | | | | | 1 | | 1 | | | | 2 | | |
| Falmouth | 45 | 74 | Davis | Job | | 1 | | | | | | 1 | | | | | 2 | | |
| Falmouth | 45 | 75 | Davis | Walter | 2 | | 1 | | | | | | 1 | | | | 4 | | |
| Falmouth | 45 | 76 | Donaldson | Hugh G. | 3 | | 1 | | 2 | 2 | 1 | | | | | | 9 | | |
| Falmouth | 45 | 77 | Dillingham | Joseph | 1 | 1 | | | | 1 | 1 | | | | | | 4 | | |
| Falmouth | 45 | 78 | Dimmick | Bradock | 2 | 2 | 1 | 1 | | 2 | 1 | | 1 | | | | 10 | | |
| Falmouth | 45 | 79 | Eldred | John | | 2 | | 1 | | 2 | | | 1 | | | | 6 | | |
| Falmouth | 45 | 80 | Eldred | Samuel | 1 | 1 | 1 | 1 | | | | | 1 | | | | 5 | | |
| Falmouth | 45 | 81 | Ellis | Nathan | 1 | | 1 | | | 3 | 1 | | 1 | | | | 7 | | |
| Falmouth | 45 | 82 | Edwards | Asa | 3 | | 2 | 1 | 1 | 2 | | 1 | | | | | 10 | | |
| Falmouth | 45 | 83 | Eldred | William | | | 1 | | | | | | | | | | 1 | | |
| Falmouth | 45 | 84 | Eldred | Ann | | | 1 | | | | | 2 | 1 | | | | 4 | | |
| Falmouth | 45 | 85 | Eldred | Ezekiel | 2 | | 1 | | | | | | 1 | | | | 4 | | |
| Falmouth | 45 | 86 | Eldred | Abiel | 1 | 1 | 1 | | 1 | | 1 | 1 | | | | | 6 | | |
| Falmouth | 45 | 87 | Eldred | Samuel | 1 | 1 | | 1 | | 1 | | | 1 | | | | 5 | | |
| Falmouth | 45 | 88 | Eldred | Thos | 2 | | 1 | | | | | | 1 | | | | 4 | | |
| Falmouth | 45 | 89 | Eldred | Experience | 1 | | 1 | | | | 1 | | 1 | | | | 4 | | |
| Falmouth | 45 | 90 | Eldred | Simeon | | 1 | | | | 1 | | | | 1 | | | 3 | | |

# 1800 Falmouth, Barnstable County, Massachusetts

| TOWN | PG# | LN# | LAST NAME | FIRST NAME | FREE WHITE MALES under 10 | 10 to 16 | 16 to 26 | 26 to 45 | 45 and over | FREE WHITE FEMALES under 10 | 10 to 16 | 16 to 26 | 26 to 45 | 45 and over | TOTAL ALL OTHER | TOTAL SLAVES | TOTALS | DISTRICT/ TOWNSHIP | NOTES |
|---|---|---|---|---|---|---|---|---|---|---|---|---|---|---|---|---|---|---|---|
| Falmouth | 45 | 91 | Gifford | Ebenz | 2 | | 1 | 1 | | 2 | 1 | | 1 | | | | 8 | | |
| Falmouth | 45 | 92 | Fisk | Samuel | | | 1 | | | 1 | | 1 | 1 | | 1 | | 5 | | |
| Falmouth | 45 | 93 | Fisk | Thomas | | | | 1 | | 1 | | | | 1 | | | 3 | | |
| Falmouth | 45 | 94 | Fisk | Abraham | | 1 | 1 | 2 | | | | 1 | | | | | 5 | | |
| Falmouth | 45 | 95 | Fisk | Ebenz | | | 2 | 1 | | | | | 2 | | | | 5 | | |
| Falmouth | 45 | 96 | Fisk | Thomas Junr | 4 | 1 | | 1 | | 3 | | | 1 | | | | 10 | | |
| Falmouth | 45 | 97 | Freeman | Thos Junr | 2 | 1 | | 1 | | 2 | | | 1 | 1 | | | 8 | | |
| Falmouth | 45 | 98 | Fisk | Rufus Junr | | 2 | 1 | | 1 | | 2 | 1 | | 1 | | | 8 | | |
| Falmouth | 45 | 99 | Fisk | Benjm | 1 | 1 | | 1 | | 2 | | | 1 | | | | 6 | | |
| Falmouth | 45 | 100 | Fisk | Saml Junr | 1 | | | 1 | | 1 | | | 1 | | | | 4 | | |
| Falmouth | 45 | 101 | Fisk | Freeman | 4 | | | | 1 | 1 | | | 1 | | | | 7 | | |
| Falmouth | 45 | 102 | Green | Solomon | 1 | 1 | | 1 | | | | | 1 | 1 | | | 5 | | |
| Falmouth | 45 | 103 | Green | Jonathan | | 1 | | 2 | 1 | | | 2 | | | | | 6 | | |
| Falmouth | 45 | 104 | Gifford | Jesse | | 1 | 3 | | 1 | 1 | 2 | 1 | 2 | 1 | | | 12 | | |
| Falmouth | 45 | 105 | Gifford | Samuel | | | | 1 | | 1 | 1 | 1 | | 1 | | | 4 | | |
| Falmouth | 45 | 106 | Gifford | Christopher | 1 | | | 1 | | | | 2 | 1 | 1 | | | 6 | | |
| Falmouth | 45 | 107 | Gifford | Silas | 1 | | 1 | | | 1 | | | 1 | | | | 4 | | |
| Falmouth | 45 | 108 | Gifford | Mordecai | | 1 | | 2 | | | | 1 | | 2 | | | 6 | | |
| Falmouth | 45 | 109 | Gifford | Prince | | 1 | 1 | | | | 1 | 2 | | 1 | | | 8 | | |
| Falmouth | 45 | 110 | Green | Christopher | | | | 1 | | | | | 3 | 1 | | | 5 | | |
| Falmouth | 45 | 111 | Gifford | Zacheus | | | 2 | | 1 | | | 1 | 2 | 2 | | | 8 | | |
| Falmouth | 45 | 112 | Gifford | Reuben | | | | 1 | | 1 | | | 1 | 1 | | | 4 | | |
| Falmouth | 45 | 113 | Gifford | Warren | | 1 | | 1 | | 2 | | | | | | | 5 | | |
| Falmouth | 45 | 114 | Gifford | David | | 1 | | 1 | | | | 1 | | 1 | | | 4 | | |
| Falmouth | 45 | 115 | Gorham | John | | 1 | 1 | 1 | | | | 1 | | 1 | | | 5 | | |
| Falmouth | 45 | 116 | Green | Lemuel | 2 | 2 | | 1 | | | | 1 | 1 | | | | 7 | | |
| Falmouth | 45 | 117 | Green | Jonathan Jun | 4 | | 1 | | | 1 | 1 | | 1 | | | | 8 | | |
| Falmouth | 45 | 118 | Green | Jonthan | | | | 1 | | | | | 2 | | | | 3 | | |
| Falmouth | 45 | 119 | Gifford | George | | | | 1 | | | | | | 1 | | | 2 | | |
| Falmouth | 46 | 120 | Gifford | Anna | | | | | | | | 1 | | | | | 1 | | |
| Falmouth | 46 | 121 | Hatch | Howes Junr | 1 | | | 1 | | 1 | | 1 | | | | | 4 | | |
| Falmouth | 46 | 122 | Hatch | Nathl | | 1 | 2 | 1 | | | | 1 | 2 | 1 | | | 9 | | |
| Falmouth | 46 | 123 | Hatch | Benjm | 1 | | 2 | 1 | | 2 | | 1 | 1 | | | | 8 | | |
| Falmouth | 46 | 124 | Handy | Elnathan Junr | 1 | | | 1 | | | 1 | | 1 | | | | 4 | | |
| Falmouth | 46 | 125 | Hatch | Samuel | | | | 1 | | | | 2 | | 1 | | | 4 | | |
| Falmouth | 46 | 126 | Hatch | Edward | | 1 | | 1 | | | | | | 1 | | | 3 | | |
| Falmouth | 46 | 127 | Hatch | Ward | | | 1 | | | 1 | | 1 | | | | | 3 | | |
| Falmouth | 46 | 128 | Hammond | John | | | 2 | 2 | 1 | | | 2 | 1 | 1 | | | 9 | | |
| Falmouth | 46 | 129 | Hatch | Moses | 1 | | | 1 | | 1 | | 1 | | | | | 4 | | |
| Falmouth | 46 | 130 | Hatch | Coleman | | | 1 | | | | | 1 | | | | | 2 | | |
| Falmouth | 46 | 131 | Hatch | David | | | 1 | | | 1 | | 1 | | | | | 3 | | |
| Falmouth | 46 | 132 | Hatch | Zadock | | | 3 | | 1 | 1 | 1 | | 1 | 1 | | | 7 | | |
| Falmouth | 46 | 133 | Harding | Samuel | | | 2 | | 1 | | | | 1 | 1 | | | 5 | | |
| Falmouth | 46 | 134 | Hatch | David Junr | | | 1 | | | 1 | | | 1 | | | | 3 | | |
| Falmouth | 46 | 135 | Hatch | Shubael Junr | 1 | 1 | | 1 | 1 | 1 | | | | 1 | | | 6 | | |
| Falmouth | 46 | 136 | Hatch | Susanna | 1 | | 1 | | | 2 | | 1 | | | | | 6 | | |
| Falmouth | 46 | 137 | Hatch | Ichabod | | | | 1 | | | 1 | | | 1 | | | 3 | | |
| Falmouth | 46 | 138 | Hammond | Barnabas | | 1 | | 1 | | 2 | 1 | | | | | | 5 | | |
| Falmouth | 46 | 139 | Hatch | Prince | | | | 1 | | | | | | | | | 1 | | |
| Falmouth | 46 | 140 | Hamblen | Seth | 2 | 1 | | 1 | | 1 | 1 | | 1 | | | | 7 | | |
| Falmouth | 46 | 141 | Hinckley | Barnabas | | 1 | 1 | 1 | | | | | | 2 | | | 4 | | |
| Falmouth | 46 | 142 | Hatch | Major | | 1 | | 1 | | 1 | | 1 | | | | | 4 | | |
| Falmouth | 46 | 143 | Hatch | Solomon | | | | 1 | | | | 1 | 1 | 1 | 1 | | 4 | | |
| Falmouth | 46 | 144 | Hatch | Moses Junr | 1 | 1 | | 1 | 1 | 1 | | 1 | 1 | 1 | | | 8 | | |
| Falmouth | 46 | 145 | Hatch | Consider | 1 | | 2 | 1 | | 2 | 1 | | 1 | | | | 8 | | |
| Falmouth | 46 | 146 | Jenkins | Weston | 1 | | | 1 | | 1 | | | | | 1 | | 5 | | |
| Falmouth | 46 | 147 | Jenkins | James | | | 1 | | 1 | | | 1 | 1 | 2 | | | 6 | | |
| Falmouth | 46 | 148 | Jones | Thomas | 1 | 1 | 2 | | 1 | 2 | 1 | | | 2 | | | 10 | | |
| Falmouth | 46 | 149 | Jenkins | Samuel | 1 | | 4 | 1 | | | | 1 | 1 | | | | 8 | | |
| Falmouth | 46 | 150 | Jenkins | Joseph | 1 | 1 | 2 | | | 1 | 1 | 1 | 1 | | | | 9 | | |
| Falmouth | 46 | 151 | Jenkins | Eli | 2 | | | 1 | | 1 | 1 | 1 | | | | | 6 | | |
| Falmouth | 46 | 152 | Jenkins | Benjm | | | 1 | | | 1 | | 1 | | | | | 3 | | |
| Falmouth | 46 | 153 | Laurence | John | | | 1 | | 1 | | | | | 1 | | | 3 | | |
| Falmouth | 46 | 154 | Laurence | Solomon | 3 | 3 | | 1 | | 1 | | | 1 | | | | 9 | | |
| Falmouth | 46 | 155 | Laurence | Joseph | 3 | 1 | | 1 | | 1 | 1 | | 1 | | | | 8 | | |
| Falmouth | 46 | 156 | Laurence | Silas | | 1 | 2 | | 1 | 2 | 1 | | 1 | | | | 8 | | |
| Falmouth | 46 | 157 | Lewis | Samuel | 3 | | | 1 | | 2 | | | 1 | | | | 7 | | |
| Falmouth | 46 | 158 | Lake | Richard | | | 1 | 1 | | | | | | 1 | | | 3 | | |
| Falmouth | 46 | 159 | Landers | Reuben | | | | 1 | | | | | | 1 | | | 2 | | |
| Falmouth | 46 | 160 | Landers | John | | | 1 | 1 | | | | | 1 | 1 | | | 4 | | |
| Falmouth | 46 | 161 | Landers | Savory | | 1 | | | | | | 1 | 1 | 1 | | | 5 | | |
| Falmouth | 46 | 162 | Lewis | Lothrop | 2 | | 1 | 1 | 1 | | 1 | 2 | | 1 | | | 9 | | |
| Falmouth | 46 | 163 | Lewis | David | 2 | | 3 | | 1 | 3 | | 2 | | 1 | | | 12 | | |
| Falmouth | 46 | 164 | Lewis | Ebenz | | 2 | | 1 | | | | | 1 | | | | 4 | | |
| Falmouth | 46 | 165 | Laurence | Shubael | 2 | | | 1 | | | | | 1 | | | | 5 | | |
| Falmouth | 46 | 166 | Lewis | Nathl | | | 1 | | | | | | 1 | | | | 2 | | |
| Falmouth | 46 | 167 | Lewis | Thatcher | | | 1 | | | | 1 | | 1 | | | | 2 | | |
| Falmouth | 46 | 168 | Lincoln | Rev Henry | 2 | | | 1 | | 3 | | | 1 | | 1 | | 8 | | |
| Falmouth | 47 | 169 | Landers | Richard | | | 1 | | | | | | 1 | 1 | | | 3 | | |
| Falmouth | 47 | 170 | Landers | Nicholas | 1 | | | 1 | | 3 | | | | 1 | | | 7 | | |
| Falmouth | 47 | 171 | Mann | Zipporah | | 1 | | | | | | | 1 | | | | 2 | | |
| Falmouth | 47 | 172 | Morse | Martha | | | | | | 1 | 1 | | 1 | | | | 3 | | |
| Falmouth | 47 | 173 | Landers | Prince | | | | | 1 | | | | | 1 | | | 2 | | |
| Falmouth | 47 | 174 | Landers | Prince Junr | 1 | | | | | | | | 1 | | | | 3 | | |
| Falmouth | 47 | 175 | Laurence | Nabby | | | | | | 1 | | | | 1 | | | 2 | | |
| Falmouth | 47 | 176 | Landers | Jabez | 1 | | | 1 | | 1 | | | 1 | | | | 4 | | |
| Falmouth | 47 | 177 | Nickerson | Elijah | 1 | 1 | | | | 1 | | | 1 | 1 | | | 5 | | |
| Falmouth | 47 | 178 | Nye | Samuel | | 1 | 3 | | 1 | | 1 | 1 | | 2 | | | 9 | | |
| Falmouth | 47 | 179 | Nye | Nathan | | | 1 | | 1 | | | | 3 | 1 | | | 6 | | |
| Falmouth | 47 | 180 | Nye | Hannah | | | 2 | | | | | 1 | | 1 | | | 4 | | |

# 1800 Falmouth, Barnstable County, Massachusetts

| TOWN | PG# | LN# | LAST NAME | FIRST NAME | FREE WHITE MALES under 10 | 10 to 16 | 16 to 26 | 26 to 45 | 45 and over | FREE WHITE FEMALES under 10 | 10 to 16 | 16 to 26 | 26 to 45 | 45 and over | TOTAL ALL OTHER | TOTAL SLAVES | TOTALS | DISTRICT/ TOWNSHIP | NOTES |
|---|---|---|---|---|---|---|---|---|---|---|---|---|---|---|---|---|---|---|---|
| Falmouth | 47 | 181 | Nickerson | Phebe | 1 | | | | | | | | 1 | | | | 2 | | |
| Falmouth | 47 | 182 | Nye | David | 2 | 1 | 1 | | 1 | 1 | | 3 | 1 | 1 | | | 11 | | |
| Falmouth | 47 | 183 | Nye | Samuel Junr | 3 | 2 | 1 | | 1 | 1 | | 1 | | 1 | | | 10 | | |
| Falmouth | 47 | 184 | Nye | John | | | 4 | 2 | 2 | | | 1 | 1 | 2 | 1 | | 13 | | |
| Falmouth | 47 | 185 | Nye | Elisha | | 2 | 1 | | 2 | | | 1 | | 1 | | | 7 | | |
| Falmouth | 47 | 186 | Nye | Elnathan | | | | 1 | 2 | | | 1 | 1 | | | | 5 | | |
| Falmouth | 47 | 187 | Nye | Solomon Junr | 3 | | | 1 | | 1 | | | 1 | | | | 6 | | |
| Falmouth | 47 | 188 | Nye | John Junr | 2 | | | 1 | | | | | 1 | | | | 4 | | |
| Falmouth | 47 | 189 | Parker | Benjm Jun | | | 1 | | | 1 | | | 1 | | | | 3 | | |
| Falmouth | 47 | 190 | Palmer | Joseph Junr | 2 | | | | 1 | 2 | 1 | 1 | 2 | 1 | | | 10 | | |
| Falmouth | 47 | 191 | Palmer | Sarah | | | | | | | | | 1 | | | | 1 | | |
| Falmouth | 47 | 192 | Pitcher | Abigail | | | | | | | | | 1 | | | | 1 | | |
| Falmouth | 47 | 193 | Price | Matthew | | 1 | | 1 | | 1 | | 1 | | | | | 4 | | |
| Falmouth | 47 | 194 | Parker | Job | | 3 | 2 | 1 | | 1 | 1 | | 1 | | | | 9 | | |
| Falmouth | 47 | 195 | Parker | Timothy | 2 | | | 1 | | | | 1 | | 1 | 1 | | 5 | | |
| Falmouth | 47 | 196 | Parker | Joseph | | | 1 | 1 | 2 | | | 2 | | 1 | | | 7 | | |
| Falmouth | 47 | 197 | Parker | Benjm | | 1 | 1 | | 1 | | | 2 | | 1 | | | 6 | | |
| Falmouth | 47 | 198 | Price | Paul | 1 | 1 | | 1 | | 3 | 1 | | 1 | | | | 8 | | |
| Falmouth | 47 | 199 | Palmer | Joseph | | | 1 | | 1 | | | 2 | | 1 | | | 5 | | |
| Falmouth | 47 | 200 | Phinney | Peter | | | 1 | 1 | | | | | 1 | | | | 3 | | |
| Falmouth | 47 | 201 | Phinney | William | | | 1 | 1 | | | | 1 | | 1 | | | 4 | | |
| Falmouth | 47 | 202 | Phinney | Jonathan | | 2 | | 1 | | 1 | | | 1 | | | | 5 | | |
| Falmouth | 47 | 203 | Phinney | Phillip | | | 1 | 1 | 2 | | | | 1 | 1 | | | 6 | | |
| Falmouth | 47 | 204 | Price | Lot | | 1 | 1 | | 1 | | 2 | 2 | | 1 | | | 8 | | |
| Falmouth | 47 | 205 | Rice | Tabitha | | | | 1 | | | | | 1 | 1 | | | 3 | | |
| Falmouth | 47 | 206 | Parker | Seth | 1 | | 1 | | | 1 | | | | 1 | | | 5 | | |
| Falmouth | 47 | 207 | Robinson | Love | | | | | | | | | 1 | | | | 1 | | |
| Falmouth | 47 | 208 | Robinson | Charles | 1 | | 1 | | 1 | | | 2 | | 1 | | | 6 | | |
| Falmouth | 47 | 209 | Robinson | Wally | 2 | 1 | | 1 | | | | 1 | 1 | | | | 6 | | |
| Falmouth | 47 | 210 | Robinson | Cornelius | 2 | | 1 | | 2 | | | | 1 | | | | 6 | | |
| Falmouth | 47 | 211 | Rowley | Mathew | | | 1 | | | | | | 1 | 1 | | | 3 | | |
| Falmouth | 47 | 212 | Rowley | Benjm | | | 1 | | 1 | 1 | | | | | | | 3 | | |
| Falmouth | 48 | 213 | Robinson | Zephariah | 3 | 1 | | 1 | | 1 | | | 1 | | | | 8 | | |
| Falmouth | 48 | 214 | Robinson | James | 2 | 1 | | 1 | | 2 | | | 1 | | | | 7 | | |
| Falmouth | 48 | 215 | Robinson | Isaac | 2 | 2 | | 1 | 1 | 1 | | 2 | | 1 | 1 | | 11 | | |
| Falmouth | 48 | 216 | Robinson | Zenas | 1 | | | 1 | | | | | | 1 | | | 3 | | |
| Falmouth | 48 | 217 | Robinson | Joseph | | | 1 | | | 1 | | | 1 | | | | 3 | | |
| Falmouth | 48 | 218 | Robinson | Ezekiel | 4 | | | 1 | 1 | | | | 1 | 1 | | | 8 | | |
| Falmouth | 48 | 219 | Robinson | Bartlett | | | 1 | | | 1 | | | 1 | | | | 3 | | |
| Falmouth | 48 | 220 | Robinson | Stephen | | | 1 | | 1 | | | | 1 | | | | 3 | | |
| Falmouth | 48 | 221 | Robinson | Seth | 3 | | | 1 | | | | | 1 | | | | 5 | | |
| Falmouth | 48 | 222 | Sanford | Benja | | 1 | | | 1 | | 1 | 3 | 2 | | | | 8 | | |
| Falmouth | 48 | 223 | Shiverick | David | | 1 | 1 | | 1 | | | 1 | 2 | | | | 6 | | |
| Falmouth | 48 | 224 | Swift | Jabez | | | | 1 | | | | | 2 | 2 | | | 5 | | |
| Falmouth | 48 | 225 | Swift | Wm | | 1 | | 1 | | | | | | 1 | | | 3 | | |
| Falmouth | 48 | 226 | Swift | Wm Junr | 2 | | | 1 | | 1 | | 1 | 1 | | | | 7 | | |
| Falmouth | 48 | 227 | Swift | John | 2 | | 1 | | | | | | 1 | | | | 4 | | |
| Falmouth | 48 | 228 | Snow | Joanna | 1 | | | | | 1 | 1 | | 1 | | | | 4 | | |
| Falmouth | 48 | 229 | Swift | Solomon | | | 1 | | 1 | | | 1 | 1 | 1 | | | 5 | | |
| Falmouth | 48 | 230 | Smalley | Joseph | | | | 1 | | | 1 | 1 | 1 | | | | 4 | | |
| Falmouth | 48 | 231 | Samuel | Shiverick | 2 | 1 | 1 | 1 | | 1 | 1 | | 1 | | | | 8 | | |
| Falmouth | 48 | 232 | Shiverick | Joseph | | 1 | | 1 | | | 2 | | | 1 | | | 5 | | |
| Falmouth | 48 | 233 | Sherman | Wm | 1 | 1 | | 1 | | 1 | | 1 | 1 | | | | 8 | | |
| Falmouth | 48 | 234 | Swift | Moses | 1 | 1 | | | | | | | 1 | | | | 4 | | |
| Falmouth | 48 | 235 | Swift | Stephen | 1 | 2 | | 1 | | 1 | | | 1 | 1 | | | 7 | | |
| Falmouth | 48 | 236 | Swift | Ephraim Junr | 1 | | 1 | | 1 | | 1 | 2 | | 1 | | | 7 | | |
| Falmouth | 48 | 237 | Swift | Ephraim | | | | 1 | | | | | 2 | | | | 3 | | |
| Falmouth | 48 | 238 | Sanford | Wm | 4 | | 3 | | 1 | 1 | 2 | 3 | 1 | | | | 15 | | |
| Falmouth | 48 | 239 | Snow | Joseph | | | 1 | | | | | | 1 | | | | 2 | | |
| Falmouth | 48 | 240 | Swift | Abiel | 2 | | | 1 | | 1 | | | 1 | | | | 5 | | |
| Falmouth | 48 | 241 | Swift | Charles | 3 | | | 1 | | 1 | | | 1 | | | | 6 | | |
| Falmouth | 48 | 242 | Swift | Silvanus | | 2 | | 2 | 1 | | 2 | | 1 | | | | 8 | | |
| Falmouth | 48 | 243 | Swift | Paul | | 2 | | | 1 | | 2 | | 1 | | | | 6 | | |
| Falmouth | 48 | 244 | Studley | Benoni | | 1 | 1 | | | | | | | 1 | | | 4 | | |
| Falmouth | 48 | 245 | Swift | David | | 1 | | 1 | | 1 | 2 | | 1 | 1 | | | 7 | | |
| Falmouth | 48 | 246 | Swift | Jetho | 1 | | 1 | 1 | | 1 | 2 | | 1 | | | | 7 | | |
| Falmouth | 48 | 247 | Swift | Elisha | | | | 1 | | | | | 1 | | | | 2 | | |
| Falmouth | 48 | 248 | Pitts | Wm | 2 | | 2 | | 1 | | 1 | | | | | | 6 | | |
| Falmouth | 48 | 249 | Small | John | 1 | 1 | 1 | | 1 | | | 2 | 1 | 1 | | | 8 | | |
| Falmouth | 49 | 250 | Shiverick | David | | 1 | | 1 | | | | | 3 | | | | 6 | | |
| Falmouth | 49 | 251 | Shiverick | Thos | | | 1 | | 3 | 1 | | 1 | 1 | | | | 7 | | |
| Falmouth | 49 | 252 | Swift | Temperance | | | 1 | | | | | 2 | | 1 | | | 4 | | |
| Falmouth | 49 | 253 | Swift | John | 1 | | | 1 | 2 | | | | 1 | | | | 5 | | |
| Falmouth | 49 | 254 | Swift | Betsey | | 1 | | | | | | | 1 | | | | 2 | | |
| Falmouth | 49 | 255 | Verily | Desire | 2 | 2 | | | 1 | | | | 1 | | | | 6 | | |
| Falmouth | 49 | 256 | Weeks | Francis | | | 1 | | | | 1 | | 1 | | | | 3 | | |
| Falmouth | 49 | 257 | Webb | Joseph | | | 1 | | | | 1 | | 1 | | | | 3 | | |
| Falmouth | 49 | 258 | Wood | David | 2 | 1 | | 1 | | | 1 | 1 | | | | | 6 | | |
| Falmouth | 49 | 259 | Weeks | Ebenz | 1 | | 1 | | 3 | | | | 1 | | | | 6 | | |
| Falmouth | 49 | 260 | Weeks | Wm Junr | | | 1 | 1 | 2 | 2 | | | | 1 | | | 7 | | |
| Falmouth | 49 | 261 | Wing | Presbury | 2 | 1 | | 2 | | 1 | 1 | | | | | | 7 | | |
| Falmouth | 49 | 262 | Weeks | Elisha | 1 | 1 | 1 | | 2 | | 1 | | | | | | 6 | | |
| Falmouth | 49 | 263 | Weeks | Richard | 1 | 1 | 1 | | 1 | 2 | | 2 | 1 | | | | 9 | | |
| Falmouth | 49 | 264 | Weeks | Levi | | | 1 | | 1 | | | 1 | | 1 | | | 4 | | |
| Falmouth | 49 | 265 | Wing | James | 2 | 2 | 1 | 1 | | 2 | | 2 | 1 | | | | 11 | | |
| Falmouth | 49 | 266 | Smith | Thos | | | 1 | 1 | | | | | 1 | 1 | 1 | | 4 | | |
| Falmouth | 49 | 267 | Smalley | John | 2 | 1 | | 1 | | 1 | | | 1 | 1 | | | 7 | | |
| Falmouth | 49 | 268 | Young | Andrew | 1 | | | 1 | | | | | 1 | | | | 3 | | |
| Falmouth | 49 | 269 | Handy | Paul | 1 | 2 | 1 | 1 | | 2 | | 1 | 1 | | | | 9 | | |
| Falmouth | 49 | 270 | Hatch | Obadiah | 1 | | | 1 | 1 | | | 1 | 1 | | | | 5 | | |

# 1800 Falmouth, Barnstable County, Massachusetts

| TOWN | PG# | LN# | LAST NAME | FIRST NAME | FREE WHITE MALES | | | | | FREE WHITE FEMALES | | | | | TOTAL ALL OTHER | TOTAL SLAVES | TOTALS | DISTRICT/ TOWNSHIP | NOTES |
|---|---|---|---|---|---|---|---|---|---|---|---|---|---|---|---|---|---|---|---|
| | | | | | under 10 | 10 to 16 | 16 to 26 | 26 to 45 | 45 and over | under 10 | 10 to 16 | 16 to 26 | 26 to 45 | 45 and over | | | | | |
| Falmouth | 49 | 271 | Butler | Mary | | | | | | 1 | 1 | 1 | | | | | 3 | | |
| Falmouth | 49 | 272 | Brown | Prince | | | | | | | | | | | 6 | | 6 | | |
| Falmouth | 49 | 273 | Bagnett | Bethiah | | | | | | | | | | | 1 | | 1 | | |
| Falmouth | 49 | 274 | Young | David | 2 | | | 1 | | | | | 1 | | | | 4 | | |
| Falmouth | 49 | 275 | Handy | Levi | | | 1 | | | 3 | | | 1 | | | | 5 | | |
| Falmouth | 49 | 276 | Handy | Elnathan | | | | 1 | | | | 1 | | 2 | | | 4 | | |
| Falmouth | 49 | 277 | Davis | Solomon | | | | 1 | | | | 1 | | 1 | | | 3 | | |
| Falmouth | 49 | 278 | Fisk | Lemuel | 2 | | 3 | 1 | | 2 | | | 1 | | | | 9 | | |
| Falmouth | 49 | 279 | Fisk | James | 1 | | | 1 | | 1 | | 1 | | | | | 4 | | |
| Falmouth | 49 | 280 | Gifford | Prince 3d | | | | 1 | | 2 | | | 1 | | | | 4 | | |
| Falmouth | 49 | 281 | Gifford | Prince Junr | 1 | | | 1 | | | | | 1 | | | | 3 | | |
| Falmouth | 49 | 282 | Hatch | Reuben | | | 1 | | 1 | | | 3 | | 1 | | | 6 | | |
| Falmouth | 49 | 283 | Hampton | Benja | | | 1 | | 1 | 1 | 1 | | | 1 | | | 5 | | |
| Falmouth | 49 | 284 | Gifford | Lot | | 1 | 2 | | 1 | 3 | 1 | | 1 | | 1 | | 10 | | |
| Falmouth | 49 | 285 | Hatch | Joseph | 2 | 1 | 2 | | 1 | 2 | 2 | | 1 | | | | 11 | | |
| Falmouth | 49 | 286 | Gifford | Alden | | | | 1 | | | | 1 | | | | | 2 | | |
| Falmouth | 49 | 287 | Lothrop | Thomas | 1 | | | 1 | | 1 | | | 1 | | | | 4 | | |
| Falmouth | 49 | 288 | Lovel | Jemimah | | | | | | | | | 1 | 1 | | | 2 | | |
| Falmouth | 49 | 289 | Morsel | Joseph | | | | | | | | | | | | | 5 | | |
| Falmouth | 49 | 290 | | Dinah | | | | | | | | | | | | | 6 | | Last name left blank |
| Falmouth | 49 | 291 | Hatch | Barnabas | 1 | 1 | | | 1 | 1 | 1 | 3 | 1 | | | | 9 | | |
| Falmouth | 49 | 292 | Hatch | Shubael | | | | 1 | | 1 | | | | 1 | | | 3 | | |
| Falmouth | 49 | 293 | Hatch | Katharine | | | | | | | | | 2 | 1 | | | 3 | | |
| Falmouth | 49 | 294 | Parker | Jonathan | 3 | | | 1 | | 1 | | | 1 | | | | 6 | | |
| Falmouth | 49 | 295 | Hatch | Elizabeth | | | | | | | | | | 1 | | | 1 | | |
| Falmouth | 49 | 296 | Small | James | 1 | | 1 | | | | | | 1 | | | | 3 | | |
| Falmouth | 49 | 297 | Hinckley | Elijah | | | 1 | | | | | | 1 | | | | 2 | | |
| Falmouth | 49 | 298 | Davis | Malachai Junr | | | 1 | | | 1 | | | | | | | 2 | | |
| Falmouth | 49 | 299 | Small | Joseph Junr | | | | 1 | | 2 | | | 1 | | | | 4 | | |
| Falmouth | 49 | 300 | Childs | Nathan | | 2 | 2 | | 1 | 1 | | 3 | | | | | 9 | | |
| Falmouth | 49 | 301 | Turner | Walter | 1 | | 1 | | | | | 1 | | | | | 3 | | |
| Falmouth | 49 | 302 | Fisk | Prince | 1 | | 2 | | 1 | 1 | 2 | 2 | | 1 | | | 10 | | |
| Falmouth | 49 | 303 | Studley | Abraham | 1 | | 1 | | | | | 1 | | | | | 3 | | |
| Falmouth | 49 | 304 | Small | John Junr | | | 1 | | | | | 1 | | | | | 2 | | |
| Falmouth | 49 | 305 | Blackford | David | | | | 1 | | | | | 1 | | | | 2 | | |
| Falmouth | 49 | 306 | Blackford | Edward | | 1 | | 1 | | 5 | | 1 | | | | | 8 | | |
| Falmouth | 49 | 307 | Burges | Reuben | 1 | | 1 | | | 1 | | 1 | | | | | 4 | | |
| Falmouth | 49 | 308 | Weeks | Silas | | | 1 | | | | | 1 | | | | | 2 | | |
| Falmouth | 49 | 309 | Davis | Prince | 4 | | 1 | | | | | 1 | | | | | 6 | | |
| Falmouth | 49 | 310 | Davis | David | 1 | | 1 | | | | | 1 | | | | | 3 | | |
| Falmouth | 49 | 311 | Small | Benoni | | 1 | | | | | | 1 | | | | | 2 | | |
| Falmouth | 49 | 312 | Smith | Lucy | | | | | | | | 1 | | | | | 1 | | |
| Falmouth | 49 | 313 | Phinney | Abishai | | 2 | 1 | | | | | 1 | | | | | 4 | | |
| Falmouth | 49 | 314 | Chadwick | Elijah | 1 | 1 | | | | | | 1 | | | | | 3 | | |
| Falmouth | 49 | 315 | Chadwick | Ancry | 1 | | 1 | | | 1 | | 1 | | | | | 4 | | |
| Falmouth | 49 | 316 | Hambl | Nathan | 2 | 1 | 2 | 1 | | | | | 2 | | | | 8 | | |
| Falmouth | 49 | 317 | Handy | Hannah | | | | | | | | 2 | | | | | 2 | | |
| Falmouth | 49 | 318 | Meiggs | Lurany | | | 1 | | | | 2 | | 1 | | | | 4 | | |
| Falmouth | 49 | 319 | Meiggs | Ruth | | | | | | | | 1 | 1 | | | | 2 | | |
| Falmouth | 51 | 320 | Pease | Barzilla | | | 1 | | | 2 | | 2 | | 1 | 1 | | 7 | | |
| Falmouth | 51 | 321 | Bonnie | Ziniel | 3 | 2 | 1 | | | 1 | | 1 | 1 | | | | 9 | | |
| Falmouth | 51 | 322 | Maher | Joseph | | 1 | 1 | | | 2 | | 1 | | | | | 5 | | |
| Falmouth | 51 | 323 | Hatch | Joseph | 1 | | 1 | | | 1 | 1 | | 1 | | | | 5 | | |
| Falmouth | 51 | 324 | Swfit | Elijah | 1 | | 1 | | | 1 | | | | | | | 4 | | |

# 1800 Harwich, Barnstable County, Massachusetts

| TOWN | PG# | LN# | LAST NAME | FIRST NAME | FREE WHITE MALES | | | | | FREE WHITE FEMALES | | | | | TOTAL ALL OTHER | TOTAL SLAVES | TOTALS | DISTRICT/ TOWNSHIP | NOTES |
|---|---|---|---|---|---|---|---|---|---|---|---|---|---|---|---|---|---|---|---|
| | | | | | under 10 | 10 to 16 | 16 to 26 | 26 to 45 | 45 and over | under 10 | 10 to 16 | 16 to 26 | 26 to 45 | 45 and over | | | | | |
| Harwich | 3 | 1 | Sears | Edward | 2 | 1 | | 1 | | 2 | | | 1 | | | | 7 | | |
| Harwich | 3 | 2 | Remick | Freeman | | 2 | 1 | 2 | | 2 | | 1 | 1 | | | | 10 | | |
| Harwich | 3 | 3 | Sears | Joseph | 1 | 1 | | 1 | 1 | 2 | | 1 | 1 | | | | 8 | | |
| Harwich | 3 | 4 | Sears | Prince | | | | 1 | | | | | | 1 | | | 2 | | |
| Harwich | 3 | 5 | Sears | Desire Wid | | | | | | | | | 1 | 1 | | | 2 | | |
| Harwich | 3 | 6 | Sears | Noah | | | | 1 | | | | | 1 | | | | 2 | | |
| Harwich | 3 | 7 | Rider | Ebenezer | | | 1 | | | 1 | | | 1 | | | | 3 | | |
| Harwich | 3 | 8 | Miller | John | 1 | | 1 | | | | | | 1 | | | | 3 | | |
| Harwich | 3 | 9 | Snow | Thomas | | 1 | | 1 | 1 | 1 | | | 1 | 1 | | | 6 | | |
| Harwich | 3 | 10 | Snow | Thomas 3d | 1 | 1 | | 1 | | 3 | | 2 | 1 | | | | 9 | | |
| Harwich | 3 | 11 | Dillingham | John | 2 | | | | 1 | 1 | 1 | 1 | 1 | 1 | | | 8 | | |
| Harwich | 3 | 12 | Dillingham | John Jun | 2 | | 1 | | | | | | 1 | | | | 4 | | |
| Harwich | 3 | 13 | Dillingham | Isaac | | 1 | | | | 1 | | | 1 | | | | 3 | | |
| Harwich | 3 | 14 | Hopkins | Roland | | | 1 | | | 2 | | | 1 | 1 | | | 5 | | |
| Harwich | 3 | 15 | Winslow | John | 1 | | 1 | | | 1 | | 1 | | | | | 4 | | |
| Harwich | 4 | 1 | Hopkins | Freeman | | | 1 | | | 1 | | | 1 | 1 | | | 4 | | |
| Harwich | 4 | 2 | Snow | Thomas Jun | | 1 | | 1 | | | | | | 1 | | | 3 | | |
| Harwich | 4 | 3 | Clark | Praland | 1 | 2 | | 1 | | 1 | | 2 | | 1 | | | 8 | | |
| Harwich | 4 | 4 | Winslow | Isaac | 3 | | 1 | | | 1 | | | 1 | | | | 6 | | |
| Harwich | 4 | 5 | Winslow | Mary Wid | | | | | | | | | 1 | 1 | | | 2 | | |
| Harwich | 4 | 6 | Winslow | Nathaniel | | | 1 | | | | | 1 | | | | | 2 | | |
| Harwich | 4 | 7 | Winslow | Abraham | | | 1 | | | 1 | | | 1 | | | | 3 | | |
| Harwich | 4 | 8 | Winslow | Kenalam | 1 | | 1 | | | | 1 | | 1 | | | | 4 | | |
| Harwich | 4 | 9 | Freeman | John | | | 1 | | | | | 2 | 1 | 1 | | | 5 | | |
| Harwich | 4 | 10 | Freeman | John Jun | 3 | | 1 | | | 1 | | | 1 | | | | 6 | | |
| Harwich | 4 | 11 | Clark | Kimbal Jun | | 1 | 1 | | | | | 1 | | | | | 3 | | |
| Harwich | 4 | 12 | Baker | Luke | 1 | | 1 | | | | | | 1 | | | | 3 | | |
| Harwich | 4 | 13 | Bangs | Elkanah | 3 | | 1 | | | | | | 1 | | | | 5 | | |
| Harwich | 4 | 14 | Snow | Silvanus | 1 | 1 | | | | | | 1 | | | | | 3 | | |
| Harwich | 4 | 15 | Winslow | Joseph | 2 | 1 | 1 | | | 2 | | 2 | | | | | 8 | | |
| Harwich | 4 | 16 | Gray | Hannah Wid | 1 | | | | | | 1 | | 1 | | | | 3 | | |
| Harwich | 4 | 17 | Winslow | Josiah | 2 | 1 | | 1 | | | | | 1 | | | | 5 | | |
| Harwich | 4 | 18 | Winslow | Nathan Jun | 2 | | | 1 | | 1 | 1 | | 1 | | | | 6 | | |
| Harwich | 4 | 19 | Crassey | Abial | 1 | | | 1 | | | | | 1 | | | | 3 | | |
| Harwich | 4 | 20 | Clark | Salomon Jun | | 1 | | | | 2 | | 1 | | | | | 4 | | |
| Harwich | 4 | 21 | Griffith | Barnabas | | 2 | 1 | | | | | 1 | 1 | | | | 5 | | |
| Harwich | 4 | 22 | Griffith | Stephen | | 1 | 1 | 1 | | | | | 2 | | | | 5 | | |
| Harwich | 4 | 23 | Phinney | Lazarus | 1 | | 1 | 1 | | | | | 1 | 1 | | | 5 | | |
| Harwich | 4 | 24 | Phinney | Gershom | | 1 | | 1 | | | 1 | | 2 | | | | 5 | | |
| Harwich | 4 | 25 | Snow | Hannah Wd | | 1 | | | | | | | 1 | | | | 2 | | |
| Harwich | 4 | 26 | Vealnough | Peter | | 1 | 1 | | | 1 | 1 | 1 | | 1 | | | 6 | | |
| Harwich | 4 | 27 | Snow | Lucy Wd | | 1 | | | | | | | 1 | | | | 2 | | |
| Harwich | 4 | 28 | Snow | Edward Jun | 2 | | | 1 | | 3 | 1 | | 1 | | | | 8 | | |
| Harwich | 4 | 29 | Crosby | Samuel | 1 | | | 1 | | 2 | | | 1 | | | | 5 | | |
| Harwich | 4 | 30 | Ray* | Crisp | | 1 | | | | | | 1 | | | | | 2 | | |
| Harwich | 4 | 31 | Crowell | Simeon | | 1 | | | | | | 1 | | | | | 2 | | |
| Harwich | 4 | 32 | Winslow | Nathan | | 1 | 1 | 1 | | | | 1 | 1 | | | | 5 | | |
| Harwich | 4 | 33 | Wing | David | | 1 | | 1 | | 1 | 2 | | 1 | | | | 6 | | |
| Harwich | 4 | 34 | Hopkins | Elkanah | | 2 | | 1 | | | | | 1 | | | | 4 | | |
| Harwich | 4 | 35 | Hopkins | John | 1 | | | 1 | | 3 | | | 1 | | | | 6 | | |
| Harwich | 4 | 36 | Jenkins | Meltiah | 2 | | | 1 | | 2 | | | 1 | 1 | | | 7 | | |
| Harwich | 4 | 37 | Habens | Abner | 1 | 1 | 1 | | | 1 | | 1 | | 1 | | | 6 | | |
| Harwich | 4 | 38 | Sears | Stephen Jun | 1 | | | | | 1 | | | 1 | | | | 4 | | |
| Harwich | 4 | 39 | Clark | Bethiah Wd | 1 | | | | | 1 | | | 1 | | | | 3 | | |
| Harwich | 4 | 40 | Walker | Benjm | 1 | | | | | 2 | | | 1 | | | | 5 | | |
| Harwich | 4 | 41 | Habens | William | | 1 | 1 | | 1 | 1 | | 1 | 2 | 1 | | | 7 | | |
| Harwich | 5 | 1 | Sears | Stephen | | 2 | | 1 | | | 1 | | | | | | 4 | | |
| Harwich | 5 | 2 | Sears | Levi | 1 | | 1 | | | | | | 1 | | | | 3 | | |
| Harwich | 5 | 3 | McClaud | Anguish | 1 | | 1 | 1 | 1 | | 1 | 2 | | 1 | | | 8 | | |
| Harwich | 5 | 4 | Sears | Reuben | 3 | 2 | | 1 | 2 | | | 2 | 1 | | | | 11 | | |
| Harwich | 5 | 5 | Mayo | Asa | 5 | 2 | 2 | | 1 | 2 | | 1 | 1 | | | | 14 | | |
| Harwich | 5 | 6 | Gray | Joshua | | 1 | 1 | 1 | | 1 | | | | 1 | | | 5 | | |
| Harwich | 5 | 7 | Cobb | Eleanor | | | 1 | 1 | | | | 2 | 1 | | | | 5 | | |
| Harwich | 5 | 8 | Pain | James | | | | 1 | | | | | 2 | | | | 3 | | |
| Harwich | 5 | 9 | Pain | Eleanor | 1 | | | 1 | | 2 | | | 1 | | | | 5 | | |
| Harwich | 5 | 10 | Pain | James Jun | 2 | 2 | | 1 | | 2 | | | 1 | | | | 8 | | |
| Harwich | 5 | 11 | Prayers | Samuel | 1 | | | 1 | | 2 | | | 1 | | | | 5 | | |
| Harwich | 5 | 12 | Pain | Silvanus | 4 | | 1 | | | | | | 1 | | | | 6 | | |
| Harwich | 5 | 13 | Atwood | David | | 1 | | 1 | | | 2 | | 1 | | | | 5 | | |
| Harwich | 5 | 14 | Atwood | Nehemiah | 1 | | 1 | 1 | | | | 1 | | | | | 4 | | |
| Harwich | 5 | 15 | Freeman | Solomon | | 1 | | 1 | | | | 1 | 1 | | | | 4 | | |
| Harwich | 5 | 16 | Freeman | Solomon Jun | 3 | | 1 | | | 1 | | 1 | | | | | 6 | | |
| Harwich | 5 | 17 | Snow | Jonathan | 1 | 3 | | 1 | | 2 | 1 | | 1 | | | | 9 | | |
| Harwich | 5 | 18 | Cobb | Barnabas | | 1 | 1 | | 1 | | | 1 | 1 | | | | 5 | | |
| Harwich | 5 | 19 | Crosby | Elisha Jun | | 1 | | | | | | 1 | | | | | 2 | | |
| Harwich | 5 | 20 | Foster | John | | 1 | 2 | 1 | | | | 1 | 1 | | | | 6 | | |
| Harwich | 5 | 21 | Crosby | Barnabas | 2 | | 1 | | | 1 | | 1 | 1 | | | | 6 | | |
| Harwich | 5 | 22 | Crosby | Lemuel | | | | 1 | | | 1 | | 1 | | | | 3 | | |
| Harwich | 5 | 23 | Foster | Isaac | 1 | | | 1 | | | | | 1 | | | | 3 | | |
| Harwich | 5 | 24 | Foster | Samuel | 1 | | 1 | | | 1 | | 1 | | | | | 4 | | |
| Harwich | 5 | 25 | Cobb | Seth | | | | 1 | | | | | 1 | | | | 2 | | |
| Harwich | 5 | 26 | Snow | Enos | | | | 1 | | | | | 1 | | | | 2 | | |
| Harwich | 5 | 27 | Gould | Joseph | | 3 | | 1 | | 1 | 1 | | 1 | | | | 7 | | |
| Harwich | 5 | 28 | Berry | Judah | | 2 | | 1 | | | | 1 | 1 | | | | 5 | | |
| Harwich | 5 | 29 | Berry | Lemuel | | | 1 | | | | | 1 | | | | | 2 | | |
| Harwich | 5 | 30 | Snow | Thankfull | | 1 | | | | | | | 2 | | | | 3 | | |
| Harwich | 5 | 31 | Mayo | Elkanah | | 2 | | 1 | | 2 | 2 | | 1 | | | | 8 | | |
| Harwich | 5 | 32 | Hopkins | Mary Wd | 1 | 2 | | | | 1 | 1 | | 1 | | | | 6 | | |
| Harwich | 5 | 33 | Foster | Nathaniel | 3 | 2 | 2 | 1 | | 1 | 2 | | 1 | | | | 12 | | |
| Harwich | 5 | 34 | Berry | Leatte | | | | | | | | | | | | | | | |

# 1800 Harwich, Barnstable County, Massachusetts

| TOWN | PG# | LN# | LAST NAME | FIRST NAME | FREE WHITE MALES under 10 | 10 to 16 | 16 to 26 | 26 to 45 | 45 and over | FREE WHITE FEMALES under 10 | 10 to 16 | 16 to 26 | 26 to 45 | 45 and over | TOTAL ALL OTHER | TOTAL SLAVES | TOTALS | DISTRICT/ TOWNSHIP | NOTES |
|---|---|---|---|---|---|---|---|---|---|---|---|---|---|---|---|---|---|---|---|
| Harwich | 5 | 35 | Berry | John D | 1 | | 1 | 1 | | | 1 | 1 | 1 | 1 | | | 7 | | |
| Harwich | 5 | 36 | Clark | Solomon | | 1 | | 1 | | | | | | | | | 2 | | |
| Harwich | 5 | 37 | Clark | Edward | | | | 1 | | | 1 | 1 | 2 | 1 | | | 6 | | |
| Harwich | 5 | 38 | Clark | Isaac | 2 | 1 | | 1 | | 2 | | | 1 | | | | 7 | | |
| Harwich | 5 | 39 | Clark | Kimbal | 1 | | 1 | 1 | | | | | | 1 | | | 4 | | |
| Harwich | 5 | 40 | Foster | Chillingworth | | | | 1 | | | 1 | 1 | | 1 | | | 4 | | |
| Harwich | 5 | 41 | Pain | Thankfull Wd | 1 | 1 | | | | | | 2 | | 1 | | | 5 | | |
| Harwich | 5 | 42 | Foster | Chillingworth Jun | | | 1 | | | 2 | | | 1 | | | | 4 | | |
| Harwich | 5 | 43 | Freeman | Seth Jun | 2 | 1 | 1 | | 1 | | | 2 | | 1 | | | 8 | | |
| Harwich | 5 | 44 | Freeman | Lemuel | 1 | 2 | | | 1 | | 1 | 3 | | 1 | | | 9 | | |
| Harwich | 6 | 1 | Freeman | Desire Wd | | | | | | | | | | 3 | | | 3 | | |
| Harwich | 6 | 2 | Lincoln | Nathaniel | 2 | | | 1 | | 1 | | | 1 | | | | 5 | | |
| Harwich | 6 | 3 | Crosby | James Jun | 2 | | | 1 | | 2 | | | 1 | | | | 6 | | |
| Harwich | 6 | 4 | Crosby | John | | 1 | 1 | 1 | | | | | 1 | 1 | | | 5 | | |
| Harwich | 6 | 5 | Crosby | Silvanus | | | | 1 | | | | | 1 | 1 | | | 3 | | |
| Harwich | 6 | 6 | Crosby | Silvanus Jun | | 1 | | | | 1 | | | 1 | | | | 3 | | |
| Harwich | 6 | 7 | Pain | Samuel | | 1 | | 1 | | | | | 1 | | | | 3 | | |
| Harwich | 6 | 8 | Foster | James | 1 | 1 | | 1 | | 1 | | | 1 | | | | 5 | | |
| Harwich | 6 | 9 | Hopkins | Lydia Wd | | | | | | | | 1 | 1 | | | | 2 | | |
| Harwich | 6 | 10 | Bangs | Silvanus | | | 1 | | | 2 | | | 1 | | | | 4 | | |
| Harwich | 6 | 11 | Bangs | Joshua | 1 | | 1 | | | 1 | | 1 | | | | | 4 | | |
| Harwich | 6 | 12 | Clark | Josiah | 3 | 1 | 1 | | | 1 | | | 1 | | | | 7 | | |
| Harwich | 6 | 13 | Clark | Anna | | 1 | | | | | | | | 2 | | | 3 | | |
| Harwich | 6 | 14 | Freeman | Simeon | 1 | 2 | | 1 | | | 1 | 1 | | 1 | | | 7 | | |
| Harwich | 6 | 15 | Killey | Samuel | 1 | 1 | 1 | 1 | | 1 | | 1 | 1 | 1 | | | 8 | | |
| Harwich | 6 | 16 | Chase | David | 1 | | | 1 | | | | | 1 | 1 | | | 4 | | |
| Harwich | 6 | 17 | Gaye | Mayo | 3 | | 2 | | | 1 | | 1 | | 1 | | | 8 | | |
| Harwich | 6 | 18 | Killey | Ebenezer | 2 | | 1 | | | | 1 | 1 | | | | | 5 | | |
| Harwich | 6 | 19 | Killey | Patrick | | | | 2 | | | | | 1 | | | | 3 | | |
| Harwich | 6 | 20 | Sears | Willard | 1 | | | 1 | | 3 | 2 | | 1 | | | | 8 | | |
| Harwich | 6 | 21 | Freeman | Isaac | | 1 | 2 | 1 | | 1 | 2 | | 1 | | | | 8 | | |
| Harwich | 6 | 22 | Read | Thomas | 1 | | | 1 | | 3 | | | 1 | | | | 6 | | |
| Harwich | 6 | 23 | Snow | Reuben | 2 | 1 | | 1 | | | | | 1 | | | | 5 | | |
| Harwich | 6 | 24 | Snow | John | | | 1 | | | | | 3 | | | | | 4 | | |
| Harwich | 6 | 25 | Mayo | Elnathan | 2 | 1 | | 1 | | 2 | 1 | 1 | 1 | | | | 9 | | |
| Harwich | 6 | 26 | Crosby | Anthony | 2 | | | 1 | | 1 | | | 1 | | | | 5 | | |
| Harwich | 6 | 27 | Mayo | Lydia Wd | | | | | | 1 | 2 | | 1 | | | | 4 | | |
| Harwich | 6 | 28 | Mayo | Moses | | | | 1 | 1 | | | | | 2 | | | 4 | | |
| Harwich | 6 | 29 | Crosby | Hemon | | 1 | 1 | 1 | | | | | 1 | 1 | | | 5 | | |
| Harwich | 6 | 30 | Small | Thomas | 2 | | | 1 | | 3 | | | 1 | | | | 7 | | |
| Harwich | 6 | 31 | Snow | Moses | 2 | | | 1 | | 2 | | | 1 | | | | 6 | | |
| Harwich | 6 | 32 | Hopkins | Zoheth | 1 | | | 1 | | 3 | 1 | | 1 | | | | 7 | | |
| Harwich | 6 | 33 | Hopkins | Hannah Wd | | | | | | | | 1 | | 1 | | | 2 | | |
| Harwich | 6 | 34 | Wexsom | Elijah | 2 | | 1 | | | | | | 1 | | | | 4 | | |
| Harwich | 6 | 35 | Mahee | Seth | 2 | 1 | | | 1 | 2 | | 1 | | 1 | | | 8 | | |
| Harwich | 6 | 36 | Freeman | Seth | 2 | 2 | 1 | | 1 | | | 2 | | 1 | | | 9 | | |
| Harwich | 6 | 37 | Bangs | Ebenezor | | | | 1 | | | | | | 1 | | | 2 | | |
| Harwich | 6 | 38 | Bangs | Ebenezor Jun | 2 | | | 1 | | 2 | | | 1 | | | | 6 | | |
| Harwich | 6 | 39 | Hopkins | Nathan | | 1 | 1 | 1 | | | | | 1 | 1 | | | 5 | | |
| Harwich | 6 | 40 | Hopkins | Nathan Jun | 1 | | 1 | | | | | | 1 | | | | 3 | | |
| Harwich | 6 | 41 | King | Roger | 3 | 2 | | 1 | | 2 | 1 | | 1 | | | | 10 | | |
| Harwich | 6 | 42 | Eldrege | Hezekiah | | 1 | | 1 | | | 1 | | 1 | | | | 4 | | |
| Harwich | 7 | 1 | Crosby | Ebenezer | | | 3 | 1 | | | 1 | 2 | | 1 | | | 8 | | |
| Harwich | 7 | 2 | Crosby | David | 3 | | 1 | | | 2 | | | 1 | | | | 7 | | |
| Harwich | 7 | 3 | Crosby | Nathaniel | | 1 | | 1 | | | | | 1 | 1 | | | 4 | | |
| Harwich | 7 | 4 | Crosby | Elisha | | 1 | | 1 | | | | 1 | | 1 | | | 4 | | |
| Harwich | 7 | 5 | Crosby | Nathan | 4 | | 1 | | | | | | 1 | | | | 6 | | |
| Harwich | 7 | 6 | Crosby | Josiah | | | | 1 | | | | 1 | | 1 | | | 3 | | |
| Harwich | 7 | 7 | Crosby | William | 1 | | | 1 | | 2 | | 1 | 1 | | | | 6 | | |
| Harwich | 7 | 8 | Atwood | Judson | | 1 | | 1 | | | 1 | | 1 | 1 | | | 5 | | |
| Harwich | 7 | 9 | Crosby | James | | 1 | | 1 | | | | | | 2 | | | 4 | | |
| Harwich | 7 | 10 | Crosby | Thomas | | | 1 | | | | | | 1 | | | | 2 | | |
| Harwich | 7 | 11 | Crosby | Seth | 1 | | 1 | 1 | | | | 2 | 1 | 1 | | | 7 | | |
| Harwich | 7 | 12 | Foster | Seth | 1 | 3 | | 1 | | 2 | 2 | 2 | | 1 | | | 12 | | |
| Harwich | 7 | 13 | Crosby | Rebecah Wd | 1 | 2 | | | | | | | | 1 | | | 4 | | |
| Harwich | 7 | 14 | Lincoln | Susanna Wd | | 1 | 1 | | | | | | 1 | 1 | | | 4 | | |
| Harwich | 7 | 15 | Dun | Peter | | 1 | | | | | | | 1 | | | | 2 | | |
| Harwich | 7 | 16 | Hopkins | Moses | 1 | | | 1 | | | | | 1 | 1 | | | 4 | | |
| Harwich | 7 | 17 | Ripley | Nathaniel | | | 1 | | | 1 | | 1 | | | | | 3 | | |
| Harwich | 7 | 18 | Freeman | Nathaniel | | | | 1 | | | | | 1 | 2 | | | 4 | | |
| Harwich | 7 | 19 | Crosby | Samuel Jun | 1 | | | 1 | | 1 | | | 1 | | | | 4 | | |
| Harwich | 7 | 20 | Lincoln | Seth | 3 | 1 | 2 | 1 | | 1 | | 1 | 1 | | | | 10 | | |
| Harwich | 7 | 21 | Snow | Joseph | | | 1 | | | 2 | | | 1 | | | | 4 | | |
| Harwich | 7 | 22 | Crocker | Joseph | | 1 | | | | 1 | | 1 | | | | | 3 | | |
| Harwich | 7 | 23 | Snow | Priscilla Wid | | 2 | | | | | | | | 1 | | | 3 | | |
| Harwich | 7 | 24 | Nickerson | David | 1 | | 1 | | | | | | 1 | | | | 3 | | |
| Harwich | 7 | 25 | Snow | Zaheth | 1 | | 1 | | | 2 | | | 1 | | | | 5 | | |
| Harwich | 7 | 26 | Atwood | Barnabas | | 2 | | | 1 | 2 | | 1 | 1 | | | | 7 | | |
| Harwich | 7 | 27 | King | Pheba Wd | | | | | | | | 1 | | 1 | | | 2 | | |
| Harwich | 7 | 28 | Clark | Reuben | | | | 1 | | | | | 1 | 2 | | | 4 | | |
| Harwich | 7 | 29 | Mayo | Edmond | 1 | 1 | 1 | | | | | | 1 | | | | 4 | | |
| Harwich | 7 | 30 | Foster | Benjm | | | 1 | | | 1 | | 1 | | | | | 3 | | |
| Harwich | 7 | 31 | Freeman | Elkanah | 3 | | | 1 | | 3 | 1 | 1 | 1 | 1 | | | 11 | | |
| Harwich | 7 | 32 | Lincoln | Silvanus | | 1 | | 1 | | 2 | | | 1 | | | | 5 | | |
| Harwich | 7 | 33 | Foster | Isaac Jun | 1 | | 1 | | | | | 1 | | | | | 3 | | |
| Harwich | 7 | 34 | Tacher | Lucy Wd | | | | | | | 1 | | | 2 | | | 3 | | |
| Harwich | 7 | 35 | Cook | Nathaniel | | | | 1 | | | | | | 1 | | | 2 | | |
| Harwich | 7 | 36 | Cook | Temperance Wd | | | | | | | | 2 | | 1 | | | 3 | | |
| Harwich | 7 | 37 | Lincoln | Isaac | 1 | | 1 | | | 1 | | 1 | | | | | 4 | | |
| Harwich | 7 | 38 | Mayo | James | | | 1 | | | | 1 | | | | | | 3 | | |

# 1800 Harwich, Barnstable County, Massachusetts

| TOWN | PG# | LN# | LAST NAME | FIRST NAME | FREE WHITE MALES | | | | | FREE WHITE FEMALES | | | | | TOTAL ALL OTHER | TOTAL SLAVES | TOTALS | DISTRICT/ TOWNSHIP | NOTES |
|---|---|---|---|---|---|---|---|---|---|---|---|---|---|---|---|---|---|---|---|
| | | | | | under 10 | 10 to 16 | 16 to 26 | 26 to 45 | 45 and over | under 10 | 10 to 16 | 16 to 26 | 26 to 45 | 45 and over | | | | | |
| Harwich | 7 | 39 | Wing | Born | | 1 | 1 | | 1 | | | 2 | | 1 | | | 6 | | |
| Harwich | 7 | 40 | Wing | Samuel | | | | | 1 | | | 1 | | 1 | | | 3 | | |
| Harwich | 7 | 41 | Berry | Jonathan | | 2 | 1 | | 1 | | 1 | 1 | 1 | 1 | | | 8 | | |
| Harwich | 8 | 1 | Bangs | Dean | 2 | 1 | 1 | 1 | | 1 | | 2 | 1 | | | | 9 | | |
| Harwich | 8 | 2 | Lincoln | David | | | 1 | | | | | | 1 | | | | 2 | | |
| Harwich | 8 | 3 | Berry | Theofelus | | | | 1 | | | | | 1 | 1 | | | 3 | | |
| Harwich | 8 | 4 | Gray | Anthony | | 1 | | 1 | | | | | 1 | | | | 3 | | |
| Harwich | 8 | 5 | Bailey | John | | | 1 | | | | | | 1 | | | | 2 | | |
| Harwich | 8 | 6 | Snow | Nathaniel | | | 1 | 1 | | 1 | | | 2 | | | | 5 | | |
| Harwich | 8 | 7 | Berry | Mercy Wd | | | 1 | | | | | | 2 | 1 | | | 4 | | |
| Harwich | 8 | 8 | Clark | Joseph | | 2 | | 1 | | | | | 1 | 1 | | | 5 | | |
| Harwich | 8 | 9 | Harding | Ruben | | | | 1 | | 2 | | | 1 | | | | 4 | | |
| Harwich | 8 | 10 | Bangs | Benjm | 3 | 1 | | 2 | | | 2 | | 1 | 2 | | | 11 | | |
| Harwich | 8 | 11 | Hopkins | John Rev | 2 | | 1 | 2 | | 2 | | | 1 | 1 | | | 9 | | |
| Harwich | 8 | 12 | Stone | Mary Wd | | | | | 2 | | | | 1 | 1 | | | 5 | | |
| Harwich | 8 | 13 | Seaburry | Thomas | 3 | | 1 | | | 3 | | | 2 | | | | 9 | | |
| Harwich | 8 | 14 | Mayo | Thomas | 3 | 2 | | 1 | | 1 | | 1 | 1 | 1 | | | 10 | | |
| Harwich | 8 | 15 | Obriant | Edward | 4 | | 1 | | | | | | 1 | | | | 6 | | |
| Harwich | 8 | 16 | Cobb | Elijah | 2 | | 1 | | | 1 | | | 1 | | | | 6 | | |
| Harwich | 8 | 17 | Higgins | Jacob | | 3 | | 1 | | | | | | 1 | | | 5 | | |
| Harwich | 8 | 18 | Higgins | Hezekiel | | 1 | | | | | | 1 | | | | | 2 | | |
| Harwich | 8 | 19 | Fessenden | William | | 1 | | 1 | | | | | 1 | 1 | | | 4 | | |
| Harwich | 8 | 20 | Fessenden | William Jun | 2 | 1 | 1 | | | | | 1 | | | | | 5 | | |
| Harwich | 8 | 21 | Eden | Samuel | | | | 1 | | 1 | 1 | | 1 | | | | 4 | | |
| Harwich | 8 | 22 | Bradford | Cornelius | 2 | 1 | | 1 | | 2 | | | 1 | | | | 7 | | |
| Harwich | 8 | 23 | Clark | Jedian | | | 3 | 1 | | 1 | | | 1 | | | | 6 | | |
| Harwich | 8 | 24 | Minich | Isaac | 2 | 1 | | 1 | | 3 | 1 | | 1 | | | | 9 | | |
| Harwich | 8 | 25 | Minich | Samuel | 3 | 1 | 2 | 1 | | | 1 | 1 | 1 | | | | 10 | | |
| Harwich | 8 | 26 | Chase | Richard | | | | 1 | | | | 2 | | 2 | | | 5 | | |
| Harwich | 8 | 27 | Clark | Silvanus | | | 1 | 1 | | 1 | | 1 | | 1 | | | 5 | | |
| Harwich | 8 | 28 | Clark | Enoch | 3 | 1 | | 1 | | 1 | 1 | 1 | 1 | | | | 9 | | |
| Harwich | 8 | 29 | Berry | David | 1 | | | | | | | | 1 | | | | 3 | | |
| Harwich | 8 | 30 | Berry | Jerusha Wd | | | | | | | | | | 1 | | | 1 | | |
| Harwich | 8 | 31 | Gray | Samuel | 1 | 3 | | 1 | | 3 | | | 1 | | | | 9 | | |
| Harwich | 8 | 32 | Gray | Lot | | 1 | | 1 | | 4 | 2 | | 1 | | | | 9 | | |
| Harwich | 8 | 33 | Gray | Zeporiah Wd | | | | 1 | | | | | | 1 | | | 2 | | |
| Harwich | 8 | 34 | Berry | Benjamin | 1 | | | 1 | | 1 | 1 | | 1 | | | | 5 | | |
| Harwich | 8 | 35 | Crosby | Josiah | 2 | | | 1 | | | | | 1 | 1 | | | 5 | | |
| Harwich | 8 | 36 | Bangs | Sarah Wd | | | | | | 1 | 1 | | | 1 | | | 3 | | |
| Harwich | 8 | 37 | Crosby | Moses | | | | 1 | | | | | 1 | 1 | | | 3 | | |
| Harwich | 8 | 38 | Rogers | Caleb | 1 | 1 | 1 | 1 | 1 | 1 | | | 1 | | | | 7 | | |
| Harwich | 8 | 39 | Foster | Seth Jun | | | 1 | | | | | | 1 | | | | 2 | | |
| Harwich | 8 | 40 | King | Uriel | 2 | 1 | 1 | | | | | | 1 | 2 | | | 8 | | |
| Harwich | 8 | 41 | King | Nathaniel | 1 | 1 | 1 | | 1 | 1 | 1 | | 1 | 1 | | | 8 | | |
| Harwich | 8 | 42 | Hopkins | Stephen | 1 | | | 1 | | | | 2 | 1 | 1 | | | 6 | | |
| Harwich | 8 | 43 | Hopkins | Nathaniel | 1 | | 1 | | | | | | 1 | | | | 3 | | |
| Harwich | 8 | 44 | Hopkins | Prince | 1 | | 1 | | | 1 | | | 1 | | | | 4 | | |
| Harwich | 8 | 45 | Hopkins | Patiance Wd | | | | | | | | | 1 | 1 | | | 2 | | |
| Harwich | 8 | 46 | Hopkins | Jonathan | | 1 | | | | | | | 1 | 1 | | | 3 | | |
| Harwich | 9 | 1 | Hopkins | Edmond | 1 | | | 1 | | 1 | | | 1 | | | | 4 | | |
| Harwich | 9 | 2 | Foster | David | 3 | | 2 | 1 | | 1 | 1 | 1 | 1 | | | | 10 | | |
| Harwich | 9 | 3 | Crosby | Elkanah | | | 1 | | 3 | 3 | | | 1 | | | | 8 | | |
| Harwich | 9 | 4 | Mayo | Joseph | 2 | 1 | | 1 | | 2 | | | 1 | | | | 8 | | |
| Harwich | 9 | 5 | Mayo | Isaac | | 1 | | 1 | | | | | 1 | 1 | | | 4 | | |
| Harwich | 9 | 6 | Mayo | Nathan | 1 | | 1 | 2 | 1 | | 1 | | 1 | 1 | | | 8 | | |
| Harwich | 9 | 7 | Gould | John | | | | 1 | | 1 | 3 | | 1 | | | | 6 | | |
| Harwich | 9 | 8 | Kindericks | Jonathan | | 2 | 1 | | 1 | | 2 | 1 | 1 | | | | 9 | | |
| Harwich | 9 | 9 | Kindericks | Edward | 1 | | 3 | 1 | | | | 2 | | | | | 7 | | |
| Harwich | 9 | 10 | Kindericks | Thomas | | 1 | 1 | 1 | | | | | 1 | 1 | | | 5 | | |
| Harwich | 9 | 11 | Kindericks | Nathan | 2 | | | 1 | | | | | 1 | | | | 5 | | |
| Harwich | 9 | 12 | Kindericks | David | 1 | | | 1 | | 1 | | | 1 | | | | 4 | | |
| Harwich | 9 | 13 | Kindericks | Jonathan Jun | | 1 | | | | | | | 1 | | | | 2 | | |
| Harwich | 9 | 14 | Rogers | Emos | 1 | | | 1 | | | | 2 | 1 | | | | 5 | | |
| Harwich | 9 | 15 | Rogers | Reuben | | | | 1 | | | | | 1 | | | | 2 | | |
| Harwich | 9 | 16 | Nickerson | Edward | | 1 | 1 | | | | | | 1 | | | | 3 | | |
| Harwich | 9 | 17 | Nickerson | Barzillos | 1 | | | 1 | | | | 2 | 1 | | | | 5 | | |
| Harwich | 9 | 18 | Nickerson | Stephen | 2 | | 3 | 1 | | | 1 | 1 | | 1 | | | 9 | | |
| Harwich | 9 | 19 | Long | William | 1 | 1 | | 1 | | | 1 | 2 | | 1 | | | 7 | | |
| Harwich | 9 | 20 | Long | William Jun | | | 1 | | | | 3 | | 1 | | | | 5 | | |
| Harwich | 9 | 21 | Long | Levi | 2 | 2 | | 1 | | 2 | 2 | | 1 | | | | 10 | | |
| Harwich | 9 | 22 | Small | Eli | 3 | | | 1 | | 1 | 1 | | 1 | | | | 7 | | |
| Harwich | 9 | 23 | Small | Zebadee | 1 | | | 1 | | 2 | | | 1 | | | | 5 | | |
| Harwich | 9 | 24 | Cahoon | Seth | 2 | 1 | 1 | 1 | | 2 | 1 | 1 | 1 | 1 | | | 11 | | |
| Harwich | 9 | 25 | Covil | James | 2 | | | | | | | | 1 | 1 | | | 4 | | |
| Harwich | 9 | 26 | Clancy | Elnathan Jun | 1 | | | 1 | | 1 | | | 1 | | | | 4 | | |
| Harwich | 9 | 27 | Cahoon | William | 1 | | 2 | 1 | | 2 | 1 | | | 1 | | | 9 | | |
| Harwich | 9 | 28 | Eldrege | Samuel | 1 | 1 | 1 | 1 | | 3 | 1 | | | 1 | | | 10 | | |
| Harwich | 9 | 29 | Cahoon | Reuben | | 1 | | 1 | | | | | | 1 | | | 3 | | |
| Harwich | 9 | 30 | Eldrege | Reuben | | | | 1 | | | | | 1 | 1 | | | 3 | | |
| Harwich | 9 | 31 | Small | Benjamin | | | | 1 | | 1 | | | | 1 | | | 3 | | |
| Harwich | 9 | 32 | Eldrege | Boruck | 1 | | 1 | | | 3 | 1 | | | | | | 6 | | |
| Harwich | 9 | 33 | Eldrege | Mary Wd | 1 | | | | | | | 1 | 1 | 1 | | | 5 | | |
| Harwich | 9 | 34 | Allen | Seth | 1 | | 2 | 1 | | 4 | 1 | | 1 | | | | 9 | | |
| Harwich | 9 | 35 | Eldrege | Daniel | 4 | | | 1 | | 1 | 1 | | 1 | | | | 8 | | |
| Harwich | 9 | 36 | Eldrege | William | 2 | 1 | 1 | 1 | | | | | | 1 | | | 7 | | |
| Harwich | 9 | 37 | Cahoon | John | | 1 | 2 | | | 3 | 1 | | 1 | | | | 8 | | |
| Harwich | 9 | 38 | Cahoon | Jesse | 1 | 2 | 1 | 1 | | | | 2 | | 1 | | | 8 | | |
| Harwich | 9 | 39 | Phillips | Jonathan | 1 | | 1 | | | 3 | 1 | | 1 | | | | 7 | | |
| Harwich | 9 | 40 | Doane | Benjm | 1 | | 1 | | | 2 | | | 1 | | | | 5 | | |
| Harwich | 9 | 41 | Long | John | 1 | | 1 | | | | | 1 | 1 | | | | 5 | | |

# 1800 Harwich, Barnstable County, Massachusetts

| TOWN | PG# | LN# | HEADS OF HOUSEHOLD | | FREE WHITE MALES | | | | | FREE WHITE FEMALES | | | | | TOTAL ALL OTHER | TOTAL SLAVES | TOTALS | DISTRICT/ TOWNSHIP | NOTES |
|---|---|---|---|---|---|---|---|---|---|---|---|---|---|---|---|---|---|---|---|
| | | | LAST NAME | FIRST NAME | under 10 | 10 to 16 | 16 to 26 | 26 to 45 | 45 and over | under 10 | 10 to 16 | 16 to 26 | 26 to 45 | 45 and over | | | | | |
| Harwich | 9 | 42 | Long | John Junr | 1 | | | 1 | | 2 | | | 1 | | | | 5 | | |
| Harwich | 10 | 1 | Young | Prince | | | | | 1 | | | | 1 | | | | 2 | | |
| Harwich | 10 | 2 | Young | John | 2 | 1 | | 1 | | 1 | 2 | 1 | 1 | | | | 9 | | |
| Harwich | 10 | 3 | Small | Edward | | | 1 | 1 | | | | | 1 | 1 | | | 4 | | |
| Harwich | 10 | 4 | Small | Reuben | | | 1 | | | 2 | | 1 | | | | | 4 | | |
| Harwich | 10 | 5 | Phillips | Joseph | 2 | | 2 | | 1 | 1 | 2 | | | 1 | | | 9 | | |
| Harwich | 10 | 6 | Eldrege | Judah | 1 | | | 1 | | | | 1 | | 1 | | | 4 | | |
| Harwich | 10 | 7 | Nickerson | Seth | 4 | 2 | 1 | 1 | | 1 | | | 1 | | | | 10 | | |
| Harwich | 10 | 8 | Walker | Jeremiah | | | | 1 | | | | | | 1 | | | 2 | | |
| Harwich | 10 | 9 | Weeks | Ebenezer | 2 | | 2 | 1 | | 1 | 1 | 2 | 1 | | | | 10 | | |
| Harwich | 10 | 10 | Chase | Ebenezer Jun | 2 | 1 | 1 | | 1 | | | 2 | | 1 | | | 8 | | |
| Harwich | 10 | 11 | Small | Edward Jun | 2 | | | 1 | | 4 | | | | 1 | | | 8 | | |
| Harwich | 10 | 12 | Snow | Knowls | 1 | | | 1 | | 1 | | | | 1 | | | 4 | | |
| Harwich | 10 | 13 | Small | Isaac | 2 | | | 1 | | | | | | 1 | | | 4 | | |
| Harwich | 10 | 14 | Small | Samuel | 1 | | 1 | | | | | 1 | | | | | 3 | | |
| Harwich | 10 | 15 | Bassett | David | 3 | 2 | | 1 | | 4 | | | 1 | | | | 11 | | |
| Harwich | 10 | 16 | Cahoon | James Jun | 1 | 1 | | | | | | 1 | | | | | 3 | | |
| Harwich | 10 | 17 | Bassett | Richard | | 1 | | 1 | | 1 | 2 | 2 | | 1 | | | 8 | | |
| Harwich | 10 | 18 | Small | William | 2 | 2 | 1 | 1 | | 2 | | 1 | 1 | | | | 10 | | |
| Harwich | 10 | 19 | Baker | Ezra | 2 | | | 1 | | 1 | | 1 | | | | | 5 | | |
| Harwich | 10 | 20 | Rider | William | | | 1 | | | 1 | | 1 | | | | | 3 | | |
| Harwich | 10 | 21 | Baxter | Nathaniel | 1 | | | 1 | | 2 | | 1 | | | | | 5 | | |
| Harwich | 10 | 22 | Mayo | Peter | | | 1 | | | 1 | | 1 | | | | | 3 | | |
| Harwich | 10 | 23 | Broadbrooks | Ebenezer Esq | 2 | | 1 | | 2 | 2 | 2 | 1 | 1 | 1 | | | 12 | | |
| Harwich | 10 | 24 | Gifford | Calvin | | | 1 | | | 3 | | 1 | | | | | 5 | | |
| Harwich | 10 | 25 | Hall | John | | | 1 | | | 3 | | 1 | | | | | 5 | | |
| Harwich | 10 | 26 | Nickerson | Benjm | 2 | | 2 | | 1 | 1 | 2 | | 1 | | | | 9 | | |
| Harwich | 10 | 27 | Ellis | John | 1 | 1 | | | 1 | 1 | 1 | | 1 | | | | 6 | | |
| Harwich | 10 | 28 | Bangs | Jonathan Jun | 1 | | 1 | | | | | 1 | | | | | 3 | | |
| Harwich | 10 | 29 | Covill | Mary Wd | | | 1 | | | | | | | 2 | | | 3 | | |
| Harwich | 10 | 30 | Hinckley | Phillip | 2 | | | 1 | | | | 1 | 1 | | | | 5 | | |
| Harwich | 10 | 31 | Trabens | Nathaniel | 1 | 3 | | 1 | | 1 | | | | 1 | | | 7 | | |
| Harwich | 10 | 32 | Trabens | Nathaniel Jun | | 1 | | 1 | | 1 | 2 | | 1 | | | | 6 | | |
| Harwich | 10 | 33 | Nickerson | Hannah Wd | | | | | | | | | | 3 | | | 3 | | |
| Harwich | 10 | 34 | Covil | Benjm | 1 | | | 1 | | 2 | | | 1 | | | | 5 | | |
| Harwich | 10 | 35 | Small | Daniel | 3 | 1 | | 1 | | 2 | 1 | | 1 | | | | 9 | | |
| Harwich | 10 | 36 | Small | Olive Wd | 1 | | | | | | 1 | 1 | | | | | 3 | | |
| Harwich | 10 | 37 | Small | Jonathan | | | | | 2 | | | 1 | | 1 | | | 4 | | |
| Harwich | 10 | 38 | Phillips | Oker Jun | 2 | | | 1 | | 1 | 1 | | 1 | | | | 6 | | |
| Harwich | 10 | 39 | Davis | Samuel | 1 | | | 1 | | 3 | | | 1 | | | | 6 | | |
| Harwich | 10 | 40 | Ellis | Barnabas | 1 | | | | | 1 | | | 1 | | | | 3 | | |
| Harwich | 10 | 41 | Weeks | Daniel | 1 | | | | 1 | 1 | | | 1 | | | | 4 | | |
| Harwich | 10 | 42 | Small | Jonah | 1 | | | 1 | | | | | 1 | | | | 3 | | |
| Harwich | 10 | 43 | Long | Zachariah | 1 | 2 | | 1 | | 4 | | | 1 | | | | 9 | | |
| Harwich | 10 | 44 | Cash | Samuel | 1 | | 2 | 1 | | 2 | 2 | | 1 | | | | 9 | | |
| Harwich | 11 | 1 | Weeks | Pheba | | | | | | | | | 1 | 1 | | | 2 | | |
| Harwich | 11 | 2 | Davis | Timothy | 1 | 1 | 1 | | 1 | 1 | 1 | | 1 | 1 | | | 8 | | |
| Harwich | 11 | 3 | Weeks | Thankfull Wd | 1 | 1 | | | | | | | | 1 | | | 3 | | |
| Harwich | 11 | 4 | Crowell | Jabez | | 1 | 1 | | | | | 1 | | | | | 3 | | |
| Harwich | 11 | 5 | Ellis | Abraham | 2 | | | 1 | | | | 1 | 1 | | | | 5 | | |
| Harwich | 11 | 6 | Ellis | Samuel | | 1 | 1 | | 1 | 2 | 2 | | 1 | | | | 8 | | |
| Harwich | 11 | 7 | Walker | Jeremiah Jun | 1 | | | 1 | | 2 | 1 | | 1 | | | | 6 | | |
| Harwich | 11 | 8 | Smith | Isaac | 4 | | | 1 | | 1 | 1 | 1 | 1 | | | | 9 | | |
| Harwich | 11 | 9 | Ellis | Nathaniel | 1 | | | 1 | | 2 | 1 | | 1 | | | | 6 | | |
| Harwich | 11 | 10 | Ellis | Phillip | 2 | | | 1 | | 3 | 1 | | 1 | | | | 8 | | |
| Harwich | 11 | 11 | Ellis | Hemon | 2 | | | 1 | | | | | 1 | | | | 4 | | |
| Harwich | 11 | 12 | Ellis | Charles | 1 | | | 1 | | | | 1 | | | | | 3 | | |
| Harwich | 11 | 13 | Rider | Nathaniel | | 1 | | | | 1 | 1 | | | | | | 3 | | |
| Harwich | 11 | 14 | Bassett | John | 3 | | | 1 | | 1 | | | 1 | | | | 6 | | |
| Harwich | 11 | 15 | Long | Edmond | 2 | | | 1 | | 2 | | | 1 | | | | 6 | | |
| Harwich | 11 | 16 | Trip | Samuel | | | | 1 | | | | | 1 | | | | 2 | | |
| Harwich | 11 | 17 | Chase | James | 3 | 1 | | 1 | | 2 | 2 | 1 | 1 | | | | 11 | | |
| Harwich | 11 | 18 | Trip | Godfrey | 1 | | | 1 | | 2 | | | 1 | | | | 5 | | |
| Harwich | 11 | 19 | Smith | William | 1 | | 1 | | | 2 | | 1 | | | | | 5 | | |
| Harwich | 11 | 20 | Chase | Mary Wd | | | | | | | | | | 1 | | | 1 | | |
| Harwich | 11 | 21 | Chase | Gemaliel | 3 | | | 1 | | 3 | | | 1 | | | | 8 | | |
| Harwich | 11 | 22 | Chase | Silvanus | 2 | 1 | | | 1 | | | 1 | | 1 | | | 6 | | |
| Harwich | 11 | 23 | Chase | John | 2 | | 1 | | | | | | 1 | | | | 4 | | |
| Harwich | 11 | 24 | Broadbrooks | Meneboh | | | 1 | | 2 | | | 1 | | 1 | | | 5 | | |
| Harwich | 11 | 25 | Doane | Nathaniel | | 2 | | | 1 | | | | 1 | | | | 4 | | |
| Harwich | 11 | 26 | Snow | Afbond | 1 | | 1 | 1 | 1 | | 2 | 2 | | 1 | | | 9 | | |
| Harwich | 11 | 27 | Trip | Mehitable Wd | | 1 | | | | 1 | | | 1 | | | | 3 | | |
| Harwich | 11 | 28 | Snow | Elisha | | 2 | 3 | | 1 | 2 | 1 | | | 1 | | | 10 | | |
| Harwich | 11 | 29 | Snow | Elisha Jun | | | | 1 | | 2 | | | 1 | | | | 4 | | |
| Harwich | 11 | 30 | Snow | Elisha 3d | | | 1 | | | | | | 1 | | | | 2 | | |
| Harwich | 11 | 31 | Doane | Daniel | 1 | 1 | | | 1 | 3 | | | 1 | | | | 7 | | |
| Harwich | 11 | 32 | Landers | Joseph | | | 1 | | | | | | | | | | 1 | | |
| Harwich | 11 | 33 | Nickerson | Phillip | 1 | | | | | 3 | 1 | | 1 | | | | 6 | | |
| Harwich | 11 | 34 | Nickerson | Hannah Wd | | | | | | | | | | 1 | | | 1 | | |
| Harwich | 11 | 35 | Hall | Nathaniel | 1 | | | 1 | | | | 1 | | | | | 3 | | |
| Harwich | 11 | 36 | Chase | Philow | | | 1 | | | | | 2 | | 1 | | | 4 | | |
| Harwich | 11 | 37 | Chase | Enoch | 3 | | | 1 | 1 | 2 | | | 1 | 1 | | | 9 | | |
| Harwich | 11 | 38 | Baker | Anthony | 3 | 3 | | 1 | | 2 | | | 1 | | | | 10 | | |
| Harwich | 11 | 39 | Eldrege | Boni | 3 | | | 1 | | 1 | 2 | | 1 | | | | 8 | | |
| Harwich | 11 | 40 | Eldrege | Obed | 3 | 3 | | 1 | | | | 1 | | | | | 8 | | |
| Harwich | 11 | 41 | Eldrege | Isaac | | | | | 1 | | | 1 | | 1 | | | 3 | | |
| Harwich | 11 | 42 | Eldrege | Thomas | | | | | 1 | | 2 | | | 1 | | | 4 | | |
| Harwich | 11 | 43 | Eldrege | Isaac Jun | 1 | 2 | 1 | 1 | | 3 | | | 1 | | | | 9 | | |
| Harwich | 11 | 44 | Trabens | Richard | 1 | | | 1 | | 1 | 3 | | 2 | | | | 8 | | |
| Harwich | 12 | 1 | Broadbrooks | Lydia Wd | | | | | | | | | 1 | 1 | | | 2 | | |

# 1800 Harwich, Barnstable County, Massachusetts

| TOWN | PG# | LN# | LAST NAME | FIRST NAME | FREE WHITE MALES under 10 | 10 to 16 | 16 to 26 | 26 to 45 | 45 and over | FREE WHITE FEMALES under 10 | 10 to 16 | 16 to 26 | 26 to 45 | 45 and over | TOTAL ALL OTHER | TOTAL SLAVES | TOTALS | DISTRICT/ TOWNSHIP | NOTES |
|---|---|---|---|---|---|---|---|---|---|---|---|---|---|---|---|---|---|---|---|
| Harwich | 12 | 2 | Young | Edmond | 1 | | | 1 | | 3 | | 1 | | | | | 6 | | |
| Harwich | 12 | 3 | Chase | Tabitha Wd | 2 | | | | | | | | 1 | | | | 3 | | |
| Harwich | 12 | 4 | Phillips | Small | 1 | 1 | 1 | | 1 | 1 | | 1 | | 1 | | | 7 | | |
| Harwich | 12 | 5 | Ellis | Nathan | 2 | 1 | | 2 | | | 2 | 1 | | | | | 8 | | |
| Harwich | 12 | 6 | Walker | Linus | 1 | | 1 | | | | | 1 | | | | | 3 | | |
| Harwich | 12 | 7 | Cahoon | James | | 1 | 2 | | 1 | 2 | 1 | 1 | | 1 | | | 9 | | |
| Harwich | 12 | 8 | Ellis | Jeremiah | 3 | | 1 | | | 1 | | | 1 | | | | 6 | | |
| Harwich | 12 | 9 | Pain | Nathaniel | 1 | | | 1 | | | | 2 | | 1 | | | 5 | | |
| Harwich | 12 | 10 | Eldrege | Ensign | | | 1 | | | 3 | | 1 | | | | | 5 | | |
| Harwich | 12 | 11 | Brigs | Daniel | 1 | | 1 | | | 1 | | 1 | | | | | 4 | | |
| Harwich | 12 | 12 | Nickerson | Basett | | 2 | 1 | | 1 | 1 | 1 | 2 | 1 | 1 | | | 10 | | |
| Harwich | 12 | 13 | Nickerson | Asa | | 1 | | 1 | | 1 | | | 1 | | | | 4 | | |
| Harwich | 12 | 14 | Nickerson | Phinehas | 1 | | 2 | 1 | | | 1 | 1 | | 1 | | | 7 | | |
| Harwich | 12 | 15 | Nickerson | John | 1 | | 1 | | | | | 1 | | | | | 3 | | |
| Harwich | 12 | 16 | Bassett | Nathaniel | 1 | 2 | | 1 | | 1 | | | | | | | 5 | | |
| Harwich | 12 | 17 | Bassett | Nathaniel Jun | | 1 | | | | | | 1 | | | | | 2 | | |
| Harwich | 12 | 18 | Nickerson | Vincent | 1 | 1 | | | | | | 1 | | | | | 3 | | |
| Harwich | 12 | 19 | Nickerson | Olden | 1 | | 1 | | | 3 | | 1 | | | | | 6 | | |
| Harwich | 12 | 20 | Clark | David | | 1 | 1 | 1 | | 2 | 1 | 1 | 1 | | | | 8 | | |
| Harwich | 12 | 21 | Phillips | Anthony | 1 | | 1 | | | 3 | 1 | 1 | | | | | 7 | | |
| Harwich | 12 | 22 | Ames | Ame*ous | | 1 | | | | 1 | | 1 | | | | | 3 | | |
| Harwich | 12 | 23 | Allen | Nathaniel | 2 | | | | | 1 | | 1 | | | | | 5 | | |
| Harwich | 12 | 24 | Covil | Abigail Wd | | | | | | | | | 1 | 1 | | | 2 | | |
| Harwich | 12 | 25 | Doane | Elisha | | 1 | 1 | 1 | | | | | | 1 | | | 4 | | |
| Harwich | 12 | 26 | Doane | Elisha Jun | 4 | | 1 | | | 1 | | 1 | | | | | 7 | | |
| Harwich | 12 | 27 | Burges | Samuel | 2 | | 1 | | | 3 | | 1 | | | | | 7 | | |
| Harwich | 12 | 28 | Burges | Jacob | | 1 | | 1 | | | 1 | 1 | | 1 | | | 5 | | |
| Harwich | 12 | 29 | Burges | Moses | 1 | | 1 | | | | | 1 | | | | | 3 | | |
| Harwich | 12 | 30 | Burges | David | | 1 | | | | 1 | | 1 | | | | | 3 | | |
| Harwich | 12 | 31 | Burges | Thomas | | | 1 | | | | | | 1 | | | | 2 | | |
| Harwich | 12 | 32 | Burges | Thomas Jun | 1 | 1 | | 1 | | | | | 1 | | | | 4 | | |
| Harwich | 12 | 33 | Burges | Seth | 1 | | | 1 | | 3 | | | 1 | | | | 6 | | |
| Harwich | 12 | 34 | Burges | Joshua | 2 | | 1 | | | | | 1 | | | | | 4 | | |
| Harwich | 12 | 35 | Allen | John | | | | 1 | | 1 | | | 1 | | | | 3 | | |
| Harwich | 12 | 36 | Allen | William | | 2 | | 1 | 1 | | | | 1 | | | | 5 | | |
| Harwich | 12 | 37 | Allen | William Jun | 1 | 1 | | | | | | 1 | | | | | 3 | | |
| Harwich | 12 | 38 | Nickerson | Enoch | 3 | | 1 | | | | | 1 | | | | | 5 | | |
| Harwich | 12 | 39 | Small | Bethiah Wd | | 3 | | | | | | | 1 | | | | 4 | | |
| Harwich | 12 | 40 | Church | Asa | | 1 | | | | | 1 | | | | | | 2 | | |
| Harwich | 12 | 41 | Burges | Jonathan | 2 | 1 | 1 | 1 | | | 2 | | 1 | | | | 8 | | |
| Harwich | 12 | 42 | Nickerson | Samuel | 1 | 2 | 1 | 1 | | | 2 | | 1 | | | | 8 | | |
| Harwich | 12 | 43 | Chase | William | 2 | 2 | 1 | | | 2 | | 1 | | | | | 8 | | |
| Harwich | 12 | 44 | Nickerson | Enos | 2 | 1 | 1 | | | 2 | 1 | | 1 | | | | 8 | | |
| Harwich | 12 | 45 | Wexsom | Job | 2 | | 1 | | | 1 | | 1 | | | | | 5 | | |
| Harwich | 12 | 46 | Chase | Archelus | 3 | | 1 | | | 2 | 1 | 1 | | | | | 8 | | |
| Harwich | 12 | 47 | Chase | Job | | | 1 | | | | | | 1 | | | | 2 | | |
| Harwich | 12 | 48 | Chase | Job Jun | 1 | | 1 | | | 1 | | 1 | | | | | 4 | | |
| Harwich | 13 | 1 | Chase | Zenus | 1 | | 1 | | | 4 | | 1 | | | | | 7 | | |
| Harwich | 13 | 2 | Chase | Josiah | 1 | 1 | 1 | | | 3 | 1 | 1 | | | | | 8 | | |
| Harwich | 13 | 3 | Smith | Obedeslun | 3 | 1 | 1 | | | 1 | 1 | 1 | | | | | 7 | | |
| Harwich | 13 | 4 | Smith | Allen | | 1 | | | | 1 | | | | | | | 2 | | |
| Harwich | 13 | 5 | Chase | Nathaniel | 2 | | 1 | | | 3 | 1 | 1 | | | | | 8 | | |
| Harwich | 13 | 6 | Smith | Samuel | | 1 | 1 | 1 | | 3 | 1 | 1 | | | | | 5 | | |
| Harwich | 13 | 7 | Allen | Elisha | | | 1 | | | 1 | | 1 | | | | | 3 | | |
| Harwich | 13 | 8 | Allen | Pain | | | 1 | | | 3 | | 1 | | | | | 5 | | |
| Harwich | 13 | 9 | Clark | Elijah | 2 | | 1 | | | 2 | | 1 | | | | | 6 | | |
| Harwich | 13 | 10 | Clark | Jonathan | 3 | | 1 | | | 2 | | 1 | 1 | | | | 8 | | |
| Harwich | 13 | 11 | Clark | Andrew | | 1 | 1 | | | 4 | | 1 | | | | | 7 | | |
| Harwich | 13 | 12 | Ellis | Isaac | | 1 | 1 | 1 | | 1 | 1 | 2 | | 2 | | | 9 | | |
| Harwich | 13 | 13 | Higgins | Joseph | 1 | 1 | | | | | | 1 | | | | | 3 | | |
| Harwich | 13 | 14 | Pain | Thankfull Wd | | 1 | | | | | | 1 | 2 | | | | 4 | | |
| Harwich | 13 | 15 | Pain | Ebenezer | 1 | | 1 | | | | | 1 | | | | | 3 | | |
| Harwich | 13 | 16 | Bassett | Micah | 2 | | 1 | | | 1 | 1 | 1 | | | | | 6 | | |
| Harwich | 13 | 17 | Pain | Isaac | 1 | | 1 | | | 2 | | 1 | | | | | 5 | | |
| Harwich | 13 | 18 | Allen | Tamsin Wd | 1 | 1 | | | | 3 | | 1 | 1 | | | | 7 | | |
| Harwich | 13 | 19 | Nickerson | Christion | | 2 | 3 | 1 | | 2 | 1 | | 1 | | | | 10 | | |
| Harwich | 13 | 20 | Bassett | Daniel | 1 | | 1 | | | 2 | | 1 | | | | | 5 | | |
| Harwich | 13 | 21 | Phillips | Benjm | 1 | 1 | 2 | 1 | | 1 | 2 | | 1 | | | | 9 | | |
| Harwich | 13 | 22 | Walker | Seth | 3 | 1 | 1 | | | | | 1 | | | | | 6 | | |
| Harwich | 13 | 23 | Walker | James | 2 | 1 | 1 | | | 2 | | 1 | | | | | 8 | | |
| Harwich | 13 | 24 | Godfrey | Benjm | | | 1 | | | | | 1 | | | | | 2 | | |
| Harwich | 13 | 25 | Eldrege | Isaiah | 1 | 1 | 1 | | | 2 | 1 | 1 | | | | | 7 | | |
| Harwich | 13 | 26 | Eldrege | Abijah | 3 | | 1 | | | 2 | | 1 | | | | | 7 | | |
| Harwich | 13 | 27 | Eldrege | Ezra | 1 | | 1 | | | 1 | | 1 | | | | | 4 | | |
| Harwich | 13 | 28 | Eldrege | Thomas Jun | | 1 | | | | 3 | | 1 | | | | | 5 | | |
| Harwich | 13 | 29 | Eldrege | Washington | | 1 | | | | | | 1 | | | | | 2 | | |
| Harwich | 13 | 30 | Eldrege | Seth | 1 | | 1 | | | | | 1 | | | | | 3 | | |
| Harwich | 13 | 31 | Snow | Edward | | 2 | 2 | 1 | | 2 | | 1 | 1 | | | | 9 | | |
| Harwich | 13 | 32 | Eldrege | Eli | 1 | | 1 | | | | | 1 | | | | | 3 | | |
| Harwich | 13 | 33 | Eldrege | Ebenezor Jun | | 1 | | | | 1 | | 1 | | | | | 3 | | |
| Harwich | 13 | 34 | Baxter | Simeon | 2 | | 1 | | | | | | 1 | 1 | | | 5 | | |
| Harwich | 13 | 35 | Gaye | Anthony | 2 | | 1 | | 1 | | | 1 | | | | | 5 | | |
| Harwich | 13 | 36 | St*l | Daniel | 1 | 1 | | | | | | 1 | | | | | 3 | | |
| Harwich | 13 | 37 | Snow | Ebenezor | | 3 | 1 | 1 | | 1 | | 1 | | 1 | | | 8 | | |
| Harwich | 13 | 38 | Rogers | Smith | 1 | 1 | | | | | | 1 | | | | | 3 | | |
| Harwich | 13 | 39 | Lues | Abner Rev | | | 1 | | | | | 1 | | | | | 2 | | |
| Harwich | 13 | 40 | Chase | Susanna Wd | | 1 | | | | 1 | | 1 | | | | | 3 | | |
| Harwich | 13 | 41 | McCarter | Dennis | 2 | | 1 | | | | 1 | | | | | | 4 | | |
| Harwich | 13 | 42 | Chase | Seth | 2 | | 1 | | | | 1 | | | | | | 4 | | |
| Harwich | 13 | 43 | Rabens | William Jun | 2 | 2 | 1 | 1 | 1 | 1 | | 1 | | 1 | | | 10 | | |

| TOWN | PG# | LN# | LAST NAME | FIRST NAME | FREE WHITE MALES | | | | | FREE WHITE FEMALES | | | | | TOTAL ALL OTHER | TOTAL SLAVES | TOTALS | DISTRICT/ TOWNSHIP | NOTES |
|---|---|---|---|---|---|---|---|---|---|---|---|---|---|---|---|---|---|---|---|
| | | | | | under 10 | 10 to 16 | 16 to 26 | 26 to 45 | 45 and over | under 10 | 10 to 16 | 16 to 26 | 26 to 45 | 45 and over | | | | | |
| Harwich | 13 | 44 | Chase | Elezor | 2 | | 1 | | | | | | 1 | | | | 4 | | |
| Harwich | 13 | 45 | Gaye | Zebulon | | | 1 | 1 | | | | | | 1 | | | 3 | | |
| Harwich | 13 | 46 | Killey | Anthony | 1 | 2 | | 1 | | 2 | 1 | 1 | 1 | | | | 9 | | |
| Harwich | 13 | 47 | Killey | Jeremaiah | | | 1 | 1 | | | | 1 | 1 | 1 | | | 5 | | |
| Harwich | 13 | 48 | Hall | Edward Jun | 3 | | | 1 | | 2 | | 1 | 1 | 1 | | | 9 | | |
| Harwich | 13 | 49 | Hall | Benjm | 2 | 1 | | | 1 | 1 | 2 | 1 | | | | | 9 | | |
| Harwich | 13 | 50 | Gipson | Robert | | | 1 | 1 | | 1 | | 1 | | | | | 4 | | |
| Harwich | 14 | 1 | Nickerson | Thomas | | | 1 | | | 2 | | 1 | | | | | 4 | | |
| Harwich | 14 | 2 | Crowell | Nathan | | | 1 | 1 | | | | | | 1 | | | 3 | | |
| Harwich | 14 | 3 | Hall | Elisha | 2 | | 1 | | | 2 | | | 1 | | | | 6 | | |
| Harwich | 14 | 4 | Hinckley | Thomas | | | | 1 | | | | 1 | | 1 | | | 3 | | |
| Harwich | 14 | 5 | Hinckley | Elijah | | 1 | | | | | | 1 | | | | | 2 | | |
| Harwich | 14 | 6 | Chase | Daniel | | 1 | | 1 | | 1 | 1 | | 1 | 1 | | | 6 | | |
| Harwich | 14 | 7 | Baker | Shubal | | 1 | 2 | 1 | | | | 2 | | 1 | | | 7 | | |
| Harwich | 14 | 8 | Ellis | Reuben | | | | 1 | | 1 | 1 | 1 | | 3 | | | 7 | | |
| Harwich | 14 | 9 | Hall | Gershom | 3 | 1 | 1 | 1 | | 2 | 5 | 2 | 1 | | | | 16 | | |
| Harwich | 14 | 10 | Hall | Edward | 1 | 3 | 1 | 1 | | 3 | | | 1 | 1 | | | 11 | | |
| Harwich | 14 | 11 | Hall | Seth | | | 1 | | | 1 | | | 1 | | | | 3 | | |
| Harwich | 14 | 12 | Hall | Jonathan | 2 | | 1 | | | 2 | | | 1 | | | | 6 | | |
| Harwich | 14 | 13 | Killey | Patrick Jun | 4 | | 2 | 1 | | | 1 | 2 | | 1 | | | 11 | | |
| Harwich | 14 | 14 | Broadbrooks | Nathan | 1 | 1 | 1 | 1 | | 5 | 1 | | 1 | | | | 11 | | |
| Harwich | 14 | 15 | Smith | John | | | 2 | 1 | | | | | 3 | 1 | | | 7 | | |
| Harwich | 14 | 16 | Underwood | Nathan Rev | 3 | | | 1 | | | | | 1 | | | | 5 | | |
| Harwich | 14 | 17 | Welch | John | | | 1 | | | 2 | | | 1 | | | | 4 | | |
| Harwich | 14 | 18 | Killey | Joseph | 2 | | 1 | | | 1 | | 1 | | | | | 5 | | |
| Harwich | 14 | 19 | Rogers | Richard | 2 | | 1 | | | | | | 1 | | | | 4 | | |
| Harwich | 14 | 20 | Lues | John | 1 | | 1 | 1 | | 1 | | | 1 | | | | 5 | | |
| Harwich | 14 | 21 | Rider | Paul | 1 | | 1 | | | | | 1 | | | | | 3 | | |
| Harwich | 14 | 22 | Chase | John | | 1 | | 1 | | 2 | 1 | | 1 | | | | 6 | | |
| Harwich | 14 | 23 | Chase | Isaac | | | | 1 | | | | | | 1 | | | 2 | | |
| Harwich | 14 | 24 | Oliver | James | 1 | 1 | | 1 | | 1 | | | 1 | | | | 5 | | |
| Harwich | 14 | 25 | Snow | Stephen | | 1 | 1 | | | 1 | 1 | | 1 | | | | 5 | | |
| Harwich | 14 | 26 | Nickerson | Solomon | 1 | 1 | | 1 | | 3 | 3 | | 1 | | | | 10 | | |
| Harwich | 14 | 27 | Baker | Shubal Jun | 2 | | | 1 | | 2 | | 1 | 1 | | | | 7 | | |
| Harwich | 14 | 28 | Nickerson | Stephen | 2 | 1 | 2 | | 1 | | | 1 | 1 | 1 | | | 9 | | |
| Harwich | 14 | 29 | Small | James | 1 | 1 | | 1 | | 4 | 2 | | 1 | | | | 10 | | |
| Harwich | 14 | 30 | Rogers | Dinah Wd | 3 | | | | | | | 1 | 1 | | | | 6 | | |
| Harwich | 14 | 31 | Eldrege | Elnathan | 1 | 1 | 1 | | 1 | | | 1 | | 1 | | | 6 | | |
| Harwich | 14 | 32 | Eldrege | Nehemiah | 2 | | 1 | | | | | | 1 | | | | 4 | | |
| Harwich | 14 | 33 | Pain | John | | | | | 1 | 1 | 2 | 1 | | 1 | | | 6 | | |
| Harwich | 14 | 34 | Cahoon | Gamaliel | | 2 | | 1 | | 3 | | | 1 | | | | 7 | | |
| Harwich | 14 | 35 | Cahoon | Peter | 2 | | | 1 | | 2 | | | 1 | | | | 6 | | |
| Harwich | 14 | 36 | Turner | Stephen | 1 | | | 1 | | 3 | | | 1 | 2 | | | 8 | | |
| Harwich | 14 | 37 | Nickerson | Henry | 1 | | 1 | | | | | | 1 | | | | 3 | | |
| Harwich | 14 | 38 | Nickerson | Silas | | 1 | 1 | | 1 | | | 1 | | 1 | | | 5 | | |
| Harwich | 14 | 39 | Nickerson | Silas Jun | | | 1 | | | 1 | | 1 | | | | | 3 | | |
| Harwich | 14 | 40 | Berge | Zadock | | | | 1 | | 1 | | | 1 | | | | 3 | | |
| Harwich | 14 | 41 | Crowell | Solomon | | | 1 | | | 1 | 1 | 1 | | 1 | | | 5 | | |
| Harwich | 14 | 42 | Nickerson | Uriel | 2 | 1 | | 1 | | 2 | 1 | 2 | 1 | | | | 10 | | |
| Harwich | 14 | 43 | Nickerson | Ebenezer | 2 | 1 | | 1 | | 3 | 1 | | 2 | | | | 10 | | |
| Harwich | 14 | 44 | Rogers | Thomas | | | 1 | | | 1 | | 1 | | | | | 3 | | |
| Harwich | 14 | 45 | Allen | John Jun | 1 | 2 | | 1 | | 3 | 2 | | 1 | | | | 10 | | |
| Harwich | 14 | 46 | McDonnell | John | 1 | 1 | | 1 | | 2 | 2 | | 1 | | | | 8 | | |
| Harwich | 14 | 47 | Eldrege | Ebenezer | 4 | | 1 | 1 | | 1 | 2 | | 1 | | | | 10 | | |
| Harwich | 14 | 48 | Nickerson | Tulley | 3 | 1 | | 1 | | 1 | | 1 | | 1 | | | 8 | | |
| Harwich | 14 | 49 | Nickerson | Jones | 3 | | | 1 | | 1 | | | 1 | | | | 6 | | |
| Harwich | 14 | 50 | Kindericks | Henry | | 1 | 3 | | 1 | 3 | 2 | 1 | | 1 | | | 12 | | |
| Harwich | 15 | 1 | Kindericks | Stephen | 2 | 1 | 2 | | 1 | 3 | | | 1 | 1 | | | 11 | | |
| Harwich | 15 | 2 | Linnel | Thomas | 1 | 2 | 1 | | 1 | | | | 2 | 1 | | | 8 | | |
| Harwich | 15 | 3 | Higgins | Thankfull Wd | 2 | 1 | 1 | | | 2 | 1 | | 1 | | | | 8 | | |
| Harwich | 15 | 4 | Hurd | Joshua | | 2 | 1 | 1 | | 3 | 1 | 1 | 1 | | | | 10 | | |
| Harwich | 15 | 5 | Hopkins | Joshua | | 2 | 1 | | 1 | 1 | 3 | | | | | | 8 | | |
| Harwich | 15 | 6 | Rogers | Elisha | | 2 | | 1 | | 3 | 1 | 1 | | | | | 8 | | |
| Harwich | 15 | 7 | Nickerson | William | 1 | | | 1 | | 1 | | | 1 | | | | 4 | | |
| Harwich | 15 | 8 | Crowell | Mary Wd | | | | | | | | | 2 | 1 | | | 3 | | |
| Harwich | 15 | 9 | Cesar | Jesse | | | | | | | | | | | 3 | | 3 | | |
| Harwich | 15 | 10 | Hornes | John | | | | | | | | | | | 8 | | 8 | | |
| Harwich | 15 | 11 | Black | Nathan | | | | | | | | | | | 5 | | 5 | | |
| Harwich | 15 | 12 | Cesar | Isaac | | | | | | | | | | | 3 | | 3 | | |
| Harwich | 15 | 13 | Fortune | Reuben | | | | | | | | | | | 5 | | 5 | | |

# 1800 Mashpee, Barnstabe County, Massachusetts

| TOWN | PG# | LN# | LAST NAME | FIRST NAME | FREE WHITE MALES under 10 | 10 to 16 | 16 to 26 | 26 to 45 | 45 and over | FREE WHITE FEMALES under 10 | 10 to 16 | 16 to 26 | 26 to 45 | 45 and over | TOTAL ALL OTHER | TOTAL SLAVES | TOTALS | DISTRICT/ TOWNSHIP | NOTES |
|---|---|---|---|---|---|---|---|---|---|---|---|---|---|---|---|---|---|---|---|
| Mashpee | 51 | 1 | Hawley | Gideon Revd | | | | 1 | 1 | | | | | 2 | | | 4 | | |
| Mashpee | 51 | 2 | Coleman | Edward | 1 | 1 | | 1 | | 2 | | | 1 | | | | 6 | | |
| Mashpee | 51 | 3 | Lovel | Silas | | 1 | 1 | 1 | | | | | | 1 | | | 4 | | |
| Mashpee | 51 | 4 | Fish | Levi | 1 | 1 | | 1 | | | 2 | 2 | | 1 | | | 8 | | |
| Mashpee | 51 | 5 | Fish | Samuel | | | | 1 | | | | | | 1 | | | 2 | | |
| Mashpee | 51 | 6 | Doty | James | 1 | | | 1 | | | | | 1 | | | | 3 | | |
| Mashpee | 51 | 7 | Bearce | Daniel | | 2 | 2 | 1 | | 1 | 1 | 1 | | | | | 8 | | |
| Mashpee | 51 | 8 | Adams | Nathl | | | 3 | 1 | | 1 | 1 | | 1 | | | | 7 | | |
| Mashpee | 51 | 9 | Wolf | Stephen | 2 | 1 | | 1 | | 1 | | | 1 | 1 | | | 7 | | |
| Mashpee | 51 | 10 | Wolf | James | | 2 | 3 | 1 | | | | | 1 | 1 | | | 8 | | |
| Mashpee | 51 | 11 | Bates | Anselon | 2 | | | 1 | | | | | 1 | | | | 4 | | |
| Mashpee | 51 | 12 | Bates | Simeon | | | | 1 | | | | | | 1 | | | 2 | | |
| Mashpee | 51 | 13 | Hatch | Joseph | | | | 1 | | | | | 1 | 1 | | | 3 | | |
| Mashpee | 51 | 14 | Hatch | Abel | | | 1 | 1 | | 2 | 3 | 2 | 1 | | | | 10 | | |
| Mashpee | 51 | 15 | Hatch | Reuben | | 1 | | 1 | | 2 | | 3 | | | | | 7 | | |
| Mashpee | 51 | 16 | Turner | Joseph | 2 | 4 | | 1 | | 1 | 1 | 1 | | 1 | | | 11 | | |
| Mashpee | 51 | 17 | Porter | Peter | | | | | | | | | | | 4 | | 4 | | |
| Mashpee | 51 | 18 | *ulcan | | | | | | | | | | | | 1 | | 1 | | First name left blank on census |
| Mashpee | 51 | 19 | Low | Anthony | | | | | | | | | | | 3 | | 3 | | |
| Mashpee | 51 | 20 | Portuges | Louis | | | | | | | | | | | 7 | | 7 | | |
| Mashpee | 51 | 21 | Clifford | | | | | | | | | | | | 6 | | 6 | | First name left blank on census |
| Mashpee | 52 | 1 | Cross | | | | | | | | | | | | 1 | | 1 | | First name left blank on census |
| Mashpee | 52 | 2 | Pollard | Stepney | | | | | | | | | | | 4 | | 4 | | |
| Mashpee | 52 | 3 | George | | | | | | | | | | | | 1 | | 1 | | First name left balnk on census |
| Mashpee | 52 | 4 | Lippit | * | | | | | | | | | | | 8 | | 8 | | |
| Mashpee | 52 | 5 | Copas | Thomas | | | | | | | | | | | 2 | | 2 | | |
| Mashpee | 52 | 6 | Wilson | Sancho | | | | | | | | | | | 2 | | 2 | | |
| Mashpee | 52 | 7 | Badger | Elizabeth | | | | | | | | 1 | | 1 | | | 2 | | |
| Mashpee | 52 | 8 | Hamblen | Jonathan | | 1 | | 1 | | 1 | | | | 1 | | | 4 | | |
| Mashpee | 52 | 9 | Phinney | Prince | 1 | | 2 | 1 | | 2 | 1 | 2 | 2 | | | | 11 | | |
| Mashpee | 52 | 10 | Bates | Stephen | 2 | | | 1 | | 2 | | | 1 | | | | 6 | | |

# 1800 Orleans, Barnstable County, Massachusetts

| TOWN | PG# | LN# | LAST NAME | FIRST NAME | FREE WHITE MALES | | | | | FREE WHITE FEMALES | | | | | TOTAL ALL OTHER | TOTAL SLAVES | TOTALS | DISTRICT/ TOWNSHIP | NOTES |
|---|---|---|---|---|---|---|---|---|---|---|---|---|---|---|---|---|---|---|---|
| | | | | | under 10 | 10 to 16 | 16 to 26 | 26 to 45 | 45 and over | under 10 | 10 to 16 | 16 to 26 | 26 to 45 | 45 and over | | | | | |
| Orleans | 21 | 1 | Freeman | John | 2 | 2 | | 1 | | 3 | 1 | | 1 | | | | 10 | | |
| Orleans | 21 | 2 | Freeman | Abner | 1 | | 2 | | 1 | 3 | 2 | 2 | 1 | | | | 12 | | |
| Orleans | 21 | 3 | Freeman | Thankful Wid | | | | | | | | | | 1 | | | 1 | | |
| Orleans | 21 | 4 | Higgins | Freeman | | 1 | | 1 | 1 | 1 | | | 2 | 1 | | | 7 | | |
| Orleans | 21 | 5 | Higgins | Rebeccah Wid | 1 | | | | | | | 1 | 1 | 1 | | | 4 | | |
| Orleans | 21 | 6 | Higgins | Aaron | | 2 | | 1 | | 1 | 3 | | | | | | 7 | | |
| Orleans | 21 | 7 | Mulford | Joshua | | | 1 | | | | | | 1 | 1 | | | 3 | | |
| Orleans | 21 | 8 | Higgins | Absalon | | | | 1 | | 4 | 1 | | | 1 | | | 7 | | |
| Orleans | 21 | 9 | Smith | Joshua | | 1 | | 1 | | | | 1 | | 1 | | | 4 | | |
| Orleans | 21 | 10 | Smith | Isaac | | | | 1 | | | | 1 | | 1 | | | 3 | | |
| Orleans | 21 | 11 | Smith | Timothy | | | 1 | | | | | | 1 | | | | 2 | | |
| Orleans | 21 | 12 | Harding | Ephraim | 1 | | 1 | | | 1 | | | 1 | | | | 4 | | |
| Orleans | 21 | 13 | Cole | Nathan | | 1 | | | | | | | 1 | | | | 2 | | |
| Orleans | 21 | 14 | Higgins | Rebeccah | | 1 | | | | | | | | 2 | | | 3 | | |
| Orleans | 21 | 15 | Snow | Moses | 2 | | 1 | | | 4 | | | | 1 | | | 8 | | |
| Orleans | 21 | 16 | Snow | Stephen | 1 | 3 | 2 | | 1 | 3 | 1 | 2 | 1 | | | | 14 | | |
| Orleans | 21 | 17 | Cole | Mary Wid | | | | | | | | | 1 | | | | 1 | | |
| Orleans | 21 | 18 | Cole | Martha | | | | | | | | | 1 | | | | 1 | | |
| Orleans | 21 | 19 | Higgins | Zachariah | 3 | 1 | | 1 | | 1 | | | 1 | | | | 7 | | |
| Orleans | 21 | 20 | Hopkins | Curtis | | | 1 | | | | | | 1 | | | | 2 | | |
| Orleans | 21 | 21 | Hopkins | Priscilla | | | | | | | | | | 1 | 1 | | 2 | | |
| Orleans | 21 | 22 | Snow | Priscilla | | | | | | | | 1 | 1 | 1 | | | 3 | | |
| Orleans | 21 | 23 | Rogers | Zenus | 2 | | 1 | | | 1 | | | 1 | 1 | | | 6 | | |
| Orleans | 21 | 24 | Rogers | Josiah | | 1 | 4 | | 1 | | | | 1 | | | | 8 | | |
| Orleans | 22 | 1 | Hooper | William | 1 | | 1 | | | 1 | | | 1 | | | | 4 | | |
| Orleans | 22 | 2 | Hopkins | Thomas | 1 | | 1 | | | | | | 1 | | | | 3 | | |
| Orleans | 22 | 3 | Rogers | Samuel | 1 | | | 1 | | | | | | 1 | | | 4 | | |
| Orleans | 22 | 4 | Higgins | Simeon | 1 | | | 1 | | 1 | | | 1 | 1 | | | 6 | | |
| Orleans | 22 | 5 | Crosby | Joseph | 4 | | 1 | | | 1 | | | 1 | | | | 7 | | |
| Orleans | 22 | 6 | Mayo | Theofelus | 2 | 2 | 1 | | | 1 | | | 1 | | | | 7 | | |
| Orleans | 22 | 7 | Cole | Jesse | 1 | | 1 | 1 | | | 1 | 1 | | 1 | | | 6 | | |
| Orleans | 22 | 8 | Rogers | Prince | | | 3 | 1 | | | | 2 | | 1 | | | 7 | | |
| Orleans | 22 | 9 | Sparrow | Josiah | | 3 | 1 | 1 | | 3 | | 1 | 1 | 1 | | | 11 | | |
| Orleans | 22 | 10 | Rogers | Joshua | | | 1 | | | | | | 1 | | | | 2 | | |
| Orleans | 22 | 11 | Higgins | Seth | 1 | 2 | | | 1 | | 2 | 2 | | 1 | | | 9 | | |
| Orleans | 22 | 12 | Kinney | Jesse | 1 | 2 | | | 1 | 1 | 1 | | | 1 | | | 7 | | |
| Orleans | 22 | 13 | Young | James | | | 1 | 1 | 1 | | | | | 1 | | | 4 | | |
| Orleans | 22 | 14 | Chase | Mary | | | | | | | | | 1 | 1 | | | 2 | | |
| Orleans | 22 | 15 | Sparrow | Seth | 1 | | 1 | | | | | | 1 | | | | 3 | | |
| Orleans | 22 | 16 | Higgins | Moses | 3 | | 1 | | | 1 | | | 1 | | | | 6 | | |
| Orleans | 22 | 17 | Gould | Josiah | | 2 | 2 | 1 | | | | 1 | | 1 | | | 7 | | |
| Orleans | 22 | 18 | Higgins | Lot | | 2 | | 1 | | | | 2 | | 1 | | | 6 | | |
| Orleans | 22 | 19 | Myrick | Hemon | 4 | | | 1 | | 1 | 1 | | | 1 | | | 8 | | |
| Orleans | 22 | 20 | Coffin | Obediah | 1 | | | 1 | | | | | | 1 | | | 3 | | |
| Orleans | 22 | 21 | Atkins | Joseph | 1 | | 1 | | | 1 | | | 1 | | | | 4 | | |
| Orleans | 22 | 22 | Kendricks | Jonathan | | | 3 | 1 | | | | | 1 | 1 | | | 6 | | |
| Orleans | 22 | 23 | Kendricks | Jonathan Jr | 2 | 2 | | 1 | | 3 | 1 | | 1 | | | | 10 | | |
| Orleans | 22 | 24 | Kendricks | Easter Wid | | | | | | | | | | 1 | | | 1 | | |
| Orleans | 22 | 25 | Rogers | Hezekiah | 3 | 1 | 1 | | 1 | 2 | 1 | | | 1 | | | 10 | | |
| Orleans | 22 | 26 | Rogers | Judah | 3 | 2 | 1 | | 1 | | 1 | 2 | 1 | 1 | | | 12 | | |
| Orleans | 22 | 27 | Linnel | Ezra | | | 1 | | | 1 | | | 1 | | | | 3 | | |
| Orleans | 22 | 28 | Nickerson | Joshua | 1 | 1 | | | 1 | 3 | 1 | 1 | | 1 | | | 9 | | |
| Orleans | 22 | 29 | Cahoon | Stephen Junr | | | 1 | | | 1 | | | 1 | | | | 3 | | |
| Orleans | 22 | 30 | Cahoon | Stephen | | 2 | | | 1 | | | 1 | 2 | 1 | | | 7 | | |
| Orleans | 22 | 31 | Rogers | Asa | | | 1 | | | | | | 1 | | | | 2 | | |
| Orleans | 22 | 32 | Eldrege | Reuben | | 2 | 1 | | 1 | | | 1 | 1 | 1 | | | 7 | | |
| Orleans | 22 | 33 | Mayo | Uriel | 1 | 1 | 1 | | 1 | 3 | | 2 | | 1 | | | 10 | | |
| Orleans | 22 | 34 | Reubens | Thomas | 1 | | | 2 | | 2 | | | 2 | 2 | | | 9 | | |
| Orleans | 22 | 35 | Eldrege | Nehemiah | 1 | | 1 | | | 1 | 1 | | | | | | 4 | | |
| Orleans | 22 | 36 | Young | Jediah | 2 | 1 | | 1 | | 3 | 2 | | 1 | | | | 10 | | |
| Orleans | 22 | 37 | Higgins | Hattel | 3 | | | 1 | | 1 | | | | 1 | | | 6 | | |
| Orleans | 22 | 38 | Higgins | Jonathan | | | | | 1 | | | | 1 | 1 | | | 3 | | |
| Orleans | 22 | 39 | Eldrege | David | | | 1 | | | | | | 1 | | | | 2 | | |
| Orleans | 22 | 40 | Hurd | John | 3 | 2 | | 1 | | | | 1 | | 1 | | | 8 | | |
| Orleans | 22 | 41 | Linnel | Hemon | | | 1 | | 1 | | | | 2 | 1 | | | 5 | | |
| Orleans | 22 | 42 | Linnel | Isaac | 1 | | 1 | | | | | | 1 | | | | 3 | | |
| Orleans | 22 | 43 | Rogers | Gideon | | | 1 | | | 1 | 1 | | 1 | 2 | | | 6 | | |
| Orleans | 22 | 44 | Linnel | Samuel | 2 | | 1 | | | 1 | 1 | | 1 | | | | 6 | | |
| Orleans | 22 | 45 | Linnel | Uriel | 3 | | 1 | | | 1 | | 1 | | 1 | | | 7 | | |
| Orleans | 22 | 46 | Gould | John | | | | 1 | 1 | | | | 1 | 1 | | | 4 | | |
| Orleans | 23 | 1 | Gould | John Junr | | | 1 | | | 2 | | | 1 | | | | 4 | | |
| Orleans | 23 | 2 | Hopkins | Elkanah | 3 | 3 | | 1 | | 2 | | | | 1 | | | 10 | | |
| Orleans | 23 | 3 | Higgins | Eliakim | 2 | 2 | | 1 | | 1 | | 2 | | 1 | | | 9 | | |
| Orleans | 23 | 4 | Higgins | Lot | 2 | 1 | 1 | | 1 | | | 1 | 2 | 1 | | | 9 | | |
| Orleans | 23 | 5 | Higgins | Richard | 1 | | | 1 | | 3 | | | | 1 | | | 6 | | |
| Orleans | 23 | 6 | Rogers | Josiah | | 1 | 2 | 1 | | | | | 1 | 1 | | | 6 | | |
| Orleans | 23 | 7 | Rogers | Zenus | 1 | | | 1 | | | | | 1 | | | | 4 | | |
| Orleans | 23 | 8 | Freeman | Isaac | | 1 | 1 | | | | | 3 | | 1 | | | 7 | | |
| Orleans | 23 | 9 | Hopkins | Elkanah | 2 | | | | | | | | 1 | | | | 4 | | |

# 1800 Orleans, Barnstable County, Massachusetts

| TOWN | PG# | LN# | HEADS OF HOUSEHOLD | | FREE WHITE MALES | | | | | FREE WHITE FEMALES | | | | | TOTAL ALL OTHER | TOTAL SLAVES | TOTALS | DISTRICT/TOWNSHIP | NOTES |
|---|---|---|---|---|---|---|---|---|---|---|---|---|---|---|---|---|---|---|---|
| | | | LAST NAME | FIRST NAME | under 10 | 10 to 16 | 16 to 26 | 26 to 45 | 45 and over | under 10 | 10 to 16 | 16 to 26 | 26 to 45 | 45 and over | | | | | |
| Orleans | 23 | 10 | Higgins | Easter Wid | | | | | | | | 2 | | 1 | | | 3 | | |
| Orleans | 23 | 11 | Higgins | Elnathan | | | | 1 | | | | | | 1 | | | 2 | | |
| Orleans | 23 | 12 | Mayo | Sears | 4 | | 1 | 1 | | 1 | | 1 | 1 | | | | 9 | | |
| Orleans | 23 | 13 | Linnel | Samuel | 1 | | | 1 | | 2 | 1 | | 1 | | | | 6 | | |
| Orleans | 23 | 14 | Rogers | Joshua Junr | 3 | | 1 | | | | | | 1 | | | | 5 | | |
| Orleans | 23 | 15 | Rogers | Elizabeth Wid | | | | | | | | 1 | 2 | 1 | | | 4 | | |
| Orleans | 23 | 16 | Linnel | Elkanah | 2 | | | 1 | | 3 | 1 | | 1 | 1 | | | 9 | | |
| Orleans | 23 | 17 | Linnel | Edmond | 2 | | | 1 | | 3 | 1 | | 1 | | | | 8 | | |
| Orleans | 23 | 18 | Rogers | Jonathan | | 1 | 2 | 1 | | | 1 | | 1 | 1 | | | 7 | | |
| Orleans | 23 | 19 | Higgins | Daniel | 1 | | | 1 | | 1 | | | 1 | | | | 4 | | |
| Orleans | 23 | 20 | Rogers | Ruth Wid | | 1 | | | | | | | | 1 | | | 2 | | |
| Orleans | 23 | 21 | Sparrow | Jabez | 2 | 1 | | 1 | | 2 | 1 | 1 | | 1 | | | 9 | | |
| Orleans | 23 | 22 | Young | Edmond | | | | 1 | | | | 1 | | 1 | | | 3 | | |
| Orleans | 23 | 23 | Snow | Edmond | 2 | 2 | | 1 | | 1 | | 1 | 1 | | | | 8 | | |
| Orleans | 23 | 24 | Sparrow | Richard | 2 | 2 | 1 | 1 | | | | 3 | 1 | | | | 10 | | |
| Orleans | 23 | 25 | Sparrow | Isaac | | | | 1 | | | | 1 | | 1 | | | 3 | | |
| Orleans | 23 | 26 | Rogers | Hesekiah | 3 | 1 | 1 | | 1 | 2 | 1 | | 1 | | | | 10 | | |
| Orleans | 23 | 27 | Rogers | James | | | | 1 | | | | | | 1 | | | 2 | | |
| Orleans | 23 | 28 | Rogers | James Jun | | | 1 | | | 1 | | 1 | | | | | 3 | | |
| Orleans | 23 | 29 | Tailor | John | 3 | 2 | | 1 | 1 | 2 | 1 | | 1 | 1 | | | 12 | | |
| Orleans | 23 | 30 | Young | Jediah | 2 | 1 | | 1 | | 3 | 2 | 1 | 1 | | | | 11 | | |
| Orleans | 23 | 31 | Young | Ebenezor | | | | 1 | | | | | | 1 | | | 2 | | |
| Orleans | 23 | 32 | Higgins | Joshua | 2 | | | 1 | | 1 | 1 | | 1 | | | | 6 | | |
| Orleans | 23 | 33 | Lewis | Edward | | 1 | 1 | | 1 | 3 | 2 | 1 | 1 | | | | 10 | | |
| Orleans | 23 | 34 | Linnel | Jopah | | 3 | 1 | | 1 | | | | 1 | 2 | | | 8 | | |
| Orleans | 23 | 35 | Linnel | Benjm | 2 | 2 | | 1 | | 2 | | | 1 | | | | 8 | | |
| Orleans | 23 | 36 | Baker | Benony | 3 | 2 | 1 | 1 | | 1 | 1 | | 1 | | | | 10 | | |
| Orleans | 23 | 37 | Snow | Aaron | 3 | 1 | | | | 3 | | | 1 | | | | 8 | | |
| Orleans | 23 | 38 | Snow | Elnathon Jun | 2 | | 1 | | | | | | 1 | | | | 4 | | |
| Orleans | 23 | 39 | Snow | Elnathon | | | | 1 | | | 1 | | | 1 | | | 3 | | |
| Orleans | 23 | 40 | Higgins | Gideon | 1 | | | 1 | | 2 | 2 | | 1 | | | | 7 | | |
| Orleans | 23 | 41 | Cole | Stephen | 1 | | | 1 | | 2 | | | 1 | | | | 5 | | |
| Orleans | 23 | 42 | Twining | Barnabes | | 1 | | 1 | | 1 | 1 | | 1 | | | | 5 | | |
| Orleans | 23 | 43 | Twining | Barnabes Jun | 1 | | | 1 | | 1 | | | 1 | | | | 4 | | |
| Orleans | 23 | 44 | Rogers | Prince | | 1 | 2 | 1 | | 1 | 1 | 2 | 1 | | | | 9 | | |
| Orleans | 23 | 45 | Rogers | Joshua | | 1 | | | | | | 1 | | | | | 2 | | |
| Orleans | 23 | 46 | Higgins | Hezekiah | 1 | | | 1 | | | | | 1 | | | | 3 | | |
| Orleans | 24 | 1 | Higgins | Asa | 4 | | | 1 | | 1 | | | 1 | | 1 | | 8 | | |
| Orleans | 24 | 2 | Higgins | Moses | 3 | | | 1 | | 1 | | | 1 | | | | 6 | | |
| Orleans | 24 | 3 | Any | Oliver | 1 | | | 1 | | | | 1 | 1 | 1 | | | 5 | | |
| Orleans | 24 | 4 | Any | Thomas | | 2 | 1 | 1 | | 3 | 1 | 1 | | 1 | | | 10 | | |
| Orleans | 24 | 5 | Rogers | Richard | 1 | | | 1 | | 2 | 1 | 1 | 1 | | | | 7 | | |
| Orleans | 24 | 6 | Sparrow | Solomon | | | | 1 | | | | 1 | | 1 | | | 3 | | |
| Orleans | 24 | 7 | Sparrow | Seth Jun | | | | 1 | | 2 | | | 1 | | | | 4 | | |
| Orleans | 24 | 8 | Kinney | Jesse Jun | | | | 1 | | 2 | | | 1 | | | | 4 | | |
| Orleans | 24 | 9 | Sparrow | John | 2 | | | 1 | | 1 | | | 1 | | | | 5 | | |
| Orleans | 24 | 10 | Young | James | | 1 | | 1 | | | | | | 1 | | | 3 | | |
| Orleans | 24 | 11 | Linnel | Gould | 1 | | | 1 | | 1 | | | 1 | | | | 4 | | |
| Orleans | 24 | 12 | Young | Phillip | | 1 | 2 | 1 | 1 | | | 1 | 2 | 1 | | | 9 | | |
| Orleans | 24 | 13 | Doane | Timothy | | 3 | 1 | 1 | 3 | 1 | 1 | 1 | | | | | 11 | | |
| Orleans | 24 | 14 | Hurd | Joseph | | 2 | 2 | 1 | | 1 | 2 | | 1 | | | | 9 | | |
| Orleans | 24 | 15 | Hurd | Benjm | 2 | | | 1 | | 1 | | | 1 | | | | 5 | | |
| Orleans | 24 | 16 | Smith | Nathan | | | | 1 | | | 2 | 2 | 1 | | | | 6 | | |
| Orleans | 24 | 17 | Smith | Lues | | | 1 | | | 2 | | | 1 | | | | 4 | | |
| Orleans | 24 | 18 | Crosby | Joshua | 2 | 1 | 2 | | 2 | 2 | | | 1 | | | | 10 | | |
| Orleans | 24 | 19 | Smith | Joseph | | | | 1 | | | | | | 1 | | | 2 | | |
| Orleans | 24 | 20 | Mayo | Jonathan | | 1 | 2 | 1 | | 2 | | | 1 | 1 | | | 8 | | |
| Orleans | 24 | 21 | Cale | Abial | 1 | 1 | | 1 | | 3 | | | 1 | | | | 7 | | |
| Orleans | 24 | 22 | Cale | Joseph | | | 1 | | | | | | 1 | | | | 2 | | |
| Orleans | 24 | 23 | Snow | Hemen Jun | 2 | 1 | | 1 | | 2 | 1 | | 1 | | | | 8 | | |
| Orleans | 24 | 24 | Nickerson | Nathaniel | | 1 | | | | | 1 | | | | | | 2 | | |
| Orleans | 24 | 25 | Smith | Ray | 3 | 2 | | 1 | | 2 | 1 | | 1 | | | | 10 | | |
| Orleans | 24 | 26 | Knowls | John | 1 | | 1 | 1 | | 2 | 1 | | 1 | | | | 7 | | |
| Orleans | 24 | 27 | Knowls | Ruth Wd | | | | | | | | 3 | 1 | | | | 4 | | |
| Orleans | 24 | 28 | Harding | Keziah | | 2 | | | | | | 1 | 1 | | | | 4 | | |
| Orleans | 24 | 29 | Bascom | Jonathan Jun | | 1 | | | | | | 1 | | | | | 2 | | |
| Orleans | 24 | 30 | Bascom | Jonathan Rev | | 1 | 1 | | | | | 1 | | 1 | | | 4 | | |
| Orleans | 24 | 31 | Tailor | Benjm | 3 | 1 | | 2 | 1 | | | 2 | | 1 | | | 10 | | |
| Orleans | 24 | 32 | Tailor | David | 2 | 1 | 1 | | | 1 | 1 | 1 | 1 | | | | 7 | | |
| Orleans | 24 | 33 | Twining | Jonathan | | 1 | 1 | 1 | | | | | | 2 | | | 5 | | |
| Orleans | 24 | 34 | Snow | Jerusha Wd | 1 | | | 1 | | | | | 1 | | | | 3 | | |
| Orleans | 24 | 35 | Young | Moses | | 1 | | | | | | 3 | 1 | 1 | | | 6 | | |
| Orleans | 24 | 36 | Snow | Hemon 3d | 1 | | 1 | | | | | 1 | | | | | 3 | | |
| Orleans | 24 | 37 | Rogers | Thomas | 1 | 1 | | 1 | 1 | | | | | | | | 4 | | |
| Orleans | 24 | 38 | Doane | Hezekiah | 2 | 2 | | 1 | 2 | 1 | | | 1 | 1 | | | 10 | | |
| Orleans | 24 | 39 | Seaburry | Joseph | 4 | 2 | 1 | 1 | | 2 | 1 | | 1 | | | | 12 | | |
| Orleans | 24 | 40 | Daycom | Timothy | | | 1 | | | 1 | 1 | 1 | | | | | 4 | | |
| Orleans | 24 | 41 | Young | Lewis | 1 | | | 1 | | | | 1 | | | | | 4 | | |
| Orleans | 24 | 42 | Higgins | Silvanus | | 1 | | 1 | | | | 2 | 1 | 1 | | | 6 | | |

# 1800 Orleans, Barnstable County, Massachusetts

| TOWN | PG# | LN# | LAST NAME | FIRST NAME | FREE WHITE MALES under 10 | 10 to 16 | 16 to 26 | 26 to 45 | 45 and over | FREE WHITE FEMALES under 10 | 10 to 16 | 16 to 26 | 26 to 45 | 45 and over | TOTAL ALL OTHER | TOTAL SLAVES | TOTALS | DISTRICT/TOWNSHIP | NOTES |
|---|---|---|---|---|---|---|---|---|---|---|---|---|---|---|---|---|---|---|---|
| Orleans | 24 | 43 | Sparrow | Seth Jun | 1 | | | 1 | | | | | 1 | | | | 3 | | |
| Orleans | 24 | 44 | McCormon | Micah | 3 | 1 | | 1 | | 1 | | | 1 | | | | 7 | | |
| Orleans | 24 | 45 | Higgins | Samuel | 1 | | | | 1 | | | 1 | | 1 | | | 5 | | |
| Orleans | 24 | 46 | Peper | Benja | | 1 | 2 | | 1 | | 1 | 1 | | 1 | | | 7 | | |
| Orleans | 25 | 1 | Peper | Simeon | 1 | | | 1 | | 2 | | | 1 | | | | 5 | | |
| Orleans | 25 | 2 | Peper | Pheba Wd | | | | | | | | 1 | | 1 | | | 2 | | |
| Orleans | 25 | 3 | Higgins | Aguella | | | 1 | | | 2 | | | 1 | | | | 4 | | |
| Orleans | 25 | 4 | Linnel | Thomas | | | | 1 | | | | 1 | | 1 | | | 3 | | |
| Orleans | 25 | 5 | Linnel | Elisha | 5 | | 1 | | | | | | 1 | | | | 7 | | |
| Orleans | 25 | 6 | Freeman | Gideon | | | | 1 | | | 1 | | | 1 | | | 3 | | |
| Orleans | 25 | 7 | Nickerson | Yates | 1 | | | 1 | | | | | 1 | 1 | | | 4 | | |
| Orleans | 25 | 8 | Higgins | Daniel | 1 | | | 1 | | 1 | | | 1 | | | | 4 | | |
| Orleans | 25 | 9 | Snow | Isaac | 1 | 1 | | 1 | | 3 | 1 | 1 | | | | | 8 | | |
| Orleans | 25 | 10 | Cale | Joshua | | 1 | 1 | | 1 | 1 | 1 | | | 1 | | | 6 | | |
| Orleans | 25 | 11 | Snow | Heman | | | 2 | | 1 | | 2 | 2 | | 1 | | | 8 | | |
| Orleans | 25 | 12 | Twining | Prince | 2 | | 1 | | 1 | | 1 | 2 | | 1 | | | 8 | | |
| Orleans | 25 | 13 | Mayo | Abner | | | 1 | | | | | 1 | | | | | 2 | | |
| Orleans | 25 | 14 | Kingman | Simeon | | 1 | | 1 | | | | 1 | 1 | | | | 4 | | |
| Orleans | 25 | 15 | Freeman | Pheba Wd | | | | | | | | | 1 | 1 | | | 2 | | |
| Orleans | 25 | 16 | Freeman | Jopah | 2 | 2 | | 1 | | 2 | 1 | | 1 | | | | 9 | | |
| Orleans | 25 | 17 | Freeman | Thomas | 1 | | | 1 | | 1 | | | 1 | | | | 4 | | |
| Orleans | 25 | 18 | Smith | Zoheth | | | | 1 | | 2 | 1 | | 1 | | | | 5 | | |
| Orleans | 25 | 19 | Snow | Prince | | 1 | 1 | | 1 | | 1 | | | 1 | | | 5 | | |
| Orleans | 25 | 20 | Knowls | Nathaniel | | 1 | 2 | | 1 | 1 | | 3 | 1 | | | | 9 | | |
| Orleans | 25 | 21 | Freeman | Eleozer | 1 | | | | 1 | 2 | 2 | | 1 | | | | 7 | | |
| Orleans | 25 | 22 | Minich | Hannah Wd | | | | | | | | | | 1 | | | 1 | | |
| Orleans | 25 | 23 | Minich | John | | | 1 | 1 | | 3 | | 1 | 1 | | | | 7 | | |
| Orleans | 25 | 24 | Knowls | Mary Wd | | 1 | | | | 1 | | | | 1 | | | 3 | | |
| Orleans | 25 | 25 | Young | Jonath | | | 1 | 1 | | | | 1 | 1 | | | | 4 | | |
| Orleans | 25 | 26 | Young | David | | | 1 | | 1 | | | 1 | 4 | 1 | | | 8 | | |
| Orleans | 25 | 27 | Snow | David | | | | 1 | | 1 | | 1 | | | | | 3 | | |
| Orleans | 25 | 28 | Smith | Elisha | 1 | | | 1 | | | | | 1 | 1 | | | 4 | | |
| Orleans | 25 | 29 | Smith | Jonah | 1 | 2 | | 1 | | 2 | 1 | | 1 | | | | 8 | | |
| Orleans | 25 | 30 | Harding | Thomas | 1 | | | | 1 | | | | | 1 | | | 3 | | |

# 1800 Provincetown, Barnstable County, Massachusetts

| TOWN | PG# | LN# | LAST NAME | FIRST NAME | FREE WHITE MALES under 10 | 10 to 16 | 16 to 26 | 26 to 45 | 45 and over | FREE WHITE FEMALES under 10 | 10 to 16 | 16 to 26 | 26 to 45 | 45 and over | TOTAL ALL OTHER | TOTAL SLAVES | TOTALS | DISTRICT/ TOWNSHIP | NOTES |
|---|---|---|---|---|---|---|---|---|---|---|---|---|---|---|---|---|---|---|---|
| Provincetown | 56 | 1 | Atwood | Joshua | 1 | 2 | | 1 | | 2 | 1 | | 1 | | | | 8 | | |
| Provincetown | 56 | 2 | Atwood | Henry Junr | 2 | | | 1 | | | | | 1 | | | | 4 | | |
| Provincetown | 56 | 3 | Atkins | Silas | 2 | 2 | | 1 | | 3 | 1 | | 1 | | | | 10 | | |
| Provincetown | 57 | 1 | Atkins | Benjamin | | 1 | | 1 | | 2 | | | 1 | | | | 5 | | |
| Provincetown | 57 | 2 | Atwood | Stephen | | | | | 1 | | | | | 1 | | | 2 | | |
| Provincetown | 57 | 3 | Atwood | Jonathan | 1 | | 1 | 1 | | 1 | | | 1 | | | | 5 | | |
| Provincetown | 57 | 4 | Adisen | Condition | | | 1 | | | 2 | | 1 | | | | | 4 | | |
| Provincetown | 57 | 5 | Bates | Simeon | 1 | 2 | | 1 | | 3 | | | 1 | | | | 8 | | |
| Provincetown | 57 | 6 | Brown | David | | 1 | 4 | 1 | | 1 | 1 | | 1 | | | | 9 | | |
| Provincetown | 57 | 7 | Bowly | Asa | 2 | | 1 | | | | | | 1 | | | | 4 | | |
| Provincetown | 57 | 8 | Conant | Samuel | 1 | | 1 | | | | | | 1 | | | | 3 | | |
| Provincetown | 57 | 9 | Briggs | Barnabas | 1 | | 1 | | 1 | | | | 1 | 1 | | | 7 | | |
| Provincetown | 57 | 10 | Brown | Cyrenius | 3 | | 1 | | | | | | 1 | | | | 5 | | |
| Provincetown | 57 | 11 | Cook | Elisha | 1 | | 1 | | | 1 | | | | | | | 3 | | |
| Provincetown | 57 | 12 | Cook | Joshua | 2 | | 1 | | | | | | 1 | | | | 4 | | |
| Provincetown | 57 | 13 | Cook | Solomon Jun | 3 | 2 | | 1 | | | | 1 | 1 | | | | 8 | | |
| Provincetown | 57 | 14 | Cook | Jonathan | | 1 | 3 | | 1 | | 1 | | | 1 | | | 7 | | |
| Provincetown | 57 | 15 | Cook | Edward | 1 | | | 1 | | | 2 | | 1 | | | | 5 | | |
| Provincetown | 57 | 16 | Cook | Solomon | | 1 | | 1 | | | 1 | | 1 | | | | 4 | | |
| Provincetown | 57 | 17 | Cook | Samuel | 1 | 2 | 3 | 1 | | 2 | | | 1 | | | | 10 | | |
| Provincetown | 57 | 18 | Cook | James | | | 1 | | | 1 | | | 1 | | | | 3 | | |
| Provincetown | 57 | 19 | Cook | John | 1 | 1 | | 1 | | 2 | | | 1 | | | | 6 | | |
| Provincetown | 57 | 20 | Cook | Paron | 1 | 1 | 1 | 1 | | 2 | 2 | | 1 | | | | 9 | | |
| Provincetown | 57 | 21 | Conant | John | | | | 1 | | | | | 1 | | | | 2 | | |
| Provincetown | 58 | 1 | Crow | Solomon | | | | 1 | | | | | 1 | | | | 2 | | |
| Provincetown | 58 | 2 | Crow | Solomon Jun | | | 1 | | | 2 | | | 1 | | | | 4 | | |
| Provincetown | 58 | 3 | Coombs | Elizabeth Wd | | | | | | | | | | 1 | | | 1 | | |
| Provincetown | 58 | 4 | Cook | Sarah Wd | 1 | | | | | 1 | 1 | | 1 | | | | 4 | | |
| Provincetown | 58 | 5 | Dyer | William | 3 | | | 1 | | 1 | | | 1 | | | | 6 | | |
| Provincetown | 58 | 6 | Dunham | Rebeccah Wd | | | | | | | | 1 | | | | | 1 | | |
| Provincetown | 58 | 7 | Dyer | Hannah Wd | | | 1 | | | | | 1 | | 1 | | | 3 | | |
| Provincetown | 58 | 8 | Freeman | Prince | | | 3 | 1 | | | | 1 | | 1 | | | 6 | | |
| Provincetown | 58 | 9 | Foble | Samuel | | | 1 | | | 1 | | | 1 | | | | 3 | | |
| Provincetown | 58 | 10 | Grosher | Freeman | 3 | | | 1 | | | | | 1 | | | | 5 | | |
| Provincetown | 58 | 11 | Gross | Alexander | | | 1 | | | 2 | | | 1 | | | | 4 | | |
| Provincetown | 58 | 12 | Ginn | Samuel | 2 | | | 1 | | | 1 | 1 | | | | | 5 | | |
| Provincetown | 58 | 13 | Hinch | Samuel | | | 1 | | | | | | 1 | | | | 2 | | |
| Provincetown | 58 | 14 | Hill | John | 1 | 1 | 2 | 1 | | 2 | | | 1 | | | | 8 | | |
| Provincetown | 58 | 15 | Harding | Knowles | 2 | | 1 | | | 1 | | | 1 | | | | 5 | | |
| Provincetown | 58 | 16 | Howes | David | 1 | 1 | 1 | | | | 2 | | | | | | 5 | | |
| Provincetown | 58 | 17 | Howes | Theophilus | 3 | | 1 | | | | | | 1 | | | | 5 | | |
| Provincetown | 58 | 18 | Higgins | Enoch | 1 | | 1 | | | 1 | | | 1 | | | | 4 | | |
| Provincetown | 58 | 19 | Hopkins | Jonathan | | | 1 | 1 | | 1 | | 1 | | | | | 4 | | |
| Provincetown | 58 | 20 | Holway | Stephen | 2 | | 2 | | | 2 | | | | | | | 6 | | |
| Provincetown | 58 | 21 | Howes | Daniel | | | 2 | | | 1 | | | 1 | | | | 4 | | |
| Provincetown | 58 | 22 | Atkins | Joseph | 2 | | 1 | | | | | | 1 | | | | 4 | | |
| Provincetown | 58 | 23 | Hopkins | Seammons | 1 | | 1 | | 1 | | | | 1 | | | | 4 | | |
| Provincetown | 58 | 24 | Knowles | Phebe Wd | 2 | 1 | | | | 2 | | | 1 | | | | 6 | | |
| Provincetown | 58 | 25 | Kinyard | Benjamin | | 1 | | 1 | | | | | | 1 | | | 3 | | |
| Provincetown | 58 | 26 | Kilborn | David | 2 | 3 | | 1 | | 2 | 2 | | 1 | | | | 11 | | |
| Provincetown | 58 | 27 | Kilborn | Samuel | 1 | 1 | | 1 | | 2 | 2 | | 1 | | | | 8 | | |
| Provincetown | 58 | 28 | Kilborn | Mahitable | | | | | | | | | 1 | | | | 1 | | |
| Provincetown | 58 | 29 | Lary | John Junr | 2 | 1 | 1 | | | 2 | | | 1 | 1 | | | 8 | | |
| Provincetown | 58 | 30 | Lary | Lewis | 1 | | 1 | | | 3 | | | 1 | | | | 6 | | |
| Provincetown | 58 | 31 | Lombard | Peter | 2 | 1 | | 1 | | 1 | | | 1 | | | | 6 | | |
| Provincetown | 58 | 32 | Miller | William | 2 | 1 | | 1 | | 2 | 1 | | 1 | | | | 8 | | |
| Provincetown | 58 | 33 | Miller | Benjamin | 2 | | 1 | | | 1 | 1 | | | | | | 5 | | |
| Provincetown | 58 | 34 | Mayo | Joshua A. | 2 | 2 | | 1 | | 1 | | 1 | 1 | | | | 8 | | |
| Provincetown | 58 | 35 | Mayo | Thomas | 1 | 1 | 2 | | 1 | 1 | 1 | 2 | | 1 | | | 10 | | |
| Provincetown | 58 | 36 | Nickerson | Stephen | 2 | 1 | 1 | 1 | | 2 | 2 | | 1 | | | | 10 | | |
| Provincetown | 58 | 37 | Nickerson | Seth Junr | 1 | | | 1 | | 4 | 1 | | 1 | | | | 8 | | |
| Provincetown | 58 | 38 | Nickerson | Ebenezer | | | 1 | | | 3 | | | 1 | | | | 6 | | |
| Provincetown | 58 | 39 | Nickerson | James | 2 | | 1 | | | 2 | | | 1 | | | | 6 | | |
| Provincetown | 58 | 40 | Nickerson | Enoch | 2 | | 1 | | | 2 | | | 1 | | | | 6 | | |
| Provincetown | 58 | 41 | Nickerson | Nehemiah | | | 1 | | | | | | 2 | | | | 3 | | |
| Provincetown | 58 | 42 | Nickerson | Jonathan | | 2 | 3 | 1 | | 3 | 1 | | 1 | | | | 11 | | |
| Provincetown | 59 | 1 | Nickerson | Phinehas | | | 1 | | | 1 | | 1 | | 1 | | | 4 | | |
| Provincetown | 59 | 2 | Nickerson | Phinehas Junr | 1 | 1 | | 1 | | 4 | | 1 | | | | | 8 | | |
| Provincetown | 59 | 3 | Nickerson | Joseph | 1 | | 2 | | | 1 | 1 | | | | | | 5 | | |
| Provincetown | 59 | 4 | Nickerson | Nehemiah Junr | 1 | 1 | | | 1 | 1 | | | | | | | 4 | | |
| Provincetown | 59 | 5 | Nickerson | Seth Junr | 3 | 1 | | 1 | | 2 | | | 1 | | | | 8 | | |
| Provincetown | 59 | 6 | Nickerson | William | | | 1 | | 1 | 1 | | | | | | | 3 | | |
| Provincetown | 59 | 7 | Nickerson | Allen | 2 | 2 | | 1 | | 2 | | 1 | 1 | | | | 9 | | |
| Provincetown | 59 | 8 | Newcomb | David | 2 | | 1 | 1 | | | 2 | | 1 | | | | 7 | | |
| Provincetown | 59 | 9 | Newcomb | Jeremiah | 1 | | 3 | 1 | | 2 | 2 | 1 | | | | | 10 | | |
| Provincetown | 59 | 10 | Nickerson | Betsy Wd | | 1 | 1 | | | | | | 1 | 1 | | | 4 | | |
| Provincetown | 59 | 11 | Nickerson | Martha Wd | | 2 | | | | | | | 1 | 1 | | | 4 | | |
| Provincetown | 59 | 12 | Nickerson | Josiah | 2 | | 1 | | | | | | | 1 | | | 4 | | |
| Provincetown | 59 | 13 | Proutt | Reuben | | 1 | | 1 | | 1 | | | 1 | | | | 4 | | |

# 1800 Provincetown, Barnstable County, Massachusetts

| TOWN | PG# | LN# | LAST NAME | FIRST NAME | M under 10 | M 10 to 16 | M 16 to 26 | M 26 to 45 | M 45 and over | F under 10 | F 10 to 16 | F 16 to 26 | F 26 to 45 | F 45 and over | TOTAL ALL OTHER | TOTAL SLAVES | TOTALS | DISTRICT/TOWNSHIP | NOTES |
|---|---|---|---|---|---|---|---|---|---|---|---|---|---|---|---|---|---|---|---|
| Provincetown | 59 | 14 | Perry | Richard | | 1 | 1 | | | 3 | | | 1 | | | | 6 | | |
| Provincetown | 59 | 15 | Paine | Henry | 3 | | | 1 | | | | | 1 | | | | 5 | | |
| Provincetown | 59 | 16 | Paine | Moses | 1 | | 1 | | | 1 | | | 1 | | | | 4 | | |
| Provincetown | 59 | 17 | Peirce | Joshua | 1 | 2 | 1 | | 1 | 1 | | 1 | 1 | | | | 8 | | |
| Provincetown | 59 | 18 | Rider | David | 4 | | 1 | 1 | | | | 1 | 1 | | | | 8 | | |
| Provincetown | 59 | 19 | Rider | Ebenezer | | | | 1 | | | | | | 2 | | | 3 | | |
| Provincetown | 59 | 20 | Rider | Ebenezer Jun | 4 | | | 1 | | | | | 1 | | | | 6 | | |
| Provincetown | 59 | 21 | Rider | Thomas | | 1 | 2 | 1 | | | | | 1 | | | | 5 | | |
| Provincetown | 59 | 22 | Rich | David | | | | 1 | | 3 | | | 1 | | | | 5 | | |
| Provincetown | 59 | 23 | Reed | William B. | 2 | 1 | | 1 | | 1 | | | 1 | | | | 6 | | |
| Provincetown | 59 | 24 | Ridly | Nathaniel | 1 | | | 1 | | 1 | | | 1 | 1 | | | 5 | | |
| Provincetown | 59 | 25 | Ridly | Thomas | 1 | | | 1 | | | | | 1 | | | | 3 | | |
| Provincetown | 59 | 26 | Smalley | Thomas | 1 | 1 | 1 | 1 | | 3 | | | 1 | | | | 8 | | |
| Provincetown | 59 | 27 | Smith | James | | | 1 | 1 | 1 | | | | | 1 | | | 4 | | |
| Provincetown | 59 | 28 | Sparks | James | 1 | | 1 | 1 | | 1 | | | 1 | | | | 5 | | |
| Provincetown | 59 | 29 | Smalley | Daniel | 1 | 1 | | 1 | | 3 | | | 1 | | | | 7 | | |
| Provincetown | 59 | 30 | Stanly | Job | | | | 1 | | 2 | | | 1 | | | | 4 | | |
| Provincetown | 59 | 31 | Savage | John | 2 | | | 1 | | 1 | | | 1 | | | | 5 | | |
| Provincetown | 59 | 32 | Smaly | Talor | 2 | 1 | | 1 | | 1 | | | 1 | | | | 6 | | |
| Provincetown | 59 | 33 | Smith | Enos | 2 | | | | 1 | 2 | | | 1 | | | | 6 | | |
| Provincetown | 59 | 34 | Smith | Seth Junr | 1 | 1 | | 1 | | 1 | | 1 | | | | | 5 | | |
| Provincetown | 59 | 35 | Smith | Edmund | 2 | 1 | | 1 | | 2 | | | 1 | | | | 7 | | |
| Provincetown | 59 | 36 | Smally | Abraham | 2 | | | 1 | | 2 | | | 1 | | | | 6 | | |
| Provincetown | 59 | 37 | Smith | Seth | | 2 | | | 1 | | 1 | | | 1 | | | 5 | | |
| Provincetown | 59 | 38 | Stockwell | Joseph | | | 1 | | | 1 | | | 1 | | | | 3 | | |
| Provincetown | 59 | 39 | Smith | Enoch | 3 | 1 | | 1 | | | | | 1 | 1 | | | 7 | | |
| Provincetown | 60 | 1 | Smaley | Samuel | 1 | | 1 | | | 1 | | 1 | | | | | 4 | | |
| Provincetown | 60 | 2 | Smith | Josha | 1 | 2 | | 1 | | 2 | | | 1 | | | | 7 | | |
| Provincetown | 60 | 3 | Snow | Ryal | | 1 | 1 | 1 | | 2 | | 1 | 1 | | | | 7 | | |
| Provincetown | 60 | 4 | Smith | Daniel | 2 | 1 | | 1 | 1 | | | 1 | | | | | 6 | | |
| Provincetown | 60 | 5 | Stubbs | Dorcas Wd | 1 | | | | | 2 | 2 | | 1 | | | | 6 | | |
| Provincetown | 60 | 6 | Durner | Joseph | 1 | 1 | 2 | | 1 | 1 | 2 | 1 | 1 | | | | 10 | | |
| Provincetown | 60 | 7 | Wharf | Samuel | 2 | | | 1 | | 1 | | | 1 | | | | 5 | | |
| Provincetown | 60 | 8 | Wharf | John | | 2 | | 1 | | 3 | 1 | 1 | 1 | | | | 9 | | |
| Provincetown | 60 | 9 | Wharf | George | | 1 | | 1 | | 3 | 1 | | 1 | | | | 7 | | |
| Provincetown | 60 | 10 | Williams | Andrew | 1 | | | 1 | 1 | 1 | | | 1 | 1 | | | 6 | | |
| Provincetown | 60 | 11 | Warren | William | 3 | | | 1 | | 1 | | | 1 | | | | 6 | | |
| Provincetown | 60 | 12 | Young | David | 2 | | | 1 | | | | | 1 | | | | 4 | | |
| Provincetown | 60 | 13 | Young | Eleazar | 3 | | | 1 | | | | 1 | 1 | | | | 6 | | |
| Provincetown | 60 | 14 | Parker | Rev Samuel | | 1 | | 1 | | | | | | | 1 | | 3 | | |
| Provincetown | 60 | 15 | Collins | Richard | | 1 | | | | | | 1 | | | | | 2 | | |
| Provincetown | 60 | 16 | Young | Elisha | 1 | 1 | | | | | | 1 | | | | | 3 | | |
| Provincetown | 60 | 17 | Hill | John Junr | | 1 | | | | | | 1 | | | | | 2 | | |
| Provincetown | 60 | 18 | Wickson | Robert | | 1 | | 1 | | | | | | 1 | | | 3 | | |
| Provincetown | 60 | 19 | Atwood | Samuel | | 1 | 1 | 1 | | | | 1 | | 1 | | | 5 | | |
| Provincetown | 60 | 20 | Smith | Samuel | 1 | | | 1 | | 1 | | | 1 | | | | 4 | | |
| Provincetown | 60 | 21 | Dyer | Ambros | | 1 | | 1 | | 3 | | | 1 | | | | 6 | | |
| Provincetown | 60 | 22 | Mores | Treat | | 1 | | | | | | | 1 | | | | 2 | | |
| Provincetown | 60 | 23 | Goodwin | Jeremiah | | | 1 | | | | | | 1 | | | | 2 | | |
| Provincetown | 60 | 24 | Smith | Reuben | 1 | | 1 | | | | | | 1 | | | | 3 | | |
| Provincetown | 60 | 25 | Rider | Isaiah | | 1 | | | | | | | 1 | | | | 2 | | |
| Provincetown | 60 | 26 | Peirce | David | 1 | | | 1 | | 2 | | | 1 | | | | 5 | | |
| Provincetown | 60 | 27 | Bowley | Oliver | | | | 1 | | 1 | | | 1 | | | | 3 | | |
| Provincetown | 60 | 28 | Howes | Lot | | | 1 | | | | | | 1 | | | | 2 | | |
| Provincetown | 60 | 29 | Aires | Joseph | 1 | | | 1 | | 2 | | | 1 | 1 | | | 6 | | |
| Provincetown | 60 | 30 | Collins | Rebeccah | | 1 | | | | | | 1 | | | | | 2 | | |
| Provincetown | 60 | 31 | Eldridge | William | 1 | 1 | | | | | | | 1 | | | | 3 | | |
| Provincetown | 60 | 32 | Freeman | Elisha | 3 | 1 | | | | | | | 1 | | | | 6 | | |
| Provincetown | 60 | 33 | Cook | David | | 1 | | | | | | | 1 | | | | 2 | | |
| Provincetown | 60 | 34 | Nickerson | Mayo | | | | 1 | | 1 | | | 1 | | | | 3 | | |
| Provincetown | 60 | 35 | Bickford | Henry | | 1 | | | | | | | | | | | 1 | | |
| Provincetown | 60 | 36 | Nickerson | Timothy | | 1 | | | | | | | 1 | | | | 2 | | |
| Provincetown | 60 | 37 | Ward | John | 2 | | | 1 | | | | | 1 | | | | 4 | | |
| Provincetown | 60 | 38 | Atwood | Henry | 2 | | | 1 | | 1 | 1 | | 1 | | | | 6 | | |
| Provincetown | 60 | 39 | Ginn | John | 1 | | 1 | | | | | | 1 | | | | 3 | | |
| Provincetown | 60 | 40 | Beedie | Gamaliel | | | 1 | | | 1 | | | 1 | | | | 3 | | |
| Provincetown | 61 | 1 | Collener | Thankful | | 1 | | | | 1 | | | 1 | | | | 3 | | |
| Provincetown | 61 | 2 | Brown | Shobel | 1 | | 1 | | | | | | 1 | | | | 3 | | |
| Provincetown | 61 | 3 | Rider | Joshua | | 1 | 1 | | | 1 | | | 1 | | | | 4 | | |
| Provincetown | 61 | 4 | Hincks | Jesse | 1 | | 1 | | | 1 | | | 1 | | | | 4 | | |
| Provincetown | 61 | 5 | Hincks | Elisha | | | 1 | | | 1 | | | 1 | | | | 3 | | |
| Provincetown | 61 | 6 | Baker | Thatcher | | | 1 | | | | | | 1 | | | | 2 | | |
| Provincetown | 61 | 7 | Nichols | James | 1 | | 1 | | | 1 | | | 1 | | | | 4 | | |
| Provincetown | 61 | 8 | Cook | Isaac | | | 1 | | | 1 | | | 1 | | | | 3 | | |
| Provincetown | 61 | 9 | Bush | William | 1 | | 1 | 1 | | 2 | 1 | 1 | 1 | | | | 8 | | |
| Provincetown | 61 | 10 | Peirce | William | 3 | | 1 | | | 1 | | | 1 | | | | 6 | | |
| Provincetown | 61 | 11 | Wizell | George Rix | | | 1 | | | 1 | | | 1 | | | | 3 | | |
| Provincetown | 61 | 12 | Feavour | Peter | | | 1 | | | | | | 1 | | | | 3 | | |
| Provincetown | 61 | 13 | Snow | Sarah Wd | | | | | | | | | | 1 | | | 1 | | |

43

# 1800 Provincetown, Barnstable County, Massachusetts

| TOWN | PG# | LN# | LAST NAME | FIRST NAME | FREE WHITE MALES | | | | | FREE WHITE FEMALES | | | | | TOTAL ALL OTHER | TOTAL SLAVES | TOTALS | DISTRICT/ TOWNSHIP | NOTES |
|---|---|---|---|---|---|---|---|---|---|---|---|---|---|---|---|---|---|---|---|
| | | | | | under 10 | 10 to 16 | 16 to 26 | 26 to 45 | 45 and over | under 10 | 10 to 16 | 16 to 26 | 26 to 45 | 45 and over | | | | | |
| Provincetown | 61 | 14 | Hayden | William | | 1 | | | | 1 | | 1 | | | | | 3 | | |
| Provincetown | 61 | 15 | Brown | David Junr | | 1 | | | | 1 | | 1 | | | | | 3 | | |
| Provincetown | 61 | 16 | Rider | Joseph | | 1 | | | | | | 1 | | | | | 2 | | |
| Provincetown | 61 | 17 | Atkins | Stephen | | 1 | | | | | | 1 | | | 3 | | 5 | | |

# 1800 Sandwich, Barnstable County, Massachusetts

| TOWN | PG# | LN# | LAST NAME | FIRST NAME | FREE WHITE MALES | | | | | FREE WHITE FEMALES | | | | | TOTAL ALL OTHER | TOTAL SLAVES | TOTALS | DISTRICT/ TOWNSHIP | NOTES |
|---|---|---|---|---|---|---|---|---|---|---|---|---|---|---|---|---|---|---|---|
| | | | | | under 10 | 10 to 16 | 16 to 26 | 26 to 45 | 45 and over | under 10 | 10 to 16 | 16 to 26 | 26 to 45 | 45 and over | | | | | |
| Sandwich | 34 | 1 | Fesenden | William | 2 | | | 2 | | 1 | | | 1 | | | | 6 | | |
| Sandwich | 34 | 2 | Sturgis | Jonathan | 2 | 1 | | | | | 2 | | 1 | | | | 6 | | |
| Sandwich | 34 | 3 | Chipman | Hatsuls | 1 | | | 1 | | 4 | | | 1 | | | | 7 | | |
| Sandwich | 34 | 4 | Jones | Josiah | 1 | 2 | 3 | | 1 | 1 | | 1 | | | | | 9 | | |
| Sandwich | 34 | 5 | Bates | David | | | 1 | | | 1 | | 1 | | | | | 3 | | |
| Sandwich | 34 | 6 | Chipman | Stephen S. | 3 | | | 1 | | | | | 1 | | | | 5 | | |
| Sandwich | 34 | 7 | Wine | Ebenezer | 3 | | | | 1 | | | 1 | | 2 | | | 7 | | |
| Sandwich | 34 | 8 | Nye | Peleg | 1 | | | | 1 | 2 | 2 | | 1 | | | | 7 | | |
| Sandwich | 34 | 9 | Weeks | Joseph | | | 1 | 1 | 1 | | | | 1 | | | | 4 | | |
| Sandwich | 34 | 10 | Lewis | Louis | | | | | | | | | 1 | | | | 1 | | |
| Sandwich | 34 | 11 | Fish | Silas | | | 1 | | 1 | | | | 1 | | | | 3 | | |
| Sandwich | 34 | 12 | Gifford | Lemuel | 2 | | | | 1 | | 3 | | 2 | | | | 8 | | |
| Sandwich | 34 | 13 | Gifford | Joseph | 1 | 2 | | 1 | | 2 | 1 | | 1 | | | | 8 | | |
| Sandwich | 34 | 14 | Purrington | Daniel | 2 | | | 1 | | 1 | | | 1 | | | | 5 | | |
| Sandwich | 34 | 15 | Wing | Joseph Jun | | 1 | 2 | | 1 | | | | | 2 | | | 6 | | |
| Sandwich | 34 | 16 | Nye | Barnabas | | | 1 | | | | | | 1 | | | | 2 | | |
| Sandwich | 34 | 17 | Wing | Mary | | | | | | | | | | 1 | | | 1 | | |
| Sandwich | 34 | 18 | Childs | Jonathan | | | | 1 | | | | 1 | | 1 | | | 3 | | |
| Sandwich | 34 | 19 | Fuller | Nathaniel | 2 | | | 1 | | 1 | | | 1 | | | | 5 | | |
| Sandwich | 34 | 20 | Crosby | Levi | | | 1 | | | | | 1 | | 1 | | | 3 | | |
| Sandwich | 34 | 21 | Bowerman | Samuel | | | 1 | | 1 | | | | | 1 | | | 3 | | |
| Sandwich | 34 | 22 | Holway | Barnabas | | | | 1 | | | | 1 | 1 | | | | 3 | | |
| Sandwich | 34 | 23 | Allen | Gideon | | | | 1 | | | | | | | | | 1 | | |
| Sandwich | 35 | 1 | Nye | Levi | 1 | | 1 | 1 | | | | 1 | | | | | 4 | | |
| Sandwich | 35 | 2 | Hall | Stephen | | | 1 | | 1 | 1 | | 1 | | 1 | | | 5 | | |
| Sandwich | 35 | 3 | Hall | Joshua | 1 | | | 1 | | | 1 | | 1 | | | | 4 | | |
| Sandwich | 35 | 4 | Hall | Joseph | 2 | | | 1 | | 1 | 1 | | 1 | | | | 6 | | |
| Sandwich | 35 | 5 | Freeman | Tabitha | | | 1 | 1 | | | | | 1 | 1 | | | 4 | | |
| Sandwich | 35 | 6 | Atkins | James | | | 1 | | 1 | | | 1 | | 1 | | | 4 | | |
| Sandwich | 35 | 7 | Freeman | Samuel | 1 | | | 1 | | | | | 1 | | | | 3 | | |
| Sandwich | 35 | 8 | Freeman | Joshua | 1 | | 1 | 1 | 1 | | 1 | 2 | | 2 | | | 9 | | |
| Sandwich | 35 | 9 | Fish | Josiah | | | | 1 | | | | | | | | | 1 | | |
| Sandwich | 35 | 10 | Fish | Edmund | | | | 1 | 1 | | | | 2 | 1 | | | 5 | | |
| Sandwich | 35 | 11 | Fish | John 2d | 3 | 1 | | | 1 | | 1 | 1 | 1 | | | | 8 | | |
| Sandwich | 35 | 12 | Wing | John 2d | | | 1 | | 1 | | | 1 | 2 | 1 | | | 6 | | |
| Sandwich | 35 | 13 | Wing | Stephen | 4 | | 1 | | 1 | | 2 | | 1 | | | | 9 | | |
| Sandwich | 35 | 14 | Hoxie | Barnabas | | | | | 1 | | 1 | | 1 | 1 | | | 4 | | |
| Sandwich | 35 | 15 | Hoxie | Joseph | 2 | | | 1 | | 1 | | | 1 | | | | 5 | | |
| Sandwich | 35 | 16 | Nye | Moses | 1 | | | 1 | | 2 | | | 1 | | | | 5 | | |
| Sandwich | 35 | 17 | Nye | Mary | | | | 2 | | | | | 1 | 2 | | | 5 | | |
| Sandwich | 35 | 18 | Holway | James | | | 1 | 1 | | 1 | 2 | | 1 | | | | 6 | | |
| Sandwich | 35 | 19 | Bassett | Lemuel | 1 | | | 1 | | 1 | | 1 | | | | | 4 | | |
| Sandwich | 35 | 20 | Nye | Jabez | 1 | | 2 | | 1 | | 2 | 1 | | 1 | | | 8 | | |
| Sandwich | 35 | 21 | Bursley | John | | 1 | | | 1 | 1 | | | 1 | 1 | | | 5 | | |
| Sandwich | 35 | 22 | Atkins | William | 1 | | 1 | | | 1 | | 1 | | | | | 4 | | |
| Sandwich | 35 | 23 | Nye | Silvanus | | 3 | | | 1 | | 1 | 2 | | 1 | | | 8 | | |
| Sandwich | 35 | 24 | Howland | Jonathan | | 1 | | | 1 | | | | 1 | 1 | | | 4 | | |
| Sandwich | 35 | 25 | Cyprus | George | | | | | | | | | | | 2 | | 2 | | |
| Sandwich | 35 | 26 | Treadwell | Cesar | | | | | | | | | 1 | | 4 | | 5 | | |
| Sandwich | 35 | 27 | Bourne | Melatiah | | 1 | 1 | | 1 | | | 1 | 1 | 1 | | | 6 | | |
| Sandwich | 35 | 28 | Dillingham | John Junr | | 2 | 1 | | 1 | | | 2 | 1 | 1 | | | 8 | | |
| Sandwich | 35 | 29 | Tobey | Nathan | 1 | | | 1 | | | | 1 | | | | | 3 | | |
| Sandwich | 35 | 30 | Tobey | Maria | | | | 1 | | | | | 1 | 1 | | | 3 | | |
| Sandwich | 35 | 31 | Dillingham | Edward | | 1 | 1 | | 1 | | 1 | | | 1 | | | 5 | | |
| Sandwich | 35 | 32 | Tobey | Silvanus | | | 1 | 1 | | 1 | | 1 | | | | | 4 | | |
| Sandwich | 35 | 33 | Fessenden | Samuel | 1 | | 1 | | 1 | 2 | 2 | 2 | | 1 | | | 10 | | |
| Sandwich | 35 | 34 | Smith | Samuel | | 1 | | | 1 | 1 | | 2 | | 1 | | | 6 | | |
| Sandwich | 35 | 35 | Howland | William | 1 | | 1 | 1 | | | | | 1 | | | | 4 | | |
| Sandwich | 35 | 36 | Burr | Jonathan Revd | 1 | | | 1 | | 1 | 1 | 1 | 1 | | | | 6 | | |
| Sandwich | 35 | 37 | Tobey | William | 1 | 1 | | | 1 | | | 2 | 1 | 1 | | | 7 | | |
| Sandwich | 35 | 38 | Tobey | Heman | 1 | | | 1 | | 2 | 1 | | 1 | | | | 6 | | |
| Sandwich | 35 | 39 | Tobey | Melatiah | 1 | | | 1 | | 1 | | | 1 | | | | 4 | | |
| Sandwich | 35 | 40 | Tobey | Timothy | 1 | | | 1 | | 2 | 1 | | 1 | 1 | | | 7 | | |
| Sandwich | 35 | 41 | Dillingham | Benjamin | 1 | 2 | 1 | | 1 | | 1 | | 1 | 1 | | | 8 | | |
| Sandwich | 35 | 42 | Allen | Samuel | | 1 | | 1 | 1 | | 1 | 1 | | 1 | | | 6 | | |
| Sandwich | 35 | 43 | Wing | Joseph | | | | 1 | | | | | 1 | | | | 2 | | |
| Sandwich | 35 | 44 | Tobey | Prince | | | | 1 | | 1 | | | 1 | 1 | | | 4 | | |
| Sandwich | 36 | 1 | Willcox | Amaziah | 1 | 1 | 1 | | 1 | 3 | 2 | | 1 | | | | 10 | | |
| Sandwich | 36 | 2 | Hood | Henry | | | | 1 | | | | 1 | | | | | 2 | | |
| Sandwich | 36 | 3 | Nye | Nathan | 1 | | 1 | | 1 | | 1 | 2 | | 1 | | | 7 | | |
| Sandwich | 36 | 4 | Nye | William Junr | 2 | 1 | | 1 | | 1 | | 2 | | 1 | | | 8 | | |
| Sandwich | 36 | 5 | Tupper | Mahitabel | | | 3 | | | | | 1 | | 1 | | | 5 | | |
| Sandwich | 36 | 6 | Nye | Nathaniel | 2 | 1 | 1 | | | 1 | | 1 | | 1 | | | 8 | | |
| Sandwich | 36 | 7 | Christie | James | 1 | 1 | | 1 | | 2 | | 1 | | 1 | | | 7 | | |
| Sandwich | 36 | 8 | Dillingham | Branch | 3 | | | 1 | | 1 | | | 2 | | | | 7 | | |
| Sandwich | 36 | 9 | Dillingham | John | | | | | 1 | | | 1 | | 1 | | | 3 | | |
| Sandwich | 36 | 10 | Kelley | Benjamin | | 1 | | | 1 | | | 1 | | 1 | | | 4 | | |
| Sandwich | 36 | 11 | Smith | John | 1 | | 1 | | 1 | 2 | 1 | 1 | | | | | 7 | | |
| Sandwich | 36 | 12 | Smith | Deborah | | | | | | | | | 1 | | | | 1 | | |

# 1800 Sandwich, Barnstable County, Massachusetts

| TOWN | PG# | LN# | LAST NAME | FIRST NAME | FREE WHITE MALES | | | | | FREE WHITE FEMALES | | | | | TOTAL ALL OTHER | TOTAL SLAVES | TOTALS | DISTRICT/ TOWNSHIP | NOTES |
|---|---|---|---|---|---|---|---|---|---|---|---|---|---|---|---|---|---|---|---|
| | | | | | under 10 | 10 to 16 | 16 to 26 | 26 to 45 | 45 and over | under 10 | 10 to 16 | 16 to 26 | 26 to 45 | 45 and over | | | | | |
| Sandwich | 36 | 13 | Weeks | James | 1 | | | 1 | | 2 | 1 | | 1 | | | | 6 | | |
| Sandwich | 36 | 14 | Bassett | William | 2 | 1 | 1 | | 1 | 1 | 1 | 1 | 1 | | | | 9 | | |
| Sandwich | 36 | 15 | Bassett | Thomas | | | | 1 | | | | | | 1 | | | 2 | | |
| Sandwich | 36 | 16 | Do*ise | Fredrick | | 1 | | 1 | | 1 | | 1 | 1 | | | | 5 | | |
| Sandwich | 36 | 17 | Chipman | Benjamin | | | 1 | 1 | | 1 | | | 2 | 1 | | | 6 | | |
| Sandwich | 36 | 18 | Chipman | Stephen | | | | 1 | | | | | | | | | 1 | | |
| Sandwich | 36 | 19 | Hoxie | Jesse | 1 | 1 | | 1 | | 3 | | 1 | 1 | 1 | | | 9 | | |
| Sandwich | 36 | 20 | Fish | Jonathan | 2 | 1 | | 1 | | 2 | | | 1 | 1 | 1 | | 9 | | |
| Sandwich | 36 | 21 | Nye | Lemuel | 2 | | | 1 | | 1 | 1 | | 1 | | | | 6 | | |
| Sandwich | 36 | 22 | Nye | Joseph | 1 | | | 1 | | | | 1 | | | | | 3 | | |
| Sandwich | 36 | 23 | Nye | Ebenezer | 2 | 2 | | | 1 | 1 | | 1 | 1 | 1 | 1 | | 10 | | |
| Sandwich | 36 | 24 | Nye | Peter | | 1 | 1 | | 1 | | | 1 | | 1 | | | 5 | | |
| Sandwich | 36 | 25 | Hamblen | Thomas | 1 | | 1 | | | | | 1 | | | | | 3 | | |
| Sandwich | 36 | 26 | Nye | Heman | | | | 1 | | | | | 1 | | | | 2 | | |
| Sandwich | 36 | 27 | Nye | John | 4 | | | 2 | 1 | 3 | 1 | 2 | 1 | | | | 14 | | |
| Sandwich | 36 | 28 | Holway | Prince | 2 | | | 1 | | 1 | | | 1 | | | | 5 | | |
| Sandwich | 36 | 29 | Hoxie | Cornelius | | | 1 | | 1 | | | 1 | | 1 | | | 4 | | |
| Sandwich | 36 | 30 | Allen | George | | 1 | | | | | | 1 | 1 | 1 | | | 4 | | |
| Sandwich | 36 | 31 | Jones | Bathseba | 1 | | 2 | | 1 | | | 1 | 1 | 4 | | | 10 | | |
| Sandwich | 36 | 32 | Swift | Silas | 1 | 1 | | | 1 | 3 | 1 | 1 | 1 | | | | 9 | | |
| Sandwich | 36 | 33 | Freeman | Benjamin | 2 | | | 1 | | 1 | | | 1 | | | | 5 | | |
| Sandwich | 36 | 34 | Allen | William | 1 | 1 | 3 | | 1 | 2 | 2 | | | 1 | | | 11 | | |
| Sandwich | 36 | 35 | Freeman | Lemuel | 2 | 1 | | 1 | | 2 | | | 1 | | | | 7 | | |
| Sandwich | 36 | 36 | Fuller | Joseph | 1 | 1 | 1 | 1 | | 2 | 1 | | 1 | | | | 8 | | |
| Sandwich | 36 | 37 | Fish | Simeon | | | | 1 | | | | | | 1 | | | 2 | | |
| Sandwich | 36 | 38 | Fish | Asa | | 1 | | 1 | | 1 | | | 1 | | 1 | | 5 | | |
| Sandwich | 36 | 39 | Bourne | James Junr | | | | 1 | | | | | 1 | | | | 2 | | |
| Sandwich | 36 | 40 | Leonard | Jonathan | 1 | | | 1 | | 1 | | | 1 | | | | 4 | | |
| Sandwich | 36 | 41 | Tobey | John | | | 1 | 1 | 1 | 1 | 1 | 1 | 1 | | | | 7 | | |
| Sandwich | 36 | 42 | Tobey | John Junr | 1 | | | 1 | | | 1 | | | | | | 3 | | |
| Sandwich | 36 | 43 | E* | Lazarus | 1 | 2 | | | 1 | 2 | | 3 | 1 | | | | 10 | | |
| Sandwich | 37 | 1 | Chase | Leonard | | | 3 | | 1 | 1 | 2 | | 1 | 1 | | | 9 | | |
| Sandwich | 37 | 2 | Percival | Thomas | 1 | 1 | 2 | 1 | | 1 | 2 | | 1 | | | | 9 | | |
| Sandwich | 37 | 3 | Ewer | Peleg | | | | 1 | | | | | 1 | | | | 2 | | |
| Sandwich | 37 | 4 | Hillard | Gideon | | | | 2 | | | | | 1 | | | | 3 | | |
| Sandwich | 37 | 5 | Crocker | Deliverance | 1 | | | 1 | | 2 | 1 | 2 | | 1 | | | 8 | | |
| Sandwich | 37 | 6 | Hoxie | Mary | | | | 1 | | | | 1 | 1 | | | | 3 | | |
| Sandwich | 37 | 7 | Blossem | Joseph | | 1 | 1 | | 1 | 1 | 1 | | 1 | | | | 7 | | |
| Sandwich | 37 | 8 | Wine | Bennett | | | | 1 | | | 1 | 1 | 1 | | | | 4 | | |
| Sandwich | 37 | 9 | Jones | Silvanus | 2 | | 2 | | 1 | | 2 | | | 1 | | | 8 | | |
| Sandwich | 37 | 10 | Hoxie | Elizabeth | | | | 1 | | | | 1 | 1 | | | | 3 | | |
| Sandwich | 37 | 11 | Nye | Abigail | | 1 | | | | | 3 | 1 | | | | | 5 | | |
| Sandwich | 37 | 12 | Smith | Mathius | 1 | | | 1 | | 1 | | 1 | | | | | 4 | | |
| Sandwich | 37 | 13 | Wine | John 2d | | 1 | 1 | | 1 | | 1 | | 1 | 1 | | | 6 | | |
| Sandwich | 37 | 14 | Wine | Edward | 1 | | 1 | | 1 | 1 | | 1 | 1 | 1 | | | 7 | | |
| Sandwich | 37 | 15 | Weeks | Zenas | | 1 | | | | 1 | | | 1 | | | | 3 | | |
| Sandwich | 37 | 16 | Banister | Nancy | | | | | | | | | | | 2 | | 2 | | |
| Sandwich | 37 | 17 | Holway | Joseph | | 2 | | 1 | | | | | 1 | | | | 4 | | |
| Sandwich | 37 | 18 | Holway | Joseph Jun | 1 | | 1 | | 2 | | | 1 | | | | | 5 | | |
| Sandwich | 37 | 19 | Lawrence | Joseph | | 3 | 1 | | | 1 | | 1 | | | | | 6 | | |
| Sandwich | 37 | 20 | Percival | James | 1 | 2 | 1 | | 2 | 3 | | 1 | 1 | | | | 11 | | |
| Sandwich | 37 | 21 | Bradley | Thomas | 2 | | 1 | | 1 | | | 1 | | | | | 5 | | |
| Sandwich | 37 | 22 | Peleg | Lawrence | 5 | 1 | 1 | | | | | 1 | | | | | 8 | | |
| Sandwich | 37 | 23 | Meiggs | Josiah | 2 | | 1 | | 1 | | | 1 | | | | | 5 | | |
| Sandwich | 37 | 24 | Percival | Benjamin | 2 | 1 | 3 | | 1 | 1 | | 1 | | 1 | | | 10 | | |
| Sandwich | 37 | 25 | Fish | Stephen | 2 | 1 | | 1 | 1 | | 1 | 1 | | 1 | | | 8 | | |
| Sandwich | 37 | 26 | Meiggs | Ralph | | 1 | | 1 | | 1 | 1 | | 1 | | | | 5 | | |
| Sandwich | 37 | 27 | Meiggs | Matthew | 1 | 1 | 1 | 1 | | | 1 | 1 | 1 | | | | 7 | | |
| Sandwich | 37 | 28 | Coombs | Abigail | 1 | | | | | 1 | | 2 | | | | | 4 | | |
| Sandwich | 37 | 29 | Jona | John | 2 | 2 | | 1 | | | | 1 | 1 | | | | 7 | | |
| Sandwich | 37 | 30 | Jones | Silvanus Junr | 2 | | 1 | 1 | | 2 | | 1 | 1 | | | | 8 | | |
| Sandwich | 37 | 31 | Jones | Remember | | | | | | | | 2 | 1 | | | | 3 | | |
| Sandwich | 37 | 32 | Hoxie | Ludwick | 1 | 2 | | 1 | | 2 | 1 | 1 | 1 | | | | 9 | | |
| Sandwich | 37 | 33 | Landers | John | 2 | 1 | 1 | | 1 | | 1 | 2 | | | | | 8 | | |
| Sandwich | 37 | 34 | Wing | Jashub | 1 | | | 1 | | 2 | | 1 | | | | | 5 | | |
| Sandwich | 37 | 35 | Hoxie | Hezekiah | 2 | 1 | | 1 | | | | 1 | 1 | | | | 6 | | |
| Sandwich | 37 | 36 | Hoxie | Abner | | 1 | 1 | | | 1 | 2 | 1 | 1 | 1 | | | 8 | | |
| Sandwich | 37 | 37 | Hoxie | James | 1 | | 3 | 1 | 1 | | | 2 | 1 | | | | 9 | | |
| Sandwich | 37 | 38 | Landers | Abigail | | | | | | | | 1 | 1 | | | | 2 | | |
| Sandwich | 37 | 39 | Howland | Lemuel | | 1 | | 1 | | 1 | 2 | | 2 | 1 | | | 8 | | |
| Sandwich | 37 | 40 | Gifford | Alden | 1 | 1 | | | | | 1 | 3 | 1 | | | | 7 | | |
| Sandwich | 37 | 41 | Howland | Nathaniel | 2 | | 1 | | 2 | | | 1 | | | | | 6 | | |
| Sandwich | 37 | 42 | Goodspeed | Walter | 4 | 1 | | 1 | | 1 | | 1 | | | | | 8 | | |
| Sandwich | 37 | 43 | Goodspeed | Joseph | | | 2 | 1 | | | | | 1 | | | | 4 | | |
| Sandwich | 37 | 44 | Percival | John | | 1 | | | 1 | | | 1 | | | | | 3 | | |
| Sandwich | 37 | 45 | Ewer | Barnabas | 2 | | | 1 | | 4 | 2 | | 1 | | | | 10 | | |
| Sandwich | 37 | 46 | Ewer | John | | 1 | 2 | 1 | 1 | | 2 | | 1 | 1 | | | 9 | | |
| Sandwich | 37 | 47 | Allen | Joseph | | | | | | | | 1 | | | | | 1 | | |
| Sandwich | 37 | 48 | Adams | Thomas | | 1 | | 1 | | | 1 | | 1 | | | | 4 | | |

# 1800 Sandwich, Barnstable County, Massachusetts

| TOWN | PG# | LN# | LAST NAME | FIRST NAME | M under 10 | M 10 to 16 | M 16 to 26 | M 26 to 45 | M 45 and over | F under 10 | F 10 to 16 | F 16 to 26 | F 26 to 45 | F 45 and over | TOTAL ALL OTHER | TOTAL SLAVES | TOTALS | DISTRICT/TOWNSHIP | NOTES |
|---|---|---|---|---|---|---|---|---|---|---|---|---|---|---|---|---|---|---|---|
| Sandwich | 38 | 1 | Bourne | Nathan | | | 1 | | | | | | | | | | 1 | | |
| Sandwich | 38 | 2 | Jones | Mikah | 1 | | 1 | | | | | | | | | | 2 | | |
| Sandwich | 38 | 3 | Coleman | James | | | | 1 | | | 2 | 1 | 1 | | | | 5 | | |
| Sandwich | 38 | 4 | Coleman | Edward | | | | | | | | | | | | | | | Enumeration left blank |
| Sandwich | 38 | 5 | Coleman | John | 1 | | 1 | | | 1 | | | 1 | | | | 4 | | |
| Sandwich | 38 | 6 | Coleman | Hezekiah | 1 | | 1 | | | | | | 1 | | | | 3 | | |
| Sandwich | 38 | 7 | Lovel | Silas | | | | | | | | | | | | | | | Enumeration left blank |
| Sandwich | 38 | 8 | Fish | Levi | | | | | | | | | | | | | | | Enumeration left blank |
| Sandwich | 38 | 9 | Fish | Lemuel | | | | | | | | | | | | | | | Enumeration left blank |
| Sandwich | 38 | 10 | Doty | James | | | | | | | | | | | | | | | Enumeration left blank |
| Sandwich | 38 | 11 | Bearce | Daniel | | | | | | | | | | | | | | | Enumeration left blank |
| Sandwich | 38 | 12 | Adams | Nathl | | | | | | | | | | | | | | | Enumeration left blank |
| Sandwich | 38 | 13 | Badger | Elizabeth | | | | | | | | | | | | | | | Enumeration left blank |
| Sandwich | 38 | 14 | Fish | Simeon Junr | 1 | | 1 | 1 | | 1 | 1 | 1 | 1 | | | | 7 | | |
| Sandwich | 38 | 15 | Fish | Silvanus | 3 | 1 | | 1 | | 2 | 1 | 3 | 1 | | | | 12 | | |
| Sandwich | 38 | 16 | Fish | Chipman | 3 | | | 1 | | 1 | | | 1 | | | | 6 | | |
| Sandwich | 38 | 17 | Fish | Prince | 1 | | | 1 | | 1 | | | 1 | | | | 4 | | |
| Sandwich | 38 | 18 | Fish | Anselm | | | 1 | | | | | | 1 | | | | 2 | | |
| Sandwich | 38 | 19 | Hamblen | Seth | 1 | | | 1 | | | | | 1 | 1 | | | 4 | | |
| Sandwich | 38 | 20 | Fish | Cornelius | | 1 | 2 | 1 | | | | | | 1 | | | 5 | | |
| Sandwich | 38 | 21 | Hall | Jonathan | 2 | | | 1 | | 1 | | 1 | 1 | 1 | | | 7 | | |
| Sandwich | 38 | 22 | Tobey | Benjm | 1 | 1 | 1 | | 1 | | | | 1 | 1 | | | 6 | | |
| Sandwich | 38 | 23 | G*th | Richard | 1 | 2 | | | 1 | 2 | 1 | | 1 | | | | 8 | | |
| Sandwich | 38 | 24 | Freeman | Seth Junr | 1 | | | | | | | 1 | 1 | | | | 5 | | |
| Sandwich | 38 | 25 | Nye | Katharine | | 2 | 2 | | 1 | 3 | 1 | 2 | | 1 | | | 12 | | |
| Sandwich | 38 | 26 | Burges | James | 1 | | | 1 | | | | | 1 | | | | 3 | | |
| Sandwich | 38 | 27 | Bates | Sarah | | | 1 | | | | | | 1 | 1 | | | 3 | | |
| Sandwich | 38 | 28 | Bodfish | Wm | 2 | 1 | | 1 | 1 | 2 | 1 | | 1 | | | | 9 | | |
| Sandwich | 38 | 29 | Nye | Nathan Junr | | 2 | 2 | | 1 | 3 | 2 | | 1 | | | | 11 | | |
| Sandwich | 38 | 30 | Tupper | Remember | | | | | | | | | | 1 | | | 1 | | |
| Sandwich | 38 | 31 | Gibbs | Samuel | | | | 1 | | | | | | 1 | | | 2 | | |
| Sandwich | 38 | 32 | Gibbs | Saml Junr | 2 | 1 | | 1 | | 2 | | | | 1 | | | 7 | | |
| Sandwich | 38 | 33 | Bowerman | Jeremiah | | 1 | | 1 | | | | 2 | | 1 | | | 5 | | |
| Sandwich | 38 | 34 | Tupper | Prince | | | 1 | | | | | | 1 | | | | 2 | | |
| Sandwich | 38 | 35 | Ellis | Malachi | | | | 1 | | | | 2 | 1 | 1 | | | 5 | | |
| Sandwich | 38 | 36 | Gibbs | Charles | 2 | 3 | | 1 | | 2 | | | 1 | | | | 9 | | |
| Sandwich | 38 | 37 | Gibbs | Warren | | | | 1 | | 1 | | | 1 | | | | 3 | | |
| Sandwich | 38 | 38 | Nye | Wm | | | | 1 | 1 | | | 1 | | 1 | | | 4 | | |
| Sandwich | 38 | 39 | Chase | David | 2 | | 1 | 1 | | 2 | 1 | | 1 | | | | 8 | | |
| Sandwich | 38 | 40 | Studley | Saml Junr | 2 | 2 | | 1 | | 1 | 1 | | 1 | | | | 8 | | |
| Sandwich | 38 | 41 | O'Brine | Mott | 1 | | | 1 | | 1 | 1 | | | 1 | | | 5 | | |
| Sandwich | 38 | 42 | Fish | Anna | | | | 1 | | | | | | 1 | | | 2 | | |
| Sandwich | 39 | 1 | Fish | Hannah | | | | | | | | | | 1 | | | 1 | | |
| Sandwich | 39 | 2 | Fish | Isiah | | | | 1 | | | | | | 1 | | | 2 | | |
| Sandwich | 39 | 3 | Tupper | Esther | | | 1 | | | | | | 1 | 1 | | | 3 | | |
| Sandwich | 39 | 4 | Bassett | Stephen | | | 1 | | | 3 | | | 1 | | 1 | | 6 | | |
| Sandwich | 39 | 5 | Tobey | Silas | | | 1 | 1 | | | | | 1 | 1 | | | 4 | | |
| Sandwich | 39 | 6 | Fannie | James | | 1 | | 1 | | | | | 1 | | | | 3 | | |
| Sandwich | 39 | 7 | Nye | Allen | 2 | | | 1 | | 2 | | | 1 | | 1 | | 7 | | |
| Sandwich | 39 | 8 | Bassett | Jonathan | 2 | | | 1 | 1 | 1 | | 1 | 1 | | | | 7 | | |
| Sandwich | 39 | 9 | Freeman | Seth | | | | 1 | 1 | | | | 1 | 1 | | | 4 | | |
| Sandwich | 39 | 10 | Bassett | Joseph | | | 1 | 1 | | 1 | | | | | | | 3 | | |
| Sandwich | 39 | 11 | Newcomb | Wm | | | 2 | 1 | 1 | 1 | | | 1 | 1 | 1 | | 8 | | |
| Sandwich | 39 | 12 | Pope | Elisha | | | 2 | 1 | 1 | | | 1 | 1 | 1 | | | 7 | | |
| Sandwich | 39 | 13 | Pope | John | 2 | 1 | | 1 | | 3 | 1 | | 1 | | | | 9 | | |
| Sandwich | 39 | 14 | Morse | Lydia | | | | | | | | | 1 | | | | 1 | | |
| Sandwich | 39 | 15 | Pope | Lemuel | | 1 | | 1 | | | | 2 | 2 | | | | 6 | | |
| Sandwich | 39 | 16 | Pope | Thos | 2 | | | 1 | | | 1 | 1 | | | | | 5 | | |
| Sandwich | 39 | 17 | Freeman | Nathl | 1 | 1 | | 1 | | | | | 1 | | | | 5 | | |
| Sandwich | 39 | 18 | Williams | Abigail | | | | | | 2 | | | 1 | | | | 3 | | |
| Sandwich | 39 | 19 | Bourne | Allen | 2 | | | 1 | | | | | 1 | | | | 4 | | |
| Sandwich | 39 | 20 | Bourne | James | | | | | 1 | | | | 1 | | | | 2 | | |
| Sandwich | 39 | 21 | Nye | Stephen | 1 | | | | 1 | | | | | 1 | | | 3 | | |
| Sandwich | 39 | 22 | Nye | Zenas | 3 | 2 | | 1 | | 2 | | | 1 | | | | 9 | | |
| Sandwich | 39 | 23 | Wing | Samuel | 1 | 1 | 2 | | | | | | 1 | | | | 5 | | |
| Sandwich | 39 | 24 | Wing | Paul | | 2 | | 1 | | | | 2 | | 1 | | | 6 | | |
| Sandwich | 39 | 25 | Simons | Jonathan | | | 1 | 1 | | 1 | 1 | | 1 | | | | 5 | | |
| Sandwich | 39 | 26 | Bassett | Elisha | 1 | | | 1 | | 1 | 1 | | 1 | | | | 5 | | |
| Sandwich | 39 | 27 | Swift | Joseph | 3 | 1 | | 1 | | 2 | 1 | | 1 | | | | 9 | | |
| Sandwich | 39 | 28 | Gibbs | David | | | | 1 | | 1 | | | 2 | 1 | | | 5 | | |
| Sandwich | 39 | 29 | Gibbs | Benjamin | 1 | 1 | | 1 | | 2 | | | 1 | | | | 7 | | |
| Sandwich | 39 | 30 | Gibbs | Thomas Junr | 2 | | | 1 | | 2 | 1 | | 1 | | | | 7 | | |
| Sandwich | 39 | 31 | Swift | Thos Junr | 1 | 1 | 1 | 1 | | 1 | | 1 | | | | | 9 | | |
| Sandwich | 39 | 32 | Ellis | Josiah | 1 | 4 | | | 1 | 1 | | | 1 | 1 | | | 9 | | |
| Sandwich | 39 | 33 | Ellis | Mary | | | | | | | | 1 | | 1 | | | 2 | | |
| Sandwich | 39 | 34 | Ellis | Stephen | 1 | 1 | 1 | | 1 | | | | 1 | | | | 5 | | |
| Sandwich | 39 | 35 | Swift | Clark | 1 | | | | 1 | 3 | | 1 | 1 | | | | 7 | | |
| Sandwich | 39 | 36 | Swift | Thomas | | | 1 | 2 | | 1 | | | | 1 | | | 6 | | |
| Sandwich | 39 | 37 | Swift | Nathaniel | 3 | 1 | | | | 1 | 1 | 1 | | | | | 8 | | |

# 1800 Sandwich, Barnstable County, Massachusetts

| TOWN | PG# | LN# | LAST NAME | FIRST NAME | FREE WHITE MALES under 10 | 10 to 16 | 16 to 26 | 26 to 45 | 45 and over | FREE WHITE FEMALES under 10 | 10 to 16 | 16 to 26 | 26 to 45 | 45 and over | TOTAL ALL OTHER | TOTAL SLAVES | TOTALS | DISTRICT/ TOWNSHIP | NOTES |
|---|---|---|---|---|---|---|---|---|---|---|---|---|---|---|---|---|---|---|---|
| Sandwich | 39 | 38 | Gibbs | Saml 3d | 1 | | 1 | | | | | | 1 | | | | 3 | | |
| Sandwich | 39 | 39 | Gibbs | Caleb Junr | 2 | | | 1 | | 1 | | | 2 | 1 | | | 7 | | |
| Sandwich | 39 | 40 | Gibbs | Pelham | 3 | | | 1 | | | | | 1 | | | | 5 | | |
| Sandwich | 39 | 41 | Gibbs | Jabez | | | | 1 | | | | | | 1 | | | 2 | | |
| Sandwich | 39 | 42 | Gibbs | Anselm | | 2 | 1 | | 1 | | | | 1 | 1 | | | 6 | | |
| Sandwich | 39 | 43 | Gibbs | Elisha | | | 1 | | | | | | 1 | | | | 2 | | |
| Sandwich | 39 | 44 | Gibbs | Thomas | 1 | | 1 | | 1 | 2 | 1 | 1 | | 1 | | | 8 | | |
| Sandwich | 39 | 45 | Burges | Elisha | 1 | 1 | 1 | | 1 | | 1 | 2 | | 1 | | | 8 | | |
| Sandwich | 39 | 46 | Gibbs | Wm | 1 | 1 | | 1 | 1 | 2 | 2 | | 1 | | | | 9 | | |
| Sandwich | 40 | 1 | Gibbs | Reuben Jun | 1 | | 1 | | 1 | 1 | 1 | | 1 | | | | 6 | | |
| Sandwich | 40 | 2 | Dunham | Samuel | 2 | | 1 | 1 | | 1 | 1 | | 1 | | | | 7 | | |
| Sandwich | 40 | 3 | Blackwell | Saml | | | 2 | | 1 | 1 | 1 | | 1 | | | | 6 | | |
| Sandwich | 40 | 4 | Ellis | Benjm | 1 | | | 1 | | 3 | 1 | 2 | 1 | | | | 9 | | |
| Sandwich | 40 | 5 | Ellis | Nathl | 1 | | 1 | | | 1 | | | 1 | | | | 4 | | |
| Sandwich | 40 | 6 | Ellis | Phillip | 1 | 1 | | 1 | | | | | | 1 | | | 4 | | |
| Sandwich | 40 | 7 | Morey | Lemuel | | | 1 | | | | | | 1 | 1 | | | 3 | | |
| Sandwich | 40 | 8 | Lovel | William | 2 | | | 1 | | | | | 1 | | | | 4 | | |
| Sandwich | 40 | 9 | Foster | Elizabeth | | | | | | | | | | 1 | | | 1 | | |
| Sandwich | 40 | 10 | Ellis | Ebenezer | | 1 | 1 | 1 | 1 | | | | 1 | 1 | | | 6 | | |
| Sandwich | 40 | 11 | Bourne | Bethuel | 3 | 1 | | 1 | | 1 | | | 1 | 1 | | | 8 | | |
| Sandwich | 40 | 12 | Fish | David | 1 | | | 1 | | 1 | | | 1 | | | | 4 | | |
| Sandwich | 40 | 13 | Hamblen | Benja | 3 | 1 | | 1 | | | | 1 | 2 | | | | 8 | | |
| Sandwich | 40 | 14 | Hamblen | Dorothy | | 2 | | | | | | 1 | | 1 | | | 4 | | |
| Sandwich | 40 | 15 | Hamblen | Ellis | 1 | | 1 | | | 2 | | | 1 | | | | 5 | | |
| Sandwich | 40 | 16 | Eldredge | Josiah | 2 | | | 1 | | | | | 1 | 1 | | | 5 | | |
| Sandwich | 40 | 17 | Hamblen | Nathl | 2 | | | 1 | | | | | 1 | 1 | | | 5 | | |
| Sandwich | 40 | 18 | Fish | Nathl | | | 1 | | 1 | | 1 | | 1 | | 1 | | 5 | | |
| Sandwich | 40 | 19 | Fuller | Samuel | | | 1 | 1 | | | | | | 1 | | | 3 | | |
| Sandwich | 40 | 20 | Gibbs | Silvanus | 3 | 1 | 1 | | 1 | 2 | 3 | 2 | | 1 | | | 14 | | |
| Sandwich | 40 | 21 | Morey | Abel | 2 | | 1 | | | | | | 1 | | | | 4 | | |
| Sandwich | 40 | 22 | Morey | Elisha | | | 1 | | | 1 | | | 1 | | | | 3 | | |
| Sandwich | 40 | 23 | Gifford | Daniel | | 1 | | 1 | | | | 2 | | 1 | | | 5 | | |
| Sandwich | 40 | 24 | Gifford | John | 2 | | 1 | | | 1 | | | 1 | | | | 5 | | |
| Sandwich | 40 | 25 | Hyes | Benja | 1 | | 1 | | | | | | 1 | | | | 3 | | |
| Sandwich | 40 | 26 | Sutton | Rogers | | | | | | | | | | | 5 | | 5 | | |
| Sandwich | 40 | 27 | Ellis | Eleazer | 1 | | 2 | 1 | | 1 | | 2 | | 1 | | | 8 | | |
| Sandwich | 40 | 28 | Gibbs | Caleb | 3 | 1 | | 1 | | | 1 | | 1 | | | | 7 | | |
| Sandwich | 40 | 29 | Persons | Baston | | | | | | | | | | | 1 | | 1 | | |
| Sandwich | 40 | 30 | Arey | Job | 1 | | 1 | | | 1 | | 1 | | | | | 4 | | |
| Sandwich | 40 | 31 | Bourne | Alvan | 1 | | 1 | 1 | | 1 | | | 1 | | | | 5 | | |
| Sandwich | 40 | 32 | Bourne | Thos Junr | | 1 | | 1 | | 1 | 2 | | 1 | | 1 | | 7 | | |
| Sandwich | 40 | 33 | Bourne | Job | 1 | | 1 | | | | | | 1 | | | | 3 | | |
| Sandwich | 40 | 34 | Bourne | Lydia | | | | | | | | | 1 | | | | 1 | | |
| Sandwich | 40 | 35 | Bourne | Wm | 2 | | 1 | | | | | | 1 | | | | 4 | | |
| Sandwich | 40 | 36 | Bourne | Thos | | 1 | | 1 | | | | | | 1 | 1 | | 4 | | |
| Sandwich | 40 | 37 | Bourne | Asa | 3 | 1 | | 1 | | 2 | 1 | | 1 | | | | 9 | | |
| Sandwich | 40 | 38 | Bourne | Benja | | 2 | 1 | | 1 | 1 | 3 | | 1 | | | | 9 | | |
| Sandwich | 40 | 39 | Freeman | Fortine | | | | | | | | | | | 1 | | 1 | | |
| Sandwich | 40 | 40 | Rogers | Isaiah | 2 | | 1 | | | | | | 1 | | | | 4 | | |
| Sandwich | 40 | 41 | Mathews | Isaiah | 1 | | | 1 | | | | | 1 | | | | 3 | | |
| Sandwich | 40 | 42 | Lawrence | David | 2 | 2 | 1 | | 1 | | 1 | 1 | | | | | 8 | | |
| Sandwich | 40 | 43 | Dimmick | David | 2 | | | 1 | 1 | | 1 | 2 | 1 | | | | 8 | | |
| Sandwich | 40 | 44 | Handy | Hannah | | | 1 | | | 1 | | 1 | 1 | 1 | | | 5 | | |
| Sandwich | 40 | 45 | Nye | Moses | | | 1 | | | | | | 1 | | | | 2 | | |
| Sandwich | 40 | 46 | Parker | Katharine | | | | | | | 1 | | 1 | | | | 2 | | |
| Sandwich | 40 | 47 | Lawrence | Jonathan | | 2 | 1 | 1 | | | 1 | 1 | 1 | | | | 7 | | |
| Sandwich | 41 | 1 | Barlow | Moses | 1 | 2 | | 1 | | 1 | | | 1 | | | | 6 | | |
| Sandwich | 41 | 2 | Swift | Heman | | 1 | | 1 | | | | | 1 | 1 | | | 4 | | |
| Sandwich | 41 | 3 | Burges | Ichabod | 2 | | 2 | 1 | 2 | 1 | 1 | 1 | | | | | 10 | | |
| Sandwich | 41 | 4 | Young | Isaiah | | | 1 | 2 | | | | | 1 | | | | 4 | | |
| Sandwich | 41 | 5 | Swift | Ward | | | 1 | | | | | | 1 | 2 | | | 4 | | |
| Sandwich | 41 | 6 | Swift | Ward Junr | 1 | | 1 | | | | | 1 | | | | | 3 | | |
| Sandwich | 41 | 7 | Swift | Moses | 2 | | 1 | | 4 | | | 1 | | | | | 8 | | |
| Sandwich | 41 | 8 | Lambord | Thomas | | 1 | 2 | 1 | | 1 | | 1 | | | | | 6 | | |
| Sandwich | 41 | 9 | Nye | Thos | 2 | | 1 | | 2 | | | | 1 | | | | 6 | | |
| Sandwich | 41 | 10 | Snow | Sarah | | 1 | | | | | | | 2 | | | | 3 | | |
| Sandwich | 41 | 11 | White | Peter | | | | | | | | | 1 | 2 | | | 3 | | |
| Sandwich | 41 | 12 | Wing | Judah | 3 | | 1 | | 1 | | | 1 | 1 | | | | 7 | | |
| Sandwich | 41 | 13 | Hamond | Joshua | 3 | 2 | 1 | | 1 | | | 1 | 1 | | | | 9 | | |
| Sandwich | 41 | 14 | Wilbour | Daniel | | | | | | | | | | | 5 | | 5 | | |
| Sandwich | 41 | 15 | | Esther | | | | | | | | | | | 1 | | 1 | | No last name given |
| Sandwich | 41 | 16 | Handy | Jonathan | | 1 | | 1 | | | 1 | 1 | | | | | 4 | | |
| Sandwich | 41 | 17 | Handy | Wm | 1 | | 1 | | 2 | | 1 | 1 | | | | | 6 | | |
| Sandwich | 41 | 18 | Gardner | John | 1 | | 1 | | | | | | 1 | | | | 3 | | |
| Sandwich | 41 | 19 | Cobb | Nicholas | 3 | | | 1 | | | 1 | 1 | | | | | 6 | | |
| Sandwich | 41 | 20 | Cobb | Seth | | | 1 | | 1 | | | | 1 | | | | 3 | | |
| Sandwich | 41 | 21 | Wing | Lemuel | 1 | 1 | 1 | 1 | | 3 | 2 | | 1 | 1 | | | 11 | | |
| Sandwich | 41 | 22 | Drandy | Samuel | 3 | 2 | 1 | | 1 | | 1 | | 1 | | | | 9 | | |
| Sandwich | 41 | 23 | Freeman | James | 3 | | 1 | | 2 | | | | 1 | | | | 7 | | |

# 1800 Sandwich, Barnstable County, Massachusetts

| TOWN | PG# | LN# | LAST NAME | FIRST NAME | FREE WHITE MALES under 10 | 10 to 16 | 16 to 26 | 26 to 45 | 45 and over | FREE WHITE FEMALES under 10 | 10 to 16 | 16 to 26 | 26 to 45 | 45 and over | TOTAL ALL OTHER | TOTAL SLAVES | TOTALS | DISTRICT/ TOWNSHIP | NOTES |
|---|---|---|---|---|---|---|---|---|---|---|---|---|---|---|---|---|---|---|---|
| Sandwich | 41 | 24 | Freeman | John | | | 1 | 1 | | | | | | 1 | | | 3 | | |
| Sandwich | 41 | 25 | Raymond | Ebenezer | | | | | 1 | | | 2 | | 1 | | | 4 | | |
| Sandwich | 41 | 26 | Wing | David | 3 | | | 1 | | 1 | | | 1 | 2 | | | 8 | | |
| Sandwich | 41 | 27 | Freeman | Samuel | | 1 | | 1 | 1 | | | | | 1 | | | 4 | | |
| Sandwich | 41 | 28 | Freeman | Edward | 1 | | | 1 | | 2 | | 1 | | | | | 5 | | |
| Sandwich | 41 | 29 | Arey | Joshua | 5 | | | 1 | | | 1 | 1 | | | | | 8 | | |
| Sandwich | 41 | 30 | Arey | Thankful | | | | | | | | | | 1 | | | 1 | | |
| Sandwich | 41 | 31 | Arey | Thos | 2 | | 1 | | | | | | 1 | | | | 4 | | |
| Sandwich | 41 | 32 | Burges | Nathl | | 1 | 1 | | 1 | | 1 | | | 1 | | | 5 | | |
| Sandwich | 41 | 33 | Wing | Nathaniel | 1 | 1 | 4 | 1 | | 1 | 1 | 1 | | 1 | | | 11 | | |
| Sandwich | 41 | 34 | Whitford | Silas | | | 1 | | | 2 | | 1 | | | | | 4 | | |
| Sandwich | 41 | 35 | Godfrey | Mercy | | 1 | 2 | | | 1 | 2 | | 1 | | | | 7 | | |
| Sandwich | 41 | 36 | Burges | Jonathan | | | | 1 | | | | 1 | | | | | 2 | | |
| Sandwich | 41 | 37 | Wight | Joseph | 1 | 1 | 1 | | 1 | 2 | 1 | | 1 | | | | 8 | | |
| Sandwich | 41 | 38 | Tobey | Mariah Junr | | 2 | 1 | | | | | | | 1 | | | 4 | | |
| Sandwich | 41 | 39 | Tobey | Wm Junr | 1 | | | 1 | | 1 | | 1 | | | | | 4 | | |
| Sandwich | 41 | 40 | Burges | Covel | 2 | 1 | 1 | 1 | | 1 | 2 | | 1 | | | | 9 | | |
| Sandwich | 41 | 41 | Bennett | Stephen Jun | 2 | | | 1 | | 1 | | | 1 | 1 | | | 6 | | |
| Sandwich | 41 | 42 | Bennett | Stephen | | | 1 | 1 | 1 | 1 | | 1 | | 1 | | | 6 | | |
| Sandwich | 41 | 43 | Lewis | David | 2 | | | 1 | 1 | 2 | 1 | | 1 | | | | 8 | | |
| Sandwich | 41 | 44 | Rogers | Henry | | | 2 | | 1 | 1 | | 3 | | 1 | | | 8 | | |
| Sandwich | 41 | 45 | Chandler | Asahel | 1 | 1 | | | 1 | 2 | 1 | | 1 | | | | 7 | | |
| Sandwich | 41 | 46 | Perry | Wm | | | | 1 | | 2 | | | 1 | | | | 4 | | |
| Sandwich | 42 | 1 | Ellis | Gideon | 1 | | | 1 | | | | | 1 | | | | 3 | | |
| Sandwich | 42 | 2 | Perry | Solomon | 1 | | | 1 | | | | 1 | | | | | 3 | | |
| Sandwich | 42 | 3 | Bourne | Samuel | 1 | 1 | | 1 | | 2 | | 1 | 1 | | | | 7 | | |
| Sandwich | 42 | 4 | Bourne | Jonathan | 2 | | | 1 | | 2 | | | 1 | | | | 6 | | |
| Sandwich | 42 | 5 | Bourne | Elisha | | 1 | | | | | | | 1 | 2 | | | 5 | | |
| Sandwich | 42 | 6 | Bourne | Charles | | | 1 | | | | | 1 | | | | | 2 | | |
| Sandwich | 42 | 7 | Bourne | Hannah | 1 | | | | | | | 1 | 1 | | | | 3 | | |
| Sandwich | 42 | 8 | Ellis | Seth | | | | 1 | | 1 | 1 | | 1 | | | | 4 | | |
| Sandwich | 42 | 9 | Fish | John | | 1 | 2 | | 1 | | | | | 1 | | | 5 | | |
| Sandwich | 42 | 10 | Fish | Ephraim | 1 | | 1 | | | | | | 1 | | | | 3 | | |
| Sandwich | 42 | 11 | Chadwick | Anselm | 4 | 1 | | | 1 | 1 | | | 1 | | | | 8 | | |
| Sandwich | 42 | 12 | Cobb | Thankful | | | | | | | | | 1 | 1 | | | 2 | | |
| Sandwich | 42 | 13 | Blackwell | Samuel Junr | | | 1 | | | | | 1 | | | | | 2 | | |
| Sandwich | 42 | 14 | Buck | Benja | 1 | 1 | | | 1 | 1 | | 1 | | 1 | | | 6 | | |
| Sandwich | 42 | 15 | Perry | John 1st | | | 1 | | 1 | | | 1 | | 1 | | | 4 | | |
| Sandwich | 42 | 16 | Perry | John 4th | 1 | 1 | | | 1 | 2 | | | 1 | | | | 6 | | |
| Sandwich | 42 | 17 | Perry | Silvanus | 1 | 1 | | | 1 | 2 | | | 1 | | | | 6 | | |
| Sandwich | 42 | 18 | Perry | Caleb | 1 | | | | 1 | 3 | | | 1 | | | | 6 | | |
| Sandwich | 42 | 19 | Perry | Seth | 1 | 1 | 2 | | 1 | 2 | 1 | | | 1 | | | 9 | | |
| Sandwich | 42 | 20 | Perry | Daniel | 2 | 1 | | 1 | | | | 2 | | 1 | | | 7 | | |
| Sandwich | 42 | 21 | Phinney | John | 1 | | 3 | | 1 | 2 | 1 | | | 1 | | | 9 | | |
| Sandwich | 42 | 22 | Perry | John 2d | 3 | | | 1 | 1 | 1 | | 1 | | | | | 7 | | |
| Sandwich | 42 | 23 | Ellis | Elnathan | | | | | 1 | | 1 | 1 | | 1 | | | 4 | | |
| Sandwich | 42 | 24 | Ellis | Nathan | | 1 | | | | | | | 1 | | | | 2 | | |
| Sandwich | 42 | 25 | Ellis | Gershom | | | 2 | | | 1 | | | 1 | | | | 4 | | |
| Sandwich | 42 | 26 | Lambord | Caleb | | | 1 | | 1 | 1 | 1 | 1 | | 1 | | | 6 | | |
| Sandwich | 42 | 27 | Perry | Elisha | 1 | | 1 | | 1 | | | | 1 | 1 | | | 5 | | |
| Sandwich | 42 | 28 | Hatch | Zacheus | | | 1 | | 1 | | | | | 1 | | | 3 | | |
| Sandwich | 42 | 29 | Perry | Ellis | 3 | | | 1 | | | | | 1 | | | | 5 | | |
| Sandwich | 42 | 30 | Perry | Susanna | | | | | | | | | 1 | 1 | | | 2 | | |
| Sandwich | 42 | 31 | Keene | Aloise | | 1 | 2 | | 1 | 1 | | | | 1 | | | 6 | | |
| Sandwich | 42 | 32 | Perry | John 3d | 2 | 2 | 2 | | 1 | 1 | 1 | | | 1 | | | 10 | | |
| Sandwich | 42 | 33 | Ellis | Elijah | | | | | 1 | | | | 1 | 1 | | | 3 | | |
| Sandwich | 42 | 34 | Nye | Samuel | | 1 | | | 1 | | | 2 | 1 | 1 | | | 6 | | |
| Sandwich | 42 | 35 | Blackwell | John | | | | | 1 | | | | | 1 | | | 2 | | |
| Sandwich | 42 | 36 | Blackwell | John Junr | | 1 | 1 | | 1 | 3 | | 1 | 1 | | | | 8 | | |
| Sandwich | 42 | 37 | Blackwell | Lucy | | 1 | | | | | | | 1 | 1 | | | 3 | | |
| Sandwich | 42 | 38 | Ellis | Abiel | 2 | 2 | | | 1 | | | | 1 | 1 | | | 7 | | |
| Sandwich | 42 | 39 | Swift | Stephen | 1 | 1 | 1 | 1 | | 1 | 2 | | 1 | | | | 8 | | |
| Sandwich | 42 | 40 | Morse | Samuel | 3 | 1 | 1 | | 1 | 1 | | | 1 | | | | 8 | | |
| Sandwich | 42 | 41 | Smith | Thomas | | | | 1 | | | | | | | | | 1 | | |
| Sandwich | 42 | 42 | Covel | Deborah | | | | | | | | 1 | | | | | 1 | | |
| Sandwich | 42 | 43 | Perry | Thankful | | | | | | | | | 1 | 1 | | | 2 | | |

# 1800 Truro, Barnstable County, Massachusetts

| TOWN | PG# | LN# | LAST NAME | FIRST NAME | FREE WHITE MALES under 10 | 10 to 16 | 16 to 26 | 26 to 45 | 45 and over | FREE WHITE FEMALES under 10 | 10 to 16 | 16 to 26 | 26 to 45 | 45 and over | TOTAL ALL OTHER | TOTAL SLAVES | TOTALS | DISTRICT/ TOWNSHIP | NOTES |
|---|---|---|---|---|---|---|---|---|---|---|---|---|---|---|---|---|---|---|---|
| Truro | 62 | 1 | Snow | Anthony | 1 | | 1 | | 1 | 2 | 2 | 1 | 1 | 1 | | | 10 | | |
| Truro | 62 | 2 | Snow | Ambros | | 1 | 2 | | | 1 | | | 1 | 1 | | | 7 | | |
| Truro | 62 | 3 | Collins | Andrew | | 1 | | 1 | 1 | | | | | 1 | | | 4 | | |
| Truro | 62 | 4 | Hinchley | Benjamin | | 2 | 2 | | 1 | | | 1 | | 1 | | | 7 | | |
| Truro | 62 | 5 | Collins | Benjamin | | 2 | 2 | | 1 | | | 2 | | 1 | | | 8 | | |
| Truro | 62 | 6 | Higgins | Martha Wd | 1 | | | | | | 1 | | 1 | | | | 3 | | |
| Truro | 62 | 7 | Knowles | Caleb | 2 | | | 1 | | 1 | 1 | | 1 | | | | 6 | | |
| Truro | 62 | 8 | Paine | Barnabas | 1 | 1 | | 1 | | 2 | 2 | | 1 | 2 | | | 10 | | |
| Truro | 62 | 9 | Dyer | Deliverance Junr | | 2 | | | | | 1 | | 1 | | | | 4 | | |
| Truro | 62 | 10 | Paine | David | | | 3 | | 1 | 1 | | | 1 | | | | 6 | | |
| Truro | 62 | 11 | Snow | David | | 1 | | 1 | | | | | 1 | | | | 3 | | |
| Truro | 62 | 12 | Omsby | Rachel Wid | 1 | | | | | 2 | | | 1 | | | | 4 | | |
| Truro | 62 | 13 | Atkins | Elizabeth Wid | 1 | | | | | 1 | | 1 | | 1 | | | 4 | | |
| Truro | 62 | 14 | Paine | Ebenezer | 2 | 1 | | 1 | | 1 | | | 1 | 1 | | | 7 | | |
| Truro | 62 | 15 | Lombard | Ebenezer | 1 | | | 1 | | 1 | | 1 | | | | | 4 | | |
| Truro | 62 | 16 | Rich | Ephraim | | 1 | 1 | 1 | | | | 1 | | 1 | | | 5 | | |
| Truro | 62 | 17 | Snow | Elisha | 1 | | | 1 | | 1 | | | 1 | | | | 4 | | |
| Truro | 62 | 18 | Davis | Ebenezer Lombard | 1 | | | | | 1 | | 1 | | | | | 3 | | |
| Truro | 63 | 1 | Raimand | Francis | 1 | | | 1 | | 1 | 1 | 1 | 1 | | | | 6 | | |
| Truro | 63 | 2 | Pike | George | | | 1 | | | 2 | 1 | | 1 | | | | 5 | | |
| Truro | 63 | 3 | Rich | Henry | 2 | | | 1 | | | | 1 | | | | | 4 | | |
| Truro | 63 | 4 | Paine | Hannah | | | | | | | | | 1 | 2 | | | 3 | | |
| Truro | 63 | 5 | Dyer | Hannah Wid | 1 | | 3 | | | | 1 | | 1 | 1 | | | 7 | | |
| Truro | 63 | 6 | Rich | Heman Smith | | | 1 | | | 1 | | | 1 | | | | 3 | | |
| Truro | 63 | 7 | Snow | Hannah Junr | | 1 | 1 | | | | | 1 | | 1 | | | 4 | | |
| Truro | 63 | 8 | Snow | Hannah Wid | | | | | | | | | | 1 | | | 1 | | |
| Truro | 63 | 9 | Hopkins | Isaac | | 2 | | 1 | | | | 1 | | 1 | | | 5 | | |
| Truro | 63 | 10 | Rich | Isaiah | 2 | | 1 | | | | | 1 | | | | | 4 | | |
| Truro | 63 | 11 | Wharf | Isaac | 1 | | 1 | | | 2 | | | 1 | | | | 5 | | |
| Truro | 63 | 12 | Dyer | Isaac | 3 | 1 | 1 | | | | 1 | | 1 | | | | 7 | | |
| Truro | 63 | 13 | Atwood | Isaac | 3 | 1 | 1 | | 1 | | 1 | 1 | 1 | | | | 9 | | |
| Truro | 63 | 14 | Rich | John Junr | 1 | 1 | | 1 | | | | 1 | 2 | | | | 6 | | |
| Truro | 63 | 15 | Pike | John Junr | 1 | | 1 | 1 | 1 | | | | | 1 | | | 5 | | |
| Truro | 63 | 16 | Collins | John Junr | 1 | 1 | 1 | | 1 | 1 | | 1 | 2 | 1 | | | 9 | | |
| Truro | 63 | 17 | Cobb | Joseph | | | 1 | | | | | 1 | | 1 | | | 3 | | |
| Truro | 63 | 18 | Lombard | James | 2 | | | 1 | | 1 | | | 1 | | | | 5 | | |
| Truro | 63 | 19 | Rich | James | | 1 | | 2 | | 1 | | | | 2 | | | 6 | | |
| Truro | 63 | 20 | Paine | Sarah Wid | | | | | | | | 2 | | 1 | | | 3 | | |
| Truro | 63 | 21 | Snow | Lydia Wid | 2 | 1 | | | | 1 | 2 | | 1 | | | | 7 | | |
| Truro | 63 | 22 | Snow | Jonathan | | 1 | 1 | | 1 | 2 | | | 1 | | | | 6 | | |
| Truro | 63 | 23 | Higgins | Jedediah | 1 | | | 1 | 1 | | | 1 | 1 | | | | 5 | | |
| Truro | 63 | 24 | Snow | Joshua | 1 | 1 | | 1 | | 1 | | | 1 | | | | 5 | | |
| Truro | 63 | 25 | Small | Joseph | | 1 | 3 | | 1 | | | 2 | 1 | | | | 9 | | |
| Truro | 63 | 26 | Gross | Jazamiah | 1 | | | 1 | | 2 | | | 1 | | | | 5 | | |
| Truro | 63 | 27 | Rich | John | 1 | 1 | 3 | | 1 | | 1 | | | 1 | | | 8 | | |
| Truro | 63 | 28 | Cobb | John | | 2 | 1 | | 1 | 1 | 1 | 1 | | 1 | | | 8 | | |
| Truro | 63 | 29 | Snow | John | 2 | | 1 | | 1 | | | | 1 | | | | 7 | | |
| Truro | 63 | 30 | Collins | Joseph | | 1 | | 1 | | | | 2 | | 1 | | | 5 | | |
| Truro | 63 | 31 | Rich | John 3d | 2 | 2 | | 1 | | 1 | | | 2 | | | | 8 | | |
| Truro | 63 | 32 | Rich | Jonathan | | | 1 | | | 1 | | | 1 | | | | 3 | | |
| Truro | 63 | 33 | Snow | John Junr | | | 1 | | | | 1 | | 1 | | | | 3 | | |
| Truro | 63 | 34 | Rich | Joseph | 1 | 1 | | 1 | | 2 | 1 | | 1 | | | | 7 | | |
| Truro | 63 | 35 | Hanling | Jonathan | 1 | 1 | 2 | | 1 | 1 | 1 | | | | | | 7 | | |
| Truro | 64 | 1 | Rich | Joshua | 1 | | 1 | | 1 | 2 | 1 | 1 | | 1 | | | 8 | | |
| Truro | 64 | 2 | Atkins | Jonah | 2 | | 1 | | | 1 | | | 1 | | | | 5 | | |
| Truro | 64 | 3 | Davis | James W | 2 | | | 1 | | | | | 1 | | | | 4 | | |
| Truro | 64 | 4 | Gross | Joshua Dyer | 1 | | | 1 | | | | 1 | | | | | 3 | | |
| Truro | 64 | 5 | Rich | Joanna Wid | | 1 | | | | | | 1 | 2 | | | | 4 | | |
| Truro | 64 | 6 | Higgins | Jonathan | | 1 | | 1 | 1 | | | | 1 | | | | 4 | | |
| Truro | 64 | 7 | Rider | Sally Wid | | | | | | | 1 | | | | | | 1 | | |
| Truro | 64 | 8 | Lombard | Lewis | | | 1 | | | | | 1 | | 1 | | | 3 | | |
| Truro | 64 | 9 | Lombard | Lewis Junr | | | 1 | | | | | 1 | | | | | 3 | | |
| Truro | 64 | 10 | Harding | Lot | | | 1 | 1 | | | | 1 | 3 | | | | 6 | | |
| Truro | 64 | 11 | Harding | Lot Junr | 2 | 1 | | 1 | | | | 1 | | | | | 5 | | |
| Truro | 64 | 12 | Cobb | Loir Wid | | 2 | | | | | 2 | | 1 | | | | 5 | | |
| Truro | 64 | 13 | Rich | Lucy Wid | | 1 | | | | | | | 1 | 1 | | | 3 | | |
| Truro | 64 | 14 | Rich | Jesse | | 2 | | 1 | | | | | 1 | 2 | | | 6 | | |
| Truro | 64 | 15 | Collins | Moses | 1 | | 1 | | | | 1 | 1 | | | | | 4 | | |
| Truro | 64 | 16 | Cobb | Mulford | 2 | 2 | 1 | | | 1 | | 1 | | | | | 7 | | |
| Truro | 64 | 17 | Mayo | Noah | | 1 | | 1 | | | | 1 | | 1 | | | 4 | | |
| Truro | 64 | 18 | Freat | Nathaniel | 2 | | 2 | 1 | 1 | 2 | 1 | | | | | | 11 | | |
| Truro | 64 | 19 | Rich | Nathaniel | 1 | 1 | 1 | | 1 | 2 | 2 | | 1 | 1 | | | 10 | | |
| Truro | 64 | 20 | Dyer | Nepthaly | 2 | | | | | | | 2 | | 1 | | | 6 | | |
| Truro | 64 | 21 | Rich | Obadiah Junr | 1 | | 1 | | | | 1 | | 1 | 1 | | | 5 | | |
| Truro | 64 | 22 | Bangs | Perez | 3 | 1 | | 1 | | 3 | 1 | | | | | | 9 | | |
| Truro | 64 | 23 | Hinchley | Allen | 1 | | 1 | 1 | | 1 | 1 | 1 | 1 | | | | 7 | | |
| Truro | 64 | 24 | Atkins | Paul | 3 | | | 1 | | | | | 1 | | | | 5 | | |
| Truro | 64 | 25 | Snow | Richard | 2 | | | | 1 | | | 1 | | | | | 4 | | |
| Truro | 64 | 26 | Cobb | Richard | | | 1 | | | | | | 1 | | | | 2 | | |

# 1800 Truro, Barnstable County, Massachusetts

| TOWN | PG# | LN# | LAST NAME | FIRST NAME | \<10 | 10–16 | 16–26 | 26–45 | 45+ | \<10 | 10–16 | 16–26 | 26–45 | 45+ | TOTAL ALL OTHER | TOTAL SLAVES | TOTALS | DISTRICT/TOWNSHIP | NOTES |
|---|---|---|---|---|---|---|---|---|---|---|---|---|---|---|---|---|---|---|---|
| | | | | | FREE WHITE MALES | | | | | FREE WHITE FEMALES | | | | | | | | | |
| Truro | 64 | 27 | Collins | Ruth | 2 | | | | | | | 1 | 1 | | | | 4 | | |
| Truro | 64 | 28 | Atkins | Ruth | | 1 | 1 | | | | | 1 | 1 | 1 | 2 | | 7 | | |
| Truro | 64 | 29 | Rich | Rebeccah Wid | | | 2 | | | | | | | 1 | | | 3 | | |
| Truro | 64 | 30 | Rich | Richard 3d | | | 1 | | 1 | 1 | 1 | | 1 | | | | 5 | | |
| Truro | 64 | 31 | Rich | Richard S. | 2 | | | 1 | | | | | 1 | | | | 4 | | |
| Truro | 64 | 32 | Rich | Richard | 1 | 1 | 2 | | 1 | | 1 | 2 | | 1 | | | 9 | | |
| Truro | 64 | 33 | Baker | Richard | 1 | | | 1 | | 2 | | | 1 | | | | 5 | | |
| Truro | 64 | 34 | Higgins | Sarah Wid | | | 1 | | | | | | 2 | 1 | | | 4 | | |
| Truro | 65 | 1 | Munson | Samuel | 2 | | | 1 | | 2 | | | 1 | | | | 6 | | |
| Truro | 65 | 2 | Lombard | Rebeccah Wid | | 1 | | | | | 1 | 1 | | 1 | | | 4 | | |
| Truro | 65 | 3 | Rider | Samuel | | | 1 | | 1 | 2 | | 2 | | 1 | | | 7 | | |
| Truro | 65 | 4 | Atkins | Sarah Junr | 1 | 1 | | | | 1 | 1 | | 1 | | | | 5 | | |
| Truro | 65 | 5 | Lombard | Simon | 3 | | | 1 | | | | | 1 | | | | 5 | | |
| Truro | 65 | 6 | Atkins | Sarah | | 1 | | | | | | | 2 | 1 | | | 4 | | |
| Truro | 65 | 7 | Snow | Silvanus | | 3 | | 1 | | 3 | 2 | 1 | | 1 | | | 11 | | |
| Truro | 65 | 8 | Rich | Silvanus | 2 | | | 1 | | | | | 1 | | | | 4 | | |
| Truro | 65 | 9 | Snow | Stephen | 3 | | | 1 | | | | | 1 | | | | 5 | | |
| Truro | 65 | 10 | Lombard | Sarah | 1 | 1 | | | | | | | | 2 | | | 4 | | |
| Truro | 65 | 11 | Brown | Silvanus | | | | 1 | | | | 3 | | 1 | | | 5 | | |
| Truro | 65 | 12 | Dyer | Silvanus | 1 | | | 1 | | 2 | | | 1 | | | | 5 | | |
| Truro | 65 | 13 | Thayer | Susannah | | 1 | | | | | | | 2 | 1 | | | 4 | | |
| Truro | 65 | 14 | Freat | Samuel | | 1 | | 2 | | 1 | | | 1 | 1 | | | 6 | | |
| Truro | 65 | 15 | Paine | Thatcher | | | 2 | 1 | | | | 3 | | 1 | | | 7 | | |
| Truro | 65 | 16 | Mayo | Thomas | 1 | | | 1 | | 1 | | | 1 | | | | 4 | | |
| Truro | 65 | 17 | Rich | Thomas | 1 | | | 1 | | 2 | | | 1 | | | | 5 | | |
| Truro | 65 | 18 | Newcomb | Theophilus | 1 | | 1 | | | | | 1 | | | | | 3 | | |
| Truro | 65 | 19 | Rich | Thatcher | 2 | | | 1 | | | | | 1 | | | | 4 | | |
| Truro | 65 | 20 | Lombard | William | 1 | | 1 | | 1 | 1 | | 1 | | 1 | | | 6 | | |
| Truro | 65 | 21 | Smith | Zocth | 2 | | | 1 | | | | | 1 | | | | 4 | | |
| Truro | 65 | 22 | Newcomb | Joseph | | | | | 1 | | 2 | | | 1 | | | 4 | | |
| Truro | 65 | 23 | Newcomb | Elisha | 1 | | 1 | | | | | 1 | | | | | 3 | | |
| Truro | 65 | 24 | Hopkins | Caleb Junr | | | | | 1 | 3 | | 1 | 1 | 1 | | | 7 | | |
| Truro | 65 | 25 | Hopkins | Caleb | 1 | 2 | | | 1 | | 2 | 2 | | 1 | | | 9 | | |
| Truro | 65 | 26 | Harding | Ephraim | | 1 | | | 1 | | | | 2 | 1 | | | 5 | | |
| Truro | 65 | 27 | Hutson | Ezra | | | | 1 | | 3 | | 1 | | | | | 5 | | |
| Truro | 65 | 28 | Knowles | Paul Junr | 4 | 1 | | 1 | | 1 | | | 1 | | | | 8 | | |
| Truro | 65 | 29 | Knowles | Mary Wid | | | | | | | | | 1 | 1 | | | 2 | | |
| Truro | 65 | 30 | Knight | Peter | | | | 1 | | 3 | | | 1 | | | | 5 | | |
| Truro | 65 | 31 | Kenney | John | | 1 | 1 | | 1 | | | | 1 | | | | 4 | | |
| Truro | 65 | 32 | Knowles | Silas | 4 | 1 | 2 | 1 | 1 | 1 | | 1 | | 1 | | | 12 | | |
| Truro | 65 | 33 | Knowles | Zacheus | 2 | | | 1 | | 1 | | | 1 | | | | 5 | | |
| Truro | 65 | 34 | Knowles | Joshua | 3 | 2 | 1 | | 1 | | 2 | | 1 | | | | 10 | | |
| Truro | 65 | 35 | Knowles | Paul | 1 | | 1 | 1 | 1 | 1 | | 1 | 1 | 1 | | | 8 | | |
| Truro | 66 | 1 | Knowles | Jesse | 1 | | | 1 | | 1 | | | 1 | 1 | | | 5 | | |
| Truro | 66 | 2 | Lombard | Cornelius | 1 | | 1 | 1 | | 2 | 1 | 2 | 1 | | | | 9 | | |
| Truro | 66 | 3 | Lombard | Rebeccah Junr | | | | | | 1 | 1 | | 1 | | | | 3 | | |
| Truro | 66 | 4 | Lombard | Simon | | | | | 1 | | | 1 | | 1 | | | 3 | | |
| Truro | 66 | 5 | Lewis | Eleazer | 3 | 1 | 2 | | | 1 | | 2 | | | | | 11 | | |
| Truro | 66 | 6 | Lombard | Ephraim | | | | | 1 | | | | 2 | 1 | | | 4 | | |
| Truro | 66 | 7 | Lewis | George | 2 | | | | 1 | 1 | 1 | 1 | | | | | 6 | | |
| Truro | 66 | 8 | Lombard | Israel | 1 | 2 | | | 1 | 1 | 2 | 2 | | 1 | | | 10 | | |
| Truro | 66 | 9 | Paine | Elisha | 1 | | | 1 | 1 | 1 | | | 1 | | | | 5 | | |
| Truro | 66 | 10 | Paine | Elkanah | 5 | | 2 | | 1 | | 2 | | | 1 | | | 11 | | |
| Truro | 66 | 11 | Paine | Jesse | | | 1 | 1 | | 2 | | 1 | 1 | 1 | | | 7 | | |
| Truro | 66 | 12 | Paine | Elizabeth Wid | | 3 | | | | | | 1 | | 1 | | | 5 | | |
| Truro | 66 | 13 | Paine | Relianu | | | | | | | | | | 1 | | | 1 | | |
| Truro | 66 | 14 | Rich | Uriah | | | | 1 | | | | | | 1 | | | 2 | | |
| Truro | 66 | 15 | Ridley | John | 1 | | | 1 | | | | | | 1 | | | 3 | | |
| Truro | 66 | 16 | Smith | Sarah Wid Junr | 2 | | | | | | | | 1 | | | | 3 | | |
| Truro | 66 | 17 | Small | John | | 1 | | 1 | | | | | 1 | | | | 3 | | |
| Truro | 66 | 18 | Small | Hix | | 1 | | 1 | | | | | 1 | | | | 3 | | |
| Truro | 66 | 19 | Small | Jesse | | | 1 | | | 2 | | | 1 | | | | 4 | | |
| Truro | 66 | 20 | Atkins | Samuel | | 1 | 5 | | 1 | | 2 | 2 | | 1 | | | 9 | | |
| Truro | 66 | 21 | Avery | John | 1 | 1 | | | 1 | | | 2 | 2 | 1 | | | 8 | | |
| Truro | 66 | 22 | Atkins | Silas | | | | | 1 | | | 1 | | 1 | | | 3 | | |
| Truro | 66 | 23 | Atkins | Lydia Wid | | | 1 | | | | | | 1 | 1 | | | 3 | | |
| Truro | 66 | 24 | Avery | Job | 2 | 2 | | | 1 | 1 | | 1 | 1 | 1 | | | 9 | | |
| Truro | 66 | 25 | Atkins | Paul | | 1 | 2 | | 1 | | | | 1 | 1 | | | 6 | | |
| Truro | 66 | 26 | Brown | William | 2 | 1 | | 1 | 1 | 1 | | 1 | | 1 | | | 9 | | |
| Truro | 66 | 27 | Bowly | Hannah Wid | | 1 | | | | | | | 1 | 1 | | | 3 | | |
| Truro | 66 | 28 | Collins | John | 2 | | 1 | | 1 | 1 | | 1 | | 1 | | | 7 | | |
| Truro | 66 | 29 | Cohan | Samuel | 2 | 1 | | 1 | | 2 | | | 1 | | | | 7 | | |
| Truro | 66 | 30 | Cohan | Benjamin | | 1 | | | | 1 | | 1 | 1 | | | | 4 | | |
| Truro | 66 | 31 | Collins | Jesse | 2 | | | 1 | | 2 | | | 1 | | | | 6 | | |
| Truro | 66 | 32 | Cohan | Shobel | | | | 1 | | 4 | | | 1 | | | | 6 | | |
| Truro | 67 | 1 | Collins | Jonathan | | | 2 | | 1 | 3 | | | 1 | | | | 7 | | |
| Truro | 67 | 2 | Dyer | Henry | 1 | | | 1 | | 1 | | 1 | 1 | | | | 5 | | |
| Truro | 67 | 3 | Dyer | Rebecah Wid | | | | | | 1 | | | 1 | | | | 2 | | |
| Truro | 67 | 4 | Dyer | Thomas | | 1 | 1 | | 1 | | 1 | 1 | | 1 | | | 6 | | |

51

| TOWN | PG# | LN# | LAST NAME | FIRST NAME | FREE WHITE MALES | | | | | FREE WHITE FEMALES | | | | | TOTAL ALL OTHER | TOTAL SLAVES | TOTALS | DISTRICT/ TOWNSHIP | NOTES |
|---|---|---|---|---|---|---|---|---|---|---|---|---|---|---|---|---|---|---|---|
| | | | | | under 10 | 10 to 16 | 16 to 26 | 26 to 45 | 45 and over | under 10 | 10 to 16 | 16 to 26 | 26 to 45 | 45 and over | | | | | |
| Truro | 67 | 5 | Dyer | Fulk | | | 2 | 1 | | | | | | 1 | 1 | | 5 | | |
| Truro | 67 | 6 | Dyer | David | 3 | 1 | | 1 | | 1 | 1 | | 1 | 1 | | | 9 | | |
| Truro | 67 | 7 | Dyer | Paul | 2 | 3 | 1 | | 1 | 1 | 1 | | 1 | 1 | | | 11 | | |
| Truro | 67 | 8 | Eldridge | Elizabeth | 1 | | 1 | | | | | 1 | | 1 | | | 4 | | |
| Truro | 67 | 9 | Freeman | Rebeccah Wid | | | | | | | | | | 1 | | | 1 | | |
| Truro | 67 | 10 | Grozher | Caleb | | | 1 | | | 1 | 1 | | 1 | 1 | | | 5 | | |
| Truro | 67 | 11 | Gross | John | 1 | | 2 | | 1 | | | 1 | | 1 | | | 6 | | |
| Truro | 67 | 12 | Hopkins | Constant | | | | | | | | | 2 | | | | 2 | | |
| Truro | 67 | 13 | Hewes | Rachall Wid | 3 | | | | | 2 | 2 | | | 1 | | | 8 | | |
| Truro | 67 | 14 | Hopkins | Samuel | 1 | | | 1 | 1 | | | | 1 | 1 | | | 5 | | |
| Truro | 67 | 15 | Hopkins | Solomon | 1 | | 2 | | 1 | | | 1 | | | | | 5 | | |
| Truro | 67 | 16 | Smith | Sarah Doane | | 1 | 1 | | | 1 | 1 | | | 1 | | | 5 | | |
| Truro | 67 | 17 | Smith | Barzilla | 1 | 1 | | | 1 | 1 | 1 | 1 | | 2 | | | 8 | | |
| Truro | 67 | 18 | Small | Alexander | 1 | | 2 | 1 | | 2 | | | 1 | 1 | | | 8 | | |
| Truro | 67 | 19 | Steavens | Levi | 1 | 1 | 1 | | 1 | | 2 | | | 1 | | | 7 | | |
| Truro | 67 | 20 | Small | Isaac | 1 | 2 | | | 1 | 1 | | | | 2 | | | 7 | | |
| Truro | 67 | 21 | Small | Francis | 1 | 2 | | | 1 | 3 | | | 1 | | | | 8 | | |
| Truro | 67 | 22 | Steavens | Betsy | | 2 | | | | | | | 2 | | | | 4 | | |
| Truro | 67 | 23 | Snow | Ruth | | | | | | | | 1 | | 1 | | | 2 | | |
| Truro | 67 | 24 | Selew | John | | 2 | | 1 | | 1 | 1 | | | 1 | | | 6 | | |
| Truro | 67 | 25 | Small | Samuel | 2 | 1 | | 1 | | 3 | | 2 | | 1 | | | 10 | | |
| Truro | 67 | 26 | Savage | Dinah | | | | | | | | | | 1 | | | 1 | | |
| Truro | 67 | 27 | Thomas | John | 2 | | | 1 | | | | | 1 | | | | 4 | | |
| Truro | 67 | 28 | Thomas | Rebeccah | 1 | | | | | 1 | | | 1 | 1 | | | 4 | | |
| Truro | 67 | 29 | Wells | Peter | 1 | 1 | 1 | | 1 | 1 | 3 | | | 1 | | | 9 | | |
| Truro | 67 | 30 | Webb | Bethiah Wid | | | | | | | | 1 | 2 | | | | 3 | | |
| Truro | 68 | 1 | Avery | John Junr | | 1 | | | | | | 1 | | | | | 2 | | |
| Truro | 68 | 2 | Chapman | Samuel | 2 | 1 | | 1 | | | | | 1 | | | | 6 | | |
| Truro | 68 | 3 | Atkins | Ebenezer | 2 | | 1 | | | 1 | | | 1 | | | | 5 | | |
| Truro | 68 | 4 | Dyer | Josha | 1 | | 1 | | | | | 1 | | | | | 3 | | |
| Truro | 68 | 5 | Chandler | Joseph | | | 1 | | | | | | 1 | | | | 2 | | |
| Truro | 68 | 6 | Harding | Benjamin | 1 | | 1 | | | 2 | | | 1 | | | | 5 | | |
| Truro | 68 | 7 | Paine | Hezekiah | 1 | | 1 | | | 1 | | 1 | 1 | | | | 5 | | |
| Truro | 68 | 8 | Rich | Polly | | | | | | 1 | | | 1 | | | | 2 | | |
| Truro | 68 | 9 | Demmond | Revd Jude | 3 | | | 1 | | | | 1 | 1 | | | | 6 | | |
| Truro | 68 | 10 | Atkins | Samuel Junr | | 1 | | | | 1 | | 1 | | | | | 3 | | |
| Truro | 68 | 11 | Lombard | Israel Junr | | 1 | | | | | | 1 | | | | | 2 | | |
| Truro | 68 | 12 | Dyer | James Harding | 1 | 1 | | 1 | | 1 | 1 | | 1 | | | | 6 | | |
| Truro | 68 | 13 | Rich | Obadiah | 1 | 1 | | | | | | 1 | | | | | 3 | | |
| Truro | 68 | 14 | Paine | Benjamin | 2 | | 1 | | | 1 | | | 1 | | | | 5 | | |
| Truro | 68 | 15 | Higgins | Joseph | | | 1 | | | 1 | | 1 | | | | | 3 | | |
| Truro | 68 | 16 | Dyer | Caleb | | | 1 | | | | | 1 | | | | | 2 | | |
| Truro | 68 | 17 | Dyer | Silvanus | 1 | | 1 | | | 3 | | | 1 | 1 | | | 7 | | |
| Truro | 68 | 18 | Atwood | Zoeth | 2 | | 1 | | | 2 | 1 | 1 | | | | | 7 | | |
| Truro | 68 | 19 | Snow | Ephraim | | 1 | | | | 1 | 1 | | | | | | 3 | | |
| Truro | 68 | 20 | Lombard | Zedediah | 2 | | 1 | | | | | | 1 | | | | 4 | | |
| Truro | 68 | 21 | Paine | Samuel | 2 | | 1 | | | 1 | | 1 | | | | | 5 | | |
| Truro | 68 | 22 | Cobb | Richard Jun | 2 | | 1 | | | 2 | | 1 | | | | | 6 | | |
| Truro | 68 | 23 | Lombard | Harding | | 1 | | | | 1 | | 1 | | | | | 3 | | |
| Truro | 68 | 24 | Rich | Mulford | 1 | | 1 | | | | | 1 | | | | | 3 | | |
| Truro | 68 | 25 | Rich | David | | | 1 | | | 1 | | 1 | | | | | 3 | | |
| Truro | 68 | 26 | Rich | James Junr | 1 | | 1 | | | | | 1 | | | | | 3 | | |
| Truro | 68 | 27 | Paine | Asa | | 1 | | | | | | 1 | | | | | 2 | | |
| Truro | 68 | 28 | Mayo | Nehemiah D. | | | 1 | | | 1 | | 1 | | | | | 3 | | |
| Truro | 68 | 29 | Nye | Timothy | 1 | | 1 | | | | | 1 | | | | | 3 | | |
| Truro | 68 | 30 | Braver | John | 1 | 1 | | | | | | 1 | | | | | 3 | | |
| Truro | 68 | 31 | Wharf | Joseph | 2 | | 1 | | | 2 | | | 1 | | | | 6 | | |
| Truro | 69 | 1 | Perry | Prince | | 1 | 1 | 1 | | 1 | 1 | | | 1 | | | 6 | | |
| Truro | 69 | 2 | Holbrook | Anthony | 1 | | 1 | | | | | 1 | | | | | 3 | | |
| Truro | 69 | 3 | Rich | Richard Junr | | 2 | 1 | 1 | | | | 2 | 1 | | | | 7 | | |
| Truro | 69 | 4 | Hopkins | Constant Junr | | 1 | 2 | 1 | | 2 | 2 | | 1 | | | | 9 | | |

# 1800 Wellfleet, Barnstable County, Massachusetts

| TOWN | PG# | LN# | LAST NAME | FIRST NAME | FREE WHITE MALES | | | | | FREE WHITE FEMALES | | | | | TOTAL ALL OTHER | SLAVES | TOTALS | DISTRICT/ TOWNSHIP | NOTES |
|---|---|---|---|---|---|---|---|---|---|---|---|---|---|---|---|---|---|---|---|
| | | | | | under 10 | 10 to 16 | 16 to 26 | 26 to 45 | 45 and over | under 10 | 10 to 16 | 16 to 26 | 26 to 45 | 45 and over | | | | | |
| Wellfleet | 69 | 1 | Arcy | Reuben | 2 | 2 | | | 1 | 3 | 1 | 1 | | 1 | | | 11 | | |
| Wellfleet | 69 | 2 | Atwood | Benjamin | 1 | | | 1 | | 2 | | | 1 | | | | 5 | | |
| Wellfleet | 69 | 3 | Atwood | Ephraim | | 1 | | 1 | | | | | 1 | | | | 3 | | |
| Wellfleet | 69 | 4 | Atwood | Azuba | | 2 | | | | 3 | | | 1 | | | | 6 | | |
| Wellfleet | 69 | 5 | Atwood | Joshua | | 1 | | 1 | | | | | 1 | | | | 3 | | |
| Wellfleet | 69 | 6 | Atkins | Daniel | | | 1 | | | 1 | | 1 | | | | | 3 | | |
| Wellfleet | 69 | 7 | Atwood | Experience | | | | | | | | | 1 | | | | 1 | | |
| Wellfleet | 69 | 8 | Atwood | David | 1 | 2 | 1 | 1 | | 2 | 1 | | 1 | | | | 9 | | |
| Wellfleet | 69 | 9 | Atwood | John | 2 | | | 1 | | | | | 1 | | | | 4 | | |
| Wellfleet | 69 | 10 | Atwood | Nathaniel | 3 | | 1 | 1 | 1 | 2 | 1 | | 1 | | | | 10 | | |
| Wellfleet | 69 | 11 | Atwood | Ebenezer | 1 | 1 | | | 1 | 4 | 1 | | 1 | | | | 9 | | |
| Wellfleet | 69 | 12 | Atwood | Hannah | | | | | | | 2 | | 1 | | | | 3 | | |
| Wellfleet | 69 | 13 | Atwood | Simeon | 1 | 1 | | 1 | | 1 | 1 | 1 | | | | | 6 | | |
| Wellfleet | 69 | 14 | Atwood | Gideon | | 1 | | 1 | | | | | 1 | | | | 3 | | |
| Wellfleet | 69 | 15 | Ellis | Ansell | | | | 1 | | | 1 | 1 | | 1 | | | 4 | | |
| Wellfleet | 69 | 16 | Bacon | Freeman | | | 1 | | | 1 | | 1 | | | | | 3 | | |
| Wellfleet | 69 | 17 | Hawes | Jeremiah | 1 | | 1 | | | 1 | | 1 | | | | | 4 | | |
| Wellfleet | 69 | 18 | Brown | Doane | 1 | | 1 | | | | | 1 | | | | | 3 | | |
| Wellfleet | 69 | 19 | Brown | Elisha | | 1 | | 1 | | 3 | 4 | | 1 | | | | 10 | | |
| Wellfleet | 70 | 1 | Brown | John | | | 1 | | | 1 | | 1 | | | | | 3 | | |
| Wellfleet | 70 | 2 | Brown | Isaac | | | 1 | | | 1 | | 1 | | | | | 3 | | |
| Wellfleet | 70 | 3 | Brown | Molly | 1 | | | | | 2 | | | 1 | | | | 4 | | |
| Wellfleet | 70 | 4 | Baker | Ruth | 1 | | | | | 3 | 1 | 1 | 1 | | | | 7 | | |
| Wellfleet | 70 | 5 | Brimhall | Robert | 1 | | 2 | 1 | | 2 | 1 | | 1 | 1 | | | 9 | | |
| Wellfleet | 70 | 6 | Brown | George | | 1 | 2 | | 1 | | 1 | 2 | | 1 | | | 8 | | |
| Wellfleet | 70 | 7 | Brown | David | | 1 | | 1 | | | | | 1 | | | | 3 | | |
| Wellfleet | 70 | 8 | Baker | Hannah | | 1 | | | | | | | 1 | 1 | | | 3 | | |
| Wellfleet | 70 | 9 | Cole | Joanna | | 1 | | 1 | | | | | 1 | | | | 4 | | |
| Wellfleet | 70 | 10 | Cohoon | Joseph | | 1 | | 1 | | | | | 1 | | | | 3 | | |
| Wellfleet | 70 | 11 | Chipman | Betty | | | 2 | | | | | | | 1 | | | 3 | | |
| Wellfleet | 70 | 12 | Covell | Reuben | | | | 1 | | | | | | 1 | | | 2 | | |
| Wellfleet | 70 | 13 | Cole | William | | | 1 | | 1 | | | | 3 | 1 | | | 6 | | |
| Wellfleet | 70 | 14 | Cole | William Junr | 2 | | 1 | 1 | | 1 | | | 1 | | | | 6 | | |
| Wellfleet | 70 | 15 | Chipman | Dorcas | | 1 | | | | 1 | | | 1 | | | | 3 | | |
| Wellfleet | 70 | 16 | Covell | Reuben Junr | 2 | | | 1 | | 1 | 1 | | 1 | | | | 6 | | |
| Wellfleet | 70 | 17 | Covell | Ruth | | | 2 | | | 1 | 1 | | 1 | | | | 5 | | |
| Wellfleet | 70 | 18 | Cole | Daniel | 1 | 2 | 2 | | 1 | 2 | | | | 1 | | | 9 | | |
| Wellfleet | 70 | 19 | Chipman | Samuel | 1 | | | 1 | | | | | 1 | | | | 3 | | |
| Wellfleet | 70 | 20 | Chipman | John | | | 1 | | | 1 | | | 1 | | | | 3 | | |
| Wellfleet | 70 | 21 | Deane | Hezekiah | | | 1 | | 1 | 1 | | | 1 | | | | 4 | | |
| Wellfleet | 70 | 22 | Dyer | Solomon | | 1 | | | 1 | 1 | 1 | 2 | | | | | 6 | | |
| Wellfleet | 70 | 23 | Dyer | Micah | 3 | | | 1 | | | | | 1 | | | | 5 | | |
| Wellfleet | 70 | 24 | Dill | James | | 1 | 1 | 1 | | | | | | 1 | | | 4 | | |
| Wellfleet | 70 | 25 | Jones | Deborah | | 2 | | | | | | 1 | 1 | | | | 4 | | |
| Wellfleet | 70 | 26 | Gill | John | 3 | | | 1 | | 2 | | | 1 | | | | 7 | | |
| Wellfleet | 70 | 27 | Graham | Deliverance | 1 | 1 | 1 | | | 2 | | 1 | 1 | | | | 7 | | |
| Wellfleet | 70 | 28 | Hatch | George | 4 | 1 | 1 | | 1 | 1 | 1 | 1 | 1 | 1 | | | 12 | | |
| Wellfleet | 70 | 29 | Higgins | Beriah | 1 | | 1 | 1 | | 2 | 1 | | 1 | | | | 7 | | |
| Wellfleet | 70 | 30 | Holbrook | Joseph | 2 | | 1 | 1 | | 1 | | | 1 | | | | 6 | | |
| Wellfleet | 70 | 31 | Holbrook | Solomon | 1 | | 1 | | | 1 | | 1 | | | | | 4 | | |
| Wellfleet | 70 | 32 | Harding | Joseph Junr | 1 | 1 | 1 | | | 1 | | 2 | | | | | 6 | | |
| Wellfleet | 70 | 33 | Hamblen | Cornelius | 1 | 1 | 3 | | 1 | | 2 | 2 | | 1 | | | 11 | | |
| Wellfleet | 70 | 34 | Whitaker | William | | | | 1 | | | | | 1 | | | | 2 | | |
| Wellfleet | 70 | 35 | Higgins | Phillip | 1 | | | 1 | | 2 | | | 1 | | | | 5 | | |
| Wellfleet | 70 | 36 | Holbrook | Jonathan | | 1 | | 1 | | 1 | 1 | | 1 | | | | 5 | | |
| Wellfleet | 70 | 37 | Hopkins | Solomon Junr | 1 | 3 | | 1 | | | | | 1 | | | | 6 | | |
| Wellfleet | 71 | 1 | Hinkley | Moses | | | 1 | | | 1 | | 1 | | | | | 3 | | |
| Wellfleet | 71 | 2 | Higgins | Hannah | | | 2 | | | | | 3 | | 1 | | | 6 | | |
| Wellfleet | 71 | 3 | Higgins | Hannah Junr | | 1 | | | | | 1 | 1 | | | | | 3 | | |
| Wellfleet | 71 | 4 | Hamlen | Lewis | 1 | | | 1 | | | | | | 1 | | | 3 | | |
| Wellfleet | 71 | 5 | Hopkins | Benjamin | 1 | | 1 | 1 | | | 1 | 1 | | | | | 5 | | |
| Wellfleet | 71 | 6 | Hawes | Hulday | | | | | | | | 1 | | 1 | | | 2 | | |
| Wellfleet | 71 | 7 | Hawes | Thomas | | | 1 | | | 1 | | 1 | | | | | 3 | | |
| Wellfleet | 71 | 8 | Holbrook | David | 1 | 1 | 1 | | 1 | | 1 | 1 | 1 | | | | 7 | | |
| Wellfleet | 71 | 9 | Hopkins | Theophilus | 2 | | | 2 | | 1 | | | 1 | | | | 6 | | |
| Wellfleet | 71 | 10 | Hopkins | Giles | | | | 1 | | 3 | | | 1 | 1 | | | 6 | | |
| Wellfleet | 71 | 11 | Graham | Talor | | 1 | | | | 1 | | | 1 | | | | 3 | | |
| Wellfleet | 71 | 12 | Higgins | Enoch | | | | 1 | | | | | 1 | 2 | | | 4 | | |
| Wellfleet | 71 | 13 | Hopkins | Solomon | 2 | | | 1 | | 2 | 1 | | 1 | | | | 7 | | |
| Wellfleet | 71 | 14 | Harding | Nathaniel | 2 | 1 | 1 | | 1 | 1 | 2 | | 1 | | | | 9 | | |
| Wellfleet | 71 | 15 | Harding | Abigail | | | 3 | | | 1 | 3 | | | 1 | | | 8 | | |
| Wellfleet | 71 | 16 | Holbrook | Thomas | | 1 | 1 | | 2 | 1 | 1 | | 1 | | | | 7 | | |
| Wellfleet | 71 | 17 | Kenurich | Warren A. | 4 | | 1 | 1 | | | | | | 2 | | | 8 | | |
| Wellfleet | 71 | 18 | King | Joanna | | | 1 | | | | | | 2 | 1 | | | 4 | | |
| Wellfleet | 71 | 19 | Kenye | Robert | 3 | 2 | 2 | | 1 | | | | 1 | | | | 9 | | |
| Wellfleet | 71 | 20 | Lewis | Moses | | 1 | 2 | | 1 | 1 | 1 | | | 1 | | | 7 | | |
| Wellfleet | 71 | 21 | Lombard | Peter | | | | 1 | | 4 | 2 | | 1 | | | | 8 | | |
| Wellfleet | 71 | 22 | Lewis | Benjamin | | | 1 | 1 | 1 | | | | | 1 | | | 4 | | |
| Wellfleet | 71 | 23 | Lewis | Sarah | | 1 | | | | | 2 | | 2 | | | | 5 | | |

# 1800 Wellfleet, Barnstable County, Massachusetts

| TOWN | PG# | LN# | LAST NAME | FIRST NAME | FREE WHITE MALES | | | | | FREE WHITE FEMALES | | | | | TOTAL ALL OTHER | SLAVES | TOTALS | DISTRICT/ TOWNSHIP | NOTES |
|------|-----|-----|-----------|------------|------|------|------|------|------|------|------|------|------|------|------|------|------|------|------|
| | | | | | under 10 | 10 to 16 | 16 to 26 | 26 to 45 | 45 and over | under 10 | 10 to 16 | 16 to 26 | 26 to 45 | 45 and over | | | | | |
| Wellfleet | 71 | 24 | Lewis | Solomon | 3 | | | 1 | | 1 | | | | 1 | | | 6 | | |
| Wellfleet | 71 | 25 | Mayo | Mary | | | | | | | | | 2 | | | | 2 | | |
| Wellfleet | 71 | 26 | Mayo | Daniel | | | 1 | | | 1 | | | 1 | | | | 3 | | |
| Wellfleet | 71 | 27 | Mayo | Abigail | | | | | | | | | 1 | 1 | | | 2 | | |
| Wellfleet | 71 | 28 | Morris | James | 1 | | | 1 | | 1 | 1 | | 2 | | | | 6 | | |
| Wellfleet | 71 | 29 | Mayo | Nathan | | | | 1 | | 1 | | | 1 | | | | 3 | | |
| Wellfleet | 71 | 30 | Newcomb | Lemuel | 1 | 2 | 2 | 1 | | | | 1 | 2 | 1 | | | 10 | | |
| Wellfleet | 71 | 31 | Newcomb | Lemuel Junr | 2 | | | 1 | | 2 | 2 | | | 1 | | | 8 | | |
| Wellfleet | 71 | 32 | Newcomb | Seth | 2 | | 1 | | | 2 | | | 1 | | | | 6 | | |
| Wellfleet | 71 | 33 | Newcomb | Simon Junr | 1 | | 1 | 1 | | | 1 | 2 | | 1 | | | 7 | | |
| Wellfleet | 71 | 34 | Newcomb | Hezekiah | 2 | | 1 | | | 1 | | | 1 | | | | 5 | | |
| Wellfleet | 71 | 35 | Newcomb | Elisha | 1 | | 1 | | | 1 | | 1 | | | | | 4 | | |
| Wellfleet | 71 | 36 | Newcomb | Sally | 1 | | | | | | 2 | | 1 | 1 | | | 5 | | |
| Wellfleet | 71 | 37 | Newcomb | James | | | 1 | 1 | | 2 | 2 | | 1 | | | | 7 | | |
| Wellfleet | 72 | 1 | Holbrook | Joseph Junr | | | 1 | | | 2 | | 2 | | | | | 5 | | |
| Wellfleet | 72 | 2 | Newcomb | Joshua | | | 1 | | | | | | | 1 | | | 2 | | |
| Wellfleet | 72 | 3 | Newcomb | Jeremiah | | 1 | 1 | | | 3 | 1 | | 1 | | | | 7 | | |
| Wellfleet | 72 | 4 | Peirce | Samuel Junr | 1 | 1 | 1 | | | 2 | | | 1 | | | | 6 | | |
| Wellfleet | 72 | 5 | Paine | Thomas Junr | 2 | | 1 | | | 1 | | | 1 | | | | 5 | | |
| Wellfleet | 72 | 6 | Peirce | Solomon | 1 | | 1 | 1 | | | | | 1 | 1 | | | 5 | | |
| Wellfleet | 72 | 7 | Peirce | Joseph Junr | 1 | 2 | 1 | 1 | | | | | 1 | | | | 6 | | |
| Wellfleet | 72 | 8 | Peirce | Isaac | | 1 | | 1 | | | 1 | | 1 | 1 | | | 5 | | |
| Wellfleet | 72 | 9 | Paine | Thomas | | 1 | | 1 | | | | | 1 | 1 | | | 4 | | |
| Wellfleet | 72 | 10 | Higgins | Joseph | | | 1 | | | 1 | | | 1 | | | | 3 | | |
| Wellfleet | 72 | 11 | Rich | Robert | 2 | | 1 | | | 2 | | | 1 | | | | 6 | | |
| Wellfleet | 72 | 12 | Rich | Hezekiah | 1 | | 1 | | | 1 | | | 1 | | | | 4 | | |
| Wellfleet | 72 | 13 | Rider | Abigail | | | | | | 1 | | | | 1 | | | 2 | | |
| Wellfleet | 72 | 14 | Rider | Matthias | | 1 | 1 | 1 | | | 1 | 2 | | 1 | | | 7 | | |
| Wellfleet | 72 | 15 | Rider | Matthias Junr | 2 | | 1 | | | 2 | | | 3 | | | | 8 | | |
| Wellfleet | 72 | 16 | Sweat | John | | 1 | | 1 | | | | | | 1 | | | 3 | | |
| Wellfleet | 72 | 17 | Sweat | Joshua | 1 | 1 | | | | | | | 1 | | | | 3 | | |
| Wellfleet | 72 | 18 | Smith | Isaac | 1 | 1 | | 1 | | 2 | | 1 | | 1 | | | 7 | | |
| Wellfleet | 72 | 19 | Snow | Joseph | | 1 | 1 | 1 | | | 2 | 1 | 1 | | | | 7 | | |
| Wellfleet | 72 | 20 | Smith | Joseph | | 1 | 1 | 1 | | | | | 2 | 1 | | | 6 | | |
| Wellfleet | 72 | 21 | Stubbs | John | | 1 | | 1 | | 1 | 1 | | 1 | | | | 5 | | |
| Wellfleet | 72 | 22 | Smith | Joshua | 1 | | | 1 | | 1 | | 1 | | | | | 4 | | |
| Wellfleet | 72 | 23 | St*t | Thomas | | | | 1 | | | | | | 1 | | | 2 | | |
| Wellfleet | 72 | 24 | Smith | Azariah | | 1 | | | | 1 | | | | 1 | | | 3 | | |
| Wellfleet | 72 | 25 | Smith | Samuel Junr | 1 | 1 | | 1 | | 2 | | | 1 | | | | 6 | | |
| Wellfleet | 72 | 26 | Snow | Solomon | 2 | 1 | | 1 | | 2 | | | 1 | 1 | | | 8 | | |
| Wellfleet | 72 | 27 | Smith | Samuel | 1 | | | 1 | | 3 | | 2 | 1 | | | | 8 | | |
| Wellfleet | 72 | 28 | Smith | Jesse | 2 | | 1 | | | | | | 1 | | | | 5 | | |
| Wellfleet | 72 | 29 | Smith | Edward | | 1 | | 1 | | | | 2 | 1 | | | | 5 | | |
| Wellfleet | 72 | 30 | Smith | George | | 2 | 1 | 1 | | | 3 | | 1 | | | | 8 | | |
| Wellfleet | 72 | 31 | Watts | Samuel | 1 | 1 | 1 | 1 | | 2 | 1 | 1 | 1 | | | | 9 | | |
| Wellfleet | 72 | 32 | Waterman | Samuel | | 1 | | 1 | | | | 2 | 1 | | | | 5 | | |
| Wellfleet | 72 | 33 | Wiley | Levi | | | | 1 | | | | 1 | 1 | | | | 3 | | |
| Wellfleet | 72 | 34 | Wiley | Levi Junr | | | 1 | | | | 2 | | 1 | | | | 4 | | |
| Wellfleet | 72 | 35 | Withrell | John | | 1 | | 1 | | | 2 | | 1 | | | | 5 | | |
| Wellfleet | 72 | 36 | Withrell | Whitfield | 1 | | 1 | | | 1 | | | 1 | | | | 4 | | |
| Wellfleet | 73 | 1 | Ward | Benjamin | 2 | 1 | 2 | 1 | | 1 | 1 | 1 | 1 | | | | 10 | | |
| Wellfleet | 73 | 2 | Whitman | Ezra | | | 1 | | | | 2 | | 1 | | | | 4 | | |
| Wellfleet | 73 | 3 | Wiley | Ebenezer | 1 | 1 | 1 | | | | 3 | | 1 | | | | 7 | | |
| Wellfleet | 73 | 4 | Wiley | David | 1 | | 1 | | | | 1 | 1 | | | | | 4 | | |
| Wellfleet | 73 | 5 | Withrell | Ruth | | 1 | 1 | | | | 3 | 1 | 1 | | | | 7 | | |
| Wellfleet | 73 | 6 | Ward | Elisha | 2 | | 1 | 1 | | 1 | 1 | | 1 | | | | 7 | | |
| Wellfleet | 73 | 7 | Ward | Benjamin | | | 1 | | | | 2 | | 1 | | | | 4 | | |
| Wellfleet | 73 | 8 | Young | Barnabus | | 1 | 1 | | | | | | | 1 | | | 3 | | |
| Wellfleet | 73 | 9 | Young | Stephen | 1 | 1 | | 1 | | 1 | | | 1 | | | | 5 | | |
| Wellfleet | 73 | 10 | Young | John Junr | | | 1 | | | 1 | 1 | 1 | | | | | 4 | | |
| Wellfleet | 73 | 11 | Young | Molly | | | | | | | 1 | | | | | | 1 | | |
| Wellfleet | 73 | 12 | Young | Moses | | 2 | | 1 | | 1 | | | 1 | | | | 5 | | |
| Wellfleet | 73 | 13 | Young | Henry | | | 1 | | | | | 1 | | | | | 2 | | |
| Wellfleet | 73 | 14 | Young | Robert | | | 1 | 1 | | | | 2 | 1 | | | | 5 | | |
| Wellfleet | 73 | 15 | Young | Naby | | | | | | | | 2 | 2 | 1 | | | 5 | | |
| Wellfleet | 73 | 16 | Freeman | Benjamin | 5 | | 1 | 1 | | | | | 1 | | | | 8 | | |
| Wellfleet | 73 | 17 | Wiley | Bethuel | | | 1 | | | | | 1 | 1 | 1 | | | 4 | | |
| Wellfleet | 73 | 18 | Baker | David | | 1 | 1 | | | | | | | 1 | | | 3 | | |
| Wellfleet | 73 | 19 | Baker | David Junr | 2 | | 1 | | | | | | 1 | | | | 4 | | |
| Wellfleet | 73 | 20 | Atwood | Ezekiel | | 1 | | 2 | | | | | 1 | | | | 4 | | |
| Wellfleet | 73 | 21 | Higgins | Ephraim | 2 | | 1 | | | | | | 1 | | | | 4 | | |
| Wellfleet | 73 | 22 | Higgins | Eleazar | 1 | 1 | | 3 | | 1 | | | 1 | | | | 8 | | |
| Wellfleet | 73 | 23 | Nisbit | Elizabeth | 1 | | 2 | | | | | 1 | | 1 | | | 5 | | |
| Wellfleet | 73 | 24 | Atwood | Eleazar | | 1 | 1 | 1 | | | | 1 | | 1 | | | 5 | | |
| Wellfleet | 73 | 25 | Rich | Elisha | 4 | 2 | 1 | 1 | 1 | | | 2 | 1 | | | | 12 | | |
| Wellfleet | 73 | 26 | Atwood | Elisha | 1 | | 1 | | | | | 2 | | 1 | | | 5 | | |
| Wellfleet | 73 | 27 | Wiley | Elisha | 2 | | | 1 | | | | 2 | 1 | | | | 6 | | |
| Wellfleet | 73 | 28 | Freeman | Edmund | 1 | 2 | 2 | | 1 | | | | 2 | 1 | | | 9 | | |
| Wellfleet | 73 | 29 | Hatch | Elisha | | | 1 | | | | | 2 | 1 | 1 | | | 5 | | |

# 1800 Wellfleet, Barnstable County, Massachusetts

| TOWN | PG# | LN# | LAST NAME | FIRST NAME | FREE WHITE MALES under 10 | 10 to 16 | 16 to 26 | 26 to 45 | 45 and over | FREE WHITE FEMALES under 10 | 10 to 16 | 16 to 26 | 26 to 45 | 45 and over | TOTAL ALL OTHER | SLAVES | TOTALS | DISTRICT/ TOWNSHIP | NOTES |
|---|---|---|---|---|---|---|---|---|---|---|---|---|---|---|---|---|---|---|---|
| Wellfleet | 73 | 30 | Atwood | Freeman | | | 1 | | | | | | 1 | | | | 2 | | |
| Wellfleet | 73 | 31 | Wiley | Hannah | 2 | | 2 | | | 1 | | | 1 | 1 | | | 7 | | |
| Wellfleet | 73 | 32 | Rich | Isaac | 3 | 2 | 1 | 1 | | 1 | 1 | | 1 | | | | 10 | | |
| Wellfleet | 73 | 33 | Atwood | Isaiah | | | 1 | 1 | | 3 | | | 1 | 1 | | | 7 | | |
| Wellfleet | 73 | 34 | Freeman | Isaac | | | 2 | | 1 | | | | | 1 | | | 4 | | |
| Wellfleet | 73 | 35 | Freeman | Isaac Junr | 2 | 4 | 1 | 1 | | | | | 1 | | | | 9 | | |
| Wellfleet | 73 | 36 | Baker | Isaiah | 1 | | | 1 | | 1 | | | 1 | | | | 4 | | |
| Wellfleet | 73 | 37 | Higgins | Jonathan | 1 | 1 | 5 | | 1 | 3 | 1 | 1 | 1 | | | | 14 | | |
| Wellfleet | 74 | 1 | Newcomb | Jonathan Younger | 1 | | 1 | | | 1 | | 1 | 1 | 1 | | | 6 | | |
| Wellfleet | 74 | 2 | Rich | Josiah | 1 | | 2 | | 1 | | | | 1 | 2 | | | 7 | | |
| Wellfleet | 74 | 3 | Hatch | Joseph | | 1 | | | 1 | | | | 3 | 1 | | | 6 | | |
| Wellfleet | 74 | 4 | Hatch | Joseph Junr | 1 | | | 1 | | 2 | | | 1 | | | | 5 | | |
| Wellfleet | 74 | 5 | Darling | John | 1 | | | 1 | | | | | 1 | | | | 3 | | |
| Wellfleet | 74 | 6 | Atkins | James | | 1 | | 1 | | 4 | 1 | | 1 | | | | 8 | | |
| Wellfleet | 74 | 7 | Dill | Moses | 2 | | | 1 | | | | 1 | | | | | 4 | | |
| Wellfleet | 74 | 8 | Sweat | Mercy | | | 1 | | | | | | | 1 | | | 2 | | |
| Wellfleet | 74 | 9 | Wiley | Nathaniel | | 2 | | 1 | | 2 | | | 1 | 1 | | | 7 | | |
| Wellfleet | 74 | 10 | Higgins | Paine | | 1 | | 1 | | 2 | 1 | 1 | 1 | | | | 7 | | |
| Wellfleet | 74 | 11 | Atwood | Richard | 4 | | 2 | 1 | | | 1 | | 1 | | | | 9 | | |
| Wellfleet | 74 | 12 | Rich | Reuben | | | | 1 | | | | | 1 | | | | 2 | | |
| Wellfleet | 74 | 13 | Higgins | Solomon Junr | 2 | 1 | | 1 | | | | | 1 | | | | 5 | | |
| Wellfleet | 74 | 14 | Higgins | Solomon | | 1 | | 1 | | | | | 1 | 1 | | | 4 | | |
| Wellfleet | 74 | 15 | Atwood | Stephen | 1 | 1 | 3 | | 1 | | | 1 | 1 | | 4 | | 12 | | |
| Wellfleet | 74 | 16 | Newcomb | Simon | | 1 | 1 | 1 | | 1 | | 1 | | 1 | 2 | | 8 | | |
| Wellfleet | 74 | 17 | Atwood | Thomas | | 1 | | 1 | | 3 | 1 | | 1 | | 3 | | 10 | | |
| Wellfleet | 74 | 18 | Higgins | Thomas | | | | 1 | | | | | | 1 | | | 2 | | |
| Wellfleet | 74 | 19 | Higgins | Thomas 3d | 1 | | 1 | 1 | | | | | 1 | | | | 4 | | |
| Wellfleet | 74 | 20 | Peirce | Thomas | 1 | | | 1 | | 1 | | | 1 | | | | 4 | | |
| Wellfleet | 74 | 21 | Newcomb | Jemima | | 1 | | | | | | 1 | 1 | | | | 3 | | |
| Wellfleet | 74 | 22 | Paine | Thomas 3d | 2 | | | 1 | | 1 | | | 1 | | | | 5 | | |
| Wellfleet | 74 | 23 | Gross | Thomas | 1 | | 3 | | 1 | 1 | 3 | 1 | | 1 | | | 11 | | |
| Wellfleet | 74 | 24 | Sweat | Thankfull | | 1 | | | | | | | 1 | 1 | | | 3 | | |
| Wellfleet | 74 | 25 | Higgins | Uriah | 2 | | | 1 | | | | 1 | 1 | 1 | | | 6 | | |
| Wellfleet | 74 | 26 | Harding | Mary | | 1 | | | | 1 | 2 | | 1 | | | | 5 | | |
| Wellfleet | 74 | 27 | Murry | Betsy | | | 1 | | | | | 1 | 1 | | | | 3 | | |
| Wellfleet | 74 | 28 | Atwood | Timothy | | 1 | | 1 | | | | | 1 | | | | 3 | | |
| Wellfleet | 74 | 29 | Atwood | Joshua Junr | | | 1 | | | | | | 1 | | | | 2 | | |
| Wellfleet | 74 | 30 | Nickerson | Hatsael | | 2 | | 1 | | 2 | | | 1 | 1 | | | 7 | | |
| Wellfleet | 74 | 31 | Rider | Seth | | | 1 | | | | | | 1 | 1 | | | 3 | | |
| Wellfleet | 74 | 32 | Rider | Samuel | 1 | | 1 | | | | | 1 | | | | | 3 | | |
| Wellfleet | 74 | 33 | Peirce | John | | 1 | 1 | | | | | | 1 | | | | 3 | | |
| Wellfleet | 74 | 34 | Higgins | Reuben | | | 1 | | | 1 | | 1 | | | | | 3 | | |
| Wellfleet | 74 | 35 | Harding | Nathaniel | | 1 | 1 | | | 1 | | 1 | | | | | 4 | | |
| Wellfleet | 74 | 36 | Atwood | Jemima | 2 | 1 | 1 | | | | | | 2 | 1 | | | 7 | | |
| Wellfleet | 74 | 37 | Corlister | Thomas | | | 1 | | | | | | 1 | | | | 2 | | |
| Wellfleet | 75 | 1 | Adams | Ephraim | 1 | | | 1 | | 3 | 1 | | 1 | | | | 7 | | |
| Wellfleet | 75 | 2 | Cookson | Mary | | | | | | | | | | 1 | | | 1 | | |
| Wellfleet | 75 | 3 | Hatch | Thomas | | | 1 | | | 1 | | | 1 | | | | 3 | | |
| Wellfleet | 75 | 4 | Snow | Samuel | | | 1 | | | | | | 1 | | | | 2 | | |
| Wellfleet | 75 | 5 | Young | John | 1 | 1 | | | 1 | 3 | 1 | | 1 | 1 | | | 9 | | |
| Wellfleet | 75 | 6 | Brown | Benjamin | | | 1 | | | | | | 1 | | | | 2 | | |
| Wellfleet | 75 | 7 | Dyer | Solomon Junr | 1 | | 1 | | | | | | 1 | | | | 3 | | |
| Wellfleet | 75 | 8 | Lewis | Uorice | | 1 | | | | | | | | 1 | | | 2 | | |
| Wellfleet | 75 | 9 | Smith | Jarad | | | 1 | | | | | | 1 | | | | 2 | | |
| Wellfleet | 75 | 10 | Rider | Silas | 3 | 1 | | 1 | | | | | 1 | | | | 6 | | |
| Wellfleet | 75 | 11 | Covell | David | 1 | | | 1 | | 1 | | | 1 | | | | 4 | | |
| Wellfleet | 75 | 12 | Hatch | James B. | | | | 1 | | 1 | | | 1 | | | | 3 | | |
| Wellfleet | 75 | 13 | Paine | Mary | | | 1 | | | | | | 1 | 1 | | | 3 | | |
| Wellfleet | 75 | 14 | Sweat | John Junr | | | 1 | | | 1 | | | 1 | | | | 3 | | |
| Wellfleet | 75 | 15 | Newcomb | Simon 3d | 1 | | 1 | | | | | | 1 | | | | 3 | | |
| Wellfleet | 75 | 16 | Atkins | David | 2 | 1 | | 1 | | 3 | 1 | | 1 | | | | 9 | | |
| Wellfleet | 75 | 17 | Paine | William | | | 1 | | | | | | 1 | | | | 2 | | |
| Wellfleet | 75 | 18 | Peirce | Joshua | | | 1 | | | | | | 1 | | | | 2 | | |
| Wellfleet | 75 | 19 | Atwood | Harding | | | 1 | | | 1 | | | | 1 | | | 3 | | |
| Wellfleet | 75 | 20 | Hawes | Edmund | 4 | | | 1 | | | | | | 1 | | | 6 | | |
| Wellfleet | 75 | 21 | Landman | Edward | | | | | 1 | | | | | 1 | | | 2 | | |
| Wellfleet | 75 | 22 | Ballard | Anna | | | | | | | | | | | 2 | | 2 | | |
| Wellfleet | 75 | 23 | Smith | David | 1 | | 1 | | | | | | 1 | | | | 3 | | |
| Wellfleet | 75 | 24 | Wiley | Henry | | 1 | | | | | | | 1 | | | | 2 | | |
| Wellfleet | 75 | 25 | S*y | Reuben Junr | | | 1 | | | | | | 1 | | | | 2 | | |
| Wellfleet | 75 | 26 | Stubbs | Richard | 4 | 1 | | 1 | | | | | | 1 | | | 7 | | |
| Wellfleet | 75 | 27 | Smith | Samuel 3d | | 1 | | | | 1 | | | 1 | | | | 3 | | |
| Wellfleet | 75 | 28 | Bointon | Gershom | | | 1 | | | 1 | | | 1 | | | | 3 | | |
| Wellfleet | 75 | 29 | Smith | John | 1 | | 1 | | | | | | 1 | | | | 3 | | |
| Wellfleet | 75 | 30 | Tailor | Solomon | 1 | | | 1 | | 1 | | | 1 | | | | 4 | | |
| Wellfleet | 75 | 31 | Cole | Ebenezer | 1 | | 1 | | | | | | 1 | | | | 3 | | |
| Wellfleet | 75 | 32 | Young | Daniel | 3 | | 1 | | | | | | | 1 | | | 5 | | |
| Wellfleet | 75 | 33 | Wiley | John | 1 | | 1 | | | | | | 1 | | | | 3 | | |
| Wellfleet | 75 | 34 | Whitman | Levi Rev | 2 | | | 1 | 1 | 3 | 1 | | 1 | | | | 9 | | |

# 1800 Yarmouth, Barnstable County, Massachusetts

| TOWN | PG# | LN# | LAST NAME | FIRST NAME | FREE WHITE MALES | | | | | FREE WHITE FEMALES | | | | | TOTAL ALL OTHER | SLAVES | TOTALS | DISTRICT/ TOWNSHIP | NOTES |
|---|---|---|---|---|---|---|---|---|---|---|---|---|---|---|---|---|---|---|---|
| | | | | | under 10 | 10 to 16 | 16 to 26 | 26 to 45 | 45 and over | under 10 | 10 to 16 | 16 to 26 | 26 to 45 | 45 and over | | | | | |
| Yarmouth | 95 | 1 | Mathews | Thankful | 1 | 1 | | | | | | 1 | 1 | | | | 4 | | |
| Yarmouth | 95 | 2 | Mathews | Atkins | 3 | | 1 | | | 1 | 2 | 1 | | | | | 8 | | |
| Yarmouth | 95 | 3 | Thacher | Ebenz | | 2 | | 1 | | 2 | | | 1 | | | | 6 | | |
| Yarmouth | 95 | 4 | Mathews | Nathl | 3 | | | 1 | | 4 | 2 | 1 | | | | | 11 | | |
| Yarmouth | 95 | 5 | Eldredge | Barna | 1 | | 1 | | | 2 | | | 1 | | | | 5 | | |
| Yarmouth | 95 | 6 | Crowell | Thankful | | | | | | | | | 1 | 1 | | | 2 | | |
| Yarmouth | 95 | 7 | Hedge | William | | 1 | | 1 | | | | | 3 | 1 | | | 6 | | |
| Yarmouth | 95 | 8 | Taylor | William | | | | 1 | | | | | | 1 | | | 2 | | |
| Yarmouth | 95 | 9 | Hawes | Prince | 2 | | 1 | | | | | | 1 | | | | 4 | | |
| Yarmouth | 95 | 10 | Rider | Edward | | | | 1 | | | | | | 1 | | | 2 | | |
| Yarmouth | 95 | 11 | Bassett | Betty | | 1 | 3 | | | | | | | 1 | | | 5 | | |
| Yarmouth | 95 | 12 | Thacher | Edmund | | | 1 | | | | | 1 | | 1 | | | 3 | | |
| Yarmouth | 95 | 13 | Hedge | Elisha | | 1 | 1 | 1 | | 1 | | 1 | | 1 | | | 6 | | |
| Yarmouth | 95 | 14 | Thacher | Josiah Jr | 2 | | 1 | | | 2 | | | 1 | | | | 6 | | |
| Yarmouth | 95 | 15 | Whelden | Jonathan | 1 | | | 1 | | 2 | 1 | | 1 | | | | 6 | | |
| Yarmouth | 95 | 16 | Mathews | John | | | | 1 | | | | | | 1 | | | 2 | | |
| Yarmouth | 95 | 17 | Gorham | Joseph | 2 | | | 1 | | | | 3 | 2 | 1 | | | 9 | | |
| Yarmouth | 95 | 18 | Griffeth | Joseph | | | | 1 | | | | | 1 | | | | 2 | | |
| Yarmouth | 95 | 19 | Taylor | Ansel | | | | 1 | | | | 3 | 2 | 1 | | | 8 | | |
| Yarmouth | 95 | 20 | Hedge | Andrew | | | 1 | | | 1 | | | | 1 | | | 3 | | |
| Yarmouth | 95 | 21 | Hedge | Barnabas | | 2 | | 1 | | 1 | | | | 1 | | | 5 | | |
| Yarmouth | 95 | 22 | Rider | Edward Jr | 2 | 2 | | 1 | | 2 | | | 1 | | | | 9 | | |
| Yarmouth | 95 | 23 | Bassett | Joseph | | 1 | | 1 | | | | | 1 | 1 | | | 4 | | |
| Yarmouth | 95 | 24 | Homer | Robert | | 1 | 1 | 1 | | | | | | 1 | | | 4 | | |
| Yarmouth | 95 | 25 | Homer | Benjamin | 2 | | 1 | | | | | | 1 | | | | 4 | | |
| Yarmouth | 95 | 26 | Homer | John | 1 | | 1 | | | | | | 1 | | | | 3 | | |
| Yarmouth | 95 | 27 | Homer | Stevens | | 1 | 1 | 1 | | | | | 1 | | | | 4 | | |
| Yarmouth | 95 | 28 | Bray | William | | 1 | | 1 | | | | | 1 | 1 | | | 4 | | |
| Yarmouth | 95 | 29 | Bray | Isaiah | | 1 | | | | | | | 1 | | | | 2 | | |
| Yarmouth | 95 | 30 | Taylor | Jorce | 1 | 1 | 3 | 1 | | 3 | 2 | | 1 | | | | 12 | | |
| Yarmouth | 95 | 31 | Bray | William Jr | | | 1 | | 3 | | | | 1 | | | | 5 | | |
| Yarmouth | 95 | 32 | Hale | Isaac | 1 | | 1 | 1 | 1 | 1 | 1 | 1 | 1 | | | | 8 | | |
| Yarmouth | 95 | 33 | Bray | Edmund | | | 2 | 1 | 1 | | | | 1 | | | | 5 | | |
| Yarmouth | 95 | 34 | Gray | Gideon | | | | 1 | | | | | 1 | 1 | | | 3 | | |
| Yarmouth | 95 | 35 | Gray | Alden | 2 | | 1 | | | | | | 1 | | | | 4 | | |
| Yarmouth | 95 | 36 | Hall | John | | 1 | 2 | 1 | 1 | | | | 1 | 1 | | | 7 | | |
| Yarmouth | 95 | 37 | Hall | Edward | | | 1 | | | | | | 1 | | | | 2 | | |
| Yarmouth | 95 | 38 | Taylor | Samuel Jr | 1 | | 1 | 1 | | 2 | 2 | 1 | | | | | 8 | | |
| Yarmouth | 95 | 39 | Hale | David | 1 | 1 | 3 | 1 | | 1 | 1 | | 1 | | | | 9 | | |
| Yarmouth | 95 | 40 | Taylor | Lothrop | 1 | | 1 | | | 3 | | 1 | | | | | 6 | | |
| Yarmouth | 95 | 41 | Gray | John | 1 | | 1 | | | 1 | | | 1 | | | | 4 | | |
| Yarmouth | 95 | 42 | Mathews | Isaac | | | 1 | | | 1 | | 1 | | | | | 3 | | |
| Yarmouth | 95 | 43 | Homer | Daniel | | 1 | | | | 1 | | 1 | | | | | 3 | | |
| Yarmouth | 95 | 44 | Rider | Elizabeth | | | | | | | | | 2 | | | | 2 | | |
| Yarmouth | 95 | 45 | Rider | Rowland | | | 1 | | | | | | 1 | | | | 3 | | |
| Yarmouth | 95 | 46 | Taylor | Howes | | 1 | | | | | | 1 | 1 | | | | 3 | | |
| Yarmouth | 95 | 47 | Rider | Tempe | | | | | | | | 1 | 1 | | | | 2 | | |
| Yarmouth | 95 | 48 | Whelden | David | 2 | 1 | 1 | 1 | | 2 | 2 | 3 | 1 | | | | 13 | | |
| Yarmouth | 95 | 49 | Whelden | Seth | | 2 | 1 | 1 | | | | | 1 | | | | 5 | | |
| Yarmouth | 95 | 50 | Gage | Ebenezer | | 1 | 2 | 1 | | 1 | 2 | 1 | | | | | 8 | | |
| Yarmouth | 95 | 51 | Taylor | Benjamin | | | 2 | 1 | | | | | 1 | | | | 4 | | |
| Yarmouth | 95 | 52 | Taylor | Edward | | | 1 | | | 3 | | | 1 | | | | 5 | | |
| Yarmouth | 95 | 53 | Mathews | Joshua | | | 3 | 1 | | 1 | 1 | 1 | | | | | 7 | | |
| Yarmouth | 95 | 54 | Mathews | Samuel | | | 1 | | | 1 | | 1 | | | | | 3 | | |
| Yarmouth | 96 | 1 | Hedge | Edward | | | 1 | | | | | | 1 | | | | 2 | | |
| Yarmouth | 96 | 2 | Mathews | Phebe | | | 2 | 1 | 1 | | | | 1 | 1 | | | 6 | | |
| Yarmouth | 96 | 3 | Mathews | Benjamin | 1 | | | 1 | | | | 1 | 1 | 1 | | | 5 | | |
| Yarmouth | 96 | 4 | Bray | John | 1 | 1 | | 1 | | | | | 1 | | | | 5 | | |
| Yarmouth | 96 | 5 | Gage | Prince | 3 | | | 1 | | 1 | | 1 | | 1 | | | 7 | | |
| Yarmouth | 96 | 6 | Hamblin | Isaac | | | | 1 | | | | | 1 | 1 | | | 3 | | |
| Yarmouth | 96 | 7 | Hamblin | Joshua | 1 | 1 | | | | | | | 1 | | | | 3 | | |
| Yarmouth | 96 | 8 | Hamblin | Isaac Jr | 1 | | 1 | | | 2 | | | 1 | | | | | | |
| Yarmouth | 96 | 9 | Hallet | Ansel | 2 | | 1 | | | 1 | | | | | | | 4 | | |
| Yarmouth | 96 | 10 | Gage | Thomas | | | 1 | | | 1 | | 1 | | | | | 3 | | |
| Yarmouth | 96 | 11 | Linnell | Elisha | | | 1 | 1 | | | | | | 1 | | | 3 | | |
| Yarmouth | 96 | 12 | Studley | Anthony | 1 | 2 | | 1 | | 1 | | 1 | | 1 | | | 7 | | |
| Yarmouth | 96 | 13 | Studley | Josiah Jr | | | | 1 | | 2 | | | 1 | | | | 4 | | |
| Yarmouth | 96 | 14 | Nickerson | John | 1 | 1 | 1 | 1 | | 2 | | 1 | | 1 | | | 8 | | |
| Yarmouth | 96 | 15 | Nickerson | Azubah | | | | 1 | | | | | | 1 | | | 2 | | |
| Yarmouth | 96 | 16 | Godfrey | Elisha | 1 | 2 | 1 | | | 1 | | 1 | 1 | | | | 7 | | |
| Yarmouth | 96 | 17 | Godfrey | Mehitable | | | | | | | | | 2 | | | | 2 | | |
| Yarmouth | 96 | 18 | Cash | Elisha | | 2 | | 1 | | 1 | | 1 | | 1 | | | 7 | | |
| Yarmouth | 96 | 19 | Webber | Prince | 1 | 3 | | 1 | | 3 | | | 1 | | | | 9 | | |
| Yarmouth | 96 | 20 | Webber | Samuel | | 1 | | 1 | | 1 | 1 | 1 | | | 5 | | 10 | | |
| Yarmouth | 96 | 21 | Webber | William | | 1 | | 1 | 1 | | | | | 1 | 6 | | 10 | | |
| Yarmouth | 96 | 22 | Taylor | Samuel | 1 | 3 | | 1 | | 1 | 1 | | 1 | | 4 | | 12 | | |
| Yarmouth | 96 | 23 | Linnell | Moses | | | 1 | | | | | | 2 | 1 | | | 5 | | |
| Yarmouth | 96 | 24 | Linnell | John | 2 | | 1 | | | | | | 1 | | | | 5 | | |
| Yarmouth | 96 | 25 | Marchant | Desire | | | 1 | | | | | 2 | 1 | 1 | | | 5 | | |

# 1800 Yarmouth, Barnstable County, Massachusetts

| TOWN | PG# | LN# | LAST NAME | FIRST NAME | FREE WHITE MALES under 10 | 10 to 16 | 16 to 26 | 26 to 45 | 45 and over | FREE WHITE FEMALES under 10 | 10 to 16 | 16 to 26 | 26 to 45 | 45 and over | TOTAL ALL OTHER | SLAVES | TOTALS | DISTRICT/ TOWNSHIP | NOTES |
|---|---|---|---|---|---|---|---|---|---|---|---|---|---|---|---|---|---|---|---|
| Yarmouth | 96 | 26 | Mathews | Ezekiel | 4 | | | 1 | | 1 | | 1 | 1 | | 1 | | 9 | | |
| Yarmouth | 96 | 27 | Mathews | Mercy Jr | 2 | | | | | | | 1 | | | | | 3 | | |
| Yarmouth | 96 | 28 | Bray | David | | | 1 | | 1 | | 1 | | | 1 | | | 4 | | |
| Yarmouth | 96 | 29 | Mathews | David | | | | | 1 | | | | 2 | 1 | | | 4 | | |
| Yarmouth | 96 | 30 | Hamblin | Seth | 1 | | | 1 | | | | | 1 | | | | 3 | | |
| Yarmouth | 96 | 31 | Hall | Isaac Jr | 1 | | | 1 | | 1 | | | 1 | | | | 4 | | |
| Yarmouth | 96 | 32 | Anderson | John | 2 | | | 1 | | 1 | 1 | | 1 | | | | 6 | | |
| Yarmouth | 96 | 33 | Mathews | Mercy | | | | | | 2 | 1 | | 1 | | | | 4 | | |
| Yarmouth | 96 | 34 | Taylor | Richard | | 2 | | 1 | | | | 2 | 1 | | | | 6 | | |
| Yarmouth | 96 | 35 | Hedge | Dinah | 1 | 1 | 1 | | | 2 | 1 | | 1 | | | | 7 | | |
| Yarmouth | 96 | 36 | Hedge | Josiah Jr | | 1 | | | | 1 | | 1 | | | | | 3 | | |
| Yarmouth | 96 | 37 | Doane | Elisha | 1 | 1 | | 1 | | 1 | 1 | | 1 | 1 | | | 7 | | |
| Yarmouth | 96 | 38 | Alden | Rev Tima | | | 2 | 1 | | | | 2 | | | | | 5 | | |
| Yarmouth | 96 | 39 | Thacher | Josiah | | 1 | | 1 | | 1 | | | 1 | 1 | | | 5 | | |
| Yarmouth | 96 | 40 | Taylor | William Jr | 2 | 2 | | 1 | | 2 | | | 1 | | | | 8 | | |
| Yarmouth | 96 | 41 | Gorham | Abigail | | 1 | | | | | | | 1 | 1 | | | 2 | | |
| Yarmouth | 96 | 42 | Thacher | James | | | 1 | | | 3 | | | 1 | | | | 5 | | |
| Yarmouth | 96 | 43 | Thacher | Susanna | | 1 | | | | | | | | 1 | | | | | |
| Yarmouth | 96 | 44 | Miller | Elisha | 4 | | | 1 | | | 1 | | 1 | | | | 7 | | |
| Yarmouth | 96 | 45 | Hallet | John | 2 | 1 | 1 | 1 | | 2 | 1 | | 2 | | | | 10 | | |
| Yarmouth | 96 | 46 | Rider | Reuben | 3 | | | 1 | | 1 | 1 | | 1 | | | | 7 | | |
| Yarmouth | 96 | 47 | Rider | John | 1 | | | 1 | 1 | | | | 1 | 1 | | | 5 | | |
| Yarmouth | 96 | 48 | Rider | Thankful | | | | | | 1 | | | 1 | | | | 2 | | |
| Yarmouth | 96 | 49 | Howes | Edward | | | | | 2 | | | | | 1 | | | 3 | | |
| Yarmouth | 97 | 1 | Gorham | Hezekiah | | | 1 | | | | | 1 | | | | | 2 | | |
| Yarmouth | 97 | 2 | Thacher | Susanna Jr | 2 | 1 | | | | 1 | | | 1 | | | | 5 | | |
| Yarmouth | 97 | 3 | Thacher | Joseph | 3 | 1 | | 1 | | 1 | | | 1 | | 2 | | 9 | | |
| Yarmouth | 97 | 4 | Hallet | Enoch | 3 | 1 | | 1 | | 2 | 1 | | | 1 | 8 | | 17 | | |
| Yarmouth | 97 | 5 | Taylor | Daniel | | | | 1 | 1 | | | | | 1 | 6 | | 9 | | |
| Yarmouth | 97 | 6 | Taylor | Daniel Jr | 1 | | | 1 | | 3 | | | 1 | | 1 | | 7 | | |
| Yarmouth | 97 | 7 | Thacher | John | 2 | | | 1 | | 2 | | | 1 | | | | 6 | | |
| Yarmouth | 97 | 8 | Killey | Silvanus | 2 | | | 1 | | | | | 1 | | | | 4 | | |
| Yarmouth | 97 | 9 | Thacher | Hannah | | 2 | 2 | | | | 1 | 1 | 1 | | | | 7 | | |
| Yarmouth | 97 | 10 | Thacher | William | | 3 | | 1 | | | 1 | | 1 | | | | 6 | | |
| Yarmouth | 97 | 11 | Killey | Benja | 1 | | | 1 | | 2 | | | | | | | 4 | | |
| Yarmouth | 97 | 12 | Thacher | Laban | 3 | | 2 | 1 | | | | 1 | 1 | | | | 8 | | |
| Yarmouth | 97 | 13 | Thacher | David | | | | 1 | | | | | | 2 | | | 3 | | |
| Yarmouth | 97 | 14 | Thacher | David Jr | 4 | 1 | | 1 | | 1 | 1 | | | 1 | | | 9 | | |
| Yarmouth | 97 | 15 | Hawes | Simeon | | 2 | 2 | | | | | 2 | 1 | | | | 7 | | |
| Yarmouth | 97 | 16 | Hawes | Benja | 1 | | 1 | | | | | 1 | | | | | 3 | | |
| Yarmouth | 97 | 17 | Thacher | Thomas | 2 | | | 1 | | 2 | 1 | | 1 | 1 | | | 8 | | |
| Yarmouth | 97 | 18 | Thacher | Peter | | | 2 | 1 | | | | | 1 | | | | 4 | | |
| Yarmouth | 97 | 19 | Sears | Ebenezer | 2 | 1 | | 1 | | 2 | | | 1 | | | | 7 | | |
| Yarmouth | 97 | 20 | Hawes | David | 1 | 4 | | 1 | | | | | 1 | 1 | | | 8 | | |
| Yarmouth | 97 | 21 | Hawes | Ebenezer | | | 1 | | 1 | | | 3 | | 2 | | | 7 | | |
| Yarmouth | 97 | 22 | Hawes | Ebenezer Jr | | | 1 | | | | | | 1 | | | | 2 | | |
| Yarmouth | 97 | 23 | Thacher | Barnabas | 3 | | 1 | 1 | | | | 1 | | | | | 7 | | |
| Yarmouth | 97 | 24 | Taylor | Joshua | 1 | 1 | 1 | 1 | | | | 1 | 1 | | | | 6 | | |
| Yarmouth | 97 | 25 | Custis | John | 1 | | 1 | 1 | | 2 | | 1 | 2 | 1 | | | 9 | | |
| Yarmouth | 97 | 26 | Howes | Ebenz | 1 | 1 | 1 | | 1 | | 1 | 1 | 1 | 1 | | | 8 | | |
| Yarmouth | 97 | 27 | Hallet | Sarah | | | 1 | | | | 1 | 1 | | 1 | | | 4 | | |
| Yarmouth | 97 | 28 | Hallet | Ebenezer Jr | 1 | 2 | 2 | | 2 | 1 | 2 | 1 | | 1 | | | 12 | | |
| Yarmouth | 97 | 29 | Crowell | Edmund Jr | | | | 1 | | | | | 1 | | | | 2 | | |
| Yarmouth | 97 | 30 | Howes | Zenas | | | 1 | | | | | | 1 | | | | 2 | | |
| Yarmouth | 97 | 31 | Hallet | Stephen | | | | | 1 | | | | | 3 | | | 4 | | |
| Yarmouth | 97 | 32 | Hallet | Ruth | | 1 | 1 | | | | | | | 1 | | | 3 | | |
| Yarmouth | 97 | 33 | Hallet | Stephen Jr | | | 1 | | | | | | 1 | | | | 2 | | |
| Yarmouth | 97 | 34 | Hallet | Charles | 2 | 1 | 1 | | 1 | | 1 | 1 | 1 | | | | 8 | | |
| Yarmouth | 97 | 35 | Hawes | Joseph | | | 1 | | | 1 | | | 1 | | | | 4 | | |
| Yarmouth | 97 | 36 | Hallet | Nathan | 1 | | | 1 | | 3 | | | 1 | 1 | | | 7 | | |
| Yarmouth | 97 | 37 | Bassett | Joshua | 2 | | | 1 | 1 | | | | 1 | | | | 5 | | |
| Yarmouth | 97 | 38 | Taylor | Ebenezer | 1 | | | 1 | | | | | 1 | | | | 3 | | |
| Yarmouth | 97 | 39 | Hallet | Andrew | | | 1 | | | 1 | | 1 | | | | | 3 | | |
| Yarmouth | 97 | 40 | Gorham | Isaac | | | 1 | | | | | | 1 | | | | 2 | | |
| Yarmouth | 97 | 41 | Bassett | John | | | | | 1 | 1 | | | 1 | | | | 3 | | |
| Yarmouth | 97 | 42 | Crowell | Prince | 2 | | | 1 | | 1 | | | 1 | | | | 5 | | |
| Yarmouth | 97 | 43 | Hallet | Abigail | | 1 | | | | | | 1 | | 1 | | | 3 | | |
| Yarmouth | 97 | 44 | Hallet | Prince | | | 1 | | | | | | | 1 | | | 2 | | |
| Yarmouth | 97 | 45 | Hallet | Ezra | 1 | | 1 | | | 1 | | | 1 | | | | 4 | | |
| Yarmouth | 97 | 46 | Eldredge | John | 1 | | 1 | | | | | 2 | | | | | 4 | | |
| Yarmouth | 97 | 47 | Howes | Prince | 1 | | 1 | | | 3 | | | 1 | | | | 6 | | |
| Yarmouth | 97 | 48 | Hallet | William | | 1 | | | | | | 1 | | | | | 2 | | |
| Yarmouth | 97 | 49 | Gray | Mary | | 1 | | | | 1 | 1 | 2 | 1 | | 1 | | 7 | | |
| Yarmouth | 97 | 50 | Gray | Joshua | | 1 | | | | | | | 1 | | | | 2 | | |
| Yarmouth | 98 | 1 | Hallet | Jonathan | | | | | 1 | | 1 | | 1 | 1 | | | 4 | | |
| Yarmouth | 98 | 2 | Hallet | Zenas | 2 | | | 1 | | | | | 1 | | | | 4 | | |
| Yarmouth | 98 | 3 | Hallet | Jonathan Jr | | 2 | | 1 | | 1 | | | 1 | 1 | | | 6 | | |
| Yarmouth | 98 | 4 | Hallet | Jeremiah | | | 1 | 1 | 1 | | | | 1 | 1 | | | 6 | | |
| Yarmouth | 98 | 5 | Hallet | Thomas | 1 | | | 1 | | | 1 | | 3 | 1 | | | 7 | | |

# 1800 Yarmouth, Barnstable County, Massachusetts

| TOWN | PG# | LN# | LAST NAME | FIRST NAME | FREE WHITE MALES under 10 | 10 to 16 | 16 to 26 | 26 to 45 | 45 and over | FREE WHITE FEMALES under 10 | 10 to 16 | 16 to 26 | 26 to 45 | 45 and over | TOTAL ALL OTHER | SLAVES | TOTALS | DISTRICT/ TOWNSHIP | NOTES |
|---|---|---|---|---|---|---|---|---|---|---|---|---|---|---|---|---|---|---|---|
| Yarmouth | 98 | 6 | Hallet | Moses | | | | | 1 | | | | 2 | 1 | | | 4 | | |
| Yarmouth | 98 | 7 | Hallet | James | 1 | | 1 | | 1 | 2 | | 2 | 1 | 1 | | | 9 | | |
| Yarmouth | 98 | 8 | Hallet | Benjamin | | | | 1 | | 1 | 1 | | 1 | | | | 4 | | |
| Yarmouth | 98 | 9 | Hallet | Isaac | | 1 | 1 | | 1 | | | 1 | | 1 | | | 5 | | |
| Yarmouth | 98 | 10 | Hallet | John Jr | | | 1 | | | | | | 1 | | | | 2 | | |
| Yarmouth | 98 | 11 | Hallet | Joshua | | | 1 | | 1 | | | | 3 | 1 | | | 6 | | |
| Yarmouth | 98 | 12 | Gray | Samuel | | 1 | 2 | 1 | 1 | 1 | | 1 | 2 | 1 | | | 10 | | |
| Yarmouth | 98 | 13 | Eldredge | Hannah | 3 | 1 | | | | | 1 | 2 | | 2 | | | 9 | | |
| Yarmouth | 98 | 14 | White | Joseph | | 1 | | | 1 | | | | 1 | 1 | | | 4 | | |
| Yarmouth | 98 | 15 | White | Joseph Jr | 3 | | | 1 | | | | | 1 | | | | 5 | | |
| Yarmouth | 98 | 16 | White | Isaac | | 1 | | | 1 | | | | 1 | | | | 3 | | |
| Yarmouth | 98 | 17 | Mathews | Phebe Jr | 1 | 1 | | | | 1 | 1 | 1 | | 1 | | | 6 | | |
| Yarmouth | 98 | 18 | White | Daniel | | 1 | | 1 | | 1 | | | | 1 | | | 4 | | |
| Yarmouth | 98 | 19 | Rogers | Solomon | 1 | 1 | | | | | | | 1 | | | | 3 | | |
| Yarmouth | 98 | 20 | Eldredge | Patience | | 1 | | | | | | | | 1 | | | 2 | | |
| Yarmouth | 98 | 21 | Eldredge | Reuben | 2 | | | 1 | | | | | 1 | | | | 4 | | |
| Yarmouth | 98 | 22 | Sears | Eliza | | | | | | | | 1 | 1 | 1 | | | 3 | | |
| Yarmouth | 98 | 23 | Sears | Enoch | | 1 | | | | | | | 1 | | | | 2 | | |
| Yarmouth | 98 | 24 | Sears | Prince | 1 | | | 1 | | | 1 | | 1 | | | | 4 | | |
| Yarmouth | 98 | 25 | Sears | Eleazer Jr | | 1 | 2 | 1 | | 1 | 1 | | 1 | 2 | | | 9 | | |
| Yarmouth | 98 | 26 | Sears | Joseph | 1 | | 1 | | | 1 | | 1 | | | | | 4 | | |
| Yarmouth | 98 | 27 | Sears | James | 1 | | | 1 | | 1 | | | 1 | | | | 4 | | |
| Yarmouth | 98 | 28 | Eldredge | David | | | 2 | | 1 | 3 | 2 | 2 | 1 | | | | 11 | | |
| Yarmouth | 98 | 29 | Black | Alexr | 2 | | | 1 | | 1 | | | 1 | | | | 5 | | |
| Yarmouth | 98 | 30 | Sears | Lewis | 2 | | | 1 | | 1 | | | 1 | | | | 5 | | |
| Yarmouth | 98 | 31 | Sears | Edward | 1 | | 1 | | | | | | 1 | | | | 3 | | |
| Yarmouth | 98 | 32 | Crowell | Joseph | 4 | 1 | | 1 | | 1 | | | 1 | | | | 8 | | |
| Yarmouth | 98 | 33 | Sears | Eleazer | | | | 1 | | 1 | | | | 1 | | | 3 | | |
| Yarmouth | 98 | 34 | Crosby | David | | | | 1 | | | | | 1 | | | | 2 | | |
| Yarmouth | 98 | 35 | Baker | Abraham | | 2 | 2 | 2 | 1 | 1 | 1 | | | 1 | | | 10 | | |
| Yarmouth | 98 | 36 | Baker | Cornelius | | 1 | | | | | | 1 | | | | | 2 | | |
| Yarmouth | 98 | 37 | Baker | Benoni | 1 | | | 1 | | | | | 1 | | | | 3 | | |
| Yarmouth | 98 | 38 | Baker | Levi | | | | 1 | | 1 | | | 3 | 1 | | | 6 | | |
| Yarmouth | 98 | 39 | Studley | Silvanus | 1 | 1 | 1 | | 1 | | | 1 | | | | | 5 | | |
| Yarmouth | 98 | 40 | Crowell | Abigail | 2 | | | 2 | 1 | | 1 | | | | | | 6 | | |
| Yarmouth | 98 | 41 | Marchent | Silvanus | 2 | | | 1 | | 1 | | 1 | | | | | 5 | | |
| Yarmouth | 98 | 42 | Baker | Elisha Jr | | | 1 | | | 2 | | 1 | | | | | 4 | | |
| Yarmouth | 98 | 43 | Baker | Moody | | 1 | 2 | 1 | | | 1 | 2 | 1 | | | | 8 | | |
| Yarmouth | 98 | 44 | Baker | Daniel Jr | 2 | | | 1 | | 1 | | | 1 | | | | 5 | | |
| Yarmouth | 98 | 45 | Baker | Daniel | | | 2 | | 1 | | | | | 1 | | | 4 | | |
| Yarmouth | 98 | 46 | Killey | Zeno | | 1 | 1 | 1 | | 1 | 1 | 1 | | | | | 6 | | |
| Yarmouth | 98 | 47 | Akins | Abiel | 2 | 1 | | | 1 | | | 1 | | | | | 6 | | |
| Yarmouth | 98 | 48 | Laha | John | 1 | | | 1 | | 2 | | | 1 | | | | 5 | | |
| Yarmouth | 98 | 49 | Killey | Meribah | 2 | | 1 | | | | | 1 | 1 | | | | 5 | | |
| Yarmouth | 98 | 50 | Farris | Samuel | 2 | 2 | 1 | | 1 | | | 1 | | 1 | | | 8 | | |
| Yarmouth | 98 | 51 | Farris | Thomas | 1 | | | 1 | | 1 | | | 1 | 1 | | | 5 | | |
| Yarmouth | 99 | 1 | Tripp | Benja | 1 | | | 1 | 1 | | | | 1 | | | | 5 | | |
| Yarmouth | 99 | 2 | Baker | Bethuel | 4 | 1 | | | | | | | 1 | | | | 7 | | |
| Yarmouth | 99 | 3 | Hopkins | Perez | 2 | | | 1 | | | 1 | | | | | | 4 | | |
| Yarmouth | 99 | 4 | Bassett | Nathan Jr | | | | 1 | | | 2 | | | | 5 | | 8 | | |
| Yarmouth | 99 | 5 | Crowell | Thomas | | 1 | | | 1 | 2 | 2 | | 1 | 1 | | | 8 | | |
| Yarmouth | 99 | 6 | Farris | Jeremiah | 1 | | | 1 | | 1 | | | 1 | | | | 4 | | |
| Yarmouth | 99 | 7 | Hedge | Abram | 1 | 1 | 1 | | | 1 | | 1 | | | | | 5 | | |
| Yarmouth | 99 | 8 | Crowell | Michael | 3 | 1 | | | 1 | 3 | | 1 | 1 | | | | 10 | | |
| Yarmouth | 99 | 9 | Crowell | Samuel | 2 | | | 1 | | 2 | | | 2 | | | | 7 | | |
| Yarmouth | 99 | 10 | Baker | Amos | 1 | 1 | | 1 | | 1 | | | 1 | | | | 5 | | |
| Yarmouth | 99 | 11 | Crocker | Isaiah | 2 | 1 | | 1 | | 1 | | | 1 | | | | 6 | | |
| Yarmouth | 99 | 12 | Killey | John | | | | 1 | | | | | 2 | | | | 3 | | |
| Yarmouth | 99 | 13 | Berry | James | | | | 1 | | | 1 | 2 | 1 | | | | 5 | | |
| Yarmouth | 99 | 14 | Baker | Elisha | 3 | 1 | 2 | | 1 | 2 | | 1 | 1 | | | | 11 | | |
| Yarmouth | 99 | 15 | Crowell | Mathew | | | | 1 | | | 1 | | | 2 | | | 4 | | |
| Yarmouth | 99 | 16 | Crowell | Lot | 2 | | | 1 | 1 | | | | 1 | | | | 5 | | |
| Yarmouth | 99 | 17 | Berry | Isaac | 2 | 1 | 1 | | | | | 2 | | 1 | | | 9 | | |
| Yarmouth | 99 | 18 | Shearman | Ichabod | | | 1 | | | | 1 | | | | | | 2 | | |
| Yarmouth | 99 | 19 | Whelden | Elisha | | 3 | 3 | 1 | | | | 2 | | 1 | | | 10 | | |
| Yarmouth | 99 | 20 | Hudson | James | | 1 | | 1 | | | | | 1 | | | | 3 | | |
| Yarmouth | 99 | 21 | Bunker | Benja | 2 | | | 1 | | | 1 | | 1 | 1 | | | 6 | | |
| Yarmouth | 99 | 22 | Baker | Obadiah | 3 | | | 1 | | | 2 | | 1 | | | | 7 | | |
| Yarmouth | 99 | 23 | Baker | Jonathan | 1 | | | 1 | | 1 | | 1 | 1 | | | | 5 | | |
| Yarmouth | 99 | 24 | Killey | Oliver | | | 2 | 1 | | | 1 | | 1 | | | | 5 | | |
| Yarmouth | 99 | 25 | Baker | Silas | | | 3 | 1 | | | 1 | | 1 | 1 | | | 6 | | |
| Yarmouth | 99 | 26 | Baker | Silas Jr | 2 | | | 1 | | 2 | 1 | | 1 | 1 | | | 8 | | |
| Yarmouth | 99 | 27 | Baker | Lemuel Jr | 2 | 1 | 1 | 3 | | | | | 1 | | | | 8 | | |
| Yarmouth | 99 | 28 | Baker | Philip | 1 | | | 1 | | 2 | | 1 | 1 | | | | 6 | | |
| Yarmouth | 99 | 29 | Baker | Marchent | 1 | | | 1 | | 2 | | 1 | 1 | | | | 6 | | |
| Yarmouth | 99 | 30 | Berry | Jeremiah | 1 | | 2 | | 1 | 2 | | 2 | | 1 | | | 9 | | |
| Yarmouth | 99 | 31 | Baker | Prince | 1 | | | 1 | | 2 | | | 1 | | | | 5 | | |
| Yarmouth | 99 | 32 | York | Nathan | | | | 1 | | 2 | | | 1 | | | | 4 | | |
| Yarmouth | 99 | 33 | Parsons | William | 1 | | | 1 | | | 3 | | 1 | | | | 7 | | |

# 1800 Yarmouth, Barnstable County, Massachusetts

| TOWN | PG# | LN# | LAST NAME | FIRST NAME | FREE WHITE MALES | | | | | FREE WHITE FEMALES | | | | | TOTAL ALL OTHER | SLAVES | TOTALS | DISTRICT/ TOWNSHIP | NOTES |
|---|---|---|---|---|---|---|---|---|---|---|---|---|---|---|---|---|---|---|---|
| | | | | | under 10 | 10 to 16 | 16 to 26 | 26 to 45 | 45 and over | under 10 | 10 to 16 | 16 to 26 | 26 to 45 | 45 and over | | | | | |
| Yarmouth | 99 | 34 | Marchent | Anne | 1 | | 1 | | | 1 | | 1 | | 1 | | | 5 | | |
| Yarmouth | 99 | 35 | Marchent | Gorham | | | 1 | | | | | 1 | | | | | 2 | | |
| Yarmouth | 99 | 36 | Marchent | Josiah | 1 | | | 1 | | | | 1 | | | | | 3 | | |
| Yarmouth | 99 | 37 | Marchent | E* | | | 3 | | 1 | 2 | 1 | | 1 | | | | 8 | | |
| Yarmouth | 99 | 38 | Baker | Lemuel | 1 | | | | 1 | 3 | | 2 | 1 | | | | 8 | | |
| Yarmouth | 99 | 39 | Baker | Edward | | | 1 | | | 1 | | 1 | | | | | 3 | | |
| Yarmouth | 99 | 40 | Bray | Edmund Jr | 3 | | | 1 | | 1 | | | 1 | | | | 6 | | |
| Yarmouth | 99 | 41 | Crowell | John Jr | 1 | 1 | | 1 | | 4 | | | 1 | | | | 8 | | |
| Yarmouth | 99 | 42 | Jerauld | Dutee | 3 | | | | 1 | | 1 | | 1 | | | | 6 | | |
| Yarmouth | 99 | 43 | Baxter | David Jr | 2 | 2 | | 1 | | 2 | | | 1 | | | | 8 | | |
| Yarmouth | 99 | 44 | Baker | Elisha | 1 | 1 | | 1 | | 2 | | | 1 | | | | 6 | | |
| Yarmouth | 99 | 45 | Gray | Richard | | 1 | | 1 | | 3 | | | 1 | | | | 6 | | |
| Yarmouth | 99 | 46 | Berry | Howes | 2 | | | 1 | | 1 | | | | | | | 4 | | |
| Yarmouth | 99 | 47 | Crowell | Eleazer | 3 | 1 | | 1 | | 1 | 1 | | 1 | | | | 8 | | |
| Yarmouth | 99 | 48 | Crowell | Silvanus | | | 1 | | | | | | | | | | 1 | | |
| Yarmouth | 99 | 49 | Ellin | James | 1 | | | 1 | | 1 | | 1 | | | | | 4 | | |
| Yarmouth | 99 | 50 | Crowell | Isaiah | 2 | | | 1 | | 1 | | | 1 | | | | 5 | | |
| Yarmouth | 99 | 51 | Baker | Jacob | | | 1 | | 1 | | | 1 | | | | | 3 | | |
| Yarmouth | 100 | 1 | Taylor | Abner | | | 1 | | 1 | | | 1 | 1 | | | | 4 | | |
| Yarmouth | 100 | 2 | Parker | Jacob | | 1 | 1 | | 1 | 1 | 1 | 1 | 1 | | | | 7 | | |
| Yarmouth | 100 | 3 | Sears | Winthrop | | | 1 | | | | | 1 | | | | | 2 | | |
| Yarmouth | 100 | 4 | Parker | Jacob Jr | | | 1 | | | | | 1 | | | | | 2 | | |
| Yarmouth | 100 | 5 | Parker | Isaiah | | | | 1 | | | | 1 | | | | | 2 | | |
| Yarmouth | 100 | 6 | Parker | Benjamin | 1 | | 1 | | | 1 | | 1 | | | | | 4 | | |
| Yarmouth | 100 | 7 | Gorham | Lydia | | | | | | | | | 2 | | | | 2 | | |
| Yarmouth | 100 | 8 | Gorham | John | | 1 | | | 1 | 1 | | | 1 | | | | 4 | | |
| Yarmouth | 100 | 9 | Crowell | Shubail | 1 | 2 | 4 | | 1 | 2 | | | 1 | | 1 | | 12 | | |
| Yarmouth | 100 | 10 | Walls | James | | 1 | | 1 | | 2 | 1 | | 1 | | | | 6 | | |
| Yarmouth | 100 | 11 | Burges | Timo | 1 | | 1 | | 1 | 3 | 3 | 1 | | 1 | | | 11 | | |
| Yarmouth | 100 | 12 | Killey | Martha | | | | | | | | | 2 | | | | 2 | | |
| Yarmouth | 100 | 13 | Crowell | Robert | | 1 | 1 | | 1 | | 1 | | 1 | | | | 5 | | |
| Yarmouth | 100 | 14 | Howes | Andrew | | | | 1 | | 1 | | | 1 | | | | 3 | | |
| Yarmouth | 100 | 15 | Crowell | Jeremiah | | 1 | 2 | | 1 | 1 | 1 | | 1 | | | | 7 | | |
| Yarmouth | 100 | 16 | Crowell | Elkanah | 1 | 1 | | | 1 | 4 | 1 | 1 | 1 | | | | 10 | | |
| Yarmouth | 100 | 17 | Crowell | Solomon | 2 | 1 | 1 | 1 | | 1 | 1 | | 1 | | | | 8 | | |
| Yarmouth | 100 | 18 | Crowell | John | 1 | | | 1 | 1 | | | | 1 | | | | 4 | | |
| Yarmouth | 100 | 19 | Crowell | Nehemiah | 2 | | | 1 | | 1 | | | 1 | | | | 5 | | |
| Yarmouth | 100 | 20 | Blish | Owen | 2 | | | 1 | | 1 | | 1 | | | | | 5 | | |
| Yarmouth | 100 | 21 | Howes | Jabez | 1 | | | 1 | | 3 | | | 1 | | | | 6 | | |
| Yarmouth | 100 | 22 | Lewis | Jabez | 1 | 1 | | | 1 | | 1 | 1 | | 1 | | | 6 | | |
| Yarmouth | 100 | 23 | Lewis | Benjamin | 1 | 1 | | 1 | | 2 | | 1 | 1 | | | | 7 | | |
| Yarmouth | 100 | 24 | Lewis | Jabez Jr | | | 1 | | | | | 1 | | | | | 2 | | |

| TOWN | PG# | LN# | LAST NAME | FIRST NAME | M <10 | M 10-16 | M 16-26 | M 26-45 | M 45+ | F <10 | F 10-16 | F 16-26 | F 26-45 | F 45+ | TOTAL ALL OTHER | TOTAL SLAVES | TOTALS | DISTRICT/ TOWNSHIP | NOTES |
|---|---|---|---|---|---|---|---|---|---|---|---|---|---|---|---|---|---|---|---|
| Mashpee | 51 | 18 | *ulcan | | | | | | | | | | | | 1 | | 1 | | First name left blank on census |
| Chatham | 19 | 24 | Abelthough | William | | | | 1 | | 2 | | | 1 | | | | 4 | | |
| Barnstable | 88 | 19 | Adams | Ansel | 5 | 3 | | 1 | | | | | 1 | 1 | | | 11 | | |
| Barnstable | 88 | 21 | Adams | Benjamin | 2 | | | 1 | | | | | 1 | | | | 4 | | |
| Barnstable | 88 | 36 | Adams | Edward | | | | 1 | | | | | 1 | 1 | | | 3 | | |
| Wellfleet | 75 | 1 | Adams | Ephraim | 1 | | | 1 | | 3 | 1 | | 1 | | | | 7 | | |
| Mashpee | 51 | 8 | Adams | Nathl | | | 3 | | 1 | | 1 | 1 | | 1 | | | 7 | | |
| Sandwich | 38 | 12 | Adams | Nathl | | | | | | | | | | | | | | | Enumeration left blank |
| Barnstable | 92 | 16 | Adams | Obed | | 1 | | 1 | | | 1 | | | 1 | | | 4 | | |
| Sandwich | 37 | 48 | Adams | Thomas | | 1 | | 1 | | | 1 | 1 | | | | | 4 | | |
| Provincetown | 57 | 4 | Adisen | Condition | | 1 | | | | 2 | 1 | | | | | | 4 | | |
| Provincetown | 60 | 29 | Aires | Joseph | 1 | | 1 | | | 2 | | | 1 | 1 | | | 6 | | |
| Yarmouth | 98 | 47 | Akins | Abiel | 2 | 1 | 1 | | | 1 | 1 | | | | | | 6 | | |
| Yarmouth | 96 | 38 | Alden | Rev Tima | | | 2 | 1 | | | 2 | | | | | | 5 | | |
| Barnstable | 91 | 35 | Allen | Andrew | | | | 1 | | | | | 1 | | | | 2 | | |
| Barnstable | 91 | 36 | Allen | David | 1 | | 1 | | | 1 | | 1 | | | | | 4 | | |
| Falmouth | 43 | 2 | Allen | David | | 1 | 1 | | 1 | | | 1 | | 1 | | | 5 | | |
| Harwich | 13 | 7 | Allen | Elisha | | | 1 | | 1 | | 1 | | | | | | 3 | | |
| Sandwich | 36 | 30 | Allen | George | | 1 | | 1 | | | 1 | 1 | | | | | 4 | | |
| Sandwich | 34 | 23 | Allen | Gideon | | | | 1 | | | | | | | | | 1 | | |
| Harwich | 12 | 35 | Allen | John | | | | 1 | | 1 | 1 | | | | | | 3 | | |
| Harwich | 14 | 45 | Allen | John Jun | 1 | 2 | | 1 | | 3 | 2 | | 1 | | | | 10 | | |
| Sandwich | 37 | 47 | Allen | Joseph | | | | 1 | | | | | | | | | 1 | | |
| Falmouth | 43 | 1 | Allen | Nathaniel | 2 | 1 | | 1 | | 1 | 1 | | | 1 | | | 7 | | |
| Harwich | 12 | 23 | Allen | Nathaniel | 2 | | | 1 | | 1 | | 1 | | | | | 5 | | |
| Barnstable | 91 | 37 | Allen | Nathl | | | 1 | | | | | | 1 | | | | 2 | | |
| Harwich | 13 | 8 | Allen | Pain | | | 1 | | 3 | | | | 1 | | | | 5 | | |
| Sandwich | 35 | 42 | Allen | Samuel | | 1 | | 1 | 1 | | 1 | 1 | | 1 | | | 6 | | |
| Harwich | 9 | 34 | Allen | Seth | 1 | | 2 | 1 | | 4 | | 1 | | | | | 9 | | |
| Harwich | 13 | 18 | Allen | Tamsin Wd | 1 | 1 | | | | 3 | | 1 | 1 | | | | 7 | | |
| Harwich | 12 | 36 | Allen | William | | 2 | 1 | 1 | | | | | 1 | | | | 5 | | |
| Sandwich | 36 | 34 | Allen | William | 1 | 1 | 3 | | 1 | 2 | 2 | | | 1 | | | 11 | | |
| Harwich | 12 | 37 | Allen | William Jun | 1 | 1 | | | | | | 1 | | | | | 3 | | |
| Barnstable | 86 | 30 | Allyn | Benjamin | 1 | | 1 | | 1 | 1 | 2 | | 1 | | | | 7 | | |
| Barnstable | 86 | 36 | Allyn | James | 1 | | | 1 | | 2 | 2 | 2 | | 1 | | | 9 | | |
| Barnstable | 86 | 31 | Allyn | Lydia | | | | | | | | | 2 | | | | 2 | | |
| Barnstable | 86 | 33 | Allyn | Samuel | | | 1 | | | 1 | | 1 | 1 | | | | 4 | | |
| Barnstable | 86 | 32 | Allyn | Thomas | | 1 | | 1 | | 2 | | | 1 | | | | 5 | | |
| Barnstable | 85 | 22 | Alten | Thomas | | 1 | | | | | | | | | | | 1 | | |
| Harwich | 12 | 22 | Ames | Ame*ous | | 1 | | | | 1 | | 1 | | | | | 3 | | |
| Barnstable | 91 | 5 | Ames | Enos | 2 | 2 | 1 | 1 | | 3 | | | | | | | 10 | | |
| Barnstable | 94 | 24 | Ames | Thomas | | 1 | 2 | | 1 | 1 | 1 | | 1 | | | | 8 | | |
| Yarmouth | 96 | 32 | Anderson | John | 2 | | | 1 | 1 | 1 | | 1 | | | | | 6 | | |
| Eastham | 76 | 5 | Anderson | William | 3 | 1 | 2 | | 1 | | 1 | 1 | | 1 | | | 10 | | |
| Eastham | 79 | 5 | Anderson | William Junr | | | 2 | 1 | | | | | 1 | | | | 4 | | |
| Barnstable | 86 | 23 | Annable | Joseph | 2 | 1 | | 1 | | | | 1 | 3 | 1 | | | 9 | | |
| Barnstable | 86 | 25 | Annable | Samuel | 1 | 1 | | | | 1 | | | 1 | | | | 4 | | |
| Orleans | 24 | 3 | Any | Oliver | 1 | | | 1 | | | 1 | 1 | 1 | | | | 5 | | |
| Orleans | 24 | 4 | Any | Thomas | | 2 | 1 | 1 | | 3 | 1 | 1 | | 1 | | | 10 | | |
| Wellfleet | 69 | 1 | Arcy | Reuben | 2 | 2 | | 1 | | 1 | 1 | | 1 | | | | 11 | | |
| Sandwich | 40 | 30 | Arey | Job | 1 | | 1 | | | 1 | | 1 | | | | | 4 | | |
| Sandwich | 41 | 29 | Arey | Joshua | 5 | | | 1 | | | 1 | 1 | | | | | 8 | | |
| Sandwich | 41 | 30 | Arey | Thankful | | | | | | | | | 1 | | | | 1 | | |
| Sandwich | 41 | 31 | Arey | Thos | 2 | | 1 | | | | | | 1 | | | | 4 | | |
| Dennis | 26 | 44 | Aspendelow | Amanuel | 1 | | 1 | | | | | | 1 | | | | 3 | | |
| Barnstable | 92 | 40 | Atkins | Asa | 4 | | | 1 | | 1 | 1 | | 1 | | | | 8 | | |
| Provincetown | 57 | 1 | Atkins | Benjamin | | 1 | | 1 | | 2 | | | 1 | | | | 5 | | |
| Wellfleet | 69 | 6 | Atkins | Daniel | | | 1 | | | 1 | | 1 | | | | | 3 | | |
| Wellfleet | 75 | 16 | Atkins | David | 2 | 1 | | 1 | | 3 | 1 | | 1 | | | | 9 | | |
| Truro | 68 | 3 | Atkins | Ebenezer | 2 | | | 1 | | | 1 | | 1 | | | | 5 | | |
| Truro | 62 | 13 | Atkins | Elizabeth Wid | 1 | | | | | 1 | | 1 | 1 | | | | 4 | | |
| Sandwich | 35 | 6 | Atkins | James | | 1 | | 1 | | | 1 | | 1 | | | | 4 | | |
| Wellfleet | 74 | 6 | Atkins | James | | 1 | | 1 | | 4 | 1 | | 1 | | | | 8 | | |
| Truro | 64 | 2 | Atkins | Jonah | 2 | | | 1 | | 1 | | 1 | | | | | 5 | | |
| Orleans | 22 | 21 | Atkins | Joseph | 1 | | | 1 | | | 1 | | 1 | | | | 4 | | |
| Provincetown | 58 | 22 | Atkins | Joseph | 2 | | | 1 | | | | | 1 | | | | 4 | | |
| Chatham | 20 | 20 | Atkins | Joshua | | 1 | | | | | 1 | | | | | | 2 | | |
| Truro | 66 | 23 | Atkins | Lydia Wid | | 1 | | | | | 1 | 1 | | | | | 3 | | |
| Truro | 64 | 24 | Atkins | Paul | 3 | | 1 | | | | 1 | | | | | | 5 | | |
| Truro | 66 | 25 | Atkins | Paul | | 1 | 2 | | 1 | | 1 | | 1 | | | | 6 | | |
| Truro | 64 | 28 | Atkins | Ruth | | 1 | 1 | | | 1 | 1 | 1 | | 2 | | | 7 | | |
| Truro | 66 | 20 | Atkins | Samuel | | 1 | 5 | 1 | | 1 | | | 1 | | | | 9 | | |
| Truro | 68 | 10 | Atkins | Samuel Junr | | 1 | | | 1 | | 1 | | | | | | 3 | | |
| Truro | 65 | 6 | Atkins | Sarah | | 1 | | | | | | 2 | 1 | | | | 4 | | |
| Truro | 65 | 4 | Atkins | Sarah Junr | 1 | 1 | | | 1 | 1 | 1 | | | | | | 5 | | |
| Provincetown | 56 | 3 | Atkins | Silas | 2 | 2 | 1 | | | 3 | 1 | 1 | | | | | 10 | | |
| Truro | 66 | 22 | Atkins | Silas | | | 1 | | | 1 | | 1 | | | | | 3 | | |
| Provincetown | 61 | 17 | Atkins | Stephen | | 1 | | | | | 1 | | | 3 | | | 5 | | |
| Sandwich | 35 | 22 | Atkins | William | 1 | | 1 | | | 1 | | | | | | | 4 | | |
| Wellfleet | 69 | 4 | Atwood | Azuba | | 2 | | | | 3 | | 1 | | | | | 6 | | |
| Eastham | 76 | 4 | Atwood | Barnabas | 1 | | 1 | 1 | | 1 | 1 | | 1 | | | | 6 | | |
| Harwich | 7 | 26 | Atwood | Barnabas | | 2 | | 1 | 2 | | 1 | 1 | | | | | 7 | | |

# 1800 Barnstable County, Massachusetts Index

| Town | PG# | LN# | Last Name | First Name | M under 10 | M 10–16 | M 16–26 | M 26–45 | M 45+ | F under 10 | F 10–16 | F 16–26 | F 26–45 | F 45+ | Total All Other | Total Slaves | Totals | District/Township | Notes |
|---|---|---|---|---|---|---|---|---|---|---|---|---|---|---|---|---|---|---|---|
| Eastham | 79 | 17 | Atwood | Barnabas Junr | | 1 | | | | | | 1 | | | | | 2 | | |
| Wellfleet | 69 | 2 | Atwood | Benjamin | 1 | | 1 | | | 2 | | | 1 | | | | 5 | | |
| Harwich | 5 | 13 | Atwood | David | | 1 | | 1 | | | | 1 | 1 | 1 | | | 5 | | |
| Wellfleet | 69 | 8 | Atwood | David | 1 | 2 | 1 | 1 | | 2 | 1 | | 1 | | | | 9 | | |
| Wellfleet | 69 | 11 | Atwood | Ebenezer | 1 | 1 | | | 1 | 4 | 1 | | | 1 | | | 9 | | |
| Wellfleet | 73 | 24 | Atwood | Eleazar | | 1 | 1 | | 1 | | | 1 | | 1 | | | 5 | | |
| Wellfleet | 73 | 26 | Atwood | Elisha | 1 | | | 1 | | 2 | | | 1 | | | | 5 | | |
| Wellfleet | 69 | 3 | Atwood | Ephraim | | 1 | | 1 | | | | | 1 | | | | 3 | | |
| Wellfleet | 69 | 7 | Atwood | Experience | | | | | | | | | | 1 | | | 1 | | |
| Wellfleet | 73 | 20 | Atwood | Ezekiel | | | 1 | | | 2 | | | 1 | | | | 4 | | |
| Wellfleet | 73 | 30 | Atwood | Freeman | | | 1 | | | | | | 1 | | | | 2 | | |
| Wellfleet | 69 | 14 | Atwood | Gideon | | 1 | 1 | | | | | | 1 | | | | 3 | | |
| Wellfleet | 69 | 12 | Atwood | Hannah | | | | | | | | 2 | | 1 | | | 3 | | |
| Wellfleet | 75 | 19 | Atwood | Harding | | 1 | | | | 1 | | | 1 | | | | 3 | | |
| Provincetown | 60 | 38 | Atwood | Henry | 2 | | 1 | | | 1 | 1 | | 1 | | | | 6 | | |
| Provincetown | 56 | 2 | Atwood | Henry Junr | 2 | | 1 | | | | | | 1 | | | | 4 | | |
| Eastham | 76 | 3 | Atwood | Hezekiah | | | 1 | | | | | | 1 | | | | 2 | | |
| Truro | 63 | 13 | Atwood | Isaac | 3 | 1 | 1 | | 1 | | 1 | 1 | 1 | | | | 9 | | |
| Wellfleet | 73 | 33 | Atwood | Isaiah | | 1 | 1 | | | 3 | | | 1 | 1 | | | 7 | | |
| Eastham | 76 | 1 | Atwood | James | | | | 1 | | | | | 1 | | | | 2 | | |
| Wellfleet | 74 | 36 | Atwood | Jemima | 2 | 1 | 1 | | | | | 2 | | 1 | | | 7 | | |
| Wellfleet | 69 | 9 | Atwood | John | 2 | | 1 | | | | | | 1 | | | | 4 | | |
| Provincetown | 57 | 3 | Atwood | Jonathan | 1 | | 1 | 1 | | 1 | | | 1 | | | | 5 | | |
| Provincetown | 56 | 1 | Atwood | Joshua | 1 | 2 | | 1 | | 2 | 1 | | 1 | | | | 8 | | |
| Wellfleet | 69 | 5 | Atwood | Joshua | | 1 | | 1 | | | | | | 1 | | | 3 | | |
| Wellfleet | 74 | 29 | Atwood | Joshua Junr | | | 1 | | | | | 1 | | | | | 2 | | |
| Harwich | 7 | 8 | Atwood | Judson | | 1 | | 1 | | | 1 | 1 | 1 | 1 | | | 5 | | |
| Wellfleet | 69 | 10 | Atwood | Nathaniel | 3 | | 1 | 1 | 1 | 2 | 1 | | | 1 | | | 10 | | |
| Harwich | 5 | 14 | Atwood | Nehemiah | 1 | | | 1 | | 1 | | | 1 | | | | 4 | | |
| Eastham | 76 | 2 | Atwood | Richard | | 1 | 2 | | 1 | | | 1 | 1 | | | | 6 | | |
| Wellfleet | 74 | 11 | Atwood | Richard | 4 | | 2 | | 1 | | 1 | | 1 | | | | 9 | | |
| Provincetown | 60 | 19 | Atwood | Samuel | | 1 | 1 | | 1 | | | 1 | | 1 | | | 5 | | |
| Chatham | 15 | 3 | Atwood | Sears | 1 | 3 | 1 | 1 | | | | | 1 | 1 | 1 | | 8 | | |
| Wellfleet | 69 | 13 | Atwood | Simeon | 1 | 1 | | 1 | | 1 | 1 | | 1 | | | | 6 | | |
| Provincetown | 57 | 2 | Atwood | Stephen | | | | 1 | | | | | 1 | | | | 2 | | |
| Wellfleet | 74 | 15 | Atwood | Stephen | 1 | 1 | 3 | | 1 | | | 1 | 1 | | 4 | | 12 | | |
| Wellfleet | 74 | 17 | Atwood | Thomas | | 1 | | 1 | | 3 | 1 | | 1 | | 3 | | 10 | | |
| Wellfleet | 74 | 28 | Atwood | Timothy | | 1 | | 1 | | | | | 1 | | | | 3 | | |
| Truro | 68 | 18 | Atwood | Zoeth | 2 | | 1 | | | 2 | 1 | | 1 | | | | 7 | | |
| Truro | 66 | 24 | Avery | Job | 2 | 2 | | 1 | | 1 | 1 | 1 | | 1 | | | 9 | | |
| Truro | 66 | 21 | Avery | John | 1 | 1 | | 1 | | | | 2 | 2 | 1 | | | 8 | | |
| Truro | 68 | 1 | Avery | John Junr | | | 1 | | | | | | 1 | | | | 2 | | |
| Barnstable | 89 | 15 | Backus | Clark | 2 | 1 | 1 | 2 | 1 | | | | 1 | 1 | | | 9 | | |
| Barnstable | 89 | 14 | Backus | Simeon | 1 | | 1 | | | | | | 1 | | | | 3 | | |
| Barnstable | 89 | 13 | Backus | Thomas | | 1 | 5 | | 1 | | 1 | 1 | 1 | 1 | | | 11 | | |
| Barnstable | 93 | 8 | Bacon | Deborah | | | | | | | | | 2 | | | | 2 | | |
| Barnstable | 85 | 50 | Bacon | Ebenz | 2 | 1 | | 1 | | 2 | 3 | 2 | 1 | 1 | 1 | | 14 | | |
| Barnstable | 85 | 49 | Bacon | Edward | | | 1 | | 1 | | | | | | | | 2 | | |
| Wellfleet | 69 | 16 | Bacon | Freeman | | | 1 | | | 1 | | 1 | | | | | 3 | | |
| Barnstable | 85 | 9 | Bacon | Isaac | | | | | 1 | | | | 2 | 2 | 1 | | 6 | | |
| Barnstable | 84 | 51 | Bacon | Issac Jr | 2 | | | 1 | | 3 | | | 1 | | | | 7 | | |
| Barnstable | 93 | 37 | Bacon | Jabez | | 1 | 2 | | 1 | 1 | | 2 | 2 | 1 | | | 10 | | |
| Barnstable | 93 | 38 | Bacon | Onan | | | 1 | | | | | | 1 | | | | 2 | | |
| Barnstable | 84 | 45 | Bacon | Orris | | | | 2 | 1 | | | | 2 | 1 | | | 6 | | |
| Barnstable | 84 | 46 | Bacon | Orris Jr | | 1 | | | | 1 | | | 1 | | | | 3 | | |
| Barnstable | 86 | 24 | Bacon | Richard | | | | | 1 | | | 1 | 1 | 1 | | | 4 | | |
| Barnstable | 86 | 9 | Bacon | Sarah | | | | | | | | | 1 | | | | 1 | | |
| Mashpee | 52 | 7 | Badger | Elizabeth | | | | | | 1 | | | 1 | | | | 2 | | |
| Sandwich | 38 | 13 | Badger | Elizabeth | | | | | | | | | | | | | | | Enumeration left blank |
| Chatham | 15 | 19 | Badshell | Caty | | | | | | 1 | | | 1 | | | | 2 | | |
| Chatham | 15 | 18 | Badshell | William Jun | 1 | | | 1 | | 2 | 1 | | 1 | | | | 6 | | |
| Falmouth | 49 | 273 | Bagnett | Bethiah | | | | | | | | | | | 1 | | 1 | | |
| Harwich | 8 | 5 | Bailey | John | | | 1 | | | | | 1 | | | | | 2 | | |
| Yarmouth | 98 | 35 | Baker | Abraham | | 2 | 2 | 2 | 1 | 1 | 1 | | | 1 | | | 10 | | |
| Dennis | 31 | 8 | Baker | Allen | 3 | | | 1 | | | 1 | | 1 | | | | 6 | | |
| Yarmouth | 99 | 10 | Baker | Amos | 1 | 1 | | 1 | | 1 | | | 1 | | | | 5 | | |
| Harwich | 11 | 38 | Baker | Anthony | 3 | 3 | | 1 | | 2 | | | 1 | | | | 10 | | |
| Dennis | 30 | 20 | Baker | Archelus | 4 | | | 1 | | 1 | 1 | | 1 | | | | 8 | | |
| Dennis | 31 | 13 | Baker | Barnabas | | | 1 | | | 1 | | 1 | | | | | 3 | | |
| Falmouth | 43 | 23 | Baker | Barnabas | 4 | | | 1 | | | | 1 | 1 | | | | 7 | | |
| Barnstable | 86 | 5 | Baker | Benjamin | 3 | | | 1 | | | | | 1 | | | | 5 | | |
| Yarmouth | 98 | 37 | Baker | Benoni | 1 | | | | | | | | 1 | 1 | | | 3 | | |
| Orleans | 23 | 36 | Baker | Benony | 3 | 2 | 1 | 1 | | 1 | 1 | | | 1 | | | 10 | | |
| Yarmouth | 99 | 2 | Baker | Bethuel | 4 | 1 | 1 | | | | | | | 1 | | | 7 | | |
| Yarmouth | 98 | 36 | Baker | Cornelius | | | 1 | | | | | | 1 | | | | 2 | | |
| Dennis | 30 | 10 | Baker | Cornelus | | | 1 | | | | | | 1 | | | | 2 | | |
| Dennis | 31 | 25 | Baker | Crowell | | | 1 | | | | | | 1 | | | | 2 | | |
| Yarmouth | 98 | 45 | Baker | Daniel | | | 2 | 1 | | | | | | 1 | | | 4 | | |
| Yarmouth | 98 | 44 | Baker | Daniel Jr | 2 | | | 1 | | 1 | | 1 | | | | | 5 | | |
| Dennis | 29 | 8 | Baker | David | | | | 1 | | 2 | | | 1 | | | | 4 | | |
| Wellfleet | 73 | 18 | Baker | David | | | 1 | 1 | | | | | | 1 | | | 3 | | |

# 1800 Barnstable County, Massachusetts Index

| TOWN | PG# | LN# | LAST NAME | FIRST NAME | M under 10 | M 10 to 16 | M 16 to 26 | M 26 to 45 | M 45 and over | F under 10 | F 10 to 16 | F 16 to 26 | F 26 to 45 | F 45 and over | TOTAL ALL OTHER | TOTAL SLAVES | TOTALS | DISTRICT/TOWNSHIP | NOTES |
|---|---|---|---|---|---|---|---|---|---|---|---|---|---|---|---|---|---|---|---|
| Wellfleet | 73 | 19 | Baker | David Junr | 2 | | | 1 | | | | | 1 | | | | 4 | | |
| Dennis | 31 | 6 | Baker | Davis | | 1 | | 1 | | 3 | | | 1 | | | | 6 | | |
| Barnstable | 85 | 30 | Baker | Ebenezer | | | | 1 | | | | 1 | 1 | | | | 3 | | |
| Dennis | 31 | 24 | Baker | Ebenezer | | | 1 | | | | | | 1 | | | | 2 | | |
| Dennis | 30 | 7 | Baker | Edward | | | 1 | | | 2 | | 2 | | | | | 5 | | |
| Yarmouth | 99 | 39 | Baker | Edward | | | 1 | | | 1 | | 1 | | | | | 3 | | |
| Dennis | 31 | 29 | Baker | Eliphalet | | | | 1 | | 2 | | | 1 | | | | 4 | | |
| Yarmouth | 99 | 14 | Baker | Elisha | 3 | 1 | 2 | | 1 | 2 | 1 | | 1 | | | | 11 | | |
| Yarmouth | 99 | 44 | Baker | Elisha | 1 | 1 | | 1 | | 2 | | | 1 | | | | 6 | | |
| Yarmouth | 98 | 42 | Baker | Elisha Jr | | | 1 | | | 2 | | 1 | | | | | 4 | | |
| Dennis | 31 | 26 | Baker | Experience Wd | | | 1 | | | | | | 1 | 2 | | | 4 | | |
| Harwich | 10 | 19 | Baker | Ezra | 2 | | | 1 | | 1 | | | 1 | | | | 5 | | |
| Dennis | 31 | 17 | Baker | Frances | | 1 | | | | 1 | | | 1 | | | | 3 | | |
| Dennis | 31 | 33 | Baker | Freeman | 1 | 1 | | | | | | | 1 | | | | 3 | | |
| Chatham | 15 | 7 | Baker | Gideon | | 1 | | | | 1 | | | 1 | | | | 3 | | |
| Dennis | 28 | 37 | Baker | Goram | 1 | 1 | | 1 | | 1 | | | 1 | | | | 5 | | |
| Wellfleet | 70 | 8 | Baker | Hannah | | 1 | | | | | | | 1 | 1 | | | 3 | | |
| Dennis | 31 | 14 | Baker | Hemon | | | 1 | | | 1 | | | 1 | | | | 3 | | |
| Dennis | 30 | 1 | Baker | Henry | 2 | | 1 | | | | | | 1 | | | | 4 | | |
| Falmouth | 44 | 27 | Baker | Henry | | | | 1 | | | 1 | 1 | | | | | 3 | | |
| Dennis | 31 | 30 | Baker | Isaac | | | 1 | | | | | | 1 | | | | 2 | | |
| Barnstable | 88 | 11 | Baker | Isaiah | 1 | 1 | 1 | | 1 | | | | 1 | 1 | | | 6 | | |
| Wellfleet | 73 | 36 | Baker | Isaiah | 1 | | | 1 | | 1 | | 1 | | | | | 4 | | |
| Yarmouth | 99 | 51 | Baker | Jacob | | 1 | | 1 | | | | | 1 | | | | 3 | | |
| Dennis | 30 | 6 | Baker | Jeremiah | | 1 | 1 | | 1 | | 1 | 1 | 1 | 1 | | | 7 | | |
| Falmouth | 44 | 24 | Baker | Job | 2 | 1 | | | 1 | | 2 | 4 | 1 | | | | 11 | | |
| Dennis | 30 | 8 | Baker | John | 2 | | 2 | | 1 | | 2 | 2 | | 2 | | | 11 | | |
| Dennis | 31 | 35 | Baker | John 3d | | | 1 | | | 2 | | | 1 | | | | 4 | | |
| Dennis | 30 | 9 | Baker | John Jun | | | 1 | | | 1 | | | 1 | | | | 3 | | |
| Yarmouth | 99 | 23 | Baker | Jonathan | 1 | | | 1 | | 1 | 1 | | 1 | | | | 5 | | |
| Dennis | 31 | 34 | Baker | Josiah | 2 | 1 | 1 | | | | | | 1 | | | | 5 | | |
| Dennis | 28 | 38 | Baker | Judah | | 1 | | | 1 | | | 1 | 1 | | | | 4 | | |
| Dennis | 31 | 16 | Baker | Judah 3d | | | | 1 | | 1 | | | 1 | | | | 3 | | |
| Dennis | 31 | 15 | Baker | Judah Jun | | 1 | 1 | | 1 | | | | 1 | 1 | | | 5 | | |
| Yarmouth | 99 | 38 | Baker | Lemuel | 1 | | | 1 | | 3 | | 2 | | 1 | | | 8 | | |
| Yarmouth | 99 | 27 | Baker | Lemuel Jr | 2 | 1 | | 1 | | 3 | | | 1 | | | | 8 | | |
| Yarmouth | 98 | 38 | Baker | Levi | | | 1 | | | 1 | | | 3 | 1 | | | 6 | | |
| Harwich | 4 | 12 | Baker | Luke | 1 | | 1 | | | | | | 1 | | | | 3 | | |
| Barnstable | 85 | 31 | Baker | Lydia | | | | | | | 1 | | | 1 | | | 2 | | |
| Yarmouth | 99 | 29 | Baker | Marchent | 1 | | | 1 | | 2 | | | 1 | 1 | | | 6 | | |
| Barnstable | 83 | 17 | Baker | Mary | | | 1 | | | | | | 1 | 1 | | | 3 | | |
| Yarmouth | 98 | 43 | Baker | Moody | | 1 | 2 | 1 | | | 1 | 2 | 1 | | | | 8 | | |
| Dennis | 28 | 39 | Baker | Nathaniel | | | 1 | | | | | | 1 | 1 | | | 3 | | |
| Yarmouth | 99 | 22 | Baker | Obadiah | 3 | | | 1 | | 2 | | | 1 | | | | 7 | | |
| Falmouth | 44 | 25 | Baker | Obediah | 3 | 2 | 1 | | 1 | 3 | 1 | 2 | 1 | | | | 14 | | |
| Dennis | 30 | 5 | Baker | Paul | 2 | 1 | 1 | | 1 | 3 | 1 | 1 | 1 | | | | 11 | | |
| Yarmouth | 99 | 28 | Baker | Philip | 1 | | | 1 | | 2 | | | 1 | 1 | | | 6 | | |
| Yarmouth | 99 | 31 | Baker | Prince | 1 | | | 1 | | 2 | | | | 1 | | | 5 | | |
| Dennis | 30 | 39 | Baker | Richard | 2 | | 1 | | | | | | 1 | | | | 4 | | |
| Truro | 64 | 33 | Baker | Richard | 1 | | | 1 | | 2 | | | 1 | | | | 5 | | |
| Wellfleet | 70 | 4 | Baker | Ruth | 1 | | | | | 3 | 1 | 1 | | 1 | | | 7 | | |
| Dennis | 30 | 29 | Baker | Samuel | 1 | | | | 1 | 1 | 1 | | 1 | | | | 6 | | |
| Barnstable | 94 | 43 | Baker | Seth | 1 | | 1 | | 1 | 2 | 3 | | | 1 | | | 9 | | |
| Dennis | 28 | 36 | Baker | Seth | | 2 | 3 | 1 | 1 | | | 1 | 2 | 1 | | | 11 | | |
| Dennis | 31 | 28 | Baker | Seth 3d | 1 | | | 1 | | | | 1 | 1 | | | | 4 | | |
| Dennis | 31 | 31 | Baker | Seth Jun | | | 1 | | | | | | 1 | | | | 4 | | |
| Harwich | 14 | 7 | Baker | Shubal | | 1 | 2 | | 1 | | | 2 | | 1 | | | 7 | | |
| Harwich | 14 | 27 | Baker | Shubal Jun | 2 | | | 1 | | 2 | | | 1 | 1 | | | 7 | | |
| Yarmouth | 99 | 25 | Baker | Silas | | | 3 | | | 1 | | 1 | 1 | | | | 6 | | |
| Yarmouth | 99 | 26 | Baker | Silas Jr | 2 | | | 1 | | 2 | | | 1 | 1 | | | 8 | | |
| Dennis | 31 | 3 | Baker | Silvanus | 2 | 1 | | | 1 | 2 | 1 | | 1 | 1 | | | 9 | | |
| Dennis | 29 | 26 | Baker | Simeon | | 1 | | 1 | | 1 | | | 1 | | | | 4 | | |
| Provincetown | 61 | 6 | Baker | Thatcher | | 1 | | | | | | | 1 | | | | 2 | | |
| Dennis | 31 | 23 | Baker | Theofelus | 1 | 1 | | | | 1 | | | 1 | | | | 3 | | |
| Barnstable | 101 | 6 | Baker | Timothy | 2 | 2 | | | 1 | | | 1 | | | | | 6 | | |
| Dennis | 31 | 5 | Baker | Timothy | | | 1 | | | | | | 1 | | | | 2 | | |
| Chatham | 15 | 6 | Baker | William | | 2 | | 3 | | | | | 1 | | | | 6 | | |
| Dennis | 31 | 27 | Baker | Zenus | 2 | 1 | 1 | | | | | | 1 | | | | 5 | | |
| Falmouth | 43 | 21 | Baley | Zacheus | 2 | | 2 | | 1 | 2 | | 1 | 1 | | | | 9 | | |
| Wellfleet | 75 | 22 | Ballard | Anna | | | | | | | | | | 2 | | | 2 | | |
| Barnstable | 92 | 52 | Balsom | Nathaniel B | | | | 1 | | | | | | 1 | 1 | | 3 | | |
| Dennis | 29 | 6 | Bangs | Allen | 2 | | | 1 | | 2 | | | 1 | | | | 6 | | |
| Harwich | 8 | 10 | Bangs | Benjm | 3 | 1 | 2 | | | 2 | | 1 | 2 | | | | 11 | | |
| Harwich | 8 | 1 | Bangs | Dean | 2 | 1 | 1 | 1 | | 1 | 2 | | 1 | | | | 9 | | |
| Harwich | 6 | 37 | Bangs | Ebenezor | | | | 1 | | | | | 1 | | | | 2 | | |
| Harwich | 6 | 38 | Bangs | Ebenezor Jun | 2 | | | 1 | | 2 | | | 1 | | | | 6 | | |
| Harwich | 4 | 13 | Bangs | Elkanah | 3 | | | 1 | | | | | 1 | | | | 5 | | |
| Dennis | 30 | 27 | Bangs | Jediah | | 1 | 2 | | 1 | 1 | | | 1 | | | | 6 | | |
| Dennis | 29 | 5 | Bangs | Jonathan | | 1 | | 1 | | | 1 | | 1 | | | | 4 | | |
| Harwich | 10 | 28 | Bangs | Jonathan Jun | 1 | | | | | | | 1 | | | | | 3 | | |
| Harwich | 6 | 11 | Bangs | Joshua | 1 | | | | | | | | | | | | 4 | | |

# 1800 Barnstable County, Massachusetts Index

| TOWN | PG# | LN# | LAST NAME | FIRST NAME | FREE WHITE MALES | | | | | FREE WHITE FEMALES | | | | | TOTAL ALL OTHER | TOTAL SLAVES | TOTALS | DISTRICT/ TOWNSHIP | NOTES |
|------|-----|-----|-----------|------------|---|---|---|---|---|---|---|---|---|---|---|---|---|---|---|
| | | | | | under 10 | 10 to 16 | 16 to 26 | 26 to 45 | 45 and over | under 10 | 10 to 16 | 16 to 26 | 26 to 45 | 45 and over | | | | | |
| Truro | 64 | 22 | Bangs | Perez | 3 | 1 | | 1 | | 3 | 1 | | | | | | 9 | | |
| Harwich | 8 | 36 | Bangs | Sarah Wd | | | | | | 1 | 1 | | 1 | | | | 3 | | |
| Dennis | 28 | 34 | Bangs | Seth | | | 1 | | | | | 1 | | | | | 2 | | |
| Harwich | 6 | 10 | Bangs | Silvanus | | | 1 | | 2 | | | 1 | | | | | 4 | | |
| Sandwich | 37 | 16 | Banister | Nancy | | | | | | | | | | | 2 | | 2 | | |
| Sandwich | 41 | 1 | Barlow | Moses | 1 | 2 | | 1 | | 1 | | 1 | | | | | 6 | | |
| Orleans | 24 | 29 | Bascom | Jonathan Jun | | | 1 | | | | | 1 | | | | | 2 | | |
| Orleans | 24 | 30 | Bascom | Jonathan Rev | | | 1 | | 1 | | | 1 | | 1 | | | 4 | | |
| Falmouth | 43 | 3 | Bassett | Berachiah | 2 | | 1 | 1 | | 1 | | 1 | 1 | | | | 7 | | |
| Yarmouth | 95 | 11 | Bassett | Betty | | 1 | 3 | | | | | | 1 | | | | 5 | | |
| Barnstable | 93 | 4 | Bassett | Daniel | 1 | | 1 | | 3 | | | 1 | | | | | 6 | | |
| Harwich | 13 | 20 | Bassett | Daniel | 1 | | 1 | | 2 | | 1 | | | | | | 5 | | |
| Harwich | 10 | 15 | Bassett | David | 3 | 2 | | 1 | | | 4 | | 1 | | | | 11 | | |
| Sandwich | 39 | 26 | Bassett | Elisha | 1 | | 1 | | 1 | 1 | 1 | | | | | | 5 | | |
| Harwich | 11 | 14 | Bassett | John | 3 | | 1 | | 1 | | 1 | | | | | | 6 | | |
| Yarmouth | 97 | 41 | Bassett | John | | | | 1 | | | | | 1 | 1 | | | 3 | | |
| Dennis | 29 | 38 | Bassett | Jonathan | 1 | | 2 | | 1 | | | 3 | | 1 | | | 8 | | |
| Sandwich | 39 | 8 | Bassett | Jonathan | 2 | | 1 | 1 | 1 | | 1 | 1 | | | | | 7 | | |
| Barnstable | 93 | 36 | Bassett | Joseph | 4 | 1 | | 1 | | 2 | 1 | 1 | | | | | 10 | | |
| Sandwich | 39 | 10 | Bassett | Joseph | | 1 | | 1 | | 1 | | | | | | | 3 | | |
| Yarmouth | 95 | 23 | Bassett | Joseph | | 1 | | 1 | | | | 1 | 1 | | | | 4 | | |
| Yarmouth | 97 | 37 | Bassett | Joshua | 2 | | 1 | 1 | | | | 1 | | | | | 5 | | |
| Sandwich | 35 | 19 | Bassett | Lemuel | 1 | | 1 | | 1 | | 1 | | | | | | 4 | | |
| Barnstable | 89 | 1 | Bassett | Luther | | 1 | | | | | | 1 | | | | | 2 | | |
| Harwich | 13 | 16 | Bassett | Micah | 2 | | 1 | | 1 | 1 | 1 | | | | | | 6 | | |
| Chatham | 15 | 14 | Bassett | Nathan Jr | 1 | | 2 | | 2 | | 1 | 1 | 1 | | | | 8 | | |
| Yarmouth | 99 | 4 | Bassett | Nathan Jr | | | 1 | | | | 2 | | | | 5 | | 8 | | |
| Harwich | 12 | 16 | Bassett | Nathaniel | 1 | 2 | | 1 | | 1 | | | | | | | 5 | | |
| Harwich | 12 | 17 | Bassett | Nathaniel Jun | | | 1 | | | | | 1 | | | | | 2 | | |
| Harwich | 10 | 17 | Bassett | Richard | | 1 | | 1 | 1 | 2 | 2 | | 1 | | | | 8 | | |
| Barnstable | 87 | 49 | Bassett | Samuel | 1 | 2 | | 1 | 1 | | 1 | | | | | | 6 | | |
| Chatham | 15 | 15 | Bassett | Samuel | 1 | | 2 | | 1 | | 2 | | 1 | | | | 7 | | |
| Barnstable | 92 | 51 | Bassett | Sarah | | | | | | | 1 | | 1 | | | | 2 | | |
| Chatham | 15 | 16 | Bassett | Sarah Wd | | | | | | | | 1 | | 1 | | | 2 | | |
| Barnstable | 93 | 3 | Bassett | Seth | 2 | | 1 | | | | | | 1 | 1 | | | 5 | | |
| Sandwich | 39 | 4 | Bassett | Stephen | | | 1 | | 3 | | | 1 | | 1 | 1 | | 6 | | |
| Sandwich | 36 | 15 | Bassett | Thomas | | | 1 | | | | | | 1 | | | | 2 | | |
| Barnstable | 88 | 52 | Bassett | William | | | 1 | | | | 1 | | 1 | | | | 3 | | |
| Sandwich | 36 | 14 | Bassett | William | 2 | 1 | 1 | | 1 | 1 | 1 | 1 | 1 | | | | 9 | | |
| Barnstable | 89 | 2 | Bassett | William Jr | 2 | | 1 | | 2 | | 1 | | | | | | 6 | | |
| Mashpee | 51 | 11 | Bates | Anselon | 2 | | 1 | | | | 1 | | | | | | 4 | | |
| Sandwich | 34 | 5 | Bates | David | | | 1 | | 1 | | 1 | | | | | | 3 | | |
| Barnstable | 88 | 38 | Bates | Hannah | | | | | | 2 | | 1 | | | | | 3 | | |
| Barnstable | 88 | 37 | Bates | Sarah | | 1 | | | | 3 | | 1 | | | | | 5 | | |
| Sandwich | 38 | 27 | Bates | Sarah | | 1 | | | | | 1 | | 1 | | | | 3 | | |
| Mashpee | 51 | 12 | Bates | Simeon | | | | 1 | | | | | 1 | | | | 2 | | |
| Provincetown | 57 | 5 | Bates | Simeon | 1 | 2 | | 1 | | 3 | | 1 | | | | | 8 | | |
| Mashpee | 52 | 10 | Bates | Stephen | 2 | | 1 | | | 2 | | 1 | | | | | 6 | | |
| Barnstable | 101 | 4 | Baxter | Alexr | 3 | | 1 | | 1 | | 1 | | | | | | 6 | | |
| Barnstable | 94 | 50 | Baxter | Barna | 2 | | 1 | | 1 | | | 1 | | | | | 5 | | |
| Dennis | 29 | 15 | Baxter | Benjm | | 1 | | 1 | | | 1 | 1 | 1 | | | | 5 | | |
| Barnstable | 101 | 3 | Baxter | Daniel | | | | 1 | | | 1 | 1 | | | | | 3 | | |
| Barnstable | 94 | 46 | Baxter | David | 2 | 2 | 3 | | 1 | | 1 | 1 | | 1 | | | 11 | | |
| Dennis | 29 | 16 | Baxter | David | 1 | | 1 | | | | 1 | | | | | | 3 | | |
| Yarmouth | 99 | 43 | Baxter | David Jr | 2 | 2 | | 1 | | 2 | | 1 | | | | | 8 | | |
| Dennis | 30 | 4 | Baxter | Ebenezer | | | 1 | | 2 | 2 | 1 | | | | | | 6 | | |
| Barnstable | 94 | 44 | Baxter | Isaac | 1 | 2 | | 1 | | 1 | | | 1 | | | | 6 | | |
| Dennis | 31 | 10 | Baxter | John | 1 | | 1 | | 1 | | 1 | | | | | | 4 | | |
| Harwich | 10 | 21 | Baxter | Nathaniel | 1 | | 1 | | 2 | | 1 | | | | | | 5 | | |
| Barnstable | 101 | 5 | Baxter | Obed | | | 1 | | | | 1 | | | | | | 2 | | |
| Dennis | 32 | 6 | Baxter | Obed | 2 | | 1 | | | | 1 | | | | | | 4 | | |
| Barnstable | 101 | 12 | Baxter | Prince | 2 | 2 | 1 | | 1 | 1 | 1 | | 1 | | | | 10 | | |
| Dennis | 31 | 9 | Baxter | Reuben | | | 1 | | 1 | | | | 1 | | | | 3 | | |
| Barnstable | 94 | 45 | Baxter | Sarah | 4 | 1 | 1 | | | | 1 | 1 | 1 | | | | 9 | | |
| Barnstable | 101 | 1 | Baxter | Shubael | 2 | | 1 | | 2 | | 1 | | | | | | 6 | | |
| Harwich | 13 | 34 | Baxter | Simeon | 2 | | 1 | | | | | | 1 | 1 | | | 5 | | |
| Barnstable | 91 | 28 | Bayman | John | | | 1 | | | | 1 | | | | | | 2 | | |
| Chatham | 15 | 23 | Bea | Isaac | | | 1 | | 1 | | 1 | | | | | | 3 | | |
| Chatham | 15 | 20 | Bea | Thomas | | 1 | | 1 | | | | | | | 2 | | 4 | | |
| Mashpee | 51 | 7 | Bearce | Daniel | | 2 | 2 | | 1 | | 1 | 1 | 1 | | | | 8 | | |
| Sandwich | 38 | 11 | Bearce | Daniel | | | | | | | | | | | | | | | Enumeration left blank |
| Barnstable | 93 | 41 | Bearse | David | 1 | | 1 | 1 | 1 | 1 | | 1 | 2 | 1 | | | 9 | | |
| Barnstable | 93 | 45 | Bearse | Edward | | 2 | | 1 | | 1 | | | 1 | | | | 5 | | |
| Barnstable | 93 | 46 | Bearse | Edward Jr | | | 1 | | | | 1 | | | | | | 2 | | |
| Barnstable | 94 | 25 | Bearse | Enoch | | 2 | 2 | | 1 | 1 | | 1 | | 1 | | | 8 | | |
| Barnstable | 93 | 20 | Bearse | Gershom | | 1 | | 1 | 1 | 1 | 1 | 1 | 1 | | | | 7 | | |
| Barnstable | 90 | 28 | Bearse | Isaac | | | | 2 | | | 1 | | | | | | 3 | | |
| Barnstable | 90 | 29 | Bearse | James | 3 | | 1 | | 1 | | | 1 | | | | | 6 | | |
| Barnstable | 93 | 17 | Bearse | Josiah | | | 1 | | 1 | | 1 | | | | | | 3 | | |
| Barnstable | 94 | 19 | Bearse | Judah | | 2 | | 1 | 1 | 1 | 1 | 1 | 1 | | | | 9 | | |
| Barnstable | 93 | 32 | Bearse | Levi | | 1 | 2 | | 1 | | 1 | | 1 | | | | 6 | | |

63

# 1800 Barnstable County, Massachusetts Index

| TOWN | PG# | LN# | LAST NAME | FIRST NAME | FREE WHITE MALES | | | | | FREE WHITE FEMALES | | | | | TOTAL ALL OTHER | TOTAL SLAVES | TOTALS | DISTRICT/ TOWNSHIP | NOTES |
|---|---|---|---|---|---|---|---|---|---|---|---|---|---|---|---|---|---|---|---|
| | | | | | under 10 | 10 to 16 | 16 to 26 | 26 to 45 | 45 and over | under 10 | 10 to 16 | 16 to 26 | 26 to 45 | 45 and over | | | | | |
| Barnstable | 94 | 21 | Bearse | Obed | 3 | 1 | | | 1 | 2 | | | 1 | | | | 8 | | |
| Barnstable | 94 | 18 | Bearse | Prince | | | | 1 | | | 1 | | | | | | 2 | | |
| Barnstable | 94 | 20 | Bearse | Prince Jr | 3 | | 2 | | 1 | 3 | 1 | | 1 | | | | 11 | | |
| Barnstable | 93 | 47 | Bearse | Samuel | 1 | | 1 | | | | | | 1 | | | | 3 | | |
| Barnstable | 101 | 10 | Bearse | Stephen | 3 | | | 1 | | 2 | | | 1 | | | | 9 | | |
| Provincetown | 60 | 40 | Beedie | Gamaliel | | 1 | | | | | 1 | 1 | | | | | 3 | | |
| Sandwich | 41 | 42 | Bennett | Stephen | | | 1 | 1 | 1 | 1 | | | 1 | 1 | | | 6 | | |
| Sandwich | 41 | 41 | Bennett | Stephen Jun | 2 | | | 1 | | 1 | | | 1 | 1 | | | 6 | | |
| Harwich | 14 | 40 | Berge | Zadock | | | 1 | | | 1 | | 1 | | | | | 3 | | |
| Chatham | 19 | 18 | Berre | David Jun | 1 | 1 | | | | | | | 1 | | | | 3 | | |
| Harwich | 8 | 34 | Berry | Benjamin | 1 | | | 1 | | 1 | 1 | | 1 | | | | 5 | | |
| Harwich | 8 | 29 | Berry | David | 1 | | 1 | | | | | | 1 | | | | 3 | | |
| Barnstable | 93 | 18 | Berry | Enoch | | 1 | | 1 | | 3 | | | 2 | 1 | | | 8 | | |
| Barnstable | 86 | 22 | Berry | Ephraim | | | | 1 | | | 1 | 1 | 2 | 1 | | | 5 | | |
| Yarmouth | 99 | 46 | Berry | Howes | 2 | | | 1 | | 1 | | | | | | | 4 | | |
| Yarmouth | 99 | 17 | Berry | Isaac | 2 | 1 | 1 | | | 1 | 1 | 2 | | 1 | | | 9 | | |
| Yarmouth | 99 | 13 | Berry | James | | | 1 | | | | 1 | 1 | 2 | 1 | | | 5 | | |
| Yarmouth | 99 | 30 | Berry | Jeremiah | 1 | | 2 | | 1 | 2 | 2 | | 1 | | | | 9 | | |
| Harwich | 8 | 30 | Berry | Jerusha Wd | | | | | | | | | | 1 | | | 1 | | |
| Harwich | 5 | 35 | Berry | John D | 1 | | 1 | 1 | | 1 | 1 | 1 | 1 | | | | 7 | | |
| Harwich | 7 | 41 | Berry | Jonathan | | 2 | 1 | | 1 | 1 | 1 | 1 | 1 | | | | 8 | | |
| Barnstable | 86 | 19 | Berry | Joseph | | 1 | | 1 | | 1 | 1 | | | | | | 4 | | |
| Harwich | 5 | 28 | Berry | Judah | | 2 | | 1 | | | | | 1 | 1 | | | 5 | | |
| Harwich | 5 | 34 | Berry | Leatte | | | | | | | | | | | | | | | |
| Harwich | 5 | 29 | Berry | Lemuel | | 1 | | | | | | | 1 | | | | 2 | | |
| Harwich | 8 | 7 | Berry | Mercy Wd | | 1 | | | | | | 2 | | 1 | | | 4 | | |
| Harwich | 8 | 3 | Berry | Theofelus | | | | 1 | | | | | 1 | 1 | | | 3 | | |
| Chatham | 15 | 24 | Berry | Willis | 1 | | 1 | | 1 | | 1 | | | | | | 4 | | |
| Chatham | 15 | 22 | Berse | Betsy | | | | 1 | | | 1 | | | | | | 2 | | |
| Chatham | 15 | 13 | Berse | Ebenezer | 2 | | 1 | | 1 | 2 | | 1 | | 1 | | | 8 | | |
| Chatham | 20 | 15 | Berse | Ezra | | 1 | | | | 3 | | | 1 | | | | 5 | | |
| Chatham | 15 | 5 | Berse | George | 1 | | | 1 | | 1 | | | 1 | | | | 4 | | |
| Chatham | 15 | 12 | Berse | Simeon | 2 | 1 | | 1 | | | | 2 | | 1 | | | 7 | | |
| Provincetown | 60 | 35 | Bickford | Henry | | 1 | | | | | | | | | | | 1 | | |
| Barnstable | 84 | 29 | Blachford | Uriah | | | 1 | 2 | | 1 | | | 1 | | | | 5 | | |
| Barnstable | 84 | 30 | Blachford | William | | | | 1 | | | | | 1 | 1 | 1 | | 3 | | |
| Yarmouth | 98 | 29 | Black | Alexr | 2 | | 1 | | | 1 | | | 1 | | | | 5 | | |
| Harwich | 15 | 11 | Black | Nathan | | | | | | | | | | | 5 | | 5 | | |
| Barnstable | 91 | 32 | Black | Thomas | 2 | 1 | | 1 | | 3 | 1 | 2 | | 1 | | | 11 | | |
| Falmouth | 49 | 305 | Blackford | David | | | | 1 | | | | | 1 | | | | 2 | | |
| Falmouth | 49 | 306 | Blackford | Edward | | 1 | | 1 | | 5 | | | 1 | | | | 8 | | |
| Sandwich | 42 | 35 | Blackwell | John | | | | 1 | | | | | 1 | | | | 2 | | |
| Sandwich | 42 | 36 | Blackwell | John Junr | | 1 | 1 | | 1 | 3 | | 1 | 1 | | | | 8 | | |
| Sandwich | 42 | 37 | Blackwell | Lucy | | 1 | | | | | | | 1 | 1 | | | 3 | | |
| Sandwich | 40 | 3 | Blackwell | Saml | | | 2 | 1 | 1 | 1 | | | | 1 | | | 6 | | |
| Sandwich | 42 | 13 | Blackwell | Samuel Junr | | | 1 | | | | | 1 | | | | | 2 | | |
| Barnstable | 88 | 1 | Blish | Ebenezer | | | | 1 | | | | | 1 | | | | 2 | | |
| Barnstable | 93 | 23 | Blish | Elisha | | | 1 | | | | | | 1 | | | | 2 | | |
| Barnstable | 88 | 2 | Blish | Joseph | | | | 2 | | | 2 | | 1 | | | | 5 | | |
| Barnstable | 88 | 3 | Blish | Joseph Jr | 4 | 1 | | 1 | | 1 | | 1 | 1 | | | | 9 | | |
| Yarmouth | 100 | 20 | Blish | Owen | 2 | | 1 | | | 1 | | | 1 | | | | 5 | | |
| Barnstable | 87 | 38 | Blish | Silas | 2 | | 1 | | | 3 | 1 | | 1 | | | | 8 | | |
| Barnstable | 89 | 44 | Blist | Achiah | 1 | | | | | | | | 1 | | | | 2 | | |
| Sandwich | 37 | 7 | Blossem | Joseph | | 1 | 1 | | 1 | 1 | 1 | 1 | | 1 | | | 7 | | |
| Barnstable | 92 | 5 | Blossom | Churchil | 1 | 1 | | 1 | 1 | 1 | | 1 | | 1 | | | 6 | | |
| Barnstable | 92 | 25 | Bodfish | Ebenz | 2 | 2 | 1 | | 1 | 2 | | 1 | 1 | | | | 10 | | |
| Barnstable | 92 | 37 | Bodfish | John | 3 | | | 1 | | | | | 1 | 1 | | | 6 | | |
| Barnstable | 92 | 36 | Bodfish | Jona | | | 3 | 1 | | | | | 1 | 1 | | | 6 | | |
| Barnstable | 92 | 28 | Bodfish | Patience | 1 | | 1 | | | | | | 1 | 1 | | | 4 | | |
| Barnstable | 93 | 1 | Bodfish | Robert | | | 1 | | 1 | | | | 1 | | | | 3 | | |
| Sandwich | 38 | 28 | Bodfish | Wm | 2 | 1 | | 1 | 1 | 2 | 1 | | 1 | | | | 9 | | |
| Chatham | 20 | 27 | Bodshell | Mulford | | 1 | | | | | | | 1 | | | | 2 | | |
| Wellfleet | 75 | 28 | Bointon | Gershom | | | 1 | | 1 | | | | 1 | | | | 3 | | |
| Falmouth | 51 | 321 | Bonnie | Ziniel | 3 | 2 | | 1 | | | 1 | | 1 | 1 | | | 9 | | |
| Dennis | 28 | 26 | Bourn | Richard | | 1 | | | 1 | | 1 | | | | | | 3 | | |
| Sandwich | 39 | 19 | Bourne | Allen | 2 | | | 1 | | | | | 1 | | | | 4 | | |
| Sandwich | 40 | 31 | Bourne | Alvan | 1 | | 1 | 1 | | 1 | | | 1 | | | | 5 | | |
| Sandwich | 40 | 37 | Bourne | Asa | 3 | 1 | | 1 | | 2 | 1 | | 1 | | | | 9 | | |
| Sandwich | 40 | 38 | Bourne | Benja | | 2 | 1 | | 1 | | 1 | 3 | | 1 | | | 9 | | |
| Sandwich | 40 | 11 | Bourne | Bethuel | 3 | 1 | | 1 | | 1 | | 1 | 1 | | | | 8 | | |
| Sandwich | 42 | 6 | Bourne | Charles | | | 1 | | | | | | 1 | | | | 2 | | |
| Falmouth | 43 | 7 | Bourne | Elijah | 2 | 1 | | 1 | | 1 | | | 1 | 1 | | | 7 | | |
| Sandwich | 42 | 5 | Bourne | Elisha | | 1 | | | 1 | | | | 1 | 2 | | | 5 | | |
| Falmouth | 44 | 33 | Bourne | Hannah | | 1 | | | | | | | | 2 | | | 3 | | |
| Sandwich | 42 | 7 | Bourne | Hannah | 1 | | | | | | | | 1 | 1 | | | 3 | | |
| Sandwich | 39 | 20 | Bourne | James | | | 1 | | | | | | 1 | | | | 2 | | |
| Sandwich | 36 | 39 | Bourne | James Junr | | | 1 | | | | | | 1 | | | | 2 | | |
| Sandwich | 40 | 33 | Bourne | Job | 1 | | 1 | | | | | 1 | | | | | 3 | | |
| Falmouth | 43 | 8 | Bourne | John | 1 | 1 | 1 | | 1 | 1 | 1 | 2 | 1 | | | | 9 | | |
| Sandwich | 42 | 4 | Bourne | Jonathan | 2 | | | 1 | | | | 2 | | 1 | | | 6 | | |
| Falmouth | 43 | 6 | Bourne | Joseph | 1 | 3 | | 1 | | 3 | | | 1 | 1 | | | 8 | | |
| Sandwich | 40 | 34 | Bourne | Lydia | | | | | | | | | 1 | | | | 1 | | |
| Sandwich | 35 | 27 | Bourne | Melatiah | | 1 | 1 | | 1 | | 1 | 1 | 1 | | | | 6 | | |

# 1800 Barnstable County, Massachusetts Index

| TOWN | PG# | LN# | LAST NAME | FIRST NAME | FWM under 10 | FWM 10 to 16 | FWM 16 to 26 | FWM 26 to 45 | FWM 45 over | FWF under 10 | FWF 10 to 16 | FWF 16 to 26 | FWF 26 to 45 | FWF 45 over | TOTAL ALL OTHER | TOTAL SLAVES | TOTALS | DISTRICT/TOWNSHIP | NOTES |
|---|---|---|---|---|---|---|---|---|---|---|---|---|---|---|---|---|---|---|---|
| Sandwich | 38 | 1 | Bourne | Nathan | | | | | | | | 1 | | | | | 1 | | |
| Falmouth | 44 | 26 | Bourne | Nathaniel | | 2 | | 1 | | 4 | 1 | 2 | 1 | | | | 11 | | |
| Falmouth | 43 | 5 | Bourne | Samuel | | 1 | 2 | 1 | | 1 | 1 | | | 1 | | | 7 | | |
| Sandwich | 42 | 3 | Bourne | Samuel | 1 | 1 | | 1 | | 2 | | 1 | 1 | | | | 7 | | |
| Falmouth | 44 | 29 | Bourne | Thomas | 1 | | | 1 | | 3 | 2 | 1 | | | | | 8 | | |
| Sandwich | 40 | 36 | Bourne | Thos | | 1 | | 1 | | | | | 1 | | 1 | | 4 | | |
| Sandwich | 40 | 32 | Bourne | Thos Junr | | | 1 | 1 | | | 1 | 2 | | 1 | 1 | | 7 | | |
| Falmouth | 43 | 4 | Bourne | Timothy | | | | 1 | | 3 | | | 1 | 1 | | | 6 | | |
| Sandwich | 40 | 35 | Bourne | Wm | 2 | | | 1 | | | | | 1 | | | | 4 | | |
| Falmouth | 43 | 11 | Bowerman | Abraham | | | 2 | | | | | | 1 | 2 | | | 5 | | |
| Falmouth | 44 | 31 | Bowerman | Clifton | 1 | | | 1 | | | | | 1 | 1 | | | 4 | | |
| Falmouth | 43 | 18 | Bowerman | Curtis | 1 | | | 1 | | | | | 1 | 2 | | | 5 | | |
| Falmouth | 43 | 15 | Bowerman | Daniel | | 1 | | 1 | | 3 | | | 2 | 1 | | | 8 | | |
| Falmouth | 43 | 17 | Bowerman | Ichabod | 3 | 1 | | 1 | | | | | 1 | | | | 6 | | |
| Sandwich | 38 | 33 | Bowerman | Jeremiah | | | 1 | | 1 | | | 2 | | 1 | | | 5 | | |
| Falmouth | 43 | 19 | Bowerman | Joseph | 2 | | 1 | | 1 | 2 | | 1 | 2 | 2 | | | 11 | | |
| Falmouth | 43 | 10 | Bowerman | Paul | | | | 1 | | 2 | | | | 1 | | | 4 | | |
| Sandwich | 34 | 21 | Bowerman | Samuel | | | 1 | | 1 | | | | | 1 | | | 3 | | |
| Falmouth | 43 | 20 | Bowerman | Seth | 3 | | | 1 | | 1 | | 2 | | | | | 7 | | |
| Falmouth | 43 | 14 | Bowerman | Stephen | 2 | | | 1 | | 1 | 1 | | 1 | | | | 6 | | |
| Falmouth | 43 | 22 | Bowerman | Stephen | 3 | 2 | | 1 | | 2 | | | 1 | | | | 9 | | |
| Provincetown | 60 | 27 | Bowley | Oliver | | | 1 | | | 1 | | | 1 | | | | 3 | | |
| Provincetown | 57 | 7 | Bowly | Asa | 2 | | | 1 | | | | | 1 | | | | 4 | | |
| Truro | 66 | 27 | Bowly | Hannah Wid | | 1 | | | | | | 1 | | 1 | | | 3 | | |
| Harwich | 8 | 22 | Bradford | Cornelius | 2 | 1 | | 1 | | 2 | | | 1 | | | | 7 | | |
| Falmouth | 44 | 28 | Bradford | Susannah | | | | | | | | | | 2 | | | 2 | | |
| Barnstable | 101 | 13 | Bradley | Abind | | | 1 | | | | 1 | | | | | | 2 | | |
| Sandwich | 37 | 21 | Bradley | Thomas | 2 | | | 1 | | 1 | | | 1 | | | | 5 | | |
| Chatham | 15 | 2 | Bradshell | William | | | 2 | | 1 | | 1 | | | 1 | | | 5 | | |
| Barnstable | 101 | 9 | Bragg | Jane | | | 2 | | | | | | | 1 | | | 3 | | |
| Truro | 68 | 30 | Braver | John | 1 | | 1 | | | | | | 1 | | | | 3 | | |
| Yarmouth | 96 | 28 | Bray | David | | | 1 | | 1 | | 1 | | | 1 | | | 4 | | |
| Yarmouth | 95 | 33 | Bray | Edmund | | | 2 | 1 | 1 | | | | | 1 | | | 5 | | |
| Yarmouth | 99 | 40 | Bray | Edmund Jr | 3 | | | 1 | | 1 | | | 1 | | | | 6 | | |
| Yarmouth | 95 | 29 | Bray | Isaiah | | | 1 | | | | | | 1 | | | | 2 | | |
| Yarmouth | 96 | 4 | Bray | John | 1 | 1 | | 1 | | 1 | | | 1 | | | | 5 | | |
| Yarmouth | 95 | 28 | Bray | William | | 1 | | | 1 | | | | 1 | 1 | | | 4 | | |
| Yarmouth | 95 | 31 | Bray | William Jr | | | 1 | | | 3 | | | 1 | | | | 5 | | |
| Provincetown | 57 | 9 | Briggs | Barnabas | 1 | | 1 | | 1 | 2 | | 1 | | 1 | | | 7 | | |
| Chatham | 15 | 10 | Briggs | Ephraim | 1 | | | | | | | 1 | 1 | 1 | | | 4 | | |
| Harwich | 12 | 11 | Brigs | Daniel | 1 | | | 1 | | 1 | | | 1 | | | | 4 | | |
| Wellfleet | 70 | 5 | Brimhall | Robert | 1 | | 2 | 1 | | 2 | 1 | | 1 | 1 | | | 9 | | |
| Harwich | 10 | 23 | Broadbrooks | Ebenezer Esq | 2 | | 1 | | 2 | 2 | 2 | 1 | 1 | 1 | | | 12 | | |
| Harwich | 12 | 1 | Broadbrooks | Lydia Wd | | | | | | | | | 1 | 1 | | | 2 | | |
| Harwich | 11 | 24 | Broadbrooks | Meneboh | | | 1 | | 2 | | | | 1 | 1 | | | 5 | | |
| Harwich | 14 | 14 | Broadbrooks | Nathan | 1 | 1 | 1 | 1 | | 5 | 1 | | 1 | | | | 11 | | |
| Wellfleet | 75 | 6 | Brown | Benjamin | | | 1 | | | | | | 1 | | | | 2 | | |
| Provincetown | 57 | 10 | Brown | Cyrenius | 3 | | 1 | | | | | | 1 | | | | 5 | | |
| Eastham | 76 | 6 | Brown | David | | 2 | 2 | | 1 | | | 1 | 1 | 1 | | | 8 | | |
| Provincetown | 57 | 6 | Brown | David | | 1 | 4 | | 1 | | | 1 | 1 | | 1 | | 9 | | |
| Wellfleet | 70 | 7 | Brown | David | | 1 | | | 1 | | | | | 1 | | | 3 | | |
| Provincetown | 61 | 15 | Brown | David Junr | | | 1 | | | 1 | | 1 | | | | | 3 | | |
| Wellfleet | 69 | 18 | Brown | Doane | 1 | | | 1 | | | | | 1 | | | | 3 | | |
| Wellfleet | 69 | 19 | Brown | Elisha | | 1 | | 1 | | 3 | 4 | | 1 | | | | 10 | | |
| Wellfleet | 70 | 6 | Brown | George | | 1 | 2 | | 1 | | 1 | 2 | | 1 | | | 8 | | |
| Eastham | 76 | 7 | Brown | Higgins | | | | 1 | | | | | 1 | | | | 2 | | |
| Wellfleet | 70 | 2 | Brown | Isaac | | | | 1 | | 1 | | | 1 | | | | 3 | | |
| Wellfleet | 70 | 1 | Brown | John | | | | 1 | | 1 | | | 1 | | | | 3 | | |
| Wellfleet | 70 | 3 | Brown | Molly | 1 | | | | | 2 | | | 1 | | | | 4 | | |
| Falmouth | 49 | 272 | Brown | Prince | | | | | | | | | | | 6 | | 6 | | |
| Provincetown | 61 | 2 | Brown | Shobel | 1 | | | | | | | 1 | | | | | 3 | | |
| Truro | 65 | 11 | Brown | Silvanus | | | | 1 | | | | 3 | | 1 | | | 5 | | |
| Barnstable | 94 | 40 | Brown | Thaddeus | 1 | 3 | 1 | 1 | | | | | 1 | | | | 7 | | |
| Truro | 66 | 26 | Brown | William | 2 | 1 | | 1 | 1 | 1 | 1 | | 1 | 1 | | | 9 | | |
| Chatham | 19 | 21 | Brussels | Phillip | 1 | | | 1 | | 1 | | | 1 | | | | 6 | | |
| Sandwich | 42 | 14 | Buck | Benja | 1 | 1 | | 1 | | 1 | | 1 | | 1 | | | 6 | | |
| Chatham | 15 | 21 | Buck | Benjm | 2 | | | 1 | | 2 | | | 1 | | | | 6 | | |
| Chatham | 15 | 4 | Buck | David | | 1 | 1 | | 1 | | | 1 | | 1 | | | 5 | | |
| Chatham | 20 | 28 | Buck | David | | 1 | | 1 | | | | 1 | | 1 | | | 4 | | |
| Chatham | 15 | 17 | Buck | Elizabeth Wd | | | | | | | 1 | 1 | 1 | 1 | | | 4 | | |
| Barnstable | 94 | 48 | Buck | John | 1 | | | 1 | | 1 | | | | 1 | | | 4 | | |
| Chatham | 15 | 11 | Buck | Joshua | 1 | | | 1 | | 2 | | | 1 | | | | 5 | | |
| Chatham | 15 | 9 | Buck | Mary Wid | 1 | | | 1 | | 1 | | | 1 | 1 | | | 6 | | |
| Barnstable | 101 | 7 | Buck | Thomas | | | 2 | | | | | 1 | | 1 | | | 4 | | |
| Yarmouth | 99 | 21 | Bunker | Benja | 2 | | | 1 | | 1 | | | 1 | 1 | | | 6 | | |
| Falmouth | 44 | 30 | Bunker | Richard | | | | | 1 | | | | 1 | 1 | | | 3 | | |
| Dennis | 26 | 41 | Burger | William | | 1 | 2 | | 1 | | 1 | | | 1 | | | 6 | | |
| Sandwich | 41 | 40 | Burges | Covel | 2 | 1 | 1 | 1 | | 1 | 2 | | 1 | | | | 9 | | |
| Harwich | 12 | 30 | Burges | David | | | 1 | | | | 1 | | 1 | | | | 3 | | |
| Sandwich | 39 | 45 | Burges | Elisha | 1 | 1 | 1 | | 1 | | | 1 | 2 | 1 | | | 8 | | |
| Sandwich | 41 | 3 | Burges | Ichabod | 2 | | | 2 | | 1 | 2 | 1 | 1 | 1 | | | 10 | | |
| Harwich | 12 | 28 | Burges | Jacob | 1 | | | 1 | | | | | 1 | | | | 5 | | |
| Sandwich | 38 | 26 | Burges | James | 1 | | | 1 | | | | | 1 | | | | 3 | | |
| Harwich | 12 | 41 | Burges | Jonathan | 2 | | 1 | 1 | | | 2 | | | 1 | | | 8 | | |

# 1800 Barnstable County, Massachusetts Index

| TOWN | PG# | LN# | LAST NAME | FIRST NAME | M under 10 | M 10 to 16 | M 16 to 26 | M 26 to 45 | M 45 and over | F under 10 | F 10 to 16 | F 16 to 26 | F 26 to 45 | F 45 and over | TOTAL ALL OTHER | TOTAL SLAVES | TOTALS | DISTRICT/ TOWNSHIP | NOTES |
|---|---|---|---|---|---|---|---|---|---|---|---|---|---|---|---|---|---|---|---|
| Sandwich | 41 | 36 | Burges | Jonathan | | | | 1 | | | | | 1 | | | | 2 | | |
| Harwich | 12 | 34 | Burges | Joshua | 2 | | | 1 | | | | | 1 | | | | 4 | | |
| Harwich | 12 | 29 | Burges | Moses | 1 | | 1 | | | | | | 1 | | | | 3 | | |
| Sandwich | 41 | 32 | Burges | Nathl | | 1 | 1 | | 1 | 1 | | | 1 | | | | 5 | | |
| Falmouth | 49 | 307 | Burges | Reuben | 1 | | | 1 | | 1 | | 1 | | | | | 4 | | |
| Harwich | 12 | 27 | Burges | Samuel | 2 | | | 1 | | 3 | | | 1 | | | | 7 | | |
| Harwich | 12 | 33 | Burges | Seth | 1 | | | 1 | | 3 | | | 1 | | | | 6 | | |
| Harwich | 12 | 31 | Burges | Thomas | | | | | 1 | | | | | 1 | | | 2 | | |
| Harwich | 12 | 32 | Burges | Thomas Jun | | 1 | 1 | | | | | 1 | | 1 | | | 4 | | |
| Yarmouth | 100 | 11 | Burges | Timo | 1 | | 1 | | 1 | 3 | 3 | 1 | 1 | | | | 11 | | |
| Sandwich | 35 | 36 | Burr | Jonathan Revd | 1 | | | 1 | | 1 | 1 | 1 | 1 | | | | 6 | | |
| Barnstable | 92 | 18 | Bursley | John | 1 | | 1 | 1 | 1 | | | | | 1 | 1 | | 6 | | |
| Sandwich | 35 | 21 | Bursley | John | | 1 | | 1 | 1 | | | | 1 | 1 | | | 5 | | |
| Barnstable | 92 | 20 | Bursley | John Jr | 3 | | | 1 | | | | | 1 | | | | 5 | | |
| Barnstable | 92 | 19 | Bursley | Lemuel | 1 | | | 1 | | 1 | | | 1 | | | | 5 | | |
| Provincetown | 61 | 9 | Bush | William | 1 | | 1 | 1 | | 2 | 1 | 1 | 1 | | | | 8 | | |
| Falmouth | 44 | 32 | Butler | Benjamin | 3 | | | 1 | | 1 | | | 1 | | | | 6 | | |
| Falmouth | 43 | 13 | Butler | David | | | 1 | 1 | | 1 | | 1 | 1 | 1 | | | 6 | | |
| Falmouth | 43 | 16 | Butler | Easten | 1 | | | 1 | | | | 1 | 3 | 1 | | | 7 | | |
| Falmouth | 49 | 271 | Butler | Mary | | | | | | | 1 | 1 | 1 | | | | 3 | | |
| Chatham | 15 | 8 | Butler | Nathaniel | 2 | | | 1 | | 1 | | | 1 | | | | 5 | | |
| Falmouth | 43 | 12 | Butler | Obedl | | 1 | | | 1 | | 2 | 1 | | 1 | | | 6 | | |
| Falmouth | 43 | 9 | Butler | Parnel | 1 | 1 | 1 | | | 1 | 1 | | 1 | | | | 6 | | |
| Harwich | 14 | 34 | Cahoon | Gamaliel | | 2 | | 1 | | 3 | | | 1 | | | | 7 | | |
| Harwich | 12 | 7 | Cahoon | James | | 1 | 2 | | 1 | 2 | 1 | 1 | | 1 | | | 9 | | |
| Harwich | 10 | 16 | Cahoon | James Jun | 1 | | 1 | | | | 1 | | | | | | 3 | | |
| Harwich | 9 | 38 | Cahoon | Jesse | 1 | 2 | 1 | 1 | | 2 | | | 1 | | | | 8 | | |
| Harwich | 9 | 37 | Cahoon | John | | 1 | | 2 | | 3 | 1 | | 1 | | | | 8 | | |
| Harwich | 14 | 35 | Cahoon | Peter | 2 | | | 1 | | 2 | | | 1 | | | | 6 | | |
| Harwich | 9 | 29 | Cahoon | Reuben | | 1 | | 1 | | | | | 1 | | | | 3 | | |
| Harwich | 9 | 24 | Cahoon | Seth | 2 | 1 | 1 | 1 | | 2 | 1 | 1 | 1 | 1 | | | 11 | | |
| Orleans | 22 | 30 | Cahoon | Stephen | | 2 | | 1 | | 1 | 2 | | 1 | | | | 7 | | |
| Orleans | 22 | 29 | Cahoon | Stephen Junr | | | 1 | | | 1 | 1 | | | | | | 3 | | |
| Harwich | 9 | 27 | Cahoon | William | 1 | | 2 | | 1 | 2 | 1 | 1 | | 1 | | | 9 | | |
| Orleans | 24 | 21 | Cale | Abial | 1 | 1 | | | 1 | 3 | | | 1 | | | | 7 | | |
| Orleans | 24 | 22 | Cale | Joseph | | | | | | 1 | | | 1 | | | | 2 | | |
| Orleans | 25 | 10 | Cale | Joshua | | 1 | 1 | | 1 | 1 | | | 1 | | | | 6 | | |
| Barnstable | 91 | 17 | Cammett | Eliza | | 1 | 1 | | | | | 1 | | 1 | | | 4 | | |
| Barnstable | 91 | 16 | Cammett | Peter | 2 | 1 | | 1 | | 1 | | 3 | 1 | | | | 9 | | |
| Dennis | 27 | 4 | Capp | John | | | | 1 | | | | 1 | | 1 | | | 3 | | |
| Barnstable | 85 | 28 | Carsley | Hannah | | | | | | | | | 2 | | | | 2 | | |
| Barnstable | 89 | 11 | Carsley | Isaac | 1 | | 1 | | 1 | 1 | 1 | | 2 | | | | 8 | | |
| Barnstable | 86 | 45 | Carsley | Lemuel | | | | 1 | | | | | 2 | | | | 3 | | |
| Barnstable | 88 | 4 | Carver | Lemuel | 1 | | | 1 | | 3 | 2 | | 1 | | | | 8 | | |
| Barnstable | 84 | 49 | Case | Ebenezer | 1 | 1 | | 1 | | 1 | 1 | | 1 | | | | 6 | | |
| Yarmouth | 96 | 18 | Cash | Elisha | 1 | | 2 | | 1 | 1 | 1 | | 1 | | | | 7 | | |
| Harwich | 10 | 44 | Cash | Samuel | 1 | | 2 | | 1 | 2 | 2 | | 1 | | | | 9 | | |
| Barnstable | 94 | 1 | Cathcart | John | | | | 1 | | | | 1 | | 1 | | | 3 | | |
| Harwich | 15 | 12 | Cesar | Isaac | | | | | | | | | | | 3 | | 3 | | |
| Harwich | 15 | 9 | Cesar | Jesse | | | | | | | | | | | 3 | | 3 | | |
| Falmouth | 49 | 315 | Chadwick | Ancry | 1 | | | 1 | | 1 | | 1 | | | | | 4 | | |
| Sandwich | 42 | 11 | Chadwick | Anselm | 4 | 1 | | 1 | | 1 | | | 1 | | | | 8 | | |
| Falmouth | 44 | 49 | Chadwick | Barnabas | 2 | | | 1 | | 1 | | | 1 | | | | 5 | | |
| Falmouth | 49 | 314 | Chadwick | Elijah | 1 | | 1 | | | | | 1 | | | | | 3 | | |
| Falmouth | 44 | 35 | Chadwick | Elizabeth | | | | | | | | | 3 | | | | 3 | | |
| Falmouth | 44 | 37 | Chadwick | Isaiah | | 1 | 1 | | 1 | 1 | 2 | | 1 | | | | 7 | | |
| Falmouth | 44 | 56 | Chadwick | Lydia | | 1 | | 1 | | | | | 1 | | | | 3 | | |
| Falmouth | 44 | 43 | Chadwick | Micajah | 2 | | | 1 | | 4 | | | 1 | | | | 8 | | |
| Falmouth | 44 | 50 | Chadwick | Reuben | | | | 1 | | 1 | | | 1 | | | | 3 | | |
| Falmouth | 44 | 53 | Chadwick | Thomas | 1 | | | 1 | | | | | 1 | | | | 3 | | |
| Sandwich | 41 | 45 | Chandler | Asahel | 1 | 1 | | 1 | | 2 | 1 | | 1 | | | | 7 | | |
| Truro | 68 | 5 | Chandler | Joseph | | | | 1 | | | | | 1 | | | | 2 | | |
| Dennis | 26 | 28 | Chapman | David | | | | | 1 | | | 1 | | 1 | | | 3 | | |
| Dennis | 26 | 30 | Chapman | John | | | | | 1 | | | | | 1 | | | 2 | | |
| Dennis | 26 | 31 | Chapman | John Jun | 1 | 1 | 1 | 1 | | 1 | 1 | | 1 | | | | 7 | | |
| Dennis | 26 | 29 | Chapman | Paul | 2 | | | 1 | | | 1 | 1 | 1 | | | | 6 | | |
| Truro | 68 | 2 | Chapman | Samuel | 2 | 1 | | 1 | | 1 | | | 1 | | | | 6 | | |
| Dennis | 30 | 12 | Chase | Abner | | 1 | | 1 | 1 | | | | 1 | | | | 4 | | |
| Barnstable | 101 | 11 | Chase | Anthony | 4 | 1 | 1 | 1 | | | 1 | 1 | 1 | | | | 10 | | |
| Harwich | 12 | 46 | Chase | Archelus | 3 | | | 1 | | 2 | 1 | | 1 | | | | 8 | | |
| Chatham | 16 | 3 | Chase | Bassett | | | | 1 | | 1 | | | 1 | | | | 3 | | |
| Dennis | 31 | 12 | Chase | Benjm | | | | 1 | | | | | 1 | | | | 2 | | |
| Harwich | 14 | 6 | Chase | Daniel | | 1 | | 1 | 1 | 1 | | | 1 | 1 | | | 6 | | |
| Harwich | 6 | 16 | Chase | David | 1 | | | 1 | | | | | 1 | 1 | | | 4 | | |
| Sandwich | 38 | 39 | Chase | David | 2 | | 1 | 1 | | 2 | 1 | | 1 | | | | 8 | | |
| Harwich | 10 | 10 | Chase | Ebenezer Jun | 2 | 1 | 1 | | 1 | | 2 | | 1 | | | | 8 | | |
| Harwich | 13 | 44 | Chase | Elezor | 2 | | 1 | | | | | 1 | | | | | 4 | | |
| Harwich | 11 | 37 | Chase | Enoch | 3 | | | 1 | 1 | 2 | | | 1 | 1 | | | 9 | | |
| Dennis | 30 | 16 | Chase | Freeman | | 1 | | | | | 1 | | | | | | 2 | | |
| Dennis | 30 | 36 | Chase | Gaurel | 1 | | | 1 | | 2 | | | 1 | | | | 5 | | |
| Harwich | 11 | 21 | Chase | Gemaliel | 3 | | | 1 | | 3 | | | 1 | | | | 8 | | |
| Harwich | 14 | 23 | Chase | Isaac | | | | 1 | | | | | 1 | | | | 2 | | |
| Harwich | 11 | 17 | Chase | James | 3 | | | 1 | | 2 | 2 | 1 | | 1 | | | 11 | | |
| Harwich | 12 | 47 | Chase | Job | | | | | 1 | | | | | 1 | | | 2 | | |
| Harwich | 12 | 48 | Chase | Job Jun | 1 | | | 1 | | 1 | | | 1 | | | | 4 | | |

# 1800 Barnstable County, Massachusetts Index

| TOWN | PG# | LN# | LAST NAME | FIRST NAME | M under 10 | M 10-16 | M 16-26 | M 26-45 | M 45 over | F under 10 | F 10-16 | F 16-26 | F 26-45 | F 45 over | TOTAL ALL OTHER | TOTAL SLAVES | TOTALS | DISTRICT/TOWNSHIP | NOTES |
|---|---|---|---|---|---|---|---|---|---|---|---|---|---|---|---|---|---|---|---|
| Harwich | 11 | 23 | Chase | John | 2 | | 1 | | | | | 1 | | | | | 4 | | |
| Harwich | 14 | 22 | Chase | John | | 1 | | 1 | | 2 | 1 | | 1 | | | | 6 | | |
| Dennis | 30 | 15 | Chase | Joseph | | | | 1 | | | | | | 2 | | | 3 | | |
| Dennis | 30 | 38 | Chase | Joseph Jun | 2 | | | 1 | | | | 2 | 1 | | | | 6 | | |
| Harwich | 13 | 2 | Chase | Josiah | 1 | 1 | | 1 | | 3 | 1 | | 1 | | | | 8 | | |
| Sandwich | 37 | 1 | Chase | Leonard | | | 3 | | 1 | 1 | 2 | | 1 | 1 | | | 9 | | |
| Dennis | 30 | 14 | Chase | Lot | 2 | | | 1 | | 2 | 2 | | 1 | | | | 8 | | |
| Dennis | 30 | 17 | Chase | Lot Jun | 2 | | | 1 | | 1 | | | 1 | | | | 5 | | |
| Orleans | 22 | 14 | Chase | Mary | | | | | | | | | 1 | 1 | | | 2 | | |
| Harwich | 11 | 20 | Chase | Mary Wd | | | | | | | | | | 1 | | | 1 | | |
| Dennis | 29 | 13 | Chase | Nathan | 1 | 2 | | 1 | | 3 | | 1 | 1 | | | | 9 | | |
| Harwich | 13 | 5 | Chase | Nathaniel | 2 | | | 1 | | 3 | 1 | | 1 | | | | 8 | | |
| Dennis | 31 | 2 | Chase | Obed | 2 | | 1 | | | 1 | | | 1 | | | | 5 | | |
| Dennis | 30 | 13 | Chase | Owen | 2 | 1 | | 1 | | 3 | | | 1 | | | | 8 | | |
| Harwich | 11 | 26 | Chase | Philow | | 1 | | | | | | | 2 | 1 | | | 4 | | |
| Harwich | 8 | 26 | Chase | Richard | | | | 1 | | 2 | | | 2 | | | | 5 | | |
| Dennis | 31 | 11 | Chase | Samuel | 1 | 2 | | 1 | | 3 | 1 | | 1 | | | | 9 | | |
| Harwich | 13 | 42 | Chase | Seth | 2 | | | 1 | | | | | 1 | | | | 4 | | |
| Harwich | 11 | 22 | Chase | Silvanus | 2 | 1 | | 1 | | | | 1 | | 1 | | | 6 | | |
| Harwich | 13 | 40 | Chase | Susanna Wd | | | 1 | | | 1 | | | | 1 | | | 3 | | |
| Harwich | 12 | 3 | Chase | Tabitha Wd | 2 | | | | | | | | 1 | | | | 3 | | |
| Dennis | 29 | 41 | Chase | Thomas | | | 1 | | | | | | | 1 | | | 2 | | |
| Dennis | 30 | 11 | Chase | Thomas Jun | 2 | | | 1 | | 2 | | | 1 | | | | 6 | | |
| Harwich | 12 | 43 | Chase | William | 2 | 2 | | 1 | | 2 | | | 1 | | | | 8 | | |
| Harwich | 13 | 1 | Chase | Zenus | 1 | | | 1 | | 4 | | | 1 | | | | 7 | | |
| Eastham | 76 | 11 | Cheven | Dorcas | | | | | | | | | 1 | 1 | | | 2 | | |
| Barnstable | 85 | 27 | Childs | David | | | | 2 | | 1 | | 1 | | 1 | | | 5 | | |
| Barnstable | 85 | 3 | Childs | Edward | 1 | | | 1 | | | 2 | | | 1 | | | 5 | | |
| Barnstable | 86 | 47 | Childs | Elijah | 1 | | | 2 | | 2 | 1 | | 1 | | | | 7 | | |
| Barnstable | 88 | 51 | Childs | James | 2 | | | 1 | | | | 1 | | 1 | | | 5 | | |
| Barnstable | 90 | 33 | Childs | Job | 2 | 2 | | 1 | | 1 | | 1 | 1 | 1 | | | 9 | | |
| Sandwich | 34 | 18 | Childs | Jonathan | | | | 1 | | | | 1 | | 1 | | | 3 | | |
| Falmouth | 44 | 52 | Childs | Joseph | 2 | 2 | 1 | | 1 | 1 | | 1 | 1 | 1 | | | 10 | | |
| Barnstable | 85 | 2 | Childs | Josiah | | | 2 | | 1 | | 2 | 1 | | 1 | | | 7 | | |
| Falmouth | 49 | 300 | Childs | Nathan | | | 2 | 2 | | 1 | 1 | | 3 | | | | 9 | | |
| Falmouth | 44 | 36 | Childs | Nathaniel | | | 2 | 2 | | 1 | 1 | | 3 | | | | 9 | | |
| Sandwich | 36 | 17 | Chipman | Benjamin | | | | 1 | 1 | 1 | | | 2 | 1 | | | 6 | | |
| Wellfleet | 70 | 11 | Chipman | Betty | | | 2 | | | | | | | 1 | | | 3 | | |
| Wellfleet | 70 | 15 | Chipman | Dorcas | | 1 | | | | 1 | | | 1 | | | | 3 | | |
| Sandwich | 34 | 3 | Chipman | Hatsuls | 1 | | | 1 | | 4 | | | 1 | | | | 7 | | |
| Barnstable | 87 | 47 | Chipman | John | | 1 | | 1 | | 3 | 1 | | 1 | | | | 7 | | |
| Wellfleet | 70 | 20 | Chipman | John | | | | 1 | | 1 | | | 1 | | | | 3 | | |
| Barnstable | 88 | 33 | Chipman | Joseph | 3 | | | 1 | | | 1 | 1 | | 1 | | | 7 | | |
| Wellfleet | 70 | 19 | Chipman | Samuel | 1 | | | 1 | | | | 1 | | | | | 3 | | |
| Sandwich | 36 | 18 | Chipman | Stephen | | | | | 1 | | | | | | | | 1 | | |
| Sandwich | 34 | 6 | Chipman | Stephen S. | 3 | | | 1 | | | | | 1 | | | | 5 | | |
| Barnstable | 87 | 48 | Chipman | Timothy | | | | 1 | | | | | 1 | 1 | | | 3 | | |
| Sandwich | 36 | 7 | Christie | James | 1 | 1 | | 1 | | 2 | 1 | | | 1 | | | 7 | | |
| Harwich | 12 | 40 | Church | Asa | | | 1 | | | | | 1 | | | | | 2 | | |
| Barnstable | 91 | 40 | Claghorn | Jabez | | 1 | | 1 | | | | | 1 | 1 | | | 4 | | |
| Harwich | 9 | 26 | Clancy | Elnathan Jun | 1 | | | 1 | | 1 | | | 1 | | | | 4 | | |
| Harwich | 13 | 11 | Clark | Andrew | | 1 | | 1 | | 4 | | | 1 | | | | 7 | | |
| Harwich | 6 | 13 | Clark | Anna | | 1 | | | | | | | | 2 | | | 3 | | |
| Harwich | 4 | 39 | Clark | Bethiah Wd | 1 | | | | | 1 | | | 1 | | | | 3 | | |
| Harwich | 12 | 20 | Clark | David | | 1 | 1 | 1 | | 2 | 1 | 1 | 1 | | | | 8 | | |
| Harwich | 5 | 37 | Clark | Edward | | | | | 1 | | 1 | 1 | 2 | 1 | | | 6 | | |
| Harwich | 13 | 9 | Clark | Elijah | 2 | | | 1 | | 2 | | | 1 | | | | 6 | | |
| Harwich | 8 | 28 | Clark | Enoch | 3 | 1 | | 1 | | 1 | 1 | 1 | 1 | | | | 9 | | |
| Harwich | 5 | 38 | Clark | Isaac | 2 | 1 | | 1 | | 2 | | | 1 | | | | 7 | | |
| Harwich | 8 | 23 | Clark | Jedian | | | 3 | | 1 | | | 1 | | 1 | | | 6 | | |
| Harwich | 13 | 10 | Clark | Jonathan | 3 | | | 1 | | 2 | | | 1 | 1 | | | 8 | | |
| Harwich | 8 | 8 | Clark | Joseph | | 2 | | 1 | | | | 1 | | 1 | | | 5 | | |
| Harwich | 6 | 12 | Clark | Josiah | 3 | 1 | | 1 | | 1 | | | 1 | | | | 7 | | |
| Harwich | 5 | 39 | Clark | Kimbal | 1 | | 1 | | | | | | | 1 | | | 4 | | |
| Harwich | 4 | 11 | Clark | Kimbal Jun | | 1 | 1 | | | | | | 1 | | | | 3 | | |
| Harwich | 4 | 3 | Clark | Praland | 1 | 2 | | 1 | | 1 | | | 2 | 1 | | | 8 | | |
| Harwich | 7 | 28 | Clark | Reuben | | | | 1 | | | | | 1 | 2 | | | 4 | | |
| Harwich | 4 | 20 | Clark | Salomon Jun | | 1 | | | | 2 | | 1 | | | | | 4 | | |
| Harwich | 8 | 27 | Clark | Silvanus | | 1 | | 1 | | 1 | | | | 1 | | | 4 | | |
| Harwich | 5 | 36 | Clark | Solomon | | 1 | | 1 | | | | | | | | | 2 | | |
| Chatham | 16 | 9 | Clark | Thomas | | 1 | | 1 | | | | 1 | | 2 | | | 5 | | |
| Eastham | 76 | 16 | Clerk | Benjamin | | 1 | 2 | | 1 | 2 | | 2 | | 1 | | | 9 | | |
| Mashpee | 51 | 21 | Clifford | | | | | | | | | | | | 6 | | 6 | | First name left blank on census |
| Harwich | 5 | 18 | Cobb | Barnabas | | | 1 | 1 | | 1 | | | 1 | 1 | | | 5 | | |
| Barnstable | 84 | 8 | Cobb | Benjamin | | | | 1 | | | | | | | | | 1 | | |
| Barnstable | 84 | 18 | Cobb | Benjamin Jn | 1 | | | 1 | | 1 | 1 | | 1 | | | | 5 | | |
| Barnstable | 84 | 22 | Cobb | Daniel | 3 | 1 | | 1 | | 1 | 2 | 1 | 1 | | | | 10 | | |
| Barnstable | 84 | 23 | Cobb | David | | 1 | 2 | | 1 | 1 | 1 | | | 1 | | | 7 | | |
| Barnstable | 85 | 5 | Cobb | Desire | 1 | | | | | | | | | 1 | | | 2 | | |
| Harwich | 5 | 7 | Cobb | Eleanor | | | 1 | 1 | | | | | 2 | | | | 5 | | |
| Barnstable | 84 | 9 | Cobb | Eleazer | 1 | | | 1 | | | 2 | | | 1 | | | 5 | | |
| Chatham | 16 | 10 | Cobb | Elezar | | 1 | 1 | | | | | | 1 | | | | 3 | | |
| Harwich | 8 | 16 | Cobb | Elijah | 2 | | | 1 | | 1 | | | | 1 | | | 6 | | |
| Eastham | 76 | 15 | Cobb | Elisha | | | 1 | | 1 | | | | | 1 | | | 3 | | |
| Eastham | 76 | 8 | Cobb | Elkanah | 1 | | 2 | 1 | | 3 | 2 | | 1 | | | | 10 | | |

# 1800 Barnstable County, Massachusetts Index

| TOWN | PG# | LN# | LAST NAME | FIRST NAME | M under 10 | M 10-16 | M 16-26 | M 26-45 | M 45+ | F under 10 | F 10-16 | F 16-26 | F 26-45 | F 45+ | TOTAL ALL OTHER | TOTAL SLAVES | TOTALS | DISTRICT/TOWNSHIP | NOTES |
|---|---|---|---|---|---|---|---|---|---|---|---|---|---|---|---|---|---|---|---|
| Barnstable | 84 | 21 | Cobb | Hary | | | | | | | | 1 | 1 | 1 | | | 3 | | |
| Barnstable | 84 | 50 | Cobb | Henry | 1 | | | 1 | | 1 | | | 1 | | | | 4 | | |
| Truro | 63 | 28 | Cobb | John | | 2 | 1 | | 1 | 1 | 1 | 1 | | 1 | | | 8 | | |
| Barnstable | 85 | 4 | Cobb | Joseph | 2 | 2 | 1 | 1 | | 3 | 1 | | 1 | | | | 11 | | |
| Truro | 63 | 17 | Cobb | Joseph | | | | 1 | | | | 1 | | 1 | | | 3 | | |
| Barnstable | 84 | 16 | Cobb | Joseph Jn | 1 | 1 | | 1 | | 1 | 1 | | 1 | | | | 6 | | |
| Truro | 64 | 12 | Cobb | Loir Wid | | 2 | | | | | 2 | | 1 | | | | 5 | | |
| Barnstable | 83 | 10 | Cobb | Martha | 1 | | | | | | | 1 | 1 | 1 | | | 4 | | |
| Truro | 64 | 16 | Cobb | Mulford | 2 | 2 | | 1 | | | | 1 | 1 | | | | 7 | | |
| Barnstable | 84 | 5 | Cobb | Nathaniel | | 1 | | 1 | | | | | | 2 | | | 4 | | |
| Sandwich | 41 | 19 | Cobb | Nicholas | 3 | | | 1 | | | | 1 | 1 | | | | 6 | | |
| Barnstable | 84 | 6 | Cobb | Orris | 1 | 1 | | 1 | | | 2 | | 1 | | | | 6 | | |
| Truro | 64 | 26 | Cobb | Richard | | | | 1 | | | | | 1 | | | | 2 | | |
| Truro | 68 | 22 | Cobb | Richard Jun | 2 | | | 1 | | | 2 | | 1 | | | | 6 | | |
| Barnstable | 84 | 17 | Cobb | Samuel | 1 | | | 1 | | 3 | | | 1 | | | | 6 | | |
| Harwich | 5 | 25 | Cobb | Seth | | | | 1 | | | | 1 | | | | | 2 | | |
| Sandwich | 41 | 20 | Cobb | Seth | | | 1 | | | 1 | | | 1 | | | | 3 | | |
| Sandwich | 42 | 12 | Cobb | Thankful | | | | | | | | 1 | 1 | | | | 2 | | |
| Barnstable | 93 | 43 | Cobb | Thomas | 1 | | | 1 | | 2 | | | 1 | | | | 5 | | |
| Eastham | 79 | 18 | Cobb | Thomas | | 1 | 1 | | 1 | | 1 | | | | | | 4 | | |
| Orleans | 22 | 20 | Coffin | Obediah | 1 | | | 1 | | | | | 1 | | | | 3 | | |
| Truro | 66 | 30 | Cohan | Benjamin | | 1 | | | | 1 | | 1 | | 1 | | | 4 | | |
| Truro | 66 | 29 | Cohan | Samuel | 2 | 1 | | 1 | | 2 | | | 1 | | | | 7 | | |
| Truro | 66 | 32 | Cohan | Shobel | | 1 | | | | 4 | | | 1 | | | | 6 | | |
| Wellfleet | 70 | 10 | Cohoon | Joseph | | 1 | | 1 | | | | | | 1 | | | 3 | | |
| Falmouth | 44 | 51 | Cohoon | Smalley | | 1 | | | | | | | | 1 | | | 2 | | |
| Eastham | 79 | 6 | Cole | Daniel | 2 | 2 | 2 | | 1 | 2 | | 1 | 1 | 1 | | | 12 | | |
| Wellfleet | 70 | 18 | Cole | Daniel | 1 | 2 | 2 | | 1 | 2 | | | | 1 | | | 9 | | |
| Wellfleet | 75 | 31 | Cole | Ebenezer | 1 | | | 1 | | | | 1 | | | | | 3 | | |
| Eastham | 76 | 10 | Cole | James | | 1 | 1 | | | | | | 1 | | | | 3 | | |
| Eastham | 77 | 2 | Cole | Jesse | 2 | | 1 | | | 2 | | | 1 | | | | 6 | | |
| Orleans | 22 | 7 | Cole | Jesse | 1 | | 1 | 1 | | | 1 | 1 | | 1 | | | 6 | | |
| Wellfleet | 70 | 9 | Cole | Joanna | | 1 | | 1 | | 1 | | | | 1 | | | 4 | | |
| Orleans | 21 | 18 | Cole | Martha | | | | | | | | | | 1 | | | 1 | | |
| Barnstable | 90 | 30 | Cole | Mary | | 1 | | | | | | | | 1 | | | 2 | | |
| Orleans | 21 | 17 | Cole | Mary Wid | | | | | | | | | | 1 | | | 1 | | |
| Orleans | 21 | 13 | Cole | Nathan | | 1 | | | | | | | 1 | | | | 2 | | |
| Orleans | 23 | 41 | Cole | Stephen | 1 | | 1 | 2 | | | | 1 | | | | | 5 | | |
| Eastham | 79 | 24 | Cole | Timothy | | 1 | | 1 | | | 1 | 1 | 1 | | | | 5 | | |
| Wellfleet | 70 | 13 | Cole | William | | 1 | 1 | | | | 3 | | 1 | | | | 6 | | |
| Wellfleet | 70 | 14 | Cole | William Junr | 2 | 1 | 1 | 1 | | | | | 1 | | | | 6 | | |
| Barnstable | 90 | 31 | Coleman | Ebenezer | | 1 | 1 | | | | | | | 1 | | | 3 | | |
| Mashpee | 51 | 2 | Coleman | Edward | 1 | 1 | | 1 | | 2 | | | 1 | | | | 6 | | |
| Sandwich | 38 | 4 | Coleman | Edward | | | | | | | | | | | | | | | Enumeration left blank |
| Sandwich | 38 | 6 | Coleman | Hezekiah | 1 | | 1 | | | | | | 1 | | | | 3 | | |
| Sandwich | 38 | 3 | Coleman | James | | | | 1 | | | 2 | 1 | 1 | | | | 5 | | |
| Chatham | 16 | 2 | Coleman | John | | | | 1 | | | | | 1 | | | | 2 | | |
| Sandwich | 38 | 5 | Coleman | John | 1 | | 1 | | | 1 | | | 1 | | | | 4 | | |
| Barnstable | 93 | 30 | Coleman | Nathaniel | 1 | 1 | 1 | 1 | | 1 | 2 | | 2 | 1 | | | 10 | | |
| Falmouth | 44 | 55 | Coleman | Thomas | 2 | 1 | | 1 | | 2 | | 1 | | | | | 7 | | |
| Provincetown | 61 | 1 | Collener | Thankful | | 1 | | | 1 | 1 | | | | | | | 3 | | |
| Truro | 62 | 3 | Collins | Andrew | | 1 | 1 | 1 | | | | | | 1 | | | 4 | | |
| Truro | 62 | 5 | Collins | Benjamin | 2 | 2 | | 2 | | | | | 2 | 1 | | | 8 | | |
| Dennis | 28 | 41 | Collins | David | | 2 | 1 | 1 | | 2 | | | 1 | | | | 7 | | |
| Truro | 66 | 31 | Collins | Jesse | 2 | | 1 | 2 | | | | | 1 | | | | 6 | | |
| Truro | 66 | 28 | Collins | John | 2 | | 1 | 1 | | 1 | | 1 | | 1 | | | 7 | | |
| Truro | 63 | 16 | Collins | John Junr | 1 | 1 | 1 | | 1 | 1 | 1 | 2 | | 1 | | | 9 | | |
| Truro | 67 | 1 | Collins | Jonathan | | 2 | 1 | 3 | | | | | 1 | | | | 7 | | |
| Eastham | 76 | 13 | Collins | Joseph | 1 | 2 | 2 | 1 | 1 | 3 | 1 | | 1 | | | | 12 | | |
| Truro | 63 | 30 | Collins | Joseph | | 1 | | 1 | | | 2 | | | 1 | | | 5 | | |
| Eastham | 77 | 1 | Collins | Michael | 2 | 2 | | 1 | | 2 | | 1 | 1 | | | | 9 | | |
| Truro | 64 | 15 | Collins | Moses | 1 | | 1 | | | | | 1 | 1 | | | | 4 | | |
| Provincetown | 60 | 30 | Collins | Rebeccah | | 1 | | | | | | | 1 | | | | 2 | | |
| Provincetown | 60 | 15 | Collins | Richard | | 1 | | | | | | | 1 | | | | 2 | | |
| Truro | 64 | 27 | Collins | Ruth | 2 | | | | | | | 1 | 1 | | | | 4 | | |
| Chatham | 15 | 26 | Collins | Samuel | 1 | | 1 | 2 | | | | | 1 | | 1 | | 6 | | |
| Barnstable | 84 | 44 | Collio | Lydia | | | | | | | 2 | | | | | | 2 | | |
| Barnstable | 92 | 31 | Conant | Asa | 2 | | | 1 | 1 | | | | 1 | | | | 5 | | |
| Barnstable | 92 | 30 | Conant | Charles | | | | 1 | | | | | 1 | | | | 2 | | |
| Provincetown | 57 | 21 | Conant | John | | | | 1 | | | | | 1 | | | | 2 | | |
| Provincetown | 57 | 8 | Conant | Samuel | 1 | | | | | | | 1 | 1 | | | | 3 | | |
| Eastham | 76 | 9 | Cook | Caleb | | | | 1 | | 2 | 2 | | 1 | | | | 6 | | |
| Provincetown | 60 | 33 | Cook | David | | 1 | | | | | | | 1 | | | | 2 | | |
| Provincetown | 57 | 15 | Cook | Edward | 1 | | | 1 | | 2 | | | 1 | | | | 5 | | |
| Provincetown | 57 | 11 | Cook | Elisha | 1 | | 1 | | 1 | | | | | | | | 3 | | |
| Provincetown | 61 | 8 | Cook | Isaac | | 1 | | | | 1 | | 1 | | | | | 3 | | |
| Provincetown | 57 | 18 | Cook | James | | | 1 | 1 | | | | | 1 | | | | 3 | | |
| Eastham | 76 | 12 | Cook | John | 2 | | 1 | 2 | | | | | 1 | | | | 6 | | |
| Provincetown | 57 | 19 | Cook | John | 1 | 1 | | 1 | | 2 | | | 1 | | | | 6 | | |
| Provincetown | 57 | 14 | Cook | Jonathan | | 1 | 3 | 1 | | 1 | | | | 1 | | | 7 | | |
| Provincetown | 57 | 12 | Cook | Joshua | 2 | | 1 | | | | | | 1 | | | | 4 | | |

# 1800 Barnstable County, Massachusetts Index

| Town | PG# | LN# | Last Name | First Name | M under 10 | M 10 to 16 | M 16 to 26 | M 26 to 45 | M 45 and over | F under 10 | F 10 to 16 | F 16 to 26 | F 26 to 45 | F 45 and over | Total All Other | Total Slaves | Totals | District/Township | Notes |
|---|---|---|---|---|---|---|---|---|---|---|---|---|---|---|---|---|---|---|---|
| Eastham | 79 | 15 | Cook | Nathaniel | | 1 | | | | 1 | | | | | | | 2 | | |
| Harwich | 7 | 35 | Cook | Nathaniel | | | | 1 | | | 1 | | | | | | 2 | | |
| Provincetown | 57 | 20 | Cook | Paron | 1 | 1 | 1 | 1 | | 2 | 2 | | 1 | | | | 9 | | |
| Eastham | 79 | 26 | Cook | Rebeccah | | | | | | | | 2 | | | | | 2 | | |
| Eastham | 76 | 14 | Cook | Samuel | 1 | 1 | | 1 | | | 1 | | 1 | | | | 5 | | |
| Provincetown | 57 | 17 | Cook | Samuel | 1 | 2 | 3 | 1 | | 2 | | | 1 | | | | 10 | | |
| Provincetown | 58 | 4 | Cook | Sarah Wd | 1 | | | | | | 1 | 1 | 1 | | | | 4 | | |
| Provincetown | 57 | 16 | Cook | Solomon | | 1 | | 1 | | | | 1 | | 1 | | | 4 | | |
| Provincetown | 57 | 13 | Cook | Solomon Jun | 3 | 2 | | 1 | | 1 | | | 1 | | | | 8 | | |
| Harwich | 7 | 36 | Cook | Temperance Wd | | | | | | | | 2 | | 1 | | | 3 | | |
| Wellfleet | 75 | 2 | Cookson | Mary | | | | | | | | | | 1 | | | 1 | | |
| Sandwich | 37 | 28 | Coombs | Abigail | 1 | | | | | 1 | | | 2 | | | | 4 | | |
| Provincetown | 58 | 3 | Coombs | Elizabeth Wd | | | | | | | | | 1 | | | | 1 | | |
| Mashpee | 52 | 5 | Copas | Thomas | | | | | | | | | | | 2 | | 2 | | |
| Wellfleet | 74 | 37 | Collister | Thomas | | 1 | | | | | 1 | | | | | | ? | | |
| Barnstable | 88 | 31 | Corsley | Seth | | 1 | | 1 | | | | | 1 | | | | 3 | | |
| Barnstable | 87 | 14 | Cotelle | Peter | | 2 | 1 | | 1 | | 1 | | 2 | | | | 7 | | |
| Sandwich | 42 | 42 | Covel | Deborah | | | | | | | | 1 | | | | | 1 | | |
| Wellfleet | 75 | 11 | Covell | David | 1 | | | 1 | | 1 | | | 1 | | | | 4 | | |
| Wellfleet | 70 | 12 | Covell | Reuben | | | | 1 | | | | | 1 | | | | 2 | | |
| Wellfleet | 70 | 16 | Covell | Reuben Junr | 2 | | | 1 | | 1 | 1 | | 1 | | | | 6 | | |
| Wellfleet | 70 | 17 | Covell | Ruth | | | 2 | | | 1 | 1 | | 1 | | | | 5 | | |
| Harwich | 12 | 24 | Covil | Abigail Wd | | | | | | | | 1 | 1 | | | | 2 | | |
| Harwich | 10 | 34 | Covil | Benjm | 1 | | | 1 | | 2 | | | 1 | | | | 5 | | |
| Harwich | 9 | 25 | Covil | James | 2 | | | 1 | | | | | 1 | | | | 4 | | |
| Dennis | 28 | 33 | Covil | John | 1 | | 1 | | | | | 1 | | | | | 3 | | |
| Dennis | 28 | 31 | Covil | Jonathan | 1 | | | 1 | | 1 | | | 1 | | | | 4 | | |
| Dennis | 28 | 32 | Covil | Nathaniel | | | 1 | 1 | 1 | | 1 | 1 | 1 | | | | 5 | | |
| Dennis | 28 | 35 | Covil | Samuel | 2 | | | 1 | | 2 | | | 1 | | | | 7 | | |
| Harwich | 10 | 29 | Covill | Mary Wd | | | 1 | | | | | | | 2 | | | 3 | | |
| Harwich | 4 | 19 | Crassey | Abial | 1 | | | 1 | | | | | 1 | | | | 3 | | |
| Barnstable | 86 | 10 | Crocker | Abiah | | | 2 | 1 | | 1 | | | | 1 | | | 5 | | |
| Barnstable | 92 | 17 | Crocker | Abner | | 1 | 1 | | 1 | | | | | 1 | | | 4 | | |
| Barnstable | 92 | 21 | Crocker | Abram | 2 | | 1 | | 1 | | | 1 | | 1 | | | 6 | | |
| Barnstable | 89 | 5 | Crocker | Alvin | 1 | | 2 | 1 | 1 | | | 2 | | 1 | 2 | | 10 | | |
| Barnstable | 89 | 19 | Crocker | Ansel | 1 | 1 | | 1 | | 2 | | | 1 | | | | 6 | | |
| Barnstable | 92 | 14 | Crocker | Barna | | | 2 | | 2 | | | 2 | 1 | | | | 7 | | |
| Barnstable | 87 | 7 | Crocker | Bathsheba | | | | 1 | | | | 1 | 1 | | | | 3 | | |
| Barnstable | 88 | 32 | Crocker | Benjamin | 1 | 2 | 2 | | 1 | | 1 | 1 | 1 | | | | 9 | | |
| Barnstable | 89 | 42 | Crocker | Benjamin Jr | 2 | 3 | 1 | | 1 | | | | 1 | 1 | | | 9 | | |
| Barnstable | 92 | 15 | Crocker | Bursley | 2 | | | | 1 | 2 | 1 | | 1 | | | | 7 | | |
| Barnstable | 89 | 30 | Crocker | Calvin | 1 | 1 | | 2 | | 3 | | | 1 | | | | 8 | | |
| Sandwich | 37 | 5 | Crocker | Deliverance | 1 | | | 2 | | 1 | 2 | 1 | | | | | 8 | | |
| Barnstable | 87 | 2 | Crocker | Ebenezr Jr | | | 2 | 1 | | 1 | 1 | | | | | | 5 | | |
| Barnstable | 88 | 50 | Crocker | Ebenz Esq | | | 2 | 1 | | | 1 | | | 1 | | | 5 | | |
| Barnstable | 87 | 42 | Crocker | Edmund | | 1 | 1 | | 1 | 1 | 1 | 3 | | 1 | | | 9 | | |
| Barnstable | 89 | 22 | Crocker | Eleazer | 2 | 1 | 3 | | 1 | 1 | 1 | | | 1 | | | 10 | | |
| Barnstable | 89 | 7 | Crocker | Elizabeth | | 1 | | | | 1 | | | 1 | | | | 3 | | |
| Barnstable | 86 | 4 | Crocker | Ezekiel | 2 | | | 1 | | 1 | | | 1 | | | | 5 | | |
| Barnstable | 92 | 22 | Crocker | Francis | | | 1 | | | | | | | | | | 1 | | |
| Barnstable | 88 | 14 | Crocker | Isaac | | | 2 | 1 | | | | 2 | | 1 | | | 6 | | |
| Barnstable | 88 | 15 | Crocker | Isaac Jr | | | 1 | | | | | | 1 | | | | 2 | | |
| Yarmouth | 99 | 11 | Crocker | Isaiah | 2 | 1 | | 1 | | 1 | | | 1 | | | | 6 | | |
| Barnstable | 92 | 46 | Crocker | John | 3 | 1 | | 1 | | 3 | | | 1 | | 1 | | 10 | | |
| Barnstable | 94 | 12 | Crocker | John | | | | 1 | | | | | 1 | | | | 2 | | |
| Barnstable | 87 | 8 | Crocker | John 3d | | 1 | 1 | | | | | 1 | | | | | 3 | | |
| Barnstable | 87 | 39 | Crocker | Joseph | | 1 | 1 | | 1 | | | | 2 | 1 | | | 6 | | |
| Falmouth | 44 | 40 | Crocker | Joseph | | 1 | 1 | | | 3 | 1 | | 1 | | 1 | | 8 | | |
| Harwich | 7 | 22 | Crocker | Joseph | | | 1 | | | 1 | | 1 | | | | | 3 | | |
| Barnstable | 87 | 20 | Crocker | Joseph 3d | 1 | 1 | | 1 | | 2 | | | 1 | | | | 6 | | |
| Barnstable | 89 | 31 | Crocker | Joseph Jr | | 2 | 2 | | 1 | | 1 | | 1 | 2 | | | 9 | | |
| Barnstable | 87 | 40 | Crocker | Moody | 3 | | 1 | 1 | | | | | 1 | | | | 6 | | |
| Barnstable | 91 | 45 | Crocker | Morton | 2 | | | | | 1 | | | 1 | | | | 5 | | |
| Barnstable | 87 | 41 | Crocker | Nathl | 1 | 1 | 1 | | 1 | 1 | | | 1 | 1 | | | 7 | | |
| Barnstable | 88 | 16 | Crocker | Reuben | | | 1 | | | 1 | | | 1 | | | | 3 | | |
| Barnstable | 86 | 13 | Crocker | Samuel | | | 1 | 1 | | | | | 1 | 1 | | | 4 | | |
| Barnstable | 84 | 24 | Crocker | Thankful | | | | | | | | | 2 | | | | 2 | | |
| Barnstable | 85 | 40 | Crocker | Thomas | | 1 | 1 | | 1 | 1 | 1 | 2 | | | | | 7 | | |
| Barnstable | 87 | 10 | Crocker | Thomas Jr | | | 1 | | | 1 | | 1 | | | | | 3 | | |
| Falmouth | 44 | 34 | Crocker | Timothy | | 1 | 2 | 1 | 1 | | | 1 | | 1 | | | 7 | | |
| Falmouth | 44 | 54 | Crocker | Timothy Junr | 1 | | | 1 | | | | | 1 | | | | 3 | | |
| Barnstable | 87 | 9 | Crocker | Walley | | | 1 | | | | | | | | | | 1 | | |
| Barnstable | 87 | 5 | Crocker | William | | | 1 | | | | | | 1 | | | | 2 | | |
| Barnstable | 87 | 6 | Crocker | William Jr | 1 | | | 1 | | 2 | | | 1 | | | | 5 | | |
| Barnstable | 87 | 18 | Crocker | Winslow | 3 | 1 | | 1 | | | | 2 | 1 | 1 | | | 9 | | |
| Barnstable | 89 | 6 | Crocker | Zenas | 2 | | | 1 | | 2 | | | 1 | 1 | 2 | | 9 | | |
| Harwich | 6 | 26 | Crocker | Anthony | 2 | | | 1 | | 1 | | | | | | | 5 | | |
| Dennis | 26 | 43 | Crosby | Barnabas | 2 | 1 | | | 1 | 1 | 2 | 1 | | 1 | | | 9 | | |
| Harwich | 5 | 21 | Crosby | Barnabas | 2 | | | 1 | | 1 | | 1 | 1 | | | | 6 | | |
| Barnstable | 91 | 14 | Crosby | Daniel | 3 | | | 1 | | 1 | | | 1 | | | | 6 | | |
| Harwich | 7 | 2 | Crosby | David | 3 | | | 1 | | 2 | | | 1 | | | | 7 | | |

| TOWN | PG# | LN# | LAST NAME | FIRST NAME | FREE WHITE MALES | | | | | FREE WHITE FEMALES | | | | | TOTAL ALL OTHER | TOTAL SLAVES | TOTALS | DISTRICT/ TOWNSHIP | NOTES |
|---|---|---|---|---|---|---|---|---|---|---|---|---|---|---|---|---|---|---|---|
| | | | | | under 10 | 10 to 16 | 16 to 26 | 26 to 45 | 45 and over | under 10 | 10 to 16 | 16 to 26 | 26 to 45 | 45 and over | | | | | |
| Yarmouth | 98 | 34 | Crosby | David | | | | 1 | | | | | | 1 | | | 2 | | |
| Harwich | 7 | 1 | Crosby | Ebenezer | | 3 | | 1 | | | 1 | 2 | | 1 | | | 8 | | |
| Harwich | 7 | 4 | Crosby | Elisha | | | 1 | 1 | | | | 1 | | 1 | | | 4 | | |
| Harwich | 5 | 19 | Crosby | Elisha Jun | | | 1 | | | | | | 1 | | | | 2 | | |
| Harwich | 9 | 3 | Crosby | Elkanah | | | | 1 | | 3 | 3 | | 1 | | | | 8 | | |
| Harwich | 6 | 29 | Crosby | Hemon | | 1 | 1 | 1 | | | | | 1 | 1 | | | 5 | | |
| Barnstable | 90 | 38 | Crosby | James | 1 | | 1 | | | | | | 1 | | | | 3 | | |
| Harwich | 7 | 9 | Crosby | James | | 1 | | 1 | | | | | 2 | | | | 4 | | |
| Harwich | 6 | 3 | Crosby | James Jun | 2 | | 1 | | | 2 | | 1 | | | | | 6 | | |
| Barnstable | 90 | 34 | Crosby | Jesse | | 1 | 1 | | | 1 | | | 1 | | | | 4 | | |
| Barnstable | 91 | 20 | Crosby | Jesse Jr | | 1 | 1 | | | 2 | | 1 | | | | | 5 | | |
| Harwich | 6 | 4 | Crosby | John | | 1 | 1 | 1 | | | | 1 | 1 | | | | 5 | | |
| Orleans | 22 | 5 | Crosby | Joseph | 4 | | 1 | | | 1 | | | 1 | | | | 7 | | |
| Orleans | 24 | 18 | Crosby | Joshua | 2 | 1 | 2 | | | 2 | 2 | | 1 | | | | 10 | | |
| Harwich | 7 | 6 | Crosby | Josiah | | | 1 | | | | 1 | | 1 | | | | 3 | | |
| Harwich | 8 | 35 | Crosby | Josiah | 2 | | | 1 | | | | 1 | 1 | | | | 5 | | |
| Harwich | 5 | 22 | Crosby | Lemuel | | | 1 | | | | | 1 | 1 | | | | 3 | | |
| Sandwich | 34 | 20 | Crosby | Levi | | | 1 | | | | | 1 | 1 | | | | 3 | | |
| Barnstable | 90 | 26 | Crosby | Lewis | | | 1 | | | | | 1 | | | | | 2 | | |
| Harwich | 8 | 37 | Crosby | Moses | | | 1 | | | | | 1 | 1 | | | | 3 | | |
| Barnstable | 91 | 38 | Crosby | Nathan | 2 | | 1 | 1 | | 3 | | | 1 | | | | 8 | | |
| Harwich | 7 | 5 | Crosby | Nathan | 4 | | 1 | | | | | | 1 | | | | 6 | | |
| Harwich | 7 | 3 | Crosby | Nathaniel | | 1 | | 1 | | | | 1 | 1 | | | | 4 | | |
| Harwich | 7 | 13 | Crosby | Rebecah Wd | 1 | 2 | | | | | | | 1 | | | | 4 | | |
| Harwich | 4 | 29 | Crosby | Samuel | 1 | | | | | | | 2 | | 1 | | | 5 | | |
| Harwich | 7 | 19 | Crosby | Samuel Jun | 1 | | 1 | | | 1 | | 1 | | | | | 4 | | |
| Harwich | 7 | 11 | Crosby | Seth | 1 | | 1 | 1 | | | 2 | 1 | 1 | | | | 7 | | |
| Harwich | 6 | 5 | Crosby | Silvanus | | | 1 | | | | | 1 | 1 | | | | 3 | | |
| Harwich | 6 | 6 | Crosby | Silvanus Jun | | 1 | | | | | 1 | 1 | | | | | 3 | | |
| Harwich | 7 | 10 | Crosby | Thomas | | 1 | | | | | | | 1 | | | | 2 | | |
| Harwich | 7 | 7 | Crosby | William | 1 | | | 1 | | 2 | | 1 | 1 | | | | 6 | | |
| Barnstable | 91 | 10 | Crosley | Samuel | | 1 | | | | | | | 1 | | | | 2 | | |
| Mashpee | 52 | 1 | Cross | | | | | | | | | | | | 1 | | 1 | | First name left blank on census |
| Falmouth | 44 | 39 | Crosswell | Sarah | 1 | | | | | 2 | 2 | 1 | | 1 | | | 7 | | |
| Provincetown | 58 | 1 | Crow | Solomon | | | 1 | | | | | | | 1 | | | 2 | | |
| Provincetown | 58 | 2 | Crow | Solomon Jun | | | 1 | | | 2 | | | | 1 | | | 4 | | |
| Falmouth | 44 | 45 | Crowel | Barnabas | | 1 | 1 | | | 1 | | | | 1 | | | 4 | | |
| Falmouth | 44 | 44 | Crowel | Benjamin | | 1 | 1 | | | | | | 1 | 1 | | | 4 | | |
| Falmouth | 44 | 38 | Crowel | David Senr | | 1 | | 1 | | 1 | | | 1 | 1 | | | 5 | | |
| Falmouth | 44 | 48 | Crowel | Joseph | | 3 | 1 | | | | 1 | | 1 | 1 | | | 7 | | |
| Falmouth | 44 | 46 | Crowel | Joshua | | | 1 | | | | | 2 | | 1 | | | 4 | | |
| Falmouth | 44 | 42 | Crowel | Lot | | 1 | 1 | 1 | | 2 | 1 | 2 | | 1 | | | 9 | | |
| Falmouth | 44 | 47 | Crowel | Stephen | 3 | | | 1 | | 2 | 1 | 1 | | 1 | | | 9 | | |
| Dennis | 27 | 13 | Crowell | Aaron | | 2 | 2 | 1 | | | | 1 | 1 | 2 | | | 9 | | |
| Yarmouth | 98 | 40 | Crowell | Abigail | 2 | | | | | | | 2 | 1 | 1 | | | 6 | | |
| Dennis | 30 | 21 | Crowell | Abner | 1 | | 1 | | | 3 | | | 1 | | | | 6 | | |
| Barnstable | 94 | 32 | Crowell | Abner Jr | | | 1 | | | | | 1 | 1 | | | | 3 | | |
| Dennis | 32 | 3 | Crowell | Anthony | 3 | | 1 | | | 1 | | | 1 | 1 | | | 7 | | |
| Barnstable | 94 | 39 | Crowell | Barnabas | | | 1 | 1 | | | | 1 | | | | | 3 | | |
| Dennis | 26 | 22 | Crowell | Christopher | | 2 | 2 | 1 | | | | | 1 | 1 | | | 7 | | |
| Barnstable | 101 | 14 | Crowell | Daniel | | 1 | 2 | 1 | | 1 | 1 | 1 | | 1 | | | 8 | | |
| Chatham | 16 | 4 | Crowell | David | | | 1 | 1 | | | | | 1 | 1 | | | 4 | | |
| Dennis | 32 | 12 | Crowell | David | 1 | 2 | 1 | 1 | | 3 | | | 1 | | | | 9 | | |
| Chatham | 19 | 36 | Crowell | David Jun | | | 1 | | | | | 1 | 1 | | | | 3 | | |
| Chatham | 20 | 17 | Crowell | David Jun | | | 1 | | | | | 2 | 1 | | | | 4 | | |
| Dennis | 32 | 14 | Crowell | Ebenezer | 1 | | 1 | | | 1 | 1 | 1 | 1 | | | | 6 | | |
| Barnstable | 94 | 30 | Crowell | Edmind | 2 | | 1 | | | 1 | 2 | 2 | | 1 | | | 9 | | |
| Dennis | 31 | 39 | Crowell | Edward | | 1 | | 1 | | | | 1 | | 1 | | | 4 | | |
| Dennis | 30 | 26 | Crowell | Edward Jun | 2 | 1 | | 1 | | 1 | | | | 1 | | | 6 | | |
| Yarmouth | 99 | 47 | Crowell | Eleazer | 3 | 1 | | 1 | | 1 | 1 | | 1 | | | | 8 | | |
| Dennis | 31 | 41 | Crowell | Elisha | 1 | | | 1 | 1 | | 2 | 1 | | 1 | | | 8 | | |
| Yarmouth | 100 | 16 | Crowell | Elkanah | 1 | 1 | | 1 | | 4 | 1 | 1 | | 1 | | | 10 | | |
| Dennis | 30 | 2 | Crowell | Ephraim | | 1 | 1 | 1 | | | | | | 2 | | | 5 | | |
| Barnstable | 86 | 15 | Crowell | Ezra | 2 | | 1 | 1 | | 2 | | | 1 | 1 | | | 8 | | |
| Chatham | 16 | 8 | Crowell | Ezra | 1 | | 1 | | | 3 | | | 1 | | | | 6 | | |
| Dennis | 32 | 1 | Crowell | Freeman | 1 | | 1 | | | | | | 1 | | | | 3 | | |
| Barnstable | 94 | 29 | Crowell | Gorham | 2 | 2 | | 1 | | 1 | | | 1 | 1 | | | 8 | | |
| Chatham | 16 | 6 | Crowell | Hallet | | | 1 | | | 2 | | | 1 | | | | 4 | | |
| Dennis | 31 | 42 | Crowell | Heman | 3 | | 2 | | | 2 | 1 | 1 | | 1 | | | 10 | | |
| Barnstable | 94 | 31 | Crowell | Isaac | 1 | 1 | | 1 | | 1 | 1 | | | 2 | | | 7 | | |
| Dennis | 32 | 2 | Crowell | Isaac | 2 | | 1 | | | | | | 1 | | | | 4 | | |
| Barnstable | 94 | 28 | Crowell | Isaac Jr | 1 | | 1 | | | | | | 1 | | | | 3 | | |
| Yarmouth | 99 | 50 | Crowell | Isaiah | 2 | | 1 | | | 1 | | | 1 | | | | 5 | | |
| Harwich | 11 | 4 | Crowell | Jabez | | 1 | 1 | | | | | 1 | | | | | 3 | | |
| Barnstable | 85 | 43 | Crowell | James | 1 | | 1 | | | | | | 1 | | | | 3 | | |
| Yarmouth | 100 | 15 | Crowell | Jeremiah | | 1 | 2 | | | 1 | 1 | 1 | | 1 | | | 7 | | |
| Chatham | 15 | 25 | Crowell | John | | | 1 | | | | | | 1 | | | | 2 | | |
| Chatham | 19 | 25 | Crowell | John | | | 1 | | | | | | 1 | | | | 2 | | |
| Chatham | 20 | 38 | Crowell | John | | 1 | | | | | | | 1 | | | | 2 | | |
| Dennis | 26 | 21 | Crowell | John | 1 | 2 | 1 | | | 1 | 2 | 1 | 1 | | | | 9 | | |
| Yarmouth | 100 | 18 | Crowell | John | 1 | | | 1 | 1 | | | | 1 | | | | 4 | | |
| Yarmouth | 99 | 41 | Crowell | John Jr | 1 | 1 | | 1 | | 4 | | | | 1 | | | 8 | | |
| Dennis | 32 | 11 | Crowell | Jonathan | | 1 | 2 | | | 2 | 1 | | | 1 | | | 8 | | |
| Yarmouth | 98 | 32 | Crowell | Joseph | 4 | 1 | | 1 | | | | | 1 | | | | 8 | | |

# 1800 Barnstable County, Massachusetts Index

| TOWN | PG# | LN# | LAST NAME | FIRST NAME | FREE WHITE MALES under 10 | 10 to 16 | 16 to 26 | 26 to 45 | 45 and over | FREE WHITE FEMALES under 10 | 10 to 16 | 16 to 26 | 26 to 45 | 45 and over | TOTAL ALL OTHER | TOTAL SLAVES | TOTALS | DISTRICT/ TOWNSHIP | NOTES |
|---|---|---|---|---|---|---|---|---|---|---|---|---|---|---|---|---|---|---|---|
| Dennis | 27 | 9 | Crowell | Josiah | | 1 | 1 | | 1 | 2 | 1 | | | 1 | | | 7 | | |
| Dennis | 32 | 7 | Crowell | Judah | 3 | 1 | | 1 | | 1 | | | 1 | | | | 7 | | |
| Yarmouth | 99 | 16 | Crowell | Lot | 2 | | | 1 | | 1 | | | 1 | | | | 5 | | |
| Harwich | 15 | 8 | Crowell | Mary Wd | | | | | | | | 2 | | 1 | | | 3 | | |
| Yarmouth | 99 | 15 | Crowell | Mathew | | | 1 | | | | 1 | | | 2 | | | 4 | | |
| Yarmouth | 99 | 8 | Crowell | Michael | 3 | 1 | | 1 | | 3 | 1 | | 1 | | | | 10 | | |
| Dennis | 27 | 1 | Crowell | Nathan | 2 | | | 1 | | 2 | | | 1 | | | | 6 | | |
| Harwich | 14 | 2 | Crowell | Nathan | | | 1 | 1 | | | | | | 1 | | | 3 | | |
| Yarmouth | 100 | 19 | Crowell | Nehemiah | 2 | | | 1 | | 1 | | | 1 | | | | 5 | | |
| Chatham | 16 | 5 | Crowell | Paul | | | | 1 | | | | | | 1 | | | 2 | | |
| Dennis | 26 | 25 | Crowell | Paul | | | 1 | | | 2 | 1 | | | | | | 4 | | |
| Yarmouth | 97 | 42 | Crowell | Prince | 2 | | | 1 | | 1 | | | 1 | | | | 5 | | |
| Dennis | 31 | 4 | Crowell | Reuben | | | | | 1 | | | 1 | 1 | 3 | | | 6 | | |
| Yarmouth | 100 | 13 | Crowell | Robert | | 1 | 1 | | 1 | | 1 | | | 1 | | | 5 | | |
| Yarmouth | 99 | 9 | Crowell | Samuel | 2 | | | 1 | | 2 | | | 2 | | | | 7 | | |
| Barnstable | 94 | 37 | Crowell | Sarah | | 1 | 1 | | 1 | | | 2 | | 1 | | | 6 | | |
| Dennis | 32 | 13 | Crowell | Sarah Wid | | 2 | | | | 2 | 1 | 3 | | 1 | | | 9 | | |
| Yarmouth | 100 | 9 | Crowell | Shubail | 1 | 2 | 4 | | 1 | 2 | | | 1 | | 1 | | 12 | | |
| Barnstable | 94 | 35 | Crowell | Silva Jr | 2 | 1 | 1 | 1 | | 3 | 1 | | 1 | | | | 10 | | |
| Yarmouth | 99 | 48 | Crowell | Silvanus | | | 1 | | | | | | | | | | 1 | | |
| Harwich | 4 | 31 | Crowell | Simeon | | | 1 | | | | | | 1 | | | | 2 | | |
| Dennis | 30 | 32 | Crowell | Solomon | | | | | 1 | | | 1 | 1 | 1 | | | 4 | | |
| Harwich | 14 | 41 | Crowell | Solomon | | | 1 | | | 1 | | 1 | 1 | 1 | | | 5 | | |
| Yarmouth | 100 | 17 | Crowell | Solomon | 2 | 1 | 1 | 1 | | 1 | | 1 | | 1 | | | 8 | | |
| Chatham | 16 | 11 | Crowell | Stetson | | 1 | 1 | | | | | | 1 | | | | 3 | | |
| Chatham | 20 | 12 | Crowell | Stetson | 3 | | 1 | | | | | | 1 | 1 | | | 6 | | |
| Yarmouth | 95 | 6 | Crowell | Thankful | | | | | | | | | 1 | 1 | | | 2 | | |
| Barnstable | 94 | 38 | Crowell | Thomas | 1 | | | 1 | | 1 | | 1 | | | | | 4 | | |
| Dennis | 31 | 40 | Crowell | Thomas | 3 | | | 1 | | 1 | 2 | | 1 | | | | 8 | | |
| Yarmouth | 99 | 5 | Crowell | Thomas | | 1 | | | 1 | 2 | 2 | | 1 | 1 | | | 8 | | |
| Dennis | 32 | 5 | Crowell | Venna | 2 | | | 1 | | | | | 1 | | | | 4 | | |
| Dennis | 26 | 24 | Crowell | William | | | | 1 | | | 1 | | | 1 | | | 3 | | |
| Dennis | 26 | 35 | Crowell | William Jun | 1 | | 1 | | | | | | 1 | | | | 3 | | |
| Chatham | 16 | 7 | Crowell | Zenus | 1 | 2 | 1 | | 1 | 2 | | 1 | 1 | 1 | | | 10 | | |
| Barnstable | 94 | 33 | Crowell | Zira | 1 | | | 1 | | | | | 1 | | | | 3 | | |
| Yarmouth | 97 | 29 | Crowell | Edmund Jr | | | 1 | | | | | | 1 | | | | 2 | | |
| Yarmouth | 97 | 25 | Custis | John | 1 | | 1 | 1 | | 2 | | 1 | 2 | 1 | | | 9 | | |
| Chatham | 16 | 1 | Cyk | Reuben | | | 1 | 1 | | | | | | 1 | | | 3 | | |
| Sandwich | 35 | 25 | Cyprus | George | | | | | | | | | | | 2 | | 2 | | |
| Barnstable | 85 | 48 | Daniel | Daniel | 2 | | | 2 | | 2 | 2 | | 1 | 2 | | | 11 | | |
| Wellfleet | 74 | 5 | Darling | John | 1 | | | 1 | | | | | 1 | | | | 3 | | |
| Falmouth | 44 | 62 | Davis | Abner | 2 | 1 | | | 1 | | | 1 | 1 | 1 | | | 7 | | |
| Chatham | 16 | 15 | Davis | Benjm | | | 1 | | | 3 | | | 1 | | | | 5 | | |
| Falmouth | 45 | 72 | Davis | Crocker | 3 | | | 1 | | 2 | | 1 | 1 | 1 | | | 9 | | |
| Falmouth | 49 | 310 | Davis | David | 1 | | | 1 | | | | | 1 | | | | 3 | | |
| Truro | 62 | 18 | Davis | Ebenezer Lomba | 1 | | | | | 1 | | 1 | | | | | 3 | | |
| Barnstable | 83 | 23 | Davis | Edward | | | | 1 | | | | | 1 | | | | 2 | | |
| Falmouth | 44 | 60 | Davis | Francis | 2 | 2 | | 1 | | 2 | 1 | 2 | 1 | | | | 11 | | |
| Falmouth | 44 | 70 | Davis | Ichabod | | | | 1 | | 2 | | 1 | | 1 | | | 5 | | |
| Barnstable | 84 | 1 | Davis | Isaac | 1 | | | 1 | | 4 | | | 1 | | | | 7 | | |
| Falmouth | 44 | 64 | Davis | Jabez | 1 | | | 1 | | | | | 1 | | | | 3 | | |
| Barnstable | 84 | 14 | Davis | James | | | 1 | | 1 | | | 1 | 2 | 1 | | | 6 | | |
| Truro | 64 | 3 | Davis | James W | 2 | | | 1 | | | | | | 1 | | | 4 | | |
| Falmouth | 45 | 73 | Davis | Joanna | | | | | | | | | 1 | 1 | | | 2 | | |
| Falmouth | 45 | 74 | Davis | Job | | 1 | | | | | | | 1 | | | | 2 | | |
| Barnstable | 84 | 13 | Davis | Job C | 1 | | | 1 | | 4 | | | 1 | | | | 7 | | |
| Barnstable | 90 | 39 | Davis | John | | | 1 | | | | | 1 | | 1 | | | 3 | | |
| Falmouth | 44 | 63 | Davis | John | 2 | 1 | | 1 | 1 | 1 | 1 | | 2 | 1 | | | 10 | | |
| Barnstable | 83 | 22 | Davis | John 3d | | 1 | | | | | | 1 | | | | | 2 | | |
| Barnstable | 84 | 47 | Davis | Jonathan | | | 1 | | | | | 1 | 1 | 1 | | | 4 | | |
| Falmouth | 44 | 68 | Davis | Joseph | 2 | 1 | | 1 | 1 | 2 | | 1 | 1 | 1 | | | 10 | | |
| Barnstable | 83 | 24 | Davis | Josiah | 1 | | | 1 | | 1 | 1 | | 1 | | | | 5 | | |
| Falmouth | 44 | 71 | Davis | Malachai | | 2 | | 1 | | | | | 1 | 1 | | | 5 | | |
| Falmouth | 49 | 298 | Davis | Malachai Junr | | 1 | | | | | | 1 | | | | | 2 | | |
| Barnstable | 85 | 35 | Davis | Mary | | | | | | 2 | 1 | | 2 | | | | 5 | | |
| Barnstable | 86 | 3 | Davis | Mehitable | | | | | | | | 1 | | 1 | | | 2 | | |
| Falmouth | 49 | 309 | Davis | Prince | 4 | | | 1 | | | | | 1 | | | | 6 | | |
| Harwich | 10 | 39 | Davis | Samuel | 1 | | | 1 | | 3 | | | 1 | | | | 6 | | |
| Falmouth | 49 | 277 | Davis | Solomon | | | | | 1 | | | 1 | | 1 | | | 3 | | |
| Falmouth | 44 | 59 | Davis | Solomon Junr | 2 | 1 | 1 | 1 | | 1 | | 1 | | | | | 7 | | |
| Falmouth | 44 | 61 | Davis | Thomas | 1 | 2 | 1 | | | 1 | | | | 1 | | | 6 | | |
| Harwich | 11 | 2 | Davis | Timothy | 1 | 1 | 1 | | 1 | 1 | | 1 | 1 | 1 | | | 8 | | |
| Falmouth | 45 | 75 | Davis | Walter | 2 | | | 1 | | | | | 1 | | | | 4 | | |
| Barnstable | 83 | 21 | Davis | Joseph | | 1 | | | 1 | | | | | 1 | | | 3 | | |
| Barnstable | 83 | 20 | Davis | Elisha T | 2 | 1 | 1 | | 1 | 2 | | | | | | | 7 | | |
| Barnstable | 83 | 6 | Davis Esq | John | | 1 | 4 | | 1 | 1 | 2 | 1 | | 1 | | | 11 | | |
| Orleans | 24 | 40 | Daycom | Timothy | | | | 1 | | 1 | | 1 | | 1 | | | 4 | | |
| Wellfleet | 70 | 21 | Deane | Hezekiah | | 1 | | 1 | | | | 1 | | 1 | | | 4 | | |
| Chatham | 16 | 18 | Deland | Ebenezer | | | 1 | | | | | | | 1 | | | 2 | | |
| Truro | 68 | 9 | Demmond | Revd Jude | 3 | | | 1 | | | | 1 | | 1 | | | 6 | | |
| Barnstable | 87 | 1 | Dexter | John | | 1 | 1 | 1 | | | | 1 | 1 | 1 | | | 6 | | |
| Chatham | 16 | 14 | Dexter | Joseph | 2 | | | 1 | | 2 | 1 | 2 | | 1 | | | 9 | | |
| Eastham | 80 | 1 | Dill | Benjamin | 3 | | | 1 | | 2 | | | 1 | | | | 7 | | |

# 1800 Barnstable County, Massachusetts Index

| TOWN | PG# | LN# | HEADS OF HOUSEHOLD | | FREE WHITE MALES | | | | | FREE WHITE FEMALES | | | | | TOTAL ALL OTHER | TOTAL SLAVES | TOTALS | DISTRICT/ TOWNSHIP | NOTES |
|---|---|---|---|---|---|---|---|---|---|---|---|---|---|---|---|---|---|---|---|
| | | | LAST NAME | FIRST NAME | under 10 | 10 to 16 | 16 to 26 | 26 to 45 | 45 and over | under 10 | 10 to 16 | 16 to 26 | 26 to 45 | 45 and over | | | | | |
| Wellfleet | 70 | 24 | Dill | James | | 1 | | 1 | 1 | | | | | 1 | | | 4 | | |
| Wellfleet | 74 | 7 | Dill | Moses | 2 | | 1 | | | | | | 1 | | | | 4 | | |
| Eastham | 77 | 16 | Dill | Thomas | 3 | 4 | | 1 | | 1 | | | | 1 | | | 10 | | |
| Sandwich | 35 | 41 | Dillingham | Benjamin | 1 | 2 | 1 | 1 | | | 1 | | 1 | 1 | | | 8 | | |
| Sandwich | 36 | 8 | Dillingham | Branch | 3 | | 1 | | | 1 | | | 2 | | | | 7 | | |
| Sandwich | 35 | 31 | Dillingham | Edward | | 1 | 1 | 1 | | | | 1 | | 1 | | | 5 | | |
| Falmouth | 44 | 65 | Dillingham | Ignatius | | | | 1 | | | | | 2 | | | | 3 | | |
| Harwich | 3 | 13 | Dillingham | Isaac | | 1 | | | | 1 | | 1 | | | | | 3 | | |
| Harwich | 3 | 11 | Dillingham | John | 2 | | | 1 | | 1 | 1 | 1 | | | 1 | | 8 | | |
| Sandwich | 36 | 9 | Dillingham | John | | | | 1 | | | | 1 | | 1 | | | 3 | | |
| Harwich | 3 | 12 | Dillingham | John Jun | 2 | | 1 | | | | | | 1 | | | | 4 | | |
| Sandwich | 35 | 28 | Dillingham | John Junr | | 2 | 1 | 1 | | | | 2 | 1 | 1 | | | 8 | | |
| Falmouth | 45 | 77 | Dillingham | Joseph | 1 | | 1 | | | | | 1 | 1 | | | | 4 | | |
| Falmouth | 44 | 69 | Dimmick | Anselm | | | 1 | | 1 | | | | 1 | | | | 3 | | |
| Falmouth | 45 | 78 | Dimmick | Bradock | 2 | 2 | 1 | 1 | | | 2 | 1 | | 1 | | | 10 | | |
| Sandwich | 40 | 43 | Dimmick | David | 2 | | | 1 | 1 | 1 | | 2 | 1 | | | | 8 | | |
| Falmouth | 44 | 67 | Dimmick | Jabez | | | 1 | | | | | | 1 | 1 | | | 3 | | |
| Falmouth | 44 | 66 | Dimmick | Joseph | | 1 | | 1 | | | | 1 | | 1 | | | 4 | | |
| Falmouth | 44 | 57 | Dimmick | Lot | 1 | 1 | | 1 | | | | | | 1 | | | 4 | | |
| Falmouth | 44 | 58 | Dimmick | Robinson | 1 | | 1 | | | | | 1 | 1 | 1 | | | 5 | | |
| Barnstable | 84 | 37 | Dimock | Charles | 1 | | 1 | | | 3 | 3 | 1 | 1 | | | | 10 | | |
| Barnstable | 84 | 36 | Dimock | Thomas | | | | 1 | | | | | 1 | 1 | | | 3 | | |
| Sandwich | 36 | 16 | Do*ise | Fredrick | | 1 | | 1 | 1 | 1 | 1 | | | | | | 5 | | |
| Harwich | 9 | 40 | Doane | Benjm | 1 | | 1 | | | 2 | | 1 | | | | | 5 | | |
| Eastham | 77 | 14 | Doane | Betty | | 1 | | | | | | | 1 | | | | 2 | | |
| Eastham | 79 | 7 | Doane | Betty | | 1 | 1 | | | | | 1 | | 1 | | | 4 | | |
| Harwich | 11 | 31 | Doane | Daniel | 1 | 1 | | 1 | | 3 | | | 1 | | | | 7 | | |
| Chatham | 19 | 15 | Doane | Elisha | | 1 | | | | | | | 1 | | | | 2 | | |
| Harwich | 12 | 25 | Doane | Elisha | | 1 | 1 | 1 | | | | | | 1 | | | 4 | | |
| Yarmouth | 96 | 37 | Doane | Elisha | 1 | | | 1 | | 1 | 1 | | 1 | | 1 | | 7 | | |
| Harwich | 12 | 26 | Doane | Elisha Jun | 4 | | 1 | 1 | | | | | 1 | | | | 7 | | |
| Eastham | 77 | 9 | Doane | Elkanah | | 1 | | 1 | | | | | | 1 | | | 3 | | |
| Eastham | 77 | 7 | Doane | Freeman | | | | 1 | | | 2 | | 1 | | | | 4 | | |
| Eastham | 77 | 4 | Doane | Herman | 3 | 2 | 1 | | | | 2 | | 1 | | | | 9 | | |
| Barnstable | 85 | 34 | Doane | Hezekiah | 1 | | 1 | | | | 1 | | 1 | | | | 4 | | |
| Chatham | 16 | 16 | Doane | Hezekiah | | 2 | 2 | 1 | | 1 | 1 | | | 1 | | | 8 | | |
| Orleans | 24 | 38 | Doane | Hezekiah | 2 | 2 | | 1 | | 2 | 1 | | 1 | 1 | | | 10 | | |
| Eastham | 77 | 5 | Doane | Isaiah | 1 | 1 | | 1 | | | | 1 | | 1 | | | 5 | | |
| Eastham | 77 | 6 | Doane | Jesse | | 1 | | 1 | | | | 1 | | 1 | | | 4 | | |
| Eastham | 79 | 8 | Doane | Jesse Junr | 1 | | 1 | 2 | | | | | 1 | | | | 5 | | |
| Chatham | 16 | 17 | Doane | John | 1 | | 1 | 1 | | | | | 1 | | | | 4 | | |
| Chatham | 16 | 13 | Doane | Joseph | | 3 | 2 | 1 | | 1 | | | | 1 | | | 8 | | |
| Eastham | 77 | 15 | Doane | Joshua | | 3 | 1 | 1 | | 1 | 2 | 1 | | 1 | | | 10 | | |
| Eastham | 77 | 3 | Doane | Lydia | | 1 | | | | | 2 | | 1 | | | | 4 | | |
| Eastham | 79 | 12 | Doane | Myrick | | | 1 | | | 1 | | 1 | | | | | 3 | | |
| Harwich | 11 | 25 | Doane | Nathaniel | | 2 | | 1 | | | | | 1 | | | | 4 | | |
| Eastham | 77 | 12 | Doane | Obadiah | 1 | | 1 | | | | 2 | | 1 | | | | 5 | | |
| Eastham | 77 | 13 | Doane | Prince | 1 | | 1 | | 1 | 1 | | 1 | | | | | 5 | | |
| Eastham | 79 | 11 | Doane | Rebecca | 1 | | | | | | | | 1 | | | | 2 | | |
| Chatham | 16 | 12 | Doane | Samuel | 2 | | | 2 | | 2 | 1 | | 1 | | | | 8 | | |
| Eastham | 79 | 16 | Doane | Samuel | 2 | | 1 | | | | | | 1 | | | | 4 | | |
| Eastham | 77 | 11 | Doane | Silvanus | | | | 1 | | | 1 | | | 1 | | | 3 | | |
| Eastham | 77 | 10 | Doane | Solomon | | 3 | | 1 | | | | | | 1 | | | 5 | | |
| Orleans | 24 | 13 | Doane | Timothy | | 3 | 1 | 1 | | 3 | 1 | 1 | 1 | | | | 11 | | |
| Eastham | 77 | 8 | Doane | Zenas | 3 | 3 | 1 | | | | | | 1 | | | | 8 | | |
| Eastham | 77 | 17 | Doanes | John | 2 | | 1 | | | | | | 1 | | | | 4 | | |
| Falmouth | 45 | 76 | Donaldson | Hugh G. | 3 | | 1 | | 2 | 2 | 1 | | | | | | 9 | | |
| Mashpee | 51 | 6 | Doty | James | 1 | | 1 | | | | | | 1 | | | | 3 | | |
| Sandwich | 38 | 10 | Doty | James | | | | | | | | | | | | | | | Enumeration left blank |
| Barnstable | 84 | 26 | Downs | Barna Jn | 1 | 1 | | 1 | | 3 | 1 | | 1 | 2 | | | 10 | | |
| Barnstable | 84 | 25 | Downs | Barnabas | | | | 1 | | | 1 | 1 | 1 | | | | 4 | | |
| Barnstable | 84 | 43 | Downs | David | 2 | | 1 | 1 | | | | | 1 | | | | 5 | | |
| Barnstable | 84 | 27 | Downs | James | | | | 1 | 2 | 2 | | | 1 | | | | 6 | | |
| Barnstable | 84 | 28 | Downs | Mary | 1 | 2 | | | | | | | 1 | | | | 5 | | |
| Sandwich | 41 | 22 | Drandy | Samuel | 3 | 2 | 1 | 1 | | | | 1 | 1 | | | | 9 | | |
| Harwich | 7 | 15 | Dun | Peter | | 1 | | | | | | | 1 | | | | 2 | | |
| Provincetown | 58 | 6 | Dunham | Rebeccah Wd | | | | | | | | | 1 | | | | 1 | | |
| Sandwich | 40 | 2 | Dunham | Samuel | 2 | | 1 | 1 | | 1 | 1 | | 1 | | | | 7 | | |
| Provincetown | 60 | 6 | Durner | Joseph | 1 | 1 | 2 | 1 | | 2 | 1 | 1 | | | | | 10 | | |
| Provincetown | 60 | 21 | Dyer | Ambros | | 1 | | 1 | 3 | | | | 1 | | | | 6 | | |
| Truro | 68 | 16 | Dyer | Caleb | | | 1 | | | | | 1 | | | | | 2 | | |
| Truro | 67 | 6 | Dyer | David | 3 | | 1 | 1 | | 1 | | 1 | 1 | | | | 9 | | |
| Truro | 62 | 9 | Dyer | Deliverance Junr | 2 | | 1 | | | | | | 1 | | | | 4 | | |
| Truro | 67 | 5 | Dyer | Fulk | | 2 | 1 | | | | | | 1 | 1 | | | 5 | | |
| Provincetown | 58 | 7 | Dyer | Hannah Wd | | 1 | | | | | | 1 | 1 | | | | 3 | | |
| Truro | 63 | 5 | Dyer | Hannah Wid | 1 | 3 | | | | | | 1 | 1 | 1 | | | 7 | | |
| Truro | 67 | 2 | Dyer | Henry | 1 | | 1 | | | | | 1 | 1 | | | | 5 | | |
| Truro | 63 | 12 | Dyer | Isaac | 3 | 1 | | 1 | | | | 1 | 1 | | | | 7 | | |
| Truro | 68 | 12 | Dyer | James Harding | 1 | 1 | | 1 | | 1 | 1 | | | | | | 6 | | |
| Truro | 68 | 4 | Dyer | Josha | 1 | | | | | | 1 | | 1 | | | | 3 | | |
| Wellfleet | 70 | 23 | Dyer | Micah | 3 | | 1 | | | | | | 1 | | | | 5 | | |
| Truro | 64 | 20 | Dyer | Nepthaly | 2 | | | 1 | | | | 2 | 1 | | | | 6 | | |
| Truro | 67 | 7 | Dyer | Paul | 2 | 3 | 1 | | | 1 | 1 | | 1 | 1 | | | 11 | | |
| Truro | 67 | 3 | Dyer | Rebecah Wid | | | | | | | | 1 | | 1 | | | 2 | | |

# 1800 Barnstable County, Massachusetts Index

| TOWN | PG# | LN# | LAST NAME | FIRST NAME | FREE WHITE MALES under 10 | 10 to 16 | 16 to 26 | 26 to 45 | 45 and over | FREE WHITE FEMALES under 10 | 10 to 16 | 16 to 26 | 26 to 45 | 45 and over | TOTAL ALL OTHER | TOTAL SLAVES | TOTALS | DISTRICT/ TOWNSHIP | NOTES |
|---|---|---|---|---|---|---|---|---|---|---|---|---|---|---|---|---|---|---|---|
| Truro | 65 | 12 | Dyer | Silvanus | 1 | | | 1 | | 2 | | | 1 | | | | 5 | | |
| Truro | 68 | 17 | Dyer | Silvanus | 1 | | | 1 | | 3 | | | 1 | 1 | | | 7 | | |
| Wellfleet | 70 | 22 | Dyer | Solomon | | 1 | | | 1 | | 1 | 1 | 2 | | | | 6 | | |
| Wellfleet | 75 | 7 | Dyer | Solomon Junr | 1 | | 1 | | | | | | 1 | | | | 3 | | |
| Truro | 67 | 4 | Dyer | Thomas | | 1 | 1 | | 1 | | 1 | 1 | | 1 | | | 6 | | |
| Provincetown | 58 | 5 | Dyer | William | 3 | | | 1 | | | 1 | | 1 | | | | 6 | | |
| Sandwich | 36 | 43 | E* | Lazarus | 1 | 2 | | | 1 | 2 | | 3 | 1 | | | | 10 | | |
| Barnstable | 83 | 15 | Easterbrook | Gorham | 1 | 1 | | 1 | 1 | 2 | 1 | | 1 | | | | 8 | | |
| Barnstable | 84 | 2 | Easterbrook | John | | | | | | | 1 | | | | | | 1 | | |
| Barnstable | 84 | 3 | Easterbrook | John Jn | 1 | | | 1 | | 3 | 1 | | 1 | | | | 7 | | |
| Barnstable | 83 | 18 | Easterbrook | Joseph | 1 | | | 1 | | 2 | | | 1 | | | | 5 | | |
| Barnstable | 84 | 4 | Easterbrook | Saml | 4 | 1 | | 1 | | | | | 1 | | | | 7 | | |
| Harwich | 8 | 21 | Eden | Samuel | | | | | 1 | | 1 | 1 | | 1 | | | 4 | | |
| Falmouth | 45 | 82 | Edwards | Asa | 3 | | 2 | | 1 | 1 | | 2 | | 1 | | | 10 | | |
| Falmouth | 45 | 86 | Eldred | Abiel | 1 | 1 | 1 | | 1 | | | 1 | 1 | | | | 6 | | |
| Falmouth | 45 | 84 | Eldred | Ann | | | 1 | | | | | 2 | 1 | | | | 4 | | |
| Falmouth | 45 | 89 | Eldred | Experience | 1 | | 1 | | | | | 1 | | 1 | | | 4 | | |
| Falmouth | 45 | 85 | Eldred | Ezekiel | 2 | | 1 | | | | | 1 | | | | | 4 | | |
| Falmouth | 45 | 79 | Eldred | John | | 2 | | 1 | | | 2 | | | 1 | | | 6 | | |
| Falmouth | 45 | 80 | Eldred | Samuel | 1 | 1 | 1 | 1 | | | | | | | | | 5 | | |
| Falmouth | 45 | 87 | Eldred | Samuel | 1 | 1 | | 1 | | | 1 | | 1 | | | | 5 | | |
| Falmouth | 45 | 90 | Eldred | Simeon | | | 1 | | | | | 1 | | | 1 | | 3 | | |
| Falmouth | 45 | 88 | Eldred | Thos | 2 | | | 1 | | | | 1 | | | | | 4 | | |
| Falmouth | 45 | 83 | Eldred | William | | | | 1 | | | | | | | | | 1 | | |
| Yarmouth | 95 | 5 | Eldredge | Barna | 1 | | | 1 | | 2 | | | 1 | | | | 5 | | |
| Yarmouth | 98 | 28 | Eldredge | David | | 2 | | 1 | | 3 | 2 | 2 | 1 | | | | 11 | | |
| Barnstable | 93 | 25 | Eldredge | Ezra | 1 | | | 1 | | 3 | | | 1 | 1 | | | 7 | | |
| Barnstable | 85 | 44 | Eldredge | Gideon | 2 | | | 1 | | | | 1 | 1 | | | | 5 | | |
| Yarmouth | 98 | 13 | Eldredge | Hannah | 3 | 1 | | | | | 1 | 2 | | 2 | | | 9 | | |
| Yarmouth | 97 | 46 | Eldredge | John | 1 | | | 1 | | | | 2 | | | | | 4 | | |
| Sandwich | 40 | 16 | Eldredge | Josiah | 2 | | | 1 | | | | 1 | | 1 | | | 5 | | |
| Yarmouth | 98 | 20 | Eldredge | Patience | | | 1 | | | | | | 1 | | | | 2 | | |
| Yarmouth | 98 | 21 | Eldredge | Reuben | 2 | | | 1 | | | | 1 | | | | | 4 | | |
| Barnstable | 94 | 7 | Eldredge | Revd Enoch | | 2 | | 1 | | 3 | 1 | | 1 | | | | 8 | | |
| Harwich | 13 | 26 | Eldrege | Abijah | 3 | | | 1 | | 2 | | | 1 | | | | 7 | | |
| Chatham | 16 | 23 | Eldrege | Anthony | 1 | | | | 1 | 1 | 1 | 2 | | 1 | | | 7 | | |
| Chatham | 20 | 14 | Eldrege | Berse | 4 | | 1 | | | 1 | | 1 | | | | | 7 | | |
| Harwich | 11 | 39 | Eldrege | Boni | 3 | | | 1 | | 1 | 2 | | 1 | | | | 8 | | |
| Harwich | 9 | 32 | Eldrege | Boruck | 1 | | 1 | | | 3 | | 1 | | | | | 6 | | |
| Chatham | 16 | 20 | Eldrege | Caleb | 1 | 1 | 1 | | | 2 | | 1 | 1 | 1 | | | 8 | | |
| Chatham | 19 | 26 | Eldrege | Caleb | 1 | 1 | | 1 | | 2 | | | 1 | | | | 6 | | |
| Chatham | 16 | 27 | Eldrege | Daniel | 2 | 1 | | 1 | | 1 | | | 1 | | | | 6 | | |
| Dennis | 28 | 2 | Eldrege | Daniel | 1 | | | 1 | | 2 | | 2 | 1 | | | | 7 | | |
| Harwich | 9 | 35 | Eldrege | Daniel | 4 | | | 1 | | 1 | 1 | | 1 | | | | 8 | | |
| Chatham | 19 | 29 | Eldrege | Daniel Jun | 1 | | | 1 | | 1 | | | 1 | | | | 4 | | |
| Orleans | 22 | 39 | Eldrege | David | | | 1 | | | | | | 1 | | | | 2 | | |
| Harwich | 14 | 47 | Eldrege | Ebenezer | 4 | | 1 | | 1 | 1 | 2 | | 1 | | | | 10 | | |
| Harwich | 13 | 33 | Eldrege | Ebenezor Jun | | 1 | | | | 1 | | 1 | | | | | 3 | | |
| Chatham | 16 | 38 | Eldrege | Edward | 1 | | 1 | | | 1 | | 1 | | | | | 4 | | |
| Harwich | 13 | 32 | Eldrege | Eli | 1 | | 1 | | | | | 1 | | | | | 3 | | |
| Chatham | 16 | 35 | Eldrege | Elisha | 4 | 2 | 1 | 1 | 1 | | | 1 | 1 | | 1 | | 12 | | |
| Chatham | 19 | 13 | Eldrege | Elnathan | | | | 1 | | 2 | 1 | | 1 | | | | 5 | | |
| Harwich | 14 | 31 | Eldrege | Elnathan | 1 | 1 | 1 | | 1 | | 1 | | | 1 | | | 6 | | |
| Chatham | 20 | 22 | Eldrege | Enos | 1 | | 1 | | | | | | 1 | | | | 3 | | |
| Harwich | 12 | 10 | Eldrege | Ensign | | | | 1 | | 3 | | | 1 | | | | 5 | | |
| Harwich | 13 | 27 | Eldrege | Ezra | 1 | | | 1 | | 1 | | | 1 | | | | 4 | | |
| Chatham | 16 | 34 | Eldrege | Hannah Wid | | | 3 | | | | 1 | 1 | | 1 | | | 6 | | |
| Harwich | 6 | 42 | Eldrege | Hezekiah | | 1 | | 1 | | | | 1 | | 1 | | | 4 | | |
| Chatham | 16 | 24 | Eldrege | Isaac | 3 | | 1 | | 1 | 1 | 1 | 2 | | 1 | | | 10 | | |
| Harwich | 11 | 41 | Eldrege | Isaac | | | | 1 | | | | 1 | 1 | | | | 3 | | |
| Chatham | 19 | 28 | Eldrege | Isaac Jun | 1 | | 1 | | | | | 1 | | | | | 3 | | |
| Harwich | 11 | 43 | Eldrege | Isaac Jun | 1 | 2 | 1 | 1 | | 3 | | | 1 | | | | 9 | | |
| Harwich | 13 | 25 | Eldrege | Isaiah | 1 | 1 | | 1 | | 2 | 1 | | 1 | | | | 7 | | |
| Chatham | 16 | 26 | Eldrege | James | 1 | | | 1 | 2 | | 1 | 1 | | 1 | | | 7 | | |
| Chatham | 19 | 27 | Eldrege | Jeremiah | | 1 | 1 | 1 | | | 1 | | | 1 | | | 5 | | |
| Chatham | 16 | 25 | Eldrege | John | 2 | 1 | 1 | 1 | | 2 | | | 1 | | | | 8 | | |
| Chatham | 16 | 30 | Eldrege | Jonathan | | 1 | 1 | | | | 1 | | 1 | | | | 4 | | |
| Chatham | 16 | 32 | Eldrege | Josiah | 4 | | | 1 | 1 | 1 | 2 | 1 | | 1 | | | 10 | | |
| Harwich | 10 | 6 | Eldrege | Judah | 1 | | | 1 | | | 1 | | | 1 | | | 4 | | |
| Chatham | 20 | 10 | Eldrege | Martha Wid | | | 1 | | | | 2 | | | 1 | | | 4 | | |
| Harwich | 9 | 33 | Eldrege | Mary Wd | 1 | | | | | | | 1 | | 1 | 1 | 1 | 5 | | |
| Chatham | 16 | 28 | Eldrege | Nathaniel | 1 | 3 | 1 | | 1 | 2 | | | 2 | | | | 11 | | |
| Chatham | 16 | 36 | Eldrege | Nathaniel Jr | 2 | | 1 | 1 | | | 2 | | | 1 | | | 7 | | |
| Harwich | 14 | 32 | Eldrege | Nehemiah | 2 | | 1 | | | | | | 1 | | | | 4 | | |
| Orleans | 22 | 35 | Eldrege | Nehemiah | 1 | | 1 | | | 1 | | | 1 | | | | 4 | | |
| Harwich | 11 | 40 | Eldrege | Obed | 3 | 3 | | 1 | | | | | 1 | | | | 8 | | |
| Dennis | 31 | 7 | Eldrege | Prince | 1 | | 1 | | | | | | 1 | | | | 3 | | |
| Harwich | 9 | 30 | Eldrege | Reuben | | | | | 1 | | | | 1 | 1 | | | 3 | | |
| Orleans | 22 | 32 | Eldrege | Reuben | | 2 | 1 | | 1 | | 1 | 1 | | 1 | | | 7 | | |
| Harwich | 9 | 28 | Eldrege | Samuel | 1 | 1 | | 1 | 1 | 3 | 1 | 1 | | 1 | | | 10 | | |
| Chatham | 16 | 19 | Eldrege | Seth | | 1 | 1 | 1 | | | 1 | | | 2 | | | 6 | | |
| Harwich | 13 | 30 | Eldrege | Seth | 1 | | 1 | | | | | 1 | | | | | 3 | | |
| Chatham | 16 | 29 | Eldrege | Stephen | | | 2 | | 1 | 2 | | | 2 | | 1 | | 6 | | |
| Chatham | 19 | 35 | Eldrege | Thankful Wid | 2 | 1 | | | | 2 | | | 1 | | | | 6 | | |
| Chatham | 16 | 37 | Eldrege | Thankfull Wid | 3 | | | | | 1 | | | 1 | | | | 5 | | |
| Chatham | 16 | 33 | Eldrege | Thomas | | | | | | 1 | | | | | | | 6 | | |

# 1800 Barnstable County, Massachusetts Index

| TOWN | PG# | LN# | LAST NAME | FIRST NAME | FREE WHITE MALES | | | | | FREE WHITE FEMALES | | | | | TOTAL ALL OTHER | TOTAL SLAVES | TOTALS | DISTRICT/ TOWNSHIP | NOTES |
|---|---|---|---|---|---|---|---|---|---|---|---|---|---|---|---|---|---|---|---|
| | | | | | under 10 | 10 to 16 | 16 to 26 | 26 to 45 | 45 and over | under 10 | 10 to 16 | 16 to 26 | 26 to 45 | 45 and over | | | | | |
| Harwich | 11 | 42 | Eldrege | Thomas | | | | 1 | | 2 | | | | 1 | | | 4 | | |
| Harwich | 13 | 28 | Eldrege | Thomas Jun | | | 1 | | | 3 | | 1 | | | | | 5 | | |
| Harwich | 13 | 29 | Eldrege | Washington | | | 1 | | | | | 1 | | | | | 2 | | |
| Chatham | 16 | 31 | Eldrege | William | 1 | | | 1 | | 2 | | | 1 | | | | 5 | | |
| Harwich | 9 | 36 | Eldrege | William | 2 | 1 | | | 1 | | | 1 | 1 | 1 | | | 7 | | |
| Chatham | 16 | 21 | Eldrege | Zephaniah | | | 1 | 1 | | | | | 1 | 1 | | | 4 | | |
| Truro | 67 | 8 | Eldridge | Elizabeth | 1 | | 1 | | | | | | 1 | 1 | | | 4 | | |
| Provincetown | 60 | 31 | Eldridge | William | 1 | | 1 | | | | | | 1 | | | | 3 | | |
| Yarmouth | 99 | 49 | Ellin | James | 1 | | | 1 | | 1 | | | 1 | | | | 4 | | |
| Sandwich | 42 | 38 | Ellis | Abiel | 2 | 2 | | 1 | | | | | 1 | 1 | | | 7 | | |
| Harwich | 11 | 5 | Ellis | Abraham | 2 | | | 1 | | | | 1 | | 1 | | | 5 | | |
| Wellfleet | 69 | 15 | Ellis | Ansell | | | 1 | | | 3 | 1 | 1 | | 1 | | | 4 | | |
| Harwich | 10 | 40 | Ellis | Barnabas | 1 | | | 1 | | | | | | 1 | | | 3 | | |
| Sandwich | 40 | 4 | Ellis | Benjm | 1 | | | 1 | | 3 | | 1 | 2 | 1 | | | 9 | | |
| Harwich | 11 | 12 | Ellis | Charles | 1 | | | 1 | | | | | 1 | | | | 3 | | |
| Dennis | 29 | 29 | Ellis | Cornelus | 1 | | | 1 | | 2 | | | 1 | | | | 5 | | |
| Sandwich | 40 | 10 | Ellis | Ebenezer | | 1 | 1 | 1 | 1 | | | | 1 | 1 | | | 6 | | |
| Sandwich | 40 | 27 | Ellis | Eleazer | 1 | | 2 | 1 | | 1 | | 2 | | 1 | | | 8 | | |
| Sandwich | 42 | 33 | Ellis | Elijah | | | | 1 | | | | | 1 | 1 | | | 3 | | |
| Sandwich | 42 | 23 | Ellis | Elnathan | | | | 1 | | | | 1 | 1 | 1 | | | 4 | | |
| Sandwich | 42 | 25 | Ellis | Gershom | | 2 | | | | 1 | | | 1 | | | | 4 | | |
| Sandwich | 42 | 1 | Ellis | Gideon | 1 | | | 1 | | | | | | 1 | | | 3 | | |
| Harwich | 11 | 11 | Ellis | Hemon | 2 | | | 1 | | | | | | 1 | | | 4 | | |
| Harwich | 13 | 12 | Ellis | Isaac | | 1 | 1 | 1 | | 1 | | 1 | 2 | 2 | | | 9 | | |
| Harwich | 12 | 8 | Ellis | Jeremiah | 3 | | | 1 | | 1 | | | 1 | | | | 6 | | |
| Harwich | 10 | 27 | Ellis | John | 1 | 1 | | 1 | | 1 | 1 | | 1 | | | | 6 | | |
| Sandwich | 39 | 32 | Ellis | Josiah | 1 | 4 | | 1 | | 1 | | | 1 | 1 | | | 9 | | |
| Dennis | 29 | 3 | Ellis | Levi | 2 | | | 1 | | 1 | | | 1 | | | | 5 | | |
| Sandwich | 38 | 35 | Ellis | Malachi | | | | 1 | | | | 2 | 1 | 1 | | | 5 | | |
| Sandwich | 39 | 33 | Ellis | Mary | | | | | | | | 1 | | 1 | | | 2 | | |
| Harwich | 12 | 5 | Ellis | Nathan | 2 | 1 | | 2 | | 2 | | | 1 | | | | 8 | | |
| Sandwich | 42 | 24 | Ellis | Nathan | | 1 | | | | | | | 1 | | | | 2 | | |
| Falmouth | 45 | 81 | Ellis | Nathan | 1 | | 1 | | | 3 | 1 | | 1 | | | | 7 | | |
| Harwich | 11 | 9 | Ellis | Nathaniel | 1 | | 1 | | | 2 | | 1 | | 1 | | | 6 | | |
| Sandwich | 40 | 5 | Ellis | Nathl | 1 | 1 | | | | | | | 1 | 1 | | | 4 | | |
| Harwich | 11 | 10 | Ellis | Phillip | 2 | | | 1 | | 3 | | 1 | | 1 | | | 8 | | |
| Sandwich | 40 | 6 | Ellis | Phillip | 1 | 1 | | 1 | | | | | | 1 | | | 4 | | |
| Harwich | 14 | 8 | Ellis | Reuben | | | 1 | 1 | | 1 | 1 | | | 3 | | | 7 | | |
| Harwich | 11 | 6 | Ellis | Samuel | | 1 | 1 | 1 | | 2 | 2 | | 1 | | | | 8 | | |
| Sandwich | 42 | 8 | Ellis | Seth | | | | 1 | | 1 | | 1 | 1 | | | | 4 | | |
| Dennis | 29 | 14 | Ellis | Stephen | 2 | | | 1 | | 1 | | | 1 | | | | 5 | | |
| Sandwich | 39 | 34 | Ellis | Stephen | 1 | 1 | 1 | | | | | 1 | 1 | | | | 5 | | |
| Dennis | 29 | 30 | Ellis | William | | | 1 | 1 | | | | 2 | | 1 | | | 5 | | |
| Chatham | 16 | 22 | Emory | John | 1 | 2 | 1 | 1 | | 2 | | 1 | 1 | 1 | | | 10 | | |
| Barnstable | 84 | 52 | Ewer | Abigail | | 1 | 1 | | | | | | 1 | 1 | | | 4 | | |
| Sandwich | 37 | 45 | Ewer | Barnabas | 2 | | | 1 | | 4 | 2 | 1 | | | | | 10 | | |
| Barnstable | 87 | 17 | Ewer | Ebenezer | | 1 | | 1 | | 1 | 1 | | 1 | | | | 5 | | |
| Sandwich | 37 | 46 | Ewer | John | | 1 | 2 | 1 | 1 | | | 2 | 1 | 1 | | | 9 | | |
| Sandwich | 37 | 3 | Ewer | Peleg | | | | 1 | | | | | | 1 | | | 2 | | |
| Sandwich | 39 | 6 | Fannie | James | | 1 | | 1 | | | | | 1 | | | | 3 | | |
| Eastham | 79 | 29 | Fararo | John | 1 | | 1 | | 1 | 2 | | | 1 | | | | 6 | | |
| Yarmouth | 99 | 6 | Farris | Jeremiah | 1 | | 1 | | | 1 | | | 1 | | | | 4 | | |
| Yarmouth | 98 | 50 | Farris | Samuel | 2 | 2 | 1 | | | | | 1 | 1 | 1 | | | 8 | | |
| Yarmouth | 98 | 51 | Farris | Thomas | 1 | | 1 | | | 1 | | | 1 | 1 | | | 5 | | |
| Provincetown | 61 | 12 | Feavour | Peter | 1 | 1 | | | | | | | 1 | | | | 3 | | |
| Sandwich | 34 | 1 | Fesenden | William | 2 | | 2 | 1 | | | | 1 | | | | | 6 | | |
| Sandwich | 35 | 33 | Fessenden | Samuel | 1 | | 1 | 1 | | 2 | 2 | 2 | | 1 | | | 10 | | |
| Harwich | 8 | 19 | Fessenden | William | | | 1 | 1 | | | | | 1 | 1 | | | 4 | | |
| Harwich | 8 | 20 | Fessenden | William Jun | 2 | 1 | | 1 | | | | | 1 | | | | 5 | | |
| Sandwich | 38 | 42 | Fish | Anna | | | 1 | | | | | | 1 | | | | 2 | | |
| Sandwich | 38 | 18 | Fish | Anselm | | 1 | | | | | | 1 | | | | | 2 | | |
| Sandwich | 36 | 38 | Fish | Asa | | 1 | | 1 | | | | 1 | 1 | 1 | | | 5 | | |
| Sandwich | 38 | 16 | Fish | Chipman | 3 | | 1 | 1 | | | | | 1 | | | | 6 | | |
| Sandwich | 38 | 20 | Fish | Cornelius | | 1 | 2 | 1 | | | | | 1 | | | | 5 | | |
| Barnstable | 89 | 9 | Fish | David | 1 | | 1 | | 1 | | | 1 | | | | | 4 | | |
| Sandwich | 40 | 12 | Fish | David | 1 | | 1 | | 1 | | | 1 | | | | | 4 | | |
| Sandwich | 35 | 10 | Fish | Edmund | | | 1 | 1 | | | | | 2 | 1 | | | 5 | | |
| Sandwich | 42 | 10 | Fish | Ephraim | 1 | | 1 | | | | | | 1 | | | | 3 | | |
| Sandwich | 39 | 1 | Fish | Hannah | | | | | | | | | 1 | | | | 1 | | |
| Barnstable | 92 | 12 | Fish | Herman | | | 1 | | | | | | 1 | | | | 2 | | |
| Sandwich | 39 | 2 | Fish | Isiah | | | 1 | | | | | | 1 | | | | 2 | | |
| Sandwich | 42 | 9 | Fish | John | | 1 | 2 | 1 | | | | | 1 | | | | 5 | | |
| Sandwich | 35 | 11 | Fish | John 2d | 3 | | | 1 | | | | 1 | 1 | 1 | | | 8 | | |
| Sandwich | 36 | 20 | Fish | Jonathan | 2 | 1 | | 1 | | | | 1 | 1 | 1 | | | 9 | | |
| Barnstable | 92 | 10 | Fish | Josiah | | 3 | | 1 | 1 | 3 | 1 | | 1 | | | | 10 | | |
| Sandwich | 35 | 9 | Fish | Josiah | | | | 1 | | | | | | | | | 1 | | |
| Sandwich | 38 | 9 | Fish | Lemuel | | | | | | | | | | | | | | | Enumeration left blank |
| Mashpee | 51 | 4 | Fish | Levi | 1 | 1 | | 1 | | | | 2 | 2 | | | | 8 | | |
| Sandwich | 38 | 8 | Fish | Levi | | | | | | | | | | | | | | | Enumeration left blank |
| Sandwich | 40 | 18 | Fish | Nathl | | 1 | | 1 | | | | 1 | 1 | 1 | | | 5 | | |
| Sandwich | 38 | 17 | Fish | Prince | 1 | | | 1 | | | | | 1 | | | | 4 | | |
| Barnstable | 92 | 11 | Fish | Reuben | | 1 | 1 | 1 | | | | 2 | | | | | 5 | | |

# 1800 Barnstable County, Massachusetts Index

| TOWN | PG# | LN# | LAST NAME | FIRST NAME | FREE WHITE MALES under 10 | 10 to 16 | 16 to 26 | 26 to 45 | 45 and over | FREE WHITE FEMALES under 10 | 10 to 16 | 16 to 26 | 26 to 45 | 45 and over | TOTAL ALL OTHER | TOTAL SLAVES | TOTALS | DISTRICT/ TOWNSHIP | NOTES |
|---|---|---|---|---|---|---|---|---|---|---|---|---|---|---|---|---|---|---|---|
| Mashpee | 51 | 5 | Fish | Samuel | | | | 1 | | | | | | 1 | | | 2 | | |
| Sandwich | 34 | 11 | Fish | Silas | | 1 | | 1 | | | | | | 1 | | | 3 | | |
| Sandwich | 38 | 15 | Fish | Silvanus | 3 | 1 | 1 | | | 2 | 1 | 3 | 1 | | | | 12 | | |
| Sandwich | 36 | 37 | Fish | Simeon | | | | 1 | | | | | | 1 | | | 2 | | |
| Sandwich | 38 | 14 | Fish | Simeon Junr | 1 | | 1 | 1 | | 1 | 1 | 1 | 1 | | | | 7 | | |
| Sandwich | 37 | 25 | Fish | Stephen | 2 | 1 | | 1 | | 1 | | 1 | 1 | | 1 | | 8 | | |
| Falmouth | 45 | 94 | Fisk | Abraham | | 1 | 1 | 2 | | | | 1 | | | | | 5 | | |
| Falmouth | 45 | 99 | Fisk | Benjm | 1 | 1 | | | | | | 2 | | 1 | | | 6 | | |
| Falmouth | 45 | 95 | Fisk | Ebenz | | | 2 | 1 | | | | | 2 | | | | 5 | | |
| Falmouth | 45 | 101 | Fisk | Freeman | 4 | | | 1 | | 1 | | | 1 | | | | 7 | | |
| Falmouth | 49 | 279 | Fisk | James | 1 | | | 1 | | 1 | | 1 | | | | | 4 | | |
| Falmouth | 49 | 278 | Fisk | Lemuel | 2 | 3 | 1 | | | 2 | | | 1 | | | | 9 | | |
| Falmouth | 49 | 302 | Fisk | Prince | 1 | | 2 | | 1 | 1 | 2 | 2 | | 1 | | | 10 | | |
| Falmouth | 45 | 98 | Fisk | Rufus Junr | | 2 | 1 | | 1 | | 2 | 1 | | 1 | | | 8 | | |
| Falmouth | 45 | 100 | Fisk | Saml Junr | 1 | | 1 | | | 1 | | | | 1 | | | 4 | | |
| Falmouth | 45 | 92 | Fisk | Samuel | | | 1 | | | 1 | | 1 | 1 | | 1 | | 5 | | |
| Falmouth | 45 | 93 | Fisk | Thomas | | | | 1 | | 1 | | | 1 | | | | 3 | | |
| Falmouth | 45 | 96 | Fisk | Thomas Junr | 4 | 1 | | 1 | | 3 | | | 1 | | | | 10 | | |
| Provincetown | 58 | 9 | Foble | Samuel | | 1 | | | | 1 | | | 1 | | | | 3 | | |
| Harwich | 15 | 13 | Fortune | Reuben | | | | | | | | | | | 5 | | 5 | | |
| Harwich | 7 | 30 | Foster | Benjm | | | 1 | | | 1 | | 1 | | | | | 3 | | |
| Harwich | 5 | 40 | Foster | Chillingworth | | | | 1 | | | 1 | 1 | | 1 | | | 4 | | |
| Harwich | 5 | 42 | Foster | Chillingworth Jun | | | 1 | | | 2 | | | 1 | | | | 4 | | |
| Harwich | 9 | 2 | Foster | David | 3 | | 2 | 1 | | 1 | 1 | 1 | 1 | | | | 10 | | |
| Sandwich | 40 | 9 | Foster | Elizabeth | | | | | | | | | 1 | | | | 1 | | |
| Harwich | 5 | 23 | Foster | Isaac | 1 | | | 1 | | | | | 1 | | | | 3 | | |
| Harwich | 7 | 33 | Foster | Isaac Jun | 1 | | 1 | | | | | 1 | | | | | 3 | | |
| Harwich | 6 | 8 | Foster | James | 1 | 1 | 1 | | | | | | 1 | 1 | | | 5 | | |
| Harwich | 5 | 20 | Foster | John | 1 | 2 | | 1 | | | | | 1 | 1 | | | 6 | | |
| Barnstable | 92 | 6 | Foster | Nathan | | | | 1 | | 1 | | | 1 | 1 | | | 4 | | |
| Harwich | 5 | 33 | Foster | Nathaniel | 3 | 2 | 2 | 1 | | | | 1 | 2 | 1 | | | 12 | | |
| Harwich | 5 | 24 | Foster | Samuel | 1 | 1 | | | | 1 | | | 1 | | | | 4 | | |
| Harwich | 7 | 12 | Foster | Seth | 1 | 3 | | 1 | | 2 | 2 | | 1 | | | | 12 | | |
| Harwich | 8 | 39 | Foster | Seth Jun | | 1 | | | | | | | 1 | | | | 2 | | |
| Truro | 64 | 18 | Freat | Nathaniel | 2 | | 2 | 1 | | 1 | 2 | 1 | | 1 | | | 11 | | |
| Truro | 65 | 14 | Freat | Samuel | | 1 | | | 2 | 1 | | | 1 | 1 | | | 6 | | |
| Orleans | 21 | 2 | Freeman | Abner | 1 | | 2 | | 1 | 3 | 2 | 2 | | 1 | | | 12 | | |
| Sandwich | 36 | 33 | Freeman | Benjamin | 2 | | 1 | | | 1 | | | | 1 | | | 5 | | |
| Wellfleet | 73 | 16 | Freeman | Benjamin | 5 | | 1 | 1 | | | | | | 1 | | | 8 | | |
| Harwich | 6 | 1 | Freeman | Desire Wd | | | | | | | | | 3 | | | | 3 | | |
| Wellfleet | 73 | 28 | Freeman | Edmund | 1 | 2 | 2 | | 1 | | | 2 | | 1 | | | 9 | | |
| Sandwich | 41 | 28 | Freeman | Edward | 1 | | | 1 | | 1 | | 2 | | | | | 5 | | |
| Orleans | 25 | 21 | Freeman | Eleozer | 1 | | | 1 | | 2 | 2 | | 1 | | | | 7 | | |
| Provincetown | 60 | 32 | Freeman | Elisha | 3 | 1 | | 1 | | | | | 1 | | | | 6 | | |
| Harwich | 7 | 31 | Freeman | Elkanah | 3 | | | 1 | | 3 | 1 | 1 | 1 | 1 | | | 11 | | |
| Sandwich | 40 | 39 | Freeman | Fortine | | | | | | | | | | | 1 | | 1 | | |
| Orleans | 25 | 6 | Freeman | Gideon | | | | 1 | | | | 1 | | 1 | | | 3 | | |
| Harwich | 6 | 21 | Freeman | Isaac | | 1 | 2 | 1 | | 1 | | 2 | | 1 | | | 8 | | |
| Orleans | 23 | 8 | Freeman | Isaac | | 1 | 1 | | 1 | | | | 3 | 1 | | | 7 | | |
| Wellfleet | 73 | 34 | Freeman | Isaac | | | 2 | | | | | | | 1 | | | 4 | | |
| Wellfleet | 73 | 35 | Freeman | Isaac Junr | 2 | 4 | 1 | | | | | | 1 | | | | 9 | | |
| Barnstable | 85 | 20 | Freeman | James | | | | 1 | | | 1 | 1 | 1 | | | | 4 | | |
| Sandwich | 41 | 23 | Freeman | James | 3 | | | 1 | | 2 | | | 1 | | | | 7 | | |
| Harwich | 4 | 9 | Freeman | John | | | | | 1 | | | | 2 | 1 | 1 | | 5 | | |
| Orleans | 21 | 1 | Freeman | John | 2 | 2 | | 1 | | 3 | 1 | | 1 | | | | 10 | | |
| Sandwich | 41 | 24 | Freeman | John | | | 1 | 1 | | | | | 1 | | | | 3 | | |
| Harwich | 4 | 10 | Freeman | John Jun | 3 | | | 1 | | 1 | | | 1 | | | | 6 | | |
| Orleans | 25 | 16 | Freeman | Jopah | 2 | 2 | | 1 | | 2 | 1 | | 1 | | | | 9 | | |
| Sandwich | 35 | 8 | Freeman | Joshua | 1 | | 1 | 1 | 1 | | 1 | 2 | | 2 | | | 9 | | |
| Harwich | 5 | 44 | Freeman | Lemuel | 1 | 2 | | 1 | | | 1 | 3 | | 1 | | | 9 | | |
| Sandwich | 36 | 35 | Freeman | Lemuel | 2 | 1 | | 1 | | 2 | | | 1 | | | | 7 | | |
| Harwich | 7 | 18 | Freeman | Nathaniel | | | | 1 | | | | | 2 | | | | 4 | | |
| Sandwich | 39 | 17 | Freeman | Nathl | 1 | 1 | 1 | 1 | | | | | 1 | | | | 5 | | |
| Orleans | 25 | 15 | Freeman | Pheba Wd | | | | | | | | | 1 | 1 | | | 2 | | |
| Provincetown | 58 | 8 | Freeman | Prince | | | 3 | 1 | | | | | 1 | 1 | | | 6 | | |
| Truro | 67 | 9 | Freeman | Rebeccah Wid | | | | | | | | | | 1 | | | 1 | | |
| Eastham | 77 | 18 | Freeman | Samuel | 2 | | | 1 | | 1 | 2 | 1 | 1 | 1 | | | 9 | | |
| Sandwich | 35 | 7 | Freeman | Samuel | 1 | | | 1 | | | | | | 1 | | | 3 | | |
| Sandwich | 41 | 27 | Freeman | Samuel | | 1 | | 1 | 1 | | | | | 1 | | | 4 | | |
| Harwich | 6 | 36 | Freeman | Seth | 2 | 2 | 1 | | 1 | | | | 2 | 1 | | | 9 | | |
| Sandwich | 39 | 9 | Freeman | Seth | | | 1 | 1 | | | | | 1 | 1 | | | 4 | | |
| Harwich | 5 | 43 | Freeman | Seth Jun | 2 | 1 | 1 | | 1 | | | | 2 | 1 | | | 8 | | |
| Sandwich | 38 | 24 | Freeman | Seth Junr | 1 | | | 1 | | 2 | | | 1 | | | | 5 | | |
| Harwich | 6 | 14 | Freeman | Simeon | 1 | 2 | | 1 | | | | 1 | 1 | 1 | | | 7 | | |
| Harwich | 5 | 15 | Freeman | Solomon | | 1 | | 1 | | | | | 1 | 1 | | | 4 | | |
| Harwich | 5 | 16 | Freeman | Solomon Jun | 3 | | | 1 | | | | | 1 | 1 | | | 6 | | |
| Sandwich | 35 | 5 | Freeman | Tabitha | | | 1 | 1 | | | | | 1 | 1 | | | 4 | | |
| Orleans | 21 | 3 | Freeman | Thankful Wid | | | | | | | | | 1 | | | | 1 | | |
| Orleans | 25 | 17 | Freeman | Thomas | 1 | | | 1 | | 1 | | | 1 | | | | 4 | | |
| Falmouth | 45 | 97 | Freeman | Thos Junr | 2 | | | 1 | | 2 | | | 1 | 1 | 1 | | 8 | | |
| Chatham | 19 | 39 | Friday | Doane | 2 | | | | | | | | | 1 | | | 3 | | |
| Barnstable | 92 | 49 | Fuller | Benjamin | | 1 | 1 | | | | | | 1 | | | | 3 | | |
| Barnstable | 92 | 47 | Fuller | James | | 1 | 1 | | 2 | | 1 | 3 | 1 | | | | 9 | | |
| Barnstable | 92 | 53 | Fuller | Jonathan | 2 | | | 1 | | | | | | 1 | | | 4 | | |

# 1800 Barnstable County, Massachusetts Index

| TOWN | PG# | LN# | LAST NAME | FIRST NAME | FREE WHITE MALES under 10 | 10 to 16 | 16 to 26 | 26 to 45 | 45 and over | FREE WHITE FEMALES under 10 | 10 to 16 | 16 to 26 | 26 to 45 | 45 and over | TOTAL ALL OTHER | TOTAL SLAVES | TOTALS | DISTRICT/ TOWNSHIP | NOTES |
|---|---|---|---|---|---|---|---|---|---|---|---|---|---|---|---|---|---|---|---|
| Barnstable | 89 | 32 | Fuller | Joseph | 2 | | | 1 | 1 | | 2 | | 1 | 1 | | | 8 | | |
| Sandwich | 36 | 36 | Fuller | Joseph | 1 | 1 | 1 | 1 | | 2 | 1 | | 1 | | | | 8 | | |
| Barnstable | 88 | 29 | Fuller | Josiah Jr | 2 | 1 | | 1 | | | | | 1 | | | | 5 | | |
| Barnstable | 92 | 38 | Fuller | Mathias | | | 1 | 1 | 1 | | | | 1 | | | | 4 | | |
| Barnstable | 92 | 39 | Fuller | Mathias Jr | 1 | | | 1 | | | | 1 | | | | | 3 | | |
| Sandwich | 34 | 19 | Fuller | Nathaniel | 2 | | | 1 | | 1 | | | 1 | | | | 5 | | |
| Barnstable | 89 | 8 | Fuller | Samuel | | | 1 | 1 | | | | | | 1 | | | 3 | | |
| Sandwich | 40 | 19 | Fuller | Samuel | | | 1 | 1 | | | | | 1 | | | | 3 | | |
| Barnstable | 88 | 47 | Fuller | Zacheus | 1 | 1 | | 1 | | 2 | 1 | | 1 | | | | 7 | | |
| Barnstable | 94 | 41 | Furnald | Benjamin | 2 | | | 1 | 1 | 1 | | | 1 | 1 | | | 7 | | |
| Sandwich | 38 | 23 | G*th | Richard | 1 | 2 | | 1 | | 2 | 1 | | | 1 | | | 8 | | |
| Yarmouth | 95 | 50 | Gage | Ebenezer | | 1 | 2 | 1 | | 1 | 2 | | 1 | | | | 8 | | |
| Dennis | 32 | 4 | Gage | James | 1 | | 1 | 1 | | 1 | 2 | | 1 | 1 | | | 8 | | |
| Barnstable | 94 | 8 | Gage | Jane | 1 | | | | | | 1 | | | 1 | | | 3 | | |
| Barnstable | 93 | 10 | Gage | Joseph | | | 1 | 1 | | | | | 1 | | | | 3 | | |
| Barnstable | 93 | 9 | Gage | Nathl | 1 | | | 1 | | 1 | 1 | | 1 | | | | 5 | | |
| Yarmouth | 96 | 5 | Gage | Prince | 3 | | | 1 | | 1 | 1 | | | 1 | | | 7 | | |
| Chatham | 16 | 46 | Gage | Reuben | 1 | | | 1 | | | | 1 | 1 | 1 | | | 5 | | |
| Yarmouth | 96 | 10 | Gage | Thomas | | | | 1 | | 1 | | 1 | | | | | 3 | | |
| Barnstable | 94 | 16 | Gage | Zenas | 1 | 1 | | 1 | | 1 | | | 1 | 1 | | | 6 | | |
| Barnstable | 90 | 7 | Gallison | John | 2 | | 1 | | 1 | 2 | 2 | | | 1 | | | 9 | | |
| Sandwich | 41 | 18 | Gardner | John | 1 | | | 1 | | | | | 1 | | | | 3 | | |
| Barnstable | 87 | 19 | Garret | Andrew | 1 | | | 1 | | | 2 | | 1 | | | | 5 | | |
| Harwich | 13 | 35 | Gaye | Anthony | 2 | | | 1 | 1 | | 1 | | | | | | 5 | | |
| Harwich | 6 | 17 | Gaye | Mayo | 3 | | | 2 | | 1 | | | 1 | 1 | | | 8 | | |
| Harwich | 13 | 45 | Gaye | Zebulon | | | 1 | 1 | | | | | | 1 | | | 3 | | |
| Mashpee | 52 | 3 | George | | | | | | | | | | | | 1 | | 1 | | First name left balnk on census |
| Dennis | 28 | 6 | Gerom | Lot | 2 | 1 | | 1 | | 2 | | | 1 | | | | 7 | | |
| Sandwich | 39 | 42 | Gibbs | Anselm | | 2 | 1 | | 1 | | | 1 | | 1 | | | 6 | | |
| Sandwich | 39 | 29 | Gibbs | Benjamin | 1 | 1 | | 1 | | 2 | 1 | | 1 | | | | 7 | | |
| Sandwich | 40 | 28 | Gibbs | Caleb | 3 | 1 | | 1 | | 1 | | | 1 | | | | 7 | | |
| Sandwich | 39 | 39 | Gibbs | Caleb Junr | 2 | | | 1 | 1 | | | 2 | 1 | | | | 7 | | |
| Sandwich | 38 | 36 | Gibbs | Charles | 2 | 3 | | 1 | | 2 | | | 1 | | | | 9 | | |
| Sandwich | 39 | 28 | Gibbs | David | | | 1 | | 1 | | | | 2 | 1 | | | 5 | | |
| Sandwich | 39 | 43 | Gibbs | Elisha | | | 1 | | | | | | 1 | | | | 2 | | |
| Sandwich | 39 | 41 | Gibbs | Jabez | | | | 1 | | | | | 1 | | | | 2 | | |
| Sandwich | 39 | 40 | Gibbs | Pelham | 3 | | 1 | | | | | 1 | | | | | 5 | | |
| Sandwich | 40 | 1 | Gibbs | Reuben Jun | 1 | | 1 | | 1 | 1 | 1 | | 1 | | | | 6 | | |
| Sandwich | 39 | 38 | Gibbs | Saml 3d | 1 | | 1 | | | | | 1 | | | | | 3 | | |
| Sandwich | 38 | 32 | Gibbs | Saml Junr | 2 | 1 | | 1 | 2 | | | | 1 | | | | 7 | | |
| Sandwich | 38 | 31 | Gibbs | Samuel | | | | 1 | | | | | | 1 | | | 2 | | |
| Sandwich | 40 | 20 | Gibbs | Silvanus | 3 | 1 | 1 | | 1 | 2 | 3 | 2 | | 1 | | | 14 | | |
| Sandwich | 39 | 44 | Gibbs | Thomas | 1 | | 1 | | 1 | 2 | 1 | 1 | | 1 | | | 8 | | |
| Sandwich | 39 | 30 | Gibbs | Thomas Junr | 2 | | | 1 | | 2 | 1 | | 1 | | | | 7 | | |
| Sandwich | 38 | 37 | Gibbs | Warren | | | 1 | | 1 | | | 1 | | 1 | | | 3 | | |
| Sandwich | 39 | 46 | Gibbs | Wm | 1 | 1 | | 1 | 1 | 2 | 2 | | | 1 | | | 9 | | |
| Falmouth | 49 | 286 | Gifford | Alden | | | 1 | | | | 1 | | | | | | 2 | | |
| Sandwich | 37 | 40 | Gifford | Alden | | 1 | 1 | | | | 1 | 3 | 1 | | | | 7 | | |
| Falmouth | 46 | 120 | Gifford | Anna | | | | | | | 1 | | | | | | 1 | | |
| Harwich | 10 | 24 | Gifford | Calvin | | | 1 | | 3 | | | | 1 | | | | 5 | | |
| Falmouth | 45 | 106 | Gifford | Christopher | 1 | | | 1 | | | 2 | 1 | 1 | | | | 6 | | |
| Sandwich | 40 | 23 | Gifford | Daniel | | 1 | | 1 | | | 2 | | 1 | | | | 5 | | |
| Falmouth | 45 | 114 | Gifford | David | | 1 | | 1 | | | 1 | | 1 | 1 | | | 4 | | |
| Falmouth | 45 | 91 | Gifford | Ebenz | 2 | | 1 | 1 | | 2 | 1 | | 1 | | | | 8 | | |
| Falmouth | 45 | 119 | Gifford | George | | | | 1 | | | | | 1 | | | | 2 | | |
| Falmouth | 45 | 104 | Gifford | Jesse | | 1 | 3 | | 1 | 1 | 2 | 1 | 2 | 1 | | | 12 | | |
| Sandwich | 40 | 24 | Gifford | John | 2 | | | 1 | | 1 | | | 1 | | | | 5 | | |
| Sandwich | 34 | 13 | Gifford | Joseph | 1 | 2 | | 1 | | 2 | 1 | | 1 | | | | 8 | | |
| Sandwich | 34 | 12 | Gifford | Lemuel | 2 | | | 1 | | 3 | 2 | | | | | | 8 | | |
| Falmouth | 49 | 284 | Gifford | Lot | | 1 | 2 | | 1 | 3 | 1 | | 1 | | 1 | | 10 | | |
| Falmouth | 45 | 108 | Gifford | Mordecai | | 1 | | 2 | | | 1 | | 2 | | | | 6 | | |
| Falmouth | 45 | 109 | Gifford | Prince | | 1 | 1 | | 1 | | 1 | 2 | | 2 | | | 8 | | |
| Falmouth | 49 | 280 | Gifford | Prince 3d | | | 1 | | 2 | | | | 1 | | | | 4 | | |
| Falmouth | 49 | 281 | Gifford | Prince Junr | 1 | | | 1 | | | | | 1 | | | | 3 | | |
| Falmouth | 45 | 112 | Gifford | Reuben | | | 1 | 1 | | | 1 | | 1 | 1 | | | 4 | | |
| Falmouth | 45 | 105 | Gifford | Samuel | | | 1 | 1 | 1 | | 1 | | 1 | | | | 4 | | |
| Falmouth | 45 | 107 | Gifford | Silas | 1 | | | 1 | | 1 | | | 1 | | | | 4 | | |
| Falmouth | 45 | 113 | Gifford | Warren | | 1 | | 1 | | 1 | 2 | | 1 | | | | 5 | | |
| Falmouth | 45 | 111 | Gifford | Zacheus | | 2 | | 1 | | | 1 | 2 | 2 | | | | 8 | | |
| Eastham | 77 | 20 | Gill | Anna | | 1 | | | | 3 | 1 | | 1 | | | | 6 | | |
| Eastham | 79 | 28 | Gill | David | 1 | 1 | | | | | 1 | | | | | | 3 | | |
| Wellfleet | 70 | 26 | Gill | John | 3 | | 1 | | 2 | | | | 1 | | | | 7 | | |
| Eastham | 77 | 21 | Gill | Scarlet | | 1 | | 1 | | | | 1 | 1 | | | | 4 | | |
| Eastham | 77 | 19 | Gill | William | 2 | | 1 | | 1 | | | | 1 | | | | 5 | | |
| Provincetown | 60 | 39 | Ginn | John | 1 | | 1 | | | | 1 | | | | | | 3 | | |
| Provincetown | 58 | 12 | Ginn | Samuel | 2 | | | 1 | | | 1 | 1 | | | | | 5 | | |
| Harwich | 13 | 50 | Gipson | Robert | | 1 | | 1 | | 1 | 1 | | | | | | 4 | | |
| Chatham | 16 | 41 | Godfrey | Benjm | 1 | | | 1 | | | | | 1 | | | | 3 | | |
| Harwich | 13 | 24 | Godfrey | Benjm | | | | 1 | | | | | 1 | | | | 2 | | |
| Chatham | 20 | 32 | Godfrey | Bethiah Wd | | | | | | | | | 1 | | | | 1 | | |
| Chatham | 16 | 42 | Godfrey | David | 2 | | 1 | 1 | | | | | 1 | | | | 5 | | |
| Yarmouth | 96 | 16 | Godfrey | Elisha | 1 | | 2 | 1 | | 1 | 1 | | 1 | | | | 7 | | |
| Chatham | 20 | 30 | Godfrey | Joshua Jun | | 1 | | 2 | | 2 | 2 | | | | | | 7 | | |

76

# 1800 Barnstable County, Massachusetts Index

| TOWN | PG# | LN# | LAST NAME | FIRST NAME | FREE WHITE MALES under 10 | 10 to 16 | 16 to 26 | 26 to 45 | 45 and over | FREE WHITE FEMALES under 10 | 10 to 16 | 16 to 26 | 26 to 45 | 45 and over | TOTAL ALL OTHER | TOTAL SLAVES | TOTALS | DISTRICT/ TOWNSHIP | NOTES |
|---|---|---|---|---|---|---|---|---|---|---|---|---|---|---|---|---|---|---|---|
| Chatham | 16 | 40 | Godfrey | Lewvi | 1 | | | 1 | | 1 | | | 1 | | | | 4 | | |
| Yarmouth | 96 | 17 | Godfrey | Mehitable | | | | | | | | | | 2 | | | 2 | | |
| Sandwich | 41 | 35 | Godfrey | Mercy | | 1 | 2 | | | | | 1 | 2 | 1 | | | 7 | | |
| Chatham | 16 | 39 | Godfrey | Rachel Wid | | | | | | | | | 1 | 1 | | | 2 | | |
| Chatham | 20 | 8 | Godfrey | Richard | 4 | 1 | | 1 | | 1 | | | 1 | | | | 8 | | |
| Barnstable | 91 | 8 | Goodspeed | Allen | 1 | | | 1 | | 1 | | | 1 | | | | 4 | | |
| Barnstable | 88 | 35 | Goodspeed | Asa | 1 | | | 1 | | 2 | | | 1 | | | | 5 | | |
| Barnstable | 92 | 23 | Goodspeed | Benjamin | | | | 1 | | 1 | | 2 | 1 | 1 | | | 6 | | |
| Sandwich | 37 | 43 | Goodspeed | Joseph | | | 2 | 1 | | | | | 1 | | | | 4 | | |
| Barnstable | 92 | 24 | Goodspeed | Joseph Jr | | 1 | | | | | | 1 | | | | | 2 | | |
| Barnstable | 89 | 35 | Goodspeed | Philemon | 1 | 1 | 1 | | 1 | 2 | 1 | 2 | 2 | 1 | | | 12 | | |
| Barnstable | 88 | 45 | Goodspeed | Rufus | | 1 | 1 | 1 | | | 1 | | 1 | | | | 5 | | |
| Barnstable | 91 | 7 | Goodspeed | Seth | | 1 | | 1 | | | | | 1 | 1 | | | 4 | | |
| Barnstable | 89 | 34 | Goodspeed | Thankful | 2 | 2 | 1 | | 1 | 1 | 1 | | 1 | 1 | | | 10 | | |
| Barnstable | 92 | 33 | Goodspeed | Timo Jr | 1 | 1 | 2 | | 1 | 2 | | | 1 | 1 | | | 9 | | |
| Sandwich | 37 | 42 | Goodspeed | Walter | 4 | 1 | | 1 | | | 1 | | 1 | | | | 8 | | |
| Barnstable | 88 | 20 | Goodspeeed | Cornelius | 2 | | | 1 | | 2 | | | 1 | | | | 6 | | |
| Barnstable | 88 | 22 | Goodspeeed | Joseph | | | | 1 | | | | | | 1 | | | 2 | | |
| Barnstable | 88 | 27 | Goodspeeed | Timothy | | | | 1 | | | | | | 1 | | | 2 | | |
| Provincetown | 60 | 23 | Goodwin | Jeremiah | | | | 1 | | | | 1 | | | | | 2 | | |
| Yarmouth | 96 | 41 | Gorham | Abigail | | 1 | | | | | | | 1 | 1 | | | 2 | | |
| Barnstable | 86 | 16 | Gorham | Deborah | | | | | | | | 1 | | 1 | | | 2 | | |
| Barnstable | 84 | 34 | Gorham | Desire | | 1 | | | | | | | | 1 | | | 2 | | |
| Barnstable | 86 | 35 | Gorham | Edward | 2 | 2 | | 1 | | 3 | 2 | | 1 | 1 | | | 12 | | |
| Barnstable | 84 | 15 | Gorham | George | 1 | 1 | | 1 | | 2 | 1 | | 1 | | | | 7 | | |
| Barnstable | 83 | 7 | Gorham | Hannah | | | | | | | | | 1 | | | | 1 | | |
| Yarmouth | 97 | 1 | Gorham | Hezekiah | | | 1 | | | | | 1 | | | | | 2 | | |
| Yarmouth | 97 | 40 | Gorham | Isaac | | | 1 | | | | | | 1 | | | | 2 | | |
| Barnstable | 83 | 13 | Gorham | James | | | | 1 | | | | | 1 | | | | 2 | | |
| Barnstable | 83 | 1 | Gorham | Job | 1 | | | 1 | | 2 | | | 1 | | | | 5 | | |
| Falmouth | 45 | 115 | Gorham | John | | 1 | 1 | 1 | | | | 1 | | 1 | | | 5 | | |
| Yarmouth | 100 | 8 | Gorham | John | | 1 | | 1 | | 1 | | | 1 | | | | 4 | | |
| Barnstable | 83 | 14 | Gorham | Jonathan | 3 | | | 1 | | 1 | 1 | | 1 | | | | 7 | | |
| Yarmouth | 95 | 17 | Gorham | Joseph | 2 | | | 1 | | | 3 | 2 | | 1 | | | 9 | | |
| Barnstable | 86 | 34 | Gorham | Josiah | 2 | | | 1 | | 2 | 1 | | 1 | 1 | | | 8 | | |
| Yarmouth | 100 | 7 | Gorham | Lydia | | | | | | | | | | 2 | | | 2 | | |
| Barnstable | 83 | 11 | Gorham | Prince | | | 2 | | 1 | | | | | 1 | | | 4 | | |
| Barnstable | 83 | 12 | Gorham | Silvanus | 1 | 2 | 1 | 2 | 1 | 1 | 1 | 1 | | 1 | | | 11 | | |
| Chatham | 19 | 34 | Gould | David | | 1 | | | | 1 | | 1 | | | | | 3 | | |
| Eastham | 77 | 22 | Gould | John | 2 | | | 1 | | 2 | | | 1 | | | | 6 | | |
| Harwich | 9 | 7 | Gould | John | | | | 1 | | | 1 | 3 | | 1 | | | 6 | | |
| Orleans | 22 | 46 | Gould | John | | | 1 | 1 | | | | 1 | 1 | | | | 4 | | |
| Orleans | 23 | 1 | Gould | John Junr | | 1 | | | | 2 | | 1 | | | | | 4 | | |
| Harwich | 5 | 27 | Gould | Joseph | | | 3 | | 1 | | 1 | 1 | | 1 | | | 7 | | |
| Chatham | 16 | 44 | Gould | Joshua Junr | | 1 | | | 1 | 2 | 2 | | 1 | | | | 7 | | |
| Chatham | 16 | 45 | Gould | Josiah | 1 | 2 | 1 | | | 2 | | | 1 | | | | 7 | | |
| Orleans | 22 | 17 | Gould | Josiah | | 2 | 2 | 1 | | | 1 | | | 1 | | | 7 | | |
| Chatham | 16 | 43 | Gould | Nathaniel | 2 | 1 | | | | 1 | | 1 | | | | | 5 | | |
| Chatham | 20 | 11 | Gould | Richard | 1 | 1 | | | | 1 | | 1 | | | | | 4 | | |
| Wellfleet | 70 | 27 | Graham | Deliverance | 1 | 1 | 1 | | | 2 | | 1 | 1 | | | | 7 | | |
| Wellfleet | 71 | 11 | Graham | Talor | | 1 | | | | 1 | | | 1 | | | | 3 | | |
| Yarmouth | 95 | 35 | Gray | Alden | 2 | | | 1 | | | | | 1 | | | | 4 | | |
| Harwich | 8 | 4 | Gray | Anthony | | 1 | | 1 | | | | 1 | | | | | 3 | | |
| Yarmouth | 95 | 34 | Gray | Gideon | | | | 1 | | | | 1 | | 1 | | | 3 | | |
| Harwich | 4 | 16 | Gray | Hannah Wid | 1 | | | | | 1 | | | 1 | | | | 3 | | |
| Yarmouth | 95 | 41 | Gray | John | 1 | | | 1 | | 1 | | | 1 | | | | 4 | | |
| Harwich | 5 | 6 | Gray | Joshua | | 1 | 1 | 1 | | | 1 | | | 1 | | | 5 | | |
| Yarmouth | 97 | 50 | Gray | Joshua | | 1 | | | | | | | 1 | | | | 2 | | |
| Harwich | 8 | 32 | Gray | Lot | | 1 | | 1 | | 4 | 2 | 1 | | | | | 9 | | |
| Yarmouth | 97 | 49 | Gray | Mary | | 1 | | | | 1 | 1 | 2 | | 1 | 1 | | 7 | | |
| Yarmouth | 99 | 45 | Gray | Richard | | 1 | | 1 | | 3 | | | 1 | | | | 6 | | |
| Harwich | 8 | 31 | Gray | Samuel | 1 | 3 | | 1 | | 3 | | | 1 | | | | 9 | | |
| Yarmouth | 98 | 12 | Gray | Samuel | | 1 | 2 | 1 | 1 | 1 | 1 | 2 | | 1 | | | 10 | | |
| Barnstable | 83 | 9 | Gray | Thomas | 2 | | | 1 | | 1 | | | 1 | | | | 5 | | |
| Harwich | 8 | 33 | Gray | Zeporiah Wd | | | 1 | | | | | | | 1 | | | 2 | | |
| Falmouth | 45 | 110 | Green | Christopher | | | | 1 | | | | | 3 | 1 | | | 5 | | |
| Barnstable | 85 | 16 | Green | Isaiah L | | | | 1 | | | | | 2 | 1 | | | 4 | | |
| Barnstable | 85 | 38 | Green | John | | 1 | 1 | | | | | | | 1 | | | 3 | | |
| Falmouth | 45 | 103 | Green | Jonathan | | 1 | 2 | 1 | | | | 2 | | | | | 6 | | |
| Falmouth | 45 | 117 | Green | Jonathan Jun | 4 | | 1 | | | 1 | 1 | | 1 | | | | 8 | | |
| Falmouth | 45 | 118 | Green | Jonthan | | | | 1 | | | | | 2 | | | | 3 | | |
| Falmouth | 45 | 116 | Green | Lemuel | 2 | 2 | | 1 | | | | | 1 | 1 | | | 7 | | |
| Falmouth | 45 | 102 | Green | Solomon | 1 | 1 | 1 | | | | | | 1 | 1 | | | 5 | | |
| Yarmouth | 95 | 18 | Griffeth | Joseph | | | | 1 | | | | | 1 | | | | 2 | | |
| Harwich | 4 | 21 | Griffith | Barnabas | | 2 | 1 | | | | | | 1 | 1 | | | 5 | | |
| Harwich | 4 | 22 | Griffith | Stephen | | 1 | 1 | | 1 | | | | 1 | 2 | | | 5 | | |
| Provincetown | 58 | 10 | Grosher | Freeman | 3 | | | 1 | | | | | 1 | | | | 5 | | |
| Provincetown | 58 | 11 | Gross | Alexander | | | | 1 | | 2 | | | | 1 | | | 4 | | |
| Truro | 63 | 26 | Gross | Jazamiah | 1 | | | 1 | | 2 | | | 1 | | | | 5 | | |
| Truro | 67 | 11 | Gross | John | 1 | | 2 | | 1 | | | 1 | | 1 | | | 6 | | |
| Truro | 64 | 4 | Gross | Joshua Dyer | 1 | | | | | | | | 1 | | | | 3 | | |
| Wellfleet | 74 | 23 | Gross | Thomas | 1 | | 3 | | 1 | 1 | 3 | 1 | | 1 | | | 11 | | |

# 1800 Barnstable County, Massachusetts Index

| TOWN | PG# | LN# | LAST NAME | FIRST NAME | M under 10 | M 10 to 16 | M 16 to 26 | M 26 to 45 | M 45 and over | F under 10 | F 10 to 16 | F 16 to 26 | F 26 to 45 | F 45 and over | TOTAL ALL OTHER | TOTAL SLAVES | TOTALS | DISTRICT/TOWNSHIP | NOTES |
|---|---|---|---|---|---|---|---|---|---|---|---|---|---|---|---|---|---|---|---|
| Truro | 67 | 10 | Grozher | Caleb | | | | 1 | | 1 | 1 | | 1 | 1 | | | 5 | | |
| Harwich | 4 | 37 | Habens | Abner | 1 | 1 | 1 | 1 | | | 1 | | | 1 | | | 6 | | |
| Harwich | 4 | 41 | Habens | William | | 1 | 1 | | 1 | 1 | | 1 | | 2 | | | 7 | | |
| Barnstable | 90 | 12 | Hadaway | Benjamin | 1 | 1 | 1 | 1 | | 2 | | | 1 | | | | 7 | | |
| Yarmouth | 95 | 39 | Hale | David | 1 | 1 | 3 | | 1 | 1 | 1 | | | 1 | | | 9 | | |
| Yarmouth | 95 | 32 | Hale | Isaac | 1 | | 1 | 1 | 1 | | 1 | 1 | 1 | 1 | | | 8 | | |
| Dennis | 27 | 10 | Hall | Anna Wid | | | | | | | | | 1 | | | | 2 | | |
| Dennis | 27 | 17 | Hall | Barnabas | | 1 | 1 | | 1 | | | | 2 | 1 | | | 6 | | |
| Dennis | 27 | 12 | Hall | Benjm | 1 | | | 1 | | 1 | | | 1 | 1 | | | 5 | | |
| Harwich | 13 | 49 | Hall | Benjm | 2 | 1 | | | 1 | 1 | 2 | 1 | 1 | | | | 9 | | |
| Dennis | 26 | 38 | Hall | Daniel | | 1 | | | | | | | 1 | 1 | | | 3 | | |
| Dennis | 27 | 11 | Hall | Donwell | | | 1 | | | | | | 1 | | | | 2 | | |
| Dennis | 26 | 42 | Hall | Edmond | 1 | | 1 | | | | | | 1 | | | | 3 | | |
| Harwich | 14 | 10 | Hall | Edward | 1 | 3 | 1 | 1 | | 3 | | | 1 | 1 | | | 11 | | |
| Yarmouth | 95 | 37 | Hall | Edward | | 1 | | | | | | | 1 | | | | 2 | | |
| Harwich | 13 | 48 | Hall | Edward Jun | 3 | | | 1 | | 2 | | 1 | 1 | 1 | | | 9 | | |
| Harwich | 14 | 3 | Hall | Elisha | 2 | | | 1 | | 2 | | | 1 | | | | 6 | | |
| Dennis | 26 | 39 | Hall | Enoch | 1 | 2 | | 1 | | 2 | 1 | | 1 | | | | 8 | | |
| Harwich | 14 | 9 | Hall | Gershom | 3 | 1 | 1 | 1 | | 2 | 5 | 2 | | 1 | | | 16 | | |
| Dennis | 27 | 23 | Hall | Henry | | 2 | | 1 | | 3 | 1 | | 1 | | | | 8 | | |
| Yarmouth | 96 | 31 | Hall | Isaac Jr | 1 | | | 1 | | 1 | | | 1 | | | | 4 | | |
| Dennis | 27 | 19 | Hall | Jesse | 1 | | | 1 | | 1 | | 1 | | | | | 4 | | |
| Harwich | 10 | 25 | Hall | John | | | 1 | | | 3 | | 1 | | | | | 5 | | |
| Yarmouth | 95 | 36 | Hall | John | | 1 | 2 | 1 | | | 1 | | | 1 | | | 7 | | |
| Harwich | 14 | 12 | Hall | Jonathan | 2 | | | 1 | | 2 | | | 1 | | | | 6 | | |
| Sandwich | 38 | 21 | Hall | Jonathan | 2 | | | 1 | | 1 | | 1 | 1 | 1 | | | 7 | | |
| Sandwich | 35 | 4 | Hall | Joseph | 2 | | | 1 | | 1 | 1 | | 1 | | | | 6 | | |
| Dennis | 27 | 16 | Hall | Joshua | 1 | | | 1 | | 1 | | 1 | | | | | 4 | | |
| Sandwich | 35 | 3 | Hall | Joshua | 1 | | | 1 | | | | | 1 | | | | 4 | | |
| Dennis | 27 | 14 | Hall | Josiah | | | 3 | | 1 | | | 1 | | 1 | | | 6 | | |
| Dennis | 27 | 27 | Hall | Josiah | | 2 | 2 | | 1 | | | 1 | | 1 | | | 7 | | |
| Dennis | 27 | 20 | Hall | Josiah Junr | | | 1 | | | | | | 1 | | | | 2 | | |
| Dennis | 27 | 15 | Hall | Nathan | 1 | 1 | 1 | 1 | | 3 | 1 | 1 | 2 | | | | 11 | | |
| Dennis | 27 | 18 | Hall | Nathaniel | | 1 | | 1 | | | | | 1 | 1 | | | 4 | | |
| Harwich | 11 | 35 | Hall | Nathaniel | 1 | | | 1 | | | | | 1 | | | | 3 | | |
| Harwich | 14 | 11 | Hall | Seth | | | 1 | | | 1 | | | 1 | | | | 3 | | |
| Dennis | 27 | 29 | Hall | Stephen | | | | 1 | | | | | | 1 | | | 2 | | |
| Sandwich | 35 | 2 | Hall | Stephen | | | 1 | | 1 | 1 | | | 1 | 1 | | | 5 | | |
| Dennis | 26 | 23 | Hall | Thomas | 1 | | 1 | | | | | | 1 | | | | 3 | | |
| Barnstable | 83 | 16 | Hall | Gorham | | | 1 | | | 3 | | | 1 | | | | 5 | | |
| Yarmouth | 97 | 43 | Hallet | Abigail | | | 1 | | | | | | 1 | 1 | | | 3 | | |
| Barnstable | 85 | 11 | Hallet | Abner | 1 | | 1 | 1 | | | | | 1 | | | | 4 | | |
| Yarmouth | 97 | 39 | Hallet | Andrew | | | 1 | | | | | 1 | 1 | | | | 3 | | |
| Yarmouth | 96 | 9 | Hallet | Ansel | 2 | | | 1 | | | | 1 | | | | | 4 | | |
| Barnstable | 91 | 13 | Hallet | Benj | 1 | 1 | | 1 | | 4 | 3 | 1 | 1 | | | | 12 | | |
| Yarmouth | 98 | 8 | Hallet | Benjamin | | | 1 | | | 1 | 1 | | 1 | | | | 4 | | |
| Barnstable | 94 | 17 | Hallet | Bethiah | 1 | | | | | | | | 1 | | | | 2 | | |
| Yarmouth | 97 | 34 | Hallet | Charles | 2 | 1 | 1 | | | | | 1 | 1 | 1 | | | 8 | | |
| Barnstable | 93 | 49 | Hallet | Daniel | | | 1 | | | 1 | | | 1 | | | | 3 | | |
| Barnstable | 94 | 22 | Hallet | David | 1 | | | 1 | | 3 | | | 1 | | 10 | | 16 | | |
| Yarmouth | 97 | 28 | Hallet | Ebenezer Jr | 1 | 2 | 2 | | 2 | 1 | 2 | 1 | | 1 | | | 12 | | |
| Barnstable | 93 | 50 | Hallet | Edward | 4 | 1 | | 1 | | | | | 1 | 1 | | | 8 | | |
| Yarmouth | 97 | 4 | Hallet | Enoch | 3 | 1 | | 1 | | 2 | | 1 | | 1 | 8 | | 17 | | |
| Yarmouth | 97 | 45 | Hallet | Ezra | 1 | | 1 | | | 1 | | | 1 | | | | 4 | | |
| Barnstable | 83 | 3 | Hallet | Isaac | 2 | | | 1 | | 2 | | 1 | | | | | 6 | | |
| Yarmouth | 98 | 9 | Hallet | Isaac | | 1 | 1 | | 1 | | 1 | | | 1 | | | 5 | | |
| Yarmouth | 98 | 7 | Hallet | James | 1 | | 1 | | 1 | 2 | 2 | 1 | 1 | | | | 9 | | |
| Yarmouth | 98 | 4 | Hallet | Jeremiah | | | 1 | 1 | 1 | 1 | | | 1 | 1 | | | 6 | | |
| Barnstable | 94 | 4 | Hallet | John | 1 | 2 | 1 | | | 2 | 1 | | 1 | | | | 9 | | |
| Yarmouth | 96 | 45 | Hallet | John | 2 | 1 | 1 | 1 | | 2 | 1 | | 2 | | | | 10 | | |
| Yarmouth | 98 | 10 | Hallet | John Jr | | 1 | | | | | | | 1 | | | | 2 | | |
| Barnstable | 93 | 51 | Hallet | Jonathan | | | | 1 | | | | | | 1 | | | 2 | | |
| Barnstable | 93 | 52 | Hallet | Jonathan | | | 1 | | | | | | 1 | | | | 2 | | |
| Yarmouth | 98 | 1 | Hallet | Jonathan | | | | 1 | | | | 1 | 1 | 1 | | | 4 | | |
| Yarmouth | 98 | 3 | Hallet | Jonathan Jr | | 2 | | 1 | | 1 | | | 1 | 1 | | | 6 | | |
| Barnstable | 94 | 10 | Hallet | Joseph | | 3 | | 1 | | | 2 | 1 | 1 | | | | 8 | | |
| Yarmouth | 98 | 11 | Hallet | Joshua | | 1 | | 1 | | | | | 3 | 1 | | | 6 | | |
| Yarmouth | 98 | 6 | Hallet | Moses | | | 1 | | | | | | 2 | 1 | | | 4 | | |
| Yarmouth | 97 | 36 | Hallet | Nathan | 1 | | | 1 | | 3 | | | 1 | 1 | | | 7 | | |
| Barnstable | 94 | 5 | Hallet | Nathaniel | 2 | 1 | 1 | | 1 | 2 | 1 | 1 | | 1 | | | 10 | | |
| Yarmouth | 97 | 44 | Hallet | Prince | | | 1 | | | | | | | 1 | | | 2 | | |
| Barnstable | 93 | 48 | Hallet | Rebecca | | | 1 | | | | | | 1 | 1 | | | 3 | | |
| Barnstable | 94 | 11 | Hallet | Rowland | 1 | 2 | 3 | 1 | | | | 2 | 2 | | | | 11 | | |
| Barnstable | 94 | 13 | Hallet | Rowland Jr | 1 | | 1 | | 2 | | | 1 | | | | | 5 | | |
| Yarmouth | 97 | 32 | Hallet | Ruth | | 1 | 1 | | | | | | | 1 | | | 3 | | |
| Barnstable | 91 | 18 | Hallet | Samuel | 1 | | 2 | 1 | 3 | | | 1 | 1 | 1 | | | 10 | | |
| Yarmouth | 97 | 27 | Hallet | Sarah | | | 1 | | | | | 1 | 1 | 1 | | | 4 | | |
| Yarmouth | 97 | 31 | Hallet | Stephen | | | | 1 | | | | | | 3 | | | 4 | | |
| Yarmouth | 97 | 33 | Hallet | Stephen Jr | | | 1 | | | | | | 1 | | | | 2 | | |
| Barnstable | 83 | 2 | Hallet | Thomas | | 1 | | 1 | | | | 1 | | | | | 3 | | |
| Yarmouth | 98 | 5 | Hallet | Thomas | 1 | | | 1 | | 1 | | | 3 | 1 | | | 7 | | |

# 1800 Barnstable County, Massachusetts Index

| Town | PG# | LN# | Last Name | First Name | Free White Males | | | | | Free White Females | | | | | Total All Other | Total Slaves | Totals | District/Township | Notes |
|---|---|---|---|---|---|---|---|---|---|---|---|---|---|---|---|---|---|---|---|
| | | | | | under 10 | 10 to 16 | 16 to 26 | 26 to 45 | 45 over | under 10 | 10 to 16 | 16 to 26 | 26 to 45 | 45 over | | | | | |
| Yarmouth | 97 | 48 | Hallet | William | | | 1 | | | | | 1 | | | | | 2 | | |
| Yarmouth | 98 | 2 | Hallet | Zenas | 2 | | 1 | | | | | 1 | | | | | 4 | | |
| Falmouth | 49 | 316 | Hambl | Nathan | 2 | 1 | 2 | 1 | | | | | 2 | | | | 8 | | |
| Sandwich | 40 | 13 | Hamblen | Benja | 3 | 1 | 1 | | | | 1 | 2 | | | | | 8 | | |
| Wellfleet | 70 | 33 | Hamblen | Cornelius | 1 | 1 | 3 | | 1 | 2 | 2 | | 1 | | | | 11 | | |
| Sandwich | 40 | 14 | Hamblen | Dorothy | | | 2 | | | | | | 1 | 1 | | | 4 | | |
| Sandwich | 40 | 15 | Hamblen | Ellis | 1 | | 1 | | | 2 | | 1 | | | | | 5 | | |
| Mashpee | 52 | 8 | Hamblen | Jonathan | | 1 | | 1 | | | 1 | | | 1 | | | 4 | | |
| Sandwich | 40 | 17 | Hamblen | Nathl | 2 | | 1 | | | | | 1 | | 1 | | | 5 | | |
| Falmouth | 46 | 140 | Hamblen | Seth | 2 | 1 | | 1 | | 1 | 1 | | 1 | | | | 7 | | |
| Sandwich | 38 | 19 | Hamblen | Seth | 1 | | 1 | | | | | 1 | | 1 | | | 4 | | |
| Sandwich | 36 | 25 | Hamblen | Thomas | 1 | 1 | | | | | | 1 | | | | | 3 | | |
| Barnstable | 93 | 24 | Hamblin | David | 2 | | 1 | | | 2 | | | 1 | | | | 6 | | |
| Yarmouth | 96 | 6 | Hamblin | Isaac | | | | 1 | | | | 1 | | 1 | | | 3 | | |
| Yarmouth | 96 | 8 | Hamblin | Isaac Jr | 1 | | 1 | | | 2 | | | 1 | | | | 5 | | |
| Barnstable | 89 | 25 | Hamblin | John | | | | 1 | | | | | | 3 | | | 4 | | |
| Barnstable | 89 | 24 | Hamblin | John Jr | 1 | | 1 | | | | | 1 | | | | | 3 | | |
| Barnstable | 89 | 41 | Hamblin | Joseph | 1 | | 1 | | | | | 1 | | | | | 3 | | |
| Barnstable | 94 | 23 | Hamblin | Joshua | 1 | 2 | 1 | | 1 | 1 | | 1 | 2 | 1 | | | 10 | | |
| Yarmouth | 96 | 7 | Hamblin | Joshua | 1 | 1 | | | | | | 1 | | | | | 3 | | |
| Barnstable | 89 | 33 | Hamblin | Lewis | 2 | | 1 | | | 2 | | | 1 | 1 | | | 7 | | |
| Barnstable | 93 | 5 | Hamblin | Martha | | | | | | | | | | 2 | | | 2 | | |
| Yarmouth | 96 | 30 | Hamblin | Seth | 1 | | 1 | | | | | | 1 | | | | 3 | | |
| Chatham | 17 | 21 | Hamilton | Benja | 4 | | 1 | | | | | | 2 | 1 | | | 8 | | |
| Chatham | 17 | 6 | Hamilton | Elizabeth | | 1 | | | | | | | | 1 | | | 2 | | |
| Chatham | 17 | 32 | Hamilton | Elizabeth | | 1 | | 1 | | | 1 | | | 1 | | | 4 | | |
| Chatham | 17 | 4 | Hamilton | Jeptha | | 1 | 1 | | 1 | 2 | 1 | | 1 | | | | 7 | | |
| Chatham | 17 | 35 | Hamilton | Jonathan | 3 | | 1 | | | | | | 1 | | | | 5 | | |
| Chatham | 17 | 31 | Hamilton | Meltiah | 1 | 2 | 1 | | | | 1 | | 1 | | | | 7 | | |
| Chatham | 17 | 5 | Hamilton | Nathaniel | | | 2 | 1 | | | 1 | | 1 | | | | 5 | | |
| Chatham | 17 | 30 | Hamilton | Nehemiah | 2 | | 1 | | | | | | 1 | | | | 4 | | |
| Chatham | 17 | 34 | Hamilton | Richard | 1 | | 1 | | 1 | 5 | 2 | | 1 | | | | 11 | | |
| Chatham | 20 | 35 | Hamilton | Samuel | | | 1 | | | 3 | | | 1 | | | | 5 | | |
| Chatham | 17 | 33 | Hamilton | Seth | 1 | | 1 | | | | | | 1 | | | | 3 | | |
| Wellfleet | 71 | 4 | Hamlen | Lewis | 1 | | | 1 | | | | | | 1 | | | 3 | | |
| Barnstable | 89 | 40 | Hamlen | Micah | | | 4 | 1 | | | 1 | | | 2 | 1 | | 9 | | |
| Barnstable | 88 | 18 | Hamlen | Shubael | 3 | 1 | | 1 | | | 1 | | | | | | 6 | | |
| Falmouth | 46 | 138 | Hammond | Barnabas | | 1 | | 1 | | 2 | | 1 | | | | | 5 | | |
| Chatham | 17 | 25 | Hammond | John | 3 | 1 | | 1 | | | 1 | | 1 | 1 | | | 8 | | |
| Falmouth | 46 | 128 | Hammond | John | | | 2 | 2 | 1 | | 2 | 1 | 1 | | | | 9 | | |
| Sandwich | 41 | 13 | Hamond | Joshua | 3 | 2 | | 1 | | 1 | 1 | 1 | | | | | 9 | | |
| Falmouth | 49 | 283 | Hampton | Benja | | 1 | | 1 | | 1 | 1 | | 1 | | | | 5 | | |
| Falmouth | 49 | 276 | Handy | Elnathan | | | | 1 | | | 1 | | 2 | | | | 4 | | |
| Falmouth | 46 | 124 | Handy | Elnathan Junr | 1 | | 1 | | | 1 | | 1 | | | | | 4 | | |
| Falmouth | 49 | 317 | Handy | Hannah | | | | | | | | 2 | | | | | 2 | | |
| Sandwich | 40 | 44 | Handy | Hannah | | | 1 | | 1 | | 1 | 1 | 1 | | | | 5 | | |
| Sandwich | 41 | 16 | Handy | Jonathan | | 1 | | 1 | | | 1 | | 1 | | | | 4 | | |
| Falmouth | 49 | 275 | Handy | Levi | | | 1 | | 3 | | | 1 | | | | | 5 | | |
| Falmouth | 49 | 269 | Handy | Paul | 1 | 2 | | 1 | | 2 | | 1 | 1 | | | | 9 | | |
| Sandwich | 41 | 17 | Handy | Wm | 1 | | 1 | | 2 | | 1 | 1 | | | | | 6 | | |
| Truro | 63 | 35 | Hanling | Jonathan | 1 | 1 | 2 | | 1 | | 1 | 1 | | | | | 7 | | |
| Wellfleet | 71 | 15 | Harding | Abigail | | 3 | | | 1 | 3 | | | 1 | | | | 8 | | |
| Chatham | 17 | 23 | Harding | Amos | 1 | 1 | | 1 | | | 1 | | | 2 | | | 6 | | |
| Truro | 68 | 6 | Harding | Benjamin | 1 | | | 1 | | 2 | | | 1 | | | | 5 | | |
| Chatham | 17 | 37 | Harding | Content Wid | | 1 | 1 | | | | 1 | 1 | | 1 | | | 5 | | |
| Eastham | 77 | 28 | Harding | Ephraim | 1 | | | 1 | | 1 | | | 1 | | | | 4 | | |
| Orleans | 21 | 12 | Harding | Ephraim | 1 | | | 1 | | 1 | | | 1 | | | | 4 | | |
| Truro | 65 | 26 | Harding | Ephraim | | 1 | | | 1 | | | | 2 | 1 | | | 5 | | |
| Chatham | 17 | 8 | Harding | John | | 2 | | | 1 | | 1 | | | 1 | | | 5 | | |
| Chatham | 19 | 22 | Harding | John Jun Widow | 1 | | 1 | | | 2 | | 1 | | | | | 5 | | |
| Wellfleet | 70 | 32 | Harding | Joseph Junr | 1 | 1 | 1 | | | 1 | | 2 | | | | | 6 | | |
| Chatham | 17 | 11 | Harding | Josiah | 4 | 1 | | 1 | | | | | 1 | | | | 7 | | |
| Orleans | 24 | 28 | Harding | Keziah | | | 2 | | | | | | 1 | 1 | | | 4 | | |
| Provincetown | 58 | 15 | Harding | Knowles | 2 | | | 1 | | 1 | | | 1 | | | | 5 | | |
| Truro | 64 | 10 | Harding | Lot | | | | 1 | 1 | | | | 1 | 3 | | | 6 | | |
| Truro | 64 | 11 | Harding | Lot Junr | 2 | 1 | | 1 | | | | | 1 | | | | 5 | | |
| Wellfleet | 74 | 26 | Harding | Mary | | 1 | | | | 1 | 2 | | 1 | | | | 5 | | |
| Chatham | 20 | 23 | Harding | Mulford | | 1 | | | | 1 | | 1 | | | | | 3 | | |
| Wellfleet | 71 | 14 | Harding | Nathaniel | 2 | 1 | 1 | | 1 | | 1 | 2 | 1 | | | | 9 | | |
| Wellfleet | 74 | 35 | Harding | Nathaniel | | 1 | 1 | | | 1 | | 1 | | | | | 4 | | |
| Chatham | 17 | 24 | Harding | Prenie | | | 1 | | 1 | 1 | | | | 1 | | | 4 | | |
| Chatham | 17 | 38 | Harding | Prince Junr | 1 | | | 1 | | 1 | | | 1 | | | | 4 | | |
| Harwich | 8 | 9 | Harding | Ruben | | | | | 1 | 2 | | | 1 | | | | 4 | | |
| Falmouth | 46 | 133 | Harding | Samuel | | | | 1 | | | | | 1 | 1 | | | 3 | | |
| Chatham | 20 | 7 | Harding | Seth | 1 | 1 | | 1 | | 2 | 1 | 1 | | 1 | | | 8 | | |
| Chatham | 17 | 29 | Harding | Seth Junr | 2 | 2 | 3 | | 1 | 1 | | | | 1 | | | 10 | | |
| Chatham | 19 | 38 | Harding | Seth Junr | 1 | | 1 | | 1 | 3 | | 1 | 1 | | | | 8 | | |
| Chatham | 17 | 28 | Harding | Silvanus | 1 | 2 | 1 | | 1 | 1 | | | 1 | | | | 9 | | |
| Chatham | 20 | 5 | Harding | Theodore | | | 1 | | | | | | 1 | | | | 2 | | |
| Chatham | 19 | 30 | Harding | Thomas | 2 | | 1 | | | 1 | | 1 | | | | | 5 | | |
| Chatham | 20 | 13 | Harding | Thomas | | 1 | 1 | | | 1 | | 1 | | | | | 5 | | |
| Orleans | 25 | 30 | Harding | Thomas | 1 | | | 1 | | | | | | 1 | | | 3 | | |
| Barnstable | 83 | 5 | Harston | Ebenzr | 1 | | | 1 | | 3 | | | 1 | | | | 6 | | |
| Barnstable | 83 | 4 | Harston | John | | | 1 | 1 | 1 | | | | 1 | | | | 5 | | |

# 1800 Barnstable County, Massachusetts Index

| TOWN | PG# | LN# | LAST NAME | FIRST NAME | FREE WHITE MALES under 10 | 10 to 16 | 16 to 26 | 26 to 45 | 45 and over | FREE WHITE FEMALES under 10 | 10 to 16 | 16 to 26 | 26 to 45 | 45 and over | TOTAL ALL OTHER | TOTAL SLAVES | TOTALS | DISTRICT/ TOWNSHIP | NOTES |
|---|---|---|---|---|---|---|---|---|---|---|---|---|---|---|---|---|---|---|---|
| Mashpee | 51 | 14 | Hatch | Abel | | | 1 | | 1 | 2 | 3 | 2 | 1 | | | | 10 | | |
| Falmouth | 49 | 291 | Hatch | Barnabas | 1 | 1 | | | 1 | 1 | 3 | 1 | | | | | 9 | | |
| Falmouth | 46 | 123 | Hatch | Benjm | 1 | | 2 | 1 | | 2 | | 1 | | 1 | | | 8 | | |
| Falmouth | 46 | 130 | Hatch | Coleman | | | 1 | | | | | 1 | | | | | 2 | | |
| Falmouth | 46 | 145 | Hatch | Consider | 1 | | 2 | 1 | | 2 | 1 | | 1 | | | | 8 | | |
| Falmouth | 46 | 131 | Hatch | David | | | 1 | | | 1 | | 1 | 1 | | | | 3 | | |
| Falmouth | 46 | 134 | Hatch | David Junr | | | 1 | | | 1 | | | 1 | | | | 3 | | |
| Falmouth | 46 | 126 | Hatch | Edward | | 1 | | 1 | | | | | | 1 | | | 3 | | |
| Wellfleet | 73 | 29 | Hatch | Elisha | | | 1 | | | 2 | | | | | | | 5 | | |
| Falmouth | 49 | 295 | Hatch | Elizabeth | | | | | | | | | 1 | | | | 1 | | |
| Wellfleet | 70 | 28 | Hatch | George | 4 | 1 | 1 | | 1 | 1 | 1 | 1 | 1 | 1 | | | 12 | | |
| Barnstable | 86 | 40 | Hatch | Gorham | | 1 | | | | | | 1 | | | | | 2 | | |
| Eastham | 77 | 25 | Hatch | Henry | 2 | | 1 | | | | | | 1 | | | | 4 | | |
| Falmouth | 46 | 121 | Hatch | Howes Junr | 1 | | | 1 | 1 | | 1 | | | | | | 4 | | |
| Falmouth | 46 | 137 | Hatch | Ichabod | | | 1 | | | 1 | | 1 | | 1 | | | 3 | | |
| Wellfleet | 75 | 12 | Hatch | James B. | | | 1 | | | 1 | | | 1 | | | | 3 | | |
| Falmouth | 49 | 285 | Hatch | Joseph | 2 | 1 | 2 | | | 2 | 2 | | 1 | | | | 11 | | |
| Falmouth | 51 | 323 | Hatch | Joseph | 1 | | | 1 | | 1 | 1 | | 1 | | | | 5 | | |
| Mashpee | 51 | 13 | Hatch | Joseph | | | 1 | | | | | 1 | | 1 | | | 3 | | |
| Wellfleet | 74 | 3 | Hatch | Joseph | | 1 | | 1 | | | | | 3 | 1 | | | 6 | | |
| Wellfleet | 74 | 4 | Hatch | Joseph Junr | 1 | | 1 | | | 2 | | | 1 | | | | 5 | | |
| Falmouth | 49 | 293 | Hatch | Katharine | | | | | | | | 2 | 1 | | | | 3 | | |
| Falmouth | 46 | 142 | Hatch | Major | | 1 | | 1 | | 1 | | 1 | | | | | 4 | | |
| Falmouth | 46 | 129 | Hatch | Moses | 1 | | | 1 | | 1 | | 1 | | | | | 4 | | |
| Falmouth | 46 | 144 | Hatch | Moses Junr | 1 | 1 | | 1 | 1 | 1 | 1 | | 1 | 1 | | | 8 | | |
| Falmouth | 46 | 122 | Hatch | Nathl | | 1 | 2 | 1 | 1 | | | 1 | 2 | 1 | | | 9 | | |
| Falmouth | 49 | 270 | Hatch | Obadiah | 1 | | | 1 | 1 | | | 1 | 1 | | | | 5 | | |
| Falmouth | 46 | 139 | Hatch | Prince | | | 1 | | | | | | | | | | 1 | | |
| Falmouth | 49 | 282 | Hatch | Reuben | | 1 | | 1 | | | | 3 | | 1 | | | 6 | | |
| Mashpee | 51 | 15 | Hatch | Reuben | | 1 | | 1 | | 2 | | 3 | | | | | 7 | | |
| Falmouth | 46 | 125 | Hatch | Samuel | | | 1 | | | | 2 | | 1 | | | | 4 | | |
| Falmouth | 49 | 292 | Hatch | Shubael | | | 1 | | | 1 | | | 1 | | | | 3 | | |
| Falmouth | 46 | 135 | Hatch | Shubael Junr | 1 | 1 | 1 | 1 | | 1 | | | 1 | | | | 6 | | |
| Falmouth | 46 | 143 | Hatch | Solomon | | | 1 | | | | 1 | | 1 | 1 | 1 | | 4 | | |
| Falmouth | 46 | 136 | Hatch | Susanna | 1 | | 1 | | | | 2 | | 1 | 1 | | | 6 | | |
| Wellfleet | 75 | 3 | Hatch | Thomas | | 1 | | | | 1 | | 1 | | | | | 3 | | |
| Falmouth | 46 | 127 | Hatch | Ward | | 1 | | | | 1 | | 1 | | | | | 3 | | |
| Sandwich | 42 | 28 | Hatch | Zacheus | | 1 | 1 | | | | | | 1 | | | | 3 | | |
| Falmouth | 46 | 132 | Hatch | Zadock | | | 3 | | 1 | 1 | 1 | | 1 | | | | 7 | | |
| Barnstable | 88 | 5 | Hathaway | Benja | | 1 | | 1 | | 1 | 1 | | 1 | | | | 5 | | |
| Barnstable | 88 | 7 | Hathaway | James | | 2 | 1 | 1 | | | | | 1 | | | | 5 | | |
| Barnstable | 90 | 44 | Hathaway | James Jr | | 1 | | 1 | | 1 | 1 | 1 | | | | | 5 | | |
| Yarmouth | 97 | 16 | Hawes | Benja | 1 | | 1 | | | | | 1 | | | | | 3 | | |
| Yarmouth | 97 | 20 | Hawes | David | 1 | 4 | | | 1 | | | 1 | | 1 | | | 8 | | |
| Yarmouth | 97 | 21 | Hawes | Ebenezer | | | 1 | | 1 | | 3 | | 2 | | | | 7 | | |
| Yarmouth | 97 | 22 | Hawes | Ebenezer Jr | | | 1 | | | | 1 | | | | | | 2 | | |
| Wellfleet | 75 | 20 | Hawes | Edmund | 4 | | 1 | | | | | | 1 | | | | 6 | | |
| Wellfleet | 71 | 6 | Hawes | Hulday | | | | | | | | 1 | | 1 | | | 2 | | |
| Wellfleet | 69 | 17 | Hawes | Jeremiah | 1 | | 1 | | 1 | 1 | | | | | | | 4 | | |
| Chatham | 17 | 22 | Hawes | John | 2 | 1 | 3 | | 1 | 1 | 1 | | 1 | 1 | | | 11 | | |
| Yarmouth | 97 | 35 | Hawes | Joseph | | 1 | | 1 | | 1 | | 1 | | | | | 4 | | |
| Barnstable | 94 | 14 | Hawes | Joshua | 2 | | 1 | | 3 | 2 | | 1 | 1 | | | | 10 | | |
| Yarmouth | 95 | 9 | Hawes | Prince | 2 | | | | | | | 1 | | | | | 4 | | |
| Yarmouth | 97 | 15 | Hawes | Simeon | | 2 | 2 | | | | 2 | 1 | | | | | 7 | | |
| Wellfleet | 71 | 7 | Hawes | Thomas | | 1 | | | | 1 | 1 | | | | | | 3 | | |
| Mashpee | 51 | 1 | Hawley | Gideon Revd | | 1 | 1 | | | | | 2 | | | | | 4 | | |
| Provincetown | 61 | 14 | Hayden | William | | 1 | | | | 1 | | 1 | | | | | 3 | | |
| Barnstable | 92 | 45 | Hayes | Hannah | | 1 | | | | | | | | | 1 | | 2 | | |
| Yarmouth | 99 | 7 | Hedge | Abram | 1 | 1 | 1 | | | | 1 | | | | | | 5 | | |
| Yarmouth | 95 | 20 | Hedge | Andrew | | | 1 | | | | 1 | | 1 | | | | 3 | | |
| Yarmouth | 95 | 21 | Hedge | Barnabas | | 2 | | 1 | | 1 | | | 1 | | | | 5 | | |
| Dennis | 28 | 1 | Hedge | Daniel | 1 | | 1 | | | 1 | | 2 | | | | | 5 | | |
| Yarmouth | 96 | 35 | Hedge | Dinah | 1 | 1 | 1 | | | 2 | 1 | | 1 | | | | 7 | | |
| Yarmouth | 96 | 1 | Hedge | Edward | | 1 | | | | | | 1 | | | | | 2 | | |
| Yarmouth | 95 | 13 | Hedge | Elisha | | 1 | 1 | | 1 | 1 | | 1 | | | | | 6 | | |
| Yarmouth | 96 | 36 | Hedge | Josiah Jr | | 1 | | | 1 | 1 | | | | | | | 3 | | |
| Yarmouth | 95 | 7 | Hedge | William | 1 | | | 1 | | 3 | | 1 | | | | | 6 | | |
| Barnstable | 88 | 17 | Hennlen | Ruth | | | | | | | | 2 | 1 | | | | 3 | | |
| Truro | 67 | 13 | Hewes | Rachall Wid | 3 | | | 2 | | 2 | | | 1 | | | | 8 | | |
| Eastham | 77 | 24 | Hickman | James | | 1 | 2 | | 2 | 2 | 3 | | 1 | | | | 11 | | |
| Orleans | 21 | 6 | Higgins | Aaron | | 2 | | 1 | | 1 | 3 | | | | | | 7 | | |
| Orleans | 21 | 8 | Higgins | Absalon | | | 1 | 4 | 1 | | 1 | | | | | | 7 | | |
| Orleans | 25 | 3 | Higgins | Aguella | | | | 1 | | | 2 | | 1 | | | | 4 | | |
| Orleans | 24 | 1 | Higgins | Asa | 4 | | | 1 | | | | 1 | | 1 | 1 | | 8 | | |
| Eastham | 79 | 30 | Higgins | Benjamin | 2 | | 1 | | | 1 | | 1 | | | | | 5 | | |
| Wellfleet | 70 | 29 | Higgins | Beriah | 1 | | 1 | 1 | | 2 | 1 | | 1 | | | | 7 | | |
| Orleans | 23 | 19 | Higgins | Daniel | 1 | | | 1 | | 1 | | 1 | | | | | 4 | | |
| Orleans | 25 | 8 | Higgins | Daniel | 1 | | | 1 | | 1 | | 1 | | | | | 4 | | |
| Orleans | 23 | 10 | Higgins | Easter Wid | | | | | | | | 2 | 1 | | | | 3 | | |
| Wellfleet | 73 | 22 | Higgins | Eleazar | 1 | 1 | | 1 | | 3 | 1 | | 1 | | | | 8 | | |
| Orleans | 23 | 3 | Higgins | Eliakim | 2 | 2 | | 1 | | 1 | 2 | | 1 | | | | 9 | | |
| Eastham | 77 | 26 | Higgins | Elkanah | | 1 | 1 | | 1 | 1 | | | | | | | 6 | | |
| Eastham | 77 | 27 | Higgins | Elkanah Junr | 2 | | 1 | | | 1 | | 1 | | | | | 6 | | |

# 1800 Barnstable County, Massachusetts Index

| TOWN | PG# | LN# | LAST NAME | FIRST NAME | FREE WHITE MALES under 10 | 10 to 16 | 16 to 26 | 26 to 45 | 45 and over | FREE WHITE FEMALES under 10 | 10 to 16 | 16 to 26 | 26 to 45 | 45 and over | TOTAL ALL OTHER | TOTAL SLAVES | TOTALS | DISTRICT/TOWNSHIP | NOTES |
|---|---|---|---|---|---|---|---|---|---|---|---|---|---|---|---|---|---|---|---|
| Orleans | 23 | 11 | Higgins | Elnathan | | | | 1 | | | | | | 1 | | | 2 | | |
| Provincetown | 58 | 18 | Higgins | Enoch | 1 | | | 1 | | 1 | | 1 | | | | | 4 | | |
| Wellfleet | 71 | 12 | Higgins | Enoch | | | | | 1 | | | | 1 | 2 | | | 4 | | |
| Wellfleet | 73 | 21 | Higgins | Ephraim | 2 | | | 1 | | | | | 1 | | | | 4 | | |
| Orleans | 21 | 4 | Higgins | Freeman | | 1 | | 1 | 1 | 1 | | | 2 | 1 | | | 7 | | |
| Orleans | 23 | 40 | Higgins | Gideon | 1 | | | 1 | | | | 2 | 2 | 1 | | | 7 | | |
| Wellfleet | 71 | 2 | Higgins | Hannah | | | 2 | | | | | | 3 | 1 | | | 6 | | |
| Wellfleet | 71 | 3 | Higgins | Hannah Junr | | 1 | | | | | | 1 | | 1 | | | 3 | | |
| Orleans | 22 | 37 | Higgins | Hattel | 3 | | | 1 | | 1 | | | 1 | | | | 6 | | |
| Orleans | 23 | 46 | Higgins | Hezekiah | 1 | | | 1 | | | | | | 1 | | | 3 | | |
| Harwich | 8 | 18 | Higgins | Hezekiel | | 1 | | | | | | | 1 | | | | 2 | | |
| Harwich | 8 | 17 | Higgins | Jacob | | 3 | | | 1 | | | | | 1 | | | 5 | | |
| Truro | 63 | 23 | Higgins | Jedediah | 1 | | | 1 | | 1 | | | 1 | 1 | | | 5 | | |
| Orleans | 22 | 38 | Higgins | Jonathan | | | | 1 | | | | 1 | | 1 | | | 3 | | |
| Wellfleet | 73 | 37 | Higgins | Jonathan | 1 | 1 | 5 | 1 | | 3 | 1 | 1 | 1 | | | | 14 | | |
| Truro | 64 | 6 | Higgins | Jonathan | | 1 | | 1 | 1 | | | | 1 | | | | 4 | | |
| Chatham | 19 | 14 | Higgins | Joseph | | | 1 | | | 1 | | | 1 | | | | 3 | | |
| Harwich | 13 | 13 | Higgins | Joseph | 1 | | 1 | | | | | | 1 | | | | 3 | | |
| Truro | 68 | 15 | Higgins | Joseph | | | | 1 | | 1 | | | 1 | | | | 3 | | |
| Wellfleet | 72 | 10 | Higgins | Joseph | | | | 1 | | 1 | | 1 | | | | | 3 | | |
| Chatham | 20 | 4 | Higgins | Joseph 3rd | | | | 1 | | 1 | | | | 1 | | | 3 | | |
| Chatham | 20 | 29 | Higgins | Joseph Jr | 2 | 1 | 1 | | 1 | 1 | 1 | | | 1 | | | 8 | | |
| Orleans | 23 | 32 | Higgins | Joshua | 2 | | | 1 | | 1 | 1 | | 1 | | | | 6 | | |
| Orleans | 22 | 18 | Higgins | Lot | | | 2 | | 1 | | | 2 | | 1 | | | 6 | | |
| Orleans | 23 | 4 | Higgins | Lot | 2 | 1 | 1 | | 1 | | 1 | 2 | 1 | | | | 9 | | |
| Truro | 62 | 6 | Higgins | Martha Wd | 1 | | | | | 1 | | | | 1 | | | 3 | | |
| Orleans | 22 | 16 | Higgins | Moses | 3 | | | 1 | | 1 | | | 1 | | | | 6 | | |
| Orleans | 24 | 2 | Higgins | Moses | 3 | | | 1 | | 1 | | | 1 | | | | 6 | | |
| Wellfleet | 74 | 10 | Higgins | Paine | | 1 | | 1 | | 2 | 1 | 1 | 1 | | | | 7 | | |
| Eastham | 79 | 33 | Higgins | Phebe | | | | | | 1 | | 1 | | 2 | | | 4 | | |
| Wellfleet | 70 | 35 | Higgins | Phillip | 1 | | | 1 | | 2 | | | 1 | | | | 5 | | |
| Orleans | 21 | 14 | Higgins | Rebeccah | | 1 | | | | | | | 2 | | | | 3 | | |
| Orleans | 21 | 5 | Higgins | Rebeccah Wid | 1 | | | | | | | 1 | 1 | 1 | | | 4 | | |
| Wellfleet | 74 | 34 | Higgins | Reuben | | | 1 | | 1 | | | 1 | | | | | 3 | | |
| Orleans | 23 | 5 | Higgins | Richard | 1 | | | 1 | | 3 | | | 1 | | | | 6 | | |
| Orleans | 24 | 45 | Higgins | Samuel | 1 | | 1 | | 1 | | 1 | | | 1 | | | 5 | | |
| Truro | 64 | 34 | Higgins | Sarah Wid | | 1 | | | | | | | 2 | 1 | | | 4 | | |
| Orleans | 22 | 11 | Higgins | Seth | 1 | 2 | | | 1 | | | 2 | 2 | 1 | | | 9 | | |
| Orleans | 24 | 42 | Higgins | Silvanus | | 1 | | 1 | | | | 2 | 1 | 1 | | | 6 | | |
| Orleans | 22 | 4 | Higgins | Simeon | 1 | | | 1 | 1 | 1 | | 1 | | 1 | | | 6 | | |
| Wellfleet | 74 | 14 | Higgins | Solomon | | 1 | | | | | | | 1 | 1 | | | 4 | | |
| Wellfleet | 74 | 13 | Higgins | Solomon Junr | 2 | 1 | | 1 | | | | | 1 | | | | 5 | | |
| Harwich | 15 | 3 | Higgins | Thankfull Wd | 2 | 1 | 1 | | | 2 | 1 | | 1 | | | | 8 | | |
| Wellfleet | 74 | 18 | Higgins | Thomas | | | | 1 | | | | | | 1 | | | 2 | | |
| Wellfleet | 74 | 19 | Higgins | Thomas 3d | 1 | | 1 | 1 | | | | | | 1 | | | 4 | | |
| Wellfleet | 74 | 25 | Higgins | Uriah | 2 | | | 1 | | | | 1 | 1 | 1 | | | 6 | | |
| Orleans | 21 | 19 | Higgins | Zachariah | 3 | 1 | | 1 | | 1 | | | 1 | | | | 7 | | |
| Provincetown | 58 | 14 | Hill | John | 1 | 1 | 2 | | 1 | 2 | | | 1 | | | | 8 | | |
| Provincetown | 60 | 17 | Hill | John Junr | | | 1 | | | | | 1 | | | | | 2 | | |
| Sandwich | 37 | 4 | Hillard | Gideon | | | | 2 | | | | | | 1 | | | 3 | | |
| Barnstable | 89 | 12 | Hilliard | George | 1 | 1 | | 1 | | 2 | 1 | 1 | 1 | | | | 8 | | |
| Provincetown | 58 | 13 | Hinch | Samuel | | | | 1 | | | | | | 1 | | | 2 | | |
| Truro | 64 | 23 | Hinchley | Allen | 1 | | 1 | 1 | | 1 | | 1 | 1 | 1 | | | 7 | | |
| Truro | 62 | 4 | Hinchley | Benjamin | | 2 | 2 | 1 | | | | | 1 | 1 | | | 7 | | |
| Barnstable | 91 | 2 | Hinckley | Abner | 1 | 1 | 2 | 1 | | | | 1 | 2 | 1 | 1 | | 10 | | |
| Barnstable | 85 | 1 | Hinckley | Adino | 3 | | | 1 | 1 | 1 | | | 1 | | | | 7 | | |
| Barnstable | 89 | 37 | Hinckley | Asa | 1 | | | 1 | | 1 | | | 1 | | | | 4 | | |
| Falmouth | 46 | 141 | Hinckley | Barnabas | | 1 | 1 | 1 | | | | | | 2 | | | 5 | | |
| Barnstable | 86 | 27 | Hinckley | Ebenezer | 1 | | | 1 | | | | 2 | | 1 | | | 6 | | |
| Falmouth | 49 | 297 | Hinckley | Elijah | | | 1 | | | | | | 1 | | | | 2 | | |
| Harwich | 14 | 5 | Hinckley | Elijah | | | 1 | | | | | | 1 | | | | 2 | | |
| Barnstable | 91 | 6 | Hinckley | Enoch | 1 | 1 | 1 | | 1 | | | 1 | 1 | 2 | | | 8 | | |
| Barnstable | 85 | 45 | Hinckley | Freeman | | 1 | 1 | | | | | | 1 | | | | 3 | | |
| Barnstable | 87 | 54 | Hinckley | Isaac Esq | | | | 1 | | | | 1 | 1 | 1 | | | 4 | | |
| Barnstable | 86 | 18 | Hinckley | Jabez | | 1 | | 1 | | | | 1 | 1 | 1 | | | 5 | | |
| Barnstable | 86 | 7 | Hinckley | James | 4 | | 1 | | | | | | 1 | | | | 6 | | |
| Barnstable | 86 | 46 | Hinckley | John | 1 | 2 | | 1 | | 1 | | 2 | | 1 | | | 8 | | |
| Barnstable | 86 | 49 | Hinckley | John | 1 | 2 | | 1 | | | | 2 | 1 | 1 | | | 8 | | |
| Barnstable | 86 | 48 | Hinckley | John 3d | | | 1 | | | | | | 1 | | | | 2 | | |
| Barnstable | 88 | 23 | Hinckley | Joseph | | | | 1 | | | | | | 1 | | | 2 | | |
| Barnstable | 90 | 17 | Hinckley | Levi | 1 | 1 | | 1 | | 3 | | | 2 | 1 | | | 9 | | |
| Barnstable | 88 | 34 | Hinckley | Nathaniel | | | 1 | 1 | 1 | | 1 | | 1 | | | | 5 | | |
| Barnstable | 91 | 15 | Hinckley | Nymphar | 2 | 2 | | 1 | | 2 | | 1 | 1 | | | | 9 | | |
| Harwich | 10 | 30 | Hinckley | Phillip | 2 | | | 1 | | | | 1 | | 1 | | | 5 | | |
| Barnstable | 88 | 9 | Hinckley | Prince | 3 | 1 | | 1 | | 2 | | | 1 | | | | 8 | | |
| Barnstable | 86 | 39 | Hinckley | Robinson | 1 | | | 1 | | 1 | | | 1 | 1 | | | 5 | | |
| Barnstable | 86 | 28 | Hinckley | Samuel | | | | 1 | | | | 1 | 1 | 2 | | | 5 | | |
| Barnstable | 90 | 16 | Hinckley | Silvanus | 3 | | | 1 | | 1 | 2 | 2 | | 1 | | | 10 | | |
| Harwich | 14 | 4 | Hinckley | Thomas | | | 1 | | | | | | 1 | 1 | | | 3 | | |
| Barnstable | 89 | 36 | Hinckley | Timo Jr | 1 | 1 | | 1 | | 1 | | | 1 | | | | 5 | | |
| Barnstable | 88 | 10 | Hinckley | Timothy | | | 4 | 1 | 1 | | | | | 1 | | | 8 | | |

# 1800 Barnstable County, Massachusetts Index

| TOWN | PG# | LN# | LAST NAME | FIRST NAME | FREE WHITE MALES | | | | | FREE WHITE FEMALES | | | | | TOTAL ALL OTHER | TOTAL SLAVES | TOTALS | DISTRICT/ TOWNSHIP | NOTES |
|---|---|---|---|---|---|---|---|---|---|---|---|---|---|---|---|---|---|---|---|
| | | | | | under 10 | 10 to 16 | 16 to 26 | 26 to 45 | 45 and over | under 10 | 10 to 16 | 16 to 26 | 26 to 45 | 45 and over | | | | | |
| Barnstable | 89 | 43 | Hinckley | Warren | 1 | | | 2 | 1 | | | 1 | | 1 | | | 6 | | |
| Barnstable | 86 | 29 | Hinckley | William | | 1 | | 1 | | 2 | 1 | | | | | | 5 | | |
| Provincetown | 61 | 5 | Hincks | Elisha | | | 1 | | | | | 1 | 1 | | | | 3 | | |
| Provincetown | 61 | 4 | Hincks | Jesse | 1 | | 1 | | | | | 1 | 1 | | | | 4 | | |
| Wellfleet | 71 | 1 | Hinkley | Moses | | | | 1 | | | | 1 | 1 | | | | 3 | | |
| Chatham | 17 | 26 | Hinkley | Shubal | | 1 | | 1 | | 2 | 2 | | 1 | | | | 7 | | |
| Barnstable | 90 | 19 | Hodges | Hex* | | | | | | | | 1 | | 1 | | | 2 | | |
| Barnstable | 90 | 20 | Hodges | Isaac | 2 | | 1 | | | 1 | | | 1 | | | | 5 | | |
| Truro | 69 | 2 | Holbrook | Anthony | 1 | | | 1 | | | | | 1 | | | | 3 | | |
| Wellfleet | 71 | 8 | Holbrook | David | 1 | 1 | 1 | 1 | | 1 | 1 | 1 | | | | | 7 | | |
| Wellfleet | 70 | 36 | Holbrook | Jonathan | | 1 | | 1 | | 1 | 1 | | | 1 | | | 5 | | |
| Wellfleet | 70 | 30 | Holbrook | Joseph | 2 | | 1 | 1 | | 1 | | | 1 | | | | 6 | | |
| Wellfleet | 72 | 1 | Holbrook | Joseph Junr | | | | 1 | | 2 | | | 2 | | | | 5 | | |
| Wellfleet | 70 | 31 | Holbrook | Solomon | 1 | | 1 | | | 1 | | | 1 | | | | 4 | | |
| Wellfleet | 71 | 16 | Holbrook | Thomas | | 1 | 1 | 2 | | 1 | 1 | | | 1 | | | 7 | | |
| Barnstable | 88 | 48 | Holmes | Bartlet | | | | 1 | | 2 | 1 | | 1 | | | | 5 | | |
| Barnstable | 91 | 22 | Holmes | Elisha | | | | | 1 | | | | 2 | 1 | | | 4 | | |
| Barnstable | 91 | 19 | Holmes | Elisha Jr | 3 | | | 1 | | 2 | | | 1 | | | | 7 | | |
| Barnstable | 91 | 23 | Holmes | Lazarus | 3 | | | 1 | | 1 | | | | 1 | | | 6 | | |
| Barnstable | 85 | 42 | Holmes | Nelson | 2 | | | 1 | | | | | 1 | | | | 4 | | |
| Barnstable | 91 | 24 | Holmes | Samuel | 1 | | | 1 | | 2 | | 1 | | | | | 5 | | |
| Sandwich | 34 | 22 | Holway | Barnabas | | | | 1 | | | | | 1 | 1 | | | 3 | | |
| Sandwich | 35 | 18 | Holway | James | | | 1 | 1 | | 1 | 2 | | 1 | | | | 6 | | |
| Sandwich | 37 | 17 | Holway | Joseph | | 2 | | 1 | | | | | | 1 | | | 4 | | |
| Sandwich | 37 | 18 | Holway | Joseph Jun | 1 | | | 1 | | 2 | | | 1 | | | | 5 | | |
| Sandwich | 36 | 28 | Holway | Prince | 2 | | | 1 | | 1 | | | 1 | | | | 5 | | |
| Provincetown | 58 | 20 | Holway | Stephen | 2 | | 2 | | | | | | 2 | | | | 6 | | |
| Yarmouth | 95 | 25 | Homer | Benjamin | 2 | | | 1 | | | | | 1 | | | | 4 | | |
| Yarmouth | 95 | 43 | Homer | Daniel | | 1 | | | | 1 | | | 1 | | | | 3 | | |
| Yarmouth | 95 | 26 | Homer | John | 1 | | | 1 | | | | | 1 | | | | 3 | | |
| Yarmouth | 95 | 24 | Homer | Robert | | 1 | 1 | 1 | | | | | | 1 | | | 4 | | |
| Dennis | 26 | 27 | Homer | Stephen | 2 | | | 1 | | 1 | | | 1 | | 1 | | 6 | | |
| Yarmouth | 95 | 27 | Homer | Stevens | | 1 | 1 | 1 | | | | | 1 | | | | 4 | | |
| Sandwich | 36 | 2 | Hood | Henry | | | | 1 | | | | | 1 | | | | 2 | | |
| Orleans | 22 | 1 | Hooper | William | 1 | | | 1 | | 1 | | | 1 | | | | 4 | | |
| Barnstable | 93 | 42 | Hope | Timothy | 2 | | | 1 | | | | | 1 | 1 | | | 5 | | |
| Wellfleet | 71 | 5 | Hopkins | Benjamin | 1 | | 1 | 1 | | 1 | 1 | | | | | | 5 | | |
| Truro | 65 | 25 | Hopkins | Caleb | 1 | 2 | | 1 | | 2 | 2 | | 1 | | | | 9 | | |
| Truro | 65 | 24 | Hopkins | Caleb Junr | | | | 1 | 3 | | | 1 | 1 | 1 | | | 7 | | |
| Truro | 67 | 12 | Hopkins | Constant | | | | | | | | | 2 | | | | 2 | | |
| Truro | 69 | 4 | Hopkins | Constant Junr | | 1 | 2 | 1 | | 2 | 2 | | 1 | | | | 9 | | |
| Orleans | 21 | 20 | Hopkins | Curtis | | | 1 | | | | | | 1 | | | | 2 | | |
| Harwich | 9 | 1 | Hopkins | Edmond | 1 | | | 1 | | 1 | | | 1 | | | | 4 | | |
| Harwich | 4 | 34 | Hopkins | Elkanah | | 2 | | 1 | | | | | | 1 | | | 4 | | |
| Orleans | 23 | 2 | Hopkins | Elkanah | 3 | 3 | | 1 | | 2 | | | 1 | | | | 10 | | |
| Orleans | 23 | 9 | Hopkins | Elkanah | 2 | | 1 | | | | | | 1 | | | | 4 | | |
| Harwich | 4 | 1 | Hopkins | Freeman | | | | 1 | | | | | 1 | 1 | 1 | | 4 | | |
| Wellfleet | 71 | 10 | Hopkins | Giles | | | | 1 | 3 | | | | 1 | 1 | | | 6 | | |
| Harwich | 6 | 33 | Hopkins | Hannah Wd | | | | | | | | | 1 | 1 | | | 2 | | |
| Truro | 63 | 9 | Hopkins | Isaac | | 2 | | 1 | | | | | 1 | 1 | | | 5 | | |
| Chatham | 17 | 27 | Hopkins | James | 1 | 1 | 1 | 1 | 5 | | | 2 | | 1 | | | 12 | | |
| Eastham | 77 | 23 | Hopkins | John | 3 | 1 | | 1 | 3 | | | | | 1 | | | 9 | | |
| Harwich | 4 | 35 | Hopkins | John | 1 | | 1 | 3 | | | | | 1 | | | | 6 | | |
| Harwich | 8 | 11 | Hopkins | John Rev | 2 | | 1 | 2 | | 2 | 1 | 1 | | | | | 9 | | |
| Harwich | 8 | 46 | Hopkins | Jonathan | | 1 | | 1 | | | | | | 1 | | | 3 | | |
| Provincetown | 58 | 19 | Hopkins | Jonathan | | 1 | | 1 | | 1 | | | | 1 | | | 4 | | |
| Harwich | 15 | 5 | Hopkins | Joshua | | 2 | 1 | 1 | 1 | 3 | | | | | | | 8 | | |
| Harwich | 6 | 9 | Hopkins | Lydia Wd | | | | | | | | | 1 | 1 | | | 2 | | |
| Harwich | 5 | 32 | Hopkins | Mary Wd | | 1 | 2 | | | 1 | 1 | | | 1 | | | 6 | | |
| Harwich | 7 | 16 | Hopkins | Moses | 1 | | | 1 | | | | | 1 | 1 | | | 4 | | |
| Harwich | 6 | 39 | Hopkins | Nathan | | 1 | 1 | | | | | | 1 | 1 | | | 5 | | |
| Harwich | 6 | 40 | Hopkins | Nathan Jun | 1 | | | 1 | | | | | 1 | | | | 3 | | |
| Harwich | 8 | 43 | Hopkins | Nathaniel | 1 | | | 1 | | | | | 1 | | | | 3 | | |
| Harwich | 8 | 45 | Hopkins | Patiance Wd | | | | | | | | | 1 | 1 | | | 2 | | |
| Yarmouth | 99 | 3 | Hopkins | Perez | 2 | | | 1 | | | | 1 | | | | | 4 | | |
| Harwich | 8 | 44 | Hopkins | Prince | 1 | | | 1 | 1 | | | | 1 | | | | 4 | | |
| Orleans | 21 | 21 | Hopkins | Priscilla | | | | | | | | | | 1 | 1 | | 2 | | |
| Harwich | 3 | 14 | Hopkins | Roland | | | 1 | 2 | | | | | 1 | 1 | | | 5 | | |
| Truro | 67 | 14 | Hopkins | Samuel | 1 | | 1 | 1 | | | | | 1 | 1 | | | 5 | | |
| Provincetown | 58 | 23 | Hopkins | Seammons | 1 | | 1 | 1 | | | | | 1 | | | | 4 | | |
| Truro | 67 | 15 | Hopkins | Solomon | 1 | 2 | | 1 | | | | 1 | | | | | 5 | | |
| Wellfleet | 71 | 13 | Hopkins | Solomon | 2 | | | 1 | | 2 | | 1 | 1 | | | | 7 | | |
| Wellfleet | 70 | 37 | Hopkins | Solomon Junr | 1 | 3 | | | | | | | 1 | | | | 6 | | |
| Harwich | 8 | 42 | Hopkins | Stephen | 1 | | | 1 | | | | 2 | 1 | 1 | | | 6 | | |
| Wellfleet | 71 | 9 | Hopkins | Theophilus | 2 | | 2 | 1 | | | | | 1 | | | | 6 | | |
| Orleans | 22 | 2 | Hopkins | Thomas | 1 | 1 | | | | | | | 1 | | | | 3 | | |
| Chatham | 19 | 12 | Hopkins | William | | | | 1 | | 2 | | 1 | 1 | | | | 5 | | |
| Chatham | 20 | 25 | Hopkins | William | | | | 1 | | 3 | | | 1 | | | | 5 | | |
| Harwich | 6 | 32 | Hopkins | Zoheth | 1 | | | 1 | 3 | 1 | | | 1 | | | | 7 | | |
| Dennis | 29 | 4 | Hording | Gidion | 3 | | | 1 | | 1 | 1 | 1 | 1 | | | | 8 | | |
| Harwich | 15 | 10 | Hornes | John | | | | | | | | | | | 8 | | 8 | | |
| Eastham | 77 | 29 | Horton | Cushing | 2 | 2 | 2 | 1 | | | | 1 | 1 | | | | 9 | | |
| Dennis | 26 | 26 | Horton | Zabina | 2 | | | 1 | | | | | 1 | | | | 4 | | |

# 1800 Barnstable County, Massachusetts Index

| TOWN | PG# | LN# | LAST NAME | FIRST NAME | FREE WHITE MALES | | | | | FREE WHITE FEMALES | | | | | TOTAL ALL OTHER | TOTAL SLAVES | TOTALS | DISTRICT/ TOWNSHIP | NOTES |
|---|---|---|---|---|---|---|---|---|---|---|---|---|---|---|---|---|---|---|---|
| | | | | | under 10 | 10 to 16 | 16 to 26 | 26 to 45 | 45 and over | under 10 | 10 to 16 | 16 to 26 | 26 to 45 | 45 and over | | | | | |
| Barnstable | 94 | 27 | Hoskins | Seth | 1 | 1 | 1 | | | 1 | | 1 | | | | | 5 | | |
| Chatham | 17 | 19 | House | Abraham | | 1 | | | | | | | 1 | 1 | | | 3 | | |
| Dennis | 27 | 38 | House | Abraham | | | | 1 | | | | | | 2 | | | 3 | | |
| Dennis | 26 | 33 | House | Barnabas | | | 1 | 1 | | | | 2 | 1 | | | | 5 | | |
| Chatham | 17 | 36 | House | Benjm | 1 | | 1 | | | 1 | | 1 | | | | | 4 | | |
| Chatham | 17 | 20 | House | Daniel | | 1 | | 1 | | 1 | | 1 | | 1 | | | 5 | | |
| Chatham | 17 | 12 | House | David | | | | 1 | | | | | | 1 | | | 2 | | |
| Dennis | 30 | 25 | House | David | 3 | | | 1 | | 1 | | | 1 | | | | 6 | | |
| Dennis | 26 | 47 | House | David 3d | | 1 | | | | | | 1 | | | | | 2 | | |
| Chatham | 17 | 2 | House | David Jun | 1 | | 1 | | | 1 | | | 1 | | | | 4 | | |
| Dennis | 28 | 17 | House | David Jun | 2 | | 1 | | | 1 | | | 1 | | | | 5 | | |
| Dennis | 28 | 24 | House | Edmand | | | | 1 | | | | | 1 | | | | 2 | | |
| Chatham | 19 | 9 | House | Elijah | | 1 | | | | | | 1 | | | | | 3 | | |
| Dennis | 27 | 25 | House | Elijah | 1 | 1 | | | | | | 1 | | | | | 3 | | |
| Dennis | 27 | 31 | House | Elisha | | | | 1 | | | | | 1 | | | | 2 | | |
| Dennis | 27 | 32 | House | Elisha 3d | 1 | | 1 | | | 2 | 1 | 1 | | 1 | | | 8 | | |
| Dennis | 28 | 13 | House | Elisha Jun | 1 | | 2 | | 1 | 2 | 1 | 2 | | 1 | | | 10 | | |
| Dennis | 27 | 33 | House | Elkanah | 1 | 1 | 2 | 1 | | | 1 | | | 1 | | | 7 | | |
| Chatham | 17 | 7 | House | Enoch | 2 | 1 | | 1 | | 2 | | | 1 | | | | 7 | | |
| Dennis | 27 | 6 | House | Ezra | 1 | | 1 | | 1 | 2 | 1 | 1 | | 1 | | | 8 | | |
| Dennis | 28 | 25 | House | Gamiel | | 1 | | | | | | 1 | | | | | 2 | | |
| Dennis | 28 | 10 | House | Ira | | 1 | | | | | | 2 | | | | | 3 | | |
| Dennis | 27 | 43 | House | Jabez | | | 1 | | | 1 | | 1 | | | | | 3 | | |
| Chatham | 17 | 14 | House | James | 1 | 1 | | 1 | | 1 | 2 | | 1 | | | | 7 | | |
| Dennis | 28 | 14 | House | James | | 3 | | 1 | | | 2 | | 1 | | | | 7 | | |
| Dennis | 28 | 8 | House | Jeremiah | 1 | | 2 | | 1 | | | 1 | 1 | | 1 | | 7 | | |
| Dennis | 28 | 3 | House | Jerusha Wd | 1 | 1 | 1 | | | | 1 | 1 | | 1 | | | 6 | | |
| Dennis | 27 | 36 | House | John | | 1 | 1 | 1 | | | | 1 | | 1 | | | 5 | | |
| Dennis | 27 | 42 | House | Jonah | | 1 | | 1 | | 1 | 1 | 1 | | | | | 6 | | |
| Dennis | 26 | 45 | House | Jonathan | | | | 1 | | | | | | 1 | | | 2 | | |
| Dennis | 28 | 9 | House | Jonathan Jun | 2 | 1 | 1 | 1 | | | | 2 | 1 | | | | 8 | | |
| Chatham | 17 | 10 | House | Joseph | | 1 | 1 | 1 | | | | 2 | | 1 | | | 6 | | |
| Dennis | 27 | 8 | House | Joseph | 1 | 2 | 1 | | 1 | | 2 | 2 | | | | | 9 | | |
| Chatham | 17 | 16 | House | Joshua | | | 1 | | 1 | | 1 | | 1 | | | | 3 | | |
| Dennis | 28 | 4 | House | Joshua | | 1 | | | | | | 1 | | | | | 3 | | |
| Chatham | 17 | 18 | House | Joshua 3d | 1 | 1 | | | | | | 1 | | | | | 3 | | |
| Chatham | 17 | 17 | House | Joshua Jun | | 1 | 1 | | | | | | 1 | | | | 3 | | |
| Dennis | 28 | 16 | House | Josiah | | 1 | | 1 | | 1 | 1 | | 1 | | | | 5 | | |
| Dennis | 27 | 40 | House | Judah | | 1 | | | | 1 | | 1 | | | | | 3 | | |
| Dennis | 26 | 46 | House | Levi | | 1 | | 1 | | | | | | 1 | | | 3 | | |
| Chatham | 20 | 42 | House | Mary Wd | 1 | | | | | 1 | | 1 | | | | | 3 | | |
| Dennis | 27 | 39 | House | Micah | | 1 | | | | | | 1 | | | | | 2 | | |
| Chatham | 17 | 9 | House | Mulford | 1 | 1 | 1 | 1 | | | | | 1 | | | | 5 | | |
| Dennis | 27 | 35 | House | Nathan Rev | | | 1 | 1 | | | 2 | | | 1 | | | 5 | | |
| Dennis | 28 | 7 | House | Nathaniel Jun | | | 1 | | | | | | 1 | | | | 2 | | |
| Dennis | 27 | 30 | House | Nehemiah | 1 | 1 | 3 | | 1 | | 2 | 1 | | | | | 9 | | |
| Dennis | 28 | 12 | House | Nehemiah | 1 | | | 1 | | 2 | | | 1 | | | | 5 | | |
| Dennis | 28 | 11 | House | Noah | | | | 1 | | 2 | 1 | | 1 | | | | 5 | | |
| Dennis | 27 | 37 | House | Obed | 2 | | | 1 | | 2 | 1 | | 1 | 1 | | | 8 | | |
| Dennis | 27 | 5 | House | Paul | | | 1 | 1 | | 2 | 2 | 1 | | 1 | | | 8 | | |
| Dennis | 28 | 5 | House | Phillip | | | | 1 | | 2 | | | 1 | | | | 4 | | |
| Dennis | 26 | 37 | House | Rebeccah Wid | | 2 | | | | | | | 1 | 1 | | | 4 | | |
| Dennis | 28 | 15 | House | Reuben | 2 | | | 1 | | 2 | | | 1 | | | | 6 | | |
| Chatham | 17 | 3 | House | Richard | | | 1 | | 1 | | | 1 | | 1 | | | 4 | | |
| Chatham | 20 | 37 | House | Salomon | 1 | | 1 | | | 1 | | 2 | | | | | 5 | | |
| Dennis | 28 | 18 | House | Samuel | | | 1 | | 1 | | | 1 | | 1 | | | 4 | | |
| Chatham | 19 | 10 | House | Seth | 2 | | | 1 | | | | | 1 | | | | 4 | | |
| Chatham | 19 | 33 | House | Seth | 2 | | | 1 | | | 1 | | 1 | | | | 5 | | |
| Dennis | 26 | 20 | House | Seth | | | | 1 | | | | | | 1 | | | 2 | | |
| Dennis | 27 | 7 | House | Seth | | 1 | 1 | 1 | | 1 | | 2 | | 1 | | | 7 | | |
| Chatham | 17 | 39 | House | Solomon | 1 | | 1 | | | 1 | | 1 | 1 | | | | 5 | | |
| Chatham | 17 | 15 | House | Stephen | 1 | | 1 | | | 3 | | 1 | | | | | 6 | | |
| Dennis | 27 | 3 | House | Stephen | 1 | | 1 | | 1 | | 2 | 2 | | 1 | | | 8 | | |
| Dennis | 26 | 34 | House | Sturges | | 1 | | | | | 1 | 1 | | 1 | | | 5 | | |
| Dennis | 27 | 34 | House | Thankfull Jun Wid | | | | | | | 1 | | | 1 | | | 2 | | |
| Dennis | 27 | 21 | House | Thankfull Wid | | | | | | | | | 1 | 1 | | | 2 | | |
| Chatham | 17 | 1 | House | Thomas Jun | | | 1 | 1 | | 1 | | | 1 | | | | 3 | | |
| Dennis | 27 | 41 | House | William | | 1 | | | | | | | 1 | | | | 2 | | |
| Yarmouth | 100 | 14 | Howes | Andrew | | | 1 | | 1 | 1 | | | 1 | | | | 3 | | |
| Provincetown | 58 | 21 | Howes | Daniel | | 2 | | | | | | 1 | 1 | | | | 4 | | |
| Provincetown | 58 | 16 | Howes | David | 1 | 1 | 1 | | | | | 2 | | | | | 5 | | |
| Yarmouth | 97 | 26 | Howes | Ebenz | 1 | 1 | 1 | 1 | | 1 | 1 | 1 | 1 | | | | 8 | | |
| Yarmouth | 96 | 49 | Howes | Edward | | | 2 | | | | | | 1 | | | | 3 | | |
| Yarmouth | 100 | 21 | Howes | Jabez | 1 | | | 1 | | 3 | | | 1 | | | | 2 | | |
| Provincetown | 60 | 28 | Howes | Lot | | | 1 | | | | | 1 | | | | | 2 | | |
| Barnstable | 86 | 21 | Howes | Martha | | | | | | | | | 1 | | | | 1 | | |
| Barnstable | 87 | 13 | Howes | Peter | | 3 | | 1 | | | 1 | | 1 | | | | 6 | | |
| Yarmouth | 97 | 47 | Howes | Prince | 1 | | | 1 | | 3 | | | 1 | | | | 6 | | |
| Provincetown | 58 | 17 | Howes | Theophilus | 3 | | | 1 | | | 1 | 1 | | | | | 2 | | |
| Yarmouth | 97 | 30 | Howes | Zenas | | | 1 | | | | | 1 | | | | | 2 | | |
| Barnstable | 87 | 43 | Howland | Ansel | | | | 1 | | | | | 1 | | | | 2 | | |
| Barnstable | 87 | 45 | Howland | Ansel Jr | 2 | | | 1 | | 1 | | 1 | | | | | 5 | | |

# 1800 Barnstable County, Massachusetts Index

| TOWN | PG# | LN# | LAST NAME | FIRST NAME | FWM <10 | FWM 10-16 | FWM 16-26 | FWM 26-45 | FWM 45+ | FWF <10 | FWF 10-16 | FWF 16-26 | FWF 26-45 | FWF 45+ | TOTAL ALL OTHER | TOTAL SLAVES | TOTALS | DISTRICT/TOWNSHIP | NOTES |
|---|---|---|---|---|---|---|---|---|---|---|---|---|---|---|---|---|---|---|---|
| Dennis | 30 | 23 | Howland | Benjamin | | 1 | 1 | | 1 | | | 1 | | 1 | | | 5 | | |
| Dennis | 31 | 32 | Howland | Benjamin Jun | | | 1 | | 1 | | | | 1 | | | | 3 | | |
| Dennis | 30 | 22 | Howland | Elisha | 1 | | 1 | | | 2 | | 1 | | | | | 5 | | |
| Barnstable | 88 | 12 | Howland | Isaac | 1 | 1 | 1 | 1 | | | | 1 | | 1 | | | 6 | | |
| Barnstable | 87 | 44 | Howland | Jabez | 1 | | 1 | | | | | 1 | | 1 | 1 | | 5 | | |
| Barnstable | 87 | 50 | Howland | John | | | | 1 | | | | 1 | 1 | | | | 3 | | |
| Sandwich | 35 | 24 | Howland | Jonathan | | 1 | | 1 | | | | | 1 | 1 | | | 4 | | |
| Dennis | 30 | 24 | Howland | Joshua | 2 | | | 1 | | | | 1 | 1 | | | | 5 | | |
| Sandwich | 37 | 39 | Howland | Lemuel | | 1 | | 1 | | 1 | 2 | | 2 | | 1 | | 8 | | |
| Barnstable | 90 | 3 | Howland | Mary | | 2 | | 1 | | | | 2 | 1 | 1 | | | 7 | | |
| Sandwich | 37 | 41 | Howland | Nathaniel | 2 | | | 1 | | 2 | | | | 1 | | | 6 | | |
| Barnstable | 88 | 13 | Howland | Samuel | | 2 | | 1 | | | | 2 | | 1 | | | 6 | | |
| Sandwich | 35 | 35 | Howland | William | 1 | 1 | 1 | | | | | 1 | | | | | 4 | | |
| Barnstable | 90 | 4 | Howland | Zacheus | 2 | | | 1 | | 1 | | | | 1 | | | 5 | | |
| Sandwich | 37 | 36 | Hoxie | Abner | | 1 | 1 | | 1 | 1 | 2 | 1 | | | | | 8 | | |
| Sandwich | 35 | 14 | Hoxie | Barnabas | | | 1 | | | | | 1 | 1 | 1 | | | 4 | | |
| Sandwich | 36 | 29 | Hoxie | Cornelius | | 1 | | 1 | | | | 1 | | 1 | | | 4 | | |
| Sandwich | 37 | 10 | Hoxie | Elizabeth | | | 1 | | | | | | 1 | 1 | | | 3 | | |
| Sandwich | 37 | 35 | Hoxie | Hezekiah | 2 | 1 | | 1 | | | | | 1 | 1 | | | 6 | | |
| Sandwich | 37 | 37 | Hoxie | James | 1 | | 3 | 1 | 1 | | | 2 | 1 | | | | 9 | | |
| Sandwich | 36 | 19 | Hoxie | Jesse | 1 | 1 | | 1 | | 3 | 1 | 1 | 1 | | | | 9 | | |
| Sandwich | 35 | 15 | Hoxie | Joseph | 2 | | | 1 | | | | 1 | | 1 | | | 5 | | |
| Sandwich | 37 | 32 | Hoxie | Ludwick | 1 | 2 | | 1 | | | | 2 | 1 | 1 | | | 9 | | |
| Sandwich | 37 | 6 | Hoxie | Mary | | | 1 | | | | | | 1 | 1 | | | 3 | | |
| Barnstable | 86 | 50 | Huckins | James | | | | 1 | | | | | | 1 | 1 | | 3 | | |
| Barnstable | 86 | 51 | Huckins | Samuel | 1 | | 2 | 1 | | 3 | 2 | 1 | 1 | | 1 | | 12 | | |
| Yarmouth | 99 | 20 | Hudson | James | | | 1 | | | 1 | | | | 1 | | | 3 | | |
| Chatham | 17 | 41 | Hunt | Edward | 1 | | 2 | 1 | | | | 1 | | 1 | | | 6 | | |
| Chatham | 17 | 13 | Hunt | Lemuel | 1 | | | 1 | | 2 | | | | 1 | | | 5 | | |
| Orleans | 24 | 15 | Hurd | Benjm | 2 | | | 1 | | 1 | | | | 1 | | | 5 | | |
| Orleans | 22 | 40 | Hurd | John | 3 | 2 | | 1 | | | | 1 | | 1 | | | 8 | | |
| Orleans | 24 | 14 | Hurd | Joseph | | 2 | 2 | 1 | | 1 | 2 | | 1 | | | | 9 | | |
| Harwich | 15 | 4 | Hurd | Joshua | | 2 | 1 | 1 | | 3 | 1 | 1 | 1 | | | | 10 | | |
| Truro | 65 | 27 | Hutson | Ezra | | | 1 | | | 3 | | | 1 | | | | 5 | | |
| Sandwich | 40 | 25 | Hyes | Benja | 1 | | | 1 | | | | | 1 | | | | 3 | | |
| Barnstable | 91 | 4 | Ishand | Herman | | 1 | | 1 | | 3 | 1 | | 1 | 1 | | | 8 | | |
| Barnstable | 91 | 3 | Ishand | Samuel | | | | 1 | | | | | 1 | | | | 2 | | |
| Chatham | 17 | 40 | Jackson | Barbara Wid | | | | | | | | | 1 | | | | 1 | | |
| Chatham | 20 | 16 | Jackson | Bassett | 2 | | | 1 | | 3 | | | | | | | 6 | | |
| Barnstable | 86 | 1 | Jackson | Richard | | 2 | | 1 | | | | | 1 | | | | 4 | | |
| Barnstable | 87 | 24 | Jenkins | Alvin | 1 | | 1 | 1 | | | | 1 | | | 1 | | 5 | | |
| Barnstable | 89 | 39 | Jenkins | Asa | 2 | | 1 | | | | 1 | 1 | | | 1 | | 6 | | |
| Falmouth | 46 | 152 | Jenkins | Benjm | | | 1 | | | 1 | | 1 | | | | | 3 | | |
| Barnstable | 87 | 32 | Jenkins | Braley | | 1 | | | | 1 | | 1 | | | | | 3 | | |
| Falmouth | 46 | 151 | Jenkins | Eli | 2 | | 1 | | | 1 | 1 | 1 | | | | | 6 | | |
| Falmouth | 46 | 147 | Jenkins | James | | 1 | | 1 | | | | 1 | 1 | 2 | | | 6 | | |
| Falmouth | 46 | 150 | Jenkins | Joseph | 1 | 1 | 2 | | 1 | 1 | 1 | 1 | 1 | | | | 9 | | |
| Barnstable | 87 | 4 | Jenkins | Joseph Jr | 1 | | 1 | | | | | 1 | 1 | | | | 4 | | |
| Barnstable | 87 | 25 | Jenkins | Joseph W. | | 1 | | 1 | | | | | 1 | 1 | | | 4 | | |
| Barnstable | 87 | 46 | Jenkins | Lot | 1 | | 1 | 1 | | 1 | | 1 | | | | | 5 | | |
| Harwich | 4 | 36 | Jenkins | Meltiah | 2 | | 1 | | | 2 | | | 1 | 1 | | | 7 | | |
| Barnstable | 87 | 29 | Jenkins | Nathl | 2 | 1 | 1 | 1 | | 1 | 1 | | 1 | 1 | | | 9 | | |
| Barnstable | 87 | 31 | Jenkins | Prince | 1 | | 1 | | | | | | 1 | | | | 3 | | |
| Falmouth | 46 | 149 | Jenkins | Samuel | 1 | 4 | | 1 | | | | 1 | | 1 | | | 8 | | |
| Barnstable | 87 | 3 | Jenkins | Sarah | 2 | | | | | | | 1 | 2 | | | | 5 | | |
| Barnstable | 87 | 30 | Jenkins | Simeon | | | | 1 | | | | 1 | | 1 | | | 3 | | |
| Barnstable | 87 | 26 | Jenkins | Simeon Jr | 1 | 1 | | 1 | | 2 | 1 | | 1 | | | | 7 | | |
| Falmouth | 46 | 146 | Jenkins | Weston | 1 | | 1 | | 1 | | | 1 | | | 1 | | 5 | | |
| Barnstable | 87 | 35 | Jenkins | Zaccheus | 1 | 1 | 1 | | 1 | | | | 1 | 1 | | | 6 | | |
| Yarmouth | 99 | 42 | Jerauld | Dutee | 3 | | | 1 | | | | 1 | 1 | | | | 6 | | |
| Sandwich | 37 | 29 | Jona | John | 2 | 2 | | 1 | | | | | 1 | 1 | | | 7 | | |
| Barnstable | 89 | 27 | Jones | Abner | 2 | 1 | | 2 | | 1 | | | 1 | 1 | | | 8 | | |
| Barnstable | 92 | 42 | Jones | Asa | 4 | 1 | | 1 | | | | 1 | | 1 | | | 8 | | |
| Sandwich | 36 | 31 | Jones | Bathseba | 1 | | 2 | 1 | | | | 1 | 1 | 4 | | | 10 | | |
| Wellfleet | 70 | 25 | Jones | Deborah | | 2 | | | | | | | 1 | 1 | | | 4 | | |
| Barnstable | 88 | 26 | Jones | Goodspeed | | | 1 | | 2 | | | | 1 | | | | 4 | | |
| Barnstable | 92 | 41 | Jones | Hannah | | | | | | | | | | 1 | | | 1 | | |
| Barnstable | 89 | 23 | Jones | Hannah Jr | | 1 | 1 | | 1 | 2 | 1 | 1 | | | | | 7 | | |
| Barnstable | 89 | 28 | Jones | Jedidiah | 2 | 1 | | 1 | | | | 1 | 1 | 1 | | | 7 | | |
| Sandwich | 34 | 4 | Jones | Josiah | 1 | 2 | 3 | 1 | 1 | | | 1 | | | | | 9 | | |
| Barnstable | 89 | 17 | Jones | Lemuel | 4 | | | 1 | | | | 1 | 1 | | | | 7 | | |
| Barnstable | 89 | 26 | Jones | Lot | 2 | | | 1 | | | | 1 | 1 | | | | 5 | | |
| Sandwich | 38 | 2 | Jones | Mikah | 1 | | | 1 | | | | | | | | | 2 | | |
| Barnstable | 89 | 20 | Jones | Nye | | 1 | | 1 | | | | | | 1 | | | 3 | | |
| Sandwich | 37 | 31 | Jones | Remember | | | | | | | | | 2 | 1 | | | 3 | | |
| Barnstable | 92 | 9 | Jones | Rosanna | | 1 | | | | | | 2 | 3 | 1 | | | 7 | | |
| Sandwich | 37 | 9 | Jones | Silvanus | 2 | | 2 | 1 | | | | 2 | | 1 | | | 8 | | |
| Sandwich | 37 | 30 | Jones | Silvanus Junr | 2 | | 1 | 1 | | 2 | | | 1 | 1 | | | 8 | | |
| Barnstable | 92 | 43 | Jones | Simon | 3 | 1 | | 1 | | 2 | 1 | | 1 | | | | 9 | | |
| Barnstable | 91 | 42 | Jones | Statson | | | 1 | | 2 | | | | 1 | | | | 4 | | |
| Barnstable | 89 | 21 | Jones | Stephen | | | | 1 | | | | | 1 | | | | 2 | | |

84

# 1800 Barnstable County, Massachusetts Index

| TOWN | PG# | LN# | LAST NAME | FIRST NAME | FREE WHITE MALES under 10 | 10 to 16 | 16 to 26 | 26 to 45 | 45 and over | FREE WHITE FEMALES under 10 | 10 to 16 | 16 to 26 | 26 to 45 | 45 and over | TOTAL ALL OTHER | TOTAL SLAVES | TOTALS | DISTRICT/ TOWNSHIP | NOTES |
|---|---|---|---|---|---|---|---|---|---|---|---|---|---|---|---|---|---|---|---|
| Falmouth | 46 | 148 | Jones | Thomas | 1 | 1 | 2 |  | 1 | 2 | 1 |  |  | 2 |  |  | 10 |  |  |
| Sandwich | 42 | 31 | Keene | Aloise |  | 1 | 2 |  | 1 |  | 1 |  |  | 1 |  |  | 6 |  |  |
| Sandwich | 36 | 10 | Kelley | Benjamin |  | 1 |  |  | 1 |  |  | 1 |  | 1 |  |  | 4 |  |  |
| Orleans | 22 | 24 | Kendricks | Easter Wid |  |  |  |  |  |  |  |  |  | 1 |  |  | 1 |  |  |
| Orleans | 22 | 22 | Kendricks | Jonathan |  |  | 3 |  | 1 |  |  | 1 |  | 1 |  |  | 6 |  |  |
| Orleans | 22 | 23 | Kendricks | Jonathan Jr | 2 | 2 |  | 1 |  | 3 | 1 | 1 |  |  |  |  | 10 |  |  |
| Truro | 65 | 31 | Kenney | John |  | 1 | 1 |  | 1 |  |  | 1 |  |  |  |  | 4 |  |  |
| Chatham | 20 | 40 | Kent | Edward | 1 | 2 |  | 1 |  | 1 |  |  | 1 |  |  |  | 6 |  |  |
| Wellfleet | 71 | 17 | Kenurich | Warren A. | 4 |  | 1 | 1 |  |  |  |  | 2 |  |  |  | 8 |  |  |
| Wellfleet | 71 | 19 | Kenye | Robert | 3 | 2 | 2 |  | 1 |  |  |  | 1 |  |  |  | 9 |  |  |
| Provincetown | 58 | 26 | Kilborn | David | 2 | 3 |  | 1 |  | 2 | 2 |  | 1 |  |  |  | 11 |  |  |
| Provincetown | 58 | 28 | Kilborn | Mahitable |  |  |  |  |  |  |  |  | 1 |  |  |  | 1 |  |  |
| Provincetown | 58 | 27 | Kilborn | Samuel | 1 | 1 |  | 1 |  | 2 | 2 |  | 1 |  |  |  | 8 |  |  |
| Dennis | 30 | 30 | Killey | Abner | 2 |  | 1 |  |  | 1 |  | 1 |  |  |  |  | 5 |  |  |
| Dennis | 31 | 37 | Killey | Amos |  | 1 |  |  |  |  |  |  | 1 |  |  |  | 2 |  |  |
| Harwich | 13 | 46 | Killey | Anthony | 1 | 2 |  | 1 |  | 2 | 1 | 1 | 1 |  |  |  | 9 |  |  |
| Yarmouth | 97 | 11 | Killey | Benja | 1 |  |  | 1 |  | 2 |  |  |  |  |  |  | 4 |  |  |
| Dennis | 32 | 9 | Killey | Brownen | 1 |  | 2 | 1 |  | 1 | 2 |  | 1 |  |  |  | 8 |  |  |
| Dennis | 30 | 40 | Killey | Daniel | 2 |  | 2 |  | 1 | 1 | 1 | 3 |  | 1 |  |  | 11 |  |  |
| Barnstable | 92 | 8 | Killey | David |  |  | 1 | 1 |  | 2 | 2 |  | 1 |  |  |  | 7 |  |  |
| Barnstable | 94 | 34 | Killey | David |  | 1 |  | 1 |  | 1 |  |  | 1 |  |  |  | 4 |  |  |
| Harwich | 6 | 18 | Killey | Ebenezer | 2 |  |  | 1 |  |  | 1 |  | 1 |  |  |  | 5 |  |  |
| Dennis | 32 | 8 | Killey | Eleazar | 1 | 1 | 1 |  | 1 | 1 |  |  | 1 | 2 |  |  | 8 |  |  |
| Barnstable | 91 | 9 | Killey | Freeman | 1 |  |  | 1 |  |  |  | 1 |  |  |  |  | 3 |  |  |
| Dennis | 28 | 44 | Killey | Hettel |  |  |  | 1 |  |  |  |  | 1 |  |  |  | 2 |  |  |
| Dennis | 29 | 1 | Killey | Hettel Jun | 2 |  | 3 | 1 |  | 2 |  | 1 |  |  |  |  | 9 |  |  |
| Dennis | 29 | 23 | Killey | Hiram | 1 |  | 1 |  |  |  |  | 1 |  |  |  |  | 3 |  |  |
| Harwich | 13 | 47 | Killey | Jeremaiah |  |  | 1 |  | 1 |  | 1 | 1 | 1 |  |  |  | 5 |  |  |
| Dennis | 30 | 18 | Killey | Jeremiah | 1 |  | 3 | 1 | 1 |  | 1 |  | 1 |  |  |  | 8 |  |  |
| Yarmouth | 99 | 12 | Killey | John |  |  |  | 1 |  |  |  |  | 2 |  |  |  | 3 |  |  |
| Dennis | 30 | 35 | Killey | Joseph |  |  |  | 1 |  |  |  |  | 2 |  |  |  | 3 |  |  |
| Harwich | 14 | 18 | Killey | Joseph | 2 |  | 1 |  |  | 1 |  | 1 |  |  |  |  | 5 |  |  |
| Dennis | 30 | 33 | Killey | Joseph Jun | 2 | 1 |  | 1 |  | 2 |  |  | 1 |  |  |  | 7 |  |  |
| Barnstable | 90 | 27 | Killey | Levi | 3 | 2 | 2 |  | 1 |  | 1 |  |  | 1 |  |  | 10 |  |  |
| Yarmouth | 100 | 12 | Killey | Martha |  |  |  |  |  |  |  |  | 2 |  |  |  | 2 |  |  |
| Yarmouth | 98 | 49 | Killey | Meribah | 2 |  | 1 |  |  |  |  |  | 1 | 1 |  |  | 5 |  |  |
| Yarmouth | 99 | 24 | Killey | Oliver |  |  | 2 |  | 1 |  | 1 | 1 |  |  |  |  | 5 |  |  |
| Harwich | 6 | 19 | Killey | Patrick |  |  |  | 2 |  |  |  |  | 1 |  |  |  | 3 |  |  |
| Harwich | 14 | 13 | Killey | Patrick Jun | 4 |  | 2 |  | 1 | 1 | 2 |  | 1 |  |  |  | 11 |  |  |
| Barnstable | 87 | 11 | Killey | Remember | 1 |  |  |  |  |  | 2 |  | 1 |  |  |  | 4 |  |  |
| Dennis | 30 | 34 | Killey | Reuben | 1 | 1 |  | 1 |  | 3 |  |  | 1 |  |  |  | 7 |  |  |
| Dennis | 30 | 19 | Killey | Richard | 1 |  |  | 1 |  |  |  |  | 1 |  |  |  | 3 |  |  |
| Harwich | 6 | 15 | Killey | Samuel | 1 | 1 | 1 | 1 |  | 1 | 1 |  | 1 | 1 |  |  | 8 |  |  |
| Dennis | 30 | 31 | Killey | Silvanus | 2 | 1 |  | 1 |  | 1 | 1 |  | 1 |  |  |  | 7 |  |  |
| Yarmouth | 97 | 8 | Killey | Silvanus | 2 |  |  | 1 |  |  |  |  | 1 |  |  |  | 4 |  |  |
| Dennis | 28 | 43 | Killey | Sy* | 1 |  |  | 1 |  | 2 |  |  | 1 |  |  |  | 5 |  |  |
| Dennis | 29 | 22 | Killey | Verna |  |  | 2 |  | 1 | 1 | 1 | 1 |  | 1 |  |  | 7 |  |  |
| Yarmouth | 98 | 46 | Killey | Zeno |  | 1 | 1 |  |  | 1 | 1 | 1 |  |  |  |  | 6 |  |  |
| Harwich | 9 | 12 | Kindericks | David | 1 |  |  | 1 |  |  | 1 |  | 1 |  |  |  | 4 |  |  |
| Harwich | 9 | 9 | Kindericks | Edward | 1 |  | 3 |  | 1 |  |  | 2 |  |  |  |  | 7 |  |  |
| Harwich | 14 | 50 | Kindericks | Henry |  | 1 | 3 |  | 1 | 3 | 2 | 1 |  | 1 |  |  | 12 |  |  |
| Harwich | 9 | 8 | Kindericks | Jonathan |  | 2 | 1 |  | 1 | 1 |  | 2 | 1 | 1 |  |  | 9 |  |  |
| Harwich | 9 | 13 | Kindericks | Jonathan Jun |  |  | 1 |  |  |  |  | 1 |  |  |  |  | 2 |  |  |
| Harwich | 9 | 11 | Kindericks | Nathan | 2 |  |  | 1 |  | 1 |  |  | 1 |  |  |  | 5 |  |  |
| Harwich | 15 | 1 | Kindericks | Stephen | 2 | 1 | 2 |  | 1 | 3 |  | 1 |  | 1 |  |  | 11 |  |  |
| Harwich | 9 | 10 | Kindericks | Thomas |  | 1 | 1 | 1 |  |  |  | 1 |  | 1 |  |  | 5 |  |  |
| Wellfleet | 71 | 18 | King | Joanna |  |  | 1 |  |  |  |  | 2 |  | 1 |  |  | 4 |  |  |
| Harwich | 8 | 41 | King | Nathaniel | 1 | 1 | 1 |  | 1 | 1 | 1 | 1 |  | 1 |  |  | 8 |  |  |
| Harwich | 7 | 27 | King | Pheba Wd |  |  |  |  |  |  |  | 1 |  | 1 |  |  | 2 |  |  |
| Harwich | 6 | 41 | King | Roger | 3 | 2 |  | 1 |  | 2 | 1 |  | 1 |  |  |  | 10 |  |  |
| Harwich | 8 | 40 | King | Uriel | 2 | 1 | 1 | 1 |  |  |  | 1 |  | 2 |  |  | 8 |  |  |
| Orleans | 25 | 14 | Kingman | Simeon |  |  | 1 | 1 |  |  |  | 1 | 1 |  |  |  | 4 |  |  |
| Orleans | 22 | 12 | Kinney | Jesse | 1 | 2 |  |  |  |  | 1 | 1 | 1 |  |  |  | 7 |  |  |
| Orleans | 24 | 8 | Kinney | Jesse Jun |  |  |  | 1 |  | 2 |  | 1 |  |  |  |  | 4 |  |  |
| Provincetown | 58 | 25 | Kinyard | Benjamin |  |  | 1 | 1 |  |  |  |  | 1 |  |  |  | 3 |  |  |
| Truro | 65 | 30 | Knight | Peter |  |  | 1 |  |  | 3 |  |  | 1 |  |  |  | 5 |  |  |
| Eastham | 77 | 33 | Knowles | Benjamin |  | 1 | 3 |  | 1 |  |  | 1 | 1 | 1 |  |  | 8 |  |  |
| Truro | 62 | 7 | Knowles | Caleb | 2 |  |  | 1 |  | 1 | 1 | 1 |  |  |  |  | 6 |  |  |
| Eastham | 78 | 3 | Knowles | David | 1 |  | 1 |  |  |  |  | 3 |  | 1 |  |  | 7 |  |  |
| Chatham | 17 | 42 | Knowles | Hannah Wid |  |  |  |  |  |  |  | 1 |  | 1 |  |  | 2 |  |  |
| Eastham | 77 | 34 | Knowles | Henry |  |  |  |  |  | 2 | 3 |  | 1 |  |  |  | 6 |  |  |
| Truro | 66 | 1 | Knowles | Jesse | 1 |  |  | 1 |  | 1 |  | 1 |  |  |  |  | 5 |  |  |
| Eastham | 78 | 2 | Knowles | John |  | 1 | 4 |  | 1 |  | 1 | 2 | 1 | 1 |  |  | 11 |  |  |
| Eastham | 78 | 5 | Knowles | Joseph |  | 1 |  |  | 1 |  |  |  | 1 | 1 |  |  | 4 |  |  |
| Truro | 65 | 34 | Knowles | Joshua | 3 | 2 | 1 |  | 1 |  | 2 |  |  | 1 |  |  | 10 |  |  |
| Truro | 65 | 29 | Knowles | Mary Wid |  |  |  |  |  |  |  |  | 1 | 1 |  |  | 2 |  |  |
| Eastham | 77 | 30 | Knowles | Obadiah |  |  |  | 1 |  | 1 |  |  | 1 |  |  |  | 3 |  |  |
| Truro | 65 | 35 | Knowles | Paul | 1 |  | 1 | 1 | 1 | 1 |  | 1 | 1 | 1 |  |  | 8 |  |  |
| Truro | 65 | 28 | Knowles | Paul Junr | 4 | 1 |  | 1 |  | 1 |  |  | 1 |  |  |  | 8 |  |  |
| Provincetown | 58 | 24 | Knowles | Phebe Wd | 2 |  |  |  |  |  |  | 2 |  |  |  |  | 6 |  |  |
| Eastham | 77 | 32 | Knowles | Rebecah |  |  |  |  |  |  |  | 1 | 1 |  |  |  | 2 |  |  |
| Eastham | 77 | 31 | Knowles | Robert |  |  | 1 |  |  | 3 |  |  | 1 |  |  |  | 5 |  |  |
| Eastham | 78 | 1 | Knowles | Seth | 2 |  |  |  | 1 | 1 |  | 1 | 2 | 1 |  |  | 9 |  |  |

| TOWN | PG# | LN# | LAST NAME | FIRST NAME | FREE WHITE MALES | | | | | FREE WHITE FEMALES | | | | | TOTAL ALL OTHER | TOTAL SLAVES | TOTALS | DISTRICT/ TOWNSHIP | NOTES |
|---|---|---|---|---|---|---|---|---|---|---|---|---|---|---|---|---|---|---|---|
| | | | | | under 10 | 10 to 16 | 16 to 26 | 26 to 45 | 45 and over | under 10 | 10 to 16 | 16 to 26 | 26 to 45 | 45 and over | | | | | |
| Truro | 65 | 32 | Knowles | Silas | 4 | 1 | 2 | 1 | 1 | 1 | | 1 | | 1 | | | 12 | | |
| Eastham | 78 | 4 | Knowles | Theophilus | 2 | | 1 | 1 | | | 1 | | 1 | | | | 7 | | |
| Eastham | 79 | 23 | Knowles | William | 1 | 1 | 1 | 1 | | 3 | 3 | | 1 | | | | 11 | | |
| Truro | 65 | 33 | Knowles | Zacheus | 2 | | | 1 | | 1 | | | 1 | | | | 5 | | |
| Orleans | 24 | 26 | Knowls | John | 1 | | 1 | | 1 | 2 | 1 | | | 1 | | | 7 | | |
| Orleans | 25 | 24 | Knowls | Mary Wd | | 1 | | | | | | | 1 | 1 | | | 3 | | |
| Orleans | 25 | 20 | Knowls | Nathaniel | | 1 | 2 | | 1 | | | 3 | 1 | | | | 9 | | |
| Orleans | 24 | 27 | Knowls | Ruth Wd | | | | | | | | | 3 | 1 | | | 4 | | |
| Yarmouth | 98 | 48 | Laha | John | 1 | | | 1 | | 2 | | | 1 | | | | 5 | | |
| Falmouth | 46 | 158 | Lake | Richard | | | 1 | 1 | | | | | | 1 | | | 3 | | |
| Sandwich | 42 | 26 | Lambord | Caleb | | | 1 | | 1 | 1 | 1 | 1 | | 1 | | | 6 | | |
| Sandwich | 41 | 8 | Lambord | Thomas | | 1 | 2 | 1 | | 1 | | | 1 | | | | 6 | | |
| Sandwich | 37 | 38 | Landers | Abigail | | | | | | | | | 1 | 1 | | | 2 | | |
| Falmouth | 47 | 176 | Landers | Jabez | 1 | | 1 | | | 1 | | | 1 | | | | 4 | | |
| Falmouth | 46 | 160 | Landers | John | | | 1 | 1 | | | | | 1 | 1 | | | 4 | | |
| Sandwich | 37 | 33 | Landers | John | 2 | 1 | 1 | | 1 | | | 1 | 2 | | | | 8 | | |
| Harwich | 11 | 32 | Landers | Joseph | | | 1 | | | | | | | | | | 1 | | |
| Falmouth | 47 | 170 | Landers | Nicholas | 1 | | 1 | | | 3 | | 1 | 1 | | | | 7 | | |
| Falmouth | 47 | 173 | Landers | Prince | | | | 1 | | | | | | 1 | | | 2 | | |
| Falmouth | 47 | 174 | Landers | Prince Junr | 1 | | | 1 | | | | | 1 | | | | 3 | | |
| Falmouth | 46 | 159 | Landers | Reuben | | | | 1 | | | | | | 1 | | | 2 | | |
| Falmouth | 47 | 169 | Landers | Richard | | | 1 | | | | | | 1 | 1 | | | 3 | | |
| Falmouth | 46 | 161 | Landers | Savory | | 1 | | 1 | | 1 | | 1 | 1 | | | | 5 | | |
| Wellfleet | 75 | 21 | Landman | Edward | | | | 1 | | | | | 1 | | | | 2 | | |
| Provincetown | 58 | 29 | Lary | John Junr | 2 | 1 | 1 | | | 2 | | | 1 | 1 | | | 8 | | |
| Provincetown | 58 | 30 | Lary | Lewis | 1 | | | 1 | | 3 | | | 1 | | | | 6 | | |
| Falmouth | 46 | 153 | Laurence | John | | | 1 | 1 | | | | | | 1 | | | 3 | | |
| Falmouth | 46 | 155 | Laurence | Joseph | 3 | 1 | | 1 | | 1 | 1 | | 1 | | | | 8 | | |
| Falmouth | 47 | 175 | Laurence | Nabby | | | | | | 1 | | | | 1 | | | 2 | | |
| Falmouth | 46 | 165 | Laurence | Shubael | 2 | 1 | | 1 | | | | | 1 | | | | 5 | | |
| Falmouth | 46 | 156 | Laurence | Silas | | 1 | 2 | | 1 | | | 2 | 1 | | | | 8 | | |
| Falmouth | 46 | 154 | Laurence | Solomon | 3 | 3 | 1 | | | 1 | | | 1 | | | | 9 | | |
| Barnstable | 89 | 3 | Lavell | Andrew | | 2 | 2 | | 1 | | | 2 | | 1 | | | 8 | | |
| Barnstable | 94 | 42 | Lavell | Gorham | | 1 | | 1 | | 2 | | 1 | 1 | | | | 6 | | |
| Barnstable | 91 | 43 | Lavell | Jacob | | | | 1 | | | | | | 1 | | | 2 | | |
| Barnstable | 91 | 44 | Lavell | Joshua | 1 | 2 | 1 | | | | | | 1 | | | | 6 | | |
| Barnstable | 93 | 12 | Lavell | Shubael | | | | 1 | | | 1 | | 1 | | | | 3 | | |
| Barnstable | 93 | 16 | Lawrence | Abigail | 2 | | | | | 1 | | | 1 | | 1 | | 5 | | |
| Sandwich | 40 | 42 | Lawrence | David | 2 | 2 | | 1 | | 1 | | 1 | 1 | | | | 8 | | |
| Sandwich | 40 | 47 | Lawrence | Jonathan | | | 2 | 1 | 1 | | | 1 | 1 | 1 | | | 7 | | |
| Sandwich | 37 | 19 | Lawrence | Joseph | | | 3 | 1 | | | | 1 | | 1 | | | 6 | | |
| Barnstable | 85 | 23 | Lawrence | Sarah | | 1 | | | | | | 1 | 1 | | | | 3 | | |
| Barnstable | 85 | 33 | Lawson | Southworth | | | | 1 | | | | | 3 | 1 | | | 5 | | |
| Sandwich | 36 | 40 | Leonard | Jonathan | 1 | | | 1 | | 1 | | 1 | | | | | 4 | | |
| Barnstable | 90 | 35 | Lewis | Asenath | | 1 | | | | | | | 3 | | | | 4 | | |
| Barnstable | 88 | 6 | Lewis | Benjamin | 3 | | | 1 | | | | | 1 | | | | 5 | | |
| Wellfleet | 71 | 22 | Lewis | Benjamin | | 1 | 1 | 1 | | | | | 1 | | | | 4 | | |
| Yarmouth | 100 | 23 | Lewis | Benjamin | 1 | 1 | | 1 | | 2 | | 1 | 1 | | | | 7 | | |
| Barnstable | 90 | 40 | Lewis | Bethiah | | | | | | | | | 1 | 2 | | | 3 | | |
| Barnstable | 90 | 45 | Lewis | Bethiah 2d | 2 | 1 | 1 | | 1 | 1 | 1 | 1 | | | | | 8 | | |
| Chatham | 17 | 43 | Lewis | Calvin | 1 | | 1 | | 1 | | | 1 | | | | | 4 | | |
| Barnstable | 85 | 21 | Lewis | David | | 1 | 1 | 1 | | | | 1 | | 1 | | | 5 | | |
| Falmouth | 46 | 163 | Lewis | David | 2 | | 3 | 1 | 3 | | | 2 | | 1 | | | 12 | | |
| Sandwich | 41 | 43 | Lewis | David | 2 | | 1 | 1 | 2 | 1 | | | 1 | | | | 8 | | |
| Falmouth | 46 | 164 | Lewis | Ebenz | | 2 | | 1 | | | | | 1 | | | | 4 | | |
| Orleans | 23 | 33 | Lewis | Edward | | 1 | 1 | | 1 | 3 | 2 | 1 | 1 | | | | 10 | | |
| Barnstable | 90 | 8 | Lewis | Edward Jr | | 1 | | | 1 | | 1 | | | | | | 3 | | |
| Truro | 66 | 5 | Lewis | Eleazer | 3 | 1 | 2 | | 1 | 1 | | | 1 | | | | 11 | | |
| Barnstable | 94 | 6 | Lewis | George | | 1 | | 1 | 3 | 1 | 3 | 1 | | | | | 10 | | |
| Truro | 66 | 7 | Lewis | George | 2 | | | 1 | 1 | 1 | 1 | | | | | | 6 | | |
| Barnstable | 85 | 17 | Lewis | Hannah | | 1 | | | | | | 1 | | 1 | | | 3 | | |
| Barnstable | 90 | 42 | Lewis | Isaac | | | 1 | | | | | | 1 | | | | 2 | | |
| Yarmouth | 100 | 22 | Lewis | Jabez | 1 | 1 | | 1 | | 1 | 1 | | 1 | | | | 6 | | |
| Barnstable | 91 | 46 | Lewis | Jesse | 1 | | 1 | | | 1 | | | 1 | | | | 4 | | |
| Barnstable | 85 | 18 | Lewis | Joseph G | 2 | | 1 | | | | | | 1 | | | | 4 | | |
| Barnstable | 94 | 2 | Lewis | Lemuel | 2 | | 1 | | 2 | 1 | | 1 | | | | | 7 | | |
| Barnstable | 93 | 40 | Lewis | Lot | 2 | 1 | | | | | | | 1 | | | | 4 | | |
| Barnstable | 90 | 43 | Lewis | Lothrop | | | 1 | | | | | | 1 | | | | 2 | | |
| Falmouth | 46 | 162 | Lewis | Lothrop | 2 | | 1 | 1 | 1 | 1 | 2 | | 1 | | | | 9 | | |
| Sandwich | 34 | 10 | Lewis | Louis | | | | | | | | | 1 | | | | 1 | | |
| Wellfleet | 71 | 20 | Lewis | Moses | | 1 | 2 | 1 | | 1 | 1 | | 1 | | | | 7 | | |
| Barnstable | 85 | 36 | Lewis | Nathl | 1 | 2 | 1 | 1 | | | | | 1 | 1 | | | 7 | | |
| Falmouth | 46 | 166 | Lewis | Nathl | | | 1 | | | | | | | 1 | | | 2 | | |
| Barnstable | 94 | 9 | Lewis | Richard | | 1 | | 1 | | | | 1 | 1 | | | | 4 | | |
| Falmouth | 46 | 157 | Lewis | Samuel | 3 | | 1 | | 2 | | | | 1 | | | | 7 | | |
| Barnstable | 93 | 39 | Lewis | Sarah | | | | | | | | | 2 | 1 | | | 3 | | |
| Wellfleet | 71 | 23 | Lewis | Sarah | | 1 | | | | 2 | | 2 | | | | | 5 | | |
| Barnstable | 85 | 29 | Lewis | Seth | | 1 | | | | | | 1 | | | | | 2 | | |
| Wellfleet | 71 | 24 | Lewis | Solomon | 3 | | 1 | 1 | | | | | 1 | | | | 6 | | |
| Barnstable | 94 | 26 | Lewis | Thankful | | 1 | | | | | | 1 | | 2 | | | 4 | | |
| Falmouth | 46 | 167 | Lewis | Thatcher | | | 1 | | | | | | 1 | | | | 2 | | |
| Barnstable | 91 | 47 | Lewis | Thomas | 2 | | 2 | 2 | 1 | | | 2 | | | | | 11 | | |

# 1800 Barnstable County, Massachusetts Index

| TOWN | PG# | LN# | LAST NAME | FIRST NAME | M<10 | M10-16 | M16-26 | M26-45 | M45+ | F<10 | F10-16 | F16-26 | F26-45 | F45+ | TOTAL ALL OTHER | TOTAL SLAVES | TOTALS | DISTRICT/TOWNSHIP | NOTES |
|---|---|---|---|---|---|---|---|---|---|---|---|---|---|---|---|---|---|---|---|
| Barnstable | 90 | 32 | Lewis | Timothy | 2 | | 1 | | | 3 | 3 | | 1 | | | | 10 | | |
| Wellfleet | 75 | 8 | Lewis | Uorice | | 1 | | | | | | | 1 | | | | 2 | | |
| Barnstable | 86 | 26 | Lewis | William | | | 1 | | | 1 | | 1 | | | | | 3 | | |
| Yarmouth | 100 | 24 | Lewis | Jabez Jr | | | 1 | | | | | 1 | | | | | 2 | | |
| Harwich | 8 | 2 | Lincoln | David | | | 1 | | | | | 1 | | | | | 2 | | |
| Harwich | 7 | 37 | Lincoln | Isaac | 1 | | 1 | | | 1 | | 1 | | | | | 4 | | |
| Harwich | 6 | 2 | Lincoln | Nathaniel | 2 | | 1 | | | 1 | | | 1 | | | | 5 | | |
| Falmouth | 46 | 168 | Lincoln | Rev Henry | 2 | | 1 | | | 3 | | 1 | | | 1 | | 8 | | |
| Harwich | 7 | 20 | Lincoln | Seth | 3 | 1 | 2 | 1 | | 1 | | 1 | 1 | | | | 10 | | |
| Harwich | 7 | 32 | Lincoln | Silvanus | | 1 | | 1 | | 2 | | 1 | | | | | 5 | | |
| Harwich | 7 | 14 | Lincoln | Susanna Wd | | 1 | 1 | | | | | 1 | | 1 | | | 4 | | |
| Eastham | 78 | 7 | Linkhornew | Joseph | | 2 | 1 | | 1 | | 1 | 2 | | 1 | | | 8 | | |
| Eastham | 79 | 34 | Linkhornew | Joseph Junr | 1 | | 1 | | | 1 | | 1 | | | | | 4 | | |
| Orleans | 23 | 35 | Linnel | Benjm | 2 | 2 | | 1 | | | | | 1 | | | | 8 | | |
| Orleans | 23 | 17 | Linnel | Edmond | 2 | | | 1 | | 3 | 1 | | 1 | | | | 8 | | |
| Orleans | 25 | 5 | Linnel | Elisha | 5 | | | 1 | | | | | 1 | | | | 7 | | |
| Orleans | 23 | 16 | Linnel | Elkanah | 2 | | | | 1 | 3 | 1 | | 1 | 1 | | | 9 | | |
| Orleans | 22 | 27 | Linnel | Ezra | | | 1 | | | 1 | | 1 | | | | | 3 | | |
| Orleans | 24 | 11 | Linnel | Gould | 1 | | | 1 | | 1 | | | 1 | | | | 4 | | |
| Orleans | 22 | 41 | Linnel | Hemon | | | 1 | | 1 | | | 2 | | 1 | | | 5 | | |
| Orleans | 22 | 42 | Linnel | Isaac | 1 | | 1 | | | | | 1 | | | | | 3 | | |
| Orleans | 23 | 34 | Linnel | Jopah | | 3 | 1 | | 1 | | | 1 | | 2 | | | 8 | | |
| Orleans | 22 | 44 | Linnel | Samuel | 2 | | | 1 | | 1 | 1 | | 1 | | | | 6 | | |
| Orleans | 23 | 13 | Linnel | Samuel | 1 | | | 1 | | 2 | 1 | | 1 | | | | 6 | | |
| Harwich | 15 | 2 | Linnel | Thomas | 1 | 2 | 1 | | 1 | | | 2 | | 1 | | | 8 | | |
| Orleans | 25 | 4 | Linnel | Thomas | | | | 1 | | | | 1 | | 1 | | | 3 | | |
| Orleans | 22 | 45 | Linnel | Uriel | 3 | | | 1 | | 1 | 1 | | 1 | | | | 7 | | |
| Barnstable | 90 | 24 | Linnell | David | 1 | | | 1 | | | | | 1 | | | | 2 | | |
| Yarmouth | 96 | 11 | Linnell | Elisha | | | 1 | 1 | | | | | 1 | | | | 3 | | |
| Barnstable | 94 | 47 | Linnell | Heman | | | 1 | | | 2 | | | 1 | 2 | | | 6 | | |
| Barnstable | 90 | 25 | Linnell | James | | 2 | | | | | | 1 | 1 | | | | 4 | | |
| Barnstable | 90 | 46 | Linnell | John | 2 | | | 1 | | 2 | | | 1 | | | | 6 | | |
| Yarmouth | 96 | 24 | Linnell | John | 2 | | | 1 | | 1 | | 1 | | | | | 5 | | |
| Barnstable | 93 | 2 | Linnell | Josiah | | | | 1 | | 1 | | | 1 | | | | 3 | | |
| Barnstable | 101 | 2 | Linnell | Levi | | | | 1 | | | 1 | 1 | 1 | | | | 4 | | |
| Yarmouth | 96 | 23 | Linnell | Moses | | | 1 | | | 2 | | 1 | | | 1 | | 5 | | |
| Mashpee | 52 | 4 | Lippit | * | | | | | | | | | | | 8 | | 8 | | |
| Eastham | 78 | 6 | Lombard | Caleb | | 2 | 1 | | 1 | | | | | 1 | | | 5 | | |
| Truro | 66 | 2 | Lombard | Cornelius | 1 | | 1 | 1 | | 2 | 1 | 2 | 1 | | | | 9 | | |
| Truro | 62 | 15 | Lombard | Ebenezer | 1 | | | 1 | | 1 | | 1 | | | | | 4 | | |
| Truro | 66 | 6 | Lombard | Ephraim | | | | 1 | | | | 2 | 1 | | | | 4 | | |
| Truro | 68 | 23 | Lombard | Harding | | 1 | | | | 1 | | 1 | | | | | 3 | | |
| Truro | 66 | 8 | Lombard | Israel | 1 | 2 | | 1 | | 1 | 2 | 2 | | 1 | | | 10 | | |
| Truro | 68 | 11 | Lombard | Israel Junr | | 1 | | | | | | 1 | | | | | 2 | | |
| Truro | 63 | 18 | Lombard | James | 2 | | | 1 | | 1 | | | 1 | | | | 5 | | |
| Truro | 64 | 8 | Lombard | Lewis | | | | 1 | | | | 1 | 1 | | | | 3 | | |
| Truro | 64 | 9 | Lombard | Lewis Junr | | | 1 | | | 1 | | | 1 | | | | 3 | | |
| Eastham | 79 | 13 | Lombard | Oliver C. | 1 | | 1 | | | | | | | | | | 2 | | |
| Provincetown | 58 | 31 | Lombard | Peter | 2 | 1 | | 1 | | 1 | | | 1 | | | | 6 | | |
| Wellfleet | 71 | 21 | Lombard | Peter | | | 1 | | | 4 | 2 | | 1 | | | | 8 | | |
| Truro | 66 | 3 | Lombard | Rebeccah Junr | | | | | | 1 | 1 | | 1 | | | | 3 | | |
| Truro | 65 | 2 | Lombard | Rebeccah Wid | | 1 | | | | | | 1 | 1 | | | | 4 | | |
| Truro | 65 | 10 | Lombard | Sarah | 1 | 1 | | | | | | | | 2 | | | 4 | | |
| Truro | 65 | 5 | Lombard | Simon | 3 | | | 1 | | | | | 1 | | | | 5 | | |
| Truro | 66 | 4 | Lombard | Simon | | | | 1 | | | | 1 | | 1 | | | 3 | | |
| Truro | 65 | 20 | Lombard | William | 1 | | 1 | | 1 | 1 | 1 | | 1 | | | | 6 | | |
| Truro | 68 | 20 | Lombard | Zedediah | 2 | | | 1 | | | | | 1 | | | | 4 | | |
| Harwich | 11 | 15 | Long | Edmond | 2 | | | 1 | | 2 | | | 1 | | | | 6 | | |
| Harwich | 9 | 41 | Long | John | 1 | | 1 | | 1 | | | | 1 | 1 | | | 5 | | |
| Harwich | 9 | 42 | Long | John Junr | 1 | | | | | 2 | | | 1 | | | | 5 | | |
| Harwich | 9 | 21 | Long | Levi | 2 | 2 | | 1 | | 2 | | 2 | 1 | | | | 10 | | |
| Harwich | 9 | 19 | Long | William | 1 | 1 | | | 1 | | 1 | 2 | | 1 | | | 7 | | |
| Harwich | 9 | 20 | Long | William Jun | | | 1 | | | 3 | | | 1 | | | | 5 | | |
| Harwich | 10 | 43 | Long | Zachariah | 1 | 2 | | 1 | | 4 | | | 1 | | | | 9 | | |
| Barnstable | 86 | 41 | Loring | Abner | | 1 | 1 | | | | | 1 | | 1 | | | 4 | | |
| Barnstable | 86 | 6 | Loring | David | 1 | | | 1 | | 1 | | | | 1 | | | 4 | | |
| Barnstable | 86 | 8 | Loring | Edward | | | 1 | | | | | 1 | | 1 | | | 3 | | |
| Barnstable | 94 | 3 | Loring | Elpalet | 2 | 1 | | 1 | | | | | 1 | | | | 5 | | |
| Barnstable | 86 | 12 | Lothrop | Benja Jr | 2 | | | 1 | | 1 | | | 1 | | | | 5 | | |
| Barnstable | 84 | 12 | Lothrop | Benjamin | | | | 1 | | 1 | | | | 1 | | | 3 | | |
| Barnstable | 94 | 49 | Lothrop | David | 1 | | | 1 | | 3 | | | 1 | | | | 6 | | |
| Barnstable | 85 | 39 | Lothrop | Ebenezer | 1 | 1 | 2 | | | | | | 2 | | | | 6 | | |
| Barnstable | 86 | 20 | Lothrop | Ebenezer | 1 | 1 | 2 | 1 | | | | 1 | 1 | | | | 7 | | |
| Barnstable | 86 | 17 | Lothrop | Eunice | | | | | | | | | 1 | | | | 1 | | |
| Barnstable | 86 | 11 | Lothrop | Isaac | 1 | | 1 | 2 | 1 | 3 | 1 | | 1 | | | | 10 | | |
| Barnstable | 84 | 10 | Lothrop | John | | | 2 | 1 | | | 2 | 2 | | 1 | | | 8 | | |
| Barnstable | 85 | 47 | Lothrop | John | | | | 1 | | 2 | | | 1 | | 2 | | 6 | | |
| Barnstable | 84 | 11 | Lothrop | Mary | | | | | | | | | 1 | | | | 1 | | |
| Barnstable | 84 | 7 | Lothrop | Nathl | | | | | | | | | 1 | | | | 2 | | |
| Barnstable | 89 | 16 | Lothrop | Prince | | | 1 | | | | | 1 | 1 | | | | 3 | | |
| Barnstable | 85 | 15 | Lothrop | Rachel | | | | | | | | | 1 | | | | 1 | | |
| Barnstable | 85 | 37 | Lothrop | Robert | | 1 | | 1 | | 3 | | 1 | 1 | | | | 7 | | |

# 1800 Barnstable County, Massachusetts Index

| TOWN | PG# | LN# | LAST NAME | FIRST NAME | FREE WHITE MALES | | | | | FREE WHITE FEMALES | | | | | TOTAL ALL OTHER | TOTAL SLAVES | TOTALS | DISTRICT/ TOWNSHIP | NOTES |
|---|---|---|---|---|---|---|---|---|---|---|---|---|---|---|---|---|---|---|---|
| | | | | | under 10 | 10 to 16 | 16 to 26 | 26 to 45 | 45 and over | under 10 | 10 to 16 | 16 to 26 | 26 to 45 | 45 and over | | | | | |
| Falmouth | 49 | 287 | Lothrop | Thomas | 1 | | | 1 | | 1 | | | 1 | | | | 4 | | |
| Falmouth | 49 | 288 | Lovel | Jemimah | | | | | | | | 1 | 1 | | | | 2 | | |
| Mashpee | 51 | 3 | Lovel | Silas | | 1 | 1 | 1 | | | | | 1 | | | | 4 | | |
| Sandwich | 38 | 7 | Lovel | Silas | | | | | | | | | | | | | | | Enumeration left blank |
| Sandwich | 40 | 8 | Lovel | William | 2 | | | 1 | | | | | 1 | | | | 4 | | |
| Chatham | 17 | 44 | Loveland | Timothy | 2 | | | 1 | 1 | | | | 1 | | | | 5 | | |
| Barnstable | 94 | 15 | Lovell | Abner W | | | | 1 | | | | 1 | 1 | 1 | | | 4 | | |
| Barnstable | 91 | 34 | Lovell | Asa | 1 | | | 1 | | 1 | | | 1 | | | | 4 | | |
| Barnstable | 84 | 35 | Lovell | Christopher | 1 | | | | 1 | 2 | | | 1 | | | | 5 | | |
| Barnstable | 91 | 30 | Lovell | Cornelius | 2 | 3 | | 1 | | 3 | | | 1 | 1 | | | 11 | | |
| Barnstable | 91 | 33 | Lovell | Daniel | | 1 | | | 1 | | 2 | | 1 | | | | 5 | | |
| Barnstable | 91 | 39 | Lovell | Elizabeth | | | | | | | | | | 2 | | | 2 | | |
| Barnstable | 89 | 38 | Lovell | Enoch | 2 | 1 | | | 1 | | 1 | 1 | 1 | | | | 7 | | |
| Barnstable | 91 | 26 | Lovell | James | 1 | 1 | 1 | | 1 | | | 1 | 1 | 1 | | | 7 | | |
| Barnstable | 91 | 27 | Lovell | James Jr | | | 1 | | | | | | 1 | | | | 2 | | |
| Barnstable | 91 | 31 | Lovell | Sarah | | | | | | | | | | 3 | | | 3 | | |
| Barnstable | 91 | 25 | Lovell | Simeon | 1 | | 2 | 1 | | 2 | | 1 | 1 | 1 | | | 9 | | |
| Mashpee | 51 | 19 | Low | Anthony | | | | | | | | | | | 3 | | 3 | | |
| Barnstable | 90 | 48 | Ludden | Asa | | | 1 | | | | | | | | | | 1 | | |
| Barnstable | 90 | 47 | Ludden | Ebenezer | | 2 | | 1 | | | | | 1 | | | | 4 | | |
| Barnstable | 90 | 49 | Ludden | Isaiah | 1 | | 1 | | | 2 | | | 1 | | | | 5 | | |
| Barnstable | 91 | 1 | Ludden | Josiah | | 1 | | | | | | | 1 | | | | 2 | | |
| Harwich | 13 | 39 | Lues | Abner Rev | | | | 1 | | | | | | 1 | | | 2 | | |
| Harwich | 14 | 20 | Lues | John | 1 | | 1 | 1 | | 1 | | | 1 | | | | 5 | | |
| Barnstable | 92 | 2 | Lumberd | Hezekiah | | | | 1 | | | | 1 | 1 | | | | 3 | | |
| Barnstable | 93 | 21 | Lumberd | Ichabod | | | | 2 | | | | 1 | 1 | | | | 4 | | |
| Barnstable | 90 | 18 | Lumberd | Joseph | | | | 1 | | | | | 1 | | | | 2 | | |
| Barnstable | 90 | 23 | Lumberd | Joshua | 1 | | | 1 | | 2 | | | 1 | | | | 5 | | |
| Barnstable | 91 | 11 | Lumberd | Joshua | | | | 1 | | | | | 1 | | | | 2 | | |
| Barnstable | 90 | 22 | Lumberd | Prince | 1 | | | 1 | | 3 | | | 1 | | | | 6 | | |
| Barnstable | 90 | 21 | Lumberd | Samuel | | 1 | | 1 | | | | | 1 | | | | 3 | * | |
| Barnstable | 90 | 15 | Lumberd | Sarah | | | | | | | | 1 | 1 | 1 | | | 3 | | |
| Barnstable | 91 | 12 | Lumberd | Simeon | 3 | | | 1 | | | | | 1 | | | | 5 | | |
| Barnstable | 93 | 22 | Lumberd | Solomon | | | | 1 | | | | 2 | | | | | 3 | | |
| Harwich | 6 | 35 | Mahee | Seth | 2 | 1 | | | 1 | 2 | | | 1 | 1 | | | 8 | | |
| Falmouth | 51 | 322 | Maher | Joseph | | 1 | 1 | | | 2 | | | 1 | | | | 5 | | |
| Falmouth | 47 | 171 | Mann | Zipporah | | 1 | | | | | | | 1 | | | | 2 | | |
| Barnstable | 92 | 1 | Marchant | Barney | | | | 1 | | | | | 1 | | | | 2 | | |
| Yarmouth | 96 | 25 | Marchant | Desire | | | | 1 | | | | 2 | | 1 | 1 | | 5 | | |
| Barnstable | 91 | 48 | Marchant | James | 1 | 1 | 1 | | 1 | 4 | 2 | 3 | 1 | 1 | | | 15 | | |
| Yarmouth | 99 | 34 | Marchent | Anne | 1 | | 1 | | | 1 | | 1 | 1 | | | | 5 | | |
| Yarmouth | 99 | 37 | Marchent | E* | | 3 | | 1 | | 2 | 1 | | 1 | | | | 8 | | |
| Yarmouth | 99 | 35 | Marchent | Gorham | | 1 | | | | | | | 1 | | | | 2 | | |
| Yarmouth | 99 | 36 | Marchent | Josiah | 1 | | | 1 | | | | | 1 | | | | 3 | | |
| Yarmouth | 98 | 41 | Marchent | Silvanus | 2 | | | 1 | | 1 | | | 1 | | | | 5 | | |
| Barnstable | 88 | 41 | Marston | Allen | 1 | | 1 | | | 1 | | | 1 | | | | 4 | | |
| Barnstable | 88 | 40 | Marston | Benjamin | 1 | | | 1 | | 1 | 1 | | 1 | | | | 5 | | |
| Barnstable | 88 | 30 | Marston | Isaiah | 2 | | 3 | | 1 | 1 | 2 | | 1 | | | | 10 | | |
| Barnstable | 88 | 46 | Marston | Nymphas | 2 | | | 1 | | | | | 1 | | | | 6 | | |
| Barnstable | 88 | 42 | Marston | Prince | | | | 1 | | | 1 | | | | | | 2 | | |
| Barnstable | 88 | 49 | Martin | Winslow | 2 | 1 | | 1 | | 1 | 1 | 1 | 1 | 1 | 1 | | 10 | | |
| Yarmouth | 95 | 2 | Mathews | Atkins | 3 | | | 1 | | 1 | 2 | | 1 | | | | 8 | | |
| Yarmouth | 96 | 3 | Mathews | Benjamin | 1 | | | 1 | | | | 1 | 1 | 1 | | | 5 | | |
| Yarmouth | 96 | 29 | Mathews | David | | | | | 1 | | | | 2 | 1 | | | 4 | | |
| Yarmouth | 96 | 26 | Mathews | Ezekiel | 4 | | | 1 | | 1 | | 1 | 1 | 1 | | | 9 | | |
| Yarmouth | 95 | 42 | Mathews | Isaac | | | 1 | | | 1 | | 1 | | | | | 3 | | |
| Sandwich | 40 | 41 | Mathews | Isaiah | 1 | | | 1 | | | | | 1 | | | | 3 | | |
| Yarmouth | 95 | 16 | Mathews | John | | | | 1 | | | | | | 1 | | | 2 | | |
| Yarmouth | 95 | 53 | Mathews | Joshua | | | 3 | | 1 | | | 1 | 1 | 1 | | | 7 | | |
| Yarmouth | 96 | 33 | Mathews | Mercy | | | | | | 2 | | 1 | 1 | | | | 4 | | |
| Yarmouth | 96 | 27 | Mathews | Mercy Jr | 2 | | | | | | | | 1 | | | | 3 | | |
| Yarmouth | 95 | 4 | Mathews | Nathl | 3 | | | 1 | | 4 | 2 | 1 | | | | | 11 | | |
| Yarmouth | 96 | 2 | Mathews | Phebe | | 2 | 1 | 1 | | | | | 1 | 1 | | | 6 | | |
| Yarmouth | 98 | 17 | Mathews | Phebe Jr | 1 | | | 1 | | | | 1 | 1 | 1 | | | 6 | | |
| Yarmouth | 95 | 54 | Mathews | Samuel | | 1 | | | | | | | 1 | | | | 3 | | |
| Yarmouth | 95 | 1 | Mathews | Thankful | 1 | 1 | | | | | | 1 | 1 | | | | 4 | | |
| Wellfleet | 71 | 27 | Mayo | Abigail | | | | | | | | | 1 | 1 | | | 2 | | |
| Eastham | 78 | 11 | Mayo | Abijah | | | 1 | | | | | | 1 | | | | 2 | | |
| Orleans | 25 | 13 | Mayo | Abner | | 1 | | | | | | | 1 | | | | 2 | | |
| Wellfleet | 71 | 26 | Mayo | Daniel | | | 1 | 1 | | | | | 1 | | | | 3 | | |
| Eastham | 78 | 12 | Mayo | Elisha | 1 | | | 1 | | | | 2 | | 1 | | | 5 | | |
| Eastham | 79 | 9 | Mayo | Hannah | 1 | | | | | | | 1 | 1 | | | | 3 | | |
| Eastham | 78 | 14 | Mayo | Henry | 1 | 1 | | | | | | | 1 | | | | 3 | | |
| Eastham | 78 | 9 | Mayo | James | 1 | | | 1 | 2 | 1 | 1 | | 1 | | | | 7 | | |
| Eastham | 78 | 15 | Mayo | James Junr | | | 1 | | | | | 1 | 1 | | | | 3 | | |
| Eastham | 78 | 10 | Mayo | John | 3 | 1 | | | 1 | 3 | 2 | 3 | | 1 | | | 14 | | |
| Orleans | 24 | 20 | Mayo | Jonathan | | 1 | 2 | 1 | | 2 | | 1 | 1 | | | | 8 | | |
| Provincetown | 58 | 34 | Mayo | Joshua A. | 2 | 2 | | 1 | | 1 | | 1 | 1 | | | | 8 | | |
| Wellfleet | 71 | 25 | Mayo | Mary | | | | | | | | | 2 | | | | 2 | | |
| Wellfleet | 71 | 29 | Mayo | Nathan | | | 1 | | | 1 | | | 1 | | | | 3 | | |
| Truro | 68 | 28 | Mayo | Nehemiah D. | | | | | | | 1 | | | | | | 3 | | |

# 1800 Barnstable County, Massachusetts Index

| TOWN | PG# | LN# | LAST NAME | FIRST NAME | FREE WHITE MALES under 10 | 10 to 16 | 16 to 26 | 26 to 45 | 45 and over | FREE WHITE FEMALES under 10 | 10 to 16 | 16 to 26 | 26 to 45 | 45 and over | TOTAL ALL OTHER | TOTAL SLAVES | TOTALS | DISTRICT/ TOWNSHIP | NOTES |
|---|---|---|---|---|---|---|---|---|---|---|---|---|---|---|---|---|---|---|---|
| Truro | 64 | 17 | Mayo | Noah | | 1 | | | 1 | | | 1 | | 1 | | | 4 | | |
| Chatham | 17 | 46 | Mayo | Paul | | | 1 | | 1 | 3 | 1 | | 1 | | | | 7 | | |
| Eastham | 79 | 10 | Mayo | Samuel | | | 1 | | | | | 1 | | | | | 2 | | |
| Eastham | 79 | 20 | Mayo | Samuel | | | 1 | | | | | 1 | | | | | 2 | | |
| Orleans | 23 | 12 | Mayo | Sears | 4 | | 1 | 1 | | 1 | | 1 | 1 | | | | 9 | | |
| Orleans | 22 | 6 | Mayo | Theofelus | 2 | | 2 | 1 | | 1 | | | 1 | | | | 7 | | |
| Provincetown | 58 | 35 | Mayo | Thomas | 1 | 1 | 2 | | 1 | 1 | 1 | 2 | | 1 | | | 10 | | |
| Truro | 65 | 16 | Mayo | Thomas | 1 | | | 1 | | 1 | | | 1 | | | | 4 | | |
| Eastham | 79 | 14 | Mayo | Timothy | | | 1 | | | | | 1 | | | | | 2 | | |
| Harwich | 5 | 5 | Mayo | Asa | 5 | 2 | 2 | | 1 | | 2 | | 1 | 1 | | | 14 | | |
| Harwich | 7 | 29 | Mayo | Edmond | 1 | 1 | | 1 | | | | 1 | | | | | 4 | | |
| Harwich | 5 | 31 | Mayo | Elkanah | | | 2 | | 1 | | 2 | 2 | | 1 | | | 8 | | |
| Harwich | 6 | 25 | Mayo | Elnathan | 2 | 1 | | 1 | | 2 | 1 | 1 | 1 | | | | 9 | | |
| Harwich | 9 | 5 | Mayo | Isaac | | | 1 | | 1 | | | 1 | 1 | | | | 3 | | |
| Harwich | 7 | 38 | Mayo | James | | | 1 | | | 1 | | 1 | | | | | 3 | | |
| Harwich | 9 | 4 | Mayo | Joseph | 2 | 1 | | 1 | | 2 | 1 | | 1 | | | | 8 | | |
| Harwich | 6 | 27 | Mayo | Lydia Wd | | | | | | 1 | 2 | | | 1 | | | 4 | | |
| Harwich | 6 | 28 | Mayo | Moses | | | 1 | 1 | | | | | 2 | | | | 4 | | |
| Harwich | 9 | 6 | Mayo | Nathan | 1 | | 1 | 2 | 1 | | 1 | 1 | 1 | | | | 8 | | |
| Harwich | 10 | 22 | Mayo | Peter | | 1 | | | | 1 | | 1 | | | | | 3 | | |
| Harwich | 8 | 14 | Mayo | Thomas | 3 | 2 | | | 1 | 1 | | 1 | 1 | 1 | | | 10 | | |
| Orleans | 22 | 33 | Mayo | Uriel | 1 | 1 | 1 | | 1 | 3 | | 2 | | 1 | | | 10 | | |
| Harwich | 13 | 41 | McCarter | Dennis | 2 | | | 1 | | | | 1 | | | | | 4 | | |
| Harwich | 5 | 3 | McClaud | Anguish | 1 | | 1 | 1 | 1 | | 1 | 2 | | 1 | | | 8 | | |
| Orleans | 24 | 44 | McCormon | Micah | 3 | | 1 | | | 1 | | | 1 | | | | 7 | | |
| Harwich | 14 | 46 | McDonnell | John | 1 | 1 | | 1 | | 2 | 2 | | 1 | | | | 8 | | |
| Sandwich | 37 | 23 | Meiggs | Josiah | 2 | | | 1 | | 1 | | | 1 | | | | 5 | | |
| Falmouth | 49 | 318 | Meiggs | Lurany | | 1 | | | | | | 2 | | 1 | | | 4 | | |
| Sandwich | 37 | 27 | Meiggs | Matthew | | 1 | 1 | 1 | 1 | | 1 | 1 | | 1 | | | 7 | | |
| Sandwich | 37 | 26 | Meiggs | Ralph | | 1 | | 1 | | 1 | 1 | | 1 | | | | 5 | | |
| Barnstable | 89 | 18 | Meiggs | Reuben | | | | 1 | | | | | 1 | | | | 2 | | |
| Falmouth | 49 | 319 | Meiggs | Ruth | | | | | | | | 1 | 1 | | | | 2 | | |
| Barnstable | 85 | 26 | Mellen | John Rev | 1 | | | | 1 | 2 | | | 1 | | | | 5 | | |
| Provincetown | 58 | 33 | Miller | Benjamin | 2 | | | 1 | | | 1 | | 1 | | | | 5 | | |
| Yarmouth | 96 | 44 | Miller | Elisha | 4 | | | 1 | | 1 | | 1 | | | | | 7 | | |
| Harwich | 3 | 8 | Miller | John | 1 | | 1 | | | | | 1 | | | | | 3 | | |
| Provincetown | 58 | 32 | Miller | William | 2 | 1 | | 1 | | 2 | 1 | | 1 | | | | 8 | | |
| Orleans | 25 | 22 | Minich | Hannah Wd | | | | | | | | | 1 | | | | 1 | | |
| Harwich | 8 | 24 | Minich | Isaac | 2 | 1 | | 1 | | 3 | 1 | | 1 | | | | 9 | | |
| Orleans | 25 | 23 | Minich | John | | | 1 | 1 | | 3 | | 1 | 1 | | | | 7 | | |
| Harwich | 8 | 25 | Minich | Samuel | 3 | 1 | 2 | 1 | | | 1 | 1 | 1 | | | | 10 | | |
| Eastham | 79 | 19 | Mores | Susannah | | | | | | | | | 2 | | | | 2 | | |
| Provincetown | 60 | 22 | Mores | Treat | | | 1 | | | | | 1 | | | | | 2 | | |
| Sandwich | 40 | 21 | Morey | Abel | 2 | | | 1 | | | | | 1 | | | | 4 | | |
| Sandwich | 40 | 22 | Morey | Elisha | | | 1 | | | 1 | | | 1 | | | | 3 | | |
| Sandwich | 40 | 7 | Morey | Lemuel | | | 1 | | | | | 1 | 1 | | | | 3 | | |
| Wellfleet | 71 | 28 | Morris | James | 1 | | | 1 | | 1 | 1 | | 2 | | | | 6 | | |
| Chatham | 17 | 45 | Morris | Lidia | | | | | | | | | 1 | | | | 1 | | |
| Sandwich | 39 | 14 | Morse | Lydia | | | | | | | | | 1 | | | | 1 | | |
| Falmouth | 47 | 172 | Morse | Martha | | | | | | | 1 | 1 | 1 | | | | 3 | | |
| Sandwich | 42 | 40 | Morse | Samuel | 3 | 1 | 1 | | 1 | 1 | | | 1 | | | | 8 | | |
| Chatham | 17 | 47 | Morse | Seth | | 2 | | | 1 | 1 | 1 | | 1 | | | | 6 | | |
| Falmouth | 49 | 289 | Morsel | Joseph | | | | | | | | | | | | | 5 | | |
| Orleans | 21 | 7 | Mulford | Joshua | | | | 1 | | | | 1 | 1 | | | | 3 | | |
| Truro | 65 | 1 | Munson | Samuel | 2 | | | 1 | | 2 | | | 1 | | | | 6 | | |
| Wellfleet | 74 | 27 | Murry | Betsy | | 1 | | | | | 1 | | 1 | | | | 3 | | |
| Orleans | 22 | 19 | Myrick | Hemon | 4 | | | 1 | | 1 | 1 | | 1 | | | | 8 | | |
| Eastham | 78 | 13 | Myrick | Isaac | 3 | 1 | 2 | | 1 | | 1 | 1 | | 1 | | | 10 | | |
| Eastham | 78 | 8 | Myrick | William | | 1 | | 1 | | | | 2 | 1 | | | | 5 | | |
| Provincetown | 59 | 8 | Newcomb | David | 2 | | 1 | | 1 | | | 2 | | 1 | | | 7 | | |
| Truro | 65 | 23 | Newcomb | Elisha | 1 | | 1 | | | | | 1 | | | | | 3 | | |
| Wellfleet | 71 | 35 | Newcomb | Elisha | 1 | | 1 | | | 1 | | 1 | | | | | 4 | | |
| Wellfleet | 71 | 34 | Newcomb | Hezekiah | 2 | | | 1 | | 1 | | | 1 | | | | 5 | | |
| Wellfleet | 71 | 37 | Newcomb | James | | | 1 | | 1 | 2 | 2 | | 1 | | | | 7 | | |
| Wellfleet | 74 | 21 | Newcomb | Jemima | | 1 | | | | | 1 | | 1 | | | | 3 | | |
| Provincetown | 59 | 9 | Newcomb | Jeremiah | 1 | | 3 | | 1 | | 2 | 2 | 1 | | | | 10 | | |
| Wellfleet | 72 | 3 | Newcomb | Jeremiah | | 1 | | 1 | | 3 | 1 | | 1 | | | | 7 | | |
| Wellfleet | 74 | 1 | Newcomb | Jonathan Young | 1 | | 1 | | | 1 | 1 | 1 | 1 | | | | 6 | | |
| Truro | 65 | 22 | Newcomb | Joseph | | | | 1 | | | 2 | | | 1 | | | 4 | | |
| Wellfleet | 72 | 2 | Newcomb | Joshua | | | | 1 | | | | | | 1 | | | 2 | | |
| Wellfleet | 71 | 30 | Newcomb | Lemuel | 1 | 2 | 2 | 1 | | | 1 | 2 | 1 | | | | 10 | | |
| Wellfleet | 71 | 31 | Newcomb | Lemuel Junr | 2 | | | 1 | | 2 | 2 | | 1 | | | | 8 | | |
| Wellfleet | 71 | 36 | Newcomb | Sally | 1 | | | | | | 2 | | 1 | 1 | | | 5 | | |
| Wellfleet | 71 | 32 | Newcomb | Seth | 2 | | | 1 | | | 2 | | 1 | | | | 6 | | |
| Wellfleet | 74 | 16 | Newcomb | Simon | | 1 | 1 | | 1 | 1 | | 1 | | 1 | 2 | | 8 | | |
| Wellfleet | 75 | 15 | Newcomb | Simon 3d | 1 | | 1 | | | | | 1 | | | | | 3 | | |
| Wellfleet | 71 | 33 | Newcomb | Simon Junr | 1 | | 1 | | 1 | | 1 | 2 | | 1 | | | 7 | | |
| Truro | 65 | 18 | Newcomb | Theophilus | 1 | | 1 | | | | | 1 | | | | | 3 | | |
| Sandwich | 39 | 11 | Newcomb | Wm | | 2 | 1 | 1 | | 1 | | | 1 | 1 | 1 | | 8 | | |
| Provincetown | 61 | 7 | Nichols | James | 1 | | 1 | | | | 1 | | 1 | | | | 4 | | |
| Dennis | 29 | 12 | Nick | Jeptha | | | 1 | | | 1 | | 1 | | | | | 3 | | |
| Provincetown | 59 | 7 | Nickerson | Allen | 2 | 2 | | 1 | | 2 | 1 | | 1 | | | | 9 | | |
| Harwich | 12 | 13 | Nickerson | Asa | | 1 | | | 1 | | | | | 1 | | | 4 | | |

# 1800 Barnstable County, Massachusetts Index

| TOWN | PG# | LN# | LAST NAME | FIRST NAME | FREE WHITE MALES under 10 | 10 to 16 | 16 to 26 | 26 to 45 | 45 and over | FREE WHITE FEMALES under 10 | 10 to 16 | 16 to 26 | 26 to 45 | 45 and over | TOTAL ALL OTHER | TOTAL SLAVES | TOTALS | DISTRICT/ TOWNSHIP | NOTES |
|---|---|---|---|---|---|---|---|---|---|---|---|---|---|---|---|---|---|---|---|
| Yarmouth | 96 | 15 | Nickerson | Azubah | | | | | | 1 | | | | 1 | | | 2 | | |
| Harwich | 9 | 17 | Nickerson | Barzillos | 1 | | | 1 | | 2 | | | 1 | | | | 5 | | |
| Harwich | 12 | 12 | Nickerson | Basett | | 2 | 1 | | 1 | 1 | 1 | 2 | 1 | 1 | | | 10 | | |
| Harwich | 10 | 26 | Nickerson | Benjm | 2 | | 2 | | 1 | 1 | 2 | | 1 | | | | 9 | | |
| Dennis | 31 | 19 | Nickerson | Betsey Wid | | 1 | 1 | | | | 1 | 1 | | 1 | | | 5 | | |
| Provincetown | 59 | 10 | Nickerson | Betsy Wd | | 1 | 1 | | | | | 1 | | 1 | | | 4 | | |
| Chatham | 18 | 2 | Nickerson | Caleb | 1 | 1 | | | 1 | | | 1 | | 1 | | | 5 | | |
| Chatham | 18 | 15 | Nickerson | Caleb Jun | 1 | | 1 | | | | | | 1 | | | | 3 | | |
| Harwich | 13 | 19 | Nickerson | Christion | | 2 | 3 | | 1 | 2 | 1 | | | 1 | | | 10 | | |
| Chatham | 18 | 7 | Nickerson | Constant | | 1 | | 2 | | | 1 | | | 1 | | | 5 | | |
| Dennis | 31 | 38 | Nickerson | Daniel | | | 1 | | | | | | 1 | | | | 2 | | |
| Chatham | 18 | 17 | Nickerson | David | 2 | | 1 | | | | | | 1 | | | | 4 | | |
| Chatham | 20 | 26 | Nickerson | David | 2 | | 1 | | | | | | 1 | | | | 4 | | |
| Dennis | 29 | 20 | Nickerson | David | | | | 1 | | 3 | | | | 1 | | | 5 | | |
| Harwich | 7 | 24 | Nickerson | David | 1 | | | 1 | | | | | | 1 | | | 3 | | |
| Harwich | 14 | 43 | Nickerson | Ebenezer | 2 | 1 | | 1 | | 3 | 1 | | 2 | | | | 10 | | |
| Provincetown | 58 | 38 | Nickerson | Ebenezer | 1 | | | 1 | | 3 | | | | 1 | | | 6 | | |
| Harwich | 9 | 16 | Nickerson | Edward | | 1 | 1 | | | | | | 1 | | | | 3 | | |
| Dennis | 29 | 24 | Nickerson | Eleazor | | | | 1 | | | | | | 2 | | | 3 | | |
| Falmouth | 47 | 177 | Nickerson | Elijah | 1 | 1 | | 1 | 1 | | | | | 1 | | | 5 | | |
| Harwich | 12 | 38 | Nickerson | Enoch | 3 | | | 1 | | | | | 1 | | | | 5 | | |
| Provincetown | 58 | 40 | Nickerson | Enoch | 2 | | | 1 | | 2 | | | | 1 | | | 6 | | |
| Harwich | 12 | 44 | Nickerson | Enos | 2 | 1 | | 1 | | 2 | 1 | | 1 | | | | 8 | | |
| Chatham | 18 | 13 | Nickerson | Ensign | 4 | 2 | | | 1 | 1 | 1 | | 1 | | | | 10 | | |
| Chatham | 18 | 9 | Nickerson | Ezra | 2 | | 1 | | | 1 | | 1 | | | | | 5 | | |
| Chatham | 20 | 41 | Nickerson | Ezra | 1 | | | 1 | | 2 | | | 1 | | | | 5 | | |
| Dennis | 31 | 20 | Nickerson | Ezrael | 2 | | | 1 | | 1 | | | 1 | | | | 5 | | |
| Chatham | 18 | 12 | Nickerson | Flathiel | | 2 | | 1 | | 5 | 2 | 1 | 1 | | | | 12 | | |
| Harwich | 10 | 33 | Nickerson | Hannah Wd | | | | | | | | | | 3 | | | 3 | | |
| Harwich | 11 | 34 | Nickerson | Hannah Wd | | | | | | | | | | 1 | | | 1 | | |
| Wellfleet | 74 | 30 | Nickerson | Hatsael | | 2 | | 1 | | 2 | | | 1 | 1 | | | 7 | | |
| Dennis | 29 | 21 | Nickerson | Heman | | | | 1 | | 1 | | | 1 | | | | 3 | | |
| Harwich | 14 | 37 | Nickerson | Henry | 1 | | 1 | | | | | | 1 | | | | 3 | | |
| Dennis | 29 | 9 | Nickerson | James | 1 | 1 | | 1 | | | | | | 1 | | | 4 | | |
| Provincetown | 58 | 39 | Nickerson | James | 2 | | | 1 | | 2 | | | 1 | | | | 6 | | |
| Dennis | 29 | 10 | Nickerson | James Jun | 1 | | | 1 | | 1 | | | 1 | | | | 4 | | |
| Chatham | 18 | 6 | Nickerson | Jememiah | | 2 | 1 | 1 | | 1 | | 1 | | 1 | | | 7 | | |
| Dennis | 29 | 25 | Nickerson | John | | 1 | 2 | 1 | | | 1 | | | 1 | | | 6 | | |
| Dennis | 31 | 21 | Nickerson | John | | 2 | 2 | 1 | | | | 1 | | 1 | | | 7 | | |
| Harwich | 12 | 15 | Nickerson | John | 1 | | 1 | | | | | | 1 | | | | 3 | | |
| Yarmouth | 96 | 14 | Nickerson | John | 1 | 1 | 1 | | 1 | 2 | 1 | | | 1 | | | 8 | | |
| Dennis | 29 | 19 | Nickerson | John Jun | 1 | 1 | | 1 | | 2 | | | 1 | | | | 6 | | |
| Chatham | 18 | 5 | Nickerson | Jonathan | | | | 1 | | 1 | | 2 | 1 | 1 | | | 6 | | |
| Dennis | 31 | 18 | Nickerson | Jonathan | | | | 1 | | 1 | | | 1 | | | | 3 | | |
| Provincetown | 58 | 42 | Nickerson | Jonathan | | 2 | 3 | 1 | | 3 | 1 | | | 1 | | | 11 | | |
| Harwich | 14 | 49 | Nickerson | Jones | 3 | | | 1 | | 1 | | | 1 | | | | 6 | | |
| Provincetown | 59 | 3 | Nickerson | Joseph | 1 | | 2 | | | | | 1 | 1 | | | | 5 | | |
| Orleans | 22 | 28 | Nickerson | Joshua | 1 | 1 | | 1 | | 3 | 1 | 1 | | 1 | | | 9 | | |
| Dennis | 31 | 22 | Nickerson | Josiah | 1 | | 1 | | | | | | 1 | | | | 3 | | |
| Provincetown | 59 | 12 | Nickerson | Josiah | 2 | | | 1 | | | | | 1 | | | | 4 | | |
| Chatham | 18 | 16 | Nickerson | Leonard | 1 | | | 1 | | 1 | 1 | | 1 | 1 | | | 5 | | |
| Chatham | 18 | 14 | Nickerson | Lumberd | | | | 1 | | | | | | 2 | | | 3 | | |
| Provincetown | 59 | 11 | Nickerson | Martha Wd | | | 2 | | | | | 1 | | 1 | | | 4 | | |
| Provincetown | 60 | 34 | Nickerson | Mayo | | | | 1 | | 1 | | 1 | | | | | 3 | | |
| Chatham | 18 | 3 | Nickerson | Minich | | | | 1 | | | 2 | | 1 | | | | 4 | | |
| Chatham | 18 | 10 | Nickerson | Moses | | 1 | 1 | | | | | 2 | | 1 | | | 6 | | |
| Chatham | 18 | 8 | Nickerson | Moses Junr | 1 | | | 1 | | 2 | 1 | 1 | | | | | 7 | | |
| Orleans | 24 | 24 | Nickerson | Nathaniel | | 1 | | | | | | 1 | | | | | 2 | | |
| Provincetown | 58 | 41 | Nickerson | Nehemiah | | | | 1 | | | | | | 2 | | | 3 | | |
| Provincetown | 59 | 4 | Nickerson | Nehemiah Junr | 1 | | 1 | | | 1 | | 1 | | | | | 4 | | |
| Harwich | 12 | 19 | Nickerson | Olden | 1 | | 1 | | | 3 | | 1 | | | | | 6 | | |
| Falmouth | 47 | 181 | Nickerson | Phebe | 1 | | | | | | 1 | | | | | | 2 | | |
| Harwich | 11 | 33 | Nickerson | Phillip | 1 | | 1 | | | 3 | 1 | | | 1 | | | 7 | | |
| Harwich | 12 | 14 | Nickerson | Phinehas | 1 | 2 | | 1 | | | 1 | 1 | | 1 | | | 7 | | |
| Provincetown | 59 | 1 | Nickerson | Phinehas | | 1 | 1 | | | | 1 | | 1 | | | | 4 | | |
| Provincetown | 59 | 2 | Nickerson | Phinehas Junr | 1 | 1 | | 1 | | 4 | | | 1 | | | | 8 | | |
| Chatham | 20 | 21 | Nickerson | Richard | 1 | 1 | | 1 | | | 1 | | 1 | | | | 5 | | |
| Harwich | 12 | 42 | Nickerson | Samuel | 1 | 2 | 1 | | 1 | | 2 | | 1 | | | | 8 | | |
| Harwich | 10 | 7 | Nickerson | Seth | 4 | 2 | 1 | 1 | | 1 | | | 1 | | | | 10 | | |
| Provincetown | 58 | 37 | Nickerson | Seth Junr | 1 | | | 1 | | 4 | 1 | | 1 | | | | 8 | | |
| Provincetown | 59 | 5 | Nickerson | Seth Junr | 3 | 1 | | | | 1 | | 2 | | 1 | | | 8 | | |
| Harwich | 14 | 38 | Nickerson | Silas | | 1 | 1 | 1 | | 1 | | | 1 | | | | 5 | | |
| Harwich | 14 | 39 | Nickerson | Silas Jun | | 1 | | 1 | | 1 | | 1 | | | | | 3 | | |
| Dennis | 29 | 17 | Nickerson | Silvanus | 2 | | | 1 | | 1 | | 1 | 1 | | | | 5 | | |
| Chatham | 18 | 1 | Nickerson | Simeon | | | 1 | | | | | | | | | | 1 | | |
| Chatham | 20 | 33 | Nickerson | Simeon | 1 | | 1 | | | | | | 1 | | | | 3 | | |
| Dennis | 32 | 10 | Nickerson | Simeon | 1 | | 1 | | | 3 | 1 | | | | | | 6 | | |
| Harwich | 14 | 26 | Nickerson | Solomon | 1 | 1 | | 1 | | 3 | 3 | | 1 | | | | 10 | | |
| Harwich | 9 | 18 | Nickerson | Stephen | 2 | 3 | 1 | | | 1 | 1 | | 1 | | | | 9 | | |
| Harwich | 14 | 28 | Nickerson | Stephen | 2 | 1 | 2 | 1 | | 1 | 1 | | 1 | | | | 9 | | |
| Provincetown | 58 | 36 | Nickerson | Stephen | 2 | 1 | 1 | 1 | | 2 | 2 | | 1 | | | | 10 | | |
| Chatham | 18 | 4 | Nickerson | Tabitha Wid | | | | 1 | | | | 2 | 1 | | | | 6 | | |
| Dennis | 29 | 18 | Nickerson | Thankfull Wid | 1 | 3 | | | | 1 | 1 | 1 | 1 | | | | 8 | | |
| Harwich | 14 | 1 | Nickerson | Thomas | | 1 | | | 2 | | | 1 | | | | | 4 | | |
| Provincetown | 60 | 36 | Nickerson | Timothy | | 1 | | | | 1 | | | | | | | 2 | | |

# 1800 Barnstable County, Massachusetts Index

| TOWN | PG# | LN# | LAST NAME | FIRST NAME | FREE WHITE MALES under 10 | 10 to 16 | 16 to 26 | 26 to 45 | 45 and over | FREE WHITE FEMALES under 10 | 10 to 16 | 16 to 26 | 26 to 45 | 45 and over | TOTAL ALL OTHER | TOTAL SLAVES | TOTALS | DISTRICT/ TOWNSHIP | NOTES |
|---|---|---|---|---|---|---|---|---|---|---|---|---|---|---|---|---|---|---|---|
| Harwich | 14 | 48 | Nickerson | Tulley | 3 | 1 |  | 1 |  | 1 |  | 1 |  | 1 |  |  | 8 |  |  |
| Eastham | 78 | 16 | Nickerson | Uriah | 4 |  |  | 1 |  | 1 | 1 |  |  | 1 |  |  | 8 |  |  |
| Harwich | 14 | 42 | Nickerson | Uriel | 2 | 1 |  | 1 |  | 2 | 1 | 2 | 1 |  |  |  | 10 |  |  |
| Harwich | 12 | 18 | Nickerson | Vincent | 1 |  | 1 |  |  |  |  |  | 1 |  |  |  | 3 |  |  |
| Harwich | 15 | 7 | Nickerson | William | 1 |  |  | 1 |  | 1 |  |  | 1 |  |  |  | 4 |  |  |
| Provincetown | 59 | 6 | Nickerson | William |  |  |  | 1 |  | 1 |  | 1 |  |  |  |  | 3 |  |  |
| Orleans | 25 | 7 | Nickerson | Yates | 1 |  |  |  | 1 |  |  |  | 1 | 1 |  |  | 4 |  |  |
| Chatham | 18 | 11 | Nickerson | Zaheth | 1 |  |  | 1 |  | 3 | 1 |  | 1 |  |  |  | 7 |  |  |
| Dennis | 29 | 2 | Nickserson | Josiah | 2 |  | 2 |  | 1 | 1 | 1 |  |  | 1 |  |  | 8 |  |  |
| Wellfleet | 73 | 23 | Nisbit | Elizabeth | 1 |  | 2 |  |  |  |  | 1 |  | 1 |  |  | 5 |  |  |
| Barnstable | 93 | 33 | Norris | Peter | 1 | 1 | 1 |  | 1 | 1 |  | 1 |  | 1 |  |  | 7 |  |  |
| Barnstable | 93 | 34 | Norris | Peter Jr |  |  | 1 |  |  |  |  | 1 |  |  |  |  | 2 |  |  |
| Sandwich | 37 | 11 | Nye | Abigail |  |  | 1 |  |  |  | 3 |  | 1 |  |  |  | 5 |  |  |
| Sandwich | 39 | 7 | Nye | Allen | 2 |  |  | 1 |  | 2 |  |  | 1 |  | 1 |  | 7 |  |  |
| Barnstable | 90 | 5 | Nye | Asa | 2 |  |  | 1 |  | 1 | 1 |  | 1 | 1 |  |  | 7 |  |  |
| Sandwich | 34 | 16 | Nye | Barnabas |  |  | 1 |  |  |  |  |  | 1 |  |  |  | 2 |  |  |
| Barnstable | 88 | 8 | Nye | Benjamin |  | 1 | 1 |  | 2 |  |  | 4 | 2 | 1 |  |  | 11 |  |  |
| Falmouth | 47 | 182 | Nye | David | 2 | 1 | 1 |  | 1 | 1 |  | 3 | 1 | 1 |  |  | 11 |  |  |
| Sandwich | 36 | 23 | Nye | Ebenezer | 2 | 2 |  |  | 1 | 1 | 1 | 1 | 1 | 1 |  |  | 10 |  |  |
| Falmouth | 47 | 185 | Nye | Elisha |  | 2 | 1 |  | 2 |  |  | 1 |  | 1 |  |  | 7 |  |  |
| Falmouth | 47 | 186 | Nye | Elnathan |  |  | 1 | 2 |  |  | 1 | 1 |  |  |  |  | 5 |  |  |
| Falmouth | 47 | 180 | Nye | Hannah |  |  | 2 |  |  |  | 1 |  |  | 1 |  |  | 4 |  |  |
| Sandwich | 36 | 26 | Nye | Heman |  |  | 1 |  |  |  |  |  | 1 |  |  |  | 2 |  |  |
| Sandwich | 35 | 20 | Nye | Jabez | 1 |  | 2 |  | 1 | 2 | 1 |  | 1 |  |  |  | 8 |  |  |
| Falmouth | 47 | 184 | Nye | John |  |  | 4 | 2 | 2 |  | 1 | 1 |  | 2 | 1 |  | 13 |  |  |
| Sandwich | 36 | 27 | Nye | John | 4 |  |  | 2 | 1 | 3 | 1 | 2 | 1 |  |  |  | 14 |  |  |
| Falmouth | 47 | 188 | Nye | John Junr | 2 |  |  | 1 |  |  |  |  | 1 |  |  |  | 4 |  |  |
| Barnstable | 87 | 36 | Nye | Jonathan | 1 | 1 |  | 1 |  | 2 |  |  | 1 | 1 |  |  | 7 |  |  |
| Sandwich | 36 | 22 | Nye | Joseph | 1 |  |  | 1 |  |  |  | 1 |  |  |  |  | 3 |  |  |
| Sandwich | 38 | 25 | Nye | Katharine |  | 2 | 2 |  | 1 | 3 | 1 | 2 |  | 1 |  |  | 12 |  |  |
| Barnstable | 87 | 33 | Nye | Lemuel |  | 1 |  | 1 |  |  |  | 1 |  | 1 |  |  | 4 |  |  |
| Sandwich | 36 | 21 | Nye | Lemuel | 2 |  |  | 1 |  | 1 | 1 |  | 1 |  |  |  | 6 |  |  |
| Barnstable | 87 | 34 | Nye | Lemuel Jr |  |  | 1 |  |  |  |  | 1 |  |  |  |  | 2 |  |  |
| Sandwich | 35 | 1 | Nye | Levi | 1 |  | 1 | 1 |  |  |  | 1 |  |  |  |  | 4 |  |  |
| Sandwich | 35 | 17 | Nye | Mary |  |  | 2 |  |  |  |  |  | 1 | 2 |  |  | 5 |  |  |
| Sandwich | 35 | 16 | Nye | Moses | 1 |  |  | 1 |  | 2 |  |  | 1 |  |  |  | 5 |  |  |
| Sandwich | 40 | 45 | Nye | Moses |  |  | 1 |  |  |  |  | 1 |  |  |  |  | 2 |  |  |
| Falmouth | 47 | 179 | Nye | Nathan |  | 1 |  | 1 |  |  |  |  | 3 | 1 |  |  | 6 |  |  |
| Sandwich | 36 | 3 | Nye | Nathan | 1 |  | 1 |  | 1 | 1 | 2 |  | 1 |  |  |  | 7 |  |  |
| Sandwich | 38 | 29 | Nye | Nathan Junr |  | 2 | 2 |  | 1 | 3 | 2 |  | 1 |  |  |  | 11 |  |  |
| Sandwich | 36 | 6 | Nye | Nathaniel | 2 | 1 | 1 |  | 1 | 1 | 1 |  |  | 1 |  |  | 8 |  |  |
| Sandwich | 34 | 8 | Nye | Peleg | 1 |  |  |  | 1 | 2 | 2 |  | 1 |  |  |  | 7 |  |  |
| Sandwich | 36 | 24 | Nye | Peter |  | 1 | 1 |  | 1 | 1 | 1 |  | 1 |  |  |  | 5 |  |  |
| Falmouth | 47 | 178 | Nye | Samuel |  | 1 | 3 |  | 1 | 1 | 1 |  |  | 2 |  |  | 9 |  |  |
| Sandwich | 42 | 34 | Nye | Samuel |  |  | 1 |  | 1 | 2 |  | 1 | 1 |  |  |  | 6 |  |  |
| Falmouth | 47 | 183 | Nye | Samuel Junr | 3 | 2 | 1 |  | 1 | 1 |  | 1 |  | 1 |  |  | 10 |  |  |
| Sandwich | 35 | 23 | Nye | Silvanus |  | 3 |  |  | 1 | 1 | 2 |  | 1 |  |  |  | 8 |  |  |
| Falmouth | 47 | 187 | Nye | Solomon Junr | 3 |  |  | 1 |  | 1 |  |  | 1 |  |  |  | 6 |  |  |
| Sandwich | 39 | 21 | Nye | Stephen | 1 |  |  |  | 1 |  |  |  | 1 |  |  |  | 3 |  |  |
| Sandwich | 41 | 9 | Nye | Thos | 2 |  |  | 1 |  | 2 |  |  | 1 |  |  |  | 6 |  |  |
| Truro | 68 | 29 | Nye | Timothy | 1 |  |  | 1 |  |  |  | 1 |  |  |  |  | 3 |  |  |
| Sandwich | 36 | 4 | Nye | William Junr | 2 | 1 |  | 1 |  | 1 | 2 |  | 1 |  |  |  | 8 |  |  |
| Sandwich | 38 | 38 | Nye | Wm |  |  | 1 | 1 |  |  |  | 1 |  | 1 |  |  | 4 |  |  |
| Sandwich | 39 | 22 | Nye | Zenas | 3 | 2 |  | 1 |  | 2 |  |  | 1 |  |  |  | 9 |  |  |
| Harwich | 8 | 15 | Obriant | Edward | 4 |  | 1 |  |  |  |  |  | 1 |  |  |  | 6 |  |  |
| Sandwich | 38 | 41 | O'Brine | Mott | 1 |  |  |  | 1 | 1 | 1 |  | 1 |  |  |  | 5 |  |  |
| Barnstable | 87 | 53 | Ohr | Joseph Esq |  | 2 |  |  | 1 |  | 1 | 1 |  | 1 |  |  | 6 |  |  |
| Harwich | 14 | 24 | Oliver | James | 1 | 1 |  | 1 |  | 1 |  |  | 1 |  |  |  | 5 |  |  |
| Truro | 62 | 12 | Omsby | Rachel Wid | 1 |  |  |  |  |  | 2 |  | 1 |  |  |  | 4 |  |  |
| Barnstable | 84 | 48 | Otis | Amos | 1 |  |  | 1 |  |  |  | 1 |  | 1 |  |  | 4 |  |  |
| Barnstable | 85 | 8 | Otis | Solomon | 1 |  |  | 1 |  |  |  | 1 |  |  |  |  | 3 |  |  |
| Dennis | 26 | 36 | Paddack | Judah |  | 1 | 2 |  | 1 | 3 |  | 2 |  | 1 |  |  | 10 |  |  |
| Dennis | 26 | 40 | Paddack | Samuel |  | 1 |  | 1 |  |  |  | 1 |  |  |  |  | 3 |  |  |
| Harwich | 13 | 15 | Pain | Ebenezer | 1 |  |  | 1 |  |  |  |  | 1 |  |  |  | 3 |  |  |
| Harwich | 5 | 9 | Pain | Eleanor | 1 |  |  | 1 |  | 2 |  |  | 1 |  |  |  | 5 |  |  |
| Harwich | 13 | 17 | Pain | Isaac | 1 |  |  | 1 |  | 2 |  |  | 1 |  |  |  | 5 |  |  |
| Harwich | 5 | 8 | Pain | James |  |  |  | 1 |  |  |  |  |  | 2 |  |  | 3 |  |  |
| Harwich | 5 | 10 | Pain | James Jun | 2 | 2 |  | 1 |  | 2 |  |  | 1 |  |  |  | 8 |  |  |
| Harwich | 14 | 33 | Pain | John |  |  |  |  | 1 | 1 | 2 | 1 |  | 1 |  |  | 6 |  |  |
| Harwich | 12 | 9 | Pain | Nathaniel | 1 |  |  | 1 |  |  |  | 2 |  | 1 |  |  | 5 |  |  |
| Harwich | 6 | 7 | Pain | Samuel |  | 1 |  | 1 |  |  |  | 1 |  | 1 |  |  | 6 |  |  |
| Harwich | 5 | 12 | Pain | Silvanus | 4 |  |  | 1 |  |  |  |  | 1 |  |  |  | 6 |  |  |
| Harwich | 5 | 41 | Pain | Thankfull Wd | 1 | 1 |  |  |  |  | 2 |  | 1 |  |  |  | 5 |  |  |
| Harwich | 13 | 14 | Pain | Thankfull Wd |  | 1 |  |  |  |  |  |  | 1 | 2 |  |  | 4 |  |  |
| Truro | 68 | 27 | Paine | Asa |  | 1 |  |  |  |  |  |  | 1 |  |  |  |  |  |  |
| Truro | 62 | 8 | Paine | Barnabas | 1 | 1 |  |  | 1 | 2 | 2 |  | 1 | 2 |  |  | 10 |  |  |
| Truro | 68 | 14 | Paine | Benjamin | 2 |  |  | 1 |  | 1 |  |  | 1 |  |  |  | 5 |  |  |
| Truro | 62 | 10 | Paine | David |  |  | 3 |  | 1 | 1 |  |  | 1 |  |  |  | 6 |  |  |
| Eastham | 78 | 20 | Paine | Ebenezer | 2 |  |  | 1 |  | 1 | 1 |  | 1 |  |  |  | 6 |  |  |
| Truro | 62 | 14 | Paine | Ebenezer | 2 | 1 |  |  |  | 1 |  |  | 1 | 1 |  |  | 7 |  |  |
| Truro | 66 | 9 | Paine | Elisha | 1 |  |  | 1 | 1 |  |  |  | 1 |  |  |  | 5 |  |  |
| Truro | 66 | 12 | Paine | Elizabeth Wid |  |  | 3 |  |  |  |  | 1 |  | 1 |  |  | 5 |  |  |
| Truro | 66 | 10 | Paine | Elkanah | 5 |  | 2 |  | 1 |  | 2 |  |  | 1 |  |  | 11 |  |  |

91

| TOWN | PG# | LN# | LAST NAME | FIRST NAME | FREE WHITE MALES under 10 | 10 to 16 | 16 to 26 | 26 to 45 | 45 and over | FREE WHITE FEMALES under 10 | 10 to 16 | 16 to 26 | 26 to 45 | 45 and over | TOTAL ALL OTHER | TOTAL SLAVES | TOTALS | DISTRICT/ TOWNSHIP | NOTES |
|---|---|---|---|---|---|---|---|---|---|---|---|---|---|---|---|---|---|---|---|
| Truro | 63 | 4 | Paine | Hannah | | | | | | | | | 1 | 2 | | | 3 | | |
| Provincetown | 59 | 15 | Paine | Henry | 3 | | | 1 | | | | | 1 | | | | 5 | | |
| Truro | 68 | 7 | Paine | Hezekiah | 1 | | 1 | | | 1 | | 1 | 1 | | | | 5 | | |
| Eastham | 78 | 19 | Paine | Isaac | | 1 | | 1 | | 1 | | | 2 | 1 | | | 6 | | |
| Truro | 66 | 11 | Paine | Jesse | | 1 | 1 | | | 2 | | 1 | 1 | 1 | | | 7 | | |
| Wellfleet | 75 | 13 | Paine | Mary | | 1 | | | | | | 1 | | 1 | | | 3 | | |
| Provincetown | 59 | 16 | Paine | Moses | 1 | | 1 | | | 1 | | | 1 | | | | 4 | | |
| Truro | 66 | 13 | Paine | Relianu | | | | | | | | | 1 | | | | 1 | | |
| Truro | 68 | 21 | Paine | Samuel | 2 | | 1 | | | 1 | | | 1 | | | | 5 | | |
| Truro | 63 | 20 | Paine | Sarah Wid | | | | | | | | 2 | | 1 | | | 3 | | |
| Truro | 65 | 15 | Paine | Thatcher | | 2 | | 1 | | | | 3 | | 1 | | | 7 | | |
| Eastham | 79 | 31 | Paine | Thomas | | | 1 | | | 3 | | | 1 | | | | 5 | | |
| Wellfleet | 72 | 9 | Paine | Thomas | | 1 | | 1 | | | | 1 | | 1 | | | 4 | | |
| Wellfleet | 74 | 22 | Paine | Thomas 3d | 2 | | | 1 | | 1 | | | 1 | | | | 5 | | |
| Wellfleet | 72 | 5 | Paine | Thomas Junr | 2 | | | 1 | | 1 | | | 1 | | | | 5 | | |
| Wellfleet | 75 | 17 | Paine | William | | 1 | | | | | | 1 | | | | | 2 | | |
| Falmouth | 47 | 199 | Palmer | Joseph | | 1 | | 1 | | | | 2 | | 1 | | | 5 | | |
| Falmouth | 47 | 190 | Palmer | Joseph Junr | 2 | | | 1 | | 2 | 1 | 1 | 2 | 1 | | | 10 | | |
| Falmouth | 47 | 191 | Palmer | Sarah | | | | | | | | | 1 | | | | 1 | | |
| Yarmouth | 100 | 6 | Parker | Benjamin | 1 | | 1 | | | 1 | | 1 | | | | | 4 | | |
| Falmouth | 47 | 197 | Parker | Benjm | | 1 | 1 | 1 | | | | 2 | | 1 | | | 6 | | |
| Falmouth | 47 | 189 | Parker | Benjm Jun | | 1 | | | | 1 | | | 1 | | | | 3 | | |
| Barnstable | 89 | 45 | Parker | Daniel | | 1 | | 1 | | | | 2 | | 1 | | | 5 | | |
| Barnstable | 89 | 46 | Parker | Daniel Jr | 1 | | | 1 | | | | 1 | | | | | 3 | | |
| Barnstable | 90 | 6 | Parker | David | 2 | 1 | 1 | | 1 | | | 1 | | 1 | 1 | | 8 | | |
| Barnstable | 87 | 22 | Parker | Desire | | | 2 | | | 1 | | | 2 | | | | 5 | | |
| Yarmouth | 100 | 5 | Parker | Isaiah | | 1 | | | | | | 1 | | | | | 2 | | |
| Barnstable | 87 | 21 | Parker | Isaiah | 2 | 2 | | | 1 | 2 | 1 | | 1 | | | | 9 | | |
| Yarmouth | 100 | 2 | Parker | Jacob | | 1 | 1 | 1 | | 1 | 1 | 1 | | 1 | | | 7 | | |
| Yarmouth | 100 | 4 | Parker | Jacob Jr | | 1 | | | | | | 1 | | | | | 2 | | |
| Barnstable | 91 | 21 | Parker | James | 2 | 1 | 2 | | 1 | 1 | 1 | 2 | 1 | 2 | | | 13 | | |
| Barnstable | 90 | 36 | Parker | Jehiel | 1 | | | 1 | | 1 | | 1 | | | | | 4 | | |
| Falmouth | 47 | 194 | Parker | Job | | 3 | 2 | 1 | | | 1 | 1 | | 1 | | | 9 | | |
| Falmouth | 49 | 294 | Parker | Jonathan | 3 | | | 1 | | | 1 | | 1 | | | | 6 | | |
| Barnstable | 90 | 1 | Parker | Joseph | 1 | | | 1 | | | | 1 | | 1 | 1 | | 4 | | |
| Falmouth | 47 | 196 | Parker | Joseph | | 1 | 1 | 2 | | | 2 | | 1 | | | | 7 | | |
| Sandwich | 40 | 46 | Parker | Katharine | | | | | | 1 | | 1 | | | | | 2 | | |
| Provincetown | 60 | 14 | Parker | Rev Samuel | | 1 | | 1 | | | | | | 1 | 1 | | 3 | | |
| Falmouth | 44 | 41 | Parker | Seth | 1 | | | 1 | | 1 | | | 1 | | | | 4 | | |
| Falmouth | 47 | 206 | Parker | Seth | 1 | 1 | | 1 | | 1 | | | 1 | | | | 5 | | |
| Falmouth | 47 | 195 | Parker | Timothy | 2 | | 1 | | | | | 1 | | 1 | 1 | | 5 | | |
| Yarmouth | 99 | 33 | Parsons | William | 1 | | | 1 | | 1 | 3 | 1 | | | | | 7 | | |
| Falmouth | 51 | 320 | Pease | Barzilla | | | 1 | | 2 | | 2 | | 1 | 1 | 1 | | 7 | | |
| Eastham | 78 | 17 | Peeks | William | 4 | 1 | | 1 | | | 1 | 1 | | 1 | | | 9 | | |
| Provincetown | 60 | 26 | Peirce | David | 1 | | | 1 | | 2 | | | 1 | | | | 5 | | |
| Wellfleet | 72 | 8 | Peirce | Isaac | | 1 | | 1 | | | 1 | 1 | 1 | | | | 5 | | |
| Wellfleet | 74 | 33 | Peirce | John | | 1 | | 1 | | | | | 1 | | | | 3 | | |
| Wellfleet | 72 | 7 | Peirce | Joseph Junr | 1 | 2 | | 1 | 1 | | | | 1 | | | | 6 | | |
| Provincetown | 59 | 17 | Peirce | Joshua | 1 | 2 | 1 | | 1 | 1 | | 1 | 1 | | | | 8 | | |
| Wellfleet | 75 | 18 | Peirce | Joshua | | 1 | | | | | | 1 | | | | | 2 | | |
| Wellfleet | 72 | 4 | Peirce | Samuel Junr | 1 | 1 | | 1 | | 2 | | | 1 | | | | 6 | | |
| Wellfleet | 72 | 6 | Peirce | Solomon | 1 | | 1 | 1 | | | | 1 | 1 | | | | 5 | | |
| Wellfleet | 74 | 20 | Peirce | Thomas | 1 | | | 1 | | 1 | | | 1 | | | | 4 | | |
| Provincetown | 61 | 10 | Peirce | William | 3 | 1 | | | | 1 | | 1 | | | | | 6 | | |
| Sandwich | 37 | 22 | Peleg | Lawrence | 5 | 1 | | 1 | | | | | 1 | | | | 8 | | |
| Orleans | 24 | 46 | Peper | Benja | | 1 | 2 | 1 | | 1 | 1 | | 1 | | | | 7 | | |
| Orleans | 25 | 2 | Peper | Pheba Wd | | | | | | 1 | | 1 | | | | | 2 | | |
| Orleans | 25 | 1 | Peper | Simeon | 1 | | | 1 | 2 | | | 1 | | | | | 5 | | |
| Eastham | 78 | 18 | Pepper | Joseph | | | 1 | 1 | | 1 | 2 | 3 | 1 | 1 | | | 10 | | |
| Sandwich | 37 | 24 | Percival | Benjamin | 2 | 1 | 3 | 1 | | 1 | | 1 | | 1 | | | 10 | | |
| Sandwich | 37 | 20 | Percival | James | 1 | | 2 | 1 | | 2 | 3 | 1 | | 1 | | | 11 | | |
| Sandwich | 37 | 44 | Percival | John | | 1 | | | | 1 | | | 1 | | | | 3 | | |
| Sandwich | 37 | 2 | Percival | Thomas | 1 | 1 | 2 | 1 | | 1 | 2 | | | 1 | | | 9 | | |
| Sandwich | 42 | 18 | Perry | Caleb | 1 | | | 1 | | 3 | | | 1 | | | | 6 | | |
| Sandwich | 42 | 20 | Perry | Daniel | 2 | 1 | | 1 | | | 2 | | 1 | | | | 7 | | |
| Sandwich | 42 | 27 | Perry | Elisha | 1 | | 1 | 1 | | | 1 | | 1 | | | | 5 | | |
| Sandwich | 42 | 29 | Perry | Ellis | 3 | | 1 | | | | | | 1 | | | | 5 | | |
| Sandwich | 42 | 15 | Perry | John 1st | | 1 | | 1 | | | 1 | | 1 | | | | 4 | | |
| Sandwich | 42 | 22 | Perry | John 2d | 3 | | 1 | 1 | | | 1 | 1 | | | | | 7 | | |
| Sandwich | 42 | 32 | Perry | John 3d | 2 | 2 | 2 | 1 | | 1 | | 1 | | 1 | | | 10 | | |
| Sandwich | 42 | 16 | Perry | John 4th | 1 | 1 | | 1 | | 2 | | | 1 | | | | 6 | | |
| Truro | 69 | 1 | Perry | Prince | | 1 | 1 | 1 | | 1 | 1 | | 1 | | | | 6 | | |
| Provincetown | 59 | 14 | Perry | Richard | | 1 | 1 | | 3 | | | 1 | | | | | 6 | | |
| Sandwich | 42 | 19 | Perry | Seth | 1 | 1 | 2 | 1 | | 2 | 1 | | 1 | | | | 9 | | |
| Sandwich | 42 | 17 | Perry | Silvanus | 1 | 1 | | 1 | | 2 | | | 1 | | | | 6 | | |
| Sandwich | 42 | 2 | Perry | Solomon | 1 | | 1 | | | | 1 | | | | | | 3 | | |
| Sandwich | 42 | 30 | Perry | Susanna | | | | | | | 1 | | 1 | | | | 2 | | |
| Sandwich | 42 | 43 | Perry | Thankful | | | | | | | 1 | 1 | | | | | 2 | | |
| Sandwich | 41 | 46 | Perry | Wm | | | 1 | | 2 | | | | | | | | 4 | | |
| Sandwich | 40 | 29 | Persons | Baston | | | | | | | | | | | 1 | | 1 | | |
| Harwich | 12 | 21 | Phillips | Anthony | 1 | | | 1 | | 3 | 1 | 1 | | | | | 7 | | |
| Harwich | 13 | 21 | Phillips | Benjm | 1 | 1 | 2 | | 1 | 1 | 2 | | 1 | | | | 9 | | |

# 1800 Barnstable County, Massachusetts Index

| TOWN | PG# | LN# | LAST NAME | FIRST NAME | \<10 | 10-16 | 16-26 | 26-45 | 45+ | \<10 | 10-16 | 16-26 | 26-45 | 45+ | TOTAL ALL OTHER | TOTAL SLAVES | TOTALS | DISTRICT/ TOWNSHIP | NOTES |
|---|---|---|---|---|---|---|---|---|---|---|---|---|---|---|---|---|---|---|---|
| Chatham | 20 | 3 | Phillips | John | 1 | | | 1 | | | | | | 1 | | | 3 | | |
| Harwich | 9 | 39 | Phillips | Jonathan | 1 | | | 1 | | 3 | 1 | | 1 | | | | 7 | | |
| Harwich | 10 | 5 | Phillips | Joseph | 2 | | 2 | | 1 | 1 | 2 | | 1 | | | | 9 | | |
| Harwich | 10 | 38 | Phillips | Oker Jun | 2 | | | 1 | | 1 | 1 | | 1 | | | | 6 | | |
| Harwich | 12 | 4 | Phillips | Small | 1 | 1 | 1 | | 1 | 1 | | 1 | | 1 | | | 7 | | |
| Falmouth | 49 | 313 | Phinney | Abishai | | 2 | | 1 | | 1 | | | 1 | | | | 4 | | |
| Barnstable | 85 | 46 | Phinney | Edward | 1 | | | 1 | | 1 | | 1 | | | | | 4 | | |
| Harwich | 4 | 24 | Phinney | Gershom | | 1 | | | 1 | | 1 | | | 2 | | | 5 | | |
| Sandwich | 42 | 21 | Phinney | John | 1 | | 3 | | 1 | | 2 | 1 | 1 | | | | 9 | | |
| Falmouth | 47 | 202 | Phinney | Jonathan | | 2 | | 1 | | 1 | | | 1 | | | | 5 | | |
| Barnstable | 90 | 9 | Phinney | Joseph | | | 1 | | 1 | | | 1 | | | | | 3 | | |
| Harwich | 4 | 23 | Phinney | Lazarus | 1 | | 1 | | 1 | | | | 1 | 1 | | | 5 | | |
| Barnstable | 90 | 14 | Phinney | Levi | 2 | | 1 | 1 | | 1 | 1 | | 1 | | | | 7 | | |
| Barnstable | 90 | 13 | Phinney | Paul | 2 | | | 1 | | 1 | 2 | | 1 | | | | 7 | | |
| Falmouth | 47 | 200 | Phinney | Peter | | | 1 | 1 | | | | | | 1 | | | 3 | | |
| Falmouth | 47 | 203 | Phinney | Phillip | | | 1 | 1 | | 2 | | | 1 | 1 | | | 6 | | |
| Mashpee | 52 | 9 | Phinney | Prince | 1 | | 2 | | 1 | 2 | 1 | 2 | 2 | | | | 11 | | |
| Barnstable | 90 | 11 | Phinney | Solomon | 3 | 1 | | 1 | | 1 | 1 | | 1 | | | | 8 | | |
| Barnstable | 85 | 19 | Phinney | Timothy | | 2 | | 1 | | 1 | 1 | 1 | | 1 | | | 7 | | |
| Barnstable | 90 | 10 | Phinney | William | 1 | | 1 | | | 1 | 1 | 1 | | | | | 5 | | |
| Falmouth | 47 | 201 | Phinney | William | | | 1 | 1 | | | | 1 | | 1 | | | 4 | | |
| Chatham | 19 | 23 | Phips | Samuel | | | 1 | | | 2 | | 1 | 1 | | | | 5 | | |
| Truro | 63 | 2 | Pike | George | | | 1 | | | 2 | 1 | | 1 | | | | 5 | | |
| Truro | 63 | 15 | Pike | John Junr | 1 | | 1 | | 1 | 1 | | | | 1 | | | 5 | | |
| Falmouth | 47 | 192 | Pitcher | Abigail | | | | | | | | | | 1 | | | 1 | | |
| Falmouth | 48 | 248 | Pitts | Wm | 2 | | 2 | | | 1 | | | 1 | | | | 6 | | |
| Mashpee | 52 | 2 | Pollard | Stepney | | | | | | | | | | | 4 | | 4 | | |
| Sandwich | 39 | 12 | Pope | Elisha | | | 2 | 1 | 1 | | 1 | 1 | | 1 | | | 7 | | |
| Sandwich | 39 | 13 | Pope | John | 2 | 1 | | 1 | | 3 | 1 | | 1 | | | | 9 | | |
| Sandwich | 39 | 15 | Pope | Lemuel | | | 1 | | 1 | | | 2 | | 2 | | | 6 | | |
| Sandwich | 39 | 16 | Pope | Thos | 2 | | | 1 | | 1 | 1 | | | | | | 5 | | |
| Mashpee | 51 | 17 | Porter | Peter | | | | | | | | | | | 4 | | 4 | | |
| Mashpee | 51 | 20 | Portuges | Louis | | | | | | | | | | | 7 | | 7 | | |
| Harwich | 5 | 11 | Prayers | Samuel | 1 | | | 1 | | 2 | | | 1 | | | | 5 | | |
| Falmouth | 47 | 204 | Price | Lot | | 1 | 1 | | 1 | | 2 | 2 | 1 | | | | 8 | | |
| Falmouth | 47 | 193 | Price | Matthew | | 1 | | 1 | | 1 | 1 | | | | | | 4 | | |
| Falmouth | 47 | 198 | Price | Paul | 1 | 1 | | 1 | | 3 | 1 | 1 | | | | | 8 | | |
| Provincetown | 59 | 13 | Proutt | Reuben | | | 1 | | 1 | | 1 | | | 1 | | | 4 | | |
| Sandwich | 34 | 14 | Purrington | Daniel | 2 | | | 1 | | 1 | | | 1 | | | | 5 | | |
| Dennis | 29 | 32 | Rabens | Eli | | | 1 | | | | 1 | | 1 | | | | 3 | | |
| Dennis | 29 | 27 | Rabens | Henry | 2 | | | 1 | | 1 | 1 | 1 | 1 | | | | 7 | | |
| Harwich | 13 | 43 | Rabens | William Jun | 2 | 2 | | 1 | 1 | 1 | 1 | | 1 | | 1 | | 10 | | |
| Truro | 63 | 1 | Raimand | Francis | 1 | | | 1 | | 1 | 1 | 1 | 1 | | | | 6 | | |
| Barnstable | 93 | 6 | Ray | Sarah | | 1 | 1 | | | | 1 | | 2 | | | | 5 | | |
| Harwich | 4 | 30 | Ray* | Crisp | | 1 | | | | | 1 | | | | | | 2 | | |
| Sandwich | 41 | 25 | Raymond | Ebenezer | | | | 1 | | | 2 | | 1 | | | | 4 | | |
| Harwich | 6 | 22 | Read | Thomas | 1 | | | 1 | | 3 | | | 1 | | | | 6 | | |
| Provincetown | 59 | 23 | Reed | William B. | 2 | 1 | | 1 | | 1 | | | 1 | | | | 6 | | |
| Harwich | 3 | 2 | Remick | Freeman | | 2 | 1 | 2 | | 2 | 1 | 1 | 1 | | | | 10 | | |
| Orleans | 22 | 34 | Reubens | Thomas | 1 | | | 2 | | 2 | | | 2 | 2 | | | 9 | | |
| Falmouth | 47 | 205 | Rice | Tabitha | | | | | 1 | | | | 1 | 1 | | | 3 | | |
| Provincetown | 59 | 22 | Rich | David | | | | 1 | | 3 | | | 1 | | | | 5 | | |
| Truro | 68 | 25 | Rich | David | | | | | 1 | 1 | | 1 | | | | | 3 | | |
| Wellfleet | 73 | 25 | Rich | Elisha | 4 | 2 | 1 | | 1 | 1 | | | 2 | 1 | | | 12 | | |
| Truro | 62 | 16 | Rich | Ephraim | | 1 | 1 | | 1 | | | | 1 | 1 | | | 5 | | |
| Truro | 63 | 6 | Rich | Heman Smith | | | | 1 | | 1 | | | 1 | | | | 3 | | |
| Truro | 63 | 3 | Rich | Henry | 2 | | | 1 | | | 1 | | | | | | 4 | | |
| Wellfleet | 72 | 12 | Rich | Hezekiah | 1 | | | 1 | | 1 | | | 1 | | | | 4 | | |
| Wellfleet | 73 | 32 | Rich | Isaac | 3 | 2 | 1 | 1 | | 1 | 1 | | 1 | | | | 10 | | |
| Truro | 63 | 10 | Rich | Isaiah | 2 | | | 1 | | | | | 1 | | | | 4 | | |
| Truro | 63 | 19 | Rich | James | | 1 | | | 2 | | 1 | | | 2 | | | 6 | | |
| Truro | 68 | 26 | Rich | James Junr | | | 1 | | | | | 1 | 1 | | | | 3 | | |
| Truro | 64 | 14 | Rich | Jesse | | | 2 | | 1 | | | | 1 | 2 | | | 6 | | |
| Truro | 64 | 5 | Rich | Joanna Wid | | 1 | | | | | | 1 | | 2 | | | 4 | | |
| Truro | 63 | 27 | Rich | John | 1 | 1 | 3 | | 1 | | 1 | | | 1 | | | 8 | | |
| Truro | 63 | 31 | Rich | John 3d | 2 | 2 | | 1 | | 1 | | | 2 | | | | 8 | | |
| Truro | 63 | 14 | Rich | John Junr | 1 | 1 | | 1 | | | | 1 | 2 | | | | 6 | | |
| Truro | 63 | 32 | Rich | Jonathan | | | | 1 | | | 1 | | | 1 | | | 3 | | |
| Truro | 63 | 34 | Rich | Joseph | 1 | 1 | | 1 | | 2 | 1 | | 1 | | | | 7 | | |
| Truro | 64 | 1 | Rich | Joshua | 1 | | 1 | | 1 | 2 | 1 | 1 | | 1 | | | 8 | | |
| Wellfleet | 74 | 2 | Rich | Josiah | 1 | | 2 | | 1 | | | | 1 | 2 | | | 7 | | |
| Truro | 64 | 13 | Rich | Lucy Wid | | | 1 | | | | | | 1 | 1 | | | 3 | | |
| Truro | 68 | 24 | Rich | Mulford | 1 | | | 1 | | | | | 1 | | | | 3 | | |
| Truro | 64 | 19 | Rich | Nathaniel | 1 | 1 | 1 | | 1 | 2 | 2 | | 1 | 1 | | | 10 | | |
| Truro | 68 | 13 | Rich | Obadiah | 1 | | 1 | | | | | | 1 | | | | 3 | | |
| Truro | 64 | 21 | Rich | Obadiah Junr | 1 | | 1 | | | | | 1 | 1 | 1 | | | 5 | | |
| Truro | 68 | 8 | Rich | Polly | | | | | | 1 | | 1 | | | | | 2 | | |
| Truro | 64 | 29 | Rich | Rebeccah Wid | | 2 | | | | | | | | 1 | | | 3 | | |
| Wellfleet | 74 | 12 | Rich | Reuben | | | | | 1 | | | 1 | | | | | 2 | | |
| Truro | 64 | 32 | Rich | Richard | 1 | | 1 | 2 | | 1 | | 1 | 2 | 1 | | | 9 | | |
| Truro | 64 | 30 | Rich | Richard 3d | | | | 1 | | | | 1 | | 1 | | | 5 | | |
| Truro | 69 | 3 | Rich | Richard Junr | | 2 | 1 | | | 1 | 1 | | | | | | 7 | | |

93

# 1800 Barnstable County, Massachusetts Index

| TOWN | PG# | LN# | LAST NAME | FIRST NAME | FWM u10 | FWM 10-16 | FWM 16-26 | FWM 26-45 | FWM 45+ | FWF u10 | FWF 10-16 | FWF 16-26 | FWF 26-45 | FWF 45+ | TOTAL ALL OTHER | TOTAL SLAVES | TOTALS | DISTRICT/TOWNSHIP | NOTES |
|---|---|---|---|---|---|---|---|---|---|---|---|---|---|---|---|---|---|---|---|
| Truro | 64 | 31 | Rich | Richard S. | 2 | | | 1 | | | | | 1 | | | | 4 | | |
| Wellfleet | 72 | 11 | Rich | Robert | 2 | | | 1 | | 2 | | | 1 | | | | 6 | | |
| Truro | 65 | 8 | Rich | Silvanus | 2 | | | 1 | | | | | 1 | | | | 4 | | |
| Truro | 65 | 19 | Rich | Thatcher | 2 | | | 1 | | | | 1 | | | | | 4 | | |
| Truro | 65 | 17 | Rich | Thomas | 1 | | | 1 | | 2 | | | 1 | | | | 5 | | |
| Truro | 66 | 14 | Rich | Uriah | | | | 1 | | | | | | 1 | | | 2 | | |
| Barnstable | 90 | 37 | Richardson | John | | | | 1 | | | | 1 | | | | | 2 | | |
| Wellfleet | 72 | 13 | Rider | Abigail | | | | | | | 1 | | | 1 | | | 2 | | |
| Provincetown | 59 | 18 | Rider | David | 4 | | 1 | 1 | | | | 1 | | 1 | | | 8 | | |
| Harwich | 3 | 7 | Rider | Ebenezer | | | 1 | | | 1 | | 1 | | | | | 3 | | |
| Provincetown | 59 | 19 | Rider | Ebenezer | | | | 1 | | | | | | 2 | | | 3 | | |
| Provincetown | 59 | 20 | Rider | Ebenezer Jun | 4 | | | 1 | | | | | 1 | | | | 6 | | |
| Yarmouth | 95 | 10 | Rider | Edward | | | 1 | | | | | | 1 | | | | 2 | | |
| Yarmouth | 95 | 22 | Rider | Edward Jr | 2 | 2 | | 1 | | 2 | 1 | | 1 | | | | 9 | | |
| Yarmouth | 95 | 44 | Rider | Elizabeth | | | | | | | | | | 2 | | | 2 | | |
| Chatham | 18 | 23 | Rider | Harding | | 1 | 1 | | 1 | | | 1 | | 1 | | | 5 | | |
| Chatham | 21 | 1 | Rider | Harding | | 1 | 1 | | 1 | | | 1 | 1 | | | | 5 | | |
| Provincetown | 60 | 25 | Rider | Isaiah | | 1 | | | | | | 1 | | | | | 2 | | |
| Chatham | 18 | 28 | Rider | James | | | | 1 | | 2 | | 1 | | | | | 4 | | |
| Chatham | 20 | 34 | Rider | James | | | | 1 | | 3 | | 1 | | | | | 5 | | |
| Chatham | 19 | 37 | Rider | John | 2 | | | 1 | | 3 | | | 1 | | | | 7 | | |
| Yarmouth | 96 | 47 | Rider | John | 1 | | | 1 | 1 | | | | 1 | 1 | | | 5 | | |
| Chatham | 18 | 18 | Rider | Joseph | 1 | 1 | 2 | | 1 | | | 2 | | 1 | | | 8 | | |
| Provincetown | 61 | 16 | Rider | Joseph | | | 1 | | | | | | 1 | | | | 2 | | |
| Provincetown | 61 | 3 | Rider | Joshua | | 1 | 1 | | 1 | | | | 1 | | | | 4 | | |
| Chatham | 18 | 21 | Rider | Josiah | | 1 | 1 | | 1 | 1 | 2 | | 1 | | | | 7 | | |
| Chatham | 18 | 25 | Rider | Kimbal | | 1 | 1 | | 1 | | | 2 | | 1 | | | 6 | | |
| Wellfleet | 72 | 14 | Rider | Matthias | | 1 | 1 | | 1 | 1 | 2 | | 1 | | | | 7 | | |
| Wellfleet | 72 | 15 | Rider | Matthias Junr | 2 | | 1 | | | 2 | | | 3 | | | | 8 | | |
| Chatham | 18 | 20 | Rider | Moses | 1 | | | 1 | | | 1 | | 1 | | | | 4 | | |
| Harwich | 11 | 13 | Rider | Nathaniel | | 1 | | | | 1 | | 1 | | | | | 3 | | |
| Harwich | 14 | 21 | Rider | Paul | 1 | 1 | | | | | | 1 | | | | | 3 | | |
| Chatham | 18 | 24 | Rider | Reuben | 3 | 1 | | | 1 | 1 | 1 | 2 | 1 | | | | 10 | | |
| Yarmouth | 96 | 46 | Rider | Reuben | 3 | | | 1 | | 1 | 1 | | 1 | | | | 7 | | |
| Yarmouth | 95 | 45 | Rider | Rowland | | | 1 | | | | | | | 1 | | | 3 | | |
| Truro | 64 | 7 | Rider | Sally Wid | | | | | | | | 1 | | | | | 1 | | |
| Truro | 65 | 3 | Rider | Samuel | | | 1 | | 1 | 2 | | 2 | | 1 | | | 7 | | |
| Wellfleet | 74 | 32 | Rider | Samuel | 1 | | | 1 | | | | | 1 | | | | 3 | | |
| Wellfleet | 74 | 31 | Rider | Seth | | | | 1 | | | | | 1 | 1 | | | 3 | | |
| Wellfleet | 75 | 10 | Rider | Silas | 3 | 1 | | 1 | | | | | | 1 | | | 6 | | |
| Chatham | 18 | 26 | Rider | Simeon | 2 | | 2 | 1 | | 2 | | | 1 | 1 | | | 9 | | |
| Chatham | 18 | 22 | Rider | Stephen | 3 | | | 1 | | 1 | | | 1 | | | | 6 | | |
| Yarmouth | 95 | 47 | Rider | Tempe | | | | | | | | 1 | | 1 | | | 2 | | |
| Chatham | 20 | 24 | Rider | Thacher | 1 | | | 1 | | 2 | | 1 | | | | | 5 | | |
| Chatham | 18 | 19 | Rider | Thacker | 1 | | | 1 | | 2 | | | | 1 | 1 | | 6 | | |
| Yarmouth | 96 | 48 | Rider | Thankful | | | | | | | | 1 | 1 | | | | 2 | | |
| Provincetown | 59 | 21 | Rider | Thomas | | 1 | 2 | 1 | | | | | 1 | | | | 5 | | |
| Chatham | 20 | 9 | Rider | William | | 1 | | | | | | 1 | 1 | | | | 3 | | |
| Dennis | 29 | 7 | Rider | William | 1 | 1 | 2 | | 1 | | | | | 1 | | | 6 | | |
| Harwich | 10 | 20 | Rider | William | | 1 | | | | 1 | | 1 | | | | | 3 | | |
| Chatham | 18 | 27 | Rider | Zenus | | | 1 | | 1 | | | 1 | | | | | 3 | | |
| Chatham | 20 | 36 | Rider | Zenus | | | 1 | | 1 | | | 1 | | | | | 3 | | |
| Truro | 66 | 15 | Ridley | John | 1 | | | 1 | | | | | 1 | | | | 3 | | |
| Provincetown | 59 | 24 | Ridly | Nathaniel | 1 | | | 1 | | 1 | | | 1 | 1 | | | 5 | | |
| Provincetown | 59 | 25 | Ridly | Thomas | 1 | | | 1 | | | | | 1 | | | | 3 | | |
| Harwich | 7 | 17 | Ripley | Nathaniel | | | 1 | | 1 | 1 | | | | | | | 3 | | |
| Barnstable | 93 | 31 | Ritcher | Jonathan | | 2 | 3 | 1 | 1 | 1 | | 1 | | 1 | | | 10 | | |
| Barnstable | 101 | 8 | Robbins | James | | 2 | | 1 | | 1 | 1 | | | 1 | | | 6 | | |
| Falmouth | 48 | 219 | Robinson | Bartlett | | | 1 | | | | 1 | | 1 | | | | 3 | | |
| Falmouth | 47 | 208 | Robinson | Charles | 1 | | 1 | 1 | | | 2 | | 1 | | | | 6 | | |
| Falmouth | 47 | 210 | Robinson | Cornelius | 2 | | | 1 | 2 | | | | 1 | | | | 6 | | |
| Falmouth | 48 | 218 | Robinson | Ezekiel | 4 | | | 1 | 1 | | | | 1 | 1 | | | 8 | | |
| Falmouth | 48 | 215 | Robinson | Isaac | 2 | 2 | | 1 | 1 | 1 | 2 | | 1 | 1 | | | 11 | | |
| Dennis | 29 | 31 | Robinson | James | 1 | | | 1 | | 1 | | 1 | | | | | 4 | | |
| Falmouth | 48 | 214 | Robinson | James | 2 | 1 | | 1 | | 2 | | | 1 | | | | 7 | | |
| Falmouth | 48 | 217 | Robinson | Joseph | | | 1 | | | 1 | | 1 | | | | | 3 | | |
| Falmouth | 47 | 207 | Robinson | Love | | | | | | | | | 1 | | | | 1 | | |
| Falmouth | 48 | 221 | Robinson | Seth | 3 | | | 1 | | | | | 1 | | | | 5 | | |
| Falmouth | 48 | 220 | Robinson | Stephen | | | | 1 | | 1 | | | 1 | | | | 3 | | |
| Falmouth | 47 | 209 | Robinson | Wally | 2 | 1 | | 1 | | | | 1 | 1 | | | | 6 | | |
| Falmouth | 48 | 216 | Robinson | Zenas | 1 | | | 1 | | | | | | 1 | | | 3 | | |
| Falmouth | 48 | 213 | Robinson | Zephariah | 3 | 1 | | | 1 | 1 | 1 | | 1 | | | | 8 | | |
| Orleans | 22 | 31 | Rogers | Asa | | 1 | | | | | 1 | | | | | | 2 | | |
| Harwich | 8 | 38 | Rogers | Caleb | 1 | 1 | 1 | 1 | 1 | 1 | | | | 1 | | | 7 | | |
| Harwich | 14 | 30 | Rogers | Dinah Wd | 3 | | | | | | 1 | 1 | 1 | | | | 6 | | |
| Harwich | 15 | 6 | Rogers | Elisha | | 2 | | 1 | | 3 | 1 | 1 | | | | | 8 | | |
| Orleans | 23 | 15 | Rogers | Elizabeth Wid | | | | | | | 1 | | 2 | 1 | | | 4 | | |
| Harwich | 9 | 14 | Rogers | Emos | 1 | | | 1 | | 2 | | | 1 | | | | 5 | | |
| Orleans | 22 | 43 | Rogers | Gideon | | | | 1 | 1 | 1 | | | 1 | 2 | | | 6 | | |
| Sandwich | 41 | 44 | Rogers | Henry | | 2 | 1 | 1 | | | | | 3 | 1 | | | 8 | | |
| Orleans | 23 | 26 | Rogers | Hesekiah | 3 | 1 | 1 | | 1 | 2 | 1 | | 1 | | | | 10 | | |
| Orleans | 22 | 25 | Rogers | Hezekiah | 3 | 1 | 1 | | 1 | 2 | 1 | | | 1 | | | 10 | | |
| Sandwich | 40 | 40 | Rogers | Isaiah | 2 | | 1 | | | | | | 1 | | | | 4 | | |
| Orleans | 23 | 27 | Rogers | James | | | | 1 | | | | | 1 | | | | 2 | | |

94

# 1800 Barnstable County, Massachusetts Index

| TOWN | PG# | LN# | LAST NAME | FIRST NAME | FREE WHITE MALES | | | | | FREE WHITE FEMALES | | | | | TOTAL ALL OTHER | TOTAL SLAVES | TOTALS | DISTRICT/ TOWNSHIP | NOTES |
|---|---|---|---|---|---|---|---|---|---|---|---|---|---|---|---|---|---|---|---|
| | | | | | under 10 | 10 to 16 | 16 to 26 | 26 to 45 | 45 and over | under 10 | 10 to 16 | 16 to 26 | 26 to 45 | 45 and over | | | | | |
| Orleans | 23 | 28 | Rogers | James Jun | | | 1 | | | 1 | | 1 | | | | | 3 | | |
| Orleans | 23 | 18 | Rogers | Jonathan | | 1 | 2 | | 1 | 1 | | | 1 | 1 | | | 7 | | |
| Orleans | 22 | 10 | Rogers | Joshua | | | 1 | | | | | | 1 | | | | 2 | | |
| Orleans | 23 | 45 | Rogers | Joshua | | | 1 | | | | | | 1 | | | | 2 | | |
| Orleans | 23 | 14 | Rogers | Joshua Junr | 3 | | 1 | | | | | | 1 | | | | 5 | | |
| Orleans | 21 | 24 | Rogers | Josiah | | 1 | 4 | | 1 | | | | 1 | 1 | | | 8 | | |
| Orleans | 23 | 6 | Rogers | Josiah | | 1 | 2 | | 1 | | | | 1 | 1 | | | 6 | | |
| Orleans | 22 | 26 | Rogers | Judah | 3 | 2 | 1 | | 1 | | 1 | 2 | 1 | 1 | | | 12 | | |
| Orleans | 22 | 8 | Rogers | Prince | | | 3 | | 1 | | | 2 | | 1 | | | 7 | | |
| Orleans | 23 | 44 | Rogers | Prince | | 1 | 2 | | 1 | 1 | 1 | 2 | | 1 | | | 9 | | |
| Harwich | 9 | 15 | Rogers | Reuben | | | | 1 | | | | | 1 | | | | 2 | | |
| Harwich | 14 | 19 | Rogers | Richard | 2 | | | 1 | | | | | 1 | | | | 4 | | |
| Orleans | 24 | 5 | Rogers | Richard | 1 | | | 1 | | 2 | 1 | 1 | 1 | | | | 7 | | |
| Orleans | 23 | 20 | Rogers | Ruth Wld | | | 1 | | | | | | | 1 | | | 2 | | |
| Orleans | 22 | 3 | Rogers | Samuel | 1 | 1 | | | 1 | | | | | 1 | | | 4 | | |
| Dennis | 29 | 39 | Rogers | Smith | 2 | 1 | 1 | | 1 | 2 | | 1 | | 1 | | | 9 | | |
| Harwich | 13 | 38 | Rogers | Smith | 1 | 1 | | | | | | | 1 | | | | 3 | | |
| Dennis | 29 | 40 | Rogers | Smith Jun | 1 | | | 1 | | | | | 1 | | | | 3 | | |
| Yarmouth | 98 | 19 | Rogers | Solomon | 1 | | 1 | | | | | | 1 | | | | 3 | | |
| Harwich | 14 | 44 | Rogers | Thomas | | | 1 | | | 1 | | | 1 | | | | 3 | | |
| Orleans | 24 | 37 | Rogers | Thomas | 1 | 1 | | | 1 | 1 | | | | | | | 4 | | |
| Orleans | 21 | 23 | Rogers | Zenus | 2 | | 1 | | | 1 | | | 1 | 1 | | | 6 | | |
| Orleans | 23 | 7 | Rogers | Zenus | 1 | | | 1 | | 1 | | | 1 | | | | 4 | | |
| Falmouth | 47 | 212 | Rowley | Benjm | | | | 1 | | 1 | 1 | | | | | | 3 | | |
| Falmouth | 47 | 211 | Rowley | Mathew | | | | | 1 | | | | 1 | 1 | | | 3 | | |
| Barnstable | 88 | 25 | Russell | Jonathan | 1 | | | 1 | | 4 | 1 | | 1 | | | | 8 | | |
| Wellfleet | 75 | 25 | S*y | Reuben Junr | | | 1 | | | | | 1 | | | | | 2 | | |
| Barnstable | 89 | 4 | Samson | Josiah | | 2 | 1 | 1 | 1 | 1 | | 1 | 2 | 1 | | | 10 | | |
| Barnstable | 85 | 14 | Samson | William | | | | 1 | | 1 | | | 1 | | | | 3 | | |
| Falmouth | 48 | 231 | Samuel | Shiverick | 2 | 1 | 1 | 1 | | 1 | 1 | | 1 | | | | 8 | | |
| Barnstable | 93 | 28 | Sands | William | 1 | | | | 1 | 3 | | 1 | 2 | | | | 8 | | |
| Falmouth | 48 | 222 | Sanford | Benja | | 1 | | | 1 | | | 1 | 3 | 2 | | | 8 | | |
| Falmouth | 48 | 238 | Sanford | Wm | 4 | | 3 | | 1 | 1 | | 2 | 3 | 1 | | | 15 | | |
| Truro | 67 | 26 | Savage | Dinah | | | | | | | | | | 1 | | | 1 | | |
| Barnstable | 84 | 40 | Savage | John | | | | 1 | | | | | | | | | 1 | | |
| Provincetown | 59 | 31 | Savage | John | 2 | | | 1 | | 1 | | | 1 | | | | 5 | | |
| Barnstable | 86 | 14 | Savage | Saml Esq | | 2 | | | 1 | 1 | | | 1 | | | | 5 | | |
| Barnstable | 93 | 11 | Scudder | David | 3 | 1 | | 1 | | 2 | | | 1 | 1 | 1 | | 10 | | |
| Barnstable | 93 | 13 | Scudder | Eleazer | | | | | 1 | | | | 1 | 1 | 1 | | 4 | | |
| Barnstable | 93 | 15 | Scudder | Eleazer Jr | 1 | | | 1 | | 1 | | | 1 | | | | 4 | | |
| Barnstable | 93 | 26 | Scudder | Lot | 2 | | | 1 | | | | | 1 | | | | 4 | | |
| Barnstable | 93 | 27 | Scudder | Samuel | | | | 1 | 1 | | | | | 1 | | | 3 | | |
| Barnstable | 85 | 32 | Scudder | Sarah | | | | | | | | | 1 | 1 | | | 2 | | |
| Barnstable | 93 | 14 | Scudder | William | 2 | | | 1 | | 1 | | | 1 | | 1 | | 6 | | |
| Orleans | 24 | 39 | Seaburry | Joseph | 4 | 2 | 1 | 1 | | 2 | 1 | | 1 | | | | 12 | | |
| Harwich | 8 | 13 | Seaburry | Thomas | 3 | | | 1 | | 3 | | 2 | | | | | 9 | | |
| Dennis | 27 | 2 | Seabury | David | | 1 | | 1 | | 2 | 1 | 1 | 1 | | | | 7 | | |
| Dennis | 26 | 19 | Sears | Christopher | 1 | 1 | | 1 | | 3 | | | 1 | 1 | | | 7 | | |
| Harwich | 3 | 5 | Sears | Desire Wid | | | | | | | | | 1 | 1 | | | 2 | | |
| Yarmouth | 97 | 19 | Sears | Ebenezer | 2 | 1 | | | 1 | 2 | | | 1 | | | | 7 | | |
| Dennis | 26 | 10 | Sears | Edmond | 1 | | 1 | | 1 | 2 | 1 | 2 | | 1 | | | 9 | | |
| Harwich | 3 | 1 | Sears | Edward | 2 | 1 | | | 1 | 2 | | | 1 | | | | 7 | | |
| Yarmouth | 98 | 31 | Sears | Edward | 1 | | 1 | | | | | | 1 | | | | 3 | | |
| Dennis | 26 | 5 | Sears | Ekkanah | 2 | | | 1 | | 3 | 1 | | 1 | | | | 8 | | |
| Yarmouth | 98 | 33 | Sears | Eleazer | | | | 1 | | 1 | | | | 1 | | | 3 | | |
| Yarmouth | 98 | 25 | Sears | Eleazer Jr | | 1 | | 2 | 1 | 1 | 1 | | 1 | 2 | | | 9 | | |
| Dennis | 26 | 1 | Sears | Elisha | 1 | | | 1 | | 1 | 1 | | 1 | | | | 5 | | |
| Yarmouth | 98 | 22 | Sears | Eliza | | | | | | | | 1 | 1 | 1 | | | 3 | | |
| Yarmouth | 98 | 23 | Sears | Enoch | | | 1 | | | | | 1 | | | | | 2 | | |
| Dennis | 26 | 6 | Sears | Hannah Wid | | | | | | | | | 1 | 1 | | | 2 | | |
| Dennis | 26 | 15 | Sears | Isaac | | 2 | | 1 | | | 1 | | 1 | | | | 5 | | |
| Dennis | 26 | 11 | Sears | Jacob | 1 | | | 1 | | | | | 1 | | | | 3 | | |
| Yarmouth | 98 | 27 | Sears | James | 1 | | | 1 | | 1 | | | 1 | | | | 4 | | |
| Dennis | 26 | 2 | Sears | John | | | | | 1 | | | | | | | | 1 | | |
| Dennis | 26 | 9 | Sears | John Jun | | 1 | 2 | | 1 | 1 | | | 3 | 1 | | | 9 | | |
| Dennis | 26 | 4 | Sears | Joseph | 2 | 2 | 1 | 1 | | 1 | 1 | | 1 | | | | 9 | | |
| Harwich | 3 | 3 | Sears | Joseph | 1 | 1 | | 1 | 1 | 2 | 1 | 1 | | | | | 8 | | |
| Yarmouth | 98 | 26 | Sears | Joseph | 1 | | 1 | | | | | 1 | | | | | 4 | | |
| Dennis | 26 | 7 | Sears | Joshua | 1 | 2 | 1 | | 1 | 3 | | | 1 | 1 | | | 10 | | |
| Dennis | 26 | 12 | Sears | Judah | | | | 1 | | 1 | | | 1 | | | | 3 | | |
| Dennis | 26 | 16 | Sears | Leonard | 2 | 1 | | 1 | | 3 | | | 1 | | | | 8 | | |
| Harwich | 5 | 2 | Sears | Levi | 1 | | | 1 | | | | | 1 | | | | 3 | | |
| Yarmouth | 98 | 30 | Sears | Lewis | 2 | | | 1 | | 1 | | | 1 | | | | 5 | | |
| Dennis | 26 | 8 | Sears | Micajah | 1 | | 1 | | 1 | | | | 1 | 1 | | | 5 | | |
| Dennis | 26 | 13 | Sears | Nathaniel | | | | 1 | | | | | | 1 | | | 2 | | |
| Dennis | 26 | 14 | Sears | Nathaniel Jun | 2 | 1 | 1 | 1 | | 1 | 1 | | 1 | | | | 8 | | |
| Harwich | 3 | 6 | Sears | Noah | | | | 1 | | | | | 1 | | | | 2 | | |
| Harwich | 3 | 4 | Sears | Prince | | | | 1 | | | | | | 1 | | | 2 | | |
| Yarmouth | 98 | 24 | Sears | Prince | 1 | | | 1 | | | 1 | | 1 | | | | 4 | | |
| Harwich | 5 | | Sears | Reuben | 3 | 2 | | | 1 | 2 | 1 | | 2 | | | | 11 | | |
| Chatham | 18 | 30 | Sears | Richard | 1 | 1 | 2 | 1 | 1 | 2 | 1 | 1 | 1 | | | | 11 | | |

# 1800 Barnstable County, Massachusetts Index

| TOWN | PG# | LN# | LAST NAME | FIRST NAME | FREE WHITE MALES | | | | | FREE WHITE FEMALES | | | | | TOTAL ALL OTHER | TOTAL SLAVES | TOTALS | DISTRICT/ TOWNSHIP | NOTES |
|---|---|---|---|---|---|---|---|---|---|---|---|---|---|---|---|---|---|---|---|
| | | | | | under 10 | 10 to 16 | 16 to 26 | 26 to 45 | 45 and over | under 10 | 10 to 16 | 16 to 26 | 26 to 45 | 45 and over | | | | | |
| Dennis | 26 | 3 | Sears | Seth | 1 | | | 1 | | 3 | | | 2 | 1 | | | 8 | | |
| Dennis | 26 | 17 | Sears | Stephen | | | | 1 | 1 | 1 | | | 1 | | | | 3 | | |
| Harwich | 5 | 1 | Sears | Stephen | | | 2 | 1 | | | | 1 | | | | | 4 | | |
| Dennis | 26 | 18 | Sears | Stephen Jun | 3 | 1 | 1 | 1 | | | 1 | 2 | 1 | | | | 10 | | |
| Harwich | 4 | 38 | Sears | Stephen Jun | 1 | | | 1 | | 1 | | | 1 | | | | 4 | | |
| Harwich | 6 | 20 | Sears | Willard | 1 | | | 1 | | 3 | 2 | | 1 | | | | 8 | | |
| Yarmouth | 100 | 3 | Sears | Winthrop | | 1 | | | | | | 1 | | | | | 2 | | |
| Truro | 67 | 24 | Selew | John | | 2 | | 1 | | | 1 | 1 | | 1 | | | 6 | | |
| Chatham | 19 | 17 | Share | James | | | 1 | | | 2 | | | 1 | | | | 4 | | |
| Eastham | 79 | 21 | Shaw | Philander Revd | | | 1 | | | | | 1 | | | | | 2 | | |
| Barnstable | 87 | 23 | Shaw | Rev Oakes | | 1 | | 1 | | | | 1 | | 1 | 6 | | 10 | | |
| Barnstable | 93 | 19 | Shaw | Samuel | 1 | | | 1 | | 1 | | | 1 | | | | 4 | | |
| Dennis | 28 | 42 | Shearman | Abraham | 1 | | 2 | | | | | | 1 | | | | 4 | | |
| Yarmouth | 99 | 18 | Shearman | Ichabod | | | 1 | | | | | 1 | | | | | 2 | | |
| Falmouth | 48 | 233 | Sherman | Wm | 1 | 1 | | 1 | | 1 | 1 | 1 | 1 | 1 | | | 8 | | |
| Falmouth | 48 | 223 | Shiverick | David | | 1 | 1 | | 1 | | | 1 | 2 | | | | 6 | | |
| Falmouth | 49 | 250 | Shiverick | David | | 1 | | 1 | 1 | | | | 3 | | | | 6 | | |
| Falmouth | 48 | 232 | Shiverick | Joseph | | 1 | | 1 | | | | 2 | | 1 | | | 5 | | |
| Barnstable | 94 | 36 | Shiverick | Thomas | 2 | 2 | 2 | 1 | | | 1 | 2 | | 1 | | | 11 | | |
| Falmouth | 49 | 251 | Shiverick | Thos | | | 1 | | | 3 | 1 | | 1 | 1 | | | 7 | | |
| Barnstable | 93 | 7 | Simmons | Silvanus | 3 | 1 | | 1 | | 1 | | | 1 | | | | 7 | | |
| Sandwich | 39 | 25 | Simons | Jonathan | | 1 | 1 | | | 1 | 1 | | 1 | | | | 5 | | |
| Provincetown | 60 | 1 | Smaley | Samuel | 1 | | 1 | | | 1 | | 1 | | | | | 4 | | |
| Truro | 67 | 18 | Small | Alexander | 1 | | 2 | 1 | | 2 | | | 1 | 1 | | | 8 | | |
| Harwich | 9 | 31 | Small | Benjamin | | | | 1 | | | 1 | | | 1 | | | 3 | | |
| Falmouth | 49 | 311 | Small | Benoni | | 1 | | | | | | 1 | | | | | 2 | | |
| Harwich | 12 | 39 | Small | Bethiah Wd | | 3 | | | | | | | 1 | | | | 4 | | |
| Harwich | 10 | 35 | Small | Daniel | 3 | 1 | | 1 | | 2 | 1 | | 1 | | | | 9 | | |
| Harwich | 10 | 3 | Small | Edward | | 1 | | 1 | | | | 1 | | 1 | | | 4 | | |
| Harwich | 10 | 11 | Small | Edward Jun | 2 | | 1 | | | 4 | | | 1 | | | | 8 | | |
| Harwich | 9 | 22 | Small | Eli | 3 | | 1 | | | 1 | 1 | | 1 | | | | 7 | | |
| Truro | 67 | 21 | Small | Francis | 1 | 2 | | 1 | | 3 | | | 1 | | | | 8 | | |
| Truro | 66 | 18 | Small | Hix | | 1 | | 1 | | | | | | 1 | | | 3 | | |
| Harwich | 10 | 13 | Small | Isaac | 2 | | 1 | | | | | | 1 | | | | 4 | | |
| Truro | 67 | 20 | Small | Isaac | 1 | 2 | | 1 | 1 | | | | 2 | | | | 7 | | |
| Falmouth | 49 | 296 | Small | James | 1 | | 1 | | | | | 1 | | | | | 3 | | |
| Harwich | 14 | 29 | Small | James | 1 | | 1 | 1 | | 4 | 2 | | 1 | | | | 10 | | |
| Truro | 66 | 19 | Small | Jesse | | | 1 | | | 2 | | | 1 | | | | 4 | | |
| Truro | 66 | 17 | Small | John | | 1 | | 1 | | | | | | 1 | | | 3 | | |
| Falmouth | 49 | 304 | Small | John Junr | | 1 | | | | | | 1 | | | | | 2 | | |
| Harwich | 10 | 42 | Small | Jonah | 1 | | 1 | | | | | | 1 | | | | 3 | | |
| Harwich | 10 | 37 | Small | Jonathan | | | 2 | 1 | | | | | 1 | | | | 4 | | |
| Truro | 63 | 25 | Small | Joseph | | 1 | 3 | 1 | | 2 | 1 | | 1 | | | | 9 | | |
| Falmouth | 49 | 299 | Small | Joseph Junr | | 1 | | 2 | | | | 1 | | | | | 4 | | |
| Harwich | 10 | 36 | Small | Olive Wd | 1 | | | | | 1 | 1 | | | | | | 3 | | |
| Harwich | 10 | 4 | Small | Reuben | | 1 | | | | 2 | | | 1 | | | | 4 | | |
| Harwich | 10 | 14 | Small | Samuel | 1 | 1 | | | | | | | 1 | | | | 3 | | |
| Truro | 67 | 25 | Small | Samuel | 2 | 1 | | 1 | | 3 | 2 | | 1 | | | | 10 | | |
| Harwich | 6 | 30 | Small | Thomas | 2 | | 1 | | | 3 | | | 1 | | | | 7 | | |
| Harwich | 10 | 18 | Small | William | 2 | 2 | 1 | 1 | | 2 | | 1 | 1 | | | | 10 | | |
| Harwich | 9 | 23 | Small | Zebadee | 1 | | | 1 | | 2 | | | 1 | | | | 5 | | |
| Falmouth | 48 | 249 | Small | John | 1 | 1 | 1 | 1 | | | 2 | 1 | 1 | | | | 8 | | |
| Provincetown | 59 | 29 | Smalley | Daniel | 1 | 1 | | 1 | | 3 | | | 1 | | | | 7 | | |
| Falmouth | 49 | 267 | Smalley | John | | 2 | 1 | | | 1 | | 1 | | 1 | | | 7 | | |
| Falmouth | 48 | 230 | Smalley | Joseph | | | 1 | | | | 1 | 1 | | 1 | | | 4 | | |
| Provincetown | 59 | 26 | Smalley | Thomas | 1 | 1 | 1 | 1 | | 3 | | 1 | | | | | 8 | | |
| Provincetown | 59 | 36 | Smally | Abraham | 2 | | 1 | | | 2 | | | 1 | | | | 6 | | |
| Provincetown | 59 | 32 | Smaly | Talor | 2 | 1 | | 1 | | 1 | | | 1 | | | | 6 | | |
| Harwich | 13 | 4 | Smith | Allen | | 1 | | | | | | 1 | | | | | 2 | | |
| Chatham | 19 | 11 | Smith | Araph | | 1 | | | | | | 2 | 1 | | | | 4 | | |
| Chatham | 19 | 32 | Smith | Asaph | | 1 | | | | | | 2 | 1 | | | | 4 | | |
| Wellfleet | 72 | 24 | Smith | Azariah | | 1 | | | | | 1 | | | 1 | | | 3 | | |
| Truro | 67 | 17 | Smith | Barzilla | 1 | 1 | | 1 | | 1 | 1 | 1 | | 2 | | | 8 | | |
| Eastham | 78 | 32 | Smith | Bathsheba | | | | | | | | | 2 | | | | 2 | | |
| Barnstable | 87 | 27 | Smith | Benjamin | 1 | | | 1 | | | | 1 | 1 | | | | 4 | | |
| Chatham | 18 | 45 | Smith | Benjm | 2 | | 1 | | | | | | 1 | | | | 4 | | |
| Barnstable | 88 | 43 | Smith | Benjmain | | 2 | | 1 | | | | 2 | | 1 | | | 6 | | |
| Provincetown | 60 | 4 | Smith | Daniel | 2 | 1 | | 1 | 1 | | | | 1 | | | | 6 | | |
| Wellfleet | 75 | 23 | Smith | David | 1 | | 1 | | | | | | 1 | | | | 3 | | |
| Chatham | 18 | 31 | Smith | Dean | | | 1 | | 3 | | 1 | | | | | | 5 | | |
| Sandwich | 36 | 12 | Smith | Deborah | | | | | | | | | 1 | | | | 1 | | |
| Barnstable | 86 | 37 | Smith | Desire | | | | | | | | | 1 | | | | 1 | | |
| Provincetown | 59 | 35 | Smith | Edmund | 2 | 1 | | 1 | | 2 | | 1 | | | | | 7 | | |
| Wellfleet | 72 | 29 | Smith | Edward | | 1 | | 1 | | | 2 | | 1 | | | | 5 | | |
| Barnstable | 86 | 42 | Smith | Elijah | 1 | | 1 | 1 | | | | 1 | 1 | | | | 5 | | |
| Orleans | 25 | 28 | Smith | Elisha | 1 | | 1 | | | | | | 1 | 1 | | | 4 | | |
| Eastham | 78 | 25 | Smith | Elkanah | | 1 | | 1 | | | 2 | 1 | 1 | | | | 6 | | |
| Provincetown | 59 | 39 | Smith | Enoch | 3 | 1 | | 1 | | | | 1 | 1 | | | | 7 | | |
| Provincetown | 59 | 33 | Smith | Enos | 2 | | | 1 | | 2 | | 1 | | | | | 6 | | |
| Wellfleet | 72 | 30 | Smith | George | | 2 | | 1 | 1 | | 3 | | 1 | | | | 8 | | |
| Chatham | 18 | 38 | Smith | Gorge | | | 1 | | | | | | 1 | | | | 2 | | |
| Chatham | 18 | 39 | Smith | Gorge Jun | 2 | 2 | | 1 | | 3 | 2 | | 1 | | | | 11 | | |
| Barnstable | 92 | 29 | Smith | Hannah | | | | | | | | | 1 | 1 | | | 2 | | |
| Eastham | 79 | 27 | Smith | Heman | | 1 | | | | | | 1 | | | | | 2 | | |

# 1800 Barnstable County, Massachusetts Index

| TOWN | PG# | LN# | LAST NAME | FIRST NAME | FREE WHITE MALES under 10 | 10 to 16 | 16 to 26 | 26 to 45 | 45 and over | FREE WHITE FEMALES under 10 | 10 to 16 | 16 to 26 | 26 to 45 | 45 and over | TOTAL ALL OTHER | TOTAL SLAVES | TOTALS | DISTRICT/ TOWNSHIP | NOTES |
|---|---|---|---|---|---|---|---|---|---|---|---|---|---|---|---|---|---|---|---|
| Eastham | 78 | 22 | Smith | Herman Junr | | | 1 | | | 1 | | | 1 | | | | 3 | | |
| Eastham | 78 | 26 | Smith | Isaac | | | | 1 | | | | 1 | | 1 | | | 3 | | |
| Harwich | 11 | 8 | Smith | Isaac | 4 | | 1 | | | 1 | 2 | | 1 | | | | 9 | | |
| Orleans | 21 | 10 | Smith | Isaac | | | | 1 | | | | 1 | | 1 | | | 3 | | |
| Wellfleet | 72 | 18 | Smith | Isaac | 1 | 1 | | 1 | | 2 | | 1 | | 1 | | | 7 | | |
| Chatham | 20 | 39 | Smith | Isaac | 1 | 1 | | 1 | | 2 | 2 | | 1 | | | | 8 | | |
| Chatham | 18 | 41 | Smith | Issac | 1 | | 1 | 1 | | 2 | 2 | | 1 | | | | 8 | | |
| Barnstable | 86 | 44 | Smith | James | | | 1 | | | | | 1 | | | | | 2 | | |
| Provincetown | 59 | 27 | Smith | James | | 1 | 1 | 1 | | | | | 1 | | | | 4 | | |
| Chatham | 18 | 32 | Smith | Jane Wd | | 1 | 1 | | | | 1 | | 1 | | | | 4 | | |
| Wellfleet | 75 | 9 | Smith | Jarad | | 1 | | | | | | 1 | | | | | 2 | | |
| Wellfleet | 72 | 28 | Smith | Jesse | 2 | 1 | | 1 | | | | 1 | | | | | 5 | | |
| Chatham | 18 | 44 | Smith | John | 2 | 1 | | 1 | | | 1 | 1 | | | | | 6 | | |
| Chatham | 20 | 18 | Smith | John | 2 | 1 | | 1 | | 2 | 1 | 1 | | | | | 8 | | |
| Eastham | 78 | 31 | Smith | John | 1 | 1 | 0 | 1 | | 1 | 1 | | 1 | | | | 9 | | |
| Harwich | 14 | 15 | Smith | John | | 2 | | 1 | | | | 3 | 1 | | | | 7 | | |
| Sandwich | 36 | 11 | Smith | John | 1 | 1 | | 1 | | 2 | | 1 | | | | | 7 | | |
| Wellfleet | 75 | 29 | Smith | John | 1 | | 1 | | | | | 1 | | | | | 3 | | |
| Orleans | 25 | 29 | Smith | Jonah | 1 | 2 | | 1 | | 2 | 1 | | 1 | | | | 8 | | |
| Barnstable | 92 | 35 | Smith | Joseph | | | | 1 | 1 | 1 | | 1 | | 1 | | | 4 | | |
| Eastham | 78 | 23 | Smith | Joseph | 3 | | | 1 | | | | | 1 | | | | 5 | | |
| Orleans | 24 | 19 | Smith | Joseph | | | | 1 | | | | | 1 | | | | 2 | | |
| Wellfleet | 72 | 20 | Smith | Joseph | | 1 | 1 | 1 | | | | 2 | | 1 | | | 6 | | |
| Provincetown | 60 | 2 | Smith | Josha | 1 | 2 | | 1 | | 2 | | | 1 | | | | 7 | | |
| Eastham | 78 | 27 | Smith | Joshua | | 1 | | 1 | | | | 1 | | 1 | | | 4 | | |
| Orleans | 21 | 9 | Smith | Joshua | | 1 | | 1 | | | | 1 | | 1 | | | 4 | | |
| Wellfleet | 72 | 22 | Smith | Joshua | 1 | | | 1 | | 1 | | 1 | | | | | 4 | | |
| Chatham | 19 | 1 | Smith | Knowles | 2 | | 1 | | | | | 1 | | | | | 4 | | |
| Barnstable | 87 | 52 | Smith | Levi | | | 1 | | | | | 1 | | | | | 2 | | |
| Falmouth | 49 | 312 | Smith | Lucy | | | | | | | | 1 | | | | | 1 | | |
| Orleans | 24 | 17 | Smith | Lues | | | 1 | | | 2 | | 1 | | | | | 4 | | |
| Barnstable | 92 | 26 | Smith | Mathias | | 2 | | 1 | | | | 1 | | | | | 4 | | |
| Sandwich | 37 | 12 | Smith | Mathius | 1 | | 1 | | | 1 | 1 | | | | | | 4 | | |
| Barnstable | 92 | 34 | Smith | Nathan | 2 | | 1 | | | 1 | | 1 | | | | | 5 | | |
| Orleans | 24 | 16 | Smith | Nathan | | | 1 | | | | 2 | 2 | 1 | | | | 6 | | |
| Barnstable | 92 | 27 | Smith | Nathaniel | 1 | | 1 | | | | | 1 | 1 | | | | 4 | | |
| Chatham | 18 | 33 | Smith | Nathaniel | 2 | 1 | | | | 1 | | 1 | | | | | 5 | | |
| Eastham | 78 | 24 | Smith | Nathaniel | 3 | | 1 | | | | | 1 | | | | | 5 | | |
| Eastham | 78 | 21 | Smith | Nehemiah | 3 | 2 | 1 | 1 | | 2 | 1 | | 1 | | | | 11 | | |
| Chatham | 18 | 40 | Smith | Obadiah | 1 | | | 1 | | | | | 1 | | | | 3 | | |
| Harwich | 13 | 3 | Smith | Obedeslun | 3 | 1 | | 1 | | 1 | | 1 | | | | | 7 | | |
| Barnstable | 87 | 37 | Smith | Patrick | | | | 1 | 3 | | | 1 | | | | | 5 | | |
| Eastham | 78 | 29 | Smith | Phillip | | 2 | | 1 | | | | 2 | 1 | | | | 6 | | |
| Orleans | 24 | 25 | Smith | Ray | 3 | 2 | | 1 | | 2 | 1 | | 1 | | | | 10 | | |
| Provincetown | 60 | 24 | Smith | Reuben | 1 | | 1 | | | | | 1 | | | | | 3 | | |
| Chatham | 18 | 43 | Smith | Richard | 4 | | | 1 | | | | 1 | | | | | 6 | | |
| Barnstable | 85 | 7 | Smith | Samuel | | | | 1 | | 1 | 1 | | | | | | 3 | | |
| Eastham | 78 | 28 | Smith | Samuel | 1 | | | 1 | | 2 | | 1 | | | | | 5 | | |
| Harwich | 13 | 6 | Smith | Samuel | | 1 | 1 | | | 3 | 1 | | 1 | | | | 5 | | |
| Provincetown | 60 | 20 | Smith | Samuel | 1 | | | 1 | | 1 | | 1 | | | | | 4 | | |
| Sandwich | 35 | 34 | Smith | Samuel | | 1 | | | 1 | 1 | | 2 | | 1 | | | 6 | | |
| Wellfleet | 72 | 27 | Smith | Samuel | 1 | | | | 1 | 3 | 2 | | 1 | | | | 8 | | |
| Wellfleet | 75 | 27 | Smith | Samuel 3d | | | 1 | | | 1 | | 1 | | | | | 3 | | |
| Wellfleet | 72 | 25 | Smith | Samuel Junr | 1 | 1 | | 1 | | 2 | | 1 | | | | | 6 | | |
| Truro | 67 | 16 | Smith | Sarah Doane | | 1 | 1 | | | 1 | 1 | | 1 | | | | 5 | | |
| Truro | 66 | 16 | Smith | Sarah Wid Junr | 2 | | | | | | | 1 | | | | | 1 | | |
| Eastham | 78 | 33 | Smith | Seth | | 1 | | 1 | | | | 1 | 1 | | | | 4 | | |
| Provincetown | 59 | 37 | Smith | Seth | | 2 | | 1 | | 1 | | | 1 | | | | 5 | | |
| Provincetown | 59 | 34 | Smith | Seth Junr | 1 | 1 | | 1 | | 1 | | 1 | | | | | 5 | | |
| Eastham | 78 | 35 | Smith | Silvanus | 1 | 1 | | 2 | | 2 | | | 1 | | | | 7 | | |
| Barnstable | 86 | 43 | Smith | Solomon | 3 | | 1 | | | | | 1 | | | | | 5 | | |
| Chatham | 18 | 42 | Smith | Stephen | 3 | | 1 | | | 3 | | | 1 | | | | 8 | | |
| Chatham | 18 | 36 | Smith | Thankful Wid | | | | | | | | | | 1 | | | 1 | | |
| Sandwich | 42 | 41 | Smith | Thomas | | | 1 | | | | | | | | | | 1 | | |
| Falmouth | 49 | 266 | Smith | Thos | | | | 1 | | 1 | | | 1 | 1 | 1 | | 4 | | |
| Eastham | 79 | 22 | Smith | Timothy | 1 | | 1 | | | | | 1 | | | | | 3 | | |
| Orleans | 21 | 11 | Smith | Timothy | | | 1 | | | | | 1 | | | | | 2 | | |
| Harwich | 11 | 19 | Smith | William | 1 | | 1 | | | 2 | 1 | | | | | | 5 | | |
| Truro | 65 | 21 | Smith | Zocth | 2 | | | 1 | | | | 1 | | | | | 4 | | |
| Orleans | 25 | 18 | Smith | Zoheth | | | | 1 | | 2 | 1 | | 1 | | | | 5 | | |
| Chatham | 18 | 34 | Snow | *uinyton | | | 1 | | | 3 | | 1 | | | | | 5 | | |
| Chatham | 18 | 37 | Snow | Aaron | | | 1 | | | 3 | 2 | 1 | | | | | 7 | | |
| Orleans | 23 | 37 | Snow | Aaron | 3 | 1 | | 1 | | 2 | | 1 | | | | | 8 | | |
| Harwich | 11 | 26 | Snow | Afbond | 1 | | 1 | 1 | 1 | | | 2 | 2 | 1 | | | 9 | | |
| Truro | 62 | 2 | Snow | Ambros | | 1 | 2 | | 1 | 1 | | | 1 | 1 | | | 7 | | |
| Truro | 62 | 1 | Snow | Anthony | 1 | | 1 | | 1 | 2 | 2 | 1 | 1 | 1 | | | 10 | | |
| Orleans | 25 | 27 | Snow | David | | | | | | 1 | 1 | | 1 | | | | 3 | | |
| Truro | 62 | 11 | Snow | David | | 1 | 1 | | | | 1 | | | | | | 3 | | |
| Harwich | 13 | 37 | Snow | Ebenezor | | 3 | 1 | | 1 | 1 | | 1 | | 1 | | | 8 | | |
| Orleans | 23 | 23 | Snow | Edmond | 2 | 2 | | 1 | | 1 | | 1 | 1 | | | | 8 | | |
| Harwich | 13 | 31 | Snow | Edward | | 2 | 2 | | 1 | 2 | | 1 | 1 | | | | 9 | | |
| Harwich | 4 | 28 | Snow | Edward Jun | 2 | | | 1 | | 3 | 1 | | 1 | | | | 8 | | |
| Truro | 62 | 17 | Snow | Elisha | 1 | | | 1 | | 1 | | | 1 | | | | 4 | | |
| Harwich | 11 | 28 | Snow | Elisha | | 2 | 3 | | 1 | 2 | 1 | | 1 | | | | 10 | | |

# 1800 Barnstable County, Massachusetts Index

| Town | PG# | LN# | Last Name | First Name | FWM under 10 | FWM 10 to 16 | FWM 16 to 26 | FWM 26 to 45 | FWM 45 and over | FWF under 10 | FWF 10 to 16 | FWF 16 to 26 | FWF 26 to 45 | FWF 45 and over | Total All Other | Total Slaves | Totals | District/ Township | Notes |
|---|---|---|---|---|---|---|---|---|---|---|---|---|---|---|---|---|---|---|---|
| Harwich | 11 | 30 | Snow | Elisha 3d | | | 1 | | | | | | 1 | | | | 2 | | |
| Harwich | 11 | 29 | Snow | Elisha Jun | | | | 1 | | 2 | | 1 | | | | | 4 | | |
| Orleans | 23 | 39 | Snow | Elnathon | | | | 1 | | | | 1 | 1 | | | | 3 | | |
| Orleans | 23 | 38 | Snow | Elnathon Jun | 2 | | 1 | | | | | | 1 | | | | 4 | | |
| Harwich | 5 | 26 | Snow | Enos | | | 1 | | | | | | 1 | | | | 2 | | |
| Truro | 68 | 19 | Snow | Ephraim | | 1 | | | | 1 | | 1 | | | | | 3 | | |
| Truro | 63 | 7 | Snow | Hannah Junr | 1 | 1 | | | | | | 1 | | 1 | | | 4 | | |
| Harwich | 4 | 25 | Snow | Hannah Wd | | 1 | | | | | | | | 1 | | | 2 | | |
| Truro | 63 | 8 | Snow | Hannah Wid | | | | | | | | | | 1 | | | 1 | | |
| Orleans | 25 | 11 | Snow | Heman | | | 2 | 1 | | 2 | 2 | | 1 | | | | 8 | | |
| Orleans | 24 | 23 | Snow | Hemen Jun | 2 | 1 | | 1 | | 2 | 1 | | 1 | | | | 8 | | |
| Orleans | 24 | 36 | Snow | Hemon 3d | 1 | | 1 | | | | | | 1 | | | | 3 | | |
| Orleans | 25 | 9 | Snow | Isaac | 1 | 1 | | 1 | | 3 | 1 | | 1 | | | | 8 | | |
| Eastham | 78 | 34 | Snow | James | | | 1 | | | | | 1 | | 1 | | | 3 | | |
| Orleans | 24 | 34 | Snow | Jerusha Wd | 1 | | | | | | | 1 | | 1 | | | 3 | | |
| Falmouth | 48 | 228 | Snow | Joanna | 1 | | | | | | | 1 | 1 | 1 | | | 4 | | |
| Harwich | 6 | 24 | Snow | John | | 1 | | | | | | | 3 | | | | 4 | | |
| Truro | 63 | 29 | Snow | John | 2 | 1 | | 1 | | 2 | | | 1 | | | | 7 | | |
| Truro | 63 | 33 | Snow | John Junr | | | | 1 | | | 1 | | 1 | | | | 3 | | |
| Harwich | 5 | 17 | Snow | Jonathan | 1 | | 3 | 1 | | 2 | 1 | | 1 | | | | 9 | | |
| Truro | 63 | 22 | Snow | Jonathan | | 1 | 1 | 1 | | 2 | | | 1 | | | | 6 | | |
| Eastham | 78 | 30 | Snow | Joseph | 3 | 1 | | 1 | | 2 | | 1 | | | | | 8 | | |
| Falmouth | 48 | 239 | Snow | Joseph | | | 1 | | | | | | 1 | | | | 2 | | |
| Harwich | 7 | 21 | Snow | Joseph | | | 1 | | | 2 | | | 1 | | | | 4 | | |
| Wellfleet | 72 | 19 | Snow | Joseph | | 1 | 1 | 1 | | 2 | 1 | | 1 | | | | 7 | | |
| Truro | 63 | 24 | Snow | Joshua | 1 | 1 | | 1 | | 1 | | | 1 | | | | 5 | | |
| Harwich | 10 | 12 | Snow | Knowls | 1 | | | 1 | | 1 | | | 1 | | | | 4 | | |
| Harwich | 4 | 27 | Snow | Lucy Wd | | 1 | | | | | | | | 1 | | | 2 | | |
| Truro | 63 | 21 | Snow | Lydia Wid | 2 | 1 | | | | 1 | 2 | | 1 | | | | 7 | | |
| Harwich | 6 | 31 | Snow | Moses | 2 | | 1 | | | 2 | | | 1 | | | | 6 | | |
| Orleans | 21 | 15 | Snow | Moses | 2 | | | 1 | | 4 | | | 1 | | | | 8 | | |
| Barnstable | 93 | 44 | Snow | Nathaniel | | 1 | 2 | 1 | 1 | 3 | | 2 | | 1 | | | 11 | | |
| Chatham | 18 | 29 | Snow | Nathaniel | 4 | | 1 | | | | 1 | | 1 | | | | 7 | | |
| Chatham | 20 | 19 | Snow | Nathaniel | 4 | | 1 | | | 1 | | | 1 | | | | 7 | | |
| Harwich | 8 | 6 | Snow | Nathaniel | | 1 | | 1 | | 1 | | | 2 | | | | 5 | | |
| Orleans | 25 | 19 | Snow | Prince | | 1 | 1 | 1 | | 1 | | | 1 | | | | 5 | | |
| Orleans | 21 | 22 | Snow | Priscilla | | | | | | | | 1 | 1 | 1 | | | 3 | | |
| Harwich | 7 | 23 | Snow | Priscilla Wid | | 2 | | | | | | | | 1 | | | 3 | | |
| Harwich | 6 | 23 | Snow | Reuben | 2 | 1 | | 1 | | | | 1 | | | | | 5 | | |
| Truro | 64 | 25 | Snow | Richard | 2 | | | 1 | | | | | 1 | | | | 4 | | |
| Truro | 67 | 23 | Snow | Ruth | | | | | | | 1 | | 1 | | | | 2 | | |
| Provincetown | 60 | 3 | Snow | Ryal | | 1 | 1 | 1 | | 2 | 1 | | 1 | | | | 7 | | |
| Barnstable | 90 | 2 | Snow | Samuel | 2 | 1 | | 1 | | 2 | 2 | | 1 | | | | 9 | | |
| Wellfleet | 75 | 4 | Snow | Samuel | | | 1 | | | | | | 1 | | | | 2 | | |
| Sandwich | 41 | 10 | Snow | Sarah | | | 1 | | | | | | 2 | | | | 3 | | |
| Provincetown | 61 | 13 | Snow | Sarah Wd | 1 | | | | | | | | 1 | | | | 1 | | |
| Harwich | 4 | 14 | Snow | Silvanus | 1 | | 1 | | | | | | 1 | | | | 3 | | |
| Truro | 65 | 7 | Snow | Silvanus | | | 3 | | 1 | 3 | 2 | 1 | 1 | | | | 11 | | |
| Wellfleet | 72 | 26 | Snow | Solomon | 2 | | 1 | | | 2 | | | 1 | 1 | | | 8 | | |
| Harwich | 14 | 25 | Snow | Stephen | | 1 | 1 | | | 1 | 1 | | 1 | | | | 5 | | |
| Orleans | 21 | 16 | Snow | Stephen | 1 | 3 | 2 | | 1 | 3 | 1 | 2 | 1 | | | | 14 | | |
| Truro | 65 | 9 | Snow | Stephen | 3 | | | 1 | | | | | 1 | | | | 5 | | |
| Harwich | 5 | 30 | Snow | Thankfull | | 1 | | | | | | | | 2 | | | 3 | | |
| Harwich | 3 | 9 | Snow | Thomas | | 1 | | 1 | 1 | 1 | | 1 | | 1 | | | 6 | | |
| Harwich | 3 | 10 | Snow | Thomas 3d | 1 | 1 | | 1 | | 3 | | 2 | 1 | | | | 9 | | |
| Harwich | 4 | 2 | Snow | Thomas Jun | | 1 | | 1 | | | | | | 1 | | | 3 | | |
| Harwich | 7 | 25 | Snow | Zaheth | 1 | | | 1 | | 2 | | | 1 | | | | 5 | | |
| Provincetown | 59 | 28 | Sparks | James | 1 | | 1 | 1 | | 1 | | | 1 | | | | 5 | | |
| Orleans | 23 | 25 | Sparrow | Isaac | | | | 1 | | | | 1 | | 1 | | | 3 | | |
| Orleans | 23 | 21 | Sparrow | Jabez | 2 | 1 | | 1 | | 2 | 1 | 1 | | 1 | | | 9 | | |
| Orleans | 24 | 9 | Sparrow | John | 2 | | | 1 | | | | 1 | | 1 | | | 5 | | |
| Orleans | 22 | 9 | Sparrow | Josiah | | 3 | 1 | | | 3 | 1 | 1 | | 1 | | | 11 | | |
| Orleans | 23 | 24 | Sparrow | Richard | 2 | 2 | 1 | 1 | | | | 3 | 1 | | | | 10 | | |
| Orleans | 22 | 15 | Sparrow | Seth | 1 | | | 1 | | | | | | 1 | | | 3 | | |
| Orleans | 24 | 7 | Sparrow | Seth Jun | | | 1 | | | 2 | | | 1 | | | | 4 | | |
| Orleans | 24 | 43 | Sparrow | Seth Jun | 1 | | 1 | | | | | | | 1 | | | 3 | | |
| Orleans | 24 | 6 | Sparrow | Solomon | | | | 1 | | | 1 | | 1 | | | | 3 | | |
| Harwich | 13 | 36 | St*l | Daniel | 1 | | 1 | | | | 1 | | | | | | 3 | | |
| Wellfleet | 72 | 23 | St*t | Thomas | | | 1 | | | | | | 1 | | | | 2 | | |
| Provincetown | 59 | 30 | Stanly | Job | | | 1 | | | 2 | | | 1 | | | | 4 | | |
| Truro | 67 | 22 | Steavens | Betsy | | 2 | | | | | | 2 | | | | | 4 | | |
| Truro | 67 | 19 | Steavens | Levi | 1 | 1 | 1 | | 1 | 2 | | | 1 | | | | 7 | | |
| Chatham | 19 | 16 | Stetson | John | 1 | | 1 | | | 2 | | 1 | | | | | 5 | | |
| Chatham | 19 | 31 | Stetson | John | 1 | | 1 | | | 2 | 1 | | | | | | 5 | | |
| Barnstable | 85 | 10 | Stetson | Thomas | 2 | | 1 | | | 1 | 1 | | 1 | | | | 6 | | |
| Barnstable | 88 | 39 | Stevens | Richard | | | 1 | | | | | | 1 | | | | 2 | | |
| Barnstable | 93 | 29 | Stewart | James | 1 | | 1 | 1 | | | | | 1 | 2 | | | 6 | | |
| Chatham | 18 | 35 | Stewart | William | | 1 | 1 | | 1 | | | 1 | | 1 | | | 4 | | |
| Provincetown | 59 | 38 | Stockwell | Joseph | | 1 | 1 | | | 1 | | | 1 | | | | 3 | | |
| Harwich | 8 | 12 | Stone | Mary Wd | | | 2 | | | | 1 | 2 | | | | | 5 | | |
| Dennis | 27 | 22 | Stone | Nathan Jun | 2 | | 1 | | | 1 | | | 1 | | | | 5 | | |
| Barnstable | 93 | 35 | Stuart | Solomon | 2 | | 1 | | | 1 | | | 1 | | | | 5 | | |
| Provincetown | 60 | 5 | Stubbs | Dorcas Wd | 1 | | | | | 2 | 2 | | 1 | | | | 6 | | |

# 1800 Barnstable County, Massachusetts Index

| TOWN | PG# | LN# | LAST NAME | FIRST NAME | M U10 | M 10-16 | M 16-26 | M 26-45 | M 45+ | F U10 | F 10-16 | F 16-26 | F 26-45 | F 45+ | TOT ALL OTHER | TOT SLAVES | TOTALS | DISTRICT/TOWNSHIP | NOTES |
|---|---|---|---|---|---|---|---|---|---|---|---|---|---|---|---|---|---|---|---|
| Wellfleet | 72 | 21 | Stubbs | John | | 1 | | | 1 | 1 | 1 | | 1 | | | | 5 | | |
| Wellfleet | 75 | 26 | Stubbs | Richard | 4 | 1 | | 1 | | | | | 1 | | | | 7 | | |
| Dennis | 29 | 34 | Studley | Abner | 1 | | 1 | | | | | | 1 | | | | 3 | | |
| Falmouth | 49 | 303 | Studley | Abraham | 1 | | 1 | | | | | | 1 | | | | 3 | | |
| Dennis | 29 | 35 | Studley | Anthony | | 1 | | 1 | | 2 | 1 | | 1 | | | | 6 | | |
| Yarmouth | 96 | 12 | Studley | Anthony | 1 | 2 | | 1 | | 1 | 1 | | | 1 | | | 7 | | |
| Falmouth | 48 | 244 | Studley | Benoni | | 1 | 1 | | | | | | | 1 | | | 4 | | |
| Dennis | 29 | 36 | Studley | Edward | | | 1 | | | | | | 1 | | | | 2 | | |
| Yarmouth | 96 | 13 | Studley | Josiah Jr | | | 1 | | | 2 | | | 1 | | | | 4 | | |
| Sandwich | 38 | 40 | Studley | Saml Junr | 2 | 2 | 1 | | | 1 | 1 | | 1 | | | | 8 | | |
| Dennis | 29 | 33 | Studley | Samuel | 2 | | 1 | | | 1 | | | 1 | | | | 5 | | |
| Dennis | 31 | 36 | Studley | Silvanus | 1 | | 1 | | | 2 | | | 1 | | | | 5 | | |
| Yarmouth | 98 | 39 | Studley | Silvanus | 1 | 1 | 1 | | 1 | | | | 1 | | | | 5 | | |
| Barnstable | 84 | 39 | Sturgis | Ebenezer | 2 | 1 | | 1 | | 2 | 1 | 2 | 1 | | | | 10 | | |
| Barnstable | 86 | 2 | Sturgis | Hannah | | 1 | | | | | | 1 | | 1 | | | 3 | | |
| Barnstable | 90 | 41 | Sturgis | John | 4 | | 3 | | 1 | 1 | 1 | 1 | | 1 | | | 12 | | |
| Sandwich | 34 | 2 | Sturgis | Jonathan | 2 | 1 | | | | | | 2 | | 1 | | | 6 | | |
| Barnstable | 92 | 7 | Sturgis | Lucretia | | | | | | | | | | 1 | | | 1 | | |
| Barnstable | 85 | 24 | Sturgis | Thomas | 1 | 1 | | 1 | | 2 | 1 | 1 | 1 | | | | 8 | | |
| Barnstable | 88 | 24 | Sudder | Ebenezer | 4 | | 1 | | | | | | 1 | | | | 6 | | |
| Sandwich | 40 | 26 | Sutton | Rogers | | | | | | | | | | | 5 | | 5 | | |
| Dennis | 30 | 28 | Swain | Desire | | | | | | | | | 1 | | | | 1 | | |
| Wellfleet | 72 | 16 | Sweat | John | | 1 | | 1 | | | | | 1 | | | | 3 | | |
| Wellfleet | 75 | 14 | Sweat | John Junr | | | 1 | | | 1 | | 1 | | | | | 3 | | |
| Wellfleet | 72 | 17 | Sweat | Joshua | 1 | 1 | | | | | | | | 1 | | | 3 | | |
| Wellfleet | 74 | 8 | Sweat | Mercy | | | 1 | | | | | | | 1 | | | 2 | | |
| Wellfleet | 74 | 24 | Sweat | Thankfull | | | 1 | | | | | | 1 | 1 | | | 3 | | |
| Falmouth | 51 | 324 | Swfit | Elijah | 1 | | | 1 | | 1 | | | | 1 | | | 4 | | |
| Falmouth | 48 | 240 | Swift | Abiel | 2 | | | 1 | | 1 | | | | 1 | | | 5 | | |
| Falmouth | 49 | 254 | Swift | Betsey | | 1 | | | | | | | | 1 | | | 2 | | |
| Falmouth | 48 | 241 | Swift | Charles | 3 | | | 1 | | 1 | | | | 1 | | | 6 | | |
| Sandwich | 39 | 35 | Swift | Clark | 1 | | | 1 | | 3 | | 1 | 1 | | | | 7 | | |
| Falmouth | 48 | 245 | Swift | David | | 1 | | 1 | | 1 | 2 | | 1 | 1 | | | 7 | | |
| Barnstable | 85 | 25 | Swift | Ebenezer | | | 1 | 1 | | | | | 1 | | | | 3 | | |
| Falmouth | 48 | 247 | Swift | Elisha | | | | | 1 | | | | | 1 | | | 2 | | |
| Falmouth | 48 | 237 | Swift | Ephraim | | | | | 1 | | | | 2 | | | | 3 | | |
| Falmouth | 48 | 236 | Swift | Ephraim Junr | 1 | | 1 | | 1 | | | 1 | 2 | 1 | | | 7 | | |
| Sandwich | 41 | 2 | Swift | Heman | | 1 | | | | 1 | | | 1 | 1 | 2 | | 5 | | |
| Falmouth | 48 | 224 | Swift | Jabez | | | | 1 | | | | | 2 | | 2 | | 5 | | |
| Falmouth | 48 | 246 | Swift | Jetho | 1 | | 1 | 1 | | 1 | 2 | | 1 | | | | 7 | | |
| Falmouth | 48 | 227 | Swift | John | 2 | 1 | | | | | | 1 | | | | | 4 | | |
| Falmouth | 49 | 253 | Swift | John | 1 | | | 1 | | 2 | | | 1 | | | | 5 | | |
| Sandwich | 39 | 27 | Swift | Joseph | 3 | 1 | | 1 | | 2 | 1 | | 1 | | | | 9 | | |
| Falmouth | 48 | 234 | Swift | Moses | 1 | 1 | | 1 | | | | | | 1 | | | 4 | | |
| Sandwich | 41 | 7 | Swift | Moses | 2 | | | 1 | | 4 | | | 1 | | | | 8 | | |
| Sandwich | 39 | 37 | Swift | Nathaniel | 3 | 1 | | 1 | | 1 | 1 | | 1 | | | | 8 | | |
| Falmouth | 48 | 243 | Swift | Paul | | 2 | | | 1 | | 2 | | 1 | | | | 6 | | |
| Sandwich | 36 | 32 | Swift | Silas | 1 | 1 | | | 1 | 3 | 1 | 1 | 1 | | | | 9 | | |
| Falmouth | 48 | 242 | Swift | Silvanus | | 2 | | 2 | 1 | | 2 | | 1 | | | | 8 | | |
| Falmouth | 48 | 229 | Swift | Solomon | | | 1 | | 1 | | | 1 | 1 | 1 | | | 5 | | |
| Falmouth | 48 | 235 | Swift | Stephen | 1 | 2 | | | 1 | | | 1 | 1 | 1 | | | 7 | | |
| Sandwich | 42 | 39 | Swift | Stephen | 1 | 1 | 1 | 1 | | 1 | 2 | | 1 | | | | 8 | | |
| Falmouth | 49 | 252 | Swift | Temperance | | 1 | | | | | | 2 | | 1 | | | 4 | | |
| Sandwich | 39 | 36 | Swift | Thomas | | 1 | 2 | | 1 | 1 | | | | 1 | | | 6 | | |
| Sandwich | 39 | 31 | Swift | Thos Junr | 1 | 1 | 1 | 1 | | 1 | | | 1 | | | | 6 | | |
| Sandwich | 41 | 5 | Swift | Ward | | | | 1 | | | | | | 1 | 2 | | 4 | | |
| Sandwich | 41 | 6 | Swift | Ward Junr | 1 | | 1 | | | | | | 1 | | | | 3 | | |
| Falmouth | 48 | 225 | Swift | Wm | | 1 | | 1 | | | | | | 1 | | | 3 | | |
| Falmouth | 48 | 226 | Swift | Wm Junr | 2 | | | 1 | | 1 | 1 | 1 | | 1 | | | 7 | | |
| Barnstable | 84 | 31 | Swinerton | Timothy | 2 | | | 1 | | 2 | | | 1 | 1 | | | 7 | | |
| Harwich | 7 | 34 | Tacher | Lucy Wd | | | | | | 1 | | | | | 2 | | 3 | | |
| Chatham | 19 | 19 | Tailor | Barnabas | | 1 | | | | 1 | | | | 1 | | | 3 | | |
| Orleans | 24 | 31 | Tailor | Benjm | 3 | 1 | | | 2 | 1 | | 2 | | 1 | | | 10 | | |
| Orleans | 24 | 32 | Tailor | David | 2 | 1 | | 1 | | 1 | 1 | | 1 | | | | 7 | | |
| Chatham | 19 | 8 | Tailor | James | 1 | | | 1 | | 1 | | | 1 | | | | 4 | | |
| Chatham | 19 | 3 | Tailor | Janye | | | | 1 | | 4 | | | 1 | | | | 6 | | |
| Chatham | 19 | 7 | Tailor | John | 1 | | | 1 | | 1 | | | 1 | | | | 4 | | |
| Dennis | 29 | 37 | Tailor | John | 1 | | | 1 | | 1 | | | 1 | | | | 4 | | |
| Orleans | 23 | 29 | Tailor | John | 3 | 2 | | 1 | 1 | 2 | 1 | | 1 | 1 | | | 12 | | |
| Chatham | 19 | 41 | Tailor | Mathew | | | | | | 1 | | | 1 | | | | 2 | | |
| Chatham | 19 | 42 | Tailor | Mathew Jun | 2 | | | 1 | | 2 | 2 | | 1 | | | | 8 | | |
| Chatham | 19 | 4 | Tailor | Reuben | 3 | | | 1 | | 3 | | | 1 | | | | 8 | | |
| Dennis | 27 | 24 | Tailor | Reuben | 2 | | | 1 | | 1 | | | 1 | | | | 5 | | |
| Chatham | 19 | 40 | Tailor | Seth | 1 | 1 | | | | | | 1 | 1 | 1 | | | 6 | | |
| Dennis | 28 | 22 | Tailor | Simeon | | | 2 | 1 | | | | | 1 | 1 | | | 5 | | |
| Dennis | 28 | 23 | Tailor | Simeon | | | 1 | | | | | | 1 | | | | 2 | | |
| Wellfleet | 75 | 30 | Tailor | Solomon | 1 | | | 1 | | 1 | | | | 1 | | | 4 | | |
| Chatham | 19 | 5 | Tailor | Thomas | 1 | | 2 | | 1 | | | 2 | | 1 | | | 7 | | |
| Chatham | 19 | 6 | Tailor | Zenas | 1 | | | 1 | | 2 | | | | 1 | | | 5 | | |
| Yarmouth | 100 | 1 | Taylor | Abner | | | 1 | | 1 | | | | 1 | 1 | | | 4 | | |
| Yarmouth | 95 | 19 | Taylor | Ansel | | | | | 1 | | 3 | 2 | 1 | 1 | | | 8 | | |
| Yarmouth | 95 | 51 | Taylor | Benjamin | | | 2 | 1 | | | | | | 1 | | | 4 | | |
| Yarmouth | 97 | 5 | Taylor | Daniel | | | 1 | 1 | | | | | | 1 | 6 | | 9 | | |

| TOWN | PG# | LN# | LAST NAME | FIRST NAME | FREE WHITE MALES under 10 | 10 to 16 | 16 to 26 | 26 to 45 | 45 and over | FREE WHITE FEMALES under 10 | 10 to 16 | 16 to 26 | 26 to 45 | 45 and over | TOTAL ALL OTHER | TOTAL SLAVES | TOTALS | DISTRICT/ TOWNSHIP | NOTES |
|---|---|---|---|---|---|---|---|---|---|---|---|---|---|---|---|---|---|---|---|
| Yarmouth | 97 | 6 | Taylor | Daniel Jr | 1 | | | 1 | | 3 | | | 1 | | 1 | | 7 | | |
| Yarmouth | 97 | 38 | Taylor | Ebenezer | 1 | | | 1 | | | | | 1 | | | | 3 | | |
| Yarmouth | 95 | 52 | Taylor | Edward | | | 1 | | | 3 | | | 1 | | | | 5 | | |
| Yarmouth | 95 | 46 | Taylor | Howes | | | 1 | | | | | 1 | | 1 | | | 3 | | |
| Yarmouth | 95 | 30 | Taylor | Jorce | 1 | 1 | 3 | | 1 | | 3 | 2 | | 1 | | | 12 | | |
| Yarmouth | 97 | 24 | Taylor | Joshua | 1 | 1 | 1 | | 1 | | | | 1 | | 1 | | 6 | | |
| Yarmouth | 95 | 40 | Taylor | Lothrop | 1 | | | 1 | | 3 | | | 1 | | | | 6 | | |
| Barnstable | 86 | 38 | Taylor | Mary | | | | | | | | | 1 | 1 | 2 | | 4 | | |
| Yarmouth | 96 | 34 | Taylor | Richard | | | 2 | | 1 | | | 2 | 1 | | | | 6 | | |
| Yarmouth | 96 | 22 | Taylor | Samuel | | 1 | 3 | | 1 | | 1 | 1 | | 1 | 4 | | 12 | | |
| Yarmouth | 95 | 38 | Taylor | Samuel Jr | 1 | | 1 | 1 | | 2 | 2 | | 1 | | | | 8 | | |
| Barnstable | 84 | 20 | Taylor | William | | 1 | | 1 | | | | | 1 | | | | 3 | | |
| Yarmouth | 95 | 8 | Taylor | William | | | | 1 | | | | | | 1 | | | 2 | | |
| Yarmouth | 96 | 40 | Taylor | William Jr | 2 | 2 | | | 1 | 2 | | | 1 | | | | 8 | | |
| Barnstable | 83 | 19 | Thacher | Anthony | | | 1 | | | | | 1 | | 1 | | | 3 | | |
| Yarmouth | 97 | 23 | Thacher | Barnabas | 3 | | 1 | 1 | | 1 | | | 1 | | | | 7 | | |
| Yarmouth | 97 | 13 | Thacher | David | | | | 1 | | | | | | 2 | | | 3 | | |
| Yarmouth | 97 | 14 | Thacher | David Jr | 4 | 1 | | 1 | | | 1 | 1 | | | 1 | | 9 | | |
| Yarmouth | 95 | 3 | Thacher | Ebenz | | 2 | | 1 | | 2 | | | 1 | | | | 6 | | |
| Yarmouth | 95 | 12 | Thacher | Edmund | | | 1 | | | 1 | | 1 | | | | | 3 | | |
| Yarmouth | 97 | 9 | Thacher | Hannah | | 2 | 2 | | | | | 1 | 1 | 1 | | | 7 | | |
| Yarmouth | 96 | 42 | Thacher | James | | | 1 | | | 3 | | | 1 | | | | 5 | | |
| Barnstable | 84 | 33 | Thacher | Jethro | | 1 | | 1 | | 2 | 1 | 1 | | 3 | | | 10 | | |
| Barnstable | 84 | 32 | Thacher | John | | 1 | 2 | | 1 | 1 | | | 1 | 1 | | | 7 | | |
| Yarmouth | 97 | 7 | Thacher | John | 2 | | | 1 | | 2 | | | 1 | | | | 6 | | |
| Yarmouth | 97 | 3 | Thacher | Joseph | 3 | 1 | | 1 | | 1 | | | 1 | | 2 | | 9 | | |
| Yarmouth | 96 | 39 | Thacher | Josiah | | 1 | | | | 1 | 1 | | 1 | 1 | | | 5 | | |
| Yarmouth | 95 | 14 | Thacher | Josiah Jr | 2 | | | 1 | | 2 | | | 1 | | | | 6 | | |
| Yarmouth | 97 | 12 | Thacher | Laban | 3 | | 2 | 1 | | | | 1 | 1 | | | | 8 | | |
| Barnstable | 85 | 6 | Thacher | Martha | 1 | | | | | | | | 1 | 1 | | | 3 | | |
| Barnstable | 83 | 8 | Thacher | Peleg | | | | 1 | | 1 | | | 1 | | | | 3 | | |
| Yarmouth | 97 | 18 | Thacher | Peter | | | 2 | | 1 | | | | | 1 | | | 4 | | |
| Yarmouth | 96 | 43 | Thacher | Susanna | | | 1 | | | | | | | 1 | | | 2 | | |
| Yarmouth | 97 | 2 | Thacher | Susanna Jr | 2 | 1 | | | | 1 | | | | 1 | | | 5 | | |
| Yarmouth | 97 | 17 | Thacher | Thomas | 2 | | | 1 | | 2 | 1 | | 1 | 1 | | | 8 | | |
| Yarmouth | 97 | 10 | Thacher | William | | 3 | | | 1 | | 1 | | | 1 | | | 6 | | |
| Truro | 65 | 13 | Thayer | Susannah | | 1 | | | | | | 2 | | 1 | | | 4 | | |
| Barnstable | 88 | 28 | Thomas | Ansel | 4 | | | 1 | | 2 | | | 1 | | | | 8 | | |
| Barnstable | 88 | 44 | Thomas | Eliza | | | 2 | | | | | 1 | | 1 | | | 4 | | |
| Truro | 67 | 27 | Thomas | John | 2 | | | 1 | | | | 1 | | | | | 4 | | |
| Barnstable | 92 | 44 | Thomas | Joseph | | | | 1 | | | 1 | | 1 | | | | 3 | | |
| Truro | 67 | 28 | Thomas | Rebeccah | 1 | | | | | | | 1 | 1 | 1 | | | 4 | | |
| Barnstable | 91 | 29 | Thomas | Samuel | 1 | | | 1 | | | | | 1 | | | | 3 | | |
| Sandwich | 38 | 22 | Tobey | Benjm | 1 | 1 | 1 | | 1 | | | 1 | | 1 | | | 6 | | |
| Sandwich | 35 | 38 | Tobey | Heman | 1 | | | 1 | | 2 | 1 | | 1 | | | | 6 | | |
| Barnstable | 91 | 41 | Tobey | James | | | 1 | 2 | | | | | 3 | 1 | | | 7 | | |
| Sandwich | 36 | 41 | Tobey | John | | | 1 | 1 | | 1 | 1 | 1 | 1 | | | | 7 | | |
| Sandwich | 36 | 42 | Tobey | John Junr | 1 | | | 1 | | | | 1 | | | | | 3 | | |
| Sandwich | 35 | 30 | Tobey | Maria | | | | 1 | | | | | 1 | 1 | | | 3 | | |
| Sandwich | 41 | 38 | Tobey | Mariah Junr | | 2 | 1 | | | | | | | 1 | | | 4 | | |
| Sandwich | 35 | 39 | Tobey | Melatiah | 1 | | | 1 | | 1 | | 1 | | | | | 4 | | |
| Sandwich | 35 | 29 | Tobey | Nathan | 1 | | | 1 | | | 1 | | | | | | 3 | | |
| Sandwich | 35 | 44 | Tobey | Prince | | | 1 | 1 | | | | 1 | 1 | | | | 4 | | |
| Sandwich | 39 | 5 | Tobey | Silas | | | 1 | 1 | | | | 1 | 1 | | | | 4 | | |
| Sandwich | 35 | 32 | Tobey | Silvanus | | 1 | 1 | | 1 | | 1 | | | | | | 4 | | |
| Sandwich | 35 | 40 | Tobey | Timothy | 1 | | | 1 | | 2 | 1 | | 1 | 1 | | | 7 | | |
| Sandwich | 35 | 37 | Tobey | William | 1 | 1 | | 1 | | | 2 | 1 | 1 | | | | 7 | | |
| Sandwich | 41 | 39 | Tobey | Wm Junr | 1 | | | 1 | | 1 | | 1 | | | | | 4 | | |
| Dennis | 28 | 20 | Toby | Seth | | | 1 | | | | | | 1 | | | | 2 | | |
| Dennis | 28 | 21 | Toby | Seth Jun | 2 | | | 1 | | 1 | 1 | | 1 | | | | 6 | | |
| Dennis | 28 | 19 | Toby | Stephen | | | | 2 | | | 1 | 1 | | | | | 4 | | |
| Eastham | 79 | 25 | Townson | Obadiah | 3 | | | 1 | | 2 | | | 1 | 1 | | | 7 | | |
| Harwich | 10 | 31 | Trabens | Nathaniel | 1 | 3 | | 1 | 1 | | | | 1 | | | | 7 | | |
| Harwich | 10 | 32 | Trabens | Nathaniel Jun | | 1 | | 1 | 2 | | 1 | | 1 | | | | 6 | | |
| Harwich | 11 | 44 | Trabens | Richard | | 1 | | 1 | 1 | 3 | | | 2 | | | | 8 | | |
| Sandwich | 35 | 26 | Treadwell | Cesar | | | | | | | | 1 | | 4 | | | 5 | | |
| Harwich | 11 | 18 | Trip | Godfrey | 1 | | | 1 | | 2 | | | 1 | | | | 5 | | |
| Chatham | 19 | 2 | Trip | Jeptha | 2 | 2 | | 1 | 1 | | 1 | | 1 | | | | 8 | | |
| Dennis | 29 | 28 | Trip | Jonathan | 1 | | 2 | 1 | | 3 | | 1 | 1 | | | | 9 | | |
| Harwich | 11 | 27 | Trip | Mehitable Wd | | 1 | | | | 1 | | | 1 | | | | 3 | | |
| Harwich | 11 | 16 | Trip | Samuel | | | 1 | | | | | | 1 | | | | 2 | | |
| Yarmouth | 99 | 1 | Tripp | Benja | 1 | | 1 | 1 | | 1 | | | 1 | | | | 5 | | |
| Barnstable | 85 | 13 | Tupper | Abigail | | | | | | | | | 1 | | | | 1 | | |
| Sandwich | 39 | 3 | Tupper | Esther | | | 1 | | | | | 1 | 1 | | | | 3 | | |
| Barnstable | 85 | 12 | Tupper | Lothrop | 2 | 1 | | 1 | | 2 | 2 | | 1 | | | | 9 | | |
| Sandwich | 36 | 5 | Tupper | Mahitabel | | | 3 | | | | 1 | | 1 | | | | 5 | | |
| Sandwich | 38 | 34 | Tupper | Prince | | | 1 | | | | | 1 | | | | | 2 | | |
| Sandwich | 38 | 30 | Tupper | Remember | | | | | | | | | 1 | | | | 1 | | |
| Mashpee | 51 | 16 | Turner | Joseph | 2 | 4 | | 1 | | 1 | 1 | 1 | 1 | | | | 11 | | |
| Harwich | 14 | 36 | Turner | Stephen | 1 | | | 1 | 3 | | | | 1 | 2 | | | 8 | | |
| Falmouth | 49 | 30 | Turner | Walter | 1 | | 1 | | | | | 1 | | | | | 3 | | |

| TOWN | PG# | LN# | LAST NAME | FIRST NAME | FREE WHITE MALES | | | | | FREE WHITE FEMALES | | | | | TOTAL ALL OTHER | TOTAL SLAVES | TOTALS | DISTRICT/ TOWNSHIP | NOTES |
|---|---|---|---|---|---|---|---|---|---|---|---|---|---|---|---|---|---|---|---|
| | | | | | under 10 | 10 to 16 | 16 to 26 | 26 to 45 | 45 and over | under 10 | 10 to 16 | 16 to 26 | 26 to 45 | 45 and over | | | | | |
| Orleans | 23 | 42 | Twining | Barnabes | | 1 | | 1 | | 1 | 1 | | | 1 | | | 5 | | |
| Orleans | 23 | 43 | Twining | Barnabes Jun | 1 | | 1 | | | 1 | | | 1 | | | | 4 | | |
| Orleans | 24 | 33 | Twining | Jonathan | | 1 | 1 | 1 | | | | | | 2 | | | 5 | | |
| Orleans | 25 | 12 | Twining | Prince | 2 | | 1 | 1 | | | 1 | 2 | | 1 | | | 8 | | |
| Harwich | 14 | 16 | Underwood | Nathan Rev | 3 | | | 1 | | | | | 1 | | | | 5 | | |
| Harwich | 4 | 26 | Vealnough | Peter | | | 1 | 1 | | 1 | 1 | 1 | | 1 | | | 6 | | |
| Falmouth | 49 | 255 | Verily | Desire | 2 | 2 | | | | 1 | | | 1 | | | | 6 | | |
| Dennis | 27 | 28 | Vincent | David | | | | 1 | | | | | | 1 | | | 2 | | |
| Dennis | 27 | 26 | Vincent | Isaac | 1 | 1 | 2 | 1 | | | 1 | | | 1 | | | 7 | | |
| Eastham | 79 | 2 | Walker | Andrew | | | | 1 | | | | | 2 | 1 | | | 4 | | |
| Harwich | 4 | 40 | Walker | Benjm | 1 | | 1 | | | 2 | | | 1 | | | | 5 | | |
| Eastham | 79 | 32 | Walker | David | 2 | | 1 | | | 2 | | | 1 | | | | 6 | | |
| Harwich | 13 | 23 | Walker | James | 2 | 1 | | 1 | | 2 | 1 | | 1 | | | | 8 | | |
| Harwich | 10 | 8 | Walker | Jeremiah | | | | 1 | | | | | 1 | | | | 2 | | |
| Harwich | 11 | 7 | Walker | Jeremiah Jun | 1 | | 1 | | | 2 | 1 | | 1 | | | | 6 | | |
| Harwich | 12 | 6 | Walker | Linus | 1 | | 1 | | | | | | 1 | | | | 3 | | |
| Eastham | 79 | 3 | Walker | Peter | | | 1 | | | 3 | | | 1 | | | | 5 | | |
| Harwich | 13 | 22 | Walker | Seth | 3 | 1 | 1 | | | | | | 1 | | | | 6 | | |
| Eastham | 79 | 1 | Walker | William | | 1 | | 1 | | | | | 1 | 1 | | | 6 | | |
| Yarmouth | 100 | 10 | Walls | James | | 1 | | 1 | | 2 | 1 | | 1 | | | | 6 | | |
| Wellfleet | 73 | 1 | Ward | Benjamin | 2 | 1 | 2 | | 1 | 1 | 1 | 1 | 1 | | | | 10 | | |
| Wellfleet | 73 | 7 | Ward | Benjamin | | | 1 | | | 2 | | | 1 | | | | 4 | | |
| Wellfleet | 73 | 6 | Ward | Elisha | 2 | | 1 | | 1 | 1 | 1 | | | 1 | | | 7 | | |
| Provincetown | 60 | 37 | Ward | John | 2 | | 1 | | | | | | 1 | | | | 4 | | |
| Dennis | 29 | 11 | Warner | Gilbert | | 1 | | | | 1 | | 1 | | | | | 3 | | |
| Provincetown | 60 | 11 | Warren | William | 3 | | 1 | | | 1 | | | 1 | | | | 6 | | |
| Wellfleet | 72 | 32 | Waterman | Samuel | | 1 | | 1 | | | | 2 | | 1 | | | 5 | | |
| Wellfleet | 72 | 31 | Watts | Samuel | 1 | 1 | 1 | | 1 | 2 | 1 | 1 | | 1 | | | 9 | | |
| Truro | 67 | 30 | Webb | Bethiah Wid | | | | | | | | 1 | | 2 | | | 3 | | |
| Falmouth | 49 | 257 | Webb | Joseph | | | 1 | | | | 1 | | 1 | | | | 3 | | |
| Yarmouth | 96 | 19 | Webber | Prince | 1 | 3 | | 1 | | 3 | | | 1 | | | | 9 | | |
| Yarmouth | 96 | 20 | Webber | Samuel | | | 1 | | | | 1 | 1 | | 1 | 5 | | 10 | | |
| Yarmouth | 96 | 21 | Webber | William | | 1 | | 1 | | 1 | | | 1 | | 6 | | 10 | | |
| Barnstable | 92 | 48 | Weeks | Barzilla | | | 2 | 1 | | | | 2 | 1 | | | | 6 | | |
| Barnstable | 92 | 50 | Weeks | Barzilla Jr | 2 | | 1 | | | | | 1 | | | | | 4 | | |
| Harwich | 10 | 41 | Weeks | Daniel | 1 | | | 1 | | 1 | | | 1 | | | | 4 | | |
| Harwich | 10 | 9 | Weeks | Ebenezer | 2 | | 2 | 1 | | 1 | 1 | 2 | 1 | | | | 10 | | |
| Falmouth | 49 | 259 | Weeks | Ebenz | 1 | | | 1 | | 3 | | | 1 | | | | 6 | | |
| Falmouth | 49 | 262 | Weeks | Elisha | 1 | 1 | | 1 | | 2 | | 1 | | | | | 6 | | |
| Falmouth | 49 | 256 | Weeks | Francis | | | | 1 | | | | 1 | 1 | | | | 3 | | |
| Sandwich | 36 | 13 | Weeks | James | 1 | | | 1 | | 2 | 1 | | 1 | | | | 6 | | |
| Sandwich | 34 | 9 | Weeks | Joseph | | 1 | 1 | 1 | | | | | | 1 | | | 4 | | |
| Falmouth | 49 | 264 | Weeks | Levi | | 1 | | 1 | | | | 1 | | 1 | | | 4 | | |
| Barnstable | 87 | 12 | Weeks | Nathan | 1 | | | 1 | | 2 | | | 1 | | | | 5 | | |
| Harwich | 11 | 1 | Weeks | Pheba | | | | | | | | | 1 | 1 | | | 2 | | |
| Falmouth | 49 | 263 | Weeks | Richard | 1 | 1 | 1 | | 1 | 2 | | | 2 | 1 | | | 9 | | |
| Falmouth | 49 | 308 | Weeks | Silas | | | 1 | | | | | | 1 | | | | 2 | | |
| Harwich | 11 | 3 | Weeks | Thankfull Wd | 1 | | 1 | | | | | | | 1 | | | 3 | | |
| Falmouth | 49 | 260 | Weeks | Wm Junr | | | 1 | 1 | | 2 | 2 | | | 1 | | | 7 | | |
| Sandwich | 37 | 15 | Weeks | Zenas | | | 1 | | | 1 | | | 1 | | | | 3 | | |
| Harwich | 14 | 17 | Welch | John | | | | 1 | | 2 | | | 1 | | | | 4 | | |
| Truro | 67 | 29 | Wells | Peter | 1 | 1 | 1 | | 1 | | | 1 | 3 | 1 | | | 9 | | |
| Dennis | 30 | 3 | Wener | Caleb | | 2 | | | 1 | 2 | 1 | | 1 | | | | 7 | | |
| Dennis | 30 | 41 | Wexsom | Barnabas | 2 | 1 | 1 | | | | | | 1 | | | | 5 | | |
| Dennis | 28 | 28 | Wexsom | Daniel | 2 | 1 | 1 | | 1 | | 1 | | | 1 | | | 7 | | |
| Dennis | 31 | 1 | Wexsom | Darcey Wid | 1 | | | | | | 2 | | 1 | 1 | | | 5 | | |
| Harwich | 6 | 34 | Wexsom | Elijah | 2 | | | 1 | | | | | 1 | | | | 4 | | |
| Harwich | 12 | 45 | Wexsom | Job | 2 | | | 1 | | 1 | | | 1 | | | | 5 | | |
| Dennis | 28 | 27 | Wexsom | Joshua | | 2 | 1 | 1 | | 4 | | 1 | 1 | | | | 10 | | |
| Dennis | 30 | 37 | Wexsom | Solomon | 1 | 1 | | 1 | | 1 | | | 1 | | | | 5 | | |
| Provincetown | 60 | 9 | Wharf | George | | 1 | | 1 | | 3 | 1 | | | 1 | | | 7 | | |
| Truro | 63 | 11 | Wharf | Isaac | 1 | | | 1 | | 2 | | | | 1 | | | 5 | | |
| Provincetown | 60 | 8 | Wharf | John | | 2 | | 1 | | 3 | 1 | 1 | | 1 | | | 9 | | |
| Truro | 68 | 31 | Wharf | Joseph | 2 | | | 1 | | 2 | | | | 1 | | | 6 | | |
| Provincetown | 60 | 7 | Wharf | Samuel | 2 | | | 1 | | 2 | | | | | | | 5 | | |
| Yarmouth | 95 | 48 | Whelden | David | 2 | 1 | 1 | | 1 | 2 | | 2 | 3 | 1 | | | 13 | | |
| Barnstable | 87 | 28 | Whelden | Eben | 2 | | | | 1 | 3 | | | 1 | 1 | | | 8 | | |
| Yarmouth | 99 | 19 | Whelden | Elisha | | 3 | 3 | | 1 | | | 2 | | 1 | | | 10 | | |
| Yarmouth | 95 | 15 | Whelden | Jonathan | 1 | | | | 1 | 2 | 1 | | 1 | | | | 6 | | |
| Barnstable | 87 | 16 | Whelden | Peter | 1 | | | | 1 | 1 | | | 1 | | | | 4 | | |
| Yarmouth | 95 | 49 | Whelden | Seth | | | 2 | 1 | 1 | | | | | 1 | | | 5 | | |
| Barnstable | 87 | 15 | Whelden | Thomas | | | | 1 | | | | | 1 | 1 | | | 3 | | |
| Dennis | 28 | 40 | Whelding | Abahail Wd | | 1 | | | | | | 1 | 1 | 1 | | | 4 | | |
| Wellfleet | 70 | 34 | Whitaker | William | | | | 1 | | | | | 1 | | | | 2 | | |
| Dennis | 28 | 29 | Whitamore | Edward | 1 | 1 | | 1 | | 3 | 1 | | | | | | 7 | | |
| Yarmouth | 98 | 18 | White | Daniel | | | 1 | | | 1 | | | 1 | | | | 4 | | |
| Yarmouth | 98 | 16 | White | Isaac | | | 1 | | | 1 | | | 1 | | | | 3 | | |
| Yarmouth | 98 | 14 | White | Joseph | | 1 | | | | | | 1 | | 1 | | | 4 | | |
| Yarmouth | 98 | 15 | White | Joseph Jr | 3 | | | 1 | | | | | 1 | | | | 5 | | |
| Sandwich | 41 | 11 | White | Peter | | | | | | | | | | 1 | 2 | | 3 | | |
| Sandwich | 41 | 34 | Whitford | Silas | | | 1 | | | 2 | | 1 | | | | | 4 | | |
| Wellfleet | 73 | 2 | Whitman | Ezra | | | 1 | | | 2 | | | 1 | | | | 4 | | |
| Barnstable | 92 | 32 | Whitman | Jonas | 3 | 1 | 1 | | 1 | 1 | | 1 | 1 | 1 | | | 10 | | |

# 1800 Barnstable County, Massachusetts Index

| Town | PG# | LN# | Last Name | First Name | FWM <10 | FWM 10-16 | FWM 16-26 | FWM 26-45 | FWM 45+ | FWF <10 | FWF 10-16 | FWF 16-26 | FWF 26-45 | FWF 45+ | Total All Other | Total Slaves | Totals | District/Township | Notes |
|---|---|---|---|---|---|---|---|---|---|---|---|---|---|---|---|---|---|---|---|
| Wellfleet | 75 | 34 | Whitman | Levi Rev | 2 | 1 | | | 1 | 3 | 1 | | 1 | | | | 9 | | |
| Provincetown | 60 | 18 | Wickson | Robert | | | 1 | | 1 | | | | | 1 | | | 3 | | |
| Sandwich | 41 | 37 | Wight | Joseph | 1 | | 1 | 1 | 1 | 2 | 1 | | 1 | | | | 8 | | |
| Sandwich | 41 | 14 | Wilbour | Daniel | | | | | | | | | | | 5 | | 5 | | |
| Wellfleet | 73 | 17 | Wiley | Bethuel | | | | 1 | | | | 1 | 1 | 1 | | | 4 | | |
| Wellfleet | 73 | 4 | Wiley | David | 1 | | | 1 | | 1 | | 1 | | | | | 4 | | |
| Wellfleet | 73 | 3 | Wiley | Ebenezer | 1 | 1 | | 1 | | 3 | | | 1 | | | | 7 | | |
| Wellfleet | 73 | 27 | Wiley | Elisha | 2 | | | 1 | | 2 | | | 1 | | | | 6 | | |
| Wellfleet | 73 | 31 | Wiley | Hannah | 2 | | 2 | | | 1 | | | 1 | 1 | | | 7 | | |
| Wellfleet | 75 | 24 | Wiley | Henry | | | | 1 | | | | | 1 | | | | 2 | | |
| Wellfleet | 75 | 33 | Wiley | John | 1 | | 1 | | | | | | 1 | | | | 3 | | |
| Wellfleet | 72 | 33 | Wiley | Levi | | | | | 1 | | | 1 | | 1 | | | 3 | | |
| Wellfleet | 72 | 34 | Wiley | Levi Junr | | | | 1 | | 2 | | | 1 | | | | 4 | | |
| Eastham | 79 | 4 | Wiley | Moses | | | | 1 | | 1 | | | 1 | | | | 3 | | |
| Wellfleet | 74 | 9 | Wiley | Nathaniel | | 2 | | 1 | | 2 | | 1 | 1 | | | | 7 | | |
| Sandwich | 36 | 1 | Willcox | Amaziah | 1 | 1 | 1 | 1 | | 3 | 2 | | 1 | | | | 10 | | |
| Sandwich | 39 | 18 | Williams | Abigail | | | | | | | 2 | | 1 | | | | 3 | | |
| Provincetown | 60 | 10 | Williams | Andrew | 1 | | | 1 | 1 | 1 | | | 1 | 1 | | | 6 | | |
| Mashpee | 52 | 6 | Wilson | Sancho | | | | | | | | | | | 2 | | 2 | | |
| Sandwich | 37 | 8 | Wine | Bennett | | | | 1 | | 1 | 1 | 1 | | | | | 4 | | |
| Sandwich | 34 | 7 | Wine | Ebenezer | 3 | | | 1 | | | | 1 | | 2 | | | 7 | | |
| Sandwich | 37 | 14 | Wine | Edward | 1 | | 1 | 1 | | 1 | 1 | 1 | 1 | | | | 7 | | |
| Sandwich | 37 | 13 | Wine | John 2d | | 1 | 1 | 1 | | 1 | | 1 | 1 | | | | 6 | | |
| Harwich | 7 | 39 | Wing | Born | | 1 | 1 | 1 | | | | 2 | | 1 | | | 6 | | |
| Dennis | 26 | 32 | Wing | David | 1 | | | 1 | | 3 | | | 1 | | | | 6 | | |
| Harwich | 4 | 33 | Wing | David | | | 1 | | | 1 | 2 | | 1 | | | | 6 | | |
| Sandwich | 41 | 26 | Wing | David | 3 | | | 1 | | 1 | | | 1 | 2 | | | 8 | | |
| Falmouth | 49 | 265 | Wing | James | 2 | 2 | 1 | 1 | | 2 | | 2 | 1 | | | | 11 | | |
| Sandwich | 37 | 34 | Wing | Jashub | 1 | | | 1 | | | 2 | | 1 | | | | 5 | | |
| Sandwich | 35 | 12 | Wing | John 2d | | | 1 | 1 | | | 1 | 2 | 1 | | | | 6 | | |
| Chatham | 19 | 43 | Wing | Joseph | | | | 1 | | | | | 1 | | | | 2 | | |
| Sandwich | 35 | 43 | Wing | Joseph | | | | 1 | | | | | 1 | | | | 2 | | |
| Sandwich | 34 | 15 | Wing | Joseph Jun | | 1 | 2 | 1 | | | | | 2 | | | | 6 | | |
| Sandwich | 41 | 12 | Wing | Judah | 3 | | | 1 | | 1 | | 1 | 1 | | | | 7 | | |
| Sandwich | 41 | 21 | Wing | Lemuel | 1 | 1 | 1 | 1 | | 3 | 2 | | 1 | 1 | | | 11 | | |
| Chatham | 19 | 44 | Wing | Levi | | | | 1 | | 1 | 1 | | 1 | | | | 4 | | |
| Sandwich | 34 | 17 | Wing | Mary | | | | | | | | | | 1 | | | 1 | | |
| Sandwich | 41 | 33 | Wing | Nathaniel | 1 | 1 | 4 | 1 | | 1 | 1 | 1 | | 1 | | | 11 | | |
| Sandwich | 39 | 24 | Wing | Paul | | 2 | | | 1 | | 2 | | 1 | | | | 6 | | |
| Falmouth | 49 | 261 | Wing | Presbury | 2 | 1 | | 2 | | 1 | | 1 | | | | | 7 | | |
| Harwich | 7 | 40 | Wing | Samuel | | | 1 | | | | 1 | | 1 | | | | 3 | | |
| Sandwich | 39 | 23 | Wing | Samuel | 1 | 1 | 2 | | | | | | 1 | | | | 5 | | |
| Sandwich | 35 | 13 | Wing | Stephen | 4 | | 1 | | | 2 | | | 1 | | | | 9 | | |
| Harwich | 4 | 7 | Winslow | Abraham | | | | 1 | | 1 | | | 1 | | | | 3 | | |
| Harwich | 4 | 4 | Winslow | Isaac | 3 | | | 1 | | 1 | | | 1 | | | | 6 | | |
| Harwich | 3 | 15 | Winslow | John | 1 | | 1 | | | 1 | | 1 | | | | | 4 | | |
| Harwich | 4 | 15 | Winslow | Joseph | 2 | | 1 | 1 | | 2 | 2 | | | | | | 8 | | |
| Harwich | 4 | 17 | Winslow | Josiah | 2 | 1 | | | | | | 1 | 1 | | | | 5 | | |
| Harwich | 4 | 8 | Winslow | Kenalam | 1 | | 1 | | | | | 1 | 1 | | | | 4 | | |
| Harwich | 4 | 5 | Winslow | Mary Wid | | | | | | | | | 1 | 1 | | | 2 | | |
| Harwich | 4 | 32 | Winslow | Nathan | | 1 | 1 | 1 | | | | 1 | | 1 | | | 5 | | |
| Harwich | 4 | 18 | Winslow | Nathan Jun | 2 | | | 1 | | 1 | 1 | | 1 | | | | 6 | | |
| Harwich | 4 | 6 | Winslow | Nathaniel | | | | 1 | | | | 1 | | | | | 2 | | |
| Dennis | 28 | 30 | Witamore | Edward Jun | 1 | 1 | | | | | | | 1 | | | | 3 | | |
| Wellfleet | 72 | 35 | Withrell | John | | 1 | | | 1 | 2 | | | 1 | | | | 5 | | |
| Wellfleet | 73 | 5 | Withrell | Ruth | | 1 | 1 | | | 3 | 1 | | 1 | | | | 7 | | |
| Wellfleet | 72 | 36 | Withrell | Whitfield | 1 | | | 1 | | 1 | | | 1 | | | | 4 | | |
| Provincetown | 61 | 11 | Wizell | George Rix | | | 1 | | | 1 | | | 1 | | | | 3 | | |
| Mashpee | 51 | 10 | Wolf | James | | 2 | 3 | 1 | | | | 1 | 1 | | | | 8 | | |
| Mashpee | 51 | 9 | Wolf | Stephen | 2 | | 1 | | | 1 | | | 1 | 1 | | | 7 | | |
| Falmouth | 49 | 258 | Wood | David | 2 | 1 | | 1 | | | 1 | | 1 | | | | 6 | | |
| Barnstable | 84 | 19 | Wood | Matthew | | | | 1 | | | | 1 | | | | | 2 | | |
| Barnstable | 92 | 13 | Wood | Francis | | | 1 | 1 | | | | | 1 | 1 | | | 5 | | |
| Barnstable | 92 | 3 | Wood | Wilson | 1 | | 1 | 1 | | | | | 1 | 1 | | | 5 | | |
| Barnstable | 92 | 4 | Wood | Zenas | | | 1 | | | | | 1 | | | | | 2 | | |
| Barnstable | 87 | 51 | Woods | Ansel | 2 | | | 1 | 3 | | | | 1 | | | | 7 | | |
| Chatham | 20 | 6 | Woodson | Wid | | 1 | | | | 1 | | | 1 | | | | 3 | | |
| Barnstable | 89 | 29 | Wright | Benjamin | | | 1 | | | 1 | | 1 | | | | | 3 | | |
| Barnstable | 89 | 10 | Wright | Martin | | 1 | | | | | | | 1 | | | | 2 | | |
| Yarmouth | 99 | 32 | York | Nathan | | | 1 | | | 2 | | | 1 | | | | 4 | | |
| Chatham | 19 | 20 | Young | *yat | | 2 | | 1 | 1 | | | | | 1 | | | 5 | | |
| Barnstable | 84 | 42 | Young | Bangs | 1 | 1 | 3 | 1 | | 3 | 2 | 1 | 1 | | | | 13 | | |
| Wellfleet | 73 | 8 | Young | Barnabus | | | 1 | | | 1 | | | | 1 | | | 3 | | |
| Wellfleet | 75 | 32 | Young | Daniel | 3 | | | 1 | | | | | 1 | | | | 5 | | |
| Orleans | 25 | 26 | Young | David | | 1 | | 1 | | | 1 | 4 | 1 | | | | 8 | | |
| Provincetown | 60 | 12 | Young | David | 2 | | | 1 | | | | | 1 | | | | 4 | | |
| Orleans | 23 | 31 | Young | Ebenezor | | | | 1 | | | | | 1 | | | | 2 | | |
| Harwich | 12 | 2 | Young | Edmond | 1 | | | 1 | 3 | | | 1 | | | | | 6 | | |
| Orleans | 23 | 22 | Young | Edmond | | | | 1 | | | | 1 | | 1 | | | 3 | | |
| Provincetown | 60 | 13 | Young | Eleazar | 3 | | | 1 | | | | 1 | 1 | | | | 6 | | |
| Provincetown | 60 | 16 | Young | Elisha | 1 | | 1 | | | | | | 1 | | | | 3 | | |
| Chatham | 20 | 2 | Young | Ezekel | | | 1 | | | | | | 1 | | | | 2 | | |

| Town | PG# | LN# | Last Name | First Name | Free White Males under 10 | 10 to 16 | 16 to 26 | 26 to 45 | 45 and over | Free White Females under 10 | 10 to 16 | 16 to 26 | 26 to 45 | 45 and over | Total All Other | Total Slaves | Totals | District/ Township | Notes |
|---|---|---|---|---|---|---|---|---|---|---|---|---|---|---|---|---|---|---|---|
| Chatham | 20 | 31 | Young | Hemon | 1 | | 2 | | 1 | | 1 | | | 1 | | | 6 | | |
| Wellfleet | 73 | 13 | Young | Henry | | | 1 | | | | 1 | | | | | | 2 | | |
| Sandwich | 41 | 4 | Young | Isaiah | | | | 1 | | 2 | | | | 1 | | | 4 | | |
| Orleans | 22 | 13 | Young | James | | | 1 | 1 | 1 | | | | | 1 | | | 4 | | |
| Orleans | 24 | 10 | Young | James | | | 1 | | 1 | | | | | 1 | | | 3 | | |
| Orleans | 22 | 36 | Young | Jediah | 2 | 1 | | 1 | | 3 | 2 | | 1 | | | | 10 | | |
| Orleans | 23 | 30 | Young | Jediah | 2 | 1 | | 1 | | 3 | 2 | 1 | | 1 | | | 11 | | |
| Chatham | 19 | 46 | Young | John | 2 | 1 | | 1 | | | | | | | | | 5 | | |
| Harwich | 10 | 2 | Young | John | 2 | 1 | | 1 | | 1 | 2 | 1 | | 1 | | | 9 | | |
| Wellfleet | 75 | 5 | Young | John | 1 | 1 | | | 1 | 3 | 1 | | 1 | 1 | | | 9 | | |
| Wellfleet | 73 | 10 | Young | John Junr | | | | 1 | | | 1 | 1 | 1 | | | | 4 | | |
| Orleans | 25 | 25 | Young | Jonath | | | 1 | 1 | | | | | 1 | 1 | | | 4 | | |
| Chatham | 20 | 1 | Young | Joseph | 1 | 1 | | 1 | | 3 | 1 | | | 1 | | | 8 | | |
| Orleans | 24 | 41 | Young | Lewis | 1 | | | 1 | | 1 | | | | 1 | | | 4 | | |
| Wellfleet | 73 | 11 | Young | Molly | | | | | | | | 1 | | | | | 1 | | |
| Barnstable | 84 | 38 | Young | Moses | | 1 | 1 | 1 | | 1 | | | | 1 | | | 5 | | |
| Orleans | 24 | 35 | Young | Moses | | | 1 | | | 3 | 1 | | 1 | | | | 6 | | |
| Wellfleet | 73 | 12 | Young | Moses | | | 2 | | 1 | | 1 | | 1 | | | | 5 | | |
| Wellfleet | 73 | 15 | Young | Naby | | | | | | 2 | 2 | | 1 | | | | 5 | | |
| Orleans | 24 | 12 | Young | Phillip | | 1 | 2 | 1 | 1 | | 1 | 2 | | 1 | | | 9 | | |
| Harwich | 10 | 1 | Young | Prince | | | | 1 | | | | | | 1 | | | 2 | | |
| Chatham | 19 | 45 | Young | Prince | 1 | 1 | | | 1 | 1 | | 1 | 1 | 1 | | | 7 | | |
| Wellfleet | 73 | 14 | Young | Robert | | | | 1 | 1 | 2 | | | | 1 | | | 5 | | |
| Chatham | 19 | 48 | Young | Samuel | 2 | | | 1 | | 2 | | 1 | 1 | | | | 7 | | |
| Chatham | 19 | 47 | Young | Simeon | 2 | | 1 | | 1 | 2 | 2 | 1 | | 1 | | | 11 | | |
| Wellfleet | 73 | 9 | Young | Stephen | 1 | 1 | | | 1 | 1 | | | | 1 | | | 5 | | |
| Barnstable | 84 | 41 | Young | Thomas | | | | 1 | | | | | | | | | 1 | | |
| Barnstable | 85 | 41 | Young | Thomas | | | 1 | | | 3 | | | | 1 | | | 5 | | |
| Falmouth | 49 | 268 | Young | Andrew | 1 | | 1 | | | | | | | 1 | | | 4 | | |
| Falmouth | 49 | 274 | Young | David | 2 | | 1 | | | | | | | 1 | | | 6 | | |
| Falmouth | 49 | 290 | | Dinah | | | | | | | | | | | | | 1 | | Last name left blank |
| Sandwich | 41 | 15 | | Esther | | | | | | | | | | | 1 | | 1 | | No last name given |

# 1800 Chilmark, Dukes County, Massachusetts

| TOWN | PG# | LN# | LAST NAME | FIRST NAME | FREE WHITE MALES under 10 | 10 to 16 | 16 to 26 | 26 to 45 | 45 and over | FREE WHITE FEMALES under 10 | 10 to 16 | 16 to 26 | 26 to 45 | 45 and over | TOTAL ALL OTHER | TOTAL SLAVES | TOTALS | DISTRICT/ TOWNSHIP | NOTES |
|---|---|---|---|---|---|---|---|---|---|---|---|---|---|---|---|---|---|---|---|
| Chilmark | 448 | 1 | Skiff | Vinal | | 1 | 1 | 1 | | 1 | | 1 | 1 | | | | 6 | | |
| Chilmark | 448 | 2 | Hamlin | Lydia | | | | | | | | | 1 | | | | 1 | | |
| Chilmark | 448 | 3 | Allen | Josiah | | | | 1 | | 1 | | 1 | 1 | | | | 4 | | |
| Chilmark | 448 | 4 | Pease | Fortunatus | | 1 | | 1 | | | | | | 1 | | | 3 | | |
| Chilmark | 448 | 5 | Pease | Fortunatus Jr | | 1 | | 1 | | 2 | 1 | | 1 | | | | 6 | | |
| Chilmark | 448 | 6 | Pease | Nathl | | | | 1 | | 2 | | 1 | | | | | 4 | | |
| Chilmark | 448 | 7 | Pease | Abishai | | 1 | | 2 | 1 | | | | | 1 | | | 5 | | |
| Chilmark | 448 | 8 | Norris | Patience | | 1 | | | | | | | 1 | | | | 2 | | |
| Chilmark | 448 | 9 | Ferguson | John | | | | 1 | | | | 1 | 1 | 1 | | | 4 | | |
| Chilmark | 448 | 10 | Ferguson | William | 2 | | 1 | | 1 | | | 1 | | | | | 5 | | |
| Chilmark | 448 | 11 | Mayhew | * | 1 | | 1 | | 1 | | | | 1 | 1 | | | 5 | | |
| Chilmark | 448 | 12 | Smith | Eunice | | 1 | | | | | | 1 | | | | | 2 | | |
| Chilmark | 448 | 13 | Jones | Daniel | | 2 | | 1 | | 1 | | | 1 | | | | 5 | | |
| Chilmark | 448 | 14 | Tillton | Stephen | 1 | | 1 | 1 | | | | | 1 | | | | 4 | | |
| Chilmark | 448 | 15 | Flanders | John | 1 | | 1 | | 2 | | | 1 | | | | | 5 | | |
| Chilmark | 448 | 16 | Hillman | Saml | | | | 1 | | | | | 1 | | | | 2 | | |
| Chilmark | 448 | 17 | Hillman | Moses | 2 | | 1 | | 1 | | | 1 | | | | | 5 | | |
| Chilmark | 448 | 18 | Cooper | Zacheus | | | | | | | | | | | 3 | | 3 | | |
| Chilmark | 448 | 19 | Adams | Mayhew | | 1 | | 1 | | 2 | 1 | 2 | | | 1 | | 8 | | |
| Chilmark | 448 | 20 | Adams | Wm | 1 | | 1 | | 1 | | | 1 | | | | | 4 | | |
| Chilmark | 448 | 21 | Adams | James | 1 | 1 | 1 | | 1 | 2 | 1 | | | | | | 8 | | |
| Chilmark | 448 | 22 | Norton | Ruth | | | | | | | | | 1 | | | | 1 | | |
| Chilmark | 448 | 23 | Norton | Shubael | 3 | | | 2 | | 2 | | | 1 | | | | 8 | | |
| Chilmark | 448 | 24 | Dunham | Abigail | | 1 | | | | | | | 1 | 1 | | | 3 | | |
| Chilmark | 448 | 25 | Cox | Thos | 2 | | | 1 | 1 | 2 | | | 1 | | | | 7 | | |
| Chilmark | 448 | 26 | Look | Job Jr | | | 1 | | 1 | | | 1 | | | | | 3 | | |
| Chilmark | 448 | 27 | Hancock | James | 2 | | 1 | 1 | | 1 | | 1 | | | | | 6 | | |
| Chilmark | 448 | 28 | Hillman | Robert | | 1 | 3 | 1 | 1 | | 1 | | 1 | 1 | | | 9 | | |
| Chilmark | 448 | 29 | Bassett | Nathl | | 1 | | 1 | 1 | | | | 1 | | | | 4 | | |
| Chilmark | 448 | 30 | Hillman | Uriel | 1 | | 1 | | 1 | | | 1 | | | | | 4 | | |
| Chilmark | 448 | 31 | Pease | John | | 1 | | 1 | | 1 | 3 | | 1 | | | | 7 | | |
| Chilmark | 448 | 32 | Bargis | Marcy | | | | | | | | 1 | | | | | 1 | | |
| Chilmark | 448 | 33 | Skiff | Nathan | | | 1 | 1 | 1 | | | 1 | 1 | 2 | | | 7 | | |
| Chilmark | 448 | 34 | Lumbert | Thos | 1 | | | 1 | 3 | | | 1 | | | | | 6 | | |
| Chilmark | 448 | 35 | Lumbert | Moses | | | 1 | | | 3 | 2 | 1 | | | | | 7 | | |
| Chilmark | 448 | 36 | Lumbert | Abishai | 2 | | 1 | 1 | 3 | 1 | | | | | | | 8 | | |
| Chilmark | 448 | 37 | Nickerson | Samuel | 1 | | 1 | | | | | | 1 | 1 | | | 4 | | |
| Chilmark | 448 | 38 | Butler | Nicholas | 2 | | 1 | | | | | | 1 | | | | 4 | | |
| Chilmark | 448 | 39 | Hanks | Uriah | | | | 1 | | | | | 1 | | | | 2 | | |
| Chilmark | 448 | 40 | Norton | Saml | | 1 | | 1 | | | | 1 | 1 | | | | 4 | | |
| Chilmark | 448 | 41 | Norton | James | | | | 1 | | | | | 1 | 1 | | | 3 | | |
| Chilmark | 448 | 42 | Norton | Wm | 1 | | 1 | | | | | | 1 | | | | 5 | | |
| Chilmark | 448 | 43 | Mayhew | Lois | | | | | | | | | 2 | | | | 2 | | |
| Chilmark | 448 | 44 | Mayhew | John | 1 | | | 1 | 2 | | | | 1 | | | | 5 | | |
| Chilmark | 448 | 45 | Allen | Robert | | 1 | | 1 | | 1 | | | 1 | | | | 4 | | |
| Chilmark | 448 | 46 | Allen | Ezra | | | | 1 | | | | | 1 | | | | 2 | | |
| Chilmark | 448 | 47 | Allen | Mathew | 1 | 1 | | 1 | | 1 | | | | | | | 4 | | |
| Chilmark | 448 | 48 | Bassett | Jona | | | | 1 | | | | | | | | | 1 | | |
| Chilmark | 448 | 49 | McColumn | Arch | 1 | | 1 | | | | | 1 | | | | | 3 | | |
| Chilmark | 449 | 1 | Smith | Jonathan | 1 | | | 1 | 1 | 1 | | 1 | | | | | 5 | | |
| Chilmark | 449 | 2 | Bassett | Wm | 2 | | | 1 | | | | 1 | 1 | | | | 5 | | |
| Chilmark | 449 | 3 | Hillman | Silas | | | | 1 | | | 3 | | 1 | | | | 5 | | |
| Chilmark | 449 | 4 | Hillman | Silas Jr | | | | 1 | | | | | 1 | | | | 2 | | |
| Chilmark | 449 | 5 | House | Work | | | | 2 | | | | | 5 | | | | 7 | | |
| Chilmark | 449 | 6 | Hillman | Ezra | 1 | 1 | | 2 | | 1 | | 1 | 1 | | 1 | | 8 | | |
| Chilmark | 449 | 7 | Bassett | Benja | 1 | 1 | | | 1 | 1 | 3 | | 2 | | | | 9 | | |
| Chilmark | 449 | 8 | Pitts | Thankful | | | | | | | | | 1 | | | | 1 | | |
| Chilmark | 449 | 9 | Mayhew | Mathew | | 1 | | 2 | | | | 1 | 1 | | | | 5 | | |
| Chilmark | 449 | 10 | Mayhew | Mathew Jr | 2 | | 1 | 1 | | 2 | 2 | 2 | 1 | | | | 11 | | |
| Chilmark | 449 | 11 | Mayhew | Allen | 1 | | | 1 | | | | | 1 | | | | 3 | | |
| Chilmark | 449 | 12 | Stewart | Wm | | | | 1 | | | | | 1 | 1 | | | 3 | | |
| Chilmark | 449 | 13 | Stewart | Wm Jr | 1 | | | 1 | | 2 | | | 1 | | | | 5 | | |
| Chilmark | 449 | 14 | Tillton | Wm | | 1 | | 1 | | | 3 | | 1 | 1 | | | 7 | | |
| Chilmark | 449 | 15 | Tillton | Beriah | 2 | 2 | 1 | 1 | | 3 | | 1 | 1 | | | | 11 | | |
| Chilmark | 449 | 16 | Tillton | Wm Jr | 1 | | | 1 | | 3 | 1 | | 1 | | | | 7 | | |
| Chilmark | 449 | 17 | Allen | Tristram | 2 | | | 1 | | | | | 1 | 1 | | | 5 | | |
| Chilmark | 449 | 18 | Allen | Deborah | 1 | | 1 | | | | | | 1 | | | | 3 | | |
| Chilmark | 449 | 19 | Mayhew | Simon | | | | 1 | | | | | 1 | | | | 2 | | |
| Chilmark | 449 | 20 | Mayhew | Oliver | | 1 | | 1 | | | | 2 | | | | | 4 | | |
| Chilmark | 449 | 21 | Mayhew | Ruth | | | | | | | | | 1 | | | | 1 | | |
| Chilmark | 449 | 22 | Hillman | Abigail | | 1 | | | | | | | 1 | | | | 2 | | |
| Chilmark | 449 | 23 | Bassett | Norton | 2 | | | 1 | | 1 | | | 1 | | | | 5 | | |
| Chilmark | 449 | 24 | Mayhew | Rachel | | | | | | | | | 2 | | | | 2 | | |
| Chilmark | 449 | 25 | Tillton | Ezra | 1 | 1 | 1 | | 1 | 1 | | 1 | 2 | | | | 8 | | |
| Chilmark | 449 | 26 | Tillton | Oliver | 2 | | 1 | 1 | | 2 | | | 1 | | | | 7 | | |
| Chilmark | 449 | 27 | Tillton | Joseph | 3 | | | 1 | 1 | 2 | 1 | | 1 | 1 | | | 10 | | |
| Chilmark | 449 | 28 | Tillton | Zilpah | | | | | | | | | 2 | | | | 2 | | |
| Chilmark | 449 | 29 | Tillton | Mathew | 1 | 1 | 1 | | 1 | 2 | | 1 | 1 | | | | 9 | | |
| Chilmark | 449 | 30 | Tillton | Daniel | 3 | | | 1 | | | | | 1 | | | | 5 | | |

# 1800 Chilmark, Dukes County, Massachusetts

| TOWN | PG# | LN# | LAST NAME | FIRST NAME | FREE WHITE MALES under 10 | 10 to 16 | 16 to 26 | 26 to 45 | 45 and over | FREE WHITE FEMALES under 10 | 10 to 16 | 16 to 26 | 26 to 45 | 45 and over | TOTAL ALL OTHER | TOTAL SLAVES | TOTALS | DISTRICT/ TOWNSHIP | NOTES |
|---|---|---|---|---|---|---|---|---|---|---|---|---|---|---|---|---|---|---|---|
| Chilmark | 449 | 31 | Tillton | Isaac | 1 | | | | 1 | 2 | | | 1 | | | | 5 | | |
| Chilmark | 449 | 32 | Allen | Samuel | | | | | 1 | | | | 1 | 2 | | | 4 | | |
| Chilmark | 449 | 33 | Allen | Ephraim | | 1 | | | 1 | | | 2 | 1 | 1 | | | 6 | | |
| Chilmark | 449 | 34 | Cottle | John | | | | | 1 | | | | | 1 | | | 2 | | |
| Chilmark | 449 | 35 | Cottle | John Jr | 2 | 1 | 1 | | 1 | 1 | 1 | 1 | 1 | | | | 9 | | |
| Chilmark | 449 | 36 | Cottle | Silas | | 1 | 1 | | 1 | | | 2 | 1 | | | | 6 | | |
| Chilmark | 449 | 37 | Tillton | Reuben | | | 2 | 2 | | 1 | | | 2 | 2 | | | 9 | | |
| Chilmark | 449 | 38 | Look | Prince | 2 | 1 | | | 1 | 1 | | 1 | | | | | 6 | | |
| Chilmark | 449 | 39 | Mayhew | Pheir | | | 1 | | | | | | | 1 | | | 2 | | |
| Chilmark | 449 | 40 | Mayhew | Mark | | 2 | | 2 | | | | | | 1 | 2 | | 7 | | |
| Chilmark | 449 | 41 | Mayhew | Abner | | 1 | 3 | | | 1 | | 1 | 1 | | 1 | | 8 | | |
| Chilmark | 449 | 42 | Mayhew | Timo | | 2 | 1 | 1 | 1 | | | 2 | | 1 | | | 8 | | |
| Chilmark | 449 | 43 | Pool | Wm | | | | 1 | | 1 | | | 1 | | | | 3 | | |
| Chilmark | 449 | 44 | Allen | James | | | | | 1 | | 1 | 1 | | 1 | | | 4 | | |
| Chilmark | 449 | 45 | Allen | James Jr | | 1 | | 1 | | 1 | | | 1 | | | | 4 | | |
| Chilmark | 449 | 46 | Allen | Sylvanus | 1 | | | 1 | | 3 | | 1 | | | | | 6 | | |
| Chilmark | 449 | 47 | Allen | Zebulon | 1 | | | 1 | | 3 | | 1 | 1 | | | | 7 | | |
| Chilmark | 449 | 48 | Smith | Elijah | | | 2 | | 1 | | | 3 | | 1 | | | 7 | | |
| Chilmark | 449 | 49 | Tillton | Nathan | | | 2 | | 1 | 1 | 1 | 1 | 1 | | | | 8 | | |
| Chilmark | 449 | 50 | Mayhew | Nathl | 2 | 2 | | 1 | | 2 | 1 | 1 | 1 | | | | 10 | | |
| Chilmark | 449 | 51 | Mayhew | Thos W. | 2 | | 1 | 2 | | 1 | 3 | | 2 | | | | 11 | | |
| Chilmark | 449 | 52 | West | Thos | 1 | 1 | | | 1 | 1 | 3 | 1 | | 1 | | | 9 | | |
| Chilmark | 450 | 1 | Mayhew | Theophilus | | | 1 | | 1 | | | 1 | | 1 | | | 4 | | |
| Chilmark | 450 | 2 | Mayhew | Seth | | | | 1 | 1 | | | 1 | | 1 | | | 4 | | |
| Chilmark | 450 | 3 | Mayhew | Benja | 2 | 2 | | | | 1 | 2 | 1 | | 1 | | | 9 | | |
| Chilmark | 450 | 4 | Mayhew | Ephm | 3 | 3 | 2 | | 1 | 1 | | 1 | | 1 | | | 12 | | |
| Chilmark | 450 | 5 | Mayhew | Simon Jr | | | | 1 | | | | | 1 | | | | 2 | | |
| Chilmark | 450 | 6 | Mayhew | Jethro | | | | 1 | | | | | | | | | 1 | | |
| Chilmark | 450 | 7 | Pool | Mary | | 1 | | | | | | 1 | | 1 | | | 3 | | |
| Chilmark | 450 | 8 | Skiff | Ebenz | 3 | | | 1 | | | | | 1 | 1 | | | 6 | | |
| Chilmark | 450 | 9 | West | George | 1 | | 1 | | | 1 | | 1 | | | | | 4 | | |
| Chilmark | 450 | 10 | Tillton | Ward | 1 | 3 | | 1 | | 1 | | | 1 | 1 | | | 8 | | |
| Chilmark | 450 | 11 | Mayhew | Hebron | 2 | | | 1 | | 1 | | 1 | | | | | 5 | | |
| Chilmark | 450 | 12 | Mayhew | Wm | 1 | | | 1 | | 1 | | 1 | | | | | 4 | | |
| Chilmark | 450 | 13 | Mayhew | Abigail | 1 | 1 | | | | | | 1 | 1 | 1 | | | 5 | | |
| Chilmark | 450 | 14 | Mayhew | Zachariah | 1 | | | 1 | 2 | 1 | | 1 | 1 | | | | 7 | | |
| Chilmark | 450 | 15 | Tillton | Pain | | | 3 | | 1 | 1 | 2 | 1 | | 1 | | | 9 | | |
| Chilmark | 450 | 16 | Luce | Mary | | | 3 | | | | | 1 | | 1 | | | 5 | | |
| Chilmark | 450 | 17 | Robinson | Paul | | 1 | 1 | 1 | | | | 1 | | 1 | | | 5 | | |
| Chilmark | 450 | 18 | Robinson | Zephh | | 2 | | 2 | | 1 | | 1 | 1 | | 1 | | 8 | | |
| Chilmark | 450 | 19 | Nye | John | | 2 | 2 | | 1 | 2 | 2 | 2 | | 1 | | | 12 | | |
| Chilmark | 450 | 20 | Robinson | Thos | 3 | 1 | | 1 | | 2 | | | | 1 | | | 8 | | |
| Chilmark | 450 | 21 | Robinson | Shadh | 1 | | 1 | 2 | | 4 | 1 | 1 | 1 | | | | 11 | | |
| Chilmark | 450 | 22 | Robinson | Elihu | 1 | | 1 | 1 | | 1 | 2 | 1 | | 1 | | | 8 | | |
| Chilmark | 450 | 23 | Gifford | Wm | 1 | 2 | 1 | | 1 | 4 | 3 | | | 2 | | | 14 | | |
| Chilmark | 450 | 24 | Gifford | Silas | 1 | | | 1 | | | | | 1 | | | | 3 | | |
| Chilmark | 450 | 25 | Slocum | Wm | 2 | | 1 | 1 | | 3 | | 1 | | | | | 8 | | |
| Chilmark | 450 | 26 | Slocum | Christr | 5 | | 1 | 1 | | 1 | | 1 | 1 | | | | 10 | | |
| Chilmark | 450 | 27 | Slocum | John | | 1 | 2 | | 1 | 1 | | 1 | | 1 | | | 7 | | |
| Chilmark | 450 | 28 | Slocum | Peleg | | 1 | | 1 | 1 | 1 | | 1 | 1 | | | | 6 | | |
| Chilmark | 450 | 29 | Peckings | Wm | 2 | 1 | | 1 | | 2 | | 1 | | | 1 | | 8 | | |
| Chilmark | 450 | 30 | Grinall | Remington | 2 | | | 1 | | | | | 1 | | | | 4 | | |
| Chilmark | 450 | 31 | Gifford | Ephm | 2 | | | 1 | | 1 | | 1 | | | | | 5 | | |
| Chilmark | 450 | 32 | Dodge | Henry | | | | | | | | | | | 2 | | 2 | | |
| Chilmark | 450 | 33 | Dodge | John | | | | | | | | | | | 3 | | 3 | | |
| Chilmark | 450 | 34 | Cooper | Thos | | | | | | | | | | | 7 | | 7 | | |
| Chilmark | 450 | 35 | Cooper | Josiah | | | | | | | | | | | 4 | | 4 | | |
| Chilmark | 450 | 36 | Cooper | Abram | | | | | | | | | | | 5 | | 5 | | |
| Chilmark | 450 | 37 | Cooper | Thos Jr | | | | | | | | | | | 3 | | 3 | | |
| Chilmark | 450 | 38 | Peters | Pero | | | | | | | | | | | 2 | | 2 | | |
| Chilmark | 450 | 39 | Tockquenett | Martha | | | | | | | | | | | 2 | | 2 | | |
| Chilmark | 450 | 40 | Jeffers | Thos | | | | | | | | | | | 5 | | 5 | | |
| Chilmark | 450 | 41 | Slocum | Jona | | | | | | | | | | | 12 | | 12 | | |
| Chilmark | 450 | 42 | de Grass | Jos | | | | | | | | | | | 6 | | 6 | | |
| Chilmark | 450 | 43 | Silvary | Emanuel | | | | | | | | | | | 3 | | 3 | | |
| Chilmark | 450 | 44 | Pero | Calo | | | | | | | | | | | 1 | | 1 | | |
| Chilmark | 450 | 45 | Sharper | Pero | | | | | | | | | | | 2 | | 2 | | |
| Chilmark | 450 | 46 | Peters | Simeon | | | | | | | | | | | 3 | | 3 | | |
| Chilmark | 450 | 47 | Swazy | Zephh | | | | | | | | | | | 4 | | 4 | | |
| Chilmark | 450 | 48 | Rogers | Joel | | | | | | | | | | | 6 | | 6 | | |
| Chilmark | 450 | 49 | Weeks | Wm | | | | | | | | | | | 2 | | 2 | | |

# 1800 Edgartown, Dukes County, Massachusetts

| TOWN | PG# | LN# | LAST NAME | FIRST NAME | FREE WHITE MALES | | | | | FREE WHITE FEMALES | | | | | TOTAL ALL OTHER | TOTAL SLAVES | TOTALS | DISTRICT/ TOWNSHIP | NOTES |
|---|---|---|---|---|---|---|---|---|---|---|---|---|---|---|---|---|---|---|---|
| | | | | | under 10 | 10 to 16 | 16 to 26 | 26 to 45 | 45 and over | under 10 | 10 to 16 | 16 to 26 | 26 to 45 | 45 and over | | | | | |
| Edgartown | 441 | 1 | Norton | Beriah | | | | 1 | 1 | | | | 1 | 1 | | | 4 | | |
| Edgartown | 441 | 2 | Norton | Dorcas | | | 1 | | | | | 1 | 1 | 1 | | | 4 | | |
| Edgartown | 441 | 3 | Worth | Benjamin | 1 | | 1 | | | 3 | | | 1 | | | | 6 | | |
| Edgartown | 441 | 4 | Thaxter | Joseph | 3 | 2 | 2 | | 1 | | 1 | 1 | 1 | | 1 | | 12 | | |
| Edgartown | 442 | 1 | Norton | Lot | 1 | 1 | 1 | | 1 | 3 | 1 | 1 | 1 | 1 | | | 11 | | |
| Edgartown | 442 | 2 | Rotch | William Jr | | | 1 | | | 2 | | 1 | | 1 | | | 5 | | |
| Edgartown | 442 | 3 | Norris | Samuel | 2 | 1 | | 1 | | 2 | 1 | 1 | 1 | | | | 9 | | |
| Edgartown | 442 | 4 | Paint | Mary | | | 3 | | | | | | 2 | 1 | | | 6 | | |
| Edgartown | 442 | 5 | Stewart | Benjamin | 1 | 1 | | 1 | | 1 | 1 | | 2 | | | | 7 | | |
| Edgartown | 442 | 6 | Norton | Tristram | 3 | | | 1 | | 2 | | | 1 | | | | 7 | | |
| Edgartown | 442 | 7 | Norton | Joseph | | 1 | 1 | | 1 | | 1 | 1 | 1 | | | | 6 | | |
| Edgartown | 442 | 8 | Norton | Noah | | 1 | 1 | 1 | | 1 | | | 1 | | | | 5 | | |
| Edgartown | 442 | 9 | Norton | Benja | | | | 2 | | 1 | | | 2 | | | | 5 | | |
| Edgartown | 442 | 10 | Smith | Ann | | 1 | | 1 | | | | | 1 | 1 | | | 4 | | |
| Edgartown | 442 | 11 | Smith | Samuel | 1 | 2 | | 1 | | 3 | 1 | | 1 | | | | 9 | | |
| Edgartown | 442 | 12 | Coffin | Uriah | 3 | | | 1 | | 1 | | | 1 | | | | 6 | | |
| Edgartown | 442 | 13 | Coffin | Elizabeth | | | | | | | | | 2 | | | | 2 | | |
| Edgartown | 442 | 14 | Beetle | Thomas | | | 1 | | 1 | | | | 2 | | | | 4 | | |
| Edgartown | 442 | 15 | Bradlee | Mary | 1 | 2 | | | | 1 | 1 | 1 | | | | | 6 | | |
| Edgartown | 442 | 16 | Mase | Zachariah | | 2 | | 1 | | | 1 | 1 | | 1 | | | 6 | | |
| Edgartown | 442 | 17 | Coffin | Edea | 1 | 1 | 1 | | 1 | 1 | 1 | 1 | | 1 | | | 8 | | |
| Edgartown | 442 | 18 | Vinson | John | | | | 1 | | | | | | | | | 1 | | |
| Edgartown | 442 | 19 | Daniel | Vinson | 3 | | | 1 | 1 | 1 | 2 | | 1 | | | | 9 | | |
| Edgartown | 442 | 20 | Vinson | Joseph | | 1 | 1 | 1 | 1 | 1 | 1 | 1 | 1 | | | | 8 | | |
| Edgartown | 442 | 21 | Vinson | Samuel | 1 | | | 1 | | 2 | | | 1 | | | | 5 | | |
| Edgartown | 442 | 22 | Vinson | Daniel Jr | 1 | | 1 | | | | 1 | 1 | | | | | 4 | | |
| Edgartown | 442 | 23 | Vinson | Jane | | | | | | | | | 1 | | | | 1 | | |
| Edgartown | 442 | 24 | Vinson | Elizabeth | | 1 | | | | 1 | | | 1 | | | | 3 | | |
| Edgartown | 442 | 25 | Duncan | Abigail | | | | | | | | 1 | 1 | | | | 2 | | |
| Edgartown | 443 | 1 | Pease | Timothy | 1 | | | 1 | | | | 1 | 1 | | | | 4 | | |
| Edgartown | 443 | 2 | Pease | Sarah | | 1 | | | | | | | 1 | | | | 2 | | |
| Edgartown | 443 | 3 | Butler | Joseph | 1 | | 1 | | | | | 1 | | | | | 3 | | |
| Edgartown | 443 | 4 | Daggett | John | 2 | | 1 | 1 | 1 | 1 | | | 1 | | | | 7 | | |
| Edgartown | 443 | 5 | Vinson | Jonathan | 1 | | | 1 | | | | 1 | 1 | 1 | | | 5 | | |
| Edgartown | 443 | 6 | Crosman | Peleg | 2 | 1 | | 1 | | 1 | 1 | | 1 | | | | 7 | | |
| Edgartown | 443 | 7 | Vinson | Barnabas | | 1 | 1 | 1 | | | | | 1 | | | | 4 | | |
| Edgartown | 443 | 8 | Lobb | Ismael | | | | 1 | | | | | 1 | | | | 2 | | |
| Edgartown | 443 | 9 | Butler | Timothy | | 2 | | 1 | | 1 | 1 | 1 | 1 | | | | 7 | | |
| Edgartown | 443 | 10 | Butler | Daniel | 2 | 1 | | 1 | 1 | 1 | 1 | | 1 | | | | 8 | | |
| Edgartown | 443 | 11 | Stewart | Thomas | | 2 | | 1 | | | 1 | 1 | 1 | | | | 6 | | |
| Edgartown | 443 | 12 | Stewart | Elijah | | 1 | | 1 | 1 | 1 | 1 | | 1 | | | | 6 | | |
| Edgartown | 443 | 13 | Vinson | Seth | | | 1 | | | | | 1 | | | | | 2 | | |
| Edgartown | 443 | 14 | Vinson | William | | 1 | 2 | | 1 | | 1 | 2 | | 1 | | | 8 | | |
| Edgartown | 443 | 15 | Vinson | Nathaniel | | 2 | 1 | | 1 | 2 | | | 1 | | | | 7 | | |
| Edgartown | 443 | 16 | Cleveland | Seth | | 1 | | | 1 | | | | | 1 | | | 3 | | |
| Edgartown | 443 | 17 | Cleveland | Joseph | 1 | | | 1 | | 1 | | | 1 | | | | 4 | | |
| Edgartown | 443 | 18 | Vinson | Benjamin | | | | 1 | | | | 1 | | | | | 2 | | |
| Edgartown | 443 | 19 | Cleveland | Ezra | | 1 | 1 | | | | 1 | 2 | | 1 | | | 7 | | |
| Edgartown | 443 | 20 | Worth | John | | | | 1 | | | | 1 | 2 | | | | 4 | | |
| Edgartown | 443 | 21 | Dunham | David | | | | 1 | | | | | 1 | | | | 2 | | |
| Edgartown | 443 | 22 | Dunham | Benajah | | | | 2 | | | | | 2 | | | | 4 | | |
| Edgartown | 443 | 23 | Mayhew | Mathew Jr | | 1 | | 1 | | | | 1 | | | | | 3 | | |
| Edgartown | 443 | 24 | Worth | Jonathan | | | 1 | | | 3 | 1 | 1 | | | | | 6 | | |
| Edgartown | 443 | 25 | Ripley | Joseph | | 1 | | 1 | | 1 | 1 | 2 | 1 | | | | 7 | | |
| Edgartown | 443 | 26 | Dunham | William | | | 1 | | | 1 | | | 1 | | | | 3 | | |
| Edgartown | 443 | 27 | Pease | Benja Jr | | | 1 | | | | | | | | | | 1 | | |
| Edgartown | 443 | 28 | Pease | Benja | | | | 1 | | | | | | | | | 1 | | |
| Edgartown | 443 | 29 | Ripley | Cornelius | | 1 | | 1 | | 1 | | | 1 | | | | 4 | | |
| Edgartown | 443 | 30 | Pease | Malatiah | 1 | | | 1 | | | | | 1 | 1 | 1 | | 4 | | |
| Edgartown | 443 | 31 | Dunham | Elisha | | 2 | | 1 | | 1 | 1 | | 1 | | | | 6 | | |
| Edgartown | 443 | 32 | Dunham | Jonathan | 1 | 1 | | 1 | | | | 1 | | | | | 4 | | |
| Edgartown | 443 | 33 | Fisher | Gamaliel | 2 | | 1 | | | 2 | | | 1 | | | | 6 | | |
| Edgartown | 443 | 34 | Pease | Elijah | | 1 | | 1 | 1 | | | 3 | | | | | 6 | | |
| Edgartown | 443 | 35 | Smith | Thomas | | 1 | | 1 | | 1 | | | 1 | | | | 4 | | |
| Edgartown | 443 | 36 | Smith | John | 1 | | 1 | | | | | | 1 | | | | 3 | | |
| Edgartown | 443 | 37 | Pease | Francis | | 2 | | 1 | | | | 1 | 1 | | | | 5 | | |
| Edgartown | 443 | 38 | Vinson | Louisa | 1 | 1 | | | | 2 | | 1 | | | | | 5 | | |
| Edgartown | 443 | 39 | Clark | John | | 2 | | 1 | | 2 | | | 1 | 1 | | | 7 | | |
| Edgartown | 443 | 40 | Livasy | Anthony | 3 | | 2 | | 1 | | | 1 | 2 | | | | 9 | | |
| Edgartown | 443 | 41 | Daggett | George | | | 1 | | | 1 | 1 | | 1 | | | | 4 | | |
| Edgartown | 443 | 42 | Parady | Emanuel | 3 | | | 1 | 1 | 1 | 2 | 1 | | | | | 8 | | |
| Edgartown | 443 | 43 | King | Robert | | 1 | | 1 | | 2 | 2 | 1 | 1 | | | | 8 | | |
| Edgartown | 443 | 44 | Fish | Henry | | | | 1 | | | | | 1 | | 1 | | 3 | | |
| Edgartown | 443 | 45 | Fish | Abner | 1 | | | 1 | | | | 2 | 1 | | | | 5 | | |
| Edgartown | 443 | 46 | Fisher | Thomas | 3 | | 1 | 1 | | 2 | 2 | | 1 | | | | 10 | | |
| Edgartown | 443 | 47 | Fish | Henry Jr | | 1 | | 1 | | 2 | | | 1 | | | | 5 | | |
| Edgartown | 443 | 48 | Fisher | Joseph | 1 | | 2 | 1 | | 1 | 1 | | 1 | | | | 7 | | |
| Edgartown | 443 | 49 | Fish | Daniel | 2 | | | 1 | | 2 | 2 | 1 | | | | | 8 | | |
| Edgartown | 443 | 50 | Fish | Amaziah | 2 | 2 | | | 3 | | | | 1 | | | | 9 | | |

# 1800 Edgartown, Dukes County, Massachusetts

| TOWN | PG# | LN# | LAST NAME | FIRST NAME | Males under 10 | 10 to 16 | 16 to 26 | 26 to 45 | 45 and over | Females under 10 | 10 to 16 | 16 to 26 | 26 to 45 | 45 and over | TOTAL ALL OTHER | TOTAL SLAVES | TOTALS | DISTRICT/ TOWNSHIP | NOTES |
|---|---|---|---|---|---|---|---|---|---|---|---|---|---|---|---|---|---|---|---|
| Edgartown | 443 | 51 | Fisher | James | 2 | | | | 1 | 1 | 3 | 1 | | 1 | | | 9 | | |
| Edgartown | 443 | 52 | Fisher | James Jr | 1 | | | 1 | | 1 | | 1 | | | | | 4 | | |
| Edgartown | 443 | 53 | Fish | Samuel | | | 1 | | | | | | | | | | 1 | | |
| Edgartown | 443 | 54 | Chadwick | Anthony | | | 1 | | 1 | 1 | 1 | | 1 | | | | 5 | | |
| Edgartown | 443 | 55 | Fisher | John | | | | 1 | | | | | 1 | | | | 2 | | |
| Edgartown | 443 | 56 | Butler | Daniel | 1 | | | 1 | | 1 | | 2 | | | | | 5 | | |
| Edgartown | 444 | 1 | Jernigan | David | 1 | | | 1 | | 1 | | 1 | | | | | 4 | | |
| Edgartown | 444 | 2 | Pease | Salathiel | 1 | 1 | | 1 | | 4 | | 1 | | | | | 8 | | |
| Edgartown | 444 | 3 | Pease | Martin | 1 | 1 | | 1 | | 2 | | 2 | | | | | 7 | | |
| Edgartown | 444 | 4 | Huxford | Joseph | | 2 | 1 | | 1 | | 1 | | | 1 | | | 6 | | |
| Edgartown | 444 | 5 | Huxford | Cornelius | | 1 | | 1 | | | 2 | 2 | | 1 | | | 7 | | |
| Edgartown | 444 | 6 | Norton | David | | 2 | 1 | | 1 | 1 | 1 | | | 1 | | | 7 | | |
| Edgartown | 444 | 7 | Merchant | Abishai | | 1 | | 1 | | | | 1 | | 1 | | | 4 | | |
| Edgartown | 444 | 8 | Ripley | Cornelius Jr | 2 | | | 1 | | 1 | | | 1 | | | | 5 | | |
| Edgartown | 444 | 9 | Dunham | Matilda | | | 1 | | | 2 | | | 1 | 1 | | | 5 | | |
| Edgartown | 444 | 10 | Dunham | Patience | | | 1 | | | 2 | 1 | | 1 | | | | 5 | | |
| Edgartown | 444 | 11 | Allen | John | | 1 | 2 | | 1 | 1 | 2 | | | 1 | 4 | | 12 | | |
| Edgartown | 444 | 12 | Kelly | William | | | 1 | | | 1 | 1 | | 1 | | | | 4 | | |
| Edgartown | 444 | 13 | Clark | John Jr | | | 1 | | | | | | 1 | | | | 2 | | |
| Edgartown | 444 | 14 | Fish | Abram | 1 | | | 1 | | 3 | | | 1 | | | | 6 | | |
| Edgartown | 444 | 15 | Swasy | Joseph | 1 | | | | 1 | | | 3 | 1 | | | | 6 | | |
| Edgartown | 444 | 16 | Smith | Benja Jr | 1 | | | 1 | | 1 | | 1 | | | | | 4 | | |
| Edgartown | 444 | 17 | Butler | Silas | | 1 | 1 | 1 | | | 1 | 2 | 1 | | | | 7 | | |
| Edgartown | 444 | 18 | Luce | Jason | 2 | 2 | | 1 | | 1 | | 1 | | 1 | | | 8 | | |
| Edgartown | 444 | 19 | Cleveland | Ichabod | 1 | 1 | 2 | 1 | | | | | | 1 | | | 6 | | |
| Edgartown | 444 | 20 | Pease | John | | | 1 | 1 | | | | 2 | 1 | 1 | | | 6 | | |
| Edgartown | 444 | 21 | Read | Amelia | | | | | | | | 2 | 1 | | | | 3 | | |
| Edgartown | 444 | 22 | Osbourne | Henry | 3 | 3 | | 1 | | 3 | 1 | 2 | 1 | | | | 14 | | |
| Edgartown | 444 | 23 | Fisher | Richard | | 1 | | | | | | 1 | | | | | 2 | | |
| Edgartown | 444 | 24 | Norton | William | 1 | | 2 | | 1 | 1 | 1 | 2 | | 1 | | | 9 | | |
| Edgartown | 444 | 25 | Norton | Wm Jr | | 1 | 1 | 1 | | | 2 | | 1 | | | | 6 | | |
| Edgartown | 444 | 26 | Butler | Ann | | | | | | | | | | 2 | | | 2 | | |
| Edgartown | 444 | 27 | Butler | John | 2 | | 1 | 1 | | 2 | 3 | | | 1 | | | 10 | | |
| Edgartown | 444 | 28 | Ewers | Isaac | | | | | 1 | | | 1 | | | | | 2 | | |
| Edgartown | 444 | 29 | Pratt | Ann | | | | | 1 | 1 | | 1 | 1 | | | | 4 | | |
| Edgartown | 444 | 30 | Pease | Noah | 2 | 1 | 1 | | 1 | | | 1 | 1 | | | | 7 | | |
| Edgartown | 444 | 31 | Whellen | Saml | 1 | | | | 1 | 1 | | 1 | | | | | 4 | | |
| Edgartown | 444 | 32 | Coffin | Sally | | 1 | 1 | | | 2 | 1 | 1 | | 1 | | | 7 | | |
| Edgartown | 444 | 33 | Kelly | Bathsheba | | | | 2 | | | | | | 2 | | | 4 | | |
| Edgartown | 444 | 34 | Kelly | Joseph | 1 | | | 1 | | | | 1 | | | | | 3 | | |
| Edgartown | 444 | 35 | Wilpenny | Robert | 1 | | | 1 | | | | 1 | | | | | 3 | | |
| Edgartown | 444 | 36 | Pease | Obed | | 1 | | | 1 | | | | | 1 | | | 3 | | |
| Edgartown | 444 | 37 | Pease | Marshall | 1 | | | 1 | | 2 | | 1 | | | | | 5 | | |
| Edgartown | 444 | 38 | Coffin | James | | 1 | 1 | | 2 | 1 | 1 | 1 | | 1 | | | 8 | | |
| Edgartown | 444 | 39 | Jernigan | William | 1 | | | 1 | | | | | 1 | 1 | | | 4 | | |
| Edgartown | 444 | 40 | Jernigan | Thomas | | 1 | 1 | 1 | | | | | | 1 | | | 4 | | |
| Edgartown | 444 | 41 | Jernigan | Wm Jr | 2 | 1 | | 1 | | 2 | 2 | | 1 | | | | 9 | | |
| Edgartown | 444 | 42 | Cottle | Sarah | | | | | | | | | 1 | 1 | | | 2 | | |
| Edgartown | 444 | 43 | Coffin | Sarah | 1 | | | | | | | | 1 | 1 | | | 3 | | |
| Edgartown | 444 | 44 | Coffin | Daniel | | | | | 1 | 1 | | | 1 | 1 | | | 4 | | |
| Edgartown | 444 | 45 | Norton | Lydia | | 1 | | | | | | | | 1 | | | 2 | | |
| Edgartown | 444 | 46 | Coffin | Beulah | | | | | | | | | | 1 | | | 1 | | |
| Edgartown | 444 | 47 | Merchant | Elihu | 1 | | | 1 | | | | | | 1 | | | 3 | | |
| Edgartown | 444 | 48 | Asey | Elijah | 1 | 1 | | | 1 | | | | 2 | 1 | | | 6 | | |
| Edgartown | 444 | 49 | Merchant | Cornl | | | | | 1 | 1 | | | 1 | 1 | | | 4 | | |
| Edgartown | 444 | 50 | Merchant | Ephm | 1 | | | 1 | | 1 | | | 1 | | | | 4 | | |
| Edgartown | 444 | 51 | Merchant | Cornels Jr | 1 | | | 1 | | | | 1 | 1 | | | | 4 | | |
| Edgartown | 444 | 52 | Worth | Jethro | 3 | 1 | | | 1 | | | | 2 | | | | 7 | | |
| Edgartown | 444 | 53 | Coffin | Timothy | 2 | | | | 1 | 2 | | 2 | 1 | | | | 8 | | |
| Edgartown | 444 | 54 | Coffin | Eunice | | | | | | | | | | 1 | 1 | | 2 | | |
| Edgartown | 444 | 55 | Weeks | Benja | 1 | | | 1 | | 1 | | | 1 | | | | 4 | | |
| Edgartown | 444 | 56 | Dunham | Elijah | | | | | 1 | | | 1 | | 1 | | | 3 | | |
| Edgartown | 444 | 57 | Sprague | John | 2 | | | | 1 | 1 | | 2 | 2 | 1 | | | 9 | | |
| Edgartown | 445 | 1 | Banning | James | 1 | 2 | 1 | | | | | 1 | | 1 | | | 7 | | |
| Edgartown | 445 | 2 | Dunham | Benajah Jr | | 2 | | 1 | | | | 1 | | 1 | | | 5 | | |
| Edgartown | 445 | 3 | Pease | Lois | | | 1 | | | | | | 1 | 1 | | | 3 | | |
| Edgartown | 445 | 4 | Mayhew | William | 1 | 4 | 1 | | 1 | 2 | | 1 | 1 | 1 | | | 12 | | |
| Edgartown | 445 | 5 | Mayhew | Thomas | | | 1 | | | 1 | | | 1 | | | | 3 | | |
| Edgartown | 445 | 6 | Coffin | Peter | 2 | | | 1 | | 2 | | | 1 | | 1 | | 7 | | |
| Edgartown | 445 | 7 | Smith | Benjamin | 1 | | 1 | 1 | | 1 | | | 1 | 1 | | | 6 | | |
| Edgartown | 445 | 8 | Mayhew | Mathew | 2 | | | 1 | | 3 | 1 | | 1 | | | | 8 | | |
| Edgartown | 445 | 9 | Pease | Jona | | | 1 | | 1 | | | 2 | | 1 | | | 5 | | |
| Edgartown | 445 | 10 | Ward | Hannah | | | | | | | | | 1 | 1 | | | 2 | | |
| Edgartown | 445 | 11 | Cooke | Thos Jr | 2 | | | 1 | | 1 | | | 1 | | | | 5 | | |
| Edgartown | 445 | 12 | Merchant | Lydia | | | 1 | | | | | 1 | | 1 | | | 3 | | |
| Edgartown | 445 | 13 | Gray | John | | | 1 | | | 1 | | | 1 | | | | 3 | | |
| Edgartown | 445 | 14 | Merchant | George | 1 | 1 | 1 | | | | | 1 | | | | | 4 | | |
| Edgartown | 445 | 15 | Fisher | Jona | 3 | 1 | 2 | | | | | 1 | 1 | | | | 9 | | |
| Edgartown | 445 | 16 | Merchant | Miriam | | | | 1 | | | | | 1 | | | | 2 | | |

# 1800 Edgartown, Dukes County, Massachusetts

| TOWN | PG# | LN# | LAST NAME | FIRST NAME | FWM under 10 | FWM 10 to 16 | FWM 16 to 26 | FWM 26 to 45 | FWM 45 and over | FWF under 10 | FWF 10 to 16 | FWF 16 to 26 | FWF 26 to 45 | FWF 45 and over | TOTAL ALL OTHER | TOTAL SLAVES | TOTALS | DISTRICT/TOWNSHIP | NOTES |
|---|---|---|---|---|---|---|---|---|---|---|---|---|---|---|---|---|---|---|---|
| Edgartown | 445 | 17 | Butler | Walter | 1 | | | 1 | | | | 1 | | | | | 3 | | |
| Edgartown | 445 | 18 | Daggett | Timothy | 1 | | | 1 | | | | 1 | | | | | 3 | | |
| Edgartown | 445 | 19 | Asey | Henry | | | 1 | | | 1 | | 1 | | | | | 3 | | |
| Edgartown | 445 | 20 | Cleveland | Tristram | | | | 1 | | 1 | | | 1 | | | | 3 | | |
| Edgartown | 445 | 21 | Gray | Rhoda | 1 | 2 | 2 | | | | | 1 | | 1 | | | 7 | | |
| Edgartown | 445 | 22 | Holley | Joseph | 1 | | | 1 | | 4 | 3 | 1 | | | | | 10 | | |
| Edgartown | 445 | 23 | Morse | Uriah | | | | 1 | | 1 | | | 1 | | | | 3 | | |
| Edgartown | 445 | 24 | Butler | Zephaniah | 2 | 1 | 1 | | 1 | | | | 1 | | | | 6 | | |
| Edgartown | 445 | 25 | Woodbee | Rebecca | | | | | | | | | | | 4 | | 4 | | |
| Edgartown | 445 | 26 | Pease | Peter | | | | 1 | | | | 1 | | 1 | | | 3 | | |
| Edgartown | 445 | 27 | Pease | Peter Jr | 3 | | | 1 | | | | 1 | | 1 | | | 6 | | |
| Edgartown | 445 | 28 | Rawson | Betsey | | | 1 | | | | | 1 | 1 | | | | 3 | | |
| Edgartown | 445 | 29 | Vinson | William Jr | | | 1 | | | 2 | | | 1 | | | | 4 | | |
| Edgartown | 445 | 30 | Norton | Martin | 3 | | | 1 | 1 | | | | 1 | | | | 6 | | |
| Edgartown | 445 | 31 | Merchant | Peter | 1 | 1 | | 1 | | 3 | 1 | | 1 | | | | 8 | | |
| Edgartown | 445 | 32 | Cooke | Thomas | 1 | | | 2 | 1 | 2 | 1 | | 2 | | | | 9 | | |
| Edgartown | 445 | 33 | Tupper | James | 2 | 3 | | 1 | | 2 | | | 1 | | | | 9 | | |
| Edgartown | 445 | 34 | Fitch | Benjamin | 1 | | | 1 | | | | | 1 | 1 | | | 4 | | |
| Edgartown | 445 | 35 | Coffin | John | | 2 | 3 | 1 | | 1 | 1 | | 1 | | | | 9 | | |
| Edgartown | 445 | 36 | Smith | Elijah | | 1 | | 1 | | | | | 1 | 2 | | | 5 | | |
| Edgartown | 445 | 37 | Norton | Prince | | | | 1 | | | | | | | | | 1 | | |
| Edgartown | 445 | 38 | Smith | David | 1 | 2 | 1 | 1 | | 1 | 1 | 1 | 1 | | | | 9 | | |
| Edgartown | 445 | 39 | Smith | Rebecca | | | | | | | | | 1 | | | | 1 | | |
| Edgartown | 445 | 40 | Norton | Nicholas | 4 | 1 | | 1 | | | | 1 | 1 | | | | 8 | | |
| Edgartown | 445 | 41 | Smith | Eunice | | | | | | | | | 1 | | | | 1 | | |
| Edgartown | 445 | 42 | Smith | John | 2 | 2 | | 1 | | 2 | 1 | | 1 | | | | 9 | | |
| Edgartown | 445 | 43 | Crosby | Harlow | | | 1 | | | 3 | | | 1 | | | | 5 | | |
| Edgartown | 445 | 44 | Coffin | Obed | | 1 | 2 | 1 | | | | | 1 | | | | 5 | | |
| Edgartown | 445 | 45 | Norton | Ichabod | | 1 | | 1 | | | | | 3 | 1 | | | 6 | | |
| Edgartown | 445 | 46 | Vinson | Reuben | | | 1 | 1 | | 1 | | | 1 | | | | 4 | | |
| Edgartown | 445 | 47 | Norton | Henry C. | | 1 | | 1 | 1 | 1 | | 1 | | | | | 5 | | |
| Edgartown | 445 | 48 | Norton | Shubael | | | | 1 | | | | 1 | 1 | 1 | 1 | | 5 | | |
| Edgartown | 445 | 49 | Norton | Isaac | | | 1 | | | 3 | | | 1 | | | | 5 | | |
| Edgartown | 445 | 50 | Daggett | Saml | | | 1 | | | 2 | | | 1 | 1 | | | 5 | | |
| Edgartown | 446 | 1 | Butler | Peter | 1 | | 1 | | | 1 | 1 | | | | | | 4 | | |
| Edgartown | 446 | 2 | Luce | Lot | | 2 | | 1 | | 2 | | | 1 | | | | 6 | | |
| Edgartown | 446 | 3 | Weeks | Solomon | | | | | | | | | | | 2 | | 2 | | |
| Edgartown | 446 | 4 | Peters | George | | | | | | | | | | | 5 | | 5 | | |
| Edgartown | 446 | 5 | Sharper | Fortune | | | | | | | | | | | 6 | | 6 | | |
| Edgartown | 446 | 6 | Luce | Elisha | 2 | 1 | 2 | | 1 | 1 | | | 1 | | | | 8 | | |
| Edgartown | 446 | 7 | Daggett | Silas | 1 | 2 | 1 | 1 | | 2 | 2 | | 2 | 1 | | | 12 | | |
| Edgartown | 446 | 8 | Luce | Jesse Jr | | | 1 | | | | | 1 | | | | | 2 | | |
| Edgartown | 446 | 9 | Dunham | Clifford | 4 | | | 1 | | | | | 1 | | | | 6 | | |
| Edgartown | 446 | 10 | Luce | Jesse Jr | | 1 | | 1 | | | | 1 | 1 | | | | 4 | | |
| Edgartown | 446 | 11 | Merry | Leonard | 1 | | 1 | | | | | 1 | | | | | 3 | | |
| Edgartown | 446 | 12 | Chace | Abram | 2 | 1 | 1 | 1 | | 2 | 1 | 1 | 1 | | | | 10 | | |
| Edgartown | 446 | 13 | Reynolds | David | 1 | 1 | 2 | 1 | 1 | 1 | 2 | 1 | | 1 | | | 11 | | |
| Edgartown | 446 | 14 | Look | Samuel | 1 | 2 | 1 | 1 | 1 | 3 | 1 | 1 | | | | | 11 | | |
| Edgartown | 447 | 1 | Norton | Obed | 1 | | 1 | | | 1 | 1 | 1 | | | 1 | | 6 | | |
| Edgartown | 447 | 2 | Courtney | Barber | | 1 | | | | | | 1 | | | | | 2 | | |
| Edgartown | 447 | 3 | Norton | Samuel | | 1 | 1 | 1 | | 1 | 1 | | 1 | | | | 6 | | |
| Edgartown | 447 | 4 | Beetle | William | 1 | | 2 | 1 | 3 | 1 | 2 | 1 | 1 | | | | 12 | | |
| Edgartown | 447 | 5 | Beetle | James | 1 | 2 | | | | | | 1 | 1 | | | | 6 | | |
| Edgartown | 447 | 6 | Davis | Benjamin | | 1 | | 1 | 1 | 1 | 1 | 1 | | | 1 | | 7 | | |
| Edgartown | 447 | 7 | Pease | Argulas | | 1 | | | | | 2 | | | | | | 3 | | |
| Edgartown | 447 | 8 | Butler | Ebenz | | | | 2 | | | | | 1 | | | | 3 | | |
| Edgartown | 447 | 9 | Norton | Baire | 1 | | | 1 | | 1 | 2 | | 1 | | | | 6 | | |
| Edgartown | 447 | 10 | Cozens | Pero | | | | | | | | | | | 8 | | 8 | | |
| Edgartown | 447 | 11 | Basset | James | | | | | | | | | | | 4 | | 4 | | |
| Edgartown | 447 | 12 | Luce | George | 3 | 1 | | 1 | 1 | 1 | | | 1 | | | | 8 | | |
| Edgartown | 447 | 13 | Norton | Darius | 1 | | 1 | 1 | | 2 | | | 1 | | | | 6 | | |
| Edgartown | 447 | 14 | Smith | Daniel | 1 | | 1 | | 1 | 1 | | | 1 | | | | 5 | | |
| Edgartown | 447 | 15 | Tillton | Abigail | | | 1 | | | | | 1 | 1 | | | | 3 | | |
| Edgartown | 447 | 16 | Linton | Joseph | | | 1 | | | | | | 1 | | | | 2 | | |
| Edgartown | 447 | 17 | Trask | Benja | 1 | | | 2 | | | | 1 | 1 | | | | 5 | | |
| Edgartown | 447 | 18 | Butler | William | 1 | | 2 | | 2 | | | | 1 | | | | 6 | | |
| Edgartown | 447 | 19 | Claghorn | Jane | | | | | | | | 1 | 1 | | | | 2 | | |
| Edgartown | 447 | 20 | Claghorn | Bartlet | 1 | | 1 | | 1 | | | | 1 | | | | 4 | | |
| Edgartown | 447 | 21 | Coffin | William | | 2 | | 1 | | 2 | 1 | 1 | | 2 | | | 9 | | |
| Edgartown | 447 | 22 | Coffin | David | | | 1 | | 1 | 1 | | | | | | | 3 | | |
| Edgartown | 447 | 23 | Davis | Rufus | | | 1 | | 2 | | | 2 | 1 | 1 | | | 7 | | |
| Edgartown | 447 | 24 | Smith | Ebenz | | 1 | 1 | | | | | 2 | 1 | | | | 5 | | |
| Edgartown | 447 | 25 | Hillman | Elijah | | | 1 | | 3 | 1 | | 1 | | | | | 6 | | |
| Edgartown | 447 | 26 | Daggett | Anna | | | | | | 1 | | | 1 | | | | 2 | | |
| Edgartown | 447 | 27 | Davis | Melatiah | 1 | 1 | 1 | | 1 | 1 | 1 | | 1 | 1 | | | 8 | | |
| Edgartown | 447 | 28 | Dexter | Joseph | 2 | 2 | 1 | 1 | | 1 | | | 1 | | | | 9 | | |
| Edgartown | 447 | 29 | Luce | Benjamin | | 1 | 2 | | 1 | | | 1 | 1 | | | | 7 | | |
| Edgartown | 447 | 30 | Luce | Levi | | | | | 1 | | | | 2 | 1 | | | 4 | | |
| Edgartown | 447 | 31 | Claghorn | Thos Jr | | | 1 | | | | | 1 | 2 | 2 | | | 6 | | |

108

# 1800 Edgartown, Dukes County, Massachusetts

| TOWN | PG# | LN# | LAST NAME | FIRST NAME | FREE WHITE MALES | | | | | FREE WHITE FEMALES | | | | | TOTAL ALL OTHER | TOTAL SLAVES | TOTALS | DISTRICT/ TOWNSHIP | NOTES |
|---|---|---|---|---|---|---|---|---|---|---|---|---|---|---|---|---|---|---|---|
| | | | | | under 10 | 10 to 16 | 16 to 26 | 26 to 45 | 45 and over | under 10 | 10 to 16 | 16 to 26 | 26 to 45 | 45 and over | | | | | |
| Edgartown | 447 | 32 | Beetle | Reuben | 3 | | 1 | | | | | | 1 | | | | 5 | | |
| Edgartown | 447 | 33 | Goodley | Phillip | | | | | | | | | | | 4 | | 4 | | |
| Edgartown | 447 | 34 | Pomidge | Simon | | | | | | | | | | | 4 | | 4 | | |
| Edgartown | 447 | 35 | Simpson | Jos | | | | | | | | | | | 7 | | 7 | | |
| Edgartown | 447 | 36 | Cooke | Lewis | | | | | | | | | | | 6 | | 6 | | |
| Edgartown | 447 | 37 | Peters | Saml | | | | | | | | | | | 6 | | 6 | | |
| Edgartown | 447 | 38 | Johnson | George | | | | | | | | | | | 2 | | 2 | | |
| Edgartown | 447 | 39 | Dimond | Jane | | | | | | | | | | | 3 | | 3 | | |
| Edgartown | 447 | 40 | Johnson | Esther | | | | | | | | | | | 3 | | 3 | | |
| Edgartown | 447 | 41 | Medicine | Charlotte | | | | | | | | | | | 4 | | 4 | | |

# 1800 Tisbury, Dukes County, Massachusetts

| TOWN | PG# | LN# | LAST NAME | FIRST NAME | FREE WHITE MALES under 10 | 10 to 16 | 16 to 26 | 26 to 45 | 45 and over | FREE WHITE FEMALES under 10 | 10 to 16 | 16 to 26 | 26 to 45 | 45 and over | TOTAL ALL OTHER | TOTAL SLAVES | TOTALS | DISTRICT/ TOWNSHIP | NOTES |
|---|---|---|---|---|---|---|---|---|---|---|---|---|---|---|---|---|---|---|---|
| Tisbury | 452 | 18 | Athearn | William | 3 | | | 1 | | 1 | | | 1 | | 1 | | 7 | | |
| Tisbury | 452 | 19 | Adams | Lydia | 1 | | | | | 1 | | | 1 | | | | 3 | | |
| Tisbury | 452 | 20 | Lumbert | Hannah | | | | | | | | | 2 | | | | 2 | | |
| Tisbury | 452 | 21 | Norton | Melatiah | | | | 1 | | 1 | | | 1 | | | | 3 | | |
| Tisbury | 452 | 22 | Look | Robert | 1 | 2 | | | 1 | 2 | 1 | 2 | 1 | | | | 10 | | |
| Tisbury | 452 | 23 | Look | Elizath | | | | | | | | | 2 | | | | 2 | | |
| Tisbury | 452 | 24 | Lewis | Saml | | | | 1 | | | | | 2 | | | | 3 | | |
| Tisbury | 452 | 25 | Lumbert | Timo | | | 3 | 1 | | | | 3 | | | | | 8 | | |
| Tisbury | 452 | 26 | Luce | Enoch | | | 1 | 1 | 1 | | | 3 | 1 | 1 | | | 8 | | |
| Tisbury | 452 | 27 | Walrond | Robert | 2 | | | 1 | | 3 | | | 1 | | | | 7 | | |
| Tisbury | 452 | 28 | Luce | Margery | | | | | | | | | 1 | | | | 1 | | |
| Tisbury | 452 | 29 | Athearn | Joseph | | 1 | 1 | 1 | | 1 | 1 | | 1 | | | | 6 | | |
| Tisbury | 452 | 30 | Athearn | Jona | | | 1 | 1 | | | | 3 | 1 | | 1 | | 7 | | |
| Tisbury | 452 | 31 | Athearn | Ezra | | | | 2 | | | | 1 | 1 | 2 | | | 6 | | |
| Tisbury | 452 | 32 | Athearn | Solomon | 1 | 1 | | 1 | | 2 | | 2 | 1 | | | | 8 | | |
| Tisbury | 452 | 33 | Luce | Benja | | | | 1 | | 2 | | | 1 | | | | 4 | | |
| Tisbury | 452 | 34 | Allen | Patience | | | | | | | | | 1 | 2 | 1 | | 4 | | |
| Tisbury | 452 | 35 | Allen | Joseph | | | 1 | | | | | | 1 | | 1 | | 3 | | |
| Tisbury | 452 | 36 | Rogers | Silas | | | 1 | 1 | | | | | 1 | 1 | 1 | | 5 | | |
| Tisbury | 452 | 37 | Luce | William | | | | 1 | | | | 2 | 1 | 2 | | | 6 | | |
| Tisbury | 452 | 38 | Luce | Jona | | | 1 | | | | | | 1 | | | | 2 | | |
| Tisbury | 452 | 39 | Luce | Joseph | | | | 1 | | | | | | | | | 1 | | |
| Tisbury | 452 | 40 | Luce | Joseph Jr | 2 | | 1 | | | | | | 1 | | | | 4 | | |
| Tisbury | 452 | 41 | Luce | Obed | | | 1 | 1 | | 1 | | 3 | 1 | | | | 6 | | |
| Tisbury | 452 | 42 | Pease | Bartlet | | 1 | | | | 1 | | 1 | | | | | 3 | | |
| Tisbury | 452 | 43 | Luce | Thos | 2 | | | 1 | | 3 | 2 | 1 | 1 | | | | 10 | | |
| Tisbury | 452 | 44 | Rotch | William | | 1 | | 1 | | | | 1 | | 1 | | | 4 | | |
| Tisbury | 452 | 45 | Lumbert | Saml | 2 | 1 | | 1 | | 2 | | 1 | 1 | | | | 8 | | |
| Tisbury | 452 | 46 | Daggett | Jos | | | 1 | 1 | | | | | 2 | 1 | | | 5 | | |
| Tisbury | 452 | 47 | Look | Jona | 1 | 1 | 1 | 1 | | | 1 | 2 | 1 | | | | 8 | | |
| Tisbury | 452 | 48 | Luce | Lucy | | | 1 | | | | | | 1 | | | | 2 | | |
| Tisbury | 452 | 49 | Lumbert | Lemuel | | | | 1 | | | | | 1 | | | | 2 | | |
| Tisbury | 452 | 50 | Daggett | Michael L. | 1 | | | 1 | | 1 | | | 1 | | | | 4 | | |
| Tisbury | 452 | 51 | Cottle | Edmund | | 1 | 1 | 1 | | 2 | | 1 | 2 | | | | 8 | | |
| Tisbury | 453 | 1 | Cottle | Shubael | | | | 1 | | | | | 1 | 1 | | | 3 | | |
| Tisbury | 453 | 2 | Luce | Dorcas | | | | | | | 1 | 1 | 1 | | | | 3 | | |
| Tisbury | 453 | 3 | Butler | David | 2 | | | 1 | | 1 | 2 | | 1 | | | | 7 | | |
| Tisbury | 453 | 4 | Cleveland | Sylvanus | 1 | 1 | | | | | | 1 | | | | | 3 | | |
| Tisbury | 453 | 5 | Avery | Zechariah | 1 | | 1 | 1 | | 2 | | | 1 | 1 | | | 7 | | |
| Tisbury | 453 | 6 | Cottle | Heppy | | 1 | | | | | 1 | 1 | 1 | | | | 4 | | |
| Tisbury | 453 | 7 | Pain | Susannah | | | | | | | | | | | 2 | | 2 | | |
| Tisbury | 453 | 8 | Chase | Joseph | | 1 | 2 | 2 | | | | | 1 | 1 | | | 7 | | |
| Tisbury | 453 | 9 | Dunham | Lydia | | | | | | | 1 | 1 | 1 | | | | 3 | | |
| Tisbury | 453 | 10 | Smith | Jona | | | | 1 | | | | | 1 | | | | 2 | | |
| Tisbury | 453 | 11 | Mantor | George | 1 | 1 | 3 | 1 | | | 1 | 2 | 1 | | | | 10 | | |
| Tisbury | 453 | 12 | Norton | Cornelius | | | | 1 | | | | | 2 | | | | 3 | | |
| Tisbury | 453 | 13 | Crosby | John | | | 3 | 1 | | | 1 | 1 | 1 | | | | 7 | | |
| Tisbury | 453 | 14 | Luce | Malatiah | | | | 1 | 1 | | | | 1 | | | | 3 | | |
| Tisbury | 453 | 15 | Luce | Elijah | | 1 | | | | | | | 1 | | | | 2 | | |
| Tisbury | 453 | 16 | Athearn | James | | | | 1 | | | | 1 | 1 | | | | 3 | | |
| Tisbury | 453 | 17 | Jones | Ebena | 1 | | | 1 | | 3 | | | 1 | | | | 6 | | |
| Tisbury | 453 | 18 | Mantor | Lois | | 1 | | | | | | 1 | | 1 | | | 3 | | |
| Tisbury | 453 | 19 | Luce | Saml | | | 1 | 1 | | 1 | | 1 | | | | | 4 | | |
| Tisbury | 453 | 20 | Cathcart | Hugh | | 1 | 1 | 1 | | 1 | 1 | 1 | | 1 | | | 7 | | |
| Tisbury | 453 | 21 | Luce | Ezekiel | | 1 | | 1 | | | | 2 | | | | 2 | 6 | | |
| Tisbury | 453 | 22 | Athearn | Jethro | | | | 1 | | | | 2 | 1 | 1 | | | 5 | | |
| Tisbury | 453 | 23 | Athearn | Timo | 1 | | | 1 | | 1 | | | 1 | | | | 4 | | |
| Tisbury | 453 | 24 | Jones | Thos | | | 1 | 1 | | | | | 1 | 1 | | | 4 | | |
| Tisbury | 453 | 25 | Norton | Peter | 3 | 1 | 1 | 1 | | 1 | | 2 | 1 | | | | 10 | | |
| Tisbury | 453 | 26 | Norton | Eliakim | | | | 1 | | | | | 1 | | | | 2 | | |
| Tisbury | 453 | 27 | Luce | Reina | | | | | | | | | 2 | | | | 2 | | |
| Tisbury | 453 | 28 | Allen | Seth | | | 1 | | | | | | 1 | | | | 2 | | |
| Tisbury | 453 | 29 | Coswell | Hannah | | | | | | | | | 1 | | | | 1 | | |
| Tisbury | 453 | 30 | Lewis | Freeman | 3 | | | 1 | | | | | 1 | | | | 5 | | |
| Tisbury | 453 | 31 | Luce | Henry | | 1 | | 1 | | | | 2 | 1 | | | | 5 | | |
| Tisbury | 453 | 32 | Merry | Elizath | | 1 | | | | | | 1 | 1 | | | | 3 | | |
| Tisbury | 453 | 33 | Dunham | Abishai | 1 | 1 | 2 | 1 | | 2 | 1 | 1 | 1 | | | | 10 | | |
| Tisbury | 453 | 34 | Coffin | Jedidah | | | 2 | | | | 2 | 1 | | 1 | | | 6 | | |
| Tisbury | 453 | 35 | Dunham | Shubael | 1 | | 1 | 1 | | 1 | 2 | | 1 | | | | 7 | | |
| Tisbury | 453 | 36 | Grinall | Oliver | 1 | | | 1 | | 2 | | | 1 | | | | 5 | | |
| Tisbury | 453 | 37 | Cottle | Robert | 2 | | | 1 | | 1 | 2 | | 1 | | | | 7 | | |
| Tisbury | 453 | 38 | Smith | Rainsford | | | | 1 | | | | 1 | 1 | | | | 3 | | |
| Tisbury | 453 | 39 | Smith | Mathew | 3 | 2 | | 1 | | 1 | 1 | 1 | 1 | | | | 10 | | |
| Tisbury | 453 | 40 | Smith | Nathan | | 1 | 1 | 1 | | | | | 1 | 1 | | | 5 | | |
| Tisbury | 453 | 41 | Daggett | Peggy | 2 | | | 1 | | | | | 1 | | | | 4 | | |
| Tisbury | 453 | 42 | Smith | Zechariah | 4 | | | 1 | 2 | 2 | | | 1 | | | | 10 | | |
| Tisbury | 453 | 43 | Smith | Thomas | | | 1 | | | | | 1 | 2 | | | | 4 | | |
| Tisbury | 453 | 44 | Walrond | Jemima | | | | | | | | | 1 | | | | 1 | | |
| Tisbury | 453 | 45 | Luce | Lemuel | | | 1 | 1 | | 1 | | | 1 | | | | 4 | | |

# 1800 Tisbury, Dukes County, Massachusetts

| TOWN | PG# | LN# | LAST NAME | FIRST NAME | FREE WHITE MALES | | | | | FREE WHITE FEMALES | | | | | TOTAL ALL OTHER | TOTAL SLAVES | TOTALS | DISTRICT/ TOWNSHIP | NOTES |
|---|---|---|---|---|---|---|---|---|---|---|---|---|---|---|---|---|---|---|---|
| | | | | | under 10 | 10 to 16 | 16 to 26 | 26 to 45 | 45 and over | under 10 | 10 to 16 | 16 to 26 | 26 to 45 | 45 and over | | | | | |
| Tisbury | 453 | 46 | Dunham | Eleazer | | | 1 | | | | | | | 1 | | | 2 | | |
| Tisbury | 453 | 47 | Smith | Frederick | 1 | | 1 | | | 2 | | | 1 | | | | 5 | | |
| Tisbury | 453 | 48 | Butler | Thomas | | 1 | 1 | 1 | | | | 1 | 1 | | | | 5 | | |
| Tisbury | 453 | 49 | Lewis | Francis | | | 2 | 1 | | | | | 1 | 1 | | | 5 | | |
| Tisbury | 454 | 1 | Luce | Rhoda | | 1 | | | | | | | 1 | | | | 2 | | |
| Tisbury | 454 | 2 | Luce | Isaac | | 1 | | 1 | | | | 1 | 1 | | | | 4 | | |
| Tisbury | 454 | 3 | Luce | Peter | | | 1 | 1 | | | | | 1 | | | | 3 | | |
| Tisbury | 454 | 4 | Luce | Malachi | 1 | 1 | 1 | | | 1 | 1 | 1 | 1 | | | | 8 | | |
| Tisbury | 454 | 5 | Weeks | William | | | | 1 | | | | | 2 | | | | 3 | | |
| Tisbury | 454 | 6 | Weeks | Nathan | | | | 1 | | | | | 1 | 1 | | | 3 | | |
| Tisbury | 454 | 7 | Weeks | James | 3 | 2 | | 1 | | 1 | 1 | | 1 | | | | 9 | | |
| Tisbury | 454 | 8 | Weeks | Saml | | | 1 | 1 | | | | | 1 | | | | 3 | | |
| Tisbury | 454 | 9 | Weeks | Shubael | | | 1 | | | | | | 1 | | | | 3 | | |
| Tisbury | 454 | 10 | Luce | Saml | 1 | | 1 | | | 2 | | 1 | | | | | 5 | | |
| Tisbury | 454 | 11 | Hammet | Abijah | 2 | | 1 | | | 2 | | | 1 | | | | 6 | | |
| Tisbury | 454 | 12 | Hammet | Mary | | | | | | | | | | 1 | | | 1 | | |
| Tisbury | 454 | 13 | Draper | Lydia | | | | | | | | | | 1 | | | 1 | | |
| Tisbury | 454 | 14 | Foster | James | 1 | | 1 | | | | | | 1 | | | | 3 | | |
| Tisbury | 454 | 15 | Hancock | Russell | | 1 | 1 | 1 | | | | 2 | 1 | | | | 6 | | |
| Tisbury | 454 | 16 | Hancock | John | 1 | | 1 | | | 2 | | 1 | | | | | 5 | | |
| Tisbury | 454 | 17 | Hancock | Jonah | | | 1 | 1 | | | | | 1 | 1 | | | 4 | | |
| Tisbury | 454 | 18 | Hancock | Mary | | | | | | | | | | 2 | | | 2 | | |
| Tisbury | 454 | 19 | Mantor | Matthew | 2 | 1 | 3 | 1 | 1 | | | | 1 | 1 | | | 10 | | |
| Tisbury | 454 | 20 | Mantor | Zeriah | | | | | 1 | | | | | 1 | | | 2 | | |
| Tisbury | 454 | 21 | Case | William | | | 2 | | 1 | | 1 | 1 | | 1 | | | 6 | | |
| Tisbury | 454 | 22 | Foster | Rebecca | | | 3 | | | | 1 | 1 | | 1 | | | 6 | | |
| Tisbury | 454 | 23 | Allen | Eleanor | | | | | | | | | 2 | 1 | 1 | | 4 | | |
| Tisbury | 454 | 24 | Allen | Benja | 1 | | 1 | | | 1 | | | 1 | | 1 | | 6 | | |
| Tisbury | 454 | 25 | Allen | Abigail | | | | | | | | | 1 | 1 | | | 2 | | |
| Tisbury | 454 | 26 | Luce | Sylvanus | 1 | | 1 | | 1 | | | 1 | 1 | 1 | | | 6 | | |
| Tisbury | 454 | 27 | Joseph | Imanuel | 1 | | | 1 | | 1 | | | 1 | | | | 4 | | |
| Tisbury | 454 | 28 | Luce | Abner | 2 | | | 1 | | | | 1 | 1 | | | | 5 | | |
| Tisbury | 454 | 29 | Dunham | Cornelius | 1 | 2 | 2 | | 1 | 2 | 1 | 1 | 1 | 1 | | | 12 | | |
| Tisbury | 454 | 30 | Jackues | Reuben | 1 | | | 1 | | 1 | | | 1 | | | | 4 | | |
| Tisbury | 454 | 31 | Gray | John | | | | 1 | | 3 | | | 1 | 1 | | | 6 | | |
| Tisbury | 454 | 32 | Gray | Mary | | | | | | | | | 1 | 1 | | | 2 | | |
| Tisbury | 454 | 33 | Gray | Abijah | 1 | | | 1 | | 4 | | | 1 | | | | 7 | | |
| Tisbury | 454 | 34 | Gray | Freeman | | | 1 | | | | | 1 | 1 | | | | 3 | | |
| Tisbury | 454 | 35 | Luce | Zephh | 1 | | | | 1 | 2 | | | 1 | | | | 5 | | |
| Tisbury | 454 | 36 | Dunham | Ephm | 2 | 1 | 1 | | 1 | 1 | 2 | 1 | 1 | | | | 10 | | |
| Tisbury | 454 | 37 | Norton | Francis | | | 2 | | 1 | | 1 | 2 | | 1 | | | 7 | | |
| Tisbury | 454 | 38 | Clifford | Varnell | 2 | 1 | | | 1 | | 1 | 1 | | | | | 6 | | |
| Tisbury | 454 | 39 | Clifford | Nathan | 2 | 1 | | 1 | | 2 | 1 | 2 | 1 | | | | 10 | | |
| Tisbury | 454 | 40 | Luce | Abishai | | | 2 | | 1 | | 1 | 1 | 2 | 1 | | | 8 | | |
| Tisbury | 454 | 41 | Cleveland | John | 1 | 2 | 2 | | 1 | | 1 | 1 | 1 | | | | 9 | | |
| Tisbury | 454 | 42 | Look | Joseph | 1 | | 2 | | 1 | | 1 | 2 | 1 | 1 | | | 9 | | |
| Tisbury | 454 | 43 | Norton | Mayhew | 2 | | 1 | | 1 | | 2 | 3 | 1 | | | | 10 | | |
| Tisbury | 454 | 44 | Luce | Ruth | | | 2 | | | | | | | | | | 2 | | |
| Tisbury | 454 | 45 | Luce | Martin | 2 | | | 1 | | 1 | | 1 | | 1 | | | 6 | | |
| Tisbury | 454 | 46 | Cleveland | Zebediah | 1 | 1 | 1 | | 1 | | 1 | 3 | | 1 | | | 9 | | |
| Tisbury | 454 | 47 | Luce | Adonijah | 3 | 2 | | | 1 | | | 2 | 1 | | | | 9 | | |
| Tisbury | 454 | 48 | Athearn | Moses | | 1 | 1 | 1 | | | | | 1 | 1 | | | 5 | | |
| Tisbury | 453 | 30 | Rogers | Lot | | 2 | 1 | | 1 | 1 | 1 | | 1 | | | | 7 | | |
| Tisbury | 453 | 31 | Rogers | Roland | | | 1 | | | | | | 1 | | | | 2 | | |
| Tisbury | 453 | 32 | Rogers | Stephen | | | | 1 | | | | | | 1 | | | 2 | | |
| Tisbury | 453 | 33 | Luce | Stephen | | | | 1 | | | | | | 1 | | | 2 | | |
| Tisbury | 453 | 34 | Luce | Timo | | | 3 | 1 | | | | 1 | | 1 | | | 6 | | |
| Tisbury | 453 | 35 | Luce | Stephen Jr | 1 | | | 1 | | | | 1 | | | | | 3 | | |
| Tisbury | 453 | 36 | Norton | Presbury | | | 1 | | | | | | 1 | | | | 2 | | |
| Tisbury | 453 | 37 | Davis | John | 1 | | 1 | | 1 | 2 | 2 | | 1 | | | | 8 | | |
| Tisbury | 453 | 38 | Crowell | Saml | | | 1 | 1 | | | | 2 | | 1 | | | 5 | | |
| Tisbury | 453 | 39 | Crowell | Barzillai | 2 | 2 | | | 1 | 1 | | 1 | 1 | | | | 8 | | |
| Tisbury | 453 | 40 | Merry | William | 2 | 1 | 3 | | 1 | | | | | 1 | | | 8 | | |
| Tisbury | 453 | 41 | Merry | Timo | 1 | | 1 | | | | 1 | | 1 | | | | 4 | | |
| Tisbury | 453 | 42 | Look | Elijah | 1 | 1 | 1 | 1 | | 2 | | 1 | 1 | 1 | | | 9 | | |
| Tisbury | 453 | 43 | Look | Job | | | 2 | 1 | | | | | | 1 | | | 4 | | |
| Tisbury | 453 | 44 | Adams | Moses | 1 | | 1 | | | | | | | 1 | | | 3 | | |
| Tisbury | 453 | 45 | Cathcart | Jona | | | | 1 | | | | 1 | 1 | | | | 3 | | |
| Tisbury | 453 | 46 | Look | Lot | 2 | | 1 | | | 1 | 2 | | 1 | | | | 7 | | |
| Tisbury | 453 | 47 | Walrond | Noah | 2 | | | 1 | | 1 | 1 | 1 | | | | | 6 | | |
| Tisbury | 453 | 48 | Walrond | Thos | | | | 1 | | | | | | 1 | | | 2 | | |
| Tisbury | 453 | 49 | Athearn | Benja | 2 | | | 1 | | | | | 1 | | | | 4 | | |
| Tisbury | 454 | 1 | Luce | Thomas | | 1 | 1 | | 1 | | | 2 | 1 | | | | 6 | | |
| Tisbury | 454 | 2 | Athearn | Jona Jr | | | | 1 | | 1 | | 1 | | | | | 3 | | |
| Tisbury | 454 | 3 | Germain | Cesar | | | | | | | | | | | 5 | | 5 | | |
| Tisbury | 454 | 4 | Spaulding | Rufus | 2 | | | 1 | | 2 | 2 | 1 | 1 | | 1 | | 10 | | |
| Tisbury | 454 | 5 | Cottle | William | 1 | | 1 | | | | | | 1 | | | | 3 | | |
| Tisbury | 454 | 6 | Daggett | William | | 1 | 1 | | 1 | 1 | | | 1 | 2 | | | 7 | | |
| Tisbury | 454 | 7 | Daggett | Seth | 1 | | 1 | | | | | | 1 | | | | 3 | | |

# 1800 Tisbury, Dukes County, Massachusetts

| TOWN | PG# | LN# | LAST NAME | FIRST NAME | FREE WHITE MALES | | | | | FREE WHITE FEMALES | | | | | TOTAL ALL OTHER | TOTAL SLAVES | TOTALS | DISTRICT/ TOWNSHIP | NOTES |
|---|---|---|---|---|---|---|---|---|---|---|---|---|---|---|---|---|---|---|---|
| | | | | | under 10 | 10 to 16 | 16 to 26 | 26 to 45 | 45 and over | under 10 | 10 to 16 | 16 to 26 | 26 to 45 | 45 and over | | | | | |
| Tisbury | 454 | 8 | Slocum | Christopher | 3 | 2 | | 1 | | 1 | | | 1 | | | | 8 | | |
| Tisbury | 454 | 9 | Manchester | John | 3 | | | 1 | | 3 | 1 | | 1 | | | | 9 | | |
| Tisbury | 454 | 10 | Dunham | David | 1 | 1 | | | 1 | | 1 | 2 | | 1 | | | 7 | | |
| Tisbury | 454 | 11 | Luce | Abijah | 1 | | 1 | 1 | | 3 | 2 | | 1 | | | | 9 | | |
| Tisbury | 454 | 12 | Manchester | Thos | | | 2 | 1 | | | | | 1 | 1 | | | 5 | | |
| Tisbury | 454 | 13 | Dunham | Thos | | | 1 | | | 2 | | 2 | | | | | 5 | | |
| Tisbury | 454 | 14 | Holmes | John | 1 | | | 1 | | 1 | 1 | | | 1 | | | 5 | | |
| Tisbury | 454 | 15 | Downes | William | 2 | | | 1 | | | | | 1 | | | | 4 | | |
| Tisbury | 454 | 16 | Daggett | Freeman | | | | 1 | | 1 | | 2 | | | | | 4 | | |
| Tisbury | 454 | 17 | Allen | Ebenz | | | | 1 | | | | | 1 | 1 | | | 3 | | |
| Tisbury | 454 | 18 | West | Jernal | 3 | 2 | 2 | 1 | | | 1 | 1 | | | | | 10 | | |
| Tisbury | 454 | 19 | West | James | 2 | | 1 | | | | 1 | | | | | | 4 | | |
| Tisbury | 454 | 20 | Winsow | James | 2 | 1 | | 1 | | | | 3 | | 1 | | | 8 | | |
| Tisbury | 454 | 21 | Merry | Jona | | | 1 | 2 | 1 | | | 1 | | 1 | | | 6 | | |
| Tisbury | 454 | 22 | Harden | Ephm | | | 3 | 1 | | 1 | 1 | | 1 | | | | 7 | | |
| Tisbury | 454 | 23 | Crepo | Jeremiah | | | | 1 | | | | | 1 | | | | 2 | | |
| Tisbury | 454 | 24 | Hillman | Jethro | | | 1 | | | | | 1 | | | | | 2 | | |
| Tisbury | 454 | 25 | Hillman | Dinah | | | | | | | | | 1 | | | | 1 | | |
| Tisbury | 454 | 26 | Daggett | Michael | | | 1 | | | 1 | | 1 | | | | | 3 | | |
| Tisbury | 454 | 27 | Winslow | Isaac | 2 | | 1 | 1 | | | | | 1 | | | | 5 | | |
| Tisbury | 454 | 28 | Luce | Warren | | | 1 | | | 1 | | 2 | | | | | 4 | | |
| Tisbury | 454 | 29 | Merry | Joseph | | | | 1 | | | | | | 1 | | | 2 | | |
| Tisbury | 454 | 30 | Chase | Timo | | | 2 | 1 | | 2 | 1 | | 1 | | | | 7 | | |
| Tisbury | 454 | 31 | Reynolds | Benja | 1 | | 1 | | | | | 1 | | | | | 3 | | |
| Tisbury | 454 | 32 | Whelden | Thos | 1 | | | 1 | | 3 | | | 1 | | | | 6 | | |
| Tisbury | 454 | 33 | Mantor | Jona | | | 2 | 1 | | | 1 | 2 | 1 | | | | 7 | | |
| Tisbury | 454 | 34 | Baxter | Rhoda | | 1 | | | | 2 | 1 | 2 | 1 | | | | 7 | | |
| Tisbury | 454 | 35 | Mantor | Thomas | | | 1 | | | 1 | | 1 | | | | | 3 | | |
| Tisbury | 454 | 36 | Mantor | Jona Jr | 2 | | | 1 | | 2 | | | 1 | | | | 6 | | |
| Tisbury | 454 | 37 | Hillman | Owen | 1 | | | 1 | | 1 | | 1 | | | | | 4 | | |
| Tisbury | 454 | 38 | Luce | Jona | 1 | | | 1 | | | | | 1 | | | | 3 | | |
| Tisbury | 454 | 39 | Worth | William | 1 | | | 1 | | 2 | 1 | | 1 | | | | 6 | | |
| Tisbury | 454 | 40 | Daggett | Isaac | | 1 | 1 | 1 | | | | | 1 | 2 | | | 6 | | |
| Tisbury | 454 | 41 | West | Peter | 2 | | | 1 | | 3 | | | 1 | | | | 7 | | |
| Tisbury | 454 | 42 | Daggett | William Jr | 1 | | | 1 | | 1 | | 1 | | | | | 4 | | |
| Tisbury | 454 | 43 | Smith | William | 3 | | 2 | 1 | | | | | 1 | | | | 7 | | |
| Tisbury | 454 | 44 | Dunham | Paul | | | 1 | | | 1 | | | 1 | | | | 3 | | |
| Tisbury | 454 | 45 | Newcomb | Sally | | 1 | | | | | | | 1 | | | | 2 | | |
| Tisbury | 454 | 46 | Claghorn | Joseph | | 1 | | 1 | | 1 | | | 2 | | | | 5 | | |
| Tisbury | 454 | 47 | Luce | Saml Jr | | | 1 | | | 1 | 1 | 1 | | | | | 4 | | |
| Tisbury | 454 | 48 | Henrit | Saml | | | | | | | | | | | 3 | | 3 | | |

112

# 1800 Dukes County, Massachusetts Index

| TOWN | PG# | LN# | LAST NAME | FIRST NAME | M under 10 | M 10 to 16 | M 16 to 26 | M 26 to 45 | M 45 and over | F under 10 | F 10 to 16 | F 16 to 26 | F 26 to 45 | F 45 and over | TOTAL ALL OTHER | TOTAL SLAVES | TOTALS | DISTRICT/ TOWNSHIP | NOTES |
|---|---|---|---|---|---|---|---|---|---|---|---|---|---|---|---|---|---|---|---|
| Chilmark | 448 | 21 | Adams | James | 1 | 1 | 1 |  | 1 | 2 | 1 |  | 1 |  |  |  | 8 |  |  |
| Tisbury | 452 | 19 | Adams | Lydia | 1 |  |  |  |  | 1 |  |  | 1 |  |  |  | 3 |  |  |
| Chilmark | 448 | 19 | Adams | Mayhew |  |  | 1 | 1 |  |  |  | 2 | 1 | 2 | 1 |  | 8 |  |  |
| Tisbury | 453 | 44 | Adams | Moses | 1 |  |  | 1 |  |  |  |  | 1 |  |  |  | 3 |  |  |
| Chilmark | 448 | 20 | Adams | Wm | 1 |  |  | 1 |  | 1 |  |  | 1 |  |  |  | 4 |  |  |
| Tisbury | 454 | 25 | Allen | Abigail |  |  |  |  |  |  |  |  | 1 | 1 |  |  | 2 |  |  |
| Tisbury | 454 | 24 | Allen | Benja | 1 | 1 |  | 1 |  | 1 |  |  | 1 |  | 1 |  | 6 |  |  |
| Chilmark | 449 | 18 | Allen | Deborah | 1 |  | 1 |  |  |  |  |  | 1 |  |  |  | 3 |  |  |
| Tisbury | 454 | 17 | Allen | Ebenz |  |  |  | 1 |  |  |  | 1 | 1 |  |  |  | 3 |  |  |
| Tisbury | 454 | 23 | Allen | Eleanor |  |  |  |  |  |  |  | 2 | 1 |  | 1 |  | 4 |  |  |
| Chilmark | 449 | 33 | Allen | Ephraim |  | 1 |  | 1 |  |  |  | 2 | 1 | 1 |  |  | 6 |  |  |
| Chilmark | 448 | 46 | Allen | Ezra |  |  |  | 1 |  |  |  |  | 1 |  |  |  | 2 |  |  |
| Chilmark | 449 | 44 | Allen | James |  |  |  | 1 |  |  | 1 | 1 | 1 |  |  |  | 4 |  |  |
| Chilmark | 449 | 45 | Allen | James Jr |  | 1 |  | 1 |  | 1 |  |  | 1 |  |  |  | 4 |  |  |
| Edgartown | 444 | 11 | Allen | John |  | 1 | 2 |  | 1 |  | 1 | 2 |  | 1 | 4 |  | 12 |  |  |
| Tisbury | 452 | 35 | Allen | Joseph |  |  | 1 |  |  |  |  |  | 1 |  | 1 |  | 3 |  |  |
| Chilmark | 448 | 3 | Allen | Josiah |  |  | 1 | 1 |  |  |  | 1 | 1 |  |  |  | 4 |  |  |
| Chilmark | 448 | 47 | Allen | Mathew | 1 | 1 |  | 1 |  |  |  |  | 1 |  |  |  | 4 |  |  |
| Tisbury | 452 | 34 | Allen | Patience |  |  |  |  |  |  |  | 1 | 2 |  | 1 |  | 4 |  |  |
| Chilmark | 448 | 45 | Allen | Robert |  | 1 |  | 1 |  |  |  | 1 | 1 |  |  |  | 4 |  |  |
| Chilmark | 449 | 32 | Allen | Samuel |  |  |  | 1 |  |  |  | 1 | 2 |  |  |  | 4 |  |  |
| Tisbury | 453 | 28 | Allen | Seth |  |  | 1 |  |  |  |  |  | 1 |  |  |  | 2 |  |  |
| Chilmark | 449 | 46 | Allen | Sylvanus | 1 |  | 1 |  |  |  |  | 3 | 1 |  |  |  | 6 |  |  |
| Chilmark | 449 | 17 | Allen | Tristram | 2 |  | 1 |  |  |  |  | 1 | 1 |  |  |  | 5 |  |  |
| Chilmark | 449 | 47 | Allen | Zebulon | 1 |  | 1 |  |  |  |  | 3 | 1 | 1 |  |  | 7 |  |  |
| Edgartown | 444 | 48 | Asey | Elijah | 1 | 1 |  | 1 |  |  |  | 2 | 1 |  |  |  | 6 |  |  |
| Edgartown | 445 | 19 | Asey | Henry |  |  | 1 |  |  | 1 |  |  | 1 |  |  |  | 3 |  |  |
| Tisbury | 453 | 49 | Athearn | Benja | 2 |  |  | 1 |  |  |  | 1 |  |  |  |  | 4 |  |  |
| Tisbury | 452 | 31 | Athearn | Ezra |  |  |  |  | 2 |  |  | 1 | 1 | 2 |  |  | 6 |  |  |
| Tisbury | 453 | 16 | Athearn | James |  |  |  | 1 |  |  |  |  | 1 | 1 |  |  | 3 |  |  |
| Tisbury | 453 | 22 | Athearn | Jethro |  |  |  | 1 |  |  |  | 2 | 1 | 1 |  |  | 5 |  |  |
| Tisbury | 452 | 30 | Athearn | Jona |  |  | 1 |  | 1 |  |  | 3 | 1 |  | 1 |  | 7 |  |  |
| Tisbury | 454 | 2 | Athearn | Jona Jr |  |  |  | 1 |  | 1 |  | 1 |  |  |  |  | 3 |  |  |
| Tisbury | 452 | 29 | Athearn | Joseph |  | 1 | 1 |  | 1 | 1 | 1 |  |  | 1 |  |  | 6 |  |  |
| Tisbury | 454 | 48 | Athearn | Moses |  |  | 1 | 1 | 1 |  |  |  | 1 | 1 |  |  | 5 |  |  |
| Tisbury | 452 | 32 | Athearn | Solomon | 1 | 1 |  | 1 |  | 2 | 2 |  | 1 |  |  |  | 8 |  |  |
| Tisbury | 453 | 23 | Athearn | Timo | 1 |  |  | 1 |  | 1 |  |  | 1 |  |  |  | 4 |  |  |
| Tisbury | 452 | 18 | Athearn | William | 3 |  |  | 1 |  | 1 |  |  | 1 |  | 1 |  | 7 |  |  |
| Tisbury | 453 | 5 | Avery | Zechariah | 1 |  | 1 | 1 |  | 2 | 1 |  | 1 |  |  |  | 7 |  |  |
| Edgartown | 445 | 1 | Banning | James | 1 | 2 | 1 |  | 1 | 1 |  |  | 1 |  |  |  | 7 |  |  |
| Chilmark | 448 | 32 | Bargis | Marcy |  |  |  |  |  |  |  |  | 1 |  |  |  | 1 |  |  |
| Edgartown | 447 | 11 | Basset | James |  |  |  |  |  |  |  |  |  |  | 4 |  | 4 |  |  |
| Chilmark | 449 | 7 | Bassett | Benja | 1 | 1 |  | 1 |  |  | 1 | 3 |  | 2 |  |  | 9 |  |  |
| Chilmark | 448 | 48 | Bassett | Jona |  |  |  | 1 |  |  |  |  |  |  |  |  | 1 |  |  |
| Chilmark | 448 | 29 | Bassett | Nathl |  | 1 |  | 1 |  | 1 |  |  | 1 |  |  |  | 4 |  |  |
| Chilmark | 449 | 23 | Bassett | Norton | 2 |  | 1 |  |  | 1 |  |  | 1 |  |  |  | 5 |  |  |
| Chilmark | 449 | 2 | Bassett | Wm | 2 |  | 1 |  |  |  |  |  | 1 | 1 |  |  | 5 |  |  |
| Tisbury | 454 | 34 | Baxter | Rhoda |  | 1 |  |  |  |  |  | 2 | 1 | 2 |  |  | 7 |  |  |
| Edgartown | 447 | 5 | Beetle | James | 1 | 2 |  | 1 |  |  |  |  | 1 |  | 1 |  | 6 |  |  |
| Edgartown | 447 | 32 | Beetle | Reuben | 3 |  |  | 1 |  |  |  |  | 1 |  |  |  | 5 |  |  |
| Edgartown | 442 | 14 | Beetle | Thomas |  |  | 1 | 1 |  |  |  |  |  | 2 |  |  | 4 |  |  |
| Edgartown | 447 | 4 | Beetle | William | 1 |  | 2 |  | 1 | 3 | 1 | 2 | 1 | 1 |  |  | 12 |  |  |
| Edgartown | 442 | 15 | Bradlee | Mary | 1 | 2 |  |  |  | 1 | 1 | 1 |  |  |  |  | 6 |  |  |
| Edgartown | 444 | 26 | Butler | Ann |  |  |  |  |  |  |  |  |  | 2 |  |  | 2 |  |  |
| Edgartown | 443 | 56 | Butler | Daniel | 1 |  |  | 1 |  | 1 |  | 2 |  |  |  |  | 5 |  |  |
| Edgartown | 443 | 10 | Butler | Daniel | 2 | 1 |  | 1 | 1 | 1 | 1 |  |  | 1 |  |  | 8 |  |  |
| Tisbury | 453 | 3 | Butler | David | 2 |  |  | 1 |  |  | 1 | 2 | 1 |  |  |  | 7 |  |  |
| Edgartown | 447 | 8 | Butler | Ebenz |  |  |  |  | 2 |  |  |  | 1 |  |  |  | 3 |  |  |
| Edgartown | 444 | 27 | Butler | John | 2 |  | 1 | 1 |  | 2 | 3 |  | 1 |  |  |  | 10 |  |  |
| Edgartown | 443 | 3 | Butler | Joseph | 1 |  | 1 |  |  |  |  |  | 1 |  |  |  | 3 |  |  |
| Chilmark | 448 | 38 | Butler | Nicholas | 2 |  | 1 |  |  |  |  |  | 1 |  |  |  | 4 |  |  |
| Edgartown | 446 | 1 | Butler | Peter | 1 |  | 1 |  |  | 1 |  |  | 1 |  |  |  | 4 |  |  |
| Edgartown | 444 | 17 | Butler | Silas |  | 1 | 1 |  | 1 |  | 1 | 2 |  | 1 |  |  | 7 |  |  |
| Tisbury | 453 | 48 | Butler | Thomas |  |  | 1 | 1 | 1 |  |  |  | 1 | 1 |  |  | 5 |  |  |
| Edgartown | 443 | 9 | Butler | Timothy |  | 2 |  | 1 |  | 1 | 1 | 1 |  | 1 |  |  | 7 |  |  |
| Edgartown | 445 | 17 | Butler | Walter | 1 |  | 1 |  |  |  |  |  | 1 |  |  |  | 3 |  |  |
| Edgartown | 447 | 18 | Butler | William | 1 |  | 2 |  |  | 2 |  |  | 1 |  |  |  | 6 |  |  |
| Edgartown | 445 | 24 | Butler | Zephaniah | 2 | 1 | 1 |  | 1 |  |  |  | 1 |  |  |  | 6 |  |  |
| Tisbury | 454 | 21 | Case | William |  |  |  | 2 | 1 |  | 1 | 1 |  | 1 |  |  | 6 |  |  |
| Tisbury | 453 | 20 | Cathcart | Hugh |  |  | 1 | 1 | 1 | 1 | 1 | 1 |  | 1 |  |  | 7 |  |  |
| Tisbury | 453 | 45 | Cathcart | Jona |  |  |  |  | 1 |  |  | 1 |  | 1 |  |  | 3 |  |  |
| Edgartown | 446 | 12 | Chace | Abram | 2 | 1 | 1 | 1 |  | 2 | 1 | 1 | 1 |  |  |  | 10 |  |  |
| Edgartown | 443 | 54 | Chadwick | Anthony |  |  | 1 | 1 |  | 1 | 1 |  |  | 1 |  |  | 5 |  |  |
| Tisbury | 453 | 8 | Chase | Joseph |  | 1 | 2 |  | 2 |  |  |  | 1 | 1 |  |  | 7 |  |  |
| Tisbury | 454 | 30 | Chase | Timo |  |  |  | 2 | 1 |  |  | 2 | 1 | 1 |  |  | 7 |  |  |
| Edgartown | 447 | 20 | Claghorn | Bartlet | 1 |  |  | 1 |  | 1 |  |  | 1 |  |  |  | 4 |  |  |
| Edgartown | 447 | 19 | Claghorn | Jane |  |  |  |  |  |  |  |  | 1 | 1 |  |  | 2 |  |  |
| Tisbury | 454 | 46 | Claghorn | Joseph |  | 1 |  |  | 1 |  |  | 1 |  | 2 |  |  | 5 |  |  |
| Edgartown | 447 | 31 | Claghorn | Thos Jr |  |  |  |  | 1 |  |  | 1 | 2 | 2 |  |  | 6 |  |  |

# 1800 Dukes County, Massachusetts Index

| TOWN | PG# | LN# | LAST NAME | FIRST NAME | FREE WHITE MALES | | | | | FREE WHITE FEMALES | | | | | TOTAL ALL OTHER | TOTAL SLAVES | TOTALS | DISTRICT/ TOWNSHIP | NOTES |
|---|---|---|---|---|---|---|---|---|---|---|---|---|---|---|---|---|---|---|---|
| | | | | | under 10 | 10 to 16 | 16 to 26 | 26 to 45 | 45 and over | under 10 | 10 to 16 | 16 to 26 | 26 to 45 | 45 and over | | | | | |
| Edgartown | 443 | 39 | Clark | John | | | 2 | 1 | 2 | | | | 1 | 1 | | | 7 | | |
| Edgartown | 444 | 13 | Clark | John Jr | | | | 1 | | | | | | 1 | | | 2 | | |
| Edgartown | 443 | 19 | Cleveland | Ezra | | 1 | 1 | | 1 | | | 1 | 2 | 1 | | | 7 | | |
| Edgartown | 444 | 19 | Cleveland | Ichabod | 1 | 1 | 2 | 1 | | | | | | 1 | | | 6 | | |
| Tisbury | 454 | 41 | Cleveland | John | 1 | 2 | 2 | 1 | | | 1 | 1 | 1 | | | | 9 | | |
| Edgartown | 443 | 17 | Cleveland | Joseph | 1 | | | 1 | | 1 | | | 1 | | | | 4 | | |
| Edgartown | 443 | 16 | Cleveland | Seth | | 1 | | 1 | | | | | 1 | | | | 3 | | |
| Tisbury | 453 | 4 | Cleveland | Sylvanus | 1 | | 1 | | | | | 1 | | | | | 3 | | |
| Edgartown | 445 | 20 | Cleveland | Tristram | | | 1 | | | 1 | | 1 | | | | | 3 | | |
| Tisbury | 454 | 46 | Cleveland | Zebediah | 1 | 1 | 1 | 1 | | | | 1 | 3 | 1 | | | 9 | | |
| Tisbury | 454 | 39 | Clifford | Nathan | 2 | 1 | | 1 | | 2 | | 1 | 2 | 1 | | | 10 | | |
| Tisbury | 454 | 38 | Clifford | Varnell | 2 | 1 | | 1 | | | | 1 | 1 | | | | 6 | | |
| Edgartown | 444 | 46 | Coffin | Beulah | | | | | | | | | 1 | | | | 1 | | |
| Edgartown | 444 | 44 | Coffin | Daniel | | | 1 | 1 | | | 1 | 1 | | | | | 4 | | |
| Edgartown | 447 | 22 | Coffin | David | | 1 | | 1 | | | | 1 | | | | | 3 | | |
| Edgartown | 442 | 17 | Coffin | Edea | 1 | 1 | 1 | | 1 | 1 | | 1 | 1 | 1 | | | 8 | | |
| Edgartown | 442 | 13 | Coffin | Elizabeth | | | | | | | | | 2 | | | | 2 | | |
| Edgartown | 444 | 54 | Coffin | Eunice | | | | | | | | | 1 | | 1 | | 2 | | |
| Edgartown | 444 | 38 | Coffin | James | | 1 | 1 | 2 | | 1 | | 1 | 1 | 1 | | | 8 | | |
| Tisbury | 453 | 34 | Coffin | Jedidah | | | 2 | | | | | 2 | 1 | 1 | | | 6 | | |
| Edgartown | 445 | 35 | Coffin | John | | 2 | 3 | 1 | | | | 1 | 1 | 1 | | | 9 | | |
| Edgartown | 445 | 44 | Coffin | Obed | | 1 | 2 | 1 | | | | | | 1 | | | 5 | | |
| Edgartown | 445 | 6 | Coffin | Peter | 2 | | | 1 | | 2 | | | | 1 | 1 | | 7 | | |
| Edgartown | 444 | 32 | Coffin | Sally | | 1 | 1 | | | 2 | | 1 | 1 | 1 | | | 7 | | |
| Edgartown | 444 | 43 | Coffin | Sarah | 1 | | | | | | | | 1 | 1 | | | 3 | | |
| Edgartown | 444 | 53 | Coffin | Timothy | 2 | | | 1 | | 2 | 2 | | 1 | | | | 8 | | |
| Edgartown | 442 | 12 | Coffin | Uriah | 3 | | | 1 | | 1 | | | 1 | | | | 6 | | |
| Edgartown | 447 | 21 | Coffin | William | | | 2 | | 1 | | | 2 | 1 | 1 | 2 | | 9 | | |
| Edgartown | 447 | 36 | Cooke | Lewis | | | | | | | | | | | 6 | | 6 | | |
| Edgartown | 445 | 32 | Cooke | Thomas | 1 | | 2 | 1 | | 2 | 1 | | | 2 | | | 9 | | |
| Edgartown | 445 | 11 | Cooke | Thos Jr | 2 | | | 1 | | 1 | | | | 1 | | | 5 | | |
| Chilmark | 450 | 36 | Cooper | Abram | | | | | | | | | | | 5 | | 5 | | |
| Chilmark | 450 | 35 | Cooper | Josiah | | | | | | | | | | | 4 | | 4 | | |
| Chilmark | 450 | 34 | Cooper | Thos | | | | | | | | | | | 7 | | 7 | | |
| Chilmark | 450 | 37 | Cooper | Thos Jr | | | | | | | | | | | 3 | | 3 | | |
| Chilmark | 448 | 18 | Cooper | Zacheus | | | | | | | | | | | 3 | | 3 | | |
| Tisbury | 453 | 29 | Coswell | Hannah | | | | | | | | | | 1 | | | 1 | | |
| Tisbury | 452 | 51 | Cottle | Edmund | | 1 | 1 | | 1 | 2 | | 1 | 2 | | | | 8 | | |
| Tisbury | 453 | 6 | Cottle | Heppy | | 1 | | | | | 1 | 1 | 1 | | | | 4 | | |
| Chilmark | 449 | 34 | Cottle | John | | | | 1 | | | | | | 1 | | | 2 | | |
| Chilmark | 449 | 35 | Cottle | John Jr | 2 | 1 | 1 | | 1 | 1 | 1 | 1 | 1 | | | | 9 | | |
| Tisbury | 453 | 37 | Cottle | Robert | 2 | | | 1 | | 1 | 2 | | 1 | | | | 7 | | |
| Edgartown | 444 | 42 | Cottle | Sarah | | | | | | | | | 1 | 1 | | | 2 | | |
| Tisbury | 453 | 1 | Cottle | Shubael | | | | 1 | | | | | 1 | 1 | | | 3 | | |
| Chilmark | 449 | 36 | Cottle | Silas | | 1 | 1 | | 1 | | | 2 | 1 | | | | 6 | | |
| Tisbury | 454 | 5 | Cottle | William | 1 | | 1 | | | | | | 1 | | | | 3 | | |
| Edgartown | 447 | 2 | Courtney | Barber | | | 1 | | | | | | 1 | | | | 2 | | |
| Chilmark | 448 | 25 | Cox | Thos | 2 | | | 1 | | 1 | 1 | | 1 | 1 | | | 7 | | |
| Edgartown | 447 | 10 | Cozens | Pero | | | | | | | | | | | 8 | | 8 | | |
| Tisbury | 454 | 23 | Crepo | Jeremiah | | | 1 | | | | | | 1 | | | | 2 | | |
| Edgartown | 445 | 43 | Crosby | Harlow | | | 1 | | | 3 | | | 1 | | | | 5 | | |
| Tisbury | 453 | 13 | Crosby | John | | 3 | 1 | | | | | 1 | 1 | 1 | | | 7 | | |
| Edgartown | 443 | 6 | Crosman | Peleg | 2 | 1 | 1 | | 1 | 1 | | 1 | 1 | | | | 7 | | |
| Tisbury | 453 | 39 | Crowell | Barzillai | 2 | 2 | | 1 | | 1 | | 1 | 1 | | | | 8 | | |
| Tisbury | 453 | 38 | Crowell | Saml | | | 1 | 1 | | | | 2 | | 1 | | | 5 | | |
| Edgartown | 447 | 26 | Daggett | Anna | | | | | | 1 | | | 1 | | | | 2 | | |
| Tisbury | 454 | 16 | Daggett | Freeman | | 1 | | | | 1 | | 2 | | | | | 4 | | |
| Edgartown | 443 | 41 | Daggett | George | | | | 1 | | | | 1 | 1 | 1 | | | 4 | | |
| Tisbury | 454 | 40 | Daggett | Isaac | | 1 | 1 | 1 | | | | | 1 | 2 | | | 6 | | |
| Edgartown | 443 | 4 | Daggett | John | 2 | | 1 | 1 | 1 | 1 | | | | 1 | | | 7 | | |
| Tisbury | 452 | 46 | Daggett | Jos | | | 1 | 1 | | | | | 2 | 1 | | | 5 | | |
| Tisbury | 454 | 26 | Daggett | Michael | | | 1 | 1 | | 1 | | | | | | | 3 | | |
| Tisbury | 452 | 50 | Daggett | Michael L. | 1 | | 1 | 1 | | | | | 1 | | | | 4 | | |
| Tisbury | 453 | 41 | Daggett | Peggy | 2 | | | 1 | | | | | 1 | | | | 4 | | |
| Edgartown | 445 | 50 | Daggett | Saml | | | 1 | 2 | | | | | 1 | 1 | | | 5 | | |
| Tisbury | 454 | 7 | Daggett | Seth | 1 | 1 | | | | | | 1 | | | | | 3 | | |
| Edgartown | 446 | 7 | Daggett | Silas | 1 | 2 | 1 | 1 | | 2 | 2 | | 2 | 1 | | | 12 | | |
| Edgartown | 445 | 18 | Daggett | Timothy | 1 | | 1 | | | | | 1 | | | | | 3 | | |
| Tisbury | 454 | 6 | Daggett | William | | 1 | 1 | 1 | | | 1 | | 1 | 2 | | | 7 | | |
| Tisbury | 454 | 42 | Daggett | William Jr | 1 | | 1 | 1 | | 1 | | | | | | | 4 | | |
| Edgartown | 442 | 19 | Daniel | Vinson | 3 | | 1 | 1 | 1 | 2 | | 1 | | | | | 9 | | |
| Edgartown | 447 | 6 | Davis | Benjamin | | 1 | | 1 | 1 | 1 | 1 | 1 | | 1 | | | 7 | | |
| Tisbury | 453 | 37 | Davis | John | 1 | | 1 | 1 | 2 | 2 | 1 | | | | | | 8 | | |
| Edgartown | 447 | 27 | Davis | Melatiah | 1 | 1 | 1 | | 1 | | | 1 | 1 | 1 | 1 | | 8 | | |
| Edgartown | 447 | 23 | Davis | Rufus | | | 1 | | 2 | | | | 2 | 1 | 1 | | 7 | | |
| Chilmark | 450 | 42 | de Grass | Jos | | | | | | | | | | | 6 | | 6 | | |
| Edgartown | 447 | 28 | Dexter | Joseph | 2 | 2 | 1 | 1 | | | 1 | | 1 | | | | 9 | | |
| Edgartown | 447 | 39 | Dimond | Jane | | | | | | | | | | 3 | | | 3 | | |
| Chilmark | 450 | 32 | Dodge | Henry | | | | | | | | | | 2 | | | 2 | | |

# 1800 Dukes County, Massachusetts Index

| TOWN | PG# | LN# | LAST NAME | FIRST NAME | FREE WHITE MALES | | | | | FREE WHITE FEMALES | | | | | TOTAL ALL OTHER | TOTAL SLAVES | TOTALS | DISTRICT/ TOWNSHIP | NOTES |
|---|---|---|---|---|---|---|---|---|---|---|---|---|---|---|---|---|---|---|---|
| | | | | | under 10 | 10 to 16 | 16 to 26 | 26 to 45 | 45 and over | under 10 | 10 to 16 | 16 to 26 | 26 to 45 | 45 and over | | | | | |
| Chilmark | 450 | 33 | Dodge | John | | | | | | | | | | | 3 | | 3 | | |
| Tisbury | 454 | 15 | Downes | William | 2 | | 1 | | | | | | 1 | | | | 4 | | |
| Tisbury | 454 | 13 | Draper | Lydia | | | | | | | | | | 1 | | | 1 | | |
| Edgartown | 442 | 25 | Duncan | Abigail | | | | | | | | | 1 | 1 | | | 2 | | |
| Chilmark | 448 | 24 | Dunham | Abigail | | 1 | | | | | | | | 1 | 1 | | 3 | | |
| Tisbury | 453 | 33 | Dunham | Abishai | 1 | 1 | 2 | | 1 | 2 | 1 | 1 | 1 | | | | 10 | | |
| Edgartown | 443 | 22 | Dunham | Benajah | | | | 2 | | | | | 2 | | | | 4 | | |
| Edgartown | 445 | 2 | Dunham | Benajah Jr | | 2 | 1 | | | | | 1 | | 1 | | | 5 | | |
| Edgartown | 446 | 9 | Dunham | Clifford | 4 | | 1 | | | | | | | 1 | | | 6 | | |
| Tisbury | 454 | 29 | Dunham | Cornelius | 1 | 2 | 2 | | 1 | 2 | 1 | 1 | 1 | 1 | | | 12 | | |
| Edgartown | 443 | 21 | Dunham | David | | | | 1 | | | | | 1 | | | | 2 | | |
| Tisbury | 454 | 10 | Dunham | David | 1 | 1 | | 1 | | | | 1 | 2 | 1 | | | 7 | | |
| Tisbury | 453 | 46 | Dunham | Eleazer | | 1 | | | | | | | | 1 | | | 2 | | |
| Edgartown | 444 | 56 | Dunham | Elijah | | | 1 | | | | | 1 | | 1 | | | 3 | | |
| Edgartown | 443 | 31 | Dunham | Elisha | | 2 | 1 | | | 1 | 1 | | 1 | | | | 6 | | |
| Tisbury | 454 | 36 | Dunham | Ephm | 2 | 1 | 1 | | 1 | 1 | 2 | 1 | 1 | | | | 10 | | |
| Edgartown | 443 | 32 | Dunham | Jonathan | 1 | | 1 | | | 1 | | | 1 | | | | 4 | | |
| Tisbury | 453 | 9 | Dunham | Lydia | | | | | | | 1 | | 1 | 1 | | | 3 | | |
| Edgartown | 444 | 9 | Dunham | Matilda | | | 1 | | | 2 | | | 1 | 1 | | | 5 | | |
| Edgartown | 444 | 10 | Dunham | Patience | | 1 | | | | 2 | 1 | | 1 | | | | 5 | | |
| Tisbury | 454 | 44 | Dunham | Paul | | 1 | | | | 1 | | | 1 | | | | 3 | | |
| Tisbury | 453 | 35 | Dunham | Shubael | 1 | | 1 | 1 | | 1 | 2 | | 1 | | | | 7 | | |
| Tisbury | 454 | 13 | Dunham | Thos | | 1 | | | | 1 | 2 | | 2 | | | | 5 | | |
| Edgartown | 443 | 26 | Dunham | William | | 1 | | | | 1 | | | 1 | | | | 3 | | |
| Edgartown | 444 | 28 | Ewers | Isaac | | | | 1 | | | | 1 | | | | | 2 | | |
| Chilmark | 448 | 9 | Ferguson | John | | | | 1 | | | | 1 | | 1 | 1 | | 4 | | |
| Chilmark | 448 | 10 | Ferguson | William | 2 | | 1 | | 1 | | | 1 | | | | | 5 | | |
| Edgartown | 444 | 14 | Fish | Abram | 1 | | 1 | | | 3 | | | 1 | | | | 6 | | |
| Edgartown | 443 | 50 | Fish | Amaziah | 2 | 2 | 1 | | | 3 | | | 1 | | | | 9 | | |
| Edgartown | 443 | 49 | Fish | Daniel | 2 | | 1 | | | 2 | 2 | 1 | | | | | 8 | | |
| Edgartown | 443 | 53 | Fish | Samuel | | | 1 | | | | | | | | | | 1 | | |
| Edgartown | 443 | 45 | Fish | Abner | 1 | | 1 | | | | | | 2 | 1 | | | 5 | | |
| Edgartown | 443 | 47 | Fish | Henry Jr | | 1 | 1 | | | 2 | | | 1 | | | | 5 | | |
| Edgartown | 443 | 44 | Fish | Henry | | | | 1 | | | | | 1 | | 1 | | 3 | | |
| Edgartown | 443 | 33 | Fisher | Gamaliel | 2 | | 1 | | | 2 | | | 1 | | | | 6 | | |
| Edgartown | 443 | 51 | Fisher | James | 2 | | | 1 | 1 | 3 | 1 | | 1 | | | | 9 | | |
| Edgartown | 443 | 52 | Fisher | James Jr | 1 | | 1 | | | 1 | | 1 | | | | | 4 | | |
| Edgartown | 443 | 55 | Fisher | John | | | | 1 | | | | | 1 | | | | 2 | | |
| Edgartown | 445 | 15 | Fisher | Jona | 3 | 1 | 2 | | 1 | | 1 | | 1 | | | | 9 | | |
| Edgartown | 443 | 48 | Fisher | Joseph | 1 | | 2 | 1 | | 1 | 1 | | 1 | | | | 7 | | |
| Edgartown | 444 | 23 | Fisher | Richard | | 1 | | | | | | 1 | | | | | 2 | | |
| Edgartown | 443 | 46 | Fisher | Thomas | 3 | | 1 | 1 | | 2 | 2 | 1 | | | | | 10 | | |
| Edgartown | 445 | 34 | Fitch | Benjamin | 1 | | | 1 | | | | | | 1 | 1 | | 4 | | |
| Chilmark | 448 | 15 | Flanders | John | 1 | | 1 | | | 2 | | | 1 | | | | 5 | | |
| Tisbury | 454 | 14 | Foster | James | 1 | | 1 | | | | | | 1 | | | | 3 | | |
| Tisbury | 454 | 22 | Foster | Rebecca | | 3 | | | | | 1 | 1 | | 1 | | | 6 | | |
| Tisbury | 454 | 3 | Germain | Cesar | | | | | | | | | | | 5 | | 5 | | |
| Chilmark | 450 | 31 | Gifford | Ephm | 2 | | | 1 | | | | 1 | | 1 | | | 5 | | |
| Chilmark | 450 | 24 | Gifford | Silas | 1 | | 1 | | | | | | 1 | | | | 3 | | |
| Chilmark | 450 | 23 | Gifford | Wm | 1 | 2 | 1 | | 1 | 4 | 3 | | | 2 | | | 14 | | |
| Edgartown | 447 | 33 | Goodley | Phillip | | | | | | | | | | | 4 | | 4 | | |
| Tisbury | 454 | 33 | Gray | Abijah | 1 | | 1 | | | 4 | | | 1 | | | | 7 | | |
| Tisbury | 454 | 34 | Gray | Freeman | | | 1 | | | 1 | | 1 | | | | | 3 | | |
| Edgartown | 445 | 13 | Gray | John | | 1 | | | | 1 | | | 1 | | | | 3 | | |
| Tisbury | 454 | 31 | Gray | John | | | 1 | | | 3 | | | 1 | 1 | | | 6 | | |
| Tisbury | 454 | 32 | Gray | Mary | | | | | | | | | 1 | 1 | | | 2 | | |
| Edgartown | 445 | 21 | Gray | Rhoda | 1 | 2 | 2 | | | | | 1 | | 1 | | | 7 | | |
| Tisbury | 453 | 36 | Grinall | Oliver | 1 | | 1 | | | 2 | | | 1 | | | | 5 | | |
| Chilmark | 450 | 30 | Grinall | Remington | 2 | | | 1 | | | | | | 1 | | | 4 | | |
| Chilmark | 448 | 2 | Hamlin | Lydia | | | | | | | | | | 1 | | | 1 | | |
| Tisbury | 454 | 11 | Hammet | Abijah | 2 | | 1 | | | 2 | | | 1 | | | | 6 | | |
| Tisbury | 454 | 12 | Hammet | Mary | | | | | | | | | | 1 | | | 1 | | |
| Chilmark | 448 | 27 | Hancock | James | 2 | | 1 | 1 | | 1 | | 1 | | | | | 6 | | |
| Tisbury | 454 | 16 | Hancock | John | 1 | | 1 | | | 2 | | | 1 | | | | 5 | | |
| Tisbury | 454 | 17 | Hancock | Jonah | | | 1 | 1 | | | | | 1 | 1 | | | 4 | | |
| Tisbury | 454 | 18 | Hancock | Mary | | | | | | | | | 2 | | | | 2 | | |
| Tisbury | 454 | 15 | Hancock | Russell | | 1 | | 1 | 1 | | | 2 | | 1 | | | 6 | | |
| Chilmark | 448 | 39 | Hanks | Uriah | | | | 1 | | | | | | 1 | | | 2 | | |
| Tisbury | 454 | 22 | Harden | Ephm | | 3 | 1 | | | 1 | 1 | | 1 | | | | 7 | | |
| Tisbury | 454 | 48 | Henrit | Saml | | | | | | | | | | | 3 | | 3 | | |
| Chilmark | 449 | 22 | Hillman | Abigail | | 1 | | | | | | | | 1 | | | 2 | | |
| Tisbury | 454 | 25 | Hillman | Dinah | | | | | | | | | | 1 | | | 1 | | |
| Edgartown | 447 | 25 | Hillman | Elijah | | | 1 | | | 3 | 1 | | 1 | | | | 6 | | |
| Chilmark | 449 | 6 | Hillman | Ezra | 1 | 1 | | 2 | | | 1 | 1 | | 1 | 1 | | 8 | | |
| Tisbury | 454 | 24 | Hillman | Jethro | | | 1 | | | | | 1 | | | | | 2 | | |
| Chilmark | 448 | 17 | Hillman | Moses | 2 | | 1 | 1 | | | | | 1 | | | | 5 | | |
| Tisbury | 454 | 37 | Hillman | Owen | 1 | | 1 | | | 1 | | | 1 | | | | 4 | | |
| Chilmark | 448 | 28 | Hillman | Robert | | 1 | 3 | 1 | 1 | | | 1 | | 1 | 1 | | 9 | | |
| Chilmark | 448 | 16 | Hillman | Saml | | | | 1 | | | | | | 1 | | | 2 | | |

115

| TOWN | PG# | LN# | LAST NAME | FIRST NAME | FREE WHITE MALES | | | | | FREE WHITE FEMALES | | | | | TOTAL ALL OTHER | TOTAL SLAVES | TOTALS | DISTRICT/ TOWNSHIP | NOTES |
|---|---|---|---|---|---|---|---|---|---|---|---|---|---|---|---|---|---|---|---|
| | | | | | under 10 | 10 to 16 | 16 to 26 | 26 to 45 | 45 and over | under 10 | 10 to 16 | 16 to 26 | 26 to 45 | 45 and over | | | | | |
| Chilmark | 449 | 3 | Hillman | Silas | | | | 1 | | | | | 3 | 1 | | | 5 | | |
| Chilmark | 449 | 4 | Hillman | Silas Jr | | | | 1 | | | | 1 | | | | | 2 | | |
| Chilmark | 448 | 30 | Hillman | Uriel | 1 | | 1 | | | 1 | | | 1 | | | | 4 | | |
| Edgartown | 445 | 22 | Holley | Joseph | 1 | | | 1 | | 4 | 3 | 1 | | | | | 10 | | |
| Tisbury | 454 | 14 | Holmes | John | 1 | | | 1 | | 1 | | 1 | | 1 | | | 5 | | |
| Chilmark | 449 | 5 | House | Work | | | 2 | | | | | | | 5 | | | 7 | | |
| Edgartown | 444 | 5 | Huxford | Cornelius | | 1 | | 1 | | 2 | 2 | | 1 | | | | 7 | | |
| Edgartown | 444 | 4 | Huxford | Joseph | | 2 | 1 | 1 | | 1 | | | 1 | | | | 6 | | |
| Tisbury | 454 | 30 | Jackues | Reuben | 1 | | 1 | | | 1 | | | 1 | | | | 4 | | |
| Chilmark | 450 | 40 | Jeffers | Thos | | | | | | | | | | | 5 | | 5 | | |
| Edgartown | 444 | 1 | Jernigan | David | 1 | | 1 | | | 1 | | 1 | | | | | 4 | | |
| Edgartown | 444 | 40 | Jernigan | Thomas | | 1 | 1 | 1 | | | | | | 1 | | | 4 | | |
| Edgartown | 444 | 39 | Jernigan | William | 1 | | | 1 | | | | | 1 | 1 | | | 4 | | |
| Edgartown | 444 | 41 | Jernigan | Wm Jr | 2 | 1 | | 1 | | 2 | 2 | 1 | | | | | 9 | | |
| Edgartown | 447 | 40 | Johnson | Esther | | | | | | | | | | | 3 | | 3 | | |
| Edgartown | 447 | 38 | Johnson | George | | | | | | | | | | | 2 | | 2 | | |
| Chilmark | 448 | 13 | Jones | Daniel | | 2 | | 1 | | 1 | | | | 1 | | | 5 | | |
| Tisbury | 453 | 17 | Jones | Ebena | 1 | | | 1 | | 3 | | | 1 | | | | 6 | | |
| Tisbury | 453 | 24 | Jones | Thos | | | 1 | 1 | | | | | 1 | 1 | | | 4 | | |
| Tisbury | 454 | 27 | Joseph | Imanuel | 1 | | | 1 | | 1 | | | 1 | | | | 4 | | |
| Edgartown | 444 | 33 | Kelly | Bathsheba | | | 2 | | | | | | | 2 | | | 4 | | |
| Edgartown | 444 | 34 | Kelly | Joseph | 1 | | | 1 | | | | | 1 | | | | 3 | | |
| Edgartown | 444 | 12 | Kelly | William | | | 1 | | | | 1 | 1 | 1 | | | | 4 | | |
| Edgartown | 443 | 43 | King | Robert | | 1 | | 1 | | 2 | 2 | 1 | 1 | | | | 8 | | |
| Tisbury | 453 | 49 | Lewis | Francis | | | 2 | 1 | | | | | 1 | 1 | | | 5 | | |
| Tisbury | 453 | 30 | Lewis | Freeman | 3 | | | 1 | | | | | 1 | | | | 5 | | |
| Tisbury | 452 | 24 | Lewis | Saml | | | | 1 | | | | | | 2 | | | 3 | | |
| Edgartown | 447 | 16 | Linton | Joseph | | | 1 | | | | | | 1 | | | | 2 | | |
| Edgartown | 443 | 40 | Livasy | Anthony | 3 | | 2 | 1 | | | | 1 | 2 | | | | 9 | | |
| Edgartown | 443 | 8 | Lobb | Ismael | | | | 1 | | | | | | 1 | | | 2 | | |
| Tisbury | 453 | 42 | Look | Elijah | 1 | 1 | 1 | 1 | | | 2 | 1 | 1 | 1 | | | 9 | | |
| Tisbury | 452 | 23 | Look | Elizath | | | | | | | | | 2 | | | | 2 | | |
| Tisbury | 453 | 43 | Look | Job | | | 2 | 1 | | | | | | 1 | | | 4 | | |
| Chilmark | 448 | 26 | Look | Job Jr | | | 1 | | | 1 | | | 1 | | | | 3 | | |
| Tisbury | 452 | 47 | Look | Jona | 1 | 1 | 1 | 1 | | | | 1 | 2 | 1 | | | 8 | | |
| Tisbury | 454 | 42 | Look | Joseph | 1 | | 2 | 1 | | | 1 | 2 | 1 | 1 | | | 9 | | |
| Tisbury | 453 | 46 | Look | Lot | 2 | | | 1 | | 1 | | 2 | 1 | | | | 7 | | |
| Chilmark | 449 | 38 | Look | Prince | 2 | 1 | | 1 | | 1 | | | 1 | | | | 6 | | |
| Tisbury | 452 | 22 | Look | Robert | 1 | 2 | | 1 | | 2 | | 1 | 2 | 1 | | | 10 | | |
| Edgartown | 446 | 14 | Look | Samuel | 1 | 2 | 1 | 1 | | 1 | | 3 | 1 | 1 | | | 11 | | |
| Tisbury | 454 | 11 | Luce | Abijah | 1 | | 1 | 1 | | 3 | 2 | | 1 | | | | 9 | | |
| Tisbury | 454 | 40 | Luce | Abishai | | | 2 | 1 | | 1 | 1 | 2 | 1 | | | | 8 | | |
| Tisbury | 454 | 28 | Luce | Abner | 2 | | 1 | | | 1 | | | 1 | | | | 5 | | |
| Tisbury | 454 | 47 | Luce | Adonijah | 3 | 2 | | 1 | | 2 | | | 1 | | | | 9 | | |
| Tisbury | 452 | 33 | Luce | Benja | | | | 1 | | 2 | | | | 1 | | | 4 | | |
| Edgartown | 447 | 29 | Luce | Benjamin | | 1 | 2 | 1 | | | | 1 | 1 | 1 | | | 7 | | |
| Tisbury | 453 | 2 | Luce | Dorcas | | | | | | | 1 | 1 | 1 | | | | 3 | | |
| Tisbury | 453 | 15 | Luce | Elijah | | 1 | | | | | | | 1 | | | | 2 | | |
| Edgartown | 446 | 6 | Luce | Elisha | 2 | 1 | 2 | 1 | | 1 | | | 1 | | | | 8 | | |
| Tisbury | 452 | 26 | Luce | Enoch | | 1 | 1 | 1 | | | 3 | 1 | 1 | | | | 8 | | |
| Tisbury | 453 | 21 | Luce | Ezekiel | | 1 | | 1 | | | 2 | | | | 2 | | 6 | | |
| Edgartown | 447 | 12 | Luce | George | 3 | 1 | | 1 | 1 | 1 | | | 1 | | | | 8 | | |
| Tisbury | 453 | 31 | Luce | Henry | | 1 | | 1 | | | 2 | 1 | | | | | 5 | | |
| Tisbury | 454 | 2 | Luce | Isaac | | 1 | 1 | | | | 1 | 1 | | | | | 4 | | |
| Edgartown | 444 | 18 | Luce | Jason | 2 | 2 | | 1 | | 1 | 1 | | 1 | | | | 8 | | |
| Edgartown | 446 | 8 | Luce | Jesse Jr | | | 1 | | | | | 1 | | | | | 2 | | |
| Edgartown | 446 | 10 | Luce | Jesse Jr | | 1 | | | | | | 1 | 1 | | | | 4 | | |
| Tisbury | 452 | 38 | Luce | Jona | | | 1 | | | | | | 1 | | | | 2 | | |
| Tisbury | 454 | 38 | Luce | Jona | 1 | | 1 | | | | | | 1 | | | | 3 | | |
| Tisbury | 452 | 39 | Luce | Joseph | | | 1 | | | | | | | | | | 1 | | |
| Tisbury | 452 | 40 | Luce | Joseph Jr | 2 | | | 1 | | | | | 1 | | | | 4 | | |
| Tisbury | 453 | 45 | Luce | Lemuel | | | 1 | | | | 1 | 1 | 1 | | | | 4 | | |
| Edgartown | 447 | 30 | Luce | Levi | | | | 1 | | | | | 2 | 1 | | | 4 | | |
| Edgartown | 446 | 2 | Luce | Lot | | 2 | | 1 | | 2 | | | 1 | | | | 6 | | |
| Tisbury | 452 | 48 | Luce | Lucy | | | 1 | | | | | | | 1 | | | 2 | | |
| Tisbury | 454 | 4 | Luce | Malachi | 1 | 1 | 1 | | | 1 | 1 | 1 | 1 | | | | 8 | | |
| Tisbury | 453 | 14 | Luce | Malatiah | | 1 | 1 | | | | | | 1 | | | | 3 | | |
| Tisbury | 452 | 28 | Luce | Margery | | | | | | | | | 1 | | | | 1 | | |
| Tisbury | 454 | 45 | Luce | Martin | 2 | | | 1 | | 1 | 1 | | 1 | | | | 6 | | |
| Chilmark | 450 | 16 | Luce | Mary | | 3 | | | | | | | 1 | 1 | | | 5 | | |
| Tisbury | 452 | 41 | Luce | Obed | | | 1 | 1 | | | 3 | | 1 | | | | 6 | | |
| Tisbury | 454 | 3 | Luce | Peter | | 1 | 1 | | | | | | 1 | | | | 3 | | |
| Tisbury | 453 | 27 | Luce | Reina | | | | | | | | | | 2 | | | 2 | | |
| Tisbury | 454 | 1 | Luce | Rhoda | | 1 | | | | | | 1 | | | | | 2 | | |
| Tisbury | 454 | 44 | Luce | Ruth | | 2 | | | | | | | | | | | 2 | | |
| Tisbury | 453 | 19 | Luce | Saml | | 1 | 1 | | | 1 | | 1 | | | | | 4 | | |
| Tisbury | 454 | 10 | Luce | Saml | 1 | | | 1 | | 2 | | 1 | | | | | 5 | | |
| Tisbury | 454 | 47 | Luce | Saml Jr | | | 1 | | | | 1 | 1 | | | | | 4 | | |
| Tisbury | 453 | 33 | Luce | Stephen | | | | 1 | | | | | 1 | | | | 2 | | |

# 1800 Dukes County, Massachusetts Index

| TOWN | PG# | LN# | LAST NAME | FIRST NAME | FREE WHITE MALES under 10 | 10 to 16 | 16 to 26 | 26 to 45 | 45 and over | FREE WHITE FEMALES under 10 | 10 to 16 | 16 to 26 | 26 to 45 | 45 and over | TOTAL ALL OTHER | TOTAL SLAVES | TOTALS | DISTRICT/ TOWNSHIP | NOTES |
|---|---|---|---|---|---|---|---|---|---|---|---|---|---|---|---|---|---|---|---|
| Tisbury | 453 | 35 | Luce | Stephen Jr | 1 | | 1 | | | | | 1 | | | | | 3 | | |
| Tisbury | 454 | 26 | Luce | Sylvanus | 1 | | 1 | 1 | | 1 | 1 | | 1 | | | | 6 | | |
| Tisbury | 454 | 1 | Luce | Thomas | | 1 | 1 | 1 | | | | 2 | | 1 | | | 6 | | |
| Tisbury | 452 | 43 | Luce | Thos | 2 | | | 1 | | 3 | 2 | 1 | 1 | | | | 10 | | |
| Tisbury | 453 | 34 | Luce | Timo | | | 3 | 1 | | | | 1 | | 1 | | | 6 | | |
| Tisbury | 454 | 28 | Luce | Warren | | | 1 | | 1 | | | 2 | | | | | 4 | | |
| Tisbury | 452 | 37 | Luce | William | | | | 1 | | | | 2 | 1 | 2 | | | 6 | | |
| Tisbury | 454 | 35 | Luce | Zephh | 1 | | | 1 | 2 | | | | 1 | | | | 5 | | |
| Chilmark | 448 | 36 | Lumbert | Abishai | 2 | | 1 | 1 | | 3 | | 1 | | | | | 8 | | |
| Tisbury | 452 | 20 | Lumbert | Hannah | | | | | | | | | | 2 | | | 2 | | |
| Tisbury | 452 | 49 | Lumbert | Lemuel | | | | 1 | | | | | | 1 | | | 2 | | |
| Chilmark | 448 | 35 | Lumbert | Moses | | | | 1 | | | 3 | 2 | 1 | | | | 7 | | |
| Tisbury | 452 | 45 | Lumbert | Saml | 2 | 1 | 1 | | | 2 | 1 | | 1 | | | | 8 | | |
| Chilmark | 448 | 34 | Lumbert | Thos | 1 | | 1 | | | 3 | | 1 | | | | | 6 | | |
| Tisbury | 452 | 25 | Lumbert | Timo | | | 3 | | | | | 3 | 1 | | | | 8 | | |
| Tisbury | 454 | 9 | Manchester | John | 3 | | 1 | | | 3 | 1 | | 1 | | | | 9 | | |
| Tisbury | 454 | 12 | Manchester | Thos | | | 2 | 1 | | | | | 1 | 1 | | | 5 | | |
| Tisbury | 453 | 11 | Mantor | George | 1 | 1 | 3 | 1 | | | 1 | 2 | | 1 | | | 10 | | |
| Tisbury | 454 | 33 | Mantor | Jona | | | 2 | 1 | | | | 1 | 2 | 1 | | | 7 | | |
| Tisbury | 454 | 36 | Mantor | Jona Jr | 2 | | | 1 | | 2 | | | 1 | | | | 6 | | |
| Tisbury | 453 | 18 | Mantor | Lois | | 1 | | | | | | 1 | 1 | | | | 3 | | |
| Tisbury | 454 | 19 | Mantor | Matthew | 2 | 1 | 3 | 1 | 1 | | | | 1 | 1 | | | 10 | | |
| Tisbury | 454 | 35 | Mantor | Thomas | | | 1 | | | 1 | | | 1 | | | | 3 | | |
| Tisbury | 454 | 20 | Mantor | Zeriah | | | | 1 | | | | | | 1 | | | 2 | | |
| Edgartown | 442 | 16 | Mase | Zachariah | | 2 | 1 | | | 1 | 1 | | | 1 | | | 6 | | |
| Chilmark | 448 | 11 | Mayhew | * | 1 | | 1 | | | 1 | | | 1 | 1 | | | 5 | | |
| Chilmark | 450 | 13 | Mayhew | Abigail | 1 | 1 | | | | 1 | 1 | | 1 | | | | 5 | | |
| Chilmark | 449 | 41 | Mayhew | Abner | | 1 | 3 | | | | 1 | 1 | 1 | | 1 | | 8 | | |
| Chilmark | 449 | 11 | Mayhew | Allen | 1 | | 1 | | | | | 1 | | | | | 3 | | |
| Chilmark | 450 | 3 | Mayhew | Benja | 2 | 2 | | 1 | | 2 | 1 | | 1 | | | | 9 | | |
| Chilmark | 450 | 4 | Mayhew | Ephm | 3 | 3 | 2 | 1 | | 1 | | 1 | 1 | | | | 12 | | |
| Chilmark | 450 | 11 | Mayhew | Hebron | 2 | | 1 | | | 1 | | 1 | | | | | 5 | | |
| Chilmark | 450 | 6 | Mayhew | Jethro | | | | 1 | | | | | | | | | 1 | | |
| Chilmark | 448 | 44 | Mayhew | John | 1 | | | 1 | | 2 | | | 1 | | | | 5 | | |
| Chilmark | 449 | 40 | Mayhew | Mark | | 2 | | 2 | | | | | 1 | | 2 | | 7 | | |
| Chilmark | 449 | 9 | Mayhew | Mathew | | | 1 | 2 | | | | 1 | 1 | | | | 5 | | |
| Edgartown | 445 | 8 | Mayhew | Mathew | 2 | | 1 | | | 3 | 1 | | 1 | | | | 8 | | |
| Chilmark | 449 | 10 | Mayhew | Mathew Jr | 2 | | 1 | 1 | | 2 | 2 | 2 | 1 | | | | 11 | | |
| Edgartown | 443 | 23 | Mayhew | Mathew Jr | | | 1 | | | | 1 | 1 | | | | | 3 | | |
| Chilmark | 449 | 50 | Mayhew | Nathl | 2 | 2 | 1 | | | 2 | 1 | 1 | 1 | | | | 10 | | |
| Chilmark | 449 | 20 | Mayhew | Oliver | | 1 | 1 | | | | | | 2 | | | | 4 | | |
| Chilmark | 449 | 39 | Mayhew | Pheir | | | 1 | | | | | | 1 | | | | 2 | | |
| Chilmark | 449 | 24 | Mayhew | Rachel | | | | | | | | | 2 | | | | 2 | | |
| Chilmark | 449 | 21 | Mayhew | Ruth | | | | | | | | | 1 | | | | 1 | | |
| Chilmark | 450 | 2 | Mayhew | Seth | | | 1 | 1 | | | | 1 | 1 | | | | 4 | | |
| Chilmark | 449 | 19 | Mayhew | Simon | | | 1 | | | | | | 1 | | | | 2 | | |
| Chilmark | 450 | 5 | Mayhew | Simon Jr | | | 1 | | | | | 1 | | | | | 2 | | |
| Chilmark | 450 | 1 | Mayhew | Theophilus | | 1 | 1 | | | 1 | 1 | | 1 | | | | 4 | | |
| Edgartown | 445 | 5 | Mayhew | Thomas | | | 1 | | 1 | | 1 | | | | | | 3 | | |
| Chilmark | 449 | 51 | Mayhew | Thos W. | 2 | | 1 | 2 | | 1 | 3 | | 2 | | | | 11 | | |
| Chilmark | 449 | 42 | Mayhew | Timo | | 2 | 1 | 1 | 1 | | | 2 | | 1 | | | 8 | | |
| Edgartown | 445 | 4 | Mayhew | William | 1 | 4 | 1 | | 1 | 2 | 1 | 1 | 1 | | | | 12 | | |
| Chilmark | 450 | 12 | Mayhew | Wm | 1 | | | 1 | | 1 | | 1 | | | | | 4 | | |
| Chilmark | 450 | 14 | Mayhew | Zachariah | 1 | | 1 | 2 | | 1 | | 1 | 1 | | | | 7 | | |
| Chilmark | 448 | 43 | Mayhew | Lois | | | | | | | | | 2 | | | | 2 | | |
| Chilmark | 448 | 49 | McColumn | Arch | 1 | | 1 | | | | | 1 | | | | | 3 | | |
| Edgartown | 447 | 41 | Medicine | Charlotte | | | | | | | | | | | 4 | | 4 | | |
| Edgartown | 444 | 7 | Merchant | Abishai | | | 1 | 1 | | | 1 | | 1 | | | | 4 | | |
| Edgartown | 444 | 51 | Merchant | Cornels Jr | 1 | | 1 | | | 1 | | 1 | | | | | 4 | | |
| Edgartown | 444 | 49 | Merchant | Cornl | | | 1 | 1 | | | 1 | | 1 | | | | 4 | | |
| Edgartown | 444 | 47 | Merchant | Elihu | 1 | | 1 | | | | | 1 | | | | | 3 | | |
| Edgartown | 444 | 50 | Merchant | Ephm | 1 | | 1 | | | 1 | | 1 | | | | | 4 | | |
| Edgartown | 445 | 14 | Merchant | George | 1 | 1 | 1 | | | | | 1 | | | | | 4 | | |
| Edgartown | 445 | 12 | Merchant | Lydia | | | 1 | | | | 1 | | 1 | | | | 3 | | |
| Edgartown | 445 | 16 | Merchant | Miriam | | | 1 | | | | | 1 | | | | | 2 | | |
| Edgartown | 445 | 31 | Merchant | Peter | 1 | 1 | 1 | | | 3 | 1 | 1 | | | | | 8 | | |
| Tisbury | 453 | 32 | Merry | Elizath | | | 1 | | | | | 1 | 1 | | | | 3 | | |
| Tisbury | 454 | 21 | Merry | Jona | | 1 | 2 | 1 | | | 1 | | 1 | | | | 6 | | |
| Tisbury | 454 | 29 | Merry | Joseph | | | | 1 | | | | | 1 | | | | 2 | | |
| Edgartown | 446 | 11 | Merry | Leonard | 1 | | 1 | | | | | 1 | | | | | 3 | | |
| Tisbury | 453 | 41 | Merry | Timo | 1 | | 1 | | | 1 | | 1 | | | | | 4 | | |
| Tisbury | 453 | 40 | Merry | William | 2 | 1 | 3 | 1 | | | | | 1 | | | | 8 | | |
| Edgartown | 445 | 23 | Morse | Uriah | | | | 1 | | 1 | | 1 | | | | | 3 | | |
| Tisbury | 454 | 45 | Newcomb | Sally | | | 1 | | | | | 1 | | | | | 2 | | |
| Chilmark | 448 | 37 | Nickerson | Samuel | 1 | | | 1 | | | | 1 | 1 | | | | 4 | | |
| Chilmark | 448 | 8 | Norris | Patience | | 1 | | | | | | | 1 | | | | 2 | | |
| Edgartown | 442 | 3 | Norris | Samuel | 2 | 1 | | 1 | | 2 | 1 | 1 | 1 | | | | 9 | | |
| Edgartown | 447 | 9 | Norton | Baire | 1 | | 1 | | | 1 | 1 | 2 | | 2 | | | 6 | | |
| Edgartown | 442 | 9 | Norton | Benja | | | | 2 | 1 | | 2 | | | | | | 5 | | |
| Edgartown | 441 | 1 | Norton | Beriah | | | 1 | 1 | | | 1 | | 1 | | | | 4 | | |

| TOWN | PG# | LN# | LAST NAME | FIRST NAME | FW MALES u10 | 10-16 | 16-26 | 26-45 | 45+ | FW FEMALES u10 | 10-16 | 16-26 | 26-45 | 45+ | TOTAL ALL OTHER | TOTAL SLAVES | TOTALS | DISTRICT/TOWNSHIP | NOTES |
|---|---|---|---|---|---|---|---|---|---|---|---|---|---|---|---|---|---|---|---|
| Tisbury | 453 | 12 | Norton | Cornelius | | | | | 1 | | | | 2 | | | | 3 | | |
| Edgartown | 447 | 13 | Norton | Darius | 1 | | 1 | 1 | | 2 | | | 1 | | | | 6 | | |
| Edgartown | 444 | 6 | Norton | David | | 2 | 1 | 1 | | | | 1 | 1 | 1 | | | 7 | | |
| Edgartown | 441 | 2 | Norton | Dorcas | | | 1 | | | | | 1 | 1 | 1 | | | 4 | | |
| Tisbury | 453 | 26 | Norton | Eliakim | | | | 1 | | | | | 1 | | | | 2 | | |
| Tisbury | 454 | 37 | Norton | Francis | | | 2 | 1 | | | | 1 | 2 | 1 | | | 7 | | |
| Edgartown | 445 | 47 | Norton | Henry C. | | 1 | 1 | 1 | | 1 | | 1 | | | | | 5 | | |
| Edgartown | 445 | 45 | Norton | Ichabod | | 1 | | 1 | | | | | 3 | | 1 | | 6 | | |
| Edgartown | 445 | 49 | Norton | Isaac | | | | 1 | | | 3 | | 1 | | | | 5 | | |
| Chilmark | 448 | 41 | Norton | James | | | | 1 | | | | | 1 | 1 | | | 3 | | |
| Edgartown | 442 | 7 | Norton | Joseph | | 1 | 1 | 1 | | | | 1 | 1 | 1 | | | 6 | | |
| Edgartown | 442 | 1 | Norton | Lot | 1 | 1 | 1 | 1 | | 3 | 1 | 1 | 1 | 1 | | | 11 | | |
| Edgartown | 445 | 45 | Norton | Lydia | 1 | | | | | | | | | 1 | | | 2 | | |
| Edgartown | 445 | 30 | Norton | Martin | 3 | | 1 | 1 | | | | | 1 | | | | 6 | | |
| Tisbury | 454 | 43 | Norton | Mayhew | 2 | | 1 | 1 | | | 2 | 3 | 1 | | | | 10 | | |
| Tisbury | 452 | 21 | Norton | Melatiah | | | 1 | | | 1 | | | 1 | | | | 3 | | |
| Edgartown | 445 | 40 | Norton | Nicholas | 4 | 1 | | 1 | | | | | 1 | 1 | | | 8 | | |
| Edgartown | 442 | 8 | Norton | Noah | | 1 | 1 | 1 | | 1 | | | 1 | | | | 5 | | |
| Edgartown | 447 | 1 | Norton | Obed | 1 | | 1 | 1 | | | | | 1 | 1 | 1 | | 6 | | |
| Tisbury | 453 | 25 | Norton | Peter | 3 | 1 | 1 | 1 | | | 1 | 2 | 1 | | | | 10 | | |
| Tisbury | 453 | 36 | Norton | Presbury | | 1 | | | | | | | 1 | | | | 2 | | |
| Edgartown | 445 | 37 | Norton | Prince | | | | 1 | | | | | | | | | 1 | | |
| Chilmark | 448 | 22 | Norton | Ruth | | | | | | | | | | 1 | | | 1 | | |
| Chilmark | 448 | 40 | Norton | Saml | | 1 | | 1 | | | | 1 | 1 | | | | 4 | | |
| Edgartown | 447 | 3 | Norton | Samuel | | 1 | 1 | 1 | | | 1 | 1 | 1 | | | | 6 | | |
| Chilmark | 448 | 23 | Norton | Shubael | 3 | | | 2 | | 2 | | | 1 | | | | 8 | | |
| Edgartown | 445 | 48 | Norton | Shubael | | | | 1 | | | | 1 | 1 | 1 | 1 | | 5 | | |
| Edgartown | 442 | 6 | Norton | Tristram | 3 | | | 1 | | | 2 | | 1 | | | | 7 | | |
| Edgartown | 444 | 24 | Norton | William | 1 | | 2 | 1 | 1 | | 1 | 2 | | 1 | | | 9 | | |
| Chilmark | 448 | 42 | Norton | Wm | 1 | | | 1 | | | 2 | | 1 | | | | 5 | | |
| Edgartown | 444 | 25 | Norton | Wm Jr | | 1 | 1 | 1 | | | | 2 | | 1 | | | 6 | | |
| Chilmark | 450 | 19 | Nye | John | | 2 | 2 | 1 | 2 | | 2 | 2 | | 1 | | | 12 | | |
| Edgartown | 444 | 22 | Osbourne | Henry | 3 | 3 | | 1 | 3 | | 1 | 2 | 1 | | | | 14 | | |
| Tisbury | 453 | 7 | Pain | Susannah | | | | | | | | | | | 2 | | 2 | | |
| Edgartown | 442 | 4 | Paint | Mary | | 3 | | | | | | | 2 | 1 | | | 6 | | |
| Edgartown | 443 | 42 | Parady | Emanuel | 3 | | | 1 | | 1 | 2 | 1 | | | | | 8 | | |
| Chilmark | 448 | 7 | Pease | Abishai | | 1 | | 2 | 1 | | | | | | 1 | | 5 | | |
| Edgartown | 447 | 7 | Pease | Argulas | | 1 | | | | | | | 2 | | | | 3 | | |
| Tisbury | 452 | 42 | Pease | Bartlet | | | 1 | | | | | 1 | 1 | | | | 3 | | |
| Edgartown | 443 | 28 | Pease | Benja | | | 1 | | | | | | | | | | 1 | | |
| Edgartown | 443 | 27 | Pease | Benja Jr | | | 1 | | | | | | | | | | 1 | | |
| Edgartown | 443 | 34 | Pease | Elijah | | 1 | | 1 | 1 | | | | 3 | | | | 6 | | |
| Chilmark | 448 | 4 | Pease | Fortunatus | | 1 | | 1 | | | | | 1 | | | | 3 | | |
| Chilmark | 448 | 5 | Pease | Fortunatus Jr | | 1 | | 1 | | | 2 | 1 | | 1 | | | 6 | | |
| Edgartown | 443 | 37 | Pease | Francis | | 2 | | 1 | | | 1 | 1 | | | | | 5 | | |
| Chilmark | 448 | 31 | Pease | John | | 1 | | 1 | | | 1 | 3 | | 1 | | | 7 | | |
| Edgartown | 444 | 20 | Pease | John | | | 1 | 1 | | | | 2 | 1 | 1 | | | 6 | | |
| Edgartown | 445 | 9 | Pease | Jona | | | 1 | | | | | 2 | 1 | 1 | | | 5 | | |
| Edgartown | 445 | 3 | Pease | Lois | | | 1 | | | | | | 1 | 1 | | | 3 | | |
| Edgartown | 443 | 30 | Pease | Malatiah | 1 | | | 1 | | | | | 1 | | 1 | | 4 | | |
| Edgartown | 444 | 37 | Pease | Marshall | 1 | | | 1 | | 2 | | 1 | | | | | 5 | | |
| Edgartown | 444 | 3 | Pease | Martin | 1 | 1 | | 1 | | 2 | | 2 | | | | | 7 | | |
| Chilmark | 448 | 6 | Pease | Nathl | | | | 1 | | 2 | | 1 | | | | | 4 | | |
| Edgartown | 444 | 30 | Pease | Noah | 2 | 1 | 1 | 1 | | 1 | | 1 | | | | | 7 | | |
| Edgartown | 444 | 36 | Pease | Obed | | 1 | | 1 | | | | | | 1 | | | 3 | | |
| Edgartown | 445 | 26 | Pease | Peter | | | | 1 | | | | 1 | | 1 | | | 3 | | |
| Edgartown | 445 | 27 | Pease | Peter Jr | 3 | | 1 | | | | 1 | 1 | | | | | 6 | | |
| Edgartown | 444 | 2 | Pease | Salathiel | 1 | 1 | | 1 | | | 4 | | 1 | | | | 8 | | |
| Edgartown | 443 | 2 | Pease | Sarah | | 1 | | | | | | | 1 | | | | 2 | | |
| Edgartown | 443 | 1 | Pease | Timothy | 1 | | | 1 | | | | 1 | 1 | | | | 4 | | |
| Chilmark | 450 | 29 | Peckings | Wm | 2 | 1 | | 1 | | 2 | | 1 | | | 1 | | 8 | | |
| Chilmark | 450 | 44 | Pero | Calo | | | | | | | | | | | 1 | | 1 | | |
| Edgartown | 446 | 4 | Peters | George | | | | | | | | | | | 5 | | 5 | | |
| Chilmark | 450 | 38 | Peters | Pero | | | | | | | | | | | 2 | | 2 | | |
| Edgartown | 447 | 37 | Peters | Saml | | | | | | | | | | | 6 | | 6 | | |
| Chilmark | 450 | 46 | Peters | Simeon | | | | | | | | | | | 3 | | 3 | | |
| Chilmark | 449 | 8 | Pitts | Thankful | | | | | | | | | 1 | | | | 1 | | |
| Edgartown | 447 | 34 | Pomidge | Simon | | | | | | | | | | | 4 | | 4 | | |
| Chilmark | 450 | 7 | Pool | Mary | | 1 | | | | 1 | | | 1 | | | | 3 | | |
| Chilmark | 449 | 43 | Pool | Wm | | | 1 | | 1 | | | | | 1 | | | 3 | | |
| Edgartown | 444 | 29 | Pratt | Ann | | | | 1 | 1 | | | | 1 | 1 | | | 4 | | |
| Edgartown | 445 | 28 | Rawson | Betsey | | 1 | | | | | | | 1 | 1 | | | 3 | | |
| Edgartown | 444 | 21 | Read | Amelia | | | | | | | | | 2 | 1 | | | 3 | | |
| Tisbury | 454 | 31 | Reynolds | Benja | 1 | | 1 | | | | | | 1 | | | | 3 | | |
| Edgartown | 446 | 13 | Reynolds | David | 1 | 1 | 2 | 1 | 1 | 1 | 2 | 1 | | 1 | | | 11 | | |
| Edgartown | 443 | 29 | Ripley | Cornelius | | 1 | | 1 | | 1 | | | 1 | | | | 4 | | |
| Edgartown | 444 | 8 | Ripley | Cornelius Jr | 2 | | | 1 | | 1 | | | 1 | | | | 5 | | |
| Edgartown | 443 | 25 | Ripley | Joseph | | 1 | | 1 | | 1 | | 1 | 2 | 1 | | | 7 | | |
| Chilmark | 450 | 22 | Robinson | Elihu | 1 | | 1 | 1 | | 1 | 2 | 1 | | 1 | | | 8 | | |

# 1800 Dukes County, Massachusetts Index

| TOWN | PG# | LN# | LAST NAME | FIRST NAME | M <10 | M 10–16 | M 16–26 | M 26–45 | M 45+ | F <10 | F 10–16 | F 16–26 | F 26–45 | F 45+ | TOTAL ALL OTHER | TOTAL SLAVES | TOTALS | DISTRICT/ TOWNSHIP | NOTES |
|---|---|---|---|---|---|---|---|---|---|---|---|---|---|---|---|---|---|---|---|
| Chilmark | 450 | 17 | Robinson | Paul | | 1 | 1 | | 1 | | | 1 | | 1 | | | 5 | | |
| Chilmark | 450 | 21 | Robinson | Shadh | 1 | | 1 | 2 | | 4 | 1 | 1 | 1 | | | | 11 | | |
| Chilmark | 450 | 20 | Robinson | Thos | 3 | 1 | | 1 | | 2 | | | 1 | | | | 8 | | |
| Chilmark | 450 | 18 | Robinson | Zephh | | 2 | | 2 | | 1 | | 1 | 1 | | 1 | | 8 | | |
| Chilmark | 450 | 48 | Rogers | Joel | | | | | | | | | | | 6 | | 6 | | |
| Tisbury | 453 | 30 | Rogers | Lot | | 2 | 1 | | 1 | 1 | 1 | | 1 | | | | 7 | | |
| Tisbury | 453 | 31 | Rogers | Roland | | | 1 | | | | | | 1 | | | | 2 | | |
| Tisbury | 452 | 36 | Rogers | Silas | | | 1 | 1 | | | | 1 | 1 | | 1 | | 5 | | |
| Tisbury | 453 | 32 | Rogers | Stephen | | | | 1 | | | | | 1 | | | | 2 | | |
| Tisbury | 452 | 44 | Rotch | William | | 1 | | 1 | | | | 1 | | 1 | | | 4 | | |
| Edgartown | 442 | 2 | Rotch | William Jr | | | 1 | | | 2 | | 1 | | 1 | | | 5 | | |
| Edgartown | 446 | 5 | Sharper | Fortune | | | | | | | | | | | 6 | | 6 | | |
| Chilmark | 450 | 45 | Sharper | Peto | | | | | | | | | | | 3 | | 3 | | |
| Chilmark | 450 | 43 | Silvary | Emanuel | | | | | | | | | | | 3 | | 3 | | |
| Edgartown | 447 | 35 | Simpson | Jos | | | | | | | | | | | 7 | | 7 | | |
| Chilmark | 450 | 8 | Skiff | Ebenz | 3 | | | | 1 | | | | 1 | 1 | | | 6 | | |
| Chilmark | 448 | 33 | Skiff | Nathan | | | 1 | 1 | | 1 | | | 1 | 1 | 2 | | 7 | | |
| Chilmark | 448 | 1 | Skiff | Vinal | | 1 | 1 | 1 | | 1 | | 1 | 1 | | | | 6 | | |
| Tisbury | 454 | 8 | Slocum | Christopher | 3 | 2 | | 1 | | 1 | | | 1 | | | | 8 | | |
| Chilmark | 450 | 26 | Slocum | Christr | 5 | | 1 | 1 | | 1 | | 1 | 1 | | | | 10 | | |
| Chilmark | 450 | 27 | Slocum | John | | 1 | 2 | | 1 | 1 | | 1 | | 1 | | | 7 | | |
| Chilmark | 450 | 41 | Slocum | Jona | | | | | | | | | | | 12 | | 12 | | |
| Chilmark | 450 | 28 | Slocum | Peleg | | 1 | | 1 | 1 | 1 | | 1 | 1 | | | | 6 | | |
| Chilmark | 450 | 25 | Slocum | Wm | 2 | | 1 | 1 | | 3 | | 1 | | | | | 8 | | |
| Edgartown | 442 | 10 | Smith | Ann | | 1 | | 1 | | | | | 1 | 1 | | | 4 | | |
| Edgartown | 444 | 16 | Smith | Benja Jr | 1 | | | 1 | | 1 | | 1 | | | | | 4 | | |
| Edgartown | 445 | 7 | Smith | Benjamin | 1 | | 1 | 1 | | 1 | | 1 | | 1 | | | 6 | | |
| Edgartown | 447 | 14 | Smith | Daniel | 1 | | | 1 | | 1 | 1 | | 1 | | | | 5 | | |
| Edgartown | 445 | 38 | Smith | David | 1 | 2 | 1 | 1 | | 1 | | 1 | 1 | 1 | | | 9 | | |
| Edgartown | 447 | 24 | Smith | Ebenz | | 1 | 1 | | | | | 2 | | 1 | | | 5 | | |
| Chilmark | 449 | 48 | Smith | Elijah | | | 2 | | 1 | | | 3 | | 1 | | | 7 | | |
| Edgartown | 445 | 36 | Smith | Elijah | | | 1 | | 1 | | | | 1 | 2 | | | 5 | | |
| Chilmark | 448 | 12 | Smith | Eunice | | | 1 | | | | | | 1 | | | | 2 | | |
| Edgartown | 445 | 41 | Smith | Eunice | | | | | | | | | | 1 | | | 1 | | |
| Tisbury | 453 | 47 | Smith | Frederick | 1 | | | 1 | | 2 | | | 1 | | | | 5 | | |
| Edgartown | 443 | 36 | Smith | John | 1 | | 1 | | | | | | 1 | | | | 3 | | |
| Edgartown | 445 | 42 | Smith | John | 2 | 2 | | 1 | | 2 | 1 | | 1 | | | | 9 | | |
| Tisbury | 453 | 10 | Smith | Jona | | | | 1 | | | | | | 1 | | | 2 | | |
| Chilmark | 449 | 1 | Smith | Jonathan | 1 | | | 1 | | 1 | 1 | | 1 | | | | 5 | | |
| Tisbury | 453 | 39 | Smith | Mathew | 3 | 2 | | 1 | | 1 | 1 | 1 | 1 | | | | 10 | | |
| Tisbury | 453 | 40 | Smith | Nathan | | 1 | 1 | | 1 | | | 1 | 1 | | | | 5 | | |
| Tisbury | 453 | 38 | Smith | Rainsford | | | 1 | | | | | 1 | | 1 | | | 3 | | |
| Edgartown | 445 | 39 | Smith | Rebecca | | | | | | | | 1 | | | | | 1 | | |
| Edgartown | 442 | 11 | Smith | Samuel | 1 | 2 | | 1 | | 3 | 1 | | 1 | | | | 9 | | |
| Edgartown | 443 | 35 | Smith | Thomas | | 1 | 1 | | | 1 | | | 1 | | | | 4 | | |
| Tisbury | 453 | 43 | Smith | Thomas | | | | 1 | | | | 1 | 2 | | | | 4 | | |
| Tisbury | 454 | 43 | Smith | William | 3 | | 2 | 1 | | | | | 1 | | | | 7 | | |
| Tisbury | 453 | 42 | Smith | Zechariah | 4 | | | 1 | | 2 | 2 | | 1 | | | | 10 | | |
| Tisbury | 454 | 4 | Spaulding | Rufus | 2 | | | 1 | | 2 | 2 | 1 | 1 | | 1 | | 10 | | |
| Edgartown | 444 | 57 | Sprague | John | 2 | | | 1 | | 1 | 2 | 2 | 1 | | | | 9 | | |
| Edgartown | 442 | 5 | Stewart | Benjamin | 1 | 1 | | 1 | | 1 | 1 | | | 2 | | | 7 | | |
| Edgartown | 443 | 12 | Stewart | Elijah | | 1 | | 1 | | 1 | 1 | 1 | | 1 | | | 6 | | |
| Edgartown | 443 | 11 | Stewart | Thomas | | 2 | | 1 | | | | 1 | 1 | | | | 6 | | |
| Chilmark | 449 | 12 | Stewart | Wm | | | | 1 | | | | | 1 | 1 | | | 3 | | |
| Chilmark | 449 | 13 | Stewart | Wm Jr | 1 | | | 1 | | 2 | | | 1 | | | | 5 | | |
| Edgartown | 444 | 15 | Swasy | Joseph | 1 | | | 1 | | | | 3 | | 1 | | | 6 | | |
| Chilmark | 450 | 47 | Swazy | Zephh | | | | | | | | | | | 4 | | 4 | | |
| Edgartown | 441 | 4 | Thaxter | Joseph | 3 | 2 | 2 | 1 | | 1 | 1 | 1 | | | 1 | | 12 | | |
| Edgartown | 447 | 15 | Tillton | Abigail | | | | | | | | 1 | 1 | 1 | | | 3 | | |
| Chilmark | 449 | 15 | Tillton | Beriah | 2 | 2 | 1 | 1 | | 3 | | | 1 | 1 | | | 11 | | |
| Chilmark | 449 | 30 | Tillton | Daniel | 3 | | | 1 | | | | | 1 | | | | 5 | | |
| Chilmark | 449 | 25 | Tillton | Ezra | 1 | 1 | 1 | | 1 | 1 | | | 1 | 2 | | | 8 | | |
| Chilmark | 449 | 31 | Tillton | Isaac | 1 | | | 1 | | 2 | | | 1 | | | | 5 | | |
| Chilmark | 449 | 27 | Tillton | Joseph | 3 | | 1 | 1 | | 2 | 1 | | 1 | 1 | | | 10 | | |
| Chilmark | 449 | 29 | Tillton | Mathew | 1 | 1 | 1 | | 1 | 2 | 1 | 1 | | 1 | | | 9 | | |
| Chilmark | 449 | 49 | Tillton | Nathan | | | 2 | | 1 | 1 | 1 | 1 | 1 | 1 | | | 8 | | |
| Chilmark | 449 | 26 | Tillton | Oliver | 2 | | 1 | 1 | | 2 | | | 1 | | | | 7 | | |
| Chilmark | 450 | 15 | Tillton | Pain | | | 3 | 1 | | 1 | 2 | 1 | | 1 | | | 9 | | |
| Chilmark | 449 | 37 | Tillton | Reuben | | | | 2 | 2 | | 1 | | 2 | 2 | | | 9 | | |
| Chilmark | 448 | 14 | Tillton | Stephen | 1 | | | 1 | 1 | | | | | 1 | | | 4 | | |
| Chilmark | 450 | 10 | Tillton | Ward | 1 | 3 | | 1 | | 1 | | | 1 | 1 | | | 8 | | |
| Chilmark | 449 | 14 | Tillton | Wm | | 1 | | 1 | | | | 3 | | 1 | 1 | | 7 | | |
| Chilmark | 449 | 16 | Tillton | Wm Jr | 1 | | | 1 | | 3 | 1 | | 1 | | | | 7 | | |
| Chilmark | 449 | 28 | Tillton | Zilpah | | | | | | | | | | 2 | | | 2 | | |
| Chilmark | 450 | 39 | Tockquenett | Martha | | | | | | | | | | | 2 | | 2 | | |
| Edgartown | 447 | 17 | Trask | Benja | 1 | | | 2 | | | 1 | 1 | | | | | 5 | | |
| Edgartown | 445 | 33 | Tupper | James | 2 | 3 | | 1 | | 2 | | | 1 | | | | 9 | | |
| Edgartown | 443 | 7 | Vinson | Barnabas | | 1 | 1 | 1 | | | | | | 1 | | | 4 | | |
| Edgartown | 443 | 18 | Vinson | Benjamin | | | | | | | | | 1 | | | | 2 | | |

# 1800 Dukes County, Massachusetts Index

| TOWN | PG# | LN# | LAST NAME | FIRST NAME | FREE WHITE MALES | | | | | FREE WHITE FEMALES | | | | | TOTAL ALL OTHER | TOTAL SLAVES | TOTALS | DISTRICT/ TOWNSHIP | NOTES |
|---|---|---|---|---|---|---|---|---|---|---|---|---|---|---|---|---|---|---|---|
| | | | | | under 10 | 10 to 16 | 16 to 26 | 26 to 45 | 45 and over | under 10 | 10 to 16 | 16 to 26 | 26 to 45 | 45 and over | | | | | |
| Edgartown | 442 | 22 | Vinson | Daniel Jr | 1 | | 1 | | | | | 1 | 1 | | | | 4 | | |
| Edgartown | 442 | 24 | Vinson | Elizabeth | | 1 | | | | 1 | | | | 1 | | | 3 | | |
| Edgartown | 442 | 23 | Vinson | Jane | | | | | | | | | | 1 | | | 1 | | |
| Edgartown | 442 | 18 | Vinson | John | | | | 1 | | | | | | | | | 1 | | |
| Edgartown | 443 | 5 | Vinson | Jonathan | 1 | | | 1 | | | | | 1 | 1 | 1 | | 5 | | |
| Edgartown | 442 | 20 | Vinson | Joseph | | 1 | 1 | 1 | 1 | 1 | 1 | 1 | 1 | | | | 8 | | |
| Edgartown | 443 | 38 | Vinson | Louisa | 1 | 1 | | | | 2 | | 1 | | | | | 5 | | |
| Edgartown | 443 | 15 | Vinson | Nathaniel | | 2 | 1 | | 1 | 2 | | | 1 | | | | 7 | | |
| Edgartown | 445 | 46 | Vinson | Reuben | | | 1 | 1 | | 1 | | | 1 | | | | 4 | | |
| Edgartown | 442 | 21 | Vinson | Samuel | 1 | | | 1 | | 2 | | | 1 | | | | 5 | | |
| Edgartown | 443 | 13 | Vinson | Seth | | | | 1 | | | | 1 | | | | | 2 | | |
| Edgartown | 443 | 14 | Vinson | William | | 1 | 2 | | 1 | 1 | 2 | | | 1 | | | 8 | | |
| Edgartown | 445 | 29 | Vinson | William Jr | | | | 1 | | 2 | | | 1 | | | | 4 | | |
| Tisbury | 453 | 44 | Walrond | Jemima | | | | | | | | | | 1 | | | 1 | | |
| Tisbury | 453 | 47 | Walrond | Noah | 2 | | | 1 | | 1 | 1 | | 1 | | | | 6 | | |
| Tisbury | 452 | 27 | Walrond | Robert | 2 | | | 1 | | 3 | | | 1 | | | | 7 | | |
| Tisbury | 453 | 48 | Walrond | Thos | | | | 1 | | | | | | 1 | | | 2 | | |
| Edgartown | 445 | 10 | Ward | Hannah | | | | | | | | | 1 | 1 | | | 2 | | |
| Edgartown | 444 | 55 | Weeks | Benja | 1 | | | 1 | | 1 | | | 1 | | | | 4 | | |
| Tisbury | 454 | 7 | Weeks | James | 3 | 2 | | 1 | | 1 | 1 | | 1 | | | | 9 | | |
| Tisbury | 454 | 6 | Weeks | Nathan | | | | 1 | | | | | 1 | 1 | | | 3 | | |
| Tisbury | 454 | 8 | Weeks | Saml | | | 1 | 1 | | | | | | 1 | | | 3 | | |
| Tisbury | 454 | 9 | Weeks | Shubael | | 1 | | | | 1 | | | 1 | | | | 3 | | |
| Edgartown | 446 | 3 | Weeks | Solomon | | | | | | | | | | | 2 | | 2 | | |
| Tisbury | 454 | 5 | Weeks | William | | | | 1 | | | | | 2 | | | | 3 | | |
| Chilmark | 450 | 49 | Weeks | Wm | | | | | | | | | | | 2 | | 2 | | |
| Chilmark | 450 | 9 | West | George | 1 | | 1 | | | 1 | | 1 | | | | | 4 | | |
| Tisbury | 454 | 19 | West | James | 2 | | 1 | | | | | 1 | | | | | 4 | | |
| Tisbury | 454 | 18 | West | Jernal | 3 | 2 | 2 | | 1 | 1 | | | 1 | | | | 10 | | |
| Tisbury | 454 | 41 | West | Peter | 2 | | | 1 | | 3 | | | 1 | | | | 7 | | |
| Chilmark | 449 | 52 | West | Thos | 1 | 1 | | | 1 | 1 | 3 | 1 | | 1 | | | 9 | | |
| Tisbury | 454 | 32 | West | Thos | 1 | | | | 1 | 3 | | | 1 | | | | 6 | | |
| Edgartown | 444 | 31 | Whellen | Saml | 1 | | | 1 | | 1 | | | 1 | | | | 4 | | |
| Edgartown | 444 | 35 | Wilpenny | Robert | 1 | | | 1 | | | | | 1 | | | | 3 | | |
| Tisbury | 454 | 27 | Winslow | Isaac | 2 | | 1 | 1 | | | | | 1 | | | | 5 | | |
| Tisbury | 454 | 20 | Winsow | James | 2 | 1 | | 1 | | | | 3 | 1 | | | | 8 | | |
| Edgartown | 445 | 25 | Woodbee | Rebecca | | | | | | | | | | | 4 | | 4 | | |
| Edgartown | 441 | 3 | Worth | Benjamin | 1 | | | 1 | | 3 | | | 1 | | | | 6 | | |
| Edgartown | 444 | 52 | Worth | Jethro | 3 | 1 | | 1 | | | | | 2 | | | | 7 | | |
| Edgartown | 443 | 20 | Worth | John | | | | 1 | | | | | 1 | 2 | | | 4 | | |
| Edgartown | 443 | 24 | Worth | Jonathan | | | 1 | | | 3 | 1 | 1 | | | | | 6 | | |
| Tisbury | 454 | 39 | Worth | William | 1 | | | 1 | | 2 | 1 | | 1 | | | | 6 | | |

# 1800 Nantucket, Nantucket County, Massachusetts

| TOWN | PG# | LN# | LAST NAME | FIRST NAME | FREE WHITE MALES | | | | | FREE WHITE FEMALES | | | | | TOTAL ALL OTHER | TOTAL SLAVES | TOTALS | DISTRICT/ TOWNSHIP | NOTES |
|---|---|---|---|---|---|---|---|---|---|---|---|---|---|---|---|---|---|---|---|
| | | | | | under 10 | 10 to 16 | 16 to 26 | 26 to 45 | 45 and over | under 10 | 10 to 16 | 16 to 26 | 26 to 45 | 45 and over | | | | | |
| Nantucket | 2 | 1 | Coffin | Simeon Junr | 1 | 2 | | 1 | | | | | | 1 | | | 5 | Not Stated | |
| Nantucket | 2 | 2 | Gardner | Rebecca | 1 | | | | | | | 1 | 1 | 1 | | | 4 | Not Stated | |
| Nantucket | 3 | 1 | Brock | William | | 1 | | 1 | | | | | 1 | | | | 3 | Not Stated | |
| Nantucket | 3 | 2 | Drew | Gershom Junr | | | 1 | | | | | 1 | 1 | | | | 3 | Not Stated | |
| Nantucket | 3 | 3 | Dixon | Edward | | | 1 | 1 | | | | | 1 | 1 | | | 4 | Not Stated | |
| Nantucket | 3 | 4 | Brown | William | | | | 1 | | 1 | 1 | 1 | 1 | 1 | | | 6 | Not Stated | |
| Nantucket | 3 | 5 | Coffin | Shubael | 1 | | | 1 | | 1 | | | | 1 | | | 4 | Not Stated | |
| Nantucket | 3 | 6 | Parker | Josiah | | | | 1 | | | | | | 1 | 6 | | 8 | Not Stated | |
| Nantucket | 3 | 7 | Spencer | Judith | 2 | | 1 | | | 1 | | | 1 | 1 | | | 6 | Not Stated | |
| Nantucket | 3 | 8 | Hosier | William | 1 | | 1 | | | 2 | 1 | | 1 | | | | 6 | Not Stated | |
| Nantucket | 3 | 9 | Macy | William | 2 | 1 | 1 | | 2 | | 1 | 6 | 1 | 1 | | | 15 | Not Stated | |
| Nantucket | 3 | 10 | Gardner | Gideon | | | 1 | | | 2 | | | 1 | 1 | | | 5 | Not Stated | |
| Nantucket | 3 | 11 | Barker | Sarah | | | | | | | | | 2 | 1 | | | 3 | Not Stated | |
| Nantucket | 3 | 12 | Macy | Lois | 2 | 1 | 1 | 1 | | 2 | 1 | | 1 | 1 | | | 10 | Not Stated | |
| Nantucket | 3 | 13 | Delano | Elizabeth | | 1 | | 1 | | | | 1 | | 1 | 1 | | 6 | Not Stated | |
| Nantucket | 3 | 14 | Brayton | Isaac | 1 | | 1 | 1 | | 1 | | 1 | 3 | | 1 | | 9 | Not Stated | |
| Nantucket | 3 | 15 | Hammatt | William | 1 | 2 | 1 | 1 | | | 1 | 1 | 1 | | | | 8 | Not Stated | |
| Nantucket | 3 | 16 | Gardner | Paul | 1 | | | 1 | 1 | | | 1 | 2 | | | | 6 | Not Stated | |
| Nantucket | 3 | 17 | Long | Peleg | | | | 1 | | | | | 2 | | | | 3 | Not Stated | |
| Nantucket | 3 | 18 | Coffin | Elizabeth | | | | | | | | | 1 | | | | 1 | Not Stated | |
| Nantucket | 3 | 19 | Gwin | James | | | 1 | | | | 1 | | 1 | | | | 3 | Not Stated | |
| Nantucket | 3 | 20 | Swain | Jonathan | | | 2 | 1 | 1 | | | | | 2 | | | 6 | Not Stated | |
| Nantucket | 3 | 21 | Folger | Joseph | 1 | | 1 | | | 2 | | 1 | 1 | | | | 6 | Not Stated | |
| Nantucket | 3 | 22 | Chadwick | Lydia | | | | | | | | | 1 | 1 | | | 2 | Not Stated | |
| Nantucket | 3 | 23 | Macy | Obed | 1 | 2 | | 1 | | 2 | | | 1 | 1 | | | 8 | Not Stated | |
| Nantucket | 3 | 24 | Barnard | Thomas 2nd | | | 1 | | | | | 1 | | | | | 2 | Not Stated | |
| Nantucket | 3 | 25 | Marshall | Obed | | 1 | 1 | 1 | | | | 1 | | 1 | | | 5 | Not Stated | |
| Nantucket | 3 | 26 | Freeborn | George | | 1 | | 1 | | | | | 1 | 1 | | | 4 | Not Stated | |
| Nantucket | 3 | 27 | Easton | Peter | 4 | | | 1 | | | | 2 | | | | | 7 | Not Stated | |
| Nantucket | 3 | 28 | Macy | Francis | 4 | 1 | | 1 | | 1 | 1 | 1 | | | | | 9 | Not Stated | |
| Nantucket | 3 | 29 | Worth | Judith | | 1 | | | | | | | 2 | 1 | | | 4 | Not Stated | |
| Nantucket | 3 | 30 | Worth | Obed | 2 | | | 1 | | | | | 1 | | | | 6 | Not Stated | |
| Nantucket | 3 | 31 | Ramsdell | James | 3 | 2 | 1 | | | | | 1 | 1 | | | | 8 | Not Stated | |
| Nantucket | 3 | 32 | Ramsdell | Silvia | | | | | | | 2 | | 1 | | | | 3 | Not Stated | |
| Nantucket | 3 | 33 | Tillingham | Parson | | 1 | | | | | 1 | 1 | | | | | 3 | Not Stated | |
| Nantucket | 3 | 34 | Chase | Thomas | 2 | | 1 | 1 | | 2 | | | 2 | 2 | | | 10 | Not Stated | |
| Nantucket | 4 | 1 | Swain | Joseph | | 1 | 2 | | | | | | | | | | 3 | Not Stated | |
| Nantucket | 4 | 2 | Gardner | Prince | 1 | 1 | 1 | | | | | | 2 | 1 | | | 6 | Not Stated | |
| Nantucket | 4 | 3 | Coffin | Abner | | 1 | 3 | | 1 | | | 2 | | 1 | | | 9 | Not Stated | |
| Nantucket | 4 | 4 | Macy | Job | 2 | | 1 | | | | | 1 | 1 | 1 | | | 6 | Not Stated | |
| Nantucket | 4 | 5 | Folger | Peregrine | 1 | | | 1 | 2 | | | 1 | 1 | | | | 6 | Not Stated | |
| Nantucket | 4 | 6 | Folger | Jonathan | 2 | | 1 | 1 | 3 | | | | 2 | | 1 | | 10 | Not Stated | |
| Nantucket | 4 | 7 | Macy | Silvanus Junr | 1 | 1 | 1 | | | 1 | 1 | 1 | | | | | 7 | Not Stated | |
| Nantucket | 4 | 8 | Barrett | Saml | | 1 | | 1 | | | | 1 | | 1 | | | 4 | Not Stated | |
| Nantucket | 4 | 9 | Coffin | Eunice | | 1 | | 1 | | | | | 1 | 1 | | | 4 | Not Stated | |
| Nantucket | 4 | 10 | Bunker | Barnabas | | 2 | | 1 | 5 | 1 | 1 | | 1 | | | | 11 | Not Stated | |
| Nantucket | 4 | 11 | Gardner | Eliakim | 2 | | 1 | | | | | | 1 | | | | 4 | Not Stated | |
| Nantucket | 4 | 12 | Bunker | James | 1 | | 1 | | | | | 1 | 1 | | | | 4 | Not Stated | |
| Nantucket | 4 | 13 | Coffin | Thankful | | 1 | | | | | | | | 1 | | | 2 | Not Stated | |
| Nantucket | 4 | 14 | Coffin | Lydia | | | 1 | | | | | | 1 | | | | 2 | Not Stated | |
| Nantucket | 4 | 15 | Coffin | Abigail | | | 1 | | | | | 1 | 1 | 1 | | | 4 | Not Stated | |
| Nantucket | 4 | 16 | Bunker | Hezekiah | 1 | 1 | | 1 | | 3 | 2 | 1 | | | | | 9 | Not Stated | |
| Nantucket | 4 | 17 | Hussey | Charles | | 2 | 1 | | | 1 | | 1 | 1 | | | | 6 | Not Stated | |
| Nantucket | 4 | 18 | Cartwright | James 2nd | 3 | | 1 | 1 | | 1 | 2 | 1 | | | | | 9 | Not Stated | |
| Nantucket | 4 | 19 | Coffin | David | | | 1 | | | | | | 1 | 1 | | | 3 | Not Stated | |
| Nantucket | 4 | 20 | Coffin | Gideon | 1 | 1 | | 1 | 3 | | | | 1 | | | | 7 | Not Stated | |
| Nantucket | 4 | 21 | Swain | Valentine | 1 | | 1 | 1 | | 2 | | 1 | | | | | 6 | Not Stated | |
| Nantucket | 4 | 22 | Macy | Silvanus Junr | 2 | 2 | 1 | | | | | 2 | 1 | | | | 8 | Not Stated | |
| Nantucket | 4 | 23 | Bunker | Seth | | | 1 | | | | | | 1 | | | | 2 | Not Stated | |
| Nantucket | 4 | 24 | Williams | Laban | | 1 | 1 | 2 | | | | | 1 | | | | 6 | Not Stated | |
| Nantucket | 4 | 25 | Chadwick | Richard | | | 1 | 1 | | | | | 1 | | | | 3 | Not Stated | |
| Nantucket | 4 | 26 | Cartwright | Thos | 1 | | 1 | | | 1 | | | | | | | 3 | Not Stated | |
| Nantucket | 4 | 27 | Starbuck | Christopher | | | 1 | 1 | | | | | 2 | | | | 4 | Not Stated | |
| Nantucket | 4 | 28 | Starbuck | Tristram | 2 | | | 2 | | | | | 1 | | | | 6 | Not Stated | |
| Nantucket | 4 | 29 | Coffin | Gilbert | 1 | 2 | 3 | 1 | | | | 1 | 1 | | | | 9 | Not Stated | |
| Nantucket | 4 | 30 | Macy | Simeon | | 1 | 1 | | | | | | 1 | | | | 3 | Not Stated | |
| Nantucket | 4 | 31 | Macy | Lydia | | | | | | | | | 1 | 1 | | | 2 | Not Stated | |
| Nantucket | 4 | 32 | Roy | Thomas | | | 1 | | | | | | 1 | | | | 2 | Not Stated | |
| Nantucket | 4 | 33 | Macy | Barnabas | 1 | 2 | | 1 | 2 | | | | 1 | | | | 7 | Not Stated | |
| Nantucket | 4 | 34 | Gardner | Mary | | | | | | | | | | 1 | | | 1 | Not Stated | |
| Nantucket | 4 | 35 | Paddack | Benjamin | | 3 | | 1 | | | | 1 | 1 | 1 | | | 7 | Not Stated | |
| Nantucket | 4 | 36 | Paddack | William | | 1 | 1 | | | | | | 1 | | | | 3 | Not Stated | |
| Nantucket | 4 | 37 | Paddack | Abishai | 3 | 1 | 3 | 1 | | | 2 | | 1 | | | | 11 | Not Stated | |
| Nantucket | 4 | 38 | Gardner | Abigail 2nd | | 1 | | | | | | 1 | | 2 | | | 4 | Not Stated | |
| Nantucket | 4 | 39 | Parker | Nathan Junr | | 1 | | | | | | | 1 | | | | 2 | Not Stated | |
| Nantucket | 4 | 40 | Barnard | Shubael | | 1 | 1 | 1 | | 1 | | | 1 | | | | 5 | Not Stated | |
| Nantucket | 4 | 41 | Whitney | Daniel | 2 | | | 1 | | 1 | | 1 | 1 | | | | 6 | Not Stated | |
| Nantucket | 4 | 42 | Coffin | Timothy | | | 1 | | | | | | 1 | 1 | | | 3 | Not Stated | |
| Nantucket | 4 | 43 | Cary | Edward Junr | 1 | | 1 | 1 | | 2 | 1 | 1 | | | | | 7 | Not Stated | |
| Nantucket | 4 | 44 | Folger | Shubael | | 1 | 1 | 2 | | | | | 1 | | | | 5 | Not Stated | |
| Nantucket | 4 | 45 | Clasby | John | | | 1 | 1 | | | | | 1 | 1 | | | 4 | Not Stated | |
| Nantucket | 4 | 46 | Clasby | John Junr | | | 1 | 1 | | | | 2 | | 1 | | | 5 | Not Stated | |
| Nantucket | 4 | 47 | Bunker | Matthew | 1 | | 1 | 1 | | 1 | | | | 1 | | | 5 | Not Stated | |
| Nantucket | 4 | 48 | Gardner | Timothy | 1 | | | 1 | 1 | | | | | 1 | | | 4 | Not Stated | |
| Nantucket | 4 | 49 | Rand | Miriam | | | 1 | | | | | | 1 | 1 | | | 3 | Not Stated | |
| Nantucket | 4 | 50 | West | Joseph | | 1 | | | | | 2 | | | | | | 3 | Not Stated | |
| Nantucket | 4 | 51 | Folger | Tristram 2nd | 1 | | | 1 | 2 | | | | 1 | | | | 5 | Not Stated | |
| Nantucket | 4 | 52 | Gardner | Thankful | | | | | | | | | 1 | 1 | | | 2 | Not Stated | |
| Nantucket | 4 | 53 | Barnard | Jonathan | 2 | 1 | | 1 | 3 | 1 | | | 1 | | | | 9 | Not Stated | |
| Nantucket | 4 | 54 | Gardner | Laban | | | 1 | 2 | 4 | 1 | | 1 | | | | | 9 | Not Stated | |

# 1800 Nantucket, Nantucket County, Massachusetts

| TOWN | PG# | LN# | LAST NAME | FIRST NAME | M under 10 | M 10-16 | M 16-26 | M 26-45 | M 45 & over | F under 10 | F 10-16 | F 16-26 | F 26-45 | F 45 & over | TOTAL ALL OTHER | TOTAL SLAVES | TOTALS | DISTRICT/TOWNSHIP | NOTES |
|---|---|---|---|---|---|---|---|---|---|---|---|---|---|---|---|---|---|---|---|
| Nantucket | 4 | 55 | Perry | Reuben | | | 1 | | 1 | 1 | | | | 1 | | | 4 | Not Stated | |
| Nantucket | 4 | 56 | Bennett | Ruth | 1 | | | | | | | | 1 | 1 | | | 3 | Not Stated | |
| Nantucket | 4 | 57 | Dow | Samuel | 2 | | 1 | | | 1 | | 1 | | | | | 5 | Not Stated | |
| Nantucket | 4 | 58 | Coffin | Gardner | 1 | | 1 | | | 1 | | | 1 | | | | 4 | Not Stated | |
| Nantucket | 4 | 59 | Folger | Charles | 3 | 2 | 2 | | 1 | 2 | 1 | | 1 | | | | 12 | Not Stated | |
| Nantucket | 4 | 60 | Hunter | John | 1 | 1 | 1 | 1 | 1 | | 1 | 1 | 2 | | | | 9 | Not Stated | |
| Nantucket | 4 | 61 | Folger | Henry | 3 | 1 | 1 | | | | | | 1 | 1 | | | 8 | Not Stated | |
| Nantucket | 4 | 62 | Folger | Miriam | | | | | | | | | 1 | | | | 1 | Not Stated | |
| Nantucket | 4 | 63 | Black | Mary | | | | | | | | | 1 | 1 | | | 2 | Not Stated | |
| Nantucket | 4 | 64 | Gardner | William 2nd | 4 | | 1 | 1 | | 1 | | 2 | 2 | 1 | | | 12 | Not Stated | |
| Nantucket | 4 | 65 | Coleman | Peleg | | | | 1 | | | | | | 1 | | | 2 | Not Stated | |
| Nantucket | 4 | 66 | Folger | Paul | | | | 1 | | | | | | 2 | | | 3 | Not Stated | |
| Nantucket | 4 | 67 | Coffin | Lydia 2nd | 1 | 2 | | | | 2 | 1 | | | 1 | | | 7 | Not Stated | |
| Nantucket | 4 | 68 | Coleman | William | | | 1 | 1 | | 1 | | | 3 | 1 | | | 4 | Not Stated | |
| Nantucket | 4 | 69 | Ellis | William | | 1 | | 1 | | | | | 3 | 1 | | | 5 | Not Stated | |
| Nantucket | 4 | 70 | Newbegin | James | | 1 | 2 | 1 | | 3 | 1 | | | 2 | | | 10 | Not Stated | |
| Nantucket | 4 | 71 | Allen | Daniel | | | | | | | | | | 1 | | | 1 | Not Stated | |
| Nantucket | 4 | 72 | Folger | Anna | | | | | | 1 | | | 2 | 1 | | | 4 | Not Stated | |
| Nantucket | 4 | 73 | Folger | Mary 2nd | | | | | | | | | 1 | 1 | | | 2 | Not Stated | |
| Nantucket | 4 | 74 | Jones | Hezhibah | | | | | | | | 1 | 1 | | | | 2 | Not Stated | |
| Nantucket | 5 | 1 | Farr | Sarah | | | 2 | | | | | | 3 | | | | 5 | Not Stated | |
| Nantucket | 5 | 2 | Merchant | Benjm | | | 2 | 1 | | | | 1 | | 1 | | | 5 | Not Stated | |
| Nantucket | 5 | 3 | Folger | Catharine | | | 1 | | | 1 | 1 | | 4 | 1 | | | 8 | Not Stated | |
| Nantucket | 5 | 4 | Clark | Wm | | | | 1 | | | | | | 1 | | | 2 | Not Stated | |
| Nantucket | 5 | 5 | Clark | William Junr | | 1 | 1 | 1 | | 1 | | | 1 | | | | 5 | Not Stated | |
| Nantucket | 5 | 6 | Clark | Joseph | | 1 | | 1 | | | | | 1 | | | | 3 | Not Stated | |
| Nantucket | 5 | 7 | Frost | Nathl | | | | 1 | | | | | | 1 | | | 2 | Not Stated | |
| Nantucket | 5 | 8 | James | Francis | 2 | 1 | 2 | 1 | | 2 | | | 1 | | | | 9 | Not Stated | |
| Nantucket | 5 | 9 | Heath | Edmund | | | | 1 | | | | | | 1 | | | 2 | Not Stated | |
| Nantucket | 5 | 10 | Hoag | Abraham | 1 | | 4 | | | 1 | | 1 | | 1 | | | 9 | Not Stated | |
| Nantucket | 5 | 11 | Marshall | Samuel | | | | 1 | | | 1 | 1 | | 1 | | | 4 | Not Stated | |
| Nantucket | 5 | 12 | Peters | John | 1 | | 1 | | | | | | 1 | | | | 3 | Not Stated | |
| Nantucket | 5 | 13 | James | Hart | 2 | | 1 | | | | | 2 | 2 | 2 | | | 9 | Not Stated | |
| Nantucket | 5 | 14 | Gardner | Nathan Junr | | 1 | | 1 | 1 | 1 | 1 | | 1 | | | | 6 | Not Stated | |
| Nantucket | 5 | 15 | Randal | Gideon | 1 | | | 1 | | 2 | | | 1 | | | | 5 | Not Stated | |
| Nantucket | 5 | 16 | Randal | Constant | | 1 | | 1 | | | | | 1 | | | | 3 | Not Stated | |
| Nantucket | 5 | 17 | Clasby | Joseph | 1 | | | 1 | | | | | 1 | | | | 3 | Not Stated | |
| Nantucket | 5 | 18 | Pinkham | Andrew | 2 | | | 1 | | | | | 1 | | | | 4 | Not Stated | |
| Nantucket | 5 | 19 | Paddack | Hephzibah | | 1 | 1 | | | | | | 1 | 1 | | | 4 | Not Stated | |
| Nantucket | 5 | 20 | Folger | Timothy | | 1 | | 1 | | 1 | 1 | | 1 | | | | 5 | Not Stated | |
| Nantucket | 5 | 21 | Paddack | Francis | | | 1 | | | | | | 1 | | | | 2 | Not Stated | |
| Nantucket | 5 | 22 | Clark | Rachel | | | | | | | | | 1 | 1 | | | 2 | Not Stated | |
| Nantucket | 5 | 23 | Starbuck | William | | 1 | | 1 | | | | | 1 | 1 | | | 4 | Not Stated | |
| Nantucket | 5 | 24 | Coffin | Ruth | 1 | 1 | | | | | | 1 | 1 | 1 | | | 5 | Not Stated | |
| Nantucket | 5 | 25 | Swain | Rebecca | | 1 | 3 | | | | | | 2 | 1 | | | 7 | Not Stated | |
| Nantucket | 5 | 26 | Starbuck | Kimbal | | | 1 | | | 2 | | | 1 | | | | 4 | Not Stated | |
| Nantucket | 5 | 27 | Starbuck | Benjamin | 2 | | 1 | | | | | | 1 | | | | 4 | Not Stated | |
| Nantucket | 5 | 28 | Starbuck | Reuben | 1 | 1 | 2 | 1 | | 3 | 1 | | 1 | | | | 10 | Not Stated | |
| Nantucket | 5 | 29 | Starbuck | Thomas | 2 | 1 | 1 | 1 | 1 | 1 | | 1 | 1 | 1 | | | 10 | Not Stated | |
| Nantucket | 5 | 30 | Coffin | Philip | 2 | 1 | | 1 | | 1 | 1 | | 1 | | | | 7 | Not Stated | |
| Nantucket | 5 | 31 | Myrick | Abigail | | | | | | | | | | 1 | | | 1 | Not Stated | |
| Nantucket | 5 | 32 | Addleton | Abigail | | | | | | | | | | 1 | | | 1 | Not Stated | |
| Nantucket | 5 | 33 | Addleton | John | 2 | | | 1 | | 2 | | | 1 | 1 | | | 7 | Not Stated | |
| Nantucket | 5 | 34 | Myrick | George | 3 | 1 | 1 | | | 2 | | | 1 | 1 | | | 10 | Not Stated | |
| Nantucket | 5 | 35 | Hayden | Zophar | | | | | | | | | 2 | | | | 3 | Not Stated | |
| Nantucket | 5 | 36 | Myrick | Andrew | | | 1 | | 1 | | | | 1 | 1 | | | 4 | Not Stated | |
| Nantucket | 5 | 37 | Ray | Isaiah | 1 | | | 1 | | | | | | 1 | | | 3 | Not Stated | |
| Nantucket | 5 | 38 | Coleman | John | | | | | 1 | | | | | 1 | | | 2 | Not Stated | |
| Nantucket | 5 | 39 | Gardner | Ammiel | | | 1 | | | 1 | | 1 | 1 | 1 | | | 5 | Not Stated | |
| Nantucket | 5 | 40 | Coffin | Elihu | 1 | | 2 | | 1 | 1 | 1 | | | 1 | | | 7 | Not Stated | |
| Nantucket | 5 | 41 | Barnard | Ruth | | 1 | 2 | 1 | | 1 | | | | 2 | | | 7 | Not Stated | |
| Nantucket | 5 | 42 | Pinkham | Bethiah | | | | | | | | | | 2 | | | 2 | Not Stated | |
| Nantucket | 5 | 43 | Coleman | Samuel | | | | 1 | | 1 | | | 1 | | | | 3 | Not Stated | |
| Nantucket | 5 | 44 | Keen | Moses | 2 | | | 1 | | | | | 1 | | | | 4 | Not Stated | |
| Nantucket | 5 | 45 | Starbuck | Joseph | | | | 1 | | 2 | | | 1 | | | | 4 | Not Stated | |
| Nantucket | 5 | 46 | Coleman | Priscilla | 1 | | 2 | 1 | | | | | | 1 | | | 5 | Not Stated | |
| Nantucket | 5 | 47 | Ellis | Nathaniel | | | | 1 | | | | | 2 | | | | 3 | Not Stated | |
| Nantucket | 5 | 48 | Coffin | John | 2 | 2 | 2 | 1 | | 1 | | | 1 | | | | 9 | Not Stated | |
| Nantucket | 5 | 49 | Ray | Alexander | 2 | | 2 | 1 | | | | | 3 | 1 | | | 9 | Not Stated | |
| Nantucket | 5 | 50 | Padduck | Benjm | 2 | 1 | | 1 | | 1 | 1 | | 1 | | | | 7 | Not Stated | |
| Nantucket | 5 | 51 | Barnard | Matthew | | | 1 | 1 | | | | 1 | 2 | 1 | | | 6 | Not Stated | |
| Nantucket | 5 | 52 | Barnard | Andrew | 1 | | | 1 | | 1 | | | 1 | | | | 4 | Not Stated | |
| Nantucket | 5 | 53 | Barnard | Libni | 3 | | | 1 | | 2 | 1 | | 1 | | | | 8 | Not Stated | |
| Nantucket | 5 | 54 | Gardner | Jeremiah | 2 | | | 1 | | 1 | | | 1 | | | | 5 | Not Stated | |
| Nantucket | 5 | 55 | Coffin | Abihu | | 1 | | 1 | | | | | | 1 | | | 3 | Not Stated | |
| Nantucket | 5 | 56 | Swain | Hannah | 1 | | 2 | 2 | | | | | 1 | 1 | | | 7 | Not Stated | |
| Nantucket | 5 | 57 | Stetson | Barzillai | | | 1 | | | 1 | | 1 | 1 | | | | 4 | Not Stated | |
| Nantucket | 5 | 58 | Briggs | Abner | | 1 | 1 | | | 1 | | | 1 | | | | 4 | Not Stated | |
| Nantucket | 5 | 59 | Hawkins | John | 1 | | 1 | | | 2 | | | 1 | 1 | | | 6 | Not Stated | |
| Nantucket | 5 | 60 | Waterman | Thaddeus | 2 | 1 | 1 | 2 | 1 | 2 | | 1 | 2 | 1 | | | 14 | Not Stated | |
| Nantucket | 5 | 61 | Barker | Saml | 1 | | 2 | 1 | | | | | 1 | 3 | | | 8 | Not Stated | |
| Nantucket | 5 | 62 | Bunker | Benjm | 1 | 1 | 3 | 1 | 1 | 1 | | 1 | 1 | 1 | | | 11 | Not Stated | |
| Nantucket | 5 | 63 | Stretton | Abigail | 1 | | | | | | | | | 1 | | | 2 | Not Stated | |
| Nantucket | 5 | 64 | Gardner | Sarah | | | | | | | | | | 1 | | | 1 | Not Stated | |
| Nantucket | 5 | 65 | Giles | Lydia | | | | | | | | 1 | 1 | | | | 2 | Not Stated | |
| Nantucket | 5 | 66 | Burrage | Rebecca | | | 2 | | | | | | 1 | 2 | | | 5 | Not Stated | |
| Nantucket | 5 | 67 | Alley | Reuben | 2 | 1 | | 1 | | 1 | | | | 2 | | | 7 | Not Stated | |
| Nantucket | 5 | 68 | Folger | Stephen | | | | | 1 | | | | | | | | 1 | Not Stated | |
| Nantucket | 6 | 1 | Alley | Jacob | | | 1 | | 1 | | | 2 | | 1 | | | 5 | Not Stated | |
| Nantucket | 6 | 2 | Brown | Francis | | | 1 | | 1 | 1 | | 2 | | 1 | | | 6 | Not Stated | |

# 1800 Nantucket, Nantucket County, Massachusetts

| TOWN | PG# | LN# | LAST NAME | FIRST NAME | M under 10 | M 10 to 16 | M 16 to 26 | M 26 to 45 | M 45 and over | F under 10 | F 10 to 16 | F 16 to 26 | F 26 to 45 | F 45 and over | TOTAL ALL OTHER | TOTAL SLAVES | TOTALS | DISTRICT/ TOWNSHIP | NOTES |
|---|---|---|---|---|---|---|---|---|---|---|---|---|---|---|---|---|---|---|---|
| Nantucket | 6 | 3 | Mitchell | Benjm | 1 | 1 | | 1 | | 3 | | 1 | | | | | 7 | Not Stated | |
| Nantucket | 6 | 4 | Mitchell | Christopher | | 1 | 1 | 1 | | 2 | 1 | 1 | | | | | 7 | Not Stated | |
| Nantucket | 6 | 5 | Briggs | Jonathan | 2 | 1 | | 1 | | | | 2 | | | | | 6 | Not Stated | |
| Nantucket | 6 | 6 | Raymond | William | | | 1 | | 1 | 1 | | 1 | 1 | 1 | | | 6 | Not Stated | |
| Nantucket | 6 | 7 | Willis | Eliakim | 1 | | | | | | | 1 | | | | | 3 | Not Stated | |
| Nantucket | 6 | 8 | Bebee | Nathan | 2 | 1 | 1 | 1 | 1 | | 3 | | 1 | | | | 10 | Not Stated | |
| Nantucket | 6 | 9 | Macy | Peleg | 3 | 1 | 1 | 1 | | 2 | 2 | | 1 | | | | 11 | Not Stated | |
| Nantucket | 6 | 10 | Parker | Francis | 2 | 2 | | 1 | | | 2 | 1 | 1 | | 2 | | 11 | Not Stated | |
| Nantucket | 6 | 11 | Davis | Joseph | | | 1 | | | | | 1 | | | | | 2 | Not Stated | |
| Nantucket | 6 | 12 | Baker | James | 1 | | | 1 | | | | 1 | | | | | 3 | Not Stated | |
| Nantucket | 6 | 13 | Coffin | William | 1 | 1 | | 1 | | 2 | 2 | 2 | 1 | | | | 10 | Not Stated | |
| Nantucket | 6 | 14 | Coleman | Richd. Lake | 2 | | | 1 | | 1 | | 2 | | | | | 6 | Not Stated | |
| Nantucket | 6 | 15 | Dow | Henry | | | 2 | | 1 | | 1 | 1 | | 2 | | | 7 | Not Stated | |
| Nantucket | 6 | 16 | Hussey | Albert | | | 1 | | | | | 1 | | | | | 2 | Not Stated | |
| Nantucket | 6 | 17 | Sherman | John | 2 | | 4 | | 1 | 2 | 1 | 1 | 1 | | | | 12 | Not Stated | |
| Nantucket | 6 | 18 | Hinckley | Elisja Mau | | | 1 | | | 2 | 1 | 2 | | 2 | | | 8 | Not Stated | |
| Nantucket | 6 | 19 | Marshall | James | 1 | | | 1 | | 1 | | | 1 | | | | 4 | Not Stated | |
| Nantucket | 6 | 20 | Russell | Elihu | 2 | | | 1 | | | 1 | | 1 | | | | 5 | Not Stated | |
| Nantucket | 6 | 21 | Coffin | William 2nd | 2 | 2 | 1 | 1 | | 2 | 1 | | 1 | | 1 | | 11 | Not Stated | |
| Nantucket | 6 | 22 | Chadwick | David | | 3 | 1 | | 1 | 1 | | | | 1 | | | 7 | Not Stated | |
| Nantucket | 6 | 23 | Chadwick | Nathaniel | 1 | | | 1 | | 2 | 2 | 3 | 1 | | | | 10 | Not Stated | |
| Nantucket | 6 | 24 | Harris | David | | | 1 | | 1 | 1 | | | 1 | | | | 4 | Not Stated | |
| Nantucket | 6 | 25 | Wright | Thomas Jackson | | | 1 | | | | | 1 | | | | | 2 | Not Stated | |
| Nantucket | 6 | 26 | Wyer | Nathaniel | | | 1 | | | | 1 | | | | | | 2 | Not Stated | |
| Nantucket | 6 | 27 | McCleve | Thos Varney | 2 | 1 | | 3 | | 4 | | | 2 | | | | 12 | Not Stated | |
| Nantucket | 6 | 28 | Giles | Paul | | | 2 | 1 | | 1 | | | 1 | | | | 5 | Not Stated | |
| Nantucket | 6 | 29 | Ellis | Silvanus Junr | | | 1 | | | | | | 2 | | | | 3 | Not Stated | |
| Nantucket | 6 | 30 | Smith | Slvanus | | | 1 | | 1 | 1 | 1 | | 1 | | | | 5 | Not Stated | |
| Nantucket | 6 | 31 | Pruff | Jane | | | 2 | | | | | 1 | 1 | | | | 4 | Not Stated | |
| Nantucket | 6 | 32 | Luce | Obed | 1 | | | 1 | | 3 | | 1 | | | | | 6 | Not Stated | |
| Nantucket | 6 | 33 | Barnard | John | | | | 1 | | | | 2 | 1 | | | | 4 | Not Stated | |
| Nantucket | 6 | 34 | Cash | Elijah | 1 | | | 1 | | 3 | | 1 | | | | | 6 | Not Stated | |
| Nantucket | 6 | 35 | Folger | David | | | | 1 | | 1 | 1 | 1 | 1 | | | | 5 | Not Stated | |
| Nantucket | 6 | 36 | Folger | Silvanus 2nd | | | 1 | | 2 | 1 | 1 | | | | | | 5 | Not Stated | |
| Nantucket | 6 | 37 | Coleman | Matthew | 1 | 2 | | | 1 | 1 | 1 | | 1 | | | | 7 | Not Stated | |
| Nantucket | 6 | 38 | Whippy | James | 1 | | 2 | | 1 | | | | 2 | | | | 6 | Not Stated | |
| Nantucket | 6 | 39 | Foye | Obed | 4 | | | 1 | | 2 | 1 | | 1 | | | | 9 | Not Stated | |
| Nantucket | 6 | 40 | Clark | James | | | 2 | | | | | 1 | | | | | 3 | Not Stated | |
| Nantucket | 6 | 41 | Gwin | Rachel | | | | | | | | | 1 | | | | 1 | Not Stated | |
| Nantucket | 6 | 42 | Hendrick | George | 1 | | | 1 | | 1 | | | 1 | | | | 4 | Not Stated | |
| Nantucket | 6 | 43 | Ray | William Junr | | 1 | | 1 | | 1 | | | 1 | | | | 4 | Not Stated | |
| Nantucket | 6 | 44 | Smith | Job Junr | 2 | | | 1 | | | | 1 | | | | | 4 | Not Stated | |
| Nantucket | 6 | 45 | Burdett | Parnell | 1 | | 3 | | | 3 | | | 1 | | | | 8 | Not Stated | |
| Nantucket | 6 | 46 | Meader | Nathl | 1 | 2 | 1 | | 1 | 1 | | 2 | 2 | 1 | | | 11 | Not Stated | |
| Nantucket | 6 | 47 | Swain | David | | 1 | 1 | 1 | | 2 | | | 1 | | | | 6 | Not Stated | |
| Nantucket | 6 | 48 | Fitzgerald | Henry | 1 | 1 | 1 | | 1 | | 1 | 1 | 1 | | | | 7 | Not Stated | |
| Nantucket | 6 | 49 | Davis | John | 1 | | | 1 | | | 1 | | | | | | 3 | Not Stated | |
| Nantucket | 6 | 50 | Starbuck | Jethro | | | 1 | | | | 1 | | 1 | | | | 3 | Not Stated | |
| Nantucket | 6 | 51 | Hussey | Daniel | 1 | | | 1 | | 1 | | | 1 | | | | 4 | Not Stated | |
| Nantucket | 6 | 52 | Coleman | Stephen | 1 | | | 1 | | | | 1 | | | | | 3 | Not Stated | |
| Nantucket | 6 | 53 | Coffin | Zebdial | 1 | | | 1 | | 2 | | 1 | | | | | 5 | Not Stated | |
| Nantucket | 6 | 54 | Swain | Abigail | 1 | | | 1 | | 2 | | | 1 | 1 | | | 6 | Not Stated | |
| Nantucket | 6 | 55 | Long | Reuben | 1 | | | | | 1 | | 1 | | | | | 3 | Not Stated | |
| Nantucket | 6 | 56 | Upham | Jonathan | | 1 | 2 | | 1 | 1 | 1 | 2 | 1 | 1 | | | 10 | Not Stated | |
| Nantucket | 6 | 57 | Coleman | Shubael | | | 1 | | | 1 | | 1 | 1 | | | | 4 | Not Stated | |
| Nantucket | 6 | 58 | Maxcy | Isaiah | 1 | 1 | | 1 | | | 2 | | 1 | | | | 6 | Not Stated | |
| Nantucket | 7 | 1 | Long | Richard | 3 | | | 1 | | | | 1 | | | | | 5 | Not Stated | |
| Nantucket | 7 | 2 | Harris | Obed | | 1 | 1 | 1 | | 1 | | 1 | | | | | 5 | Not Stated | |
| Nantucket | 7 | 3 | Fitzgerald | James | | | 1 | | 2 | | | 1 | | | | | 4 | Not Stated | |
| Nantucket | 7 | 4 | Ellis | Elisha | | 1 | | 1 | | | | 1 | | | | | 3 | Not Stated | |
| Nantucket | 7 | 5 | Manter | Joseph | | | 1 | 1 | | | 1 | 2 | 1 | | | | 6 | Not Stated | |
| Nantucket | 7 | 6 | Ramsdell | Priscilla | 1 | | 1 | 1 | | 1 | | 1 | 1 | 1 | | | 7 | Not Stated | |
| Nantucket | 7 | 7 | Smith | Abigail | | 1 | 1 | | 1 | | 1 | 1 | 2 | 2 | | | 9 | Not Stated | |
| Nantucket | 7 | 8 | Bunker | Tristram | | | | 1 | | | | 1 | | | | | 2 | Not Stated | |
| Nantucket | 7 | 9 | Hussey | Simeon | 2 | 2 | | 1 | | | | 1 | 1 | | | | 7 | Not Stated | |
| Nantucket | 7 | 10 | Baxter | Christopher | | | 1 | 1 | 1 | | | 1 | | | | | 4 | Not Stated | |
| Nantucket | 7 | 11 | Lawrence | Jeremiah | 2 | | | 1 | | | | 1 | | | | | 4 | Not Stated | |
| Nantucket | 7 | 12 | Coleman | Barzillai | 1 | 1 | 2 | | 1 | 1 | | | 2 | | | | 8 | Not Stated | |
| Nantucket | 7 | 13 | Whitehouse | James | | 1 | | 1 | | | | 1 | | | | | 3 | Not Stated | |
| Nantucket | 7 | 14 | Marshall | Green | | 1 | 2 | | 1 | 1 | | 1 | 1 | | | | 7 | Not Stated | |
| Nantucket | 7 | 15 | Harris | Humphrey | | | 1 | | 1 | 1 | | 1 | 1 | | | | 5 | Not Stated | |
| Nantucket | 7 | 16 | Manter | Benjamin | 2 | | | 1 | | | 1 | | 1 | | | | 5 | Not Stated | |
| Nantucket | 7 | 17 | Cash | Reuben | | | 1 | | | | 1 | | | | | | 2 | Not Stated | |
| Nantucket | 7 | 18 | Maxcy | Reuben | | | 1 | 1 | | | | 1 | | | | | 3 | Not Stated | |
| Nantucket | 7 | 19 | Cleaveland | Seth | 2 | 1 | | 1 | | 1 | 1 | | 1 | | | | 7 | Not Stated | |
| Nantucket | 7 | 20 | Hartshorn | John Woodman | | | 1 | | | | | 1 | | | | | 2 | Not Stated | |
| Nantucket | 7 | 21 | Ellis | Freeman | 1 | | 1 | 1 | | 1 | | | 1 | | | | 5 | Not Stated | |
| Nantucket | 7 | 22 | Bunker | Uriah | | | 2 | 1 | | | | 1 | 1 | | | | 6 | Not Stated | |
| Nantucket | 7 | 23 | Bunker | Obed | | 1 | 3 | 1 | 2 | 1 | 2 | 1 | 1 | | | | 12 | Not Stated | |
| Nantucket | 7 | 24 | Swain | Abishai | 2 | | 2 | 1 | 1 | 2 | | 1 | 2 | 1 | | | 12 | Not Stated | |
| Nantucket | 7 | 25 | Cathcart | Gershom | 1 | 1 | 5 | 1 | | 2 | 1 | | 1 | | | | 12 | Not Stated | |
| Nantucket | 7 | 26 | Manter | George | 1 | | 1 | | | | | 1 | | | | | 3 | Not Stated | |
| Nantucket | 7 | 27 | Chadwick | William | | | 3 | 1 | | | | | 1 | | | | 5 | Not Stated | |
| Nantucket | 7 | 28 | Folger | Solomon | | | 1 | 1 | | | | | 1 | | | | 3 | Not Stated | |
| Nantucket | 7 | 29 | Swain | Simeon | | 1 | 1 | 1 | 1 | 1 | 1 | 1 | 1 | | | | 8 | Not Stated | |
| Nantucket | 7 | 30 | Cleaveland | Aaron | | | | 1 | | | | 1 | 1 | | | | 3 | Not Stated | |
| Nantucket | 7 | 31 | Cash | William | 1 | | | 1 | 1 | | | 1 | 1 | | | | 5 | Not Stated | |
| Nantucket | 7 | 32 | Cleaveland | Susanna | | | | | | | | 1 | 1 | | | | 2 | Not Stated | |
| Nantucket | 7 | 33 | Crosby | Saml | 1 | 1 | 1 | 1 | | 1 | | 2 | 1 | 1 | | | 9 | Not Stated | |
| Nantucket | 7 | 34 | Cartwright | Deborah | | | | | | | | | 1 | | | | 1 | Not Stated | |

# 1800 Nantucket, Nantucket County, Massachusetts

| Town | PG# | LN# | Last Name | First Name | FREE WHITE MALES under 10 | 10 to 16 | 16 to 26 | 26 to 45 | 45 and over | FREE WHITE FEMALES under 10 | 10 to 16 | 16 to 26 | 26 to 45 | 45 and over | Total All Other | Total Slaves | Totals | District/Township | Notes |
|---|---|---|---|---|---|---|---|---|---|---|---|---|---|---|---|---|---|---|---|
| Nantucket | 7 | 35 | Wyer | Hephzibah | 1 |  | 2 |  |  |  | 1 | 1 | 2 | 1 |  |  | 8 | Not Stated |  |
| Nantucket | 7 | 36 | Wyer | Edward | 2 |  |  | 1 | 1 |  | 1 |  | 2 | 1 |  |  | 8 | Not Stated |  |
| Nantucket | 7 | 37 | Perkins | Gilbert | 1 |  | 1 |  |  | 2 |  |  | 1 |  |  |  | 5 | Not Stated |  |
| Nantucket | 7 | 38 | Perkins | John |  | 1 |  | 1 |  | 1 |  | 1 | 1 |  |  |  | 5 | Not Stated |  |
| Nantucket | 7 | 39 | Whippy | Nathaniel |  | 1 | 1 | 1 | 1 |  |  | 1 | 1 |  | 1 |  | 7 | Not Stated |  |
| Nantucket | 7 | 40 | Marshall | Josiah |  | 1 | 2 |  | 1 |  |  |  | 1 |  |  |  | 6 | Not Stated |  |
| Nantucket | 7 | 41 | Cash | Phebe | 1 |  |  |  |  |  |  | 1 | 1 | 1 |  |  | 4 | Not Stated |  |
| Nantucket | 7 | 42 | Creasy | Edward | 2 |  |  | 1 |  |  | 1 |  | 1 |  |  |  | 5 | Not Stated |  |
| Nantucket | 7 | 43 | Morslander | Linzey | 2 |  |  | 1 |  |  |  |  | 1 |  |  |  | 4 | Not Stated |  |
| Nantucket | 7 | 44 | Chase | Issac | 1 | 3 |  | 1 |  |  |  |  | 1 | 1 |  |  | 7 | Not Stated |  |
| Nantucket | 7 | 45 | Chase | Jonathan | 1 |  | 1 | 1 |  |  | 1 |  | 1 |  |  |  | 5 | Not Stated |  |
| Nantucket | 7 | 46 | Quin | Mary | 1 |  |  |  |  |  |  | 1 | 1 | 1 |  |  | 4 | Not Stated |  |
| Nantucket | 7 | 47 | Derrik | John |  |  |  | 1 |  |  |  | 1 |  | 1 |  |  | 3 | Not Stated |  |
| Nantucket | 7 | 48 | Bowcot | Sarah | 2 | 1 |  | 3 |  |  | 1 |  | 3 | 1 |  |  | 11 | Not Stated |  |
| Nantucket | 7 | 49 | Morslander | Cornelius Junr | 2 |  |  | 1 |  | 1 | 2 |  |  | 1 |  |  | 7 | Not Stated |  |
| Nantucket | 7 | 50 | Allen | John Junr | 2 |  | 2 |  |  | 1 | 3 | 1 |  |  |  |  | 12 | Not Stated |  |
| Nantucket | 7 | 51 | Swain | Paltiah | 2 | 1 | 1 |  |  |  |  |  | 2 |  |  |  | 6 | Not Stated |  |
| Nantucket | 7 | 52 | Fitzgerald | Jonathan |  | 1 | 1 |  | 1 |  | 1 | 1 |  | 1 |  |  | 6 | Not Stated |  |
| Nantucket | 7 | 53 | Cotton | Josiah | 2 |  | 1 |  |  |  |  |  | 1 |  |  |  | 4 | Not Stated |  |
| Nantucket | 7 | 54 | Baker | Catharine |  |  |  | 1 |  |  | 1 |  | 2 | 1 |  |  | 5 | Not Stated |  |
| Nantucket | 7 | 55 | Harrax | Thomas |  |  | 1 | 1 | 1 |  |  | 1 | 2 | 1 |  |  | 7 | Not Stated |  |
| Nantucket | 7 | 56 | Morslander | Cornelius |  |  | 1 |  | 1 |  |  | 1 |  | 1 |  |  | 4 | Not Stated |  |
| Nantucket | 7 | 57 | Allen | John |  |  |  | 1 |  |  |  |  | 1 |  |  |  | 2 | Not Stated |  |
| Nantucket | 7 | 58 | Allen | Reuben | 2 |  |  | 1 |  | 1 |  |  | 1 |  |  |  | 5 | Not Stated |  |
| Nantucket | 8 | 1 | Russell | Hezkiah |  | 1 | 1 |  |  |  |  |  | 1 | 1 |  |  | 4 | Not Stated |  |
| Nantucket | 8 | 2 | Weeks | Joseph | 2 |  |  |  |  |  |  |  | 1 | 1 |  |  | 4 | Not Stated |  |
| Nantucket | 8 | 3 | Waldron | Nathan | 1 |  | 2 | 1 | 1 |  |  | 1 | 2 | 1 |  |  | 9 | Not Stated |  |
| Nantucket | 8 | 4 | Folger | Silvanus |  |  | 1 |  |  |  |  |  |  | 1 |  |  | 2 | Not Stated |  |
| Nantucket | 8 | 5 | Swain | Charles | 1 |  | 1 | 1 |  |  |  |  | 1 | 1 |  |  | 5 | Not Stated |  |
| Nantucket | 8 | 6 | Brown | William | 3 |  |  | 1 |  |  |  |  | 1 | 1 |  |  | 6 | Not Stated |  |
| Nantucket | 8 | 7 | Brown | George |  | 2 | 1 |  | 1 | 1 | 1 | 1 |  |  |  |  | 7 | Not Stated |  |
| Nantucket | 8 | 8 | Brown | James |  |  |  | 1 |  |  |  | 1 | 1 |  |  |  | 3 | Not Stated |  |
| Nantucket | 8 | 9 | Worth | Francis |  | 2 |  |  | 1 | 1 | 1 | 1 | 1 |  |  |  | 7 | Not Stated |  |
| Nantucket | 8 | 10 | Cathcart | Jonathan | 1 |  |  | 1 |  | 2 |  |  | 1 |  |  |  | 5 | Not Stated |  |
| Nantucket | 8 | 11 | cash | Wheelden |  |  |  | 1 |  |  |  |  | 1 |  |  |  | 2 | Not Stated |  |
| Nantucket | 8 | 12 | Snow | James | 1 |  |  | 1 |  | 3 |  |  | 1 |  |  |  | 6 | Not Stated |  |
| Nantucket | 8 | 13 | Swain | Ebenezer |  |  | 3 |  | 1 |  |  |  | 1 | 1 |  |  | 6 | Not Stated |  |
| Nantucket | 8 | 14 | West | Stephen |  |  |  | 1 |  |  |  |  | 1 |  |  |  | 2 | Not Stated |  |
| Nantucket | 8 | 15 | Kellog | Seth | 1 |  |  | 1 |  |  |  |  | 1 |  |  |  | 3 | Not Stated |  |
| Nantucket | 8 | 16 | Perry | William | 1 |  |  | 1 |  | 1 |  |  | 1 |  |  |  | 4 | Not Stated |  |
| Nantucket | 8 | 17 | Williams | Anna |  |  |  |  |  |  |  |  |  | 1 |  |  | 1 | Not Stated |  |
| Nantucket | 8 | 18 | Wyer | Zaccariah |  |  |  | 1 |  |  |  |  | 1 | 1 |  |  | 3 | Not Stated |  |
| Nantucket | 8 | 19 | Chadwick | Wickliff | 1 | 1 | 3 | 2 | 1 |  | 1 | 3 |  | 1 |  |  | 13 | Not Stated |  |
| Nantucket | 8 | 20 | Bunker | Nathaniel | 5 | 2 | 1 |  |  |  |  | 1 | 1 |  |  |  | 11 | Not Stated |  |
| Nantucket | 8 | 21 | Myrick | Sarah |  | 1 | 3 | 1 |  | 1 |  |  |  | 1 |  |  | 7 | Not Stated |  |
| Nantucket | 8 | 22 | Harris | Lydia |  |  |  |  |  |  |  |  | 1 |  |  |  | 1 | Not Stated |  |
| Nantucket | 8 | 23 | Russell | Silvanus | 1 |  |  | 1 | 1 |  |  | 1 |  | 1 |  |  | 5 | Not Stated |  |
| Nantucket | 8 | 24 | Wilson | Abigail |  |  |  |  |  | 2 |  |  | 1 |  |  |  | 3 | Not Stated |  |
| Nantucket | 8 | 25 | Stretton | Obed |  |  | 1 |  |  |  |  |  | 1 |  |  |  | 2 | Not Stated |  |
| Nantucket | 8 | 26 | Russell | Reuben |  |  | 2 | 1 |  |  | 1 | 2 | 1 |  |  |  | 7 | Not Stated |  |
| Nantucket | 8 | 27 | Swain | Timothy Junr | 1 |  |  | 1 |  | 2 |  |  | 1 |  |  |  | 5 | Not Stated |  |
| Nantucket | 8 | 28 | Gardner | Abigail |  |  |  |  |  |  |  |  | 1 | 1 |  |  | 2 | Not Stated |  |
| Nantucket | 8 | 29 | Swain | Timothy |  |  | 1 | 1 |  |  |  |  | 1 | 1 |  |  | 4 | Not Stated |  |
| Nantucket | 8 | 30 | Ellis | Elisha Junr | 1 |  |  | 1 |  | 2 |  |  | 1 |  |  |  | 5 | Not Stated |  |
| Nantucket | 8 | 31 | Whippy | Davis | 1 |  |  | 1 |  | 2 |  | 2 |  |  |  |  | 6 | Not Stated |  |
| Nantucket | 8 | 32 | Worth | Shubael | 1 | 1 |  | 1 |  |  |  | 1 |  |  |  |  | 4 | Not Stated |  |
| Nantucket | 8 | 33 | Worth | Richard | 2 |  |  | 1 |  | 1 |  |  | 1 |  |  |  | 5 | Not Stated |  |
| Nantucket | 8 | 34 | Cathcart | Joseph | 1 | 3 | 2 | 1 |  |  |  |  |  | 1 |  |  | 8 | Not Stated |  |
| Nantucket | 8 | 35 | Swain | Franklin |  |  |  | 1 |  | 2 |  |  | 1 |  |  |  | 4 | Not Stated |  |
| Nantucket | 8 | 36 | Wyer | David | 1 |  |  | 1 |  | 2 |  |  | 1 |  |  |  | 5 | Not Stated |  |
| Nantucket | 8 | 37 | Wyer | William |  |  | 1 | 1 |  |  |  |  |  | 1 |  |  | 3 | Not Stated |  |
| Nantucket | 8 | 38 | Worth | George | 2 |  |  | 1 |  | 1 |  |  | 1 |  |  |  | 5 | Not Stated |  |
| Nantucket | 8 | 39 | Smith | Solomon | 2 |  | 2 | 1 | 1 | 1 |  |  | 1 |  |  |  | 8 | Not Stated |  |
| Nantucket | 8 | 40 | Ellis | Francis | 1 |  | 1 | 1 |  |  |  | 2 |  | 1 |  |  | 6 | Not Stated |  |
| Nantucket | 8 | 41 | Perkins | William | 1 |  |  | 1 |  | 2 | 1 |  | 1 |  |  |  | 6 | Not Stated |  |
| Nantucket | 8 | 42 | Stretton | Naomi |  |  |  |  |  |  |  |  |  | 1 |  |  | 1 | Not Stated |  |
| Nantucket | 8 | 43 | Higgins | Sabra |  |  |  |  |  |  |  |  | 1 |  |  |  | 1 | Not Stated |  |
| Nantucket | 8 | 44 | Ellis | Raymond | 2 |  |  | 1 |  |  |  | 1 |  |  |  |  | 4 | Not Stated |  |
| Nantucket | 8 | 45 | Alby | Mary |  |  |  |  |  |  |  |  | 1 |  |  |  | 1 | Not Stated |  |
| Nantucket | 8 | 46 | Coleman | Jeremiah |  |  |  |  | 1 |  |  |  | 1 | 1 |  |  | 3 | Not Stated |  |
| Nantucket | 8 | 47 | Coleman | Jonathan |  |  | 1 | 1 |  |  |  |  |  | 1 |  |  | 3 | Not Stated |  |
| Nantucket | 8 | 48 | Coleman | David 2nd |  |  |  | 2 |  | 2 | 1 |  | 1 |  |  |  | 6 | Not Stated |  |
| Nantucket | 8 | 49 | Swain | Jonathan 2nd |  | 1 |  | 1 |  |  |  | 1 |  | 2 |  |  | 5 | Not Stated |  |
| Nantucket | 8 | 50 | Slade | Benjn |  | 1 | 1 |  | 1 | 1 | 1 |  | 1 |  |  |  | 6 | Not Stated |  |
| Nantucket | 8 | 51 | Coffin | Asa |  |  |  | 1 |  |  |  | 1 | 1 |  |  |  | 3 | Not Stated |  |
| Nantucket | 8 | 52 | Russell | Charles | 3 |  |  | 1 |  |  |  | 1 | 1 |  | 1 |  | 7 | Not Stated |  |
| Nantucket | 8 | 53 | Burgess | Ebenezer |  | 1 |  |  |  |  |  | 1 | 1 |  |  |  | 3 | Not Stated |  |
| Nantucket | 8 | 54 | Coffin | Francis | 1 |  |  | 1 |  |  |  |  | 1 |  |  |  | 3 | Not Stated |  |
| Nantucket | 8 | 55 | Worth | David | 1 |  |  | 1 |  |  |  |  |  | 2 |  |  | 4 | Not Stated |  |
| Nantucket | 8 | 56 | Burnell | Jemima |  | 1 |  |  |  |  |  | 3 | 1 | 1 |  |  | 6 | Not Stated |  |
| Nantucket | 8 | 57 | Wyer | Obed | 2 |  |  | 1 |  |  |  |  | 1 |  |  |  | 5 | Not Stated |  |
| Nantucket | 8 | 58 | Clark | William 3rd |  | 1 |  | 1 |  | 1 | 1 | 1 |  |  |  |  | 5 | Not Stated |  |
| Nantucket | 9 | 1 | Coffin | Ephraim | 2 |  |  | 2 | 1 | 1 |  |  | 1 | 1 |  |  | 8 | Not Stated |  |
| Nantucket | 9 | 2 | Meader | Nicholas | 3 | 1 | 2 |  | 1 |  |  | 2 | 1 | 1 |  |  | 11 | Not Stated |  |
| Nantucket | 9 | 3 | Smith | Armstrong | 3 |  |  | 1 |  |  |  | 1 |  | 1 |  |  | 6 | Not Stated |  |
| Nantucket | 9 | 4 | Butler | Mary |  |  |  |  |  |  |  |  | 1 | 1 |  |  | 2 | Not Stated |  |
| Nantucket | 9 | 5 | Sandford | Samuel | 3 |  |  | 1 |  | 3 | 1 |  |  | 2 |  |  | 9 | Not Stated |  |
| Nantucket | 9 | 6 | Coffin | Abigail |  |  |  |  |  |  |  |  |  | 2 |  |  | 2 | Not Stated |  |
| Nantucket | 9 | 7 | Chase | George | 2 | 1 |  | 1 |  | 3 |  |  | 1 |  |  |  | 8 | Not Stated |  |
| Nantucket | 9 | 8 | Chase | Charles Junr | 3 |  |  | 1 |  | 2 |  |  | 1 |  |  |  | 7 | Not Stated |  |

# 1800 Nantucket, Nantucket County, Massachusetts

| TOWN | PG# | LN# | LAST NAME | FIRST NAME | FREE WHITE MALES under 10 | 10 to 16 | 16 to 26 | 26 to 45 | 45 and over | FREE WHITE FEMALES under 10 | 10 to 16 | 16 to 26 | 26 to 45 | 45 and over | TOTAL ALL OTHER | TOTAL SLAVES | TOTALS | DISTRICT/ TOWNSHIP | NOTES |
|---|---|---|---|---|---|---|---|---|---|---|---|---|---|---|---|---|---|---|---|
| Nantucket | 9 | 9 | Coffin | Daniel | 3 | | | 1 | | 1 | 1 | | 1 | | | | 7 | Not Stated | |
| Nantucket | 9 | 10 | Gardner | Apphia | | | 3 | | | | 1 | | | 1 | | | 5 | Not Stated | |
| Nantucket | 9 | 11 | Coleman | Prince | | 1 | | 1 | | | 1 | | 1 | | | | 4 | Not Stated | |
| Nantucket | 9 | 12 | Folger | Clement | | | | 1 | | | | 1 | | | | | 2 | Not Stated | |
| Nantucket | 9 | 13 | Ray | Enoch | | | 2 | 1 | | | | | | 1 | | | 4 | Not Stated | |
| Nantucket | 9 | 14 | Folger | Elisha | 1 | 1 | 1 | 1 | | 1 | | 3 | | 1 | | | 9 | Not Stated | |
| Nantucket | 9 | 15 | Folger | David Junr | | 1 | 1 | 1 | | 2 | | | 2 | | | | 7 | Not Stated | |
| Nantucket | 9 | 16 | Coffin | Andrew | | | | 1 | | | | 1 | | | | | 2 | Not Stated | |
| Nantucket | 9 | 17 | Barnard | Nathl | | | 1 | 2 | 1 | | | | | 1 | | | 5 | Not Stated | |
| Nantucket | 9 | 18 | Barnard | Christopher | | | 1 | | | | | | 1 | | | | 2 | Not Stated | |
| Nantucket | 9 | 19 | Folger | Elisha Junr | | | | 1 | | | | | 1 | | | | 2 | Not Stated | |
| Nantucket | 9 | 20 | Folger | Elisha | 3 | | | 1 | | | | | 1 | | | | 5 | Not Stated | |
| Nantucket | 9 | 21 | Barney | Daniel | 2 | 1 | | 1 | | 1 | | 1 | 2 | 1 | | | 9 | Not Stated | |
| Nantucket | 9 | 22 | Russell | Seth | 1 | 1 | 1 | | 1 | 2 | 1 | | | 1 | | | 8 | Not Stated | |
| Nantucket | 9 | 23 | Caswell | Levi | | 1 | | 1 | | 1 | | | | 1 | | | 4 | Not Stated | |
| Nantucket | 9 | 24 | Silver | John | 1 | | 1 | | | 1 | | 1 | | | | | 4 | Not Stated | |
| Nantucket | 9 | 25 | Christian | Peter | 2 | | 1 | | | | | 1 | | | | | 4 | Not Stated | |
| Nantucket | 9 | 26 | Swain | Job | 1 | 1 | 1 | 1 | | | 2 | | 1 | | | | 7 | Not Stated | |
| Nantucket | 9 | 27 | Coffin | Bartlett | 1 | | | 1 | | 2 | 1 | | 1 | | | | 6 | Not Stated | |
| Nantucket | 9 | 28 | Russell | Hephzibah | | | | | | | | | 1 | | | | 1 | Not Stated | |
| Nantucket | 9 | 29 | Smith | Job Junr | 2 | | 1 | 1 | | 1 | 1 | | 1 | | | | 7 | Not Stated | |
| Nantucket | 9 | 30 | Coleman | Francis | | 1 | 1 | | | | | 1 | 3 | 1 | | | 7 | Not Stated | |
| Nantucket | 9 | 31 | Allen | Abigail | | 1 | | | | 1 | 1 | 1 | 1 | 1 | | | 6 | Not Stated | |
| Nantucket | 9 | 32 | Allen | Joseph | | | 1 | | | 2 | | 1 | | | | | 4 | Not Stated | |
| Nantucket | 9 | 33 | Coffin | Seth | | 1 | 1 | 1 | | | | | 1 | | | | 4 | Not Stated | |
| Nantucket | 9 | 34 | Gifford | Luthern | | | | 1 | | 1 | | | 1 | | | | 3 | Not Stated | |
| Nantucket | 9 | 35 | Gardner | Crispus | | | 1 | 1 | | | | 3 | | 1 | | | 6 | Not Stated | |
| Nantucket | 9 | 36 | Irish | Thomas | 1 | | 1 | | | | | | 1 | | | | 3 | Not Stated | |
| Nantucket | 9 | 37 | Whiters | James | | 3 | 1 | 1 | | | | 2 | | 1 | | | 8 | Not Stated | |
| Nantucket | 9 | 38 | Swain | Mercy | | | | | | | 1 | | 1 | | | | 2 | Not Stated | |
| Nantucket | 9 | 39 | Coffin | David | 1 | | 1 | | | | | 1 | | | | | 3 | Not Stated | |
| Nantucket | 9 | 40 | Swain | Elizabeth 3 | | | 2 | | | | | | | 1 | | | 3 | Not Stated | |
| Nantucket | 9 | 41 | Swain | Grafton | 3 | 1 | | 1 | | | 1 | | 1 | | | | 7 | Not Stated | |
| Nantucket | 9 | 42 | Ellis | Deborah | | 1 | | | | 1 | | 1 | 1 | | | | 4 | Not Stated | |
| Nantucket | 9 | 43 | Swain | James | 2 | 1 | | 1 | | 1 | | | 1 | | | | 6 | Not Stated | |
| Nantucket | 9 | 44 | Austin | Benjamin Junr | 2 | | | 1 | | 2 | 1 | | 1 | | | | 7 | Not Stated | |
| Nantucket | 9 | 45 | Coffin | Jonathan 2nd | | 1 | 1 | 1 | | 1 | | 2 | 1 | | | | 7 | Not Stated | |
| Nantucket | 9 | 46 | Coffin | Thomas | | 1 | | 1 | 1 | | | | | 1 | | | 4 | Not Stated | |
| Nantucket | 9 | 47 | Coffin | Francis | 1 | | | | | | | 1 | | | | | 3 | Not Stated | |
| Nantucket | 9 | 48 | Clisby | William | | 2 | 1 | 1 | | | | 2 | 1 | | | | 7 | Not Stated | |
| Nantucket | 9 | 49 | Fitch | Beriah | 1 | | 1 | 1 | | 1 | 1 | 1 | | | | | 6 | Not Stated | |
| Nantucket | 9 | 50 | Brown | John | 1 | | | 1 | | 2 | 1 | | 1 | | | | 6 | Not Stated | |
| Nantucket | 9 | 51 | Pollard | Peter | 2 | | | 1 | | 2 | 1 | | 1 | | | | 7 | Not Stated | |
| Nantucket | 9 | 52 | Barnard Orpin | John | 1 | | 1 | | | 1 | | 1 | | | | | 4 | Not Stated | |
| Nantucket | 9 | 53 | Andrews | Jacob | 2 | | 1 | | | | | 1 | | | | | 4 | Not Stated | |
| Nantucket | 9 | 54 | Gardner | Silvanus | 1 | | 2 | 1 | | | | 1 | | | | | 5 | Not Stated | |
| Nantucket | 9 | 55 | Wotton | William | | | 1 | | | | | 1 | 1 | | | | 3 | Not Stated | |
| Nantucket | 9 | 56 | Pinkham | Jethro | | 1 | 1 | 1 | | 1 | | 2 | 1 | | | | 7 | Not Stated | |
| Nantucket | 9 | 57 | Coffin | Benjamin | | 1 | 1 | 1 | | | 2 | 2 | | 1 | | | 8 | Not Stated | |
| Nantucket | 9 | 58 | Folger | Simeon | 1 | | | 1 | | | 2 | 1 | | | | | 5 | Not Stated | |
| Nantucket | 10 | 1 | Coffin | Miriam | | | | | | | | | | 1 | | | 1 | Not Stated | |
| Nantucket | 10 | 2 | Pitts | Obed | 3 | | 1 | | | 1 | | 1 | | | | | 6 | Not Stated | |
| Nantucket | 10 | 3 | Swain | Christopher | | | 1 | | | | 2 | | 1 | | | | 4 | Not Stated | |
| Nantucket | 10 | 4 | Bennett | William | 1 | | 1 | | | | | 1 | | | | | 3 | Not Stated | |
| Nantucket | 10 | 5 | Ellis | Phebe | | | | | 1 | | | 1 | | | | | 2 | Not Stated | |
| Nantucket | 10 | 6 | Hussey | Reuben | | 1 | | 1 | 1 | 1 | 2 | | 1 | | | | 7 | Not Stated | |
| Nantucket | 10 | 7 | Macy | Abigail | | | | | | | | | 1 | | | | 1 | Not Stated | |
| Nantucket | 10 | 8 | Brown | Elizabeth | | | | | | | | | 1 | | | | 1 | Not Stated | |
| Nantucket | 10 | 9 | Worth | Miriam | | | | | | | | | 1 | | | | 1 | Not Stated | |
| Nantucket | 10 | 10 | Coffin | Paul | 1 | | | 1 | | | | 2 | 1 | | | | 5 | Not Stated | |
| Nantucket | 10 | 11 | Allen | David | 4 | 1 | | 2 | | | 1 | 1 | 1 | | | | 10 | Not Stated | |
| Nantucket | 10 | 12 | Folger | Mary | | | | | | | | | 1 | | | | 1 | Not Stated | |
| Nantucket | 10 | 13 | Johnson | Daniel | | | | 1 | | | | | | | | | 1 | Not Stated | |
| Nantucket | 10 | 14 | Cleveland | Lydia | | | 1 | 1 | | | | 2 | | | | | 4 | Not Stated | |
| Nantucket | 10 | 15 | Paul | Phebe | | 1 | | 2 | | 2 | 1 | | | | | | 6 | Not Stated | |
| Nantucket | 10 | 16 | Hull | Phebe | | 1 | | 2 | | 1 | 1 | 1 | | | | | 6 | Not Stated | |
| Nantucket | 10 | 17 | Gardner | Jonathan | | | | 1 | | | | 1 | | | | | 2 | Not Stated | |
| Nantucket | 10 | 18 | Barney | Matthew | 1 | | 1 | 1 | | 3 | | | 1 | | | | 7 | Not Stated | |
| Nantucket | 10 | 19 | Macy | George | | | 1 | | | | | 1 | | | | | 2 | Not Stated | |
| Nantucket | 10 | 20 | Gardner | Jared | 1 | 1 | | | | | 1 | | | | | | 3 | Not Stated | |
| Nantucket | 10 | 21 | Folger | Walter Junr | 3 | 1 | | 1 | | 2 | | 1 | | | | | 8 | Not Stated | |
| Nantucket | 10 | 22 | Coleman | Reuben | | | | 1 | | | | | 1 | | | | 2 | Not Stated | |
| Nantucket | 10 | 23 | Russell | Simeon | | 1 | | 1 | | 1 | | 1 | | | | | 4 | Not Stated | |
| Nantucket | 10 | 24 | Allen | Edwd | | 1 | | 1 | | | | | 1 | | | | 3 | Not Stated | |
| Nantucket | 10 | 25 | Parker | Elizabeth | 1 | | | | | | | 1 | 1 | | | | 3 | Not Stated | |
| Nantucket | 10 | 26 | Gardner | Alexander | 1 | 1 | 1 | | | 4 | 1 | | 1 | | | | 9 | Not Stated | |
| Nantucket | 10 | 27 | Gardner | Tristram Junr | 1 | | 1 | | | | | 1 | | | | | 3 | Not Stated | |
| Nantucket | 10 | 28 | Clark | Thaddeus | 2 | | 1 | | | | | | 1 | | | | 4 | Not Stated | |
| Nantucket | 10 | 29 | Shaw | John | 1 | | 1 | 2 | | | | 1 | | | | | 5 | Not Stated | |
| Nantucket | 10 | 30 | Gardner | Abigail | | | | | | | | | 1 | | | | 1 | Not Stated | |
| Nantucket | 10 | 31 | Bunker | Uriah Junr | 2 | | | 1 | | | | 1 | | | | | 4 | Not Stated | |
| Nantucket | 10 | 32 | Swain | Susanna | | | | | | | | 1 | 1 | | | | 2 | Not Stated | |
| Nantucket | 10 | 33 | Coffin | Joseph 2nd | | 1 | 1 | 1 | | | 1 | | 1 | | | | 5 | Not Stated | |
| Nantucket | 10 | 34 | Paddack | Barnabas | | 1 | | 1 | | | | 1 | | | | | 3 | Not Stated | |
| Nantucket | 10 | 35 | Chase | Joseph | 3 | | 1 | 2 | | 1 | 2 | 1 | | 1 | | | 11 | Not Stated | |
| Nantucket | 10 | 36 | Chase | Joseph Junr | | 1 | | 2 | | 2 | | | | | | | 5 | Not Stated | |
| Nantucket | 10 | 37 | Bunker | Peleg | | | 1 | 1 | | 2 | | 1 | | | | | 5 | Not Stated | |
| Nantucket | 10 | 38 | Paddack | Peter | 1 | | 1 | 1 | | 1 | | | | | | | 4 | Not Stated | |
| Nantucket | 10 | 39 | Folger | Richard | | 1 | | | | | 1 | | | | | | 2 | Not Stated | |
| Nantucket | 10 | 40 | Bunker | Christopher Jr | 1 | 1 | | 1 | | | 1 | | 2 | | | | 6 | Not Stated | |

| TOWN | PG# | LN# | LAST NAME | FIRST NAME | M u10 | M 10-16 | M 16-26 | M 26-45 | M 45+ | F u10 | F 10-16 | F 16-26 | F 26-45 | F 45+ | TOTAL ALL OTHER | TOTAL SLAVES | TOTALS | DISTRICT/ TOWNSHIP |
|---|---|---|---|---|---|---|---|---|---|---|---|---|---|---|---|---|---|---|
| Nantucket | 10 | 41 | Russell | Joseph | | 1 | 2 | | 1 | 1 | | 2 | 1 | | | | 8 | Not Stated |
| Nantucket | 10 | 42 | Mitchell | Elizabeth | | | | | | | | | 1 | | | | 1 | Not Stated |
| Nantucket | 10 | 43 | Bunker | Charles | | | 2 | | 1 | | | | 1 | 1 | | | 5 | Not Stated |
| Nantucket | 10 | 44 | Ray | Nathl | 2 | | | 1 | | | | 1 | | | | | 4 | Not Stated |
| Nantucket | 10 | 45 | Coffin | Zenas | | 1 | | 1 | | 2 | 1 | | 1 | | | | 6 | Not Stated |
| Nantucket | 10 | 46 | Coffin | Micajah | | | | 1 | | | | | | 1 | | | 2 | Not Stated |
| Nantucket | 10 | 47 | Coffin | Jonathan | | | 2 | | 1 | | | 1 | | 1 | | | 5 | Not Stated |
| Nantucket | 10 | 48 | Coffin | Isaiah | 2 | 1 | 2 | | 1 | 1 | | | 2 | | | | 9 | Not Stated |
| Nantucket | 10 | 49 | Macy | Elisha | | 1 | 1 | | | | | | 1 | 1 | | | 5 | Not Stated |
| Nantucket | 10 | 50 | Dunham | Jethro | 1 | | | | 1 | 1 | | | | 1 | | | 6 | Not Stated |
| Nantucket | 10 | 51 | Coffin | Reuben | | | | | 1 | | | | | 1 | | | 2 | Not Stated |
| Nantucket | 10 | 52 | Coffin | Benjamin 3rd | 1 | | 1 | | | | | | 1 | | | | 3 | Not Stated |
| Nantucket | 10 | 53 | Coffin | Solomon | | 2 | 1 | | 1 | 1 | 1 | | | 1 | | | 7 | Not Stated |
| Nantucket | 10 | 54 | Ramsdell | William | | 2 | 1 | | | | | | | 1 | | | 4 | Not Stated |
| Nantucket | 10 | 55 | Coffin | John | 2 | 1 | | 1 | | 1 | 1 | 3 | | 1 | | | 10 | Not Stated |
| Nantucket | 10 | 56 | Mayo | Rachel | | 1 | | | | | | | 1 | 1 | | | 3 | Not Stated |
| Nantucket | 10 | 57 | Starbuck | Levi | 2 | | | 1 | | 1 | | | 1 | | | | 5 | Not Stated |
| Nantucket | 10 | 58 | Calder | Josiah | 2 | | | 1 | | | | 2 | 1 | | | | 6 | Not Stated |
| Nantucket | 10 | 59 | Mooers | Abigail | | | | | | | | | | 1 | | | 1 | Not Stated |
| Nantucket | 11 | 1 | Swain | Hannah | | | | | | | | | 1 | 2 | | | 3 | Not Stated |
| Nantucket | 11 | 2 | Folger | John | | | | 2 | | | | | | 1 | | | 3 | Not Stated |
| Nantucket | 11 | 3 | Jenkins | Lydia | | | | | | | | | | 1 | | | 1 | Not Stated |
| Nantucket | 11 | 4 | Macy | Job Junr | 2 | | 1 | | | 1 | | | 1 | | | | 5 | Not Stated |
| Nantucket | 11 | 5 | Macy | Stephen | 1 | | 1 | 1 | | | | | | 1 | | | 4 | Not Stated |
| Nantucket | 11 | 6 | Macy | Job | 1 | | 1 | | | 2 | | | 1 | | | | 5 | Not Stated |
| Nantucket | 11 | 7 | Way | Lydia | | | | | | | | | | 1 | | | 1 | Not Stated |
| Nantucket | 11 | 8 | Macy | Shubael | | 1 | | 1 | | | 1 | 2 | 2 | 1 | | | 8 | Not Stated |
| Nantucket | 11 | 9 | Bunker | Moses | | | 1 | | | 1 | | | 1 | | | | 3 | Not Stated |
| Nantucket | 11 | 10 | Russell | Silvanus Junr | | 1 | | | | 2 | | 1 | | | | | 4 | Not Stated |
| Nantucket | 11 | 11 | Coffin | Hannah | | | | | | | | | 1 | | 1 | | 2 | Not Stated |
| Nantucket | 11 | 12 | Cartwright | James | | 1 | | 1 | | | | | 1 | | | | 3 | Not Stated |
| Nantucket | 11 | 13 | Barnard | Henry | 1 | | | 1 | | | | | 1 | | | | 3 | Not Stated |
| Nantucket | 11 | 14 | Thurston | Job | | | | 1 | | | | | 1 | | | | 2 | Not Stated |
| Nantucket | 11 | 15 | Swain | Tristram | 1 | 1 | 1 | | 1 | 1 | | 2 | | 1 | | | 9 | Not Stated |
| Nantucket | 11 | 16 | Morris | Jonathan | | | 2 | 1 | | | 1 | | 1 | | | | 5 | Not Stated |
| Nantucket | 11 | 17 | Morris | Jacob | 1 | | | 1 | | 1 | | | | 1 | | | 4 | Not Stated |
| Nantucket | 11 | 18 | Swain | Silas | | | 1 | | | 2 | | | 1 | | | | 4 | Not Stated |
| Nantucket | 11 | 19 | Joy | Reuben | 3 | | | 1 | | 2 | | | 1 | 1 | | | 8 | Not Stated |
| Nantucket | 11 | 20 | Swain | Rebecca | | 1 | 1 | | | | | | 3 | 1 | | | 6 | Not Stated |
| Nantucket | 11 | 21 | Marshall | William | | 1 | | | | | | | 1 | | | | 2 | Not Stated |
| Nantucket | 11 | 22 | Macy | Peter | 1 | 1 | | 1 | | 1 | | 1 | 1 | | | | 6 | Not Stated |
| Nantucket | 11 | 23 | Long | Jonathan | | | | 1 | | | | | | 1 | | | 2 | Not Stated |
| Nantucket | 11 | 24 | Russell | Nathaniel | | 1 | 1 | | 1 | | 1 | 1 | | 1 | 1 | | 7 | Not Stated |
| Nantucket | 11 | 25 | Russell | Fanna | 1 | | | | | | 1 | | 1 | | | | 3 | Not Stated |
| Nantucket | 11 | 26 | Coffin | Charles | | 1 | 2 | 1 | | | 1 | | 1 | | | | 6 | Not Stated |
| Nantucket | 11 | 27 | Bunker | George | | 1 | | 1 | | | | 2 | | 1 | | | 5 | Not Stated |
| Nantucket | 11 | 28 | Coffin | Paul Junr | 1 | 1 | | | | 1 | | | | | | | 3 | Not Stated |
| Nantucket | 11 | 29 | Whippy | Benjamin | | 1 | 2 | 1 | | 1 | | 2 | | 1 | | | 9 | Not Stated |
| Nantucket | 11 | 30 | Coffin | Isaac | 1 | 2 | | 1 | | 3 | 1 | | 1 | | | | 9 | Not Stated |
| Nantucket | 11 | 31 | Starbuck | Deborah | | | | | | | | | 1 | 1 | | | 2 | Not Stated |
| Nantucket | 11 | 32 | Macy | Jonathan | 3 | | 1 | | 1 | | 1 | 1 | 1 | 1 | 1 | | 9 | Not Stated |
| Nantucket | 11 | 33 | Coffin | Thomas Junr | 1 | | | 1 | | 3 | 1 | | 2 | | | | 8 | Not Stated |
| Nantucket | 11 | 34 | Folger | William | | | | 1 | | | | | 1 | | | | 2 | Not Stated |
| Nantucket | 11 | 35 | Folger | William Junr | | | | 1 | | 2 | | 1 | 1 | | | | 5 | Not Stated |
| Nantucket | 11 | 36 | Nye | Nathan | | 1 | 1 | | | | | | 1 | | | | 3 | Not Stated |
| Nantucket | 11 | 37 | Folger | Aaron | 1 | | 1 | | | | | 2 | | 1 | | | 5 | Not Stated |
| Nantucket | 11 | 38 | Gardner | Elizabeth | | 2 | | | | | 1 | 1 | 1 | | | | 5 | Not Stated |
| Nantucket | 11 | 39 | Coffin | Elizabeth | | | | | | | | | 1 | 1 | | | 2 | Not Stated |
| Nantucket | 11 | 40 | Swain | Moses | 3 | | | 1 | | 1 | | | | 1 | | | 6 | Not Stated |
| Nantucket | 11 | 41 | Parker | Silas | | 1 | | 1 | | | | | 1 | 1 | | | 4 | Not Stated |
| Nantucket | 11 | 42 | Hern | Elizabeth | | | | | | 1 | | | | 1 | | | 2 | Not Stated |
| Nantucket | 11 | 43 | Elkins | Joseph | 1 | | 1 | | | | | 1 | | | | | 3 | Not Stated |
| Nantucket | 11 | 44 | Paddack | Jonathan | 3 | | | 1 | | 3 | | | 1 | | | | 8 | Not Stated |
| Nantucket | 11 | 45 | Coleman | Silas | 2 | | | 1 | | 1 | | | 1 | | | | 5 | Not Stated |
| Nantucket | 11 | 46 | Chase | William | | | | 1 | | 1 | | | 1 | | | | 3 | Not Stated |
| Nantucket | 11 | 47 | Bunker | Mary | | | | | | 2 | | 1 | | | | | 3 | Not Stated |
| Nantucket | 11 | 48 | Gardner | Latham | | 2 | 1 | 1 | | | | | 2 | 1 | 1 | | 8 | Not Stated |
| Nantucket | 11 | 49 | Gardner | Anna | | | | | | | 1 | | | 1 | | | 2 | Not Stated |
| Nantucket | 11 | 50 | Barnard | Thomas | 1 | | | 1 | | 1 | | | 1 | | | | 4 | Not Stated |
| Nantucket | 11 | 51 | Folger | Reuben | | | | | 1 | | | | 1 | 1 | | | 3 | Not Stated |
| Nantucket | 11 | 52 | Gurrel | John | | | | 1 | | 2 | | | 1 | | | | 5 | Not Stated |
| Nantucket | 11 | 53 | Russell | George | 1 | 1 | | | 1 | | | 1 | | 1 | | | 5 | Not Stated |
| Nantucket | 11 | 54 | Riddell | Saml | 1 | | 1 | 1 | 1 | 2 | 1 | | | 1 | 1 | | 9 | Not Stated |
| Nantucket | 11 | 55 | Pinkham | Uriah | | 1 | | 1 | | | | 2 | 1 | | | | 5 | Not Stated |
| Nantucket | 11 | 56 | Pinkham | Peleg | | | | 1 | | | | | | 1 | | | 2 | Not Stated |
| Nantucket | 11 | 57 | Black | Patty | | | | | | | | | 1 | | | | 1 | Not Stated |
| Nantucket | 11 | 58 | Glover | Lydia | | | | | | 1 | 1 | | 1 | 1 | | | 4 | Not Stated |
| Nantucket | 11 | 59 | Black | Daniel | | | | | 1 | | | | 1 | 1 | | | 3 | Not Stated |
| Nantucket | 12 | 1 | Flag | Benjamin | | | 1 | | | | | | 1 | | | | 2 | Not Stated |
| Nantucket | 12 | 2 | Coffin | Robert | | | 1 | | | | | 1 | 1 | | | | 3 | Not Stated |
| Nantucket | 12 | 3 | Black | Cleophas | 1 | | 1 | | | | | | 1 | | | | 3 | Not Stated |
| Nantucket | 12 | 4 | Ray | George | | | | 1 | | | | | | 1 | | | 2 | Not Stated |
| Nantucket | 12 | 5 | Swain | Hows | | | 1 | | | 1 | | | 1 | | | | 3 | Not Stated |
| Nantucket | 12 | 6 | Ray | John | 2 | 2 | | 1 | | | | | | 1 | | | 6 | Not Stated |
| Nantucket | 12 | 7 | Hull | Thomas | | | 1 | | | | | | 1 | | | | 2 | Not Stated |
| Nantucket | 12 | 8 | Annis | Stephen | 1 | | 1 | 1 | | 4 | | | 1 | | | | 8 | Not Stated |
| Nantucket | 12 | 9 | James | Bejamin 2nd | | | 1 | | | 1 | | | 1 | | | | 3 | Not Stated |
| Nantucket | 12 | 10 | Skinner | Mary | | | 2 | | | | | | | 1 | | | 3 | Not Stated |
| Nantucket | 12 | 11 | Watson | Elizabeth | 1 | | | | | | | | 1 | | | | 3 | Not Stated |
| Nantucket | 12 | 12 | Macy | Nathl | | | 3 | 1 | | 1 | | 1 | 1 | | | | 7 | Not Stated |

# 1800 Nantucket, Nantucket County, Massachusetts

| TOWN | PG# | LN# | LAST NAME | FIRST NAME | FREE WHITE MALES | | | | | FREE WHITE FEMALES | | | | | TOTAL ALL OTHER | TOTAL SLAVES | TOTALS | DISTRICT/ TOWNSHIP | NOTES |
|---|---|---|---|---|---|---|---|---|---|---|---|---|---|---|---|---|---|---|---|
| | | | | | under 10 | 10 to 16 | 16 to 26 | 26 to 45 | 45 and over | under 10 | 10 to 16 | 16 to 26 | 26 to 45 | 45 and over | | | | | |
| Nantucket | 12 | 13 | House | John | 2 | 1 | 1 | | 1 | 3 | | 2 | | 1 | | | 11 | Not Stated | |
| Nantucket | 12 | 14 | Barnes | William | 1 | | 1 | | | | | 1 | | | | | 3 | Not Stated | |
| Nantucket | 12 | 15 | Arpin | Issac | | | 1 | | | 1 | | 1 | | | | | 3 | Not Stated | |
| Nantucket | 12 | 16 | Rice | Phebe | | | | | | | | | 1 | | | | 1 | Not Stated | |
| Nantucket | 12 | 17 | Briggs | Stephen | | | 1 | 1 | | | | 1 | 1 | | | | 4 | Not Stated | |
| Nantucket | 12 | 18 | Folger | Timothy Junr | 3 | | | 1 | | | 1 | 1 | 1 | | | | 7 | Not Stated | |
| Nantucket | 12 | 19 | Hammatt | John | 1 | | 1 | | | 1 | | 2 | | | | | 5 | Not Stated | |
| Nantucket | 12 | 20 | Cary | Edward | | 2 | 1 | | 1 | | 1 | 1 | | 1 | 3 | | 10 | Not Stated | |
| Nantucket | 12 | 21 | Cary | Samuel | 2 | | | 1 | | 1 | | | | | | | 4 | Not Stated | |
| Nantucket | 12 | 22 | Coggeshall | Peleg | | | | 1 | | | 1 | | 1 | | | | 3 | Not Stated | |
| Nantucket | 12 | 23 | Ray | William | | | | 1 | | | 1 | | 1 | | | | 3 | Not Stated | |
| Nantucket | 12 | 24 | Raymond | Elisha | 2 | | 1 | 1 | | 1 | | | 1 | | | | 6 | Not Stated | |
| Nantucket | 12 | 25 | Ray | David Junr | 1 | | | 1 | | 2 | | 1 | | | | | 5 | Not Stated | |
| Nantucket | 12 | 26 | Long | Samuel | | 1 | 1 | 1 | | | | | 1 | | | | 4 | Not Stated | |
| Nantucket | 12 | 27 | Newbegin | George | | | 1 | | | 3 | | | 1 | | | | 5 | Not Stated | |
| Nantucket | 12 | 28 | Fairweather | Anna | | | | | | | | | 1 | | | | 1 | Not Stated | |
| Nantucket | 12 | 29 | Pinkham | Jemima | | | | | | | | | 1 | | | | 1 | Not Stated | |
| Nantucket | 12 | 30 | Hulsey | Albert Jr | 1 | | 1 | | | | | 1 | | | | | 3 | | |
| Nantucket | 12 | 31 | Hulsey | Seth Jenkins | | 1 | | | | 2 | | 1 | | | | | 4 | | |
| Nantucket | 12 | 32 | Worth | Elihu | 1 | | 1 | | | | | 1 | | | | | 3 | | |
| Nantucket | 12 | 33 | Townsend | Thomas | | 1 | | | | 3 | | 1 | | | | | 5 | | |
| Nantucket | 12 | 34 | Morton | William | 1 | | | 1 | | | | 1 | | | | | 3 | | |
| Nantucket | 12 | 35 | Sinclair | Abigail | | | | | | | | 1 | 1 | | | | 2 | | |
| Nantucket | 12 | 36 | Morton | Ruth | | | | | | | | | 1 | | | | 1 | | |
| Nantucket | 12 | 37 | Burnell | Polly | 2 | | | | | | | 1 | | | | | 3 | | |
| Nantucket | 12 | 38 | Coleman | Silvanus 2nd | | 2 | | 1 | | | | | 1 | | | | 4 | | |
| Nantucket | 12 | 39 | Coleman | Silvanus 3rd | 1 | | 1 | | | | | 1 | | | | | 3 | | |
| Nantucket | 12 | 40 | Gardner | Abishai | | | 1 | | | | | 1 | | | | | 2 | | |
| Nantucket | 12 | 41 | Chase | Francis | | 3 | 1 | | | 1 | | | 1 | | | | 6 | | |
| Nantucket | 12 | 42 | Hulsey | Naomi | 1 | | | | | | 1 | | 1 | | | | 3 | | |
| Nantucket | 12 | 43 | Coffin | Shuebael 2nd | 1 | | | 1 | 1 | | 1 | 1 | 1 | | | | 6 | | |
| Nantucket | 12 | 44 | Bunker | Desire | | | | | | | | | 2 | | | | 2 | | |
| Nantucket | 12 | 45 | Coffin | Henry | | 1 | | 1 | | | | | 1 | | | | 3 | | |
| Nantucket | 12 | 46 | Coffin | Hannah 2nd | | | | | | 1 | | 1 | | | | | 2 | | |
| Nantucket | 12 | 47 | Fitch | Jonathan Gorham | 1 | 3 | | 1 | | 1 | | | 1 | | | | 7 | | |
| Nantucket | 12 | 48 | Chase | Charles | 1 | | | 1 | | | | 1 | 1 | | | | 4 | | |
| Nantucket | 12 | 49 | Bay | David | | | 1 | | | | | | 1 | | | | 2 | | |
| Nantucket | 12 | 50 | Whippy | Reuben | 1 | | | 1 | | 2 | | | 1 | | | | 5 | | |
| Nantucket | 12 | 51 | Clark | Uriah | 2 | | | 1 | | | | | 1 | | | | 4 | | |
| Nantucket | 12 | 52 | Raymond | Ebenezer | 1 | | | 1 | | 2 | | 2 | | | | | 6 | | |
| Nantucket | 12 | 53 | Baxter | Lydia | | | | | | | 1 | 1 | | | | | 2 | | |
| Nantucket | 12 | 54 | Long | Simeon | | 2 | | 1 | | 2 | 1 | 1 | 1 | | | | 8 | | |
| Nantucket | 12 | 55 | Coffin | Silvanus | | | | 1 | | | 1 | 1 | 1 | | 1 | | 5 | | |
| Nantucket | 12 | 56 | Hiller | Thomas | 2 | | 1 | 1 | | 1 | 2 | 1 | 1 | | | | 9 | | |
| Nantucket | 12 | 57 | Folger | Isaac | 1 | 1 | 2 | 1 | | 1 | | | 1 | | | | 7 | | |
| Nantucket | 12 | 58 | Jackson | Timothy | | | 1 | | | | | | 1 | | | | 2 | | |
| Nantucket | 12 | 59 | Gardner | Ebenezer | 2 | | | 1 | | 2 | 2 | | 1 | | | | 8 | | |
| Nantucket | 12 | 60 | Giles | David W | 2 | | | 1 | | 1 | | | 1 | | | | 5 | | |
| Nantucket | 12 | 61 | Gardner | Ruth | | | | | | | | 1 | 1 | | | | 2 | | |
| Nantucket | 12 | 62 | Kimberlin | Jedida | | | | | | | 1 | | 1 | | | | 2 | | |
| Nantucket | 12 | 63 | Alley | Richard | 1 | 1 | 2 | | 1 | 3 | 3 | 1 | 1 | | | | 13 | | |
| Nantucket | 12 | 64 | Glover | Benjamin | 2 | | | 1 | | 1 | 1 | | 1 | 1 | | | 7 | | |
| Nantucket | 12 | 65 | Swain | Myer | | 1 | | 1 | | 3 | | | 1 | | | | 6 | | |
| Nantucket | 12 | 66 | Wyer | Robert | | 1 | | 1 | | | | 1 | | | | | 3 | | |
| Nantucket | 12 | 67 | Wyer | Owen | 1 | | 1 | | | | | 1 | | | | | 3 | | |
| Nantucket | 13 | 1 | Wyer | Timothy | 1 | | 1 | 1 | | 1 | | 2 | | | | | 6 | | |
| Nantucket | 13 | 2 | Chase | Stephen | 3 | | 1 | | | | | | 1 | | | | 5 | | |
| Nantucket | 13 | 3 | Folger | Seth | | 1 | 1 | | | | | 1 | | | | | 3 | | |
| Nantucket | 13 | 4 | Beard | John | | 1 | 1 | | | | 2 | 1 | | | | | 5 | | |
| Nantucket | 13 | 5 | Coffin | Eliel | 1 | | | 1 | | 2 | | 1 | | | | | 5 | | |
| Nantucket | 13 | 6 | Coffin | Joseph | | | 1 | | | | 1 | 1 | | | | | 3 | | |
| Nantucket | 13 | 7 | Coffin | Matilda | | 1 | 4 | | | | | 1 | | | | | 6 | | |
| Nantucket | 13 | 8 | Coffin | Thaddeus | | 1 | | 1 | | 2 | 1 | 2 | 1 | | | | 8 | | |
| Nantucket | 13 | 9 | Folger | Seth 3rd | 1 | | | 1 | | | | 1 | | | | | 3 | | |
| Nantucket | 13 | 10 | Davis | Joseph | | 1 | | 1 | | | 1 | | | | | | 3 | | |
| Nantucket | 13 | 11 | Myrick | Jonathan Gorham | | | 1 | | | | 1 | 1 | | | | | 3 | | |
| Nantucket | 13 | 12 | Bunker | Joshua | 1 | 1 | 1 | | | | | 1 | | | | | 4 | | |
| Nantucket | 13 | 13 | Myrick | James | | 1 | | | | | | 1 | | | | | 2 | | |
| Nantucket | 13 | 14 | Waterman | Mary | | | | | | | | 2 | | | | | 2 | | |
| Nantucket | 13 | 15 | Waterman | Sarah | 1 | | | | | | | | 1 | | | | 3 | | |
| Nantucket | 13 | 16 | Marshall | Thomas | | 1 | 1 | | | 3 | | 1 | 1 | | | | 7 | | |
| Nantucket | 13 | 17 | Mooers | Lucinda | 1 | | | | | 1 | | | 1 | | | | 3 | | |
| Nantucket | 13 | 18 | Wyer | Obed Junr | | | 1 | | | | | | 1 | | | | 2 | | |
| Nantucket | 13 | 19 | Beard | Elizabeth | 1 | | 1 | | | | | 2 | | | | | 4 | | |
| Nantucket | 13 | 20 | Gardner | Joseph 2nd | | 1 | | | | 1 | | 1 | | | | | 3 | | |
| Nantucket | 13 | 21 | Bunker | Abishai | 1 | | 1 | 1 | | | | | 1 | | | | 4 | | |
| Nantucket | 13 | 22 | Myrick | Hannah | | | | | | | | 1 | 1 | | | | 2 | | |
| Nantucket | 13 | 23 | Russell | Reuben 2nd | 1 | | 1 | | | 1 | | 1 | | | | | 4 | | |
| Nantucket | 13 | 24 | Myrick | Andrew | 1 | | 1 | 1 | | 2 | 1 | | 1 | | | | 7 | | |
| Nantucket | 13 | 25 | Bunker | Latham | | 1 | 1 | | 1 | 3 | | 1 | 1 | | 2 | | 10 | | |
| Nantucket | 13 | 26 | Hulsey | Christopher | | 3 | | 2 | | 3 | 1 | | 1 | 1 | | | 11 | | |
| Nantucket | 13 | 27 | Cornell | William | | 1 | | | | | | 1 | | | | | 2 | | |
| Nantucket | 13 | 28 | Gardner | Albert | 3 | 2 | | 1 | | | 2 | 1 | | | | | 9 | | |
| Nantucket | 13 | 29 | Macy | Stephen Junr | 1 | | 1 | | 1 | 1 | 1 | 1 | | | | | 6 | | |
| Nantucket | 13 | 30 | Barnard | Tristram | 2 | | 1 | | | | | 1 | | | | | 4 | | |
| Nantucket | 13 | 31 | Taber | Antipas | 1 | 2 | | 1 | | 2 | 1 | 1 | | | | | 8 | | |
| Nantucket | 13 | 32 | Clark | Reuben | | 1 | | | | | | 2 | | | | | 3 | | |
| Nantucket | 13 | 33 | Bartlett | Oliver C. | 1 | | 1 | | | 2 | 1 | 1 | | | | | 6 | | |
| Nantucket | 13 | 34 | Gardner | Jared | | 1 | | 2 | | | | 1 | 1 | | | | 5 | | |
| Nantucket | 13 | 35 | Barrett | Abigail | 1 | | | | | | 1 | 1 | | | | | 3 | | |

# 1800 Nantucket, Nantucket County, Massachusetts

| TOWN | PG# | LN# | LAST NAME | FIRST NAME | M under 10 | M 10 to 16 | M 16 to 26 | M 26 to 45 | M 45 and over | F under 10 | F 10 to 16 | F 16 to 26 | F 26 to 45 | F 45 and over | TOTAL ALL OTHER | TOTAL SLAVES | TOTALS | DISTRICT/ TOWNSHIP | NOTES |
|---|---|---|---|---|---|---|---|---|---|---|---|---|---|---|---|---|---|---|---|
| Nantucket | 13 | 36 | Spooner | Dinah | | | | | | | | | 1 | 1 | | | 2 | | |
| Nantucket | 13 | 37 | Swain | George | 1 | | 1 | | | 1 | | | 1 | | | | 4 | | |
| Nantucket | 13 | 38 | Coffin | Seth 2nd | | 2 | 2 | | 1 | | | 1 | 1 | 1 | | | 8 | | |
| Nantucket | 13 | 39 | Barker | Latham | | | | 1 | | 1 | | | | 2 | | | 4 | | |
| Nantucket | 13 | 40 | Fanning | Kezia | 2 | | | 1 | | | | 1 | 1 | | | | 5 | | |
| Nantucket | 13 | 41 | Gardner | Elizabeth | | | | | | | | | | 1 | | | 1 | | |
| Nantucket | 13 | 42 | Coggeshall | Peleg Junr | 1 | | | 1 | | 2 | | | 1 | | | | 5 | | |
| Nantucket | 13 | 43 | Emmit | Elizabeth | | | | | | | | | | 1 | | | 1 | | |
| Nantucket | 13 | 44 | Emmit | John | | | 1 | | | | | | 1 | | | | 2 | | |
| Nantucket | 13 | 45 | Riddell | Henry | | 2 | | 1 | | 2 | 1 | | 1 | | | | 7 | | |
| Nantucket | 13 | 46 | Ames | Anna | | | | | | | | | | 1 | | | 1 | | |
| Nantucket | 13 | 47 | Swain | Valentine | 1 | | | 1 | | 1 | | | 1 | | | | 4 | | |
| Nantucket | 13 | 48 | Mooers | Jonathan | | | 1 | 1 | 1 | 1 | 1 | 1 | | 2 | | | 9 | | |
| Nantucket | 13 | 49 | Coffin | Latham | 1 | 1 | 1 | 1 | | | | | | 1 | | | 5 | | |
| Nantucket | 13 | 50 | Gary | Richard | | 1 | 1 | | | | | 1 | 1 | | | | 4 | | |
| Nantucket | 13 | 51 | Mitchell | Peleg | 1 | 1 | 2 | 1 | | 2 | 3 | 1 | 1 | | | | 12 | | |
| Nantucket | 13 | 52 | Barney | Jonathan | 3 | 3 | 1 | 1 | | 1 | | | 1 | | | | 10 | | |
| Nantucket | 13 | 53 | Freeman | Edward | | | | 1 | | | | | 1 | | | | 2 | | |
| Nantucket | 13 | 54 | Gebston | Rowlan | | 1 | 1 | 1 | | 1 | | 2 | | 1 | 2 | | 9 | | |
| Nantucket | 13 | 55 | Swain | Uriah | 2 | | 2 | 1 | 1 | 2 | | 1 | 1 | 1 | 1 | | 12 | | |
| Nantucket | 13 | 56 | Myrick | Jemima | 1 | | | | | | | 2 | 1 | | | | 4 | | |
| Nantucket | 13 | 57 | Wiederhold | John | 2 | | 1 | | | | | | 1 | | | | 4 | | |
| Nantucket | 13 | 58 | Wyer | John | 1 | | 1 | | | 1 | | | 1 | | | | 4 | | |
| Nantucket | 13 | 59 | Barney | Robert | | 1 | 2 | 1 | | | | | | 1 | | | 5 | | |
| Nantucket | 13 | 60 | Cottell | Obed Junr | | | 1 | | | 1 | 1 | | 1 | | | | 4 | | |
| Nantucket | 13 | 61 | Marshall | Joseph | | | 1 | | | | | | | 1 | | | 2 | | |
| Nantucket | 13 | 62 | Worth | Paul | | | 1 | | | 1 | | | 1 | 1 | | | 4 | | |
| Nantucket | 13 | 63 | Hulsey | Cyrus | 1 | | 1 | | | 1 | 2 | | | | | | 5 | | |
| Nantucket | 13 | 64 | Stanbuck | David | 1 | 2 | 1 | | | 2 | | | 1 | | | | 7 | | |
| Nantucket | 13 | 65 | Stanbuck | Silvanus | | | | 1 | | | | 2 | 1 | | | | 4 | | |
| Nantucket | 13 | 66 | Macy | Abigail | | | | | | | 1 | | 1 | 1 | | | 3 | | |
| Nantucket | 13 | 67 | Hutsey | Robert | 1 | | 1 | 1 | | 1 | | 1 | | | | | 5 | | |
| Nantucket | 13 | 68 | Macy | Abishai | 1 | | | | | | | | 1 | | | | 3 | | |
| Nantucket | 13 | 69 | Coleman | David | 2 | | 1 | 1 | | 3 | 1 | 1 | 1 | | | | 10 | | |
| Nantucket | 13 | 70 | Folger | Walter | | 1 | 1 | | 1 | | | | 1 | 1 | | | 5 | | |
| Nantucket | 13 | 71 | Folger | Alexander | | | 1 | | | | | | 1 | | | | 2 | | |
| Nantucket | 13 | 72 | Gardner | Phebe | | | | | | | | | | 1 | | | 1 | | |
| Nantucket | 13 | 73 | Fosdick | Peter | 1 | | | 1 | | 1 | 2 | | 2 | 1 | | | 8 | | |
| Nantucket | 13 | 74 | Fosdick | Benjamin | | | 1 | 1 | | | | | 1 | 1 | | | 4 | | |
| Nantucket | 13 | 75 | Gardner | Tristram | | | 1 | 1 | 1 | | | | 2 | 1 | | | 6 | | |
| Nantucket | 13 | 76 | Jones | Silas | | 1 | 2 | 1 | | | | 1 | 1 | 1 | | | 7 | | |
| Nantucket | 13 | 77 | * | Benjamin | | 2 | | 1 | | | | | 1 | 1 | | | 5 | | |
| Nantucket | 14 | 1 | Gardner | Richard | 3 | 1 | | 1 | 1 | | | | 1 | 1 | | | 8 | | |
| Nantucket | 14 | 2 | Perry | Saml | | 1 | 2 | 1 | | 1 | | 1 | 2 | 1 | | | 9 | | |
| Nantucket | 14 | 3 | Wilson | Elihu | 1 | | 1 | | | 1 | | | 1 | | | | 4 | | |
| Nantucket | 14 | 4 | Cathcart | Robert | 1 | | | 1 | | 1 | | | 1 | | | | 4 | | |
| Nantucket | 14 | 5 | Alley | William | 1 | | 1 | | | | | | | 1 | | | 3 | | |
| Nantucket | 14 | 6 | Gardner | Stephen | | | 1 | | 2 | | | | | 1 | | | 4 | | |
| Nantucket | 14 | 7 | Pitts | William | | | 1 | | | | | | 1 | | | | 2 | | |
| Nantucket | 14 | 8 | Bunker | Owen | | | 1 | | | | | | 1 | | | | 2 | | |
| Nantucket | 14 | 9 | Allen | Abigail | | | | | | 1 | | | 1 | | | | 2 | | |
| Nantucket | 14 | 10 | Swain | Solomon | 2 | | 1 | | | 1 | | | 1 | | | | 5 | | |
| Nantucket | 14 | 11 | Clark | Simon | | | | 1 | | | | | | 1 | | | 2 | | |
| Nantucket | 14 | 12 | Barnard | Charles | | 1 | | | | | | | 1 | | | | 2 | | |
| Nantucket | 14 | 13 | Gardner | George | | | | 1 | | 4 | 2 | | 1 | | | | 8 | | |
| Nantucket | 14 | 14 | McMurphy | James | 1 | | 1 | | | 1 | | | 1 | | | | 4 | | |
| Nantucket | 14 | 15 | Coleman | Simeon | 1 | 1 | 2 | 1 | | | | | 1 | 1 | | | 7 | | |
| Nantucket | 14 | 16 | Chase | Reuben | | | 1 | 1 | | 2 | 2 | | 1 | | | | 7 | | |
| Nantucket | 14 | 17 | Macy | Richard | | 1 | 1 | 1 | | | | 1 | 1 | 1 | | | 6 | | |
| Nantucket | 14 | 18 | Barnard | James | 2 | | | 1 | | 1 | | 1 | 1 | | | | 6 | | |
| Nantucket | 14 | 19 | Macy | Zaccheus | 1 | | | 1 | | 1 | 1 | | 1 | | | | 5 | | |
| Nantucket | 14 | 20 | Johnson | Polly | | | | | | 1 | | 3 | 1 | | | | 5 | | |
| Nantucket | 14 | 21 | Ray | Paul | 1 | | 1 | 1 | | 2 | | | 1 | | | | 6 | | |
| Nantucket | 14 | 22 | Gardner | James | | | | 1 | | | | | | 1 | | | 2 | | |
| Nantucket | 14 | 23 | Aldridge | Ichabod | | | | 1 | | | | 1 | | 1 | | | 3 | | |
| Nantucket | 14 | 24 | Aldridge | Ichabod Junr | | | 1 | | | 1 | | | | 1 | | | 3 | | |
| Nantucket | 14 | 25 | Rawson | Stephen | 3 | | | 1 | | 1 | 1 | | 1 | | | | 7 | | |
| Nantucket | 14 | 26 | Ames | Benjamin | | | | 1 | | 2 | | | 1 | 1 | | | 5 | | |
| Nantucket | 14 | 27 | Gardner | Grindal | 1 | 2 | 4 | 1 | | 1 | | | 1 | 1 | | | 11 | | |
| Nantucket | 14 | 28 | Coffin | Absalon | | | 1 | | | | | | 1 | | | | 3 | | |
| Nantucket | 14 | 29 | Gardner | Anna | | | 2 | | | | | 1 | 1 | 1 | | | 6 | | |
| Nantucket | 14 | 30 | Swain | Noah | 1 | | | 1 | | 2 | | | 1 | | | | 5 | | |
| Nantucket | 14 | 31 | Bunker | Caleb | | | | | 2 | | | | 1 | 2 | | | 5 | | |
| Nantucket | 14 | 32 | Delano | Jeffry | 1 | | | 1 | | 1 | | | 1 | 1 | | | 5 | | |
| Nantucket | 14 | 33 | Swain | Peter | | | | 1 | | | | | | 2 | | | 3 | | |
| Nantucket | 14 | 34 | Tuckerman | Stephen | 2 | | | 1 | | 1 | | | 1 | | | | 5 | | |
| Nantucket | 14 | 35 | Brock | Andrew | | | | 1 | | | | | | | 1 | | 2 | | |
| Nantucket | 14 | 36 | Aldridge | Obed Junr | | | | 1 | | 2 | | 2 | 2 | | | | 7 | | |
| Nantucket | 14 | 37 | Gardner | Peleg 2nd | 3 | 1 | 1 | 1 | | | | | 1 | | | | 7 | | |
| Nantucket | 14 | 38 | Perry | Jonath | 1 | 1 | 1 | | 1 | 1 | | 2 | 1 | 1 | | | 9 | | |
| Nantucket | 14 | 39 | Arthur | Stephen | 1 | 2 | 1 | | 1 | 1 | | | 1 | 1 | | | 8 | | |
| Nantucket | 14 | 40 | Pinkham | Matthew | 1 | 2 | 1 | | | | | | | 1 | | | 6 | | |
| Nantucket | 14 | 41 | Gardner | Lydia | | | | 1 | | | | | 1 | 1 | | | 3 | | |
| Nantucket | 14 | 42 | Gardner | Freeman | | | 1 | | | 2 | | | 1 | | | | 4 | | |
| Nantucket | 14 | 43 | Pease | David | 1 | | 1 | | | | | | 1 | | | | 3 | | |
| Nantucket | 14 | 44 | Coleman | Simeon Jun | 1 | | 1 | | | | | | 1 | | | | 3 | | |
| Nantucket | 14 | 45 | Coleman | Solomon | | 2 | 1 | 1 | | 3 | | | 2 | | | | 9 | | |
| Nantucket | 14 | 46 | Coffin | Zachariah | | 1 | 1 | | | 1 | | | 1 | 1 | | | 5 | | |
| Nantucket | 14 | 47 | Paddack | Joseph | 2 | | | 1 | | 2 | | 1 | 1 | 1 | | | 8 | | |
| Nantucket | 14 | 48 | Gardner | Silas | 1 | 1 | | 1 | | 2 | | 2 | 1 | | | | 8 | | |

129

# 1800 Nantucket, Nantucket County, Massachusetts

| TOWN | PG# | LN# | LAST NAME | FIRST NAME | FREE WHITE MALES under 10 | 10 to 16 | 16 to 26 | 26 to 45 | 45 and over | FREE WHITE FEMALES under 10 | 10 to 16 | 16 to 26 | 26 to 45 | 45 and over | TOTAL ALL OTHER | TOTAL SLAVES | TOTALS | DISTRICT/ TOWNSHIP | NOTES |
|---|---|---|---|---|---|---|---|---|---|---|---|---|---|---|---|---|---|---|---|
| Nantucket | 14 | 49 | Gardner | Elihu | | | | | 1 | | | 1 | | 1 | | | 3 | | |
| Nantucket | 14 | 50 | Paddack | Eliphalet | 1 | | 2 | 1 | | 1 | | 3 | | 1 | | | 9 | | |
| Nantucket | 14 | 51 | Grew | Samuel | 3 | | 1 | 1 | | | | 1 | | 1 | | | 7 | | |
| Nantucket | 14 | 52 | Holmes | William | 1 | | 1 | 1 | | 2 | | | | 1 | | | 6 | | |
| Nantucket | 14 | 53 | Manter | William | 3 | | | 1 | | | | | 2 | | | | 6 | | |
| Nantucket | 14 | 54 | Bunker | Christopher | | | | 1 | | | | | | 1 | | | 2 | | |
| Nantucket | 14 | 55 | Gardner | Gideon Junr | 1 | | | 1 | | 1 | | | 1 | | | | 4 | | |
| Nantucket | 14 | 56 | Worth | Henry | | | 1 | | | 2 | | | 1 | | | | 4 | | |
| Nantucket | 14 | 57 | Coleman | Daniel | | | | 1 | | | | | | 1 | | | 2 | | |
| Nantucket | 14 | 58 | Coleman | Job | | | 1 | | | 1 | | | 1 | | | | 3 | | |
| Nantucket | 14 | 59 | Gardner | Zephaniah | | | | 1 | | | | 1 | | 1 | | | 3 | | |
| Nantucket | 14 | 60 | Clark | Benjamin Junr | | | 1 | 2 | | | 1 | 2 | | 1 | | | 7 | | |
| Nantucket | 14 | 61 | Gifford | Joseph | 1 | | 1 | | | | | 1 | | | | | 3 | | |
| Nantucket | 14 | 62 | Bunker | Phebe | | | | | | | | | 2 | 1 | | | 3 | | |
| Nantucket | 14 | 63 | Barnard | Stephen | | | | 1 | | | | | | | | | 1 | | |
| Nantucket | 14 | 64 | Wilcox | Hannah | | | | | | | | | 2 | 1 | | | 3 | | |
| Nantucket | 14 | 65 | Brock | John | | 1 | | 1 | | | | | 1 | 1 | | | 4 | | |
| Nantucket | 14 | 66 | Brooks | William | 1 | | | 1 | | 3 | | 1 | | | | | 6 | | |
| Nantucket | 14 | 67 | Worth | John | | | | 1 | | | | | | 2 | | | 3 | | |
| Nantucket | 14 | 68 | Allen | Tristram | 1 | | 1 | | | 3 | | 1 | | | | | 6 | | |
| Nantucket | 14 | 69 | Chase | Nathan | 1 | | | 1 | | | | 1 | | | | | 3 | | |
| Nantucket | 14 | 70 | Worth | Matthew | | | 2 | 1 | | | | | 1 | | | | 4 | | |
| Nantucket | 14 | 71 | Sherman | Nathaniel | 1 | | 1 | | | | | | 1 | | | | 3 | | |
| Nantucket | 14 | 72 | Worth | Jonah | | | | 1 | | | | | | | | | 1 | | |
| Nantucket | 14 | 73 | Calder | Robert | 4 | 3 | 1 | | | | | | 1 | | | | 9 | | |
| Nantucket | 14 | 74 | Folger | Susanna | 2 | | | | | | 1 | 1 | 1 | | | | 5 | | |
| Nantucket | 14 | 75 | Coffin | Josiah | | 1 | | 1 | | | | | 1 | 1 | | | 4 | | |
| Nantucket | 14 | 76 | Coffin | Edward | 1 | 1 | | 1 | | | | | 1 | 1 | | | 5 | | |
| Nantucket | 14 | 77 | Brock | Thomas | 2 | 1 | 2 | 1 | | 1 | 1 | | 1 | 1 | | | 10 | | |
| Nantucket | 15 | 1 | Hammond | Lydia | 1 | | | | | | | 1 | 2 | 1 | | | 5 | | |
| Nantucket | 15 | 2 | Wilber | John | 1 | | | 1 | 3 | 1 | | | | 1 | | | 7 | | |
| Nantucket | 15 | 3 | Clasby | Robert | | | 1 | | | | | | | 1 | | | 2 | | |
| Nantucket | 15 | 4 | Clasby | Abraham | 2 | | | 1 | | 1 | 1 | 1 | | | | | 6 | | |
| Nantucket | 15 | 5 | Gardner | John | 1 | 1 | 1 | 1 | | | | 2 | | 1 | | | 7 | | |
| Nantucket | 15 | 6 | Fosdick | John | 2 | | 1 | 1 | 1 | | | | 1 | 1 | | | 7 | | |
| Nantucket | 15 | 7 | Gardner | Francis | | 1 | 2 | 1 | | 1 | | | 1 | 2 | | | 8 | | |
| Nantucket | 15 | 8 | Paddack | Nathaniel | 2 | | | 1 | | 1 | | 2 | 1 | | | | 7 | | |
| Nantucket | 15 | 9 | Pease | Valentine | 2 | | | 1 | | 3 | | 2 | | | | | 8 | | |
| Nantucket | 15 | 10 | Barrett | Nathaniel | 2 | 1 | 1 | 1 | | | | 3 | | 1 | | | 9 | | |
| Nantucket | 15 | 11 | Fosdick | Philip | 2 | | 1 | 2 | | | | 1 | | | | | 6 | | |
| Nantucket | 15 | 12 | Brock | Peter | 1 | | 1 | | | | | 1 | | | | | 3 | | |
| Nantucket | 15 | 13 | Cartwright | Benjamin | 1 | | 2 | 1 | | | 1 | | 1 | | | | 6 | | |
| Nantucket | 15 | 14 | Clark | Sarah | | | | | | | | | 1 | 1 | | | 2 | | |
| Nantucket | 15 | 15 | Turner | Baker | 2 | | 1 | | | 2 | | | 1 | | | | 6 | | |
| Nantucket | 15 | 16 | Pinkham | Tristram | 2 | 1 | 2 | 1 | | 1 | | 3 | | 1 | | | 11 | | |
| Nantucket | 15 | 17 | Chase | Jerusha | | | | | | | | | 1 | 1 | | | 2 | | |
| Nantucket | 15 | 18 | Brayton | Robert | 1 | 1 | 1 | 1 | | 1 | | | 1 | | | | 6 | | |
| Nantucket | 15 | 19 | Coffin | Eunice | | 1 | | | | | 1 | | 1 | | | | 3 | | |
| Nantucket | 15 | 20 | Hulsey | John | 3 | 3 | | 1 | | 2 | | 1 | 1 | | | | 11 | | |
| Nantucket | 15 | 21 | Hussey | Thomas | 2 | 1 | | 1 | | 1 | | | 1 | | | | 6 | | |
| Nantucket | 15 | 22 | Gardner | Thomas | | 1 | | 1 | | | | | | 1 | | | 3 | | |
| Nantucket | 15 | 23 | Jones | Benjm | 3 | | 3 | | 1 | 1 | 1 | 1 | | | | | 11 | | |
| Nantucket | 15 | 24 | Coffin | Brown | | | | | | | | | | | | | | | Enumeration left blank |
| Nantucket | 15 | 25 | Coffin | Ebenezer | | 1 | | 1 | | 1 | | | | 2 | | | 5 | | |
| Nantucket | 15 | 26 | Coffin | Albert | | 1 | | | | | | | 1 | | | | 2 | | |
| Nantucket | 15 | 27 | Jenkins | Tristram | 1 | 1 | 3 | 1 | | 1 | 1 | | | 1 | | | 10 | | |
| Nantucket | 15 | 28 | Chase | James | | 1 | 2 | 1 | | 1 | 1 | | | 1 | | | 7 | | |
| Nantucket | 15 | 29 | McCleave | Joseph | 1 | | 1 | | | 1 | | 1 | | | | | 4 | | |
| Nantucket | 15 | 30 | Reilley | Daniel | 2 | | 2 | 1 | | | 1 | 3 | | 1 | | | 10 | | |
| Nantucket | 15 | 31 | Earl | Joseph | 2 | | 1 | | 1 | 1 | 1 | 1 | 1 | | | | 9 | | |
| Nantucket | 15 | 32 | Fitch | Ebenezer | 2 | | 1 | | 1 | 1 | 1 | 1 | 1 | | | | 9 | | |
| Nantucket | 15 | 33 | Folger | Owen | | 1 | 1 | 1 | | | | | 1 | 1 | | | 6 | | |
| Nantucket | 15 | 34 | Worth | Benjm | 2 | 1 | | 1 | | 2 | | | 1 | | | | 7 | | |
| Nantucket | 15 | 35 | Folger | Thaddeus | | | | 1 | | 3 | 1 | | 1 | | | | 6 | | |
| Nantucket | 15 | 36 | Folger | Obediah | | 1 | 1 | 1 | | | | 1 | 1 | 1 | | | 6 | | |
| Nantucket | 15 | 37 | Folger | Barrillia | | 1 | | 1 | | | | 1 | 1 | | | | 4 | | |
| Nantucket | 15 | 38 | Russell | Saml | | | | | | | | 1 | 1 | | | | 3 | | |
| Nantucket | 15 | 39 | Brown | Benjamin | 2 | 1 | | 1 | | | 1 | | 2 | | | | 7 | | |
| Nantucket | 15 | 40 | Barnard | Judith | | | | 1 | | | 2 | 1 | 2 | | | | 6 | | |
| Nantucket | 15 | 41 | Easton | Wm | 2 | 2 | 1 | 1 | | | | | 1 | | | | 7 | | |
| Nantucket | 15 | 42 | Joy | Francis | 1 | | 1 | 1 | | 2 | 1 | 1 | 1 | | | | 8 | | |
| Nantucket | 15 | 43 | Clark | Obed | | | 1 | | | | | | 1 | | | | 2 | | |
| Nantucket | 15 | 44 | Cottell | David | | 1 | | | | | | 1 | | | | | 2 | | |
| Nantucket | 15 | 45 | Cob | Wm | 1 | 1 | 1 | 1 | | 2 | | | | | | | 6 | | |
| Nantucket | 15 | 46 | Gardner | Thos Junr | | 1 | | | | | | 1 | | | | | 2 | | |
| Nantucket | 15 | 47 | Barney | Jonathan | | 2 | | 1 | | | | 1 | 1 | 2 | | | 7 | | |
| Nantucket | 15 | 48 | Barney | Jonathan Junr | 4 | 2 | 2 | 1 | | 2 | | 1 | 1 | 1 | | | 14 | | |
| Nantucket | 15 | 49 | Barney | William | 1 | | | 1 | | 1 | | 1 | | | | | 4 | | |
| Nantucket | 15 | 50 | Coffin | James | | | 2 | | 1 | | | 1 | | 1 | | | 5 | | |
| Nantucket | 15 | 51 | Fitch | John | | | 1 | | | 1 | | | 1 | | | | 3 | | |
| Nantucket | 15 | 52 | Pinkham | Shubael | 2 | | | 1 | | 2 | | 1 | | | | | 6 | | |
| Nantucket | 15 | 53 | Raymond | Wm | 1 | | 1 | 1 | | 1 | | 1 | | | | | 5 | | |
| Nantucket | 15 | 54 | Wood | Amos | 2 | 2 | 1 | | | | | 1 | | | | | 6 | | |
| Nantucket | 15 | 55 | Nye | Maltiah | 1 | | 1 | | | | 1 | 1 | | | | | 4 | | |
| Nantucket | 15 | 56 | Russell | Saml | | 1 | | 1 | | | | | 1 | 1 | | | 4 | | |
| Nantucket | 15 | 57 | Easton | Peleg | | 2 | 1 | 1 | | 2 | 2 | 1 | 1 | | | | 10 | | |
| Nantucket | 15 | 58 | Sisson | Isaac | | | 1 | | 3 | | | | 1 | | | | 5 | | |
| Nantucket | 15 | 59 | Gardner | Zenas | 1 | 1 | | 3 | | | | | 2 | | | | 8 | | |
| Nantucket | 15 | 60 | Gardner | Libni | | 1 | 1 | | | | | | 2 | | | | 4 | | |
| Nantucket | 15 | 61 | Stubbs | Saml | 1 | 1 | | 1 | | 1 | 1 | | 1 | 1 | | | 7 | | |

# 1800 Nantucket, Nantucket County, Massachusetts

| Town | PG# | LN# | Last Name | First Name | Free White Males under 10 | 10 to 16 | 16 to 26 | 26 to 45 | 45 and over | Free White Females under 10 | 10 to 16 | 16 to 26 | 26 to 45 | 45 and over | Total All Other | Total Slaves | Totals | District/ Township | Notes |
|---|---|---|---|---|---|---|---|---|---|---|---|---|---|---|---|---|---|---|---|
| Nantucket | 15 | 62 | Coffin | James | | 1 | 1 | 1 | | 1 | | 3 | 1 | 1 | | | 9 | | |
| Nantucket | 15 | 63 | Gardner | Benjm | | 1 | | | | 1 | 1 | 1 | | 1 | | | 5 | | |
| Nantucket | 15 | 64 | Crosby | Silvanus | 1 | | | 1 | | | | 1 | | 1 | 1 | | 5 | | |
| Nantucket | 15 | 65 | Whippy | Benjm Junr | | 1 | | | | | | 1 | | | | | 2 | | |
| Nantucket | 15 | 66 | Folger | Peter | | 1 | 2 | 1 | | | | 2 | | 1 | | | 7 | | |
| Nantucket | 15 | 67 | Joy | Thaddeus | 1 | | 1 | | | 1 | | 1 | | | | | 4 | | |
| Nantucket | 15 | 68 | Whippy | Coffin | 2 | 1 | | 1 | | 1 | | | 1 | | | | 6 | | |
| Nantucket | 15 | 69 | Joy | Obed | 1 | | | 1 | | 2 | | | 1 | | | | 5 | | |
| Nantucket | 15 | 70 | Joy | David | | 2 | 1 | | 1 | | 1 | 1 | 1 | | | | 7 | | |
| Nantucket | 15 | 71 | Ross | L* | 1 | 1 | | | | 1 | | | 1 | | | | 5 | | |
| Nantucket | 15 | 72 | Clark | George | | | 1 | | | 1 | | | 1 | | | | 3 | | |
| Nantucket | 15 | 73 | Sanford | Giles | | | 1 | | | 1 | | 1 | | | | | 3 | | |
| Nantucket | 15 | 74 | Pitman | Saml | 1 | | | 1 | | 1 | | | 1 | | | | 4 | | |
| Nantucket | 15 | 75 | Pitman | Charles | | | 1 | | | | | | 1 | 1 | | | 3 | | |
| Nantucket | 15 | 76 | Coffin | Owen | | | 1 | | | | | | 1 | | | | 2 | | |
| Nantucket | 15 | 77 | Clark | S*t | 2 | | | 1 | | 1 | | | 1 | | | | 5 | | |
| Nantucket | 16 | 1 | Gardner | Shubael | | | | 1 | | | | | | 1 | | | 2 | | |
| Nantucket | 16 | 2 | Gardner | Caty | | | | | | | | | | 3 | | | 3 | | |
| Nantucket | 16 | 3 | Coffin | Enoch | | | | 1 | | | | | | | | | 1 | | |
| Nantucket | 16 | 4 | Joy | Anna | | | | | | | | | 1 | 1 | | | 2 | | |
| Nantucket | 16 | 5 | Smith | Thos | | | | 1 | | | 1 | | | 1 | | | 3 | | |
| Nantucket | 16 | 6 | Smith | Hepzibeh | | 1 | | | | | | | 2 | 1 | | | 4 | | |
| Nantucket | 16 | 7 | Fitch | Jedediah | | | 1 | | | | | | 1 | | | | 2 | | |
| Nantucket | 16 | 8 | Guerney | James | 1 | | 1 | | | 1 | | | 1 | | | | 3 | | |
| Nantucket | 16 | 9 | Gardner | Robert | | 1 | | 1 | | | | | | 1 | | | 3 | | |
| Nantucket | 16 | 10 | Coffin | Nathaniel | | 1 | 1 | 1 | | | | 1 | 1 | 1 | | | 6 | | |
| Nantucket | 16 | 11 | Coffin | Joshua | | 1 | | 1 | | | 1 | 1 | 1 | | | | 5 | | |
| Nantucket | 16 | 12 | Gardner | Enoch | | | | 1 | | | | | 1 | | | | 2 | | |
| Nantucket | 16 | 13 | Nichols | Joseph | | | | 1 | | | | | | 1 | | | 2 | | |
| Nantucket | 16 | 14 | Coleman | Wm | | | | 1 | | | | 1 | | 1 | | | 3 | | |
| Nantucket | 16 | 15 | Narbeth | John | | 1 | 1 | 1 | | | | | 2 | | | | 5 | | |
| Nantucket | 16 | 16 | Hussey | Nathl | 1 | | 1 | | | | | | 1 | | 1 | | 4 | | |
| Nantucket | 16 | 17 | Calef | Ebenezer | 2 | 1 | | 1 | | 2 | | | 1 | 1 | | | 8 | | |
| Nantucket | 16 | 18 | Hussey | George G | 1 | 1 | | 1 | | 1 | | | 1 | | | | 5 | | |
| Nantucket | 16 | 19 | Hussey | Peter | | 1 | | 1 | | 1 | | | 1 | 1 | | | 5 | | |
| Nantucket | 16 | 20 | Hussey | Batchelor | | | | 1 | | | | 1 | | 1 | | | 3 | | |
| Nantucket | 16 | 21 | Clark | Love | 1 | | | | | 1 | | | 1 | | | | 3 | | |
| Nantucket | 16 | 22 | Brock | John | | | 1 | | | | | 2 | 1 | | | | 4 | | |
| Nantucket | 16 | 23 | Headen | Zoaph | | | 1 | | | | | 2 | | | | | 3 | | |
| Nantucket | 16 | 24 | Hathaway | Mary | | | | | | | | | 1 | | | | 1 | | |
| Nantucket | 16 | 25 | Stubs | Wm | | 1 | | 1 | | | | | 1 | | | | 3 | | |
| Nantucket | 16 | 26 | Coggeshall | Paul | | | 2 | 1 | | 2 | | | | 1 | | | 6 | | |
| Nantucket | 16 | 27 | Hussey | Judah | | | | | | | | | | 1 | | | 1 | | |
| Nantucket | 16 | 28 | Hussey | David | | 1 | 2 | 1 | | 3 | 1 | 1 | | | | | 9 | | |
| Nantucket | 16 | 29 | Mirick | Coffin | | | 1 | | | 1 | | 1 | | 1 | | | 4 | | |
| Nantucket | 16 | 30 | Swain | Eunice | 2 | | | | | | | | 1 | | | | 3 | | |
| Nantucket | 16 | 31 | Coffin | Alpheus | 3 | | 1 | 1 | | | | | 1 | | | | 6 | | |
| Nantucket | 16 | 32 | Hussey | Peleg | | | 2 | | | 1 | | 1 | 1 | | | | 5 | | |
| Nantucket | 16 | 33 | Mirick | Jonathan Junr | 1 | 1 | 1 | 1 | | 2 | | 1 | 1 | | | | 8 | | |
| Nantucket | 16 | 34 | Barn | Mary | | | | 1 | | | | | 1 | 1 | | | 3 | | |
| Nantucket | 16 | 35 | Hussey | Tristram | | 1 | 3 | 1 | | 1 | | 2 | | 1 | | | 9 | | |
| Nantucket | 16 | 36 | Hussey | Wm | | | | 1 | | | | 1 | 1 | 1 | | | 4 | | |
| Nantucket | 16 | 37 | Chase | Peter | 4 | 1 | | 1 | | 1 | | | 1 | | | | 8 | | |
| Nantucket | 16 | 38 | Ewers | Silvanus | | | 1 | | | | | | 1 | | | | 2 | | |
| Nantucket | 16 | 39 | Folger | Albert | 2 | | | | | | | | 1 | | | | 4 | | |
| Nantucket | 16 | 40 | Chase | James | | 1 | | 1 | | 1 | | 1 | | 1 | | | 5 | | |
| Nantucket | 16 | 41 | Hussey | Albert | | 2 | 1 | 1 | | | | | 1 | | | | 5 | | |
| Nantucket | 16 | 42 | Hussey | James | 1 | | | 1 | | 1 | 1 | | | | | | 5 | | |
| Nantucket | 16 | 43 | Hussey | Stephen | | 2 | | 1 | | | | 2 | 1 | 1 | | | 7 | | |
| Nantucket | 16 | 44 | Hussey | Danl | | | 1 | | | | | | 1 | | | | 2 | | |
| Nantucket | 16 | 45 | Barnard | Obed | 2 | 2 | | 1 | | 1 | | | 1 | | | | 7 | | |
| Nantucket | 16 | 46 | Glover | Reuben | | | 1 | | | | | 1 | 1 | | | | 3 | | |
| Nantucket | 16 | 47 | Gardner | Grafton | 1 | | | 1 | | 4 | | | 1 | | | | 7 | | |
| Nantucket | 16 | 48 | Laurence | George | | 1 | | 1 | | | | 1 | | 1 | | | 4 | | |
| Nantucket | 16 | 49 | Coffin | Stephen | | 1 | | 1 | 1 | | | 1 | | 1 | | | 5 | | |
| Nantucket | 16 | 50 | Macy | Solomon | 2 | 1 | 1 | 1 | | | | 2 | | 2 | | | 9 | | |
| Nantucket | 16 | 51 | Coleman | Nathl | 1 | | 1 | 1 | 1 | | | | 2 | 1 | | | 7 | | |
| Nantucket | 16 | 52 | Swain | Barnabas | 1 | 1 | 1 | | | 1 | 1 | | | 1 | | | 7 | | |
| Nantucket | 16 | 53 | Swain | John | | 2 | | 1 | | 1 | | 1 | | 1 | | | 6 | | |
| Nantucket | 16 | 54 | Horsfield | Timothy | 4 | | 1 | 1 | | | 1 | | 1 | | | | 8 | | |
| Nantucket | 16 | 55 | Swain | Howland | | | 1 | 1 | | 1 | | 2 | | | | | 5 | | |
| Nantucket | 16 | 56 | Morris | John | | 1 | | 1 | | 3 | | | 1 | | | | 6 | | |
| Nantucket | 16 | 57 | Hussey | Latham | 1 | | | 1 | | 1 | | | 1 | | | | 4 | | |
| Nantucket | 16 | 58 | Hussey | Elizabeth | | 2 | | | | | | | | 1 | | | 3 | | |
| Nantucket | 16 | 59 | Barnard | Wm | | | | 1 | 1 | 4 | 1 | 2 | 1 | | | | 10 | | |
| Nantucket | 16 | 60 | Rand | Ebenezer | | 1 | 2 | 1 | 1 | 1 | 1 | | 1 | 1 | | | 9 | | |
| Nantucket | 16 | 61 | Jenkins | John | 1 | 1 | 1 | 1 | | 3 | | | 1 | | | | 8 | | |
| Nantucket | 16 | 62 | Norris | Charles | | | 1 | 1 | | 2 | | 1 | 1 | | | | 6 | | |
| Nantucket | 16 | 63 | Folger | Robert | | 1 | 1 | 1 | | 1 | | 1 | | 1 | | | 6 | | |
| Nantucket | 16 | 64 | Swift | Benjm | 1 | | | 1 | | 1 | | 1 | | 2 | | | 6 | | |
| Nantucket | 16 | 65 | Winslow | Benjm | | 1 | | 1 | | 1 | | 2 | | | | | 5 | | |
| Nantucket | 16 | 66 | Swain | Gilbert | 1 | | | 1 | | 1 | | | 1 | | | | 4 | | |
| Nantucket | 16 | 67 | Jones | Reuben | | | | 1 | | | 1 | | | | | | 2 | | |
| Nantucket | 16 | 68 | Gardner | Robert Junr | 1 | | | 1 | | | | 2 | | | | | 4 | | |
| Nantucket | 16 | 69 | Bunker | Uriah 2nd | | 2 | 1 | | | | 1 | 1 | 1 | | | | 7 | | |
| Nantucket | 16 | 70 | Coffin | Eber | | | 1 | | | | | | | 1 | | | 2 | | |
| Nantucket | 16 | 71 | Pitts | Silvanus | 1 | | 1 | | | 1 | | | 1 | | | | 4 | | |
| Nantucket | 16 | 72 | Brock | Andrew Junr | 1 | | 1 | | | 1 | | | 1 | | | | 4 | | |
| Nantucket | 16 | 73 | Jones | Danl | | 1 | | | | | | | | | | | 4 | | |
| Nantucket | 16 | 74 | Giles | David | 1 | | | 1 | 1 | | | | | | | | 4 | | |

| TOWN | PG# | LN# | LAST NAME | FIRST NAME | FREE WHITE MALES under 10 | 10 to 16 | 16 to 26 | 26 to 45 | 45 and over | FREE WHITE FEMALES under 10 | 10 to 16 | 16 to 26 | 26 to 45 | 45 and over | TOTAL ALL OTHER | TOTAL SLAVES | TOTALS | DISTRICT/TOWNSHIP | NOTES |
|---|---|---|---|---|---|---|---|---|---|---|---|---|---|---|---|---|---|---|---|
| Nantucket | 16 | 75 | Hussey | Eiab | | | | | | | | | 1 | | | | 1 | | |
| Nantucket | 16 | 76 | West | Peleg | | | 1 | | | 1 | 1 | | 1 | | | | 4 | | |
| Nantucket | 17 | 1 | Bunker | Thos | 2 | | 1 | | | 2 | | | 1 | | | | 6 | | |
| Nantucket | 17 | 2 | Barnard | Laban | | | 1 | | | | | | 1 | | | | 2 | | |
| Nantucket | 17 | 3 | Clasby | Charles | 1 | | 1 | | | | | 1 | 1 | | | | 4 | | |
| Nantucket | 17 | 4 | Gardner | Hepzibeh 2nd | | | | | | | | | 1 | 1 | | | 2 | | |
| Nantucket | 17 | 5 | Farr | Stephen | | | 1 | | | | | 1 | 1 | | | | 3 | | |
| Nantucket | 17 | 6 | Jenkins | Perus | 1 | 1 | | 1 | 1 | | | | 1 | | | | 5 | | |
| Nantucket | 17 | 7 | Rothbon | Jonathan | | 1 | 1 | 1 | | | | | 1 | | | | 4 | | |
| Nantucket | 17 | 8 | Hammond | Sally | | | | | | | | | 1 | | | | 1 | | |
| Nantucket | 17 | 9 | Ary | Jabez | | | | 1 | | | | 1 | | 2 | | | 4 | | |
| Nantucket | 17 | 10 | Nichols | Horatio | 2 | | 1 | | | 1 | | | 1 | | | | 5 | | |
| Nantucket | 17 | 11 | Hayden | Abishai | | 1 | | | | 2 | 2 | 1 | 1 | | | | 7 | | |
| Nantucket | 17 | 12 | Pinkham | Henry | | 1 | | | | 1 | 1 | 1 | | | | | 4 | | |
| Nantucket | 17 | 13 | Perry | Jonathan Junr | 1 | | 1 | 1 | | 1 | | | 1 | 1 | | | 6 | | |
| Nantucket | 17 | 14 | Hayden | Rebecca | | 1 | | | | | | | | 1 | | | 2 | | |
| Nantucket | 17 | 15 | Bunker | John | 2 | 1 | | 1 | | 1 | | | 1 | 1 | | | 7 | | |
| Nantucket | 17 | 16 | Bunker | Elizabeth | | | | | | | | | | 1 | | | 1 | | |
| Nantucket | 17 | 17 | Pinkham | Peter | | | 1 | | | 1 | | 1 | 1 | | | | 4 | | |
| Nantucket | 17 | 18 | Gardner | Peter | | | 2 | | | | | 1 | 2 | | | | 5 | | |
| Nantucket | 17 | 19 | Swain | Francis | 1 | 1 | 2 | | 1 | 1 | | 1 | | 1 | | | 8 | | |
| Nantucket | 17 | 20 | Barker | James | 2 | 2 | 1 | | | | | 1 | 1 | | | | 7 | | |
| Nantucket | 17 | 21 | Barnard | Lydia | | | 2 | | | | | | 1 | 1 | | | 4 | | |
| Nantucket | 17 | 22 | Russell | George Junr | 1 | | 1 | | | 1 | | | 1 | | | | 4 | | |
| Nantucket | 17 | 23 | Pinkham | Wm | | | | 1 | | | | | 1 | | | | 2 | | |
| Nantucket | 17 | 24 | Long | Nathan | | | 1 | | | 2 | 1 | 1 | | | | | 5 | | |
| Nantucket | 17 | 25 | Murphy | David | | | 1 | | | 2 | 1 | 1 | | | | | 5 | | |
| Nantucket | 17 | 26 | West | Charles | | 2 | 1 | | | | | 1 | 1 | 1 | | | 6 | | |
| Nantucket | 17 | 27 | Paddock | Anna | | | 1 | | | | | 1 | 1 | 2 | | | 5 | | |
| Nantucket | 17 | 28 | Coffin | Mary | | 1 | 1 | | | | | | | 1 | | | 3 | | |
| Nantucket | 17 | 29 | Barney | Griffin | | | 1 | | | | | | | 1 | | | 2 | | |
| Nantucket | 17 | 30 | Cook | Naomi | 2 | | | | | | | 1 | 1 | 1 | | | 5 | | |
| Nantucket | 17 | 31 | Coffin | Simeon | 1 | | | 1 | | 2 | | 1 | 1 | | | | 6 | | |
| Nantucket | 17 | 32 | Coffin | Margaret | | 1 | | | | | | | 1 | 1 | | | 3 | | |
| Nantucket | 17 | 33 | Starbuck | Reuben | | 1 | | 1 | | | | | 1 | | | | 3 | | |
| Nantucket | 17 | 34 | Coleman | Lydia | | 2 | 1 | 1 | | | | 1 | | 1 | | | 6 | | |
| Nantucket | 17 | 35 | Swain | Lewis | | | 1 | 2 | | | | | 1 | | | | 4 | | |
| Nantucket | 17 | 36 | Jarwood | John | | 1 | | | | | | | 1 | | | | 2 | | |
| Nantucket | 17 | 37 | Swain | Thaddeus | 3 | | | 1 | 1 | 1 | | | 1 | 1 | | | 8 | | |
| Nantucket | 17 | 38 | Cartwright | John | 2 | 1 | 1 | | 1 | 3 | 2 | 2 | 2 | | | | 14 | | |
| Nantucket | 17 | 39 | Swain | Thomas | 1 | | | 1 | | 3 | 1 | | 1 | 1 | | | 8 | | |
| Nantucket | 17 | 40 | Barney | Sarah | | | | | | | | | | 2 | | | 2 | | |
| Nantucket | 17 | 41 | Barker | Josiah Junr | | 2 | | 1 | | 3 | | | 1 | 1 | | | 8 | | |
| Nantucket | 17 | 42 | Pease | Elijah | | 2 | 1 | | 1 | | | 1 | 1 | 1 | | | 6 | | |
| Nantucket | 17 | 43 | Ewers | David | | 1 | | | | | | | 1 | | | | 2 | | |
| Nantucket | 17 | 44 | Rice | Randal | 2 | | 1 | 1 | | 1 | | 2 | 1 | | | | 8 | | |
| Nantucket | 17 | 45 | Walcutt | Benjamin | 1 | 1 | | 1 | | | | 1 | 1 | | 1 | | 6 | | |
| Nantucket | 17 | 46 | Coleman | Davis | | 1 | | 1 | | | | | 1 | 1 | | | 4 | | |
| Nantucket | 17 | 47 | Folger | Seth Junr | | 1 | 1 | 1 | | 1 | 1 | 1 | 1 | | | | 7 | | |
| Nantucket | 17 | 48 | Swain | Saml | 4 | | 1 | | | 2 | | 1 | 1 | | | | 9 | | |
| Nantucket | 17 | 49 | Drew | Gershom | 1 | 2 | 3 | 1 | | | | 2 | | 1 | | | 10 | | |
| Nantucket | 17 | 50 | Hussey | William Junr | | 1 | | 1 | | | | | 1 | | | | 3 | | |
| Nantucket | 17 | 51 | Brock | Jethro | | | 1 | | | | | | 1 | | | | 2 | | |
| Nantucket | 17 | 52 | Drew | Ebenezer | 1 | 1 | | 1 | | | | | | 1 | | | 4 | | |
| Nantucket | 17 | 53 | Hussey | Paul | 2 | 1 | | 1 | | 1 | | 1 | 1 | 1 | | | 8 | | |
| Nantucket | 17 | 54 | Coleman | Silvanus | | 1 | 1 | | 1 | | 2 | | 1 | | 1 | | 7 | | |
| Nantucket | 17 | 55 | Cartwright | Joseph | 1 | | | 1 | | | | 1 | 1 | | | | 4 | | |
| Nantucket | 17 | 56 | Starbuck | Nathl | 1 | | | 1 | | | | 1 | 1 | 1 | | | 5 | | |
| Nantucket | 17 | 57 | Rand | David | | 1 | | | | | | | 1 | | | | 2 | | |
| Nantucket | 17 | 58 | Russell | John | 1 | | 1 | 1 | 4 | 2 | 2 | 1 | | | | | 12 | | |
| Nantucket | 17 | 59 | Barney | Peter | | 1 | 3 | 1 | | | | 1 | 1 | 1 | | | 8 | | |
| Nantucket | 17 | 60 | Folger | George Junr | 3 | 1 | 1 | 1 | | 1 | | 1 | 1 | | | | 9 | | |
| Nantucket | 17 | 61 | Coleman | Elizabeth | 2 | 1 | 1 | | | 1 | | 1 | 1 | 1 | | | 8 | | |
| Nantucket | 17 | 62 | Whippy | George | | 1 | | | | | | | 1 | | | | 2 | | |
| Nantucket | 17 | 63 | Joy | William | 3 | | 1 | | 2 | | | | 1 | | | | 7 | | |
| Nantucket | 17 | 64 | Jenkins | Jonathan | 1 | 1 | | 1 | 1 | 2 | 1 | 1 | 1 | | | | 9 | | |
| Nantucket | 17 | 65 | Mitchell | David | 1 | 1 | | 1 | | 2 | | 2 | 1 | | | | 8 | | |
| Nantucket | 17 | 66 | Coleman | Barnabas | 2 | 1 | | 1 | | | | 2 | 1 | | | | 7 | | |
| Nantucket | 17 | 67 | Coleman | John | | 1 | | | | | | 1 | | | | | 2 | | |
| Nantucket | 17 | 68 | Pinkham | Charles | 1 | 1 | | 1 | | | | 2 | 1 | | | | 6 | | |
| Nantucket | 17 | 69 | Pinkham | Obed | | 1 | 1 | | 1 | | | | 1 | | | | 4 | | |
| Nantucket | 17 | 70 | Rawson | Abel | 1 | | 1 | 1 | | 2 | 1 | 1 | | | | | 7 | | |
| Nantucket | 17 | 71 | Wyer | Joseph | 1 | | 1 | | | | | | | | 1 | | 3 | | |
| Nantucket | 17 | 72 | Rawson | Wilson | 1 | 2 | 3 | 1 | | 1 | | | 1 | | | | 9 | | |
| Nantucket | 17 | 73 | Osborn | Saml | 3 | | 1 | | 1 | 1 | | | 1 | | | | 7 | | |
| Nantucket | 17 | 74 | Coffin | Obed | | 1 | 3 | 1 | | 1 | | | 1 | 1 | | | 8 | | |
| Nantucket | 17 | 75 | Rawson | Deborah | | | | | | | | | 1 | 1 | | | 2 | | |
| Nantucket | 18 | 1 | Colesworthy | Jonathan | 1 | | 1 | | | | | | 1 | | | | 3 | | |
| Nantucket | 18 | 2 | Ross | Isaac | | | | 1 | 1 | 2 | | | 1 | | | | 5 | | |
| Nantucket | 18 | 3 | Nichols | William | 3 | | 2 | 1 | | | 1 | 1 | 1 | | | | 9 | | |
| Nantucket | 18 | 4 | Fisher | Freeborn | | 1 | | | | | | | 1 | | | | 2 | | |
| Nantucket | 18 | 5 | Pinkham | John | | | | 1 | | | | | 1 | 1 | | | 3 | | |
| Nantucket | 18 | 6 | Coffin | Jas. Josiah | 2 | 1 | 1 | 1 | | 1 | | 1 | 1 | | | | 7 | | |
| Nantucket | 18 | 7 | Hussey | Jethro | | 1 | 1 | 1 | | | 1 | | 1 | 1 | | | 6 | | |
| Nantucket | 18 | 8 | Plum | Urial | | 1 | | | | | | | 1 | | | | 2 | | |
| Nantucket | 18 | 9 | Bunker | Love | 1 | 1 | | | | | | | 1 | 1 | | | 4 | | |
| Nantucket | 18 | 10 | Riddell | William | 2 | | | 1 | | 1 | | 1 | | | | | 5 | | |
| Nantucket | 18 | 11 | Mitchell | Laban | 2 | 1 | 1 | 1 | | 1 | | 1 | 1 | | | | 8 | | |
| Nantucket | 18 | 12 | Mitchell | Paul | 3 | 2 | | 1 | | 2 | 1 | 1 | | | | | 10 | | |
| Nantucket | 18 | 13 | Mitchell | Richard | | 1 | | 1 | | | | 1 | 1 | | | | 4 | | |

# 1800 Nantucket, Nantucket County, Massachusetts

| TOWN | PG# | LN# | LAST NAME | FIRST NAME | Free White Males under 10 | 10 to 16 | 16 to 26 | 26 to 45 | 45 and over | Free White Females under 10 | 10 to 16 | 16 to 26 | 26 to 45 | 45 and over | TOTAL ALL OTHER | TOTAL SLAVES | TOTALS | DISTRICT/ TOWNSHIP | NOTES |
|---|---|---|---|---|---|---|---|---|---|---|---|---|---|---|---|---|---|---|---|
| Nantucket | 18 | 14 | Elkins | John | | 2 | 1 | 1 | 1 | | | 1 | | 1 | 1 | | 8 | | |
| Nantucket | 18 | 15 | Chase | Job | | 1 | | 2 | | 3 | | | 2 | 1 | | | 9 | | |
| Nantucket | 18 | 16 | Hussey | Silvanus | | | 1 | | | 1 | 1 | | 1 | | | | 4 | | |
| Nantucket | 18 | 17 | Gorham | Parnell | 1 | 1 | 1 | | | | | 2 | 1 | | | | 6 | | |
| Nantucket | 18 | 18 | Pinkham | Shubael | | 1 | | 1 | | 2 | | | 1 | | | | 5 | | |
| Nantucket | 18 | 19 | Fitch | Anna | | | | | | | | | | 1 | | | 1 | | |
| Nantucket | 18 | 20 | Cumstock | John | | | | 1 | | | 1 | 2 | 1 | | | | 5 | | |
| Nantucket | 18 | 21 | Gardner | Antipas | | | | 1 | | | | | 1 | | | | 2 | | |
| Nantucket | 18 | 22 | Colesworthy | Jonathan Waldo | 1 | | | 1 | | | 1 | | 1 | | | | 4 | | |
| Nantucket | 18 | 23 | Colesworthy | Waldo | | 1 | | | | 1 | | 1 | | | | | 3 | | |
| Nantucket | 18 | 24 | Burnell | Samuel | | 1 | | | | | | | 1 | | | | 2 | | |
| Nantucket | 18 | 25 | Gardner | Peleg | 2 | 1 | | 1 | | 3 | | | 1 | | | | 8 | | |
| Nantucket | 18 | 26 | Kidder | Benjamin | | | 1 | | | | | | 1 | | | | 2 | | |
| Nantucket | 18 | 27 | Barker | Saml. Junr | 1 | 1 | | 1 | | 2 | | 1 | 1 | | | | 7 | | |
| Nantucket | 18 | 28 | Gardner | Amaziah | | | 1 | | | 2 | | | 1 | | | | 4 | | |
| Nantucket | 18 | 29 | Gardner | Micajah | | 1 | | | | | | | 1 | | | | 2 | | |
| Nantucket | 18 | 30 | Coffin | Judith | | 1 | | | | | | 1 | 1 | 1 | | | 4 | | |
| Nantucket | 18 | 31 | Bennett | reuben | | 1 | | | | 2 | | | 1 | | | | 4 | | |
| Nantucket | 18 | 32 | Meade | George | | 1 | | | | | | | 1 | | | | 2 | | |
| Nantucket | 18 | 33 | Mitchell | Aaron | 1 | 1 | | | | | | 2 | | 1 | | | 5 | | |
| Nantucket | 18 | 34 | Gardner | Paul Junr | | 1 | 1 | | | 2 | | 1 | | | | | 5 | | |
| Nantucket | 18 | 35 | Mitchell | Obed | 3 | 1 | | 1 | 1 | 3 | | 1 | | 1 | | | 11 | | |
| Nantucket | 18 | 36 | Mitchell | Jethro | | 1 | 2 | | 1 | 1 | 1 | | | 1 | | | 7 | | |
| Nantucket | 18 | 37 | Mitchell | Moses | | 1 | | 1 | | | | | 1 | | | | 3 | | |
| Nantucket | 18 | 38 | Barnard | Elisha | | | 2 | 1 | | | | 1 | 1 | | | | 5 | | |
| Nantucket | 18 | 39 | Brown | Joseph Junr | 1 | 1 | 2 | | 1 | | 1 | 1 | 1 | | | | 8 | | |
| Nantucket | 18 | 40 | Worth | Silvanus | | | | 1 | | | | | 1 | | | | 2 | | |
| Nantucket | 18 | 41 | Folger | Isaiah | | | 1 | 1 | | | | | 1 | | | | 3 | | |
| Nantucket | 18 | 42 | Worth | Christopher | | | | 1 | | | | | 1 | | | | 2 | | |
| Nantucket | 18 | 43 | Worth | Uriah | 4 | 1 | | 1 | | | | | 1 | | | | 7 | | |
| Nantucket | 18 | 44 | Folger | George | | | | 1 | | 1 | | | | 1 | 1 | | 4 | | |
| Nantucket | 18 | 45 | Macy | Uriah | 1 | | | 1 | | 3 | 1 | | 1 | | | | 7 | | |
| Nantucket | 18 | 46 | Barney | Benjamin | | | | 1 | | | | | 1 | | | | 2 | | |
| Nantucket | 18 | 47 | Wyer | Hugh | 1 | | | 1 | | 2 | 1 | | 1 | | | | 6 | | |
| Nantucket | 18 | 48 | Gardner | Hephzibah | | | | | | | | | 1 | 1 | | | 2 | | |
| Nantucket | 18 | 49 | Clark | Thomas | | | | 1 | | | | 2 | | | | | 3 | | |
| Nantucket | 18 | 50 | Remson | Arnold | 1 | | | 1 | | 1 | | | 1 | | | | 4 | | |
| Nantucket | 18 | 51 | Hussey | Urial | 2 | 1 | | 1 | | 2 | 1 | | 1 | | 1 | | 9 | | |
| Nantucket | 18 | 52 | Hussey | George | | 1 | 1 | | 1 | | | 2 | | 2 | | | 7 | | |
| Nantucket | 18 | 53 | Brown | Frederic | | 1 | | | 1 | | | | 1 | | | | 3 | | |
| Nantucket | 18 | 54 | Fish | Ruth | | | | | | 1 | | | 1 | | | | 2 | | |
| Nantucket | 18 | 55 | Fish | Stephen | | | 2 | | | | | | 1 | | | | 3 | | |
| Nantucket | 18 | 56 | Swain | Hezekiah | 1 | | 1 | | | 1 | | 1 | | | | | 4 | | |
| Nantucket | 18 | 57 | Folger | Tristram | | | | | 1 | 2 | 1 | | 1 | | | | 5 | | |
| Nantucket | 18 | 58 | Mitchell | Mary | | | | | | | | | | 1 | | | 1 | | |
| Nantucket | 18 | 59 | Swain | Jonathan Junr | 3 | | | 1 | | 2 | | | 1 | 1 | | | 8 | | |
| Nantucket | 18 | 60 | Stubbs | James | 1 | | 2 | | 1 | 3 | 2 | | 1 | | | | 10 | | |
| Nantucket | 18 | 61 | Ellis | Moses | | | 1 | | | 1 | | 1 | | | | | 3 | | |
| Nantucket | 18 | 62 | Hussey | Zaccheus | 2 | | 2 | 1 | | 3 | 2 | | 1 | | 1 | | 12 | | |
| Nantucket | 18 | 63 | Swain | Richard | | 1 | | 1 | 1 | | | | 1 | 1 | | | 5 | | |
| Nantucket | 18 | 64 | Swain | Gardner | | | 1 | | | | | 1 | | | | | 2 | | |
| Nantucket | 18 | 65 | Fitch | Obed | 1 | | | 1 | | | | 1 | 1 | | | | 4 | | |
| Nantucket | 18 | 66 | Folger | Gilbert | | | 2 | | 1 | | | 1 | 1 | 1 | | | 6 | | |
| Nantucket | 18 | 67 | Brock | Walter | | | | 1 | | | | | | 1 | 1 | | 3 | | |
| Nantucket | 18 | 68 | Riddell | Linzey | | 1 | | | | | | | 1 | | | | 2 | | |
| Nantucket | 18 | 69 | Pinkham | Hezekiah | | 1 | | | | 1 | | | 1 | | | | 3 | | |
| Nantucket | 18 | 70 | Ray | Reuben | | 1 | 1 | 1 | | | | 1 | 1 | | | | 5 | | |
| Nantucket | 18 | 71 | Coffin | Catharine | | | | | | | | | | 1 | | | 1 | | |
| Nantucket | 18 | 72 | Coffin | Saml | 2 | 1 | | 1 | 1 | | | 1 | 2 | 1 | | | 9 | | |
| Nantucket | 18 | 73 | Coffin | Barzillia | | 1 | | | | | | | 1 | | | | 2 | | |
| Nantucket | 18 | 74 | Hatch | Charles | 2 | | | 1 | | | | | 1 | | | | 4 | | |
| Nantucket | 18 | 75 | Jones | Ebenezer | 1 | | | 1 | | | | | 1 | 1 | | | 4 | | |
| Nantucket | 18 | 76 | Gardner | Wm | | | | 1 | | | | | | 1 | | | 2 | | |
| Nantucket | 19 | 1 | Starbuck | Simeon | 1 | | | 1 | | | | 1 | | 2 | | | 5 | | |
| Nantucket | 19 | 2 | Freebon | Thomas | 1 | | 1 | | | 2 | | 1 | | | | | 5 | | |
| Nantucket | 19 | 3 | Raymond | Benjm | 2 | | | 1 | | 2 | | | 1 | | | | 6 | | |
| Nantucket | 19 | 4 | Sheffield | Josiah | | | 1 | | | | | | 1 | | | | 2 | | |
| Nantucket | 19 | 5 | Robins | John | 2 | 1 | | 1 | | 1 | 1 | | 1 | | | | 7 | | |
| Nantucket | 19 | 6 | Swain | Benjm | 1 | 1 | | 1 | | 1 | 2 | | 1 | | | | 7 | | |
| Nantucket | 19 | 7 | Swain | Benjm Junr | | | 1 | | | | | | 1 | | | | 2 | | |
| Nantucket | 19 | 8 | Robinson | Saml | 1 | 1 | | 1 | | 1 | | | 1 | 1 | | | 6 | | |
| Nantucket | 19 | 9 | Chase | Judah | 3 | 1 | | 1 | | 1 | | | 1 | 1 | | | 8 | | |
| Nantucket | 19 | 10 | Foster | James | | 1 | | 1 | | | | | 1 | | | | 3 | | |
| Nantucket | 19 | 11 | Parker | Jonathan | 1 | | | 1 | | | | | 1 | | | | 3 | | |
| Nantucket | 19 | 12 | Black | Rowland | | | 1 | | | 1 | | | | 1 | | | 3 | | |
| Nantucket | 19 | 13 | Parker | Nathan | | 2 | 1 | | 1 | | | | 1 | 1 | | | 6 | | |
| Nantucket | 19 | 14 | Swain | Paul | | | 1 | 1 | | | | | | 1 | | | 3 | | |
| Nantucket | 19 | 15 | Swain | Batchelor | | | 1 | | | | | 1 | | | | | 3 | | |
| Nantucket | 19 | 16 | Swain | Reuben | 1 | 1 | | | 1 | 1 | | | 1 | 2 | 1 | | 8 | | |
| Nantucket | 19 | 17 | Baker | James | 1 | 2 | 1 | | 1 | 1 | | | 1 | 1 | | | 8 | | |
| Nantucket | 19 | 18 | Swain | Thankful | | | 1 | | | 2 | 1 | | 1 | | | | 5 | | |
| Nantucket | 19 | 19 | Fisher | Nathl | 1 | 1 | | | 1 | 1 | | | | 1 | | | 5 | | |
| Nantucket | 19 | 20 | Cottle | Lot | 2 | 2 | 2 | | 1 | 1 | | | | 1 | | | 9 | | |
| Nantucket | 19 | 21 | Luce | Elijah | 3 | 1 | 2 | | | 2 | 2 | | 1 | | | | 11 | | |
| Nantucket | 19 | 22 | Swain | George | | 1 | | | 1 | 2 | 1 | 1 | 1 | | | | 7 | | |
| Nantucket | 19 | 23 | Bissell | Abigail | | | | | | 1 | | | 1 | | | | 2 | | |
| Nantucket | 19 | 24 | Edwards | Asa | | | 1 | | | 1 | | | 1 | | | | 3 | | |
| Nantucket | 19 | 25 | Gardner | Bethuel | | | | 1 | | | | | 1 | | | | 2 | | |
| Nantucket | 19 | 26 | Pollard | George | 2 | | | 1 | 1 | 1 | | | 1 | | | | 7 | | |
| Nantucket | 19 | 27 | Dunham | Ebenezer | 2 | 2 | | 1 | | 3 | | 1 | 1 | | | | 10 | | |

133

| TOWN | PG# | LN# | HEADS OF HOUSEHOLD LAST NAME | FIRST NAME | FREE WHITE MALES under 10 | 10 to 16 | 16 to 26 | 26 to 45 | 45 and over | FREE WHITE FEMALES under 10 | 10 to 16 | 16 to 26 | 26 to 45 | 45 and over | TOTAL ALL OTHER | TOTAL SLAVES | TOTALS | DISTRICT/ TOWNSHIP | NOTES |
|---|---|---|---|---|---|---|---|---|---|---|---|---|---|---|---|---|---|---|---|
| Nantucket | 19 | 28 | Painter | Joseph | | | | | | | | | | | 5 | | 5 | | |
| Nantucket | 19 | 29 | Toby | Jemima | | | | | | | | | | | 4 | | 4 | | |
| Nantucket | 19 | 30 | Boston | Peter | | | | | | | | | | | 5 | | 5 | | |
| Nantucket | 19 | 31 | Quary | Joseph | | | | | | | | | | | 4 | | 4 | | |
| Nantucket | 19 | 32 | Warren | Paul | | | | | | | | | | | 5 | | 5 | | |
| Nantucket | 19 | 33 | Burden | Simon | | | | | | | | | | | 4 | | 4 | | |
| Nantucket | 19 | 34 | Dier | Samson | | | | | | | | | | | 6 | | 6 | | |
| Nantucket | 19 | 35 | Brock | Robin | | | | | | | | | | | 2 | | 2 | | |
| Nantucket | 19 | 36 | Fortune | Absalon | | | | | | | | | | | 3 | | 3 | | |
| Nantucket | 19 | 37 | Waterman | Prince | | | | | | | | | | | 4 | | 4 | | |
| Nantucket | 19 | 38 | Lee | Mike | | | | | | | | | | | 3 | | 3 | | |
| Nantucket | 19 | 39 | Nation | London | | | | | | | | | | | 3 | | 3 | | |
| Nantucket | 19 | 40 | Pompy | George | | | | | | | | | | | 3 | | 3 | | |
| Nantucket | 19 | 41 | Limas | Prince | | | | | | | | | | | 3 | | 3 | | |
| Nantucket | 19 | 42 | Plato | James | | | | | | | | | | | 2 | | 2 | | |
| Nantucket | 19 | 43 | Currington | Godfrey | | | | | | | | | | | 7 | | 7 | | |
| Nantucket | 19 | 44 | Hero | Saml | | | | | | | | | | | 4 | | 4 | | |
| Nantucket | 19 | 45 | Simons | Jeffry | | | | | | | | | | | 6 | | 6 | | |
| Nantucket | 19 | 46 | Thomas | John | | | | | | | | | | | 3 | | 3 | | |
| Nantucket | 19 | 47 | Wamsley | Benjm | | | | | | | | | | | 8 | | 8 | | |
| Nantucket | 19 | 48 | Gutridge | Michael | | | | | | | | | | | 2 | | 2 | | |
| Nantucket | 19 | 49 | Quady | Abram | | | | | | | | | | | 3 | | 3 | | |
| Nantucket | 19 | 50 | Isop | Sarah | | | | | | | | | | | 1 | | 1 | | |
| Nantucket | 19 | 51 | Abel | Mary | | | | | | | | | | | 2 | | 2 | | |
| Nantucket | 19 | 52 | Freeman | Issac | | | | | | | | | | | 3 | | 3 | | |
| Nantucket | 19 | 53 | Cheagers | Joshia | | | | | | | | | | | 2 | | 2 | | |
| Nantucket | 19 | 54 | Pheniz | George | | | | | | | | | | | 4 | | 4 | | |
| Nantucket | 19 | 55 | Garlow | Danl | | | | | | | | | | | 9 | | 9 | | |
| Nantucket | 19 | 56 | Godfrey | Cesar | | | | | | | | | | | 4 | | 4 | | |
| Nantucket | 19 | 57 | Jourden | Simon | | | | | | | | | | | 2 | | 2 | | |
| Nantucket | 19 | 58 | Antone | St | | | | | | | | | | | 4 | | 4 | | |
| Nantucket | 19 | 59 | Burden | Simon | | | | | | | | | | | 3 | | 3 | | |
| Nantucket | 19 | 60 | Dier | James | | | | | | | | | | | 3 | | 3 | | |
| Nantucket | 19 | 61 | Summons | Cesar | | | | | | | | | | | 8 | | 8 | | |
| Nantucket | 19 | 62 | Boston | Essex | | | | | | | | | | | 3 | | 3 | | |
| Nantucket | 19 | 63 | Boston | John | | | | | | | | | | | 2 | | 2 | | |
| Nantucket | 19 | 64 | Boston | Phillis | | | | | | | | | | | 1 | | 1 | | |
| Nantucket | 20 | 1 | Winslow | Philip | | | | | | | | | | | 4 | | 4 | | |
| Nantucket | 20 | 2 | Weeden | Charles | | | | | | | | | | | 4 | | 4 | | |
| Nantucket | 20 | 3 | Simons | Ephraim | | | | | | | | | | | 3 | | 3 | | |
| Nantucket | 20 | 4 | Jones | Edmond | | | | | | | | | | | 2 | | 2 | | |
| Nantucket | 20 | 5 | Hawkins | Ebenezer | | | | | | | | | | | 4 | | 4 | | |
| Nantucket | 20 | 6 | Simmons | Toby | | | | | | | | | | | 2 | | 2 | | |
| Nantucket | 20 | 7 | Roberts | Benjm | | | | | | | | | | | 3 | | 3 | | |
| Nantucket | 20 | 8 | Barlow | Cato | | | | | | | | | | | 7 | | 7 | | |
| Nantucket | 20 | 9 | Boston | Seneca | | | | | | | | | | | 6 | | 6 | | |
| Nantucket | 20 | 10 | Pompey | Dinah | | | | | | | | | | | 6 | | 6 | | |
| Nantucket | 20 | 11 | Ross | Matthew | 1 | | | | | | | | | | 2 | | 2 | | |
| Nantucket | 20 | 12 | Arnold | Cyrus | | | | | | | | | | | 2 | | 2 | | |
| Nantucket | 20 | 13 | Thompson | George | | | | | | | | | | | 2 | | 2 | | |
| Nantucket | 20 | 14 | Quam* | Nimrod | | | | | | | | | | | 3 | | 3 | | |

# 1800 Nantucket County, Massachusetts Index

| TOWN | PG# | LN# | LAST NAME | FIRST NAME | FREE WHITE MALES under 10 | 10 to 16 | 16 to 26 | 26 to 45 | 45 and over | FREE WHITE FEMALES under 10 | 10 to 16 | 16 to 26 | 26 to 45 | 45 and over | TOTAL ALL OTHER | TOTAL SLAVES | TOTALS | DISTRICT/ TOWNSHIP | NOTES |
|---|---|---|---|---|---|---|---|---|---|---|---|---|---|---|---|---|---|---|---|
| Nantucket | 13 | 77 | * | Benjamin | | | 2 | 1 | | | | | 1 | 1 | | | 5 | | |
| Nantucket | 19 | 51 | Abel | Mary | | | | | | | | | | | 2 | | 2 | Not Stated | |
| Nantucket | 5 | 32 | Addleton | Abigail | | | | | | | | | | 1 | | | 1 | Not Stated | |
| Nantucket | 5 | 33 | Addleton | John | 2 | | | 1 | | 2 | 1 | | 1 | | | | 7 | Not Stated | |
| Nantucket | 8 | 45 | Alby | Mary | | | | | | | | | 1 | | | | 1 | Not Stated | |
| Nantucket | 14 | 23 | Aldridge | Ichabod | | | | 1 | | | | 1 | | 1 | | | 3 | | |
| Nantucket | 14 | 24 | Aldridge | Ichabod Junr | | | 1 | | | 1 | | | 1 | | | | 3 | | |
| Nantucket | 14 | 36 | Aldridge | Obed Junr | | | 1 | | | 2 | 2 | | 2 | | | | 7 | | |
| Nantucket | 9 | 31 | Allen | Abigail | | 1 | | | | 1 | 1 | 1 | 1 | | | | 6 | Not Stated | |
| Nantucket | 14 | 9 | Allen | Abigail | | | | | | 1 | | 1 | | | | | 2 | | |
| Nantucket | 4 | 71 | Allen | Daniel | | 1 | 2 | 1 | | 3 | 1 | | | 2 | | | 10 | Not Stated | |
| Nantucket | 10 | 11 | Allen | David | 4 | 1 | | 2 | | | 1 | 1 | 1 | | | | 10 | Not Stated | |
| Nantucket | 10 | 24 | Allen | Edwd | | 1 | | | 1 | | | | | 1 | | | 3 | Not Stated | |
| Nantucket | 7 | 57 | Allen | John | | | | | 1 | | | | | 1 | | | 2 | Not Stated | |
| Nantucket | 7 | 50 | Allen | John Junr | 2 | 1 | 2 | | 1 | 1 | 1 | 3 | 1 | | | | 12 | Not Stated | |
| Nantucket | 5 | 31 | Allen | Joseph | | | 1 | | | 2 | 1 | | | | | | 4 | Not Stated | |
| Nantucket | 7 | 58 | Allen | Reuben | 2 | | 1 | | | 1 | | 1 | | | | | 5 | Not Stated | |
| Nantucket | 14 | 68 | Allen | Tristram | 1 | | 1 | | | 3 | | 1 | | | | | 6 | | |
| Nantucket | 6 | 1 | Alley | Jacob | | | 1 | | 1 | | | 2 | 1 | | | | 5 | Not Stated | |
| Nantucket | 5 | 67 | Alley | Reuben | 2 | 1 | | 1 | | 1 | | | 2 | | | | 7 | Not Stated | |
| Nantucket | 12 | 63 | Alley | Richard | 1 | 1 | 2 | | 1 | 3 | 3 | 1 | 1 | | | | 13 | | |
| Nantucket | 14 | 5 | Alley | William | 1 | | 1 | | | | | | 1 | | | | 3 | | |
| Nantucket | 13 | 46 | Ames | Anna | | | | | | | | | | 1 | | | 1 | | |
| Nantucket | 14 | 26 | Ames | Benjamin | | | 1 | | | 2 | 1 | | 1 | | | | 5 | | |
| Nantucket | 9 | 53 | Andrews | Jacob | 2 | 1 | | | | | | 1 | | | | | 4 | Not Stated | |
| Nantucket | 12 | 8 | Annis | Stephen | 1 | 1 | 1 | | | 4 | | | 1 | | | | 8 | Not Stated | |
| Nantucket | 19 | 58 | Antone | St | | | | | | | | | | | 4 | | 4 | | |
| Nantucket | 20 | 12 | Arnold | Cyrus | | | | | | | | | | | 2 | | 2 | | |
| Nantucket | 12 | 15 | Arpin | Issac | | | 1 | | | 1 | | 1 | | | | | 3 | Not Stated | |
| Nantucket | 14 | 39 | Arthur | Stephen | 1 | 2 | 1 | 1 | | 1 | | 1 | | 1 | | | 8 | | |
| Nantucket | 17 | 9 | Ary | Jabez | | | 1 | | | | 1 | | | 2 | | | 4 | | |
| Nantucket | 9 | 44 | Austin | Benjamin Junr | 2 | | 1 | | | 2 | 1 | 1 | | | | | 7 | Not Stated | |
| Nantucket | 7 | 54 | Baker | Catharine | | | 1 | | | | | 2 | 1 | | | | 5 | Not Stated | |
| Nantucket | 6 | 12 | Baker | James | 1 | | 1 | | | | | 1 | | | | | 3 | Not Stated | |
| Nantucket | 19 | 17 | Baker | James | 1 | 2 | 1 | | 1 | 1 | | 1 | | 1 | | | 8 | | |
| Nantucket | 17 | 20 | Barker | James | 2 | 2 | 1 | | | | | 1 | 1 | | | | 7 | | |
| Nantucket | 17 | 41 | Barker | Josiah Junr | | 2 | | 1 | | 3 | | 1 | 1 | | | | 8 | | |
| Nantucket | 13 | 39 | Barker | Latham | | | | 1 | | 1 | | | | 2 | | | 4 | | |
| Nantucket | 5 | 61 | Barker | Saml | 1 | | 2 | 1 | | | | | 1 | 3 | | | 8 | Not Stated | |
| Nantucket | 18 | 27 | Barker | Saml. Junr | 1 | 1 | | 1 | | 2 | | 1 | 1 | | | | 7 | | |
| Nantucket | 3 | 11 | Barker | Sarah | | | | | | | | | 2 | 1 | | | 3 | Not Stated | |
| Nantucket | 20 | 8 | Barlow | Cato | | | | | | | | | | | 7 | | 7 | | |
| Nantucket | 16 | 34 | Barn | Mary | | | | 1 | | | | | 1 | 1 | | | 3 | | |
| Nantucket | 5 | 52 | Barnard | Andrew | 1 | | | 1 | | 1 | | | 1 | | | | 4 | Not Stated | |
| Nantucket | 14 | 12 | Barnard | Charles | | | 1 | | | | | | 1 | | | | 2 | | |
| Nantucket | 9 | 18 | Barnard | Christopher | | | 1 | | | | | | 1 | | | | 2 | Not Stated | |
| Nantucket | 18 | 38 | Barnard | Elisha | | | 2 | 1 | | | | 1 | | 1 | | | 5 | | |
| Nantucket | 11 | 13 | Barnard | Henry | 1 | | 1 | | | | | | 1 | | | | 3 | Not Stated | |
| Nantucket | 14 | 18 | Barnard | James | 2 | | 1 | | | 1 | | 1 | 1 | | | | 6 | | |
| Nantucket | 6 | 33 | Barnard | John | | | | 1 | | | | 2 | 1 | | | | 4 | Not Stated | |
| Nantucket | 4 | 53 | Barnard | Jonathan | 2 | 1 | | | | 3 | 1 | | 1 | | | | 9 | Not Stated | |
| Nantucket | 15 | 40 | Barnard | Judith | | | | | | 1 | | 2 | 1 | 2 | | | 6 | | |
| Nantucket | 17 | 2 | Barnard | Laban | | | 1 | | | | | | 1 | | | | 2 | | |
| Nantucket | 5 | 53 | Barnard | Libni | 3 | | | | | 2 | | 1 | 1 | 1 | | | 8 | Not Stated | |
| Nantucket | 17 | 21 | Barnard | Lydia | | 2 | | | | | | 1 | | 1 | | | 4 | | |
| Nantucket | 5 | 51 | Barnard | Matthew | | | 1 | | 1 | 1 | 2 | 1 | | | | | 6 | Not Stated | |
| Nantucket | 9 | 17 | Barnard | Nathl | | | 1 | 2 | 1 | | | | | 1 | | | 5 | Not Stated | |
| Nantucket | 16 | 45 | Barnard | Obed | 2 | 2 | | | | 1 | | | 1 | | | | 7 | | |
| Nantucket | 5 | 41 | Barnard | Ruth | | 1 | 2 | 1 | | 1 | | 1 | 1 | | | | 7 | Not Stated | |
| Nantucket | 4 | 40 | Barnard | Shubael | | 1 | 1 | | 1 | 1 | | | 1 | | | | 5 | Not Stated | |
| Nantucket | 14 | 63 | Barnard | Stephen | | | | 1 | | | | | | | | | 1 | | |
| Nantucket | 11 | 50 | Barnard | Thomas | 1 | | | 1 | | 1 | | | 1 | | | | 4 | Not Stated | |
| Nantucket | 3 | 24 | Barnard | Thomas 2nd | | | 1 | | | | | | 1 | | | | 2 | Not Stated | |
| Nantucket | 13 | 30 | Barnard | Tristram | 2 | | | 1 | | | | | 1 | | | | 4 | | |
| Nantucket | 16 | 59 | Barnard | Wm | | | 1 | 1 | | 4 | 1 | 2 | 1 | | | | 10 | | |
| Nantucket | 9 | 52 | Barnard Orpin | John | 1 | | | 1 | | 1 | | | 1 | | | | 4 | Not Stated | |
| Nantucket | 12 | 14 | Barnes | William | 1 | | 1 | | | | | | 1 | | | | 3 | Not Stated | |
| Nantucket | 18 | 46 | Barney | Benjamin | | | | 1 | | | | | | 1 | | | 2 | | |
| Nantucket | 9 | 21 | Barney | Daniel | 2 | 1 | | 1 | | 1 | | 1 | 2 | 1 | | | 9 | Not Stated | |
| Nantucket | 17 | 29 | Barney | Griffin | | | 1 | | | | | | | 1 | | | 2 | | |
| Nantucket | 13 | 52 | Barney | Jonathan | 3 | 3 | 1 | | | 1 | | | 1 | | | | 10 | | |
| Nantucket | 15 | 47 | Barney | Jonathan | | | 2 | 1 | | | | 1 | 1 | 2 | | | 7 | | |
| Nantucket | 15 | 48 | Barney | Jonathan Junr | 4 | 2 | 2 | 1 | | 2 | | 1 | 1 | 1 | | | 14 | | |
| Nantucket | 10 | 18 | Barney | Matthew | 1 | | 1 | 1 | | 3 | | | 1 | | | | 7 | Not Stated | |
| Nantucket | 17 | 59 | Barney | Peter | | | 3 | | | | 1 | 1 | 1 | | | | 8 | | |
| Nantucket | 13 | 59 | Barney | Robert | | 1 | 2 | | 1 | | | | | 1 | | | 5 | | |
| Nantucket | 17 | 40 | Barney | Sarah | | | | | | | | | | 2 | | | 2 | | |
| Nantucket | 15 | 49 | Barney | William | 1 | | | 1 | | 1 | | | 1 | | | | 4 | | |
| Nantucket | 13 | 35 | Barrett | Abigail | 1 | | | | | | | 1 | 1 | | | | 3 | | |
| Nantucket | 15 | 10 | Barrett | Nathaniel | 2 | 1 | 1 | | 1 | | | 3 | | 1 | | | 9 | | |
| Nantucket | 4 | 8 | Barrett | Saml | | | 1 | | | | | 1 | 1 | | | | 4 | Not Stated | |
| Nantucket | 13 | 33 | Bartlett | Oliver C. | 1 | | 1 | | | 2 | 1 | | | | | | 6 | | |
| Nantucket | 7 | 10 | Baxter | Christopher | | | 1 | 1 | | 1 | | | | 1 | | | 4 | Not Stated | |
| Nantucket | 12 | 53 | Baxter | Lydia | | | | | | | | 1 | 1 | | | | 2 | | |
| Nantucket | 12 | 49 | Bay | David | | | | 1 | | | | | | 1 | | | 2 | | |
| Nantucket | 13 | 19 | Beard | Elizabeth | 1 | | 1 | | | | | | 2 | | | | 4 | | |
| Nantucket | 13 | 4 | Beard | John | | | 1 | | 1 | | | | 2 | 1 | | | 5 | | |
| Nantucket | 6 | 8 | Bebee | Nathan | 2 | | 1 | 1 | 1 | | | 3 | | 1 | | | 10 | Not Stated | |
| Nantucket | 18 | 31 | Bennett | reuben | | 1 | | | | | 2 | | | | | | 4 | Not Stated | |
| Nantucket | 4 | 56 | Bennett | Ruth | 1 | | | | | | | | 1 | 1 | | | 3 | Not Stated | |

# 1800 Nantucket County, Massachusetts Index

| TOWN | PG# | LN# | LAST NAME | FIRST NAME | M<10 | M10-16 | M16-26 | M26-45 | M45+ | F<10 | F10-16 | F16-26 | F26-45 | F45+ | TOTAL ALL OTHER | TOTAL SLAVES | TOTALS | DISTRICT/ TOWNSHIP | NOTES |
|---|---|---|---|---|---|---|---|---|---|---|---|---|---|---|---|---|---|---|---|
| Nantucket | 10 | 4 | Bennett | William | 1 | | | 1 | | | | | | 1 | | | 3 | Not Stated | |
| Nantucket | 19 | 23 | Bissell | Abigail | | | | | | | | 1 | | 1 | | | 2 | | |
| Nantucket | 12 | 3 | Black | Cleophas | 1 | | 1 | | | | | | 1 | | | | 3 | Not Stated | |
| Nantucket | 11 | 59 | Black | Daniel | | | | 1 | | | | | 1 | 1 | | | 3 | Not Stated | |
| Nantucket | 11 | 63 | Black | Mary | | | | | | | | | 1 | 1 | | | 2 | Not Stated | |
| Nantucket | 11 | 57 | Black | Patty | | | | | | | | | 1 | | | | 1 | Not Stated | |
| Nantucket | 19 | 12 | Black | Rowland | | | 1 | | | 1 | | | | 1 | | | 3 | | |
| Nantucket | 19 | 62 | Boston | Essex | | | | | | | | | | | 3 | | 3 | | |
| Nantucket | 19 | 63 | Boston | John | | | | | | | | | | | 2 | | 2 | | |
| Nantucket | 19 | 30 | Boston | Peter | | | | | | | | | | | 5 | | 5 | | |
| Nantucket | 19 | 64 | Boston | Phillis | | | | | | | | | | | 1 | | 1 | | |
| Nantucket | 20 | 9 | Boston | Seneca | | | | | | | | | | | 6 | | 6 | | |
| Nantucket | 7 | 48 | Bowcot | Sarah | 2 | 1 | | 3 | | | | 1 | 3 | 1 | | | 11 | Not Stated | |
| Nantucket | 3 | 14 | Brayton | Isaac | 1 | | 1 | 1 | | 1 | | | 1 | 3 | 1 | | 9 | Not Stated | |
| Nantucket | 15 | 18 | Brayton | Robert | 1 | 1 | 1 | 1 | | 1 | | | 1 | | | | 6 | | |
| Nantucket | 5 | 58 | Briggs | Abner | | 1 | | 1 | | | | | 1 | 1 | | | 4 | Not Stated | |
| Nantucket | 6 | 5 | Briggs | Jonathan | 2 | 1 | | 1 | | | | | 2 | | | | 6 | Not Stated | |
| Nantucket | 12 | 17 | Briggs | Stephen | | 1 | 1 | | | | | | 1 | 1 | | | 4 | Not Stated | |
| Nantucket | 14 | 35 | Brock | Andrew | | | | 1 | | | | | | 1 | | | 2 | | |
| Nantucket | 16 | 72 | Brock | Andrew Junr | 1 | | 1 | | | | | 1 | 1 | | | | 4 | | |
| Nantucket | 17 | 51 | Brock | Jethro | | 1 | | | | | | 1 | | | | | 2 | | |
| Nantucket | 14 | 65 | Brock | John | | 1 | | 1 | | | | | 1 | 1 | | | 4 | | |
| Nantucket | 16 | 22 | Brock | John | | 1 | | | | | | | 2 | 1 | | | 4 | | |
| Nantucket | 15 | 12 | Brock | Peter | 1 | | 1 | | | | | | 1 | | | | 3 | | |
| Nantucket | 19 | 35 | Brock | Robin | | | | | | | | | | | 2 | | 2 | | |
| Nantucket | 14 | 77 | Brock | Thomas | 2 | 1 | 2 | 1 | | 1 | 1 | | 1 | 1 | | | 10 | | |
| Nantucket | 18 | 67 | Brock | Walter | | | | 1 | | | | | | 1 | 1 | | 3 | | |
| Nantucket | 3 | 1 | Brock | William | | 1 | 1 | | | | | | 1 | | | | 3 | Not Stated | |
| Nantucket | 14 | 66 | Brooks | William | 1 | | 1 | | | 3 | | 1 | | | | | 6 | | |
| Nantucket | 15 | 39 | Brown | Benjamin | 2 | 1 | | 1 | | | | 1 | 2 | | | | 7 | | |
| Nantucket | 10 | 8 | Brown | Elizabeth | | | | | | | | | 1 | | | | 1 | Not Stated | |
| Nantucket | 6 | 2 | Brown | Francis | | 1 | | 1 | | 1 | | 2 | | 1 | | | 6 | Not Stated | |
| Nantucket | 18 | 53 | Brown | Frederic | | 1 | | 1 | | | | | | 1 | | | 3 | | |
| Nantucket | 8 | 7 | Brown | George | | 2 | 1 | 1 | | | | 1 | 1 | 1 | | | 7 | Not Stated | |
| Nantucket | 8 | 8 | Brown | James | | | | 1 | | | | 1 | 1 | | | | 3 | Not Stated | |
| Nantucket | 9 | 50 | Brown | John | 1 | | | 1 | | 2 | | 1 | | 1 | | | 6 | Not Stated | |
| Nantucket | 18 | 39 | Brown | Joseph Junr | 1 | 1 | 2 | 1 | | | | 1 | 1 | 1 | | | 8 | | |
| Nantucket | 3 | 4 | Brown | William | | | | 1 | | 1 | | 1 | 1 | 1 | | | 6 | Not Stated | |
| Nantucket | 8 | 6 | Brown | William | 3 | | | 1 | | 1 | | | 1 | | | | 6 | Not Stated | |
| Nantucket | 13 | 21 | Bunker | Abishai | | 1 | 1 | 1 | | | | | | 1 | | | 4 | | |
| Nantucket | 4 | 10 | Bunker | Barnabas | | 2 | | 1 | | 5 | 1 | 1 | 1 | | | | 11 | Not Stated | |
| Nantucket | 5 | 62 | Bunker | Benjm | 1 | 1 | 3 | 1 | 1 | 1 | | 1 | 1 | 1 | | | 11 | Not Stated | |
| Nantucket | 14 | 31 | Bunker | Caleb | | | 2 | | | | | | 1 | 2 | | | 5 | | |
| Nantucket | 10 | 43 | Bunker | Charles | | 2 | | 1 | | | | | 1 | 1 | | | 5 | Not Stated | |
| Nantucket | 14 | 54 | Bunker | Christopher | | | | 1 | | | | | | 1 | | | 2 | | |
| Nantucket | 10 | 40 | Bunker | Christopher Junr | 1 | 1 | | 1 | | 1 | | | 2 | | | | 6 | Not Stated | |
| Nantucket | 12 | 44 | Bunker | Desire | | | | | | | | | 2 | | | | 2 | | |
| Nantucket | 17 | 16 | Bunker | Elizabeth | | | | | | | | | 1 | | | | 1 | | |
| Nantucket | 11 | 27 | Bunker | George | | 1 | | 1 | | | | 2 | | 1 | | | 5 | Not Stated | |
| Nantucket | 4 | 16 | Bunker | Hezekiah | 1 | 1 | | 1 | | 3 | 2 | | 1 | | | | 9 | Not Stated | |
| Nantucket | 4 | 12 | Bunker | James | 1 | | 1 | | | | | 1 | 1 | | | | 4 | Not Stated | |
| Nantucket | 17 | 15 | Bunker | John | 2 | 1 | | 1 | | 1 | | | 1 | 1 | | | 7 | | |
| Nantucket | 13 | 12 | Bunker | Joshua | | 1 | 1 | 1 | | | | | | 1 | | | 4 | | |
| Nantucket | 13 | 25 | Bunker | Latham | | 1 | 1 | 1 | | 3 | | | 1 | 1 | | 2 | 10 | | |
| Nantucket | 18 | 9 | Bunker | Love | 1 | 1 | | | | | | | 1 | 1 | | | 4 | | |
| Nantucket | 11 | 47 | Bunker | Mary | | | | | | 2 | | 1 | | | | | 3 | Not Stated | |
| Nantucket | 4 | 47 | Bunker | Matthew | 1 | | 1 | | | 1 | | 1 | | 1 | | | 5 | Not Stated | |
| Nantucket | 11 | 9 | Bunker | Moses | | | 1 | | | 1 | | 1 | | | | | 3 | Not Stated | |
| Nantucket | 8 | 20 | Bunker | Nathaniel | 5 | 2 | 1 | 1 | | | | 1 | 1 | | | | 11 | Not Stated | |
| Nantucket | 7 | 23 | Bunker | Obed | | 1 | 3 | 1 | | 2 | 1 | 2 | 1 | 1 | | | 12 | Not Stated | |
| Nantucket | 14 | 8 | Bunker | Owen | | | 1 | | | | | 1 | | | | | 2 | | |
| Nantucket | 10 | 37 | Bunker | Peleg | | | | 1 | | 1 | | 2 | | 1 | | | 5 | Not Stated | |
| Nantucket | 14 | 62 | Bunker | Phebe | | | | | | | | | 2 | 1 | | | 3 | | |
| Nantucket | 4 | 23 | Bunker | Seth | | | | 1 | | | | | 1 | | | | 2 | Not Stated | |
| Nantucket | 17 | 1 | Bunker | Thos | 2 | | 1 | | | 2 | | | 1 | | | | 6 | | |
| Nantucket | 7 | 8 | Bunker | Tristram | | | | 1 | | | | | | 1 | | | 2 | Not Stated | |
| Nantucket | 7 | 22 | Bunker | Uriah | | 2 | 1 | 1 | | | | 1 | 1 | | | | 6 | Not Stated | |
| Nantucket | 16 | 69 | Bunker | Uriah 2nd | | 2 | 1 | | | 1 | 1 | 1 | | | | | 7 | | |
| Nantucket | 10 | 31 | Bunker | Uriah Junr | 2 | | 1 | | | | | | 1 | | | | 4 | Not Stated | |
| Nantucket | 19 | 33 | Burden | Simon | | | | | | | | | | | | 4 | 4 | | |
| Nantucket | 19 | 59 | Burden | Simon | | | | | | | | | | | | 3 | 3 | | |
| Nantucket | 6 | 45 | Burdett | Parnell | 1 | | 3 | | | 3 | | | 1 | | | | 8 | Not Stated | |
| Nantucket | 8 | 53 | Burgess | Ebenezer | | 1 | | 1 | | 1 | | | | | | | 3 | Not Stated | |
| Nantucket | 8 | 56 | Burnell | Jemima | | 1 | | | | | | 3 | 1 | 1 | | | 6 | Not Stated | |
| Nantucket | 12 | 37 | Burnell | Polly | 2 | | | | | | | | 1 | | | | 3 | | |
| Nantucket | 18 | 24 | Burnell | Samuel | | 1 | | | | | | | 1 | | | | 2 | | |
| Nantucket | 5 | 66 | Burrage | Rebecca | | | | | | 2 | | | 1 | 2 | | | 5 | Not Stated | |
| Nantucket | 9 | 4 | Butler | Mary | | | | | | | | 1 | | 1 | | | 2 | Not Stated | |
| Nantucket | 10 | 58 | Calder | Josiah | 2 | | | 1 | | 2 | | | 1 | | | | 6 | Not Stated | |
| Nantucket | 14 | 73 | Calder | Robert | 4 | 3 | 1 | | | | | | 1 | | | | 9 | | |
| Nantucket | 16 | 17 | Calef | Ebenezer | 2 | | 1 | | 1 | | | 2 | 1 | 1 | | | 8 | | |
| Nantucket | 15 | 13 | Cartwright | Benjamin | 1 | 2 | 1 | | | | | 1 | 1 | | | | 6 | | |
| Nantucket | 7 | 34 | Cartwright | Deborah | | | | | | | | | 1 | | | | 1 | Not Stated | |
| Nantucket | 11 | 12 | Cartwright | James | | 1 | 1 | | | | | | | 1 | | | 3 | Not Stated | |
| Nantucket | 4 | 18 | Cartwright | James 2nd | 3 | | 1 | 1 | | 2 | 1 | 1 | | | | | 9 | Not Stated | |
| Nantucket | 17 | 38 | Cartwright | John | 2 | 1 | 1 | 1 | | 3 | 2 | 2 | 2 | | | | 14 | | |
| Nantucket | 17 | 55 | Cartwright | Joseph | 1 | 1 | | | | | | 1 | 1 | | | | 4 | | |
| Nantucket | 4 | 26 | Cartwright | Thos | 1 | 1 | | | | | | | 1 | | | | 3 | Not Stated | |
| Nantucket | 12 | 20 | Cary | Edward | | 2 | 1 | 1 | | | | 1 | 1 | 1 | 3 | | 10 | Not Stated | |
| Nantucket | 4 | 43 | Cary | Edward Junr | 1 | | 1 | 1 | | 2 | 1 | 1 | | | | | 7 | Not Stated | |

# 1800 Nantucket County, Massachusetts Index

| TOWN | PG# | LN# | LAST NAME | FIRST NAME | FWM under 10 | FWM 10 to 16 | FWM 16 to 26 | FWM 26 to 45 | FWM 45 and over | FWF under 10 | FWF 10 to 16 | FWF 16 to 26 | FWF 26 to 45 | FWF 45 and over | TOTAL ALL OTHER | TOTAL SLAVES | TOTALS | DISTRICT/ TOWNSHIP | NOTES |
|---|---|---|---|---|---|---|---|---|---|---|---|---|---|---|---|---|---|---|---|
| Nantucket | 13 | 50 | Cary | Richard | | | 1 | 1 | | | | | 1 | 1 | | | 4 | | |
| Nantucket | 12 | 21 | Cary | Samuel | 2 | | | 1 | | 1 | | | | | | | 4 | Not Stated | |
| Nantucket | 6 | 34 | Cash | Elijah | 1 | | | 1 | | 3 | | | 1 | | | | 6 | Not Stated | |
| Nantucket | 7 | 41 | Cash | Phebe | 1 | | | | | 1 | 1 | | 1 | | | | 4 | Not Stated | |
| Nantucket | 7 | 17 | Cash | Reuben | | 1 | | | | | | 1 | | | | | 2 | Not Stated | |
| Nantucket | 8 | 11 | cash | Wheelden | | | | 1 | | | | | 1 | | | | 2 | Not Stated | |
| Nantucket | 7 | 31 | Cash | William | 1 | | | 1 | 1 | | | | 1 | 1 | | | 5 | Not Stated | |
| Nantucket | 9 | 23 | Caswell | Levi | | 1 | | 1 | | 1 | | | | 1 | | | 4 | Not Stated | |
| Nantucket | 7 | 25 | Cathcart | Gershom | 1 | 1 | 5 | | 1 | | 2 | 1 | | 1 | | | 12 | Not Stated | |
| Nantucket | 8 | 10 | Cathcart | Jonathan | 1 | | | 1 | | 2 | | | 1 | | | | 5 | Not Stated | |
| Nantucket | 8 | 34 | Cathcart | Joseph | 1 | 3 | 2 | | 1 | | | | | 1 | | | 8 | Not Stated | |
| Nantucket | 14 | 4 | Cathcart | Robert | 1 | | | 1 | | 1 | | 1 | | | | | 4 | | |
| Nantucket | 6 | 22 | Chadwick | David | | 3 | 1 | | 1 | 1 | | | | 1 | | | 7 | Not Stated | |
| Nantucket | 3 | 22 | Chadwick | Lydia | | | | | | | | | 1 | 1 | | | 2 | Not Stated | |
| Nantucket | 6 | 23 | Chadwick | Nathaniel | 1 | | | | 1 | 2 | 2 | 3 | 1 | | | | 10 | Not Stated | |
| Nantucket | 4 | 25 | Chadwick | Richard | | | | 1 | | 1 | | | 1 | | | | 3 | Not Stated | |
| Nantucket | 8 | 19 | Chadwick | Wickliff | 1 | 1 | 3 | 2 | 1 | | 1 | 3 | | 1 | | | 13 | Not Stated | |
| Nantucket | 7 | 27 | Chadwick | William | | 3 | | 1 | | | | | | 1 | | | 5 | Not Stated | |
| Nantucket | 12 | 48 | Chase | Charles | 1 | | | 1 | | | | | 1 | 1 | | | 4 | | |
| Nantucket | 9 | 8 | Chase | Charles Junr | 3 | | | 1 | | 2 | | | 1 | | | | 7 | Not Stated | |
| Nantucket | 12 | 41 | Chase | Francis | | | 3 | | 1 | | 1 | | | 1 | | | 6 | | |
| Nantucket | 9 | 7 | Chase | George | 2 | 1 | | 1 | | 3 | | | 1 | | | | 8 | Not Stated | |
| Nantucket | 7 | 44 | Chase | Issac | 1 | 3 | | | 1 | | | 1 | 1 | | | | 7 | Not Stated | |
| Nantucket | 15 | 28 | Chase | James | | 1 | 2 | | 1 | 1 | | 1 | | 1 | | | 7 | | |
| Nantucket | 16 | 40 | Chase | James | | 1 | | | 1 | 1 | | 1 | | 1 | | | 5 | | |
| Nantucket | 15 | 17 | Chase | Jerusha | | | | | | | | | 1 | 1 | | | 2 | | |
| Nantucket | 18 | 15 | Chase | Job | | 1 | | 2 | | 3 | | | 2 | 1 | | | 9 | | |
| Nantucket | 7 | 45 | Chase | Jonathan | 1 | | 1 | | 1 | | 1 | | 1 | | | | 5 | Not Stated | |
| Nantucket | 10 | 35 | Chase | Joseph | 3 | | 1 | | 2 | | 1 | 2 | 1 | | 1 | | 11 | Not Stated | |
| Nantucket | 10 | 36 | Chase | Joseph Junr | | | 1 | | | 2 | | | 2 | | | | 5 | Not Stated | |
| Nantucket | 19 | 9 | Chase | Judah | 3 | 1 | | 1 | | 1 | | 1 | 1 | | | | 8 | | |
| Nantucket | 14 | 69 | Chase | Nathan | 1 | | | 1 | | | | 1 | | | | | 3 | | |
| Nantucket | 16 | 37 | Chase | Peter | 4 | 1 | | 1 | | 1 | | | 1 | | | | 8 | | |
| Nantucket | 14 | 16 | Chase | Reuben | | | 1 | | 1 | 2 | 2 | | 1 | | | | 7 | | |
| Nantucket | 13 | 2 | Chase | Stephen | 3 | | | 1 | | | | | 1 | | | | 5 | | |
| Nantucket | 3 | 34 | Chase | Thomas | 2 | | | 1 | 1 | 2 | | | 2 | 2 | | | 10 | Not Stated | |
| Nantucket | 11 | 46 | Chase | William | | | | 1 | | 1 | | | 1 | | | | 3 | Not Stated | |
| Nantucket | 19 | 53 | Cheagers | Joshia | | | | | | | | | | | 2 | | 2 | | |
| Nantucket | 9 | 25 | Christian | Peter | 2 | | | 1 | | | | | 1 | | | | 4 | Not Stated | |
| Nantucket | 14 | 60 | Clark | Benjamin Junr | | | 1 | | 2 | | 1 | 2 | | 1 | | | 7 | | |
| Nantucket | 15 | 72 | Clark | George | | | | 1 | | 1 | | | 1 | | | | 3 | | |
| Nantucket | 6 | 40 | Clark | James | | | | 2 | | | | | 1 | | | | 3 | Not Stated | |
| Nantucket | 5 | 6 | Clark | Joseph | | | 1 | | 1 | | | | 1 | | | | 3 | Not Stated | |
| Nantucket | 16 | 21 | Clark | Love | 1 | | | | | 1 | | | 1 | | | | 2 | | |
| Nantucket | 15 | 43 | Clark | Obed | | | 1 | | | | | | 1 | | | | 2 | | |
| Nantucket | 5 | 22 | Clark | Rachel | | | | | | | 1 | 1 | | | | | 2 | Not Stated | |
| Nantucket | 13 | 32 | Clark | Reuben | | | 1 | | | | | | 2 | | | | 3 | | |
| Nantucket | 15 | 77 | Clark | S*t | 2 | | 1 | | | 1 | | | 1 | | | | 5 | | |
| Nantucket | 15 | 14 | Clark | Sarah | | | | | | | | 1 | 1 | | | | 2 | | |
| Nantucket | 14 | 11 | Clark | Simon | | | | 1 | | | | | | 1 | | | 2 | | |
| Nantucket | 10 | 28 | Clark | Thaddeus | 2 | | 1 | | | | | | 1 | | | | 4 | Not Stated | |
| Nantucket | 18 | 49 | Clark | Thomas | | | | 1 | | | | 2 | | | | | 3 | | |
| Nantucket | 12 | 51 | Clark | Uriah | 2 | | 1 | | | | | | 1 | | | | 4 | | |
| Nantucket | 8 | 58 | Clark | William 3rd | | 1 | | 1 | | 1 | 1 | 1 | | | | | 5 | Not Stated | |
| Nantucket | 5 | 5 | Clark | William Junr | | 1 | 1 | 1 | | 1 | | | 1 | | | | 5 | Not Stated | |
| Nantucket | 5 | 4 | Clark | Wm | | | | 1 | | | | | | 1 | | | 2 | Not Stated | |
| Nantucket | 15 | 4 | Clasby | Abraham | 2 | | | 1 | | 1 | 1 | | 1 | | | | 6 | | |
| Nantucket | 17 | 3 | Clasby | Charles | 1 | | 1 | | | | 1 | 1 | | | | | 4 | | |
| Nantucket | 4 | 45 | Clasby | John | | | 1 | | 1 | | | 1 | | 1 | | | 4 | Not Stated | |
| Nantucket | 4 | 46 | Clasby | John Junr | | | 1 | 1 | | 2 | | | 1 | | | | 5 | Not Stated | |
| Nantucket | 5 | 17 | Clasby | Joseph | 1 | | | 1 | | | | | 1 | | | | 3 | Not Stated | |
| Nantucket | 15 | 3 | Clasby | Robert | | | | 1 | | | | | | 1 | | | 2 | | |
| Nantucket | 7 | 30 | Cleaveland | Aaron | | | | 1 | | | | | 1 | 1 | | | 3 | Not Stated | |
| Nantucket | 7 | 19 | Cleaveland | Seth | 2 | 1 | | 1 | | 1 | 1 | | 1 | | | | 7 | Not Stated | |
| Nantucket | 7 | 32 | Cleaveland | Susanna | | | | | | | | | 1 | 1 | | | 2 | Not Stated | |
| Nantucket | 10 | 14 | Cleveland | Lydia | | | | 1 | | 1 | | | 2 | | | | 4 | Not Stated | |
| Nantucket | 9 | 48 | Clisby | William | | 2 | 1 | | 1 | | | 2 | 1 | | | | 7 | Not Stated | |
| Nantucket | 15 | 45 | Cob | Wm | 1 | 1 | 1 | 1 | | 2 | | | | | | | 6 | | |
| Nantucket | 4 | 15 | Coffin | Abigail | | | | 1 | | | | 1 | 1 | 1 | | | 4 | Not Stated | |
| Nantucket | 9 | 6 | Coffin | Abigail | | | | | | | | | | 2 | | | 2 | Not Stated | |
| Nantucket | 5 | 55 | Coffin | Abihu | | 1 | | | | | | | 1 | | | | 3 | Not Stated | |
| Nantucket | 4 | 3 | Coffin | Abner | | 1 | 3 | | 1 | 1 | | 2 | | 1 | | | 9 | Not Stated | |
| Nantucket | 14 | 28 | Coffin | Absalon | | | 1 | | | 1 | | | 1 | | | | 3 | | |
| Nantucket | 15 | 26 | Coffin | Albert | | 1 | | | | | | | 1 | | | | 2 | | |
| Nantucket | 16 | 31 | Coffin | Alpheus | 3 | | 1 | 1 | | | | | 1 | | | | 6 | | |
| Nantucket | 9 | 16 | Coffin | Andrew | | | 1 | | | | | 1 | | | | | 2 | Not Stated | |
| Nantucket | 8 | 51 | Coffin | Asa | | | 1 | | | | 1 | | 1 | | | | 3 | Not Stated | |
| Nantucket | 9 | 27 | Coffin | Bartlett | 1 | | | 1 | | 2 | | 1 | 1 | | | | 6 | Not Stated | |
| Nantucket | 18 | 73 | Coffin | Barzillia | | 1 | | | | | | | 1 | | | | 2 | | |
| Nantucket | 9 | 57 | Coffin | Benjamin | | 1 | 1 | | 1 | | | 2 | 2 | | 1 | | 8 | Not Stated | |
| Nantucket | 10 | 52 | Coffin | Benjamin 3rd | 1 | | | 1 | | | | | 1 | | | | 3 | Not Stated | |
| Nantucket | 15 | 24 | Coffin | Brown | | | | | | | | | | | | | | | Enumeration left blank |
| Nantucket | 18 | 71 | Coffin | Catharine | | | | | | | | | | 1 | | | 1 | | |
| Nantucket | 11 | 26 | Coffin | Charles | | 1 | 2 | 1 | | | 1 | | 1 | | | | 6 | Not Stated | |
| Nantucket | 9 | 9 | Coffin | Daniel | 3 | | | 1 | | 1 | 1 | | 1 | | | | 7 | Not Stated | |
| Nantucket | 4 | 19 | Coffin | David | | | | | 1 | | | | 1 | 1 | | | 3 | Not Stated | |
| Nantucket | 9 | 39 | Coffin | David | 1 | | 1 | | | | | 1 | | | | | 3 | Not Stated | |
| Nantucket | 15 | 25 | Coffin | Ebenezer | | | 1 | | 1 | | | | 1 | 2 | | | 5 | | |
| Nantucket | 16 | 70 | Coffin | Eber | | | | 1 | | | | | 1 | | | | 2 | | |
| Nantucket | 14 | 76 | Coffin | Edward | 1 | 1 | | 1 | | | | 1 | 1 | | | | 5 | | |

| TOWN | PG# | LN# | LAST NAME | FIRST NAME | FREE WHITE MALES | | | | | FREE WHITE FEMALES | | | | | TOTAL ALL OTHER | TOTAL SLAVES | TOTALS | DISTRICT/ TOWNSHIP | NOTES |
|---|---|---|---|---|---|---|---|---|---|---|---|---|---|---|---|---|---|---|---|
| | | | | | under 10 | 10 to 16 | 16 to 26 | 26 to 45 | 45 and over | under 10 | 10 to 16 | 16 to 26 | 26 to 45 | 45 and over | | | | | |
| Nantucket | 13 | 5 | Coffin | Eliel | 1 | | | 1 | | 2 | | | 1 | | | | 5 | | |
| Nantucket | 5 | 40 | Coffin | Elihu | 1 | | 2 | 1 | | 1 | 1 | | 1 | | | | 7 | Not Stated | |
| Nantucket | 3 | 18 | Coffin | Elizabeth | | | | | | | | | 1 | | | | 1 | Not Stated | |
| Nantucket | 11 | 39 | Coffin | Elizabeth | | | | | | | | | 1 | 1 | | | 2 | Not Stated | |
| Nantucket | 16 | 3 | Coffin | Enoch | | | | 1 | | | | | | | | | 1 | | |
| Nantucket | 9 | 1 | Coffin | Ephraim | 2 | | 2 | 1 | | 1 | | 1 | 1 | | | | 8 | Not Stated | |
| Nantucket | 4 | 9 | Coffin | Eunice | | 1 | | | | 1 | | 1 | 1 | | | | 4 | Not Stated | |
| Nantucket | 15 | 19 | Coffin | Eunice | | 1 | | | | | | | 1 | 1 | | | 3 | | |
| Nantucket | 8 | 54 | Coffin | Francis | 1 | | | 1 | | | | | 1 | | | | 3 | Not Stated | |
| Nantucket | 9 | 47 | Coffin | Francis | 1 | | | 1 | | | | | 1 | | | | 3 | Not Stated | |
| Nantucket | 4 | 58 | Coffin | Gardner | 1 | | | 1 | | 1 | | | 1 | | | | 4 | Not Stated | |
| Nantucket | 4 | 20 | Coffin | Gideon | 1 | 1 | | 1 | | 3 | | | 1 | | | | 7 | Not Stated | |
| Nantucket | 4 | 29 | Coffin | Gilbert | 1 | 2 | 3 | 1 | | 1 | | | 1 | | | | 9 | Not Stated | |
| Nantucket | 11 | 11 | Coffin | Hannah | | | | | | | | | 1 | 1 | 1 | | 2 | Not Stated | |
| Nantucket | 12 | 46 | Coffin | Hannah 2nd | | | | | | 1 | | 1 | | | | | 2 | | |
| Nantucket | 12 | 45 | Coffin | Henry | | | 1 | 1 | | | | | 1 | | | | 3 | | |
| Nantucket | 11 | 30 | Coffin | Isaac | 1 | 2 | | 1 | | 3 | 1 | | 1 | | | | 9 | Not Stated | |
| Nantucket | 10 | 48 | Coffin | Isaiah | 2 | 1 | 2 | | 1 | 1 | | | 2 | | | | 9 | Not Stated | |
| Nantucket | 15 | 50 | Coffin | James | | | 2 | | 1 | | | 1 | | 1 | | | 5 | | |
| Nantucket | 15 | 62 | Coffin | James | | 1 | 1 | 1 | | 1 | | 3 | 1 | 1 | | | 9 | | |
| Nantucket | 18 | 6 | Coffin | Jas. Josiah | 2 | 1 | 1 | 1 | | | | 1 | 1 | | | | 7 | | |
| Nantucket | 5 | 48 | Coffin | John | 2 | 2 | 2 | 1 | | 1 | | | 1 | | | | 9 | Not Stated | |
| Nantucket | 10 | 55 | Coffin | John | | 2 | 1 | 1 | | 1 | 1 | 3 | 1 | | | | 10 | Not Stated | |
| Nantucket | 10 | 47 | Coffin | Jonathan | | | 2 | | | | | | 1 | 1 | | | 5 | Not Stated | |
| Nantucket | 9 | 45 | Coffin | Jonathan 2nd | | 1 | 1 | 1 | | 1 | | | 2 | 1 | | | 7 | Not Stated | |
| Nantucket | 13 | 6 | Coffin | Joseph | | | | 1 | | | | | 1 | 1 | | | 3 | | |
| Nantucket | 10 | 33 | Coffin | Joseph 2nd | | 1 | 1 | 1 | | 1 | | | 1 | | | | 5 | Not Stated | |
| Nantucket | 16 | 11 | Coffin | Joshua | | 1 | | 1 | | 1 | 1 | 1 | | | | | 5 | | |
| Nantucket | 14 | 75 | Coffin | Josiah | | 1 | | 1 | | | | | 1 | 1 | | | 4 | | |
| Nantucket | 18 | 30 | Coffin | Judith | | 1 | | | | | | | 1 | 1 | | | 4 | | |
| Nantucket | 13 | 49 | Coffin | Latham | 1 | 1 | 1 | 1 | | | | | 1 | | | | 5 | | |
| Nantucket | 4 | 14 | Coffin | Lydia | | | 1 | | | | | | | 1 | | | 2 | Not Stated | |
| Nantucket | 4 | 67 | Coffin | Lydia 2nd | 1 | 2 | | | | 2 | 1 | | 1 | | | | 7 | Not Stated | |
| Nantucket | 17 | 32 | Coffin | Margaret | | | 1 | | | | 1 | | | 1 | | | 3 | | |
| Nantucket | 17 | 28 | Coffin | Mary | | | 1 | 1 | | | | | | 1 | | | 3 | | |
| Nantucket | 13 | 7 | Coffin | Matilda | | 1 | 4 | | | | | | | 1 | | | 6 | | |
| Nantucket | 10 | 46 | Coffin | Micajah | | | | 1 | | | | | | 1 | | | 2 | Not Stated | |
| Nantucket | 10 | 1 | Coffin | Miriam | | | | | | | | | | 1 | | | 1 | Not Stated | |
| Nantucket | 16 | 10 | Coffin | Nathaniel | | 1 | 1 | | 1 | | | 1 | 1 | 1 | | | 6 | | |
| Nantucket | 17 | 74 | Coffin | Obed | | 1 | 3 | | 1 | 1 | | | 1 | 1 | | | 8 | | |
| Nantucket | 15 | 76 | Coffin | Owen | | 1 | | | | | | 1 | | | | | 2 | | |
| Nantucket | 10 | 10 | Coffin | Paul | 1 | | | 1 | | | | | 2 | 1 | | | 5 | Not Stated | |
| Nantucket | 11 | 28 | Coffin | Paul Junr | | 1 | 1 | | | | | | 1 | | | | 3 | Not Stated | |
| Nantucket | 5 | 30 | Coffin | Philip | 2 | 1 | | 1 | | 1 | 1 | | 1 | | | | 7 | Not Stated | |
| Nantucket | 10 | 51 | Coffin | Reuben | | | | 1 | | | | | | 1 | | | 2 | Not Stated | |
| Nantucket | 12 | 2 | Coffin | Robert | | | | 1 | | | | | 1 | 1 | | | 3 | Not Stated | |
| Nantucket | 5 | 24 | Coffin | Ruth | 1 | 1 | | | | | | 1 | 1 | 1 | | | 5 | Not Stated | |
| Nantucket | 18 | 72 | Coffin | Saml | 2 | 1 | | 1 | 1 | | | 1 | 2 | | | | 9 | | |
| Nantucket | 9 | 33 | Coffin | Seth | | 1 | 1 | 1 | | | | | | 1 | | | 4 | Not Stated | |
| Nantucket | 13 | 38 | Coffin | Seth 2nd | 2 | 2 | | 1 | | | | 1 | 1 | 1 | | | 8 | | |
| Nantucket | 3 | 5 | Coffin | Shubael | 1 | | | 1 | 1 | | | | | 1 | | | 4 | Not Stated | |
| Nantucket | 12 | 43 | Coffin | Shuebael 2nd | 1 | | | 1 | 1 | | | 1 | 1 | 1 | | | 6 | | |
| Nantucket | 12 | 55 | Coffin | Silvanus | | | 1 | | | | | 1 | 1 | 1 | 1 | | 5 | | |
| Nantucket | 17 | 31 | Coffin | Simeon | 1 | | | 1 | | 2 | 1 | 1 | | | | | 6 | | |
| Nantucket | 2 | 1 | Coffin | Simeon Junr | 1 | 2 | | 1 | | | | | | 1 | | | 5 | Not Stated | |
| Nantucket | 10 | 53 | Coffin | Solomon | | 2 | 1 | 1 | | 1 | | | 1 | 1 | | | 7 | Not Stated | |
| Nantucket | 16 | 49 | Coffin | Stephen | 1 | | 1 | 1 | | 1 | | | | 1 | | | 5 | | |
| Nantucket | 13 | 8 | Coffin | Thaddeus | | 1 | | 1 | 2 | 1 | 2 | 1 | | | | | 8 | | |
| Nantucket | 4 | 13 | Coffin | Thankful | | 1 | | | | | | | | 1 | | | 2 | Not Stated | |
| Nantucket | 9 | 46 | Coffin | Thomas | | 1 | | 1 | 1 | | | | | 1 | | | 4 | Not Stated | |
| Nantucket | 11 | 33 | Coffin | Thomas Junr | 1 | | | 1 | | 3 | 1 | | 2 | | | | 8 | Not Stated | |
| Nantucket | 4 | 42 | Coffin | Timothy | | | 1 | | | | 1 | | 1 | | | | 3 | Not Stated | |
| Nantucket | 6 | 13 | Coffin | William | 1 | 1 | | 1 | | 2 | 2 | 2 | 1 | | | | 10 | Not Stated | |
| Nantucket | 6 | 21 | Coffin | William 2nd | 2 | 2 | 1 | 1 | | 2 | 1 | | 1 | 1 | 1 | | 11 | Not Stated | |
| Nantucket | 14 | 46 | Coffin | Zachariah | | 1 | 1 | 1 | | | | 1 | | 1 | | | 5 | | |
| Nantucket | 6 | 53 | Coffin | Zebdial | 1 | | | 1 | | 2 | | | 1 | | | | 5 | Not Stated | |
| Nantucket | 10 | 45 | Coffin | Zenas | | 1 | | 1 | | 2 | 1 | 1 | | | | | 6 | Not Stated | |
| Nantucket | 16 | 26 | Coggeshall | Paul | | 2 | | 1 | | 2 | | | 1 | | | | 6 | | |
| Nantucket | 12 | 22 | Coggeshall | Peleg | | | | 1 | | | | 1 | | 1 | | | 3 | Not Stated | |
| Nantucket | 13 | 42 | Coggeshall | Peleg Junr | 1 | | | 1 | | 2 | | | 1 | | | | 5 | | |
| Nantucket | 17 | 66 | Coleman | Barnabas | 2 | 1 | | | | | | | 2 | 1 | | | 7 | | |
| Nantucket | 7 | 12 | Coleman | Barzillai | 1 | 1 | 2 | | 1 | | | 1 | | 2 | | | 8 | Not Stated | |
| Nantucket | 14 | 57 | Coleman | Daniel | | | | 1 | | | | | | 1 | | | 2 | | |
| Nantucket | 13 | 69 | Coleman | David | 2 | | 1 | | 3 | 1 | 1 | 1 | | | | | 10 | | |
| Nantucket | 8 | 48 | Coleman | David 2nd | | | 2 | | | 2 | 1 | 1 | | | | | 6 | Not Stated | |
| Nantucket | 17 | 46 | Coleman | Davis | | 1 | | 1 | | | | | 1 | 1 | | | 4 | | |
| Nantucket | 17 | 61 | Coleman | Elizabeth | 2 | 1 | 1 | | | 1 | | 1 | 1 | 1 | | | 8 | | |
| Nantucket | 9 | 30 | Coleman | Francis | | 1 | | 1 | | | | 1 | 3 | 1 | | | 7 | Not Stated | |
| Nantucket | 8 | 46 | Coleman | Jeremiah | | | | 1 | | | | | 1 | 1 | | | 3 | Not Stated | |
| Nantucket | 14 | 58 | Coleman | Job | | | 1 | | 1 | | | | 1 | | | | 3 | | |
| Nantucket | 5 | 38 | Coleman | John | | | | 1 | | | | | | 1 | | | 2 | Not Stated | |
| Nantucket | 17 | 67 | Coleman | John | | 1 | | | | | | 1 | | | | | 2 | | |
| Nantucket | 8 | 47 | Coleman | Jonathan | | 1 | 1 | | | | | | 1 | | | | 3 | Not Stated | |
| Nantucket | 17 | 34 | Coleman | Lydia | | 2 | 1 | | | 1 | | 1 | | 1 | | | 6 | | |
| Nantucket | 6 | 37 | Coleman | Matthew | 1 | 2 | | 1 | | | | 1 | 1 | 1 | | | 7 | Not Stated | |
| Nantucket | 16 | 51 | Coleman | Nathl | 1 | 1 | 1 | 1 | | | | 2 | | 1 | | | 7 | | |
| Nantucket | 4 | 65 | Coleman | Peleg | | | | 1 | | | | | | 1 | | | 2 | Not Stated | |
| Nantucket | 9 | 11 | Coleman | Prince | | | | 1 | | | | 1 | 1 | 1 | | | 4 | Not Stated | |
| Nantucket | 5 | 46 | Coleman | Priscilla | 1 | | 2 | 1 | | | | | | 1 | | | 5 | Not Stated | |
| Nantucket | 10 | 22 | Coleman | Reuben | | | | 1 | | | | | | 1 | | | 2 | Not Stated | |

# 1800 Nantucket County, Massachusetts Index

| TOWN | PG# | LN# | LAST NAME | FIRST NAME | FREE WHITE MALES under 10 | 10 to 16 | 16 to 26 | 26 to 45 | 45 and over | FREE WHITE FEMALES under 10 | 10 to 16 | 16 to 26 | 26 to 45 | 45 and over | TOTAL ALL OTHER | TOTAL SLAVES | TOTALS | DISTRICT/TOWNSHIP | NOTES |
|---|---|---|---|---|---|---|---|---|---|---|---|---|---|---|---|---|---|---|---|
| Nantucket | 6 | 14 | Coleman | Richd. Lake | 2 | | | 1 | | 1 | | 2 | | | | | 6 | Not Stated | |
| Nantucket | 5 | 43 | Coleman | Samuel | | | 1 | | | 1 | | | 1 | | | | 3 | Not Stated | |
| Nantucket | 6 | 57 | Coleman | Shubael | | | | 1 | | | 1 | | 1 | 1 | | | 4 | Not Stated | |
| Nantucket | 11 | 45 | Coleman | Silas | 2 | | 1 | | | 1 | | | 1 | | | | 5 | Not Stated | |
| Nantucket | 17 | 54 | Coleman | Silvanus | | 1 | 1 | 1 | | | 2 | | 1 | | 1 | | 7 | | |
| Nantucket | 12 | 38 | Coleman | Silvanus 2nd | | 2 | | 1 | | | | | 1 | | | | 4 | | |
| Nantucket | 12 | 39 | Coleman | Silvanus 3rd | 1 | | 1 | | | | | | 1 | | | | 3 | | |
| Nantucket | 14 | 15 | Coleman | Simeon | 1 | 1 | 2 | 1 | | | | | 1 | 1 | | | 7 | | |
| Nantucket | 14 | 44 | Coleman | Simeon Jun | 1 | | | | | | | | 1 | | | | 3 | | |
| Nantucket | 14 | 45 | Coleman | Solomon | | 2 | 1 | 1 | | 3 | | 2 | | | | | 9 | | |
| Nantucket | 6 | 52 | Coleman | Stephen | 1 | | 1 | | | | | | 1 | | | | 3 | Not Stated | |
| Nantucket | 4 | 68 | Coleman | William | | | 1 | 1 | | 1 | | | 3 | 1 | | | 7 | Not Stated | |
| Nantucket | 16 | 14 | Coleman | Wm | | | | 1 | | | 1 | | 1 | | | | 3 | | |
| Nantucket | 18 | 1 | Colesworthy | Jonathan | 1 | | 1 | | | | | | 1 | | | | 3 | | |
| Nantucket | 18 | 22 | Colesworthy | Jonathan Waldo | 1 | | | 1 | | 1 | | | 1 | | | | 4 | | |
| Nantucket | 18 | 23 | Colesworthy | Walds | | 1 | | | | 1 | | 1 | | | | | 3 | | |
| Nantucket | 17 | 30 | Cook | Naomi | 2 | | | | | | 1 | 1 | 1 | | | | 5 | | |
| Nantucket | 13 | 27 | Cornell | William | | 1 | | | | | | | 1 | | | | 2 | | |
| Nantucket | 15 | 44 | Cottell | David | | 1 | | | | | | | 1 | | | | 2 | | |
| Nantucket | 13 | 60 | Cottell | Obed Junr | | | 1 | | | 1 | | 1 | | | | | 4 | | |
| Nantucket | 19 | 20 | Cottle | Lot | 2 | 2 | 2 | 1 | | 1 | | | 1 | | | | 9 | | |
| Nantucket | 7 | 53 | Cotton | Josiah | 2 | | 1 | | | | | | 1 | | | | 4 | Not Stated | |
| Nantucket | 7 | 42 | Creasy | Edward | 2 | | 1 | | | 1 | | | 1 | | | | 5 | Not Stated | |
| Nantucket | 7 | 33 | Crosby | Saml | | 1 | 1 | 1 | 1 | 1 | | 2 | 1 | 1 | | | 9 | | |
| Nantucket | 15 | 64 | Crosby | Silvanus | 1 | | | 1 | | | | 1 | | 1 | 1 | | 5 | | |
| Nantucket | 18 | 20 | Cumstock | John | | | | 1 | | 1 | 2 | | 1 | | | | 5 | | |
| Nantucket | 19 | 43 | Currington | Godfrey | | | | | | | | | | | 7 | | 7 | | |
| Nantucket | 6 | 49 | Davis | John | 1 | | 1 | | | | | | 1 | | | | 3 | Not Stated | |
| Nantucket | 6 | 11 | Davis | Joseph | | 1 | | | | | | | 1 | | | | 2 | Not Stated | |
| Nantucket | 13 | 10 | Davis | Joseph | | | 1 | | | 1 | | | 1 | | | | 3 | | |
| Nantucket | 3 | 13 | Delano | Elizabeth | | 1 | | 1 | | | 1 | 1 | | 1 | 1 | | 6 | Not Stated | |
| Nantucket | 14 | 32 | Delano | Jeffry | 1 | | | 1 | | 1 | | | 1 | 1 | | | 5 | | |
| Nantucket | 7 | 47 | Derrik | John | | | 1 | | | 1 | | | 1 | | | | 3 | Not Stated | |
| Nantucket | 19 | 60 | Dier | James | | | | | | | | | | | 3 | | 3 | | |
| Nantucket | 19 | 34 | Dier | Samson | | | | | | | | | | | 6 | | 6 | | |
| Nantucket | 3 | 3 | Dixon | Edward | | 1 | | 1 | | | | 1 | | 1 | | | 4 | Not Stated | |
| Nantucket | 6 | 15 | Dow | Henry | | 2 | | 1 | | | 1 | 1 | | 2 | | | 7 | Not Stated | |
| Nantucket | 4 | 57 | Dow | Samuel | 2 | | 1 | | | 1 | | | 1 | | | | 5 | Not Stated | |
| Nantucket | 17 | 52 | Drew | Ebenezer | | 1 | 1 | 1 | | | | | | 1 | | | 4 | | |
| Nantucket | 17 | 49 | Drew | Gershom | 1 | 2 | 3 | 1 | | | | 2 | 1 | | | | 10 | | |
| Nantucket | 3 | 2 | Drew | Gershom Junr | | | 1 | | | | 1 | 1 | | | | | 3 | Not Stated | |
| Nantucket | 19 | 27 | Dunham | Ebenezer | 2 | 2 | | 1 | | 3 | 1 | | 1 | | | | 10 | | |
| Nantucket | 10 | 50 | Dunham | Jethro | 1 | 2 | | 1 | | 1 | | | 1 | | | | 6 | Not Stated | |
| Nantucket | 15 | 31 | Earl | Joseph | 2 | | 1 | 1 | | 1 | 1 | 1 | 1 | | | | 9 | | |
| Nantucket | 15 | 57 | Easton | Peleg | | 2 | 1 | | 1 | 2 | 2 | 1 | 1 | | | | 10 | | |
| Nantucket | 3 | 27 | Easton | Peter | 4 | | | 1 | | | | 2 | | | | | 7 | Not Stated | |
| Nantucket | 15 | 41 | Easton | Wm | 2 | 2 | 1 | 1 | | | | | 1 | | | | 7 | | |
| Nantucket | 19 | 24 | Edwards | Asa | | 1 | | | | 1 | | 1 | | | | | 3 | | |
| Nantucket | 18 | 14 | Elkins | John | | 2 | 1 | 1 | 1 | | 1 | | | 1 | 1 | | 8 | | |
| Nantucket | 11 | 43 | Elkins | Joseph | 1 | | 1 | | | | | | 1 | | | | 3 | Not Stated | |
| Nantucket | 9 | 42 | Ellis | Deborah | | 1 | | | | 1 | | 1 | 1 | | | | 4 | Not Stated | |
| Nantucket | 7 | 4 | Ellis | Elisha | | 1 | | 1 | | | | | 1 | | | | 3 | Not Stated | |
| Nantucket | 8 | 30 | Ellis | Elisha Junr | 1 | | | 1 | | 2 | | | 1 | | | | 5 | Not Stated | |
| Nantucket | 8 | 40 | Ellis | Francis | 1 | | 1 | 1 | | | | 2 | 1 | | | | 7 | Not Stated | |
| Nantucket | 7 | 21 | Ellis | Freeman | 1 | | 1 | 1 | | | | | 1 | | | | 5 | Not Stated | |
| Nantucket | 18 | 61 | Ellis | Moses | | 1 | | | | 1 | | 1 | | | | | 3 | | |
| Nantucket | 5 | 47 | Ellis | Nathaniel | | | | 1 | | | | | 2 | | | | 3 | Not Stated | |
| Nantucket | 10 | 5 | Ellis | Phebe | | | | | | 1 | | | 1 | | | | 2 | Not Stated | |
| Nantucket | 8 | 44 | Ellis | Raymond | 2 | | | 1 | | | | | 1 | | | | 4 | Not Stated | |
| Nantucket | 6 | 29 | Ellis | Silvanus Junr | | | | 1 | | | | | | 2 | | | 3 | Not Stated | |
| Nantucket | 4 | 69 | Ellis | William | | 1 | | 1 | | | | | 1 | 1 | | | 4 | Not Stated | |
| Nantucket | 13 | 43 | Emmit | Elizabeth | | | | | | | | | | 1 | | | 1 | | |
| Nantucket | 13 | 44 | Emmit | John | | 1 | | | | | | | 1 | | | | 2 | | |
| Nantucket | 17 | 43 | Ewers | David | | 1 | | | | | | | 1 | | | | 2 | | |
| Nantucket | 16 | 38 | Ewers | Silvanus | | | 1 | | | | | | 1 | | | | 2 | | |
| Nantucket | 12 | 28 | Fairweather | Anna | | | | | | | | | 1 | | | | 1 | Not Stated | |
| Nantucket | 13 | 40 | Fanning | Kezia | 2 | | 1 | | | | | | 1 | 1 | | | 5 | | |
| Nantucket | 5 | 1 | Farr | Sarah | | 2 | | | | | | | | 3 | | | 5 | Not Stated | |
| Nantucket | 17 | 5 | Farr | Stephen | | 1 | | | | 1 | | | 1 | | | | 3 | | |
| Nantucket | 18 | 54 | Fish | Ruth | | | | | | 1 | | | | 1 | | | 2 | | |
| Nantucket | 18 | 55 | Fish | Stephen | | 2 | | | | | | | 1 | | | | 3 | | |
| Nantucket | 18 | 4 | Fisher | Freeborn | | 1 | | | | | | | 1 | | | | 2 | | |
| Nantucket | 19 | 19 | Fisher | Nathl | 1 | 1 | | 1 | | | | 1 | | 1 | | | 5 | | |
| Nantucket | 18 | 19 | Fitch | Anna | | | | | | | | | | 1 | | | 1 | | |
| Nantucket | 9 | 49 | Fitch | Beriah | 1 | | 1 | 1 | | 1 | 1 | 1 | | | | | 6 | Not Stated | |
| Nantucket | 15 | 32 | Fitch | Ebenezer | 2 | | 1 | | 1 | 1 | 1 | 1 | 1 | 1 | | | 9 | | |
| Nantucket | 16 | 7 | Fitch | Jedediah | | | 1 | | | | | | 1 | | | | 2 | | |
| Nantucket | 15 | 51 | Fitch | John | 1 | | 1 | | | 1 | | | 1 | | | | 3 | | |
| Nantucket | 12 | 47 | Fitch | Jonathan Gorham | | 1 | 3 | 1 | | | 1 | | | 1 | | | 7 | | |
| Nantucket | 18 | 65 | Fitch | Obed | 1 | | 1 | | | | 1 | | 1 | | | | 4 | | |
| Nantucket | 6 | 48 | Fitzgerald | Henry | 1 | 1 | 1 | | | | 1 | 1 | 1 | | | | 7 | Not Stated | |
| Nantucket | 7 | 3 | Fitzgerald | James | | | 1 | | | 2 | | | 1 | | | | 4 | Not Stated | |
| Nantucket | 7 | 52 | Fitzgerald | Jonathan | | 1 | 1 | 1 | | | 1 | 1 | | 1 | | | 6 | Not Stated | |
| Nantucket | 12 | 1 | Flag | Benjamin | | 1 | | | | | | | 1 | | | | 2 | Not Stated | |
| Nantucket | 11 | 37 | Folger | Aaron | 1 | | 1 | | | | | | 2 | 1 | | | 5 | Not Stated | |
| Nantucket | 16 | 39 | Folger | Albert | 2 | | 1 | | | | | | 1 | | | | 4 | | |
| Nantucket | 13 | 71 | Folger | Alexander | | | 1 | | | | | 1 | | | | | 2 | | |
| Nantucket | 4 | 72 | Folger | Anna | | | | | | | | | | 1 | | | 1 | Not Stated | |
| Nantucket | 15 | 37 | Folger | Barrillia | | 1 | | 1 | | | | | 1 | 1 | | | 4 | | |
| Nantucket | 5 | 3 | Folger | Catharine | | | 1 | | | 1 | | | 4 | 1 | | | 8 | Not Stated | |

# 1800 Nantucket County, Massachusetts Index

| TOWN | PG# | LN# | LAST NAME | FIRST NAME | FREE WHITE MALES | | | | | FREE WHITE FEMALES | | | | | TOTAL ALL OTHER | TOTAL SLAVES | TOTALS | DISTRICT/ TOWNSHIP | NOTES |
|---|---|---|---|---|---|---|---|---|---|---|---|---|---|---|---|---|---|---|---|
| | | | | | under 10 | 10 to 16 | 16 to 26 | 26 to 45 | 45 and over | under 10 | 10 to 16 | 16 to 26 | 26 to 45 | 45 and over | | | | | |
| Nantucket | 4 | 59 | Folger | Charles | 3 | 2 | 2 | | 1 | 2 | 1 | | 1 | | | | 12 | Not Stated | |
| Nantucket | 9 | 12 | Folger | Clement | | | 1 | | | | | | 1 | | | | 2 | Not Stated | |
| Nantucket | 6 | 35 | Folger | David | | | | | 1 | | 1 | 1 | 1 | 1 | | | 5 | Not Stated | |
| Nantucket | 9 | 15 | Folger | David Junr | | 1 | 1 | 1 | | 2 | | | 2 | | | | 7 | Not Stated | |
| Nantucket | 9 | 14 | Folger | Elisha | 1 | 1 | 1 | 1 | | 1 | | 3 | | 1 | | | 9 | Not Stated | |
| Nantucket | 9 | 20 | Folger | Elisha | 3 | | | 1 | | | | | 1 | | | | 5 | Not Stated | |
| Nantucket | 9 | 19 | Folger | Elisha Junr | | | | 1 | | | | | 1 | | | | 2 | Not Stated | |
| Nantucket | 18 | 44 | Folger | George | | | | 1 | | 1 | | | 1 | | 1 | | 4 | | |
| Nantucket | 17 | 60 | Folger | George Junr | 3 | 1 | 1 | 1 | | | 1 | 1 | 1 | | | | 9 | | |
| Nantucket | 18 | 66 | Folger | Gilbert | | 2 | | 1 | | 1 | 1 | | 1 | | | | 6 | | |
| Nantucket | 4 | 61 | Folger | Henry | 3 | 1 | 1 | 1 | | | | 1 | 1 | | | | 8 | Not Stated | |
| Nantucket | 12 | 57 | Folger | Isaac | 1 | 1 | 2 | 1 | | 1 | | | 1 | | | | 7 | | |
| Nantucket | 18 | 41 | Folger | Isaiah | | 1 | 1 | | | | | | 1 | | | | 3 | | |
| Nantucket | 11 | 2 | Folger | John | | | | 2 | | | | | 1 | | | | 3 | Not Stated | |
| Nantucket | 4 | 6 | Folger | Jonathan | 2 | | 1 | 1 | | 3 | | | 2 | | 1 | | 10 | Not Stated | |
| Nantucket | 3 | 21 | Folger | Joseph | 1 | | 1 | | | 2 | 1 | 1 | | | | | 6 | Not Stated | |
| Nantucket | 10 | 12 | Folger | Mary | | | | | | | | | 1 | | | | 1 | Not Stated | |
| Nantucket | 4 | 73 | Folger | Mary 2nd | | | | | | 1 | | 2 | 1 | | | | 4 | Not Stated | |
| Nantucket | 4 | 62 | Folger | Miriam | | | | | | | | | 1 | | | | 1 | Not Stated | |
| Nantucket | 15 | 36 | Folger | Obediah | | 1 | 1 | | 1 | | 1 | 1 | 1 | | | | 6 | | |
| Nantucket | 15 | 33 | Folger | Owen | | 1 | 1 | 1 | 1 | | | 1 | 1 | | | | 6 | | |
| Nantucket | 4 | 66 | Folger | Paul | | | | 1 | | | | | 2 | | | | 3 | Not Stated | |
| Nantucket | 4 | 5 | Folger | Peregrine | 1 | | | 1 | | 2 | | 1 | 1 | | | | 6 | Not Stated | |
| Nantucket | 15 | 66 | Folger | Peter | | 1 | 2 | 1 | | | 2 | | 1 | | | | 7 | | |
| Nantucket | 11 | 51 | Folger | Reuben | | | | 1 | | | 1 | 1 | | | | | 3 | Not Stated | |
| Nantucket | 10 | 39 | Folger | Richard | | 1 | | | | | 1 | | | | | | 2 | Not Stated | |
| Nantucket | 16 | 63 | Folger | Robert | | 1 | 1 | 1 | | 1 | 1 | | 1 | | | | 6 | | |
| Nantucket | 13 | 3 | Folger | Seth | | 1 | | 1 | | | | | 1 | | | | 3 | | |
| Nantucket | 13 | 9 | Folger | Seth 3rd | 1 | | | 1 | | | | | 1 | | | | 3 | | |
| Nantucket | 17 | 47 | Folger | Seth Junr | | 1 | 1 | | 1 | 1 | 1 | 1 | 1 | | | | 7 | | |
| Nantucket | 4 | 44 | Folger | Shubael | | 1 | | 1 | | 2 | | | 1 | | | | 5 | Not Stated | |
| Nantucket | 8 | 4 | Folger | Silvanus | | | 1 | | | | | | 1 | | | | 2 | Not Stated | |
| Nantucket | 6 | 36 | Folger | Silvanus 2nd | | | 1 | | 2 | 1 | | 1 | | | | | 5 | Not Stated | |
| Nantucket | 9 | 58 | Folger | Simeon | 1 | | 1 | | 2 | | 1 | | | | | | 5 | Not Stated | |
| Nantucket | 7 | 28 | Folger | Solomon | | 1 | | 1 | | | | | | 1 | | | 3 | Not Stated | |
| Nantucket | 5 | 68 | Folger | Stephen | | | 1 | | | | | | | | | | 1 | Not Stated | |
| Nantucket | 14 | 74 | Folger | Susanna | 2 | | | | | 1 | 1 | 1 | | | | | 5 | | |
| Nantucket | 15 | 35 | Folger | Thaddeus | | 1 | | 1 | | 3 | 1 | | 1 | | | | 6 | | |
| Nantucket | 5 | 20 | Folger | Timothy | | 1 | | 1 | | 1 | 1 | | 1 | | | | 5 | Not Stated | |
| Nantucket | 12 | 18 | Folger | Timothy Junr | 3 | | 1 | | | 1 | 1 | 1 | | | | | 7 | Not Stated | |
| Nantucket | 18 | 57 | Folger | Tristram | | | 1 | | 2 | 1 | | 1 | | | | | 5 | | |
| Nantucket | 4 | 51 | Folger | Tristram 2nd | 1 | | 1 | | 2 | | 1 | | | | | | 5 | Not Stated | |
| Nantucket | 13 | 70 | Folger | Walter | | 1 | 1 | | | | 1 | 1 | | | | | 5 | | |
| Nantucket | 10 | 21 | Folger | Walter Junr | 3 | | 1 | | 2 | | 1 | | | | | | 8 | Not Stated | |
| Nantucket | 11 | 34 | Folger | William | | | 1 | | | | | | 1 | | | | 2 | Not Stated | |
| Nantucket | 11 | 35 | Folger | William Junr | | | 1 | | 2 | | 1 | 1 | | | | | 5 | Not Stated | |
| Nantucket | 19 | 36 | Fortune | Absalon | | | | | | | | | | | 3 | | 3 | | |
| Nantucket | 13 | 74 | Fosdick | Benjamin | | | 1 | 1 | | | 1 | 1 | | | | | 4 | | |
| Nantucket | 15 | 6 | Fosdick | John | 2 | 1 | 1 | 1 | | | 1 | 1 | | | | | 7 | | |
| Nantucket | 13 | 73 | Fosdick | Peter | 1 | | 1 | | 1 | 2 | 2 | 1 | | | | | 8 | | |
| Nantucket | 15 | 11 | Fosdick | Philip | 2 | | 1 | | 2 | | 1 | | | | | | 6 | | |
| Nantucket | 19 | 10 | Foster | James | | 1 | | 1 | | | | 1 | | | | | 3 | | |
| Nantucket | 6 | 39 | Foye | Obed | 4 | | 1 | | 2 | 1 | 1 | | | | | | 9 | Not Stated | |
| Nantucket | 19 | 2 | Freebon | Thomas | 1 | | 1 | | 2 | | 1 | | | | | | 5 | | |
| Nantucket | 3 | 26 | Freeborn | George | | 1 | | 1 | | | 1 | | 1 | | | | 4 | Not Stated | |
| Nantucket | 13 | 53 | Freeman | Edward | | | 1 | | | | | | 1 | | | | 2 | | |
| Nantucket | 19 | 52 | Freeman | Issac | | | | | | | | | | | 3 | | 3 | | |
| Nantucket | 5 | 7 | Frost | Nathl | | | 1 | | | | | | 1 | | | | 2 | Not Stated | |
| Nantucket | 8 | 28 | Gardner | Abigail | | | | | | | 1 | 1 | | | | | 2 | Not Stated | |
| Nantucket | 10 | 30 | Gardner | Abigail | | | | | | | | 1 | | | | | 1 | Not Stated | |
| Nantucket | 4 | 38 | Gardner | Abigail 2nd | | 1 | | | 1 | | 2 | | | | | | 4 | Not Stated | |
| Nantucket | 12 | 40 | Gardner | Abishai | | 1 | | | 1 | | | | | | | | 2 | | |
| Nantucket | 13 | 28 | Gardner | Albert | 3 | 2 | 1 | | | 2 | 1 | | | | | | 9 | | |
| Nantucket | 10 | 26 | Gardner | Alexander | 1 | 1 | 1 | | 4 | 1 | 1 | | | | | | 9 | Not Stated | |
| Nantucket | 18 | 28 | Gardner | Amaziah | | | 1 | | 2 | | 1 | | | | | | 4 | | |
| Nantucket | 5 | 39 | Gardner | Ammiel | | | 1 | | 1 | 1 | 1 | 1 | | | | | 5 | Not Stated | |
| Nantucket | 11 | 49 | Gardner | Anna | | | | | | | 1 | | 1 | | | | 2 | Not Stated | |
| Nantucket | 14 | 29 | Gardner | Anna | | 2 | | | 1 | 1 | 1 | 1 | | | | | 6 | | |
| Nantucket | 18 | 21 | Gardner | Antipas | | | 1 | | | | | | 1 | | | | 2 | | |
| Nantucket | 9 | 10 | Gardner | Apphia | | 3 | | | 1 | | | 1 | | | | | 5 | Not Stated | |
| Nantucket | 15 | 63 | Gardner | Benjm | | 1 | | | 1 | 1 | 1 | | | | | | 5 | | |
| Nantucket | 19 | 25 | Gardner | Bethuel | | 1 | | | | 1 | | | | | | | 2 | | |
| Nantucket | 16 | 2 | Gardner | Caty | | | | | | | | | 3 | | | | 3 | | |
| Nantucket | 9 | 35 | Gardner | Crispus | | 1 | | 1 | | 3 | | 1 | | | | | 6 | Not Stated | |
| Nantucket | 12 | 59 | Gardner | Ebenezer | 2 | | 1 | | 2 | 2 | 1 | | | | | | 8 | | |
| Nantucket | 4 | 11 | Gardner | Eliakim | 2 | | 1 | | | 1 | | | | | | | 4 | Not Stated | |
| Nantucket | 14 | 49 | Gardner | Elihu | | | 1 | | 1 | | 1 | | | | | | 3 | | |
| Nantucket | 11 | 38 | Gardner | Elizabeth | | 2 | | | 1 | 1 | 1 | | | | | | 5 | Not Stated | |
| Nantucket | 13 | 41 | Gardner | Elizabeth | | | | | | | | 1 | | | | | 1 | | |
| Nantucket | 16 | 12 | Gardner | Enoch | | | 1 | | | | 1 | | | | | | 2 | | |
| Nantucket | 15 | 7 | Gardner | Francis | | 1 | 2 | 1 | | 1 | | 1 | 2 | | | | 8 | | |
| Nantucket | 14 | 42 | Gardner | Freeman | | 1 | | | 2 | 1 | | | | | | | 4 | | |
| Nantucket | 14 | 13 | Gardner | George | | | 1 | | 4 | 2 | 1 | | | | | | 8 | | |
| Nantucket | 3 | 10 | Gardner | Gideon | | 1 | | | 2 | 1 | 1 | | | | | | 5 | Not Stated | |
| Nantucket | 14 | 55 | Gardner | Gideon Junr | 1 | | 1 | | 1 | | 1 | | | | | | 4 | | |
| Nantucket | 16 | 47 | Gardner | Grafton | 1 | | 1 | | 4 | | 1 | | | | | | 7 | | |
| Nantucket | 14 | 27 | Gardner | Grindal | 1 | 2 | 4 | 1 | | 1 | 1 | 1 | | | | | 11 | | |
| Nantucket | 18 | 48 | Gardner | Hephzibah | | | | | | | 1 | 1 | | | | | 2 | | |
| Nantucket | 17 | 4 | Gardner | Hepzibeh 2nd | | | | | | | 1 | | 1 | | | | 2 | | |
| Nantucket | 14 | 22 | Gardner | James | | | 1 | | | | | 1 | | | | | 2 | | |

# 1800 Nantucket County, Massachusetts Index

| TOWN | PG# | LN# | LAST NAME | FIRST NAME | FWM under 10 | FWM 10-16 | FWM 16-26 | FWM 26-45 | FWM 45+ | FWF under 10 | FWF 10-16 | FWF 16-26 | FWF 26-45 | FWF 45+ | TOTAL ALL OTHER | TOTAL SLAVES | TOTALS | DISTRICT/TOWNSHIP | NOTES |
|---|---|---|---|---|---|---|---|---|---|---|---|---|---|---|---|---|---|---|---|
| Nantucket | 10 | 20 | Gardner | Jared | 1 | | 1 | | | | | | 1 | | | | 3 | Not Stated | |
| Nantucket | 13 | 34 | Gardner | Jared | | | 1 | | | 2 | | | 1 | 1 | | | 5 | | |
| Nantucket | 5 | 54 | Gardner | Jeremiah | 2 | | 1 | | | 1 | | | 1 | | | | 5 | Not Stated | |
| Nantucket | 15 | 5 | Gardner | John | 1 | 1 | 1 | | 1 | | | 2 | | 1 | | | 7 | | |
| Nantucket | 10 | 17 | Gardner | Jonathan | | | | 1 | | | | | 1 | | | | 2 | Not Stated | |
| Nantucket | 13 | 20 | Gardner | Joseph 2nd | | | 1 | | | 1 | | 1 | | | | | 3 | | |
| Nantucket | 4 | 54 | Gardner | Laban | | | 1 | 2 | | 4 | | 1 | 1 | | | | 9 | Not Stated | |
| Nantucket | 11 | 48 | Gardner | Latham | | 2 | 1 | 1 | | | | 2 | 1 | | 1 | | 8 | Not Stated | |
| Nantucket | 15 | 60 | Gardner | Libni | | 1 | | 1 | | | | 2 | | | | | 4 | | |
| Nantucket | 14 | 41 | Gardner | Lydia | | | | 1 | | | | 1 | | 1 | | | 3 | | |
| Nantucket | 4 | 34 | Gardner | Mary | | | | | | | | | | 1 | | | 1 | Not Stated | |
| Nantucket | 18 | 29 | Gardner | Micajah | | | 1 | | | | | 1 | | | | | 2 | | |
| Nantucket | 5 | 14 | Gardner | Nathan Junr | | 1 | | 1 | 1 | 1 | 1 | | 1 | | | | 6 | Not Stated | |
| Nantucket | 3 | 16 | Gardner | Paul | 1 | | | 1 | 1 | | | 1 | 2 | | | | 6 | Not Stated | |
| Nantucket | 18 | 34 | Gardner | Paul Junr | | 1 | | 1 | | 2 | | 1 | | | | | 5 | | |
| Nantucket | 18 | 25 | Gardner | Peleg | 2 | | | 1 | 1 | 3 | | 1 | | | | | 8 | | |
| Nantucket | 14 | 37 | Gardner | Peleg 2nd | 3 | 1 | 1 | 1 | | | | 1 | | | | | 7 | | |
| Nantucket | 17 | 18 | Gardner | Peter | | | 2 | | | 1 | | 2 | | | | | 5 | | |
| Nantucket | 13 | 72 | Gardner | Phebe | | | | | | | | | | 1 | | | 1 | | |
| Nantucket | 4 | 2 | Gardner | Prince | 1 | 1 | 1 | | | | | 2 | 1 | | | | 6 | Not Stated | |
| Nantucket | 2 | 2 | Gardner | Rebecca | 1 | | | | | | 1 | 1 | 1 | | | | 4 | Not Stated | |
| Nantucket | 14 | 1 | Gardner | Richard | 3 | 1 | | 1 | 1 | | | 1 | 1 | | | | 8 | | |
| Nantucket | 16 | 9 | Gardner | Robert | | 1 | | 1 | | | | | 1 | | | | 3 | | |
| Nantucket | 16 | 68 | Gardner | Robert Junr | 1 | | | 1 | | | | 2 | | | | | 4 | | |
| Nantucket | 12 | 61 | Gardner | Ruth | | | | | | | | 1 | 1 | | | | 2 | | |
| Nantucket | 5 | 64 | Gardner | Sarah | | | | | | | | | | 1 | | | 1 | Not Stated | |
| Nantucket | 16 | 1 | Gardner | Shubael | | | | 1 | | | | | | 1 | | | 2 | | |
| Nantucket | 14 | 48 | Gardner | Silas | 1 | 1 | | 1 | | 2 | 2 | | 1 | | | | 8 | | |
| Nantucket | 9 | 54 | Gardner | Silvanus | 1 | | 2 | 1 | | | | | 1 | | | | 5 | Not Stated | |
| Nantucket | 14 | 6 | Gardner | Stephen | | 1 | | 2 | | | | | 1 | | | | 4 | | |
| Nantucket | 4 | 52 | Gardner | Thankful | | | | | | | | 1 | 1 | | | | 2 | Not Stated | |
| Nantucket | 15 | 22 | Gardner | Thomas | | 1 | | 1 | | | | | 1 | | | | 3 | | |
| Nantucket | 15 | 46 | Gardner | Thos Junr | | 1 | | | | | 1 | | | | | | 2 | | |
| Nantucket | 4 | 48 | Gardner | Timothy | 1 | | 1 | 1 | | | | | 1 | | | | 4 | Not Stated | |
| Nantucket | 13 | 75 | Gardner | Tristram | | 1 | 1 | 1 | | | 2 | | 1 | | | | 6 | | |
| Nantucket | 10 | 27 | Gardner | Tristram Junr | 1 | | | 1 | | | | 1 | | | | | 3 | Not Stated | |
| Nantucket | 4 | 64 | Gardner | William 2nd | 4 | | 1 | 1 | | 1 | 2 | 2 | 1 | | | | 12 | Not Stated | |
| Nantucket | 18 | 76 | Gardner | Wm | | | | 1 | | | | | 1 | | | | 2 | | |
| Nantucket | 15 | 59 | Gardner | Zenas | 1 | 1 | | 1 | | 3 | | | 2 | | | | 8 | | |
| Nantucket | 14 | 59 | Gardner | Zephaniah | | | 1 | | | | 1 | | 1 | | | | 3 | | |
| Nantucket | 19 | 55 | Garlow | Danl | | | | | | | | | | | 9 | | 9 | | |
| Nantucket | 13 | 54 | Gebston | Rowlan | | 1 | 1 | 1 | | 1 | | 2 | 1 | | 2 | | 9 | | |
| Nantucket | 14 | 61 | Gifford | Joseph | 1 | | 1 | | | | | 1 | | | | | 3 | | |
| Nantucket | 9 | 34 | Gifford | Luthern | | | 1 | | | 1 | | | 1 | | | | 3 | Not Stated | |
| Nantucket | 16 | 74 | Giles | David | 1 | | | 1 | 1 | | | | 1 | | | | 4 | | |
| Nantucket | 12 | 60 | Giles | David W | 2 | | | 1 | | 1 | | | 1 | | | | 5 | | |
| Nantucket | 5 | 65 | Giles | Lydia | | | | | | | 1 | | 1 | | | | 2 | Not Stated | |
| Nantucket | 6 | 28 | Giles | Paul | | | 2 | 1 | | 1 | | | | 1 | | | 5 | Not Stated | |
| Nantucket | 12 | 64 | Glover | Benjamin | 2 | | | 1 | | 1 | 1 | | 1 | 1 | | | 7 | | |
| Nantucket | 11 | 58 | Glover | Lydia | | | | | | 1 | 1 | | 1 | 1 | | | 4 | Not Stated | |
| Nantucket | 16 | 46 | Glover | Reuben | | | | 1 | | | | 1 | 1 | | | | 3 | | |
| Nantucket | 19 | 56 | Godfrey | Cesar | | | | | | | | | | | 4 | | 4 | | |
| Nantucket | 18 | 17 | Gorham | Parnell | 1 | 1 | 1 | | | | 2 | 1 | | | | | 6 | | |
| Nantucket | 14 | 51 | Grew | Samuel | 3 | | 1 | 1 | | | | 1 | 1 | | | | 7 | | |
| Nantucket | 16 | 8 | Guerney | James | 1 | | 1 | | | 1 | | | | | | | 3 | | |
| Nantucket | 11 | 52 | Gurrel | John | 1 | | | 1 | | 2 | | 1 | | | | | 5 | Not Stated | |
| Nantucket | 19 | 48 | Gutridge | Michael | | | | | | | | | | | 2 | | 2 | | |
| Nantucket | 3 | 19 | Gwin | James | | | | 1 | | | 1 | | 1 | | | | 3 | Not Stated | |
| Nantucket | 6 | 41 | Gwin | Rachel | | | | | | | | | | 1 | | | 1 | Not Stated | |
| Nantucket | 12 | 19 | Hammatt | John | 1 | | 1 | | | 1 | | 2 | | | | | 5 | Not Stated | |
| Nantucket | 3 | 15 | Hammatt | William | 1 | 2 | 1 | 1 | | | 1 | 1 | 1 | | | | 8 | Not Stated | |
| Nantucket | 15 | 1 | Hammond | Lydia | 1 | | | | | | | 1 | 2 | 1 | | | 5 | | |
| Nantucket | 17 | 8 | Hammond | Sally | | | | | | | | | 1 | | | | 1 | | |
| Nantucket | 7 | 55 | Harrax | Thomas | | | 1 | 1 | 1 | | | 1 | 2 | 1 | | | 7 | Not Stated | |
| Nantucket | 6 | 24 | Harris | David | 1 | | 1 | | | 1 | | | 1 | | | | 4 | Not Stated | |
| Nantucket | 7 | 15 | Harris | Humphrey | | 1 | | 1 | | 1 | | 1 | | 1 | | | 5 | Not Stated | |
| Nantucket | 8 | 22 | Harris | Lydia | | | | | | | | 1 | | | | | 1 | Not Stated | |
| Nantucket | 7 | 2 | Harris | Obed | | 1 | 1 | 1 | | 1 | | | 1 | | | | 5 | Not Stated | |
| Nantucket | 7 | 20 | Hartshorn | John Woodman | | | | 1 | | | | | 1 | | | | 2 | Not Stated | |
| Nantucket | 18 | 74 | Hatch | Charles | 2 | | | 1 | | | | | 1 | | | | 4 | | |
| Nantucket | 16 | 24 | Hathaway | Mary | | | | | | | | | 1 | | | | 1 | | |
| Nantucket | 20 | 5 | Hawkins | Ebenezer | | | | | | | | | | | 4 | | 4 | | |
| Nantucket | 5 | 59 | Hawkins | John | 1 | | | 1 | | 2 | | | 1 | 1 | | | 6 | Not Stated | |
| Nantucket | 17 | 11 | Hayden | Abishai | | | | 1 | | 2 | 2 | 1 | 1 | | | | 7 | | |
| Nantucket | 17 | 14 | Hayden | Rebecca | | | 1 | | | | | | 1 | | | | 2 | | |
| Nantucket | 5 | 35 | Hayden | Zophar | | | 1 | | | | | 2 | | | | | 3 | Not Stated | |
| Nantucket | 16 | 23 | Headen | Zoaph | | | 1 | | | | | 2 | | | | | 3 | | |
| Nantucket | 5 | 9 | Heath | Edmund | | | | | 1 | | | | 1 | | | | 2 | Not Stated | |
| Nantucket | 6 | 42 | Hendrick | George | 1 | | | 1 | | 1 | | | 1 | | | | 4 | Not Stated | |
| Nantucket | 11 | 42 | Hern | Elizabeth | | | | | | 1 | | | 1 | | | | 2 | Not Stated | |
| Nantucket | 19 | 44 | Hero | Saml | | | | | | | | | | | 4 | | 4 | Not Stated | |
| Nantucket | 8 | 43 | Higgins | Sabra | | | | | | | | | | 1 | | | 1 | | |
| Nantucket | 12 | 56 | Hiller | Thomas | 2 | | 1 | 1 | | 1 | 2 | 1 | 1 | | | | 9 | | |
| Nantucket | 6 | 18 | Hinckley | Elisja Mau | | | 1 | | | 2 | 1 | 2 | | | 2 | | 8 | Not Stated | |
| Nantucket | 5 | 10 | Hoag | Abraham | 1 | 4 | | | 1 | 1 | | 1 | | 1 | | | 9 | Not Stated | |
| Nantucket | 14 | 52 | Holmes | William | 1 | | 1 | | 1 | 2 | | | | 1 | | | 6 | | |
| Nantucket | 16 | 54 | Horsfield | Timothy | 4 | 1 | 1 | | | | | 1 | 1 | | | | 8 | | |
| Nantucket | 3 | 8 | Hosier | William | 1 | | | 1 | | 2 | | 1 | | 1 | | | 6 | Not Stated | |
| Nantucket | 12 | 13 | House | John | 2 | 1 | | | 1 | 3 | | 2 | | 1 | | | 11 | Not Stated | |
| Nantucket | 10 | 16 | Hull | Phebe | | | 1 | | | 2 | | 1 | 1 | 1 | | | 6 | Not Stated | |

# 1800 Nantucket County, Massachusetts Index

| TOWN | PG# | LN# | LAST NAME | FIRST NAME | \<10 | 10-16 | 16-26 | 26-45 | 45+ | \<10 | 10-16 | 16-26 | 26-45 | 45+ | TOTAL ALL OTHER | TOTAL SLAVES | TOTALS | DISTRICT/ TOWNSHIP | NOTES |
|---|---|---|---|---|---|---|---|---|---|---|---|---|---|---|---|---|---|---|---|
| Nantucket | 12 | 7 | Hull | Thomas | | | | 1 | | | | | 1 | | | | 2 | Not Stated | |
| Nantucket | 12 | 30 | Hulsey | Albert Jr | 1 | | 1 | | | | | | 1 | | | | 3 | | |
| Nantucket | 13 | 26 | Hulsey | Christopher | | 3 | | | 2 | 3 | 1 | 1 | 1 | | | | 11 | | |
| Nantucket | 13 | 63 | Hulsey | Cyrus | 1 | | | 1 | | 1 | | 2 | | | | | 5 | | |
| Nantucket | 15 | 20 | Hulsey | John | 3 | 3 | | 1 | | 2 | | 1 | 1 | | | | 11 | | |
| Nantucket | 12 | 42 | Hulsey | Naomi | 1 | | | | | 1 | | | 1 | | | | 3 | | |
| Nantucket | 12 | 31 | Hulsey | Seth Jenkins | | | 1 | | | 2 | | 1 | | | | | 4 | | |
| Nantucket | 4 | 60 | Hunter | John | 1 | 1 | 1 | 1 | 1 | | | 1 | 1 | 2 | | | 9 | Not Stated | |
| Nantucket | 6 | 16 | Hussey | Albert | | 1 | | | | | | | 1 | | | | 2 | Not Stated | |
| Nantucket | 16 | 41 | Hussey | Albert | | 2 | 1 | | 1 | | | | 1 | | | | 5 | | |
| Nantucket | 16 | 20 | Hussey | Batchelor | | | | 1 | | | | | 1 | 1 | | | 3 | | |
| Nantucket | 4 | 17 | Hussey | Charles | | 2 | 1 | | | 1 | | 1 | 1 | | | | 6 | Not Stated | |
| Nantucket | 6 | 51 | Hussey | Daniel | 1 | | | 1 | | 1 | | | 1 | | | | 4 | Not Stated | |
| Nantucket | 16 | 44 | Hussey | Danl | | | 1 | | | | | | 1 | | | | 2 | | |
| Nantucket | 16 | 28 | Hussey | David | | 1 | 2 | | 1 | | 3 | 1 | 1 | | | | 9 | | |
| Nantucket | 16 | 75 | Hussey | Eiab | | | | | | | | | 1 | | | | 1 | | |
| Nantucket | 16 | 58 | Hussey | Elizabeth | | 2 | | | | | | | | 1 | | | 3 | | |
| Nantucket | 18 | 52 | Hussey | George | | 1 | 1 | | 1 | | | 2 | | 2 | | | 7 | | |
| Nantucket | 16 | 18 | Hussey | George G | 1 | | 1 | | 1 | 1 | | | 1 | | | | 5 | | |
| Nantucket | 16 | 42 | Hussey | James | 1 | | 1 | | | 1 | 1 | | 1 | | | | 5 | | |
| Nantucket | 18 | 7 | Hussey | Jethro | | | 1 | 1 | 1 | | | 1 | | 1 | 1 | | 6 | | |
| Nantucket | 16 | 27 | Hussey | Judah | | | | | | | | | | 1 | | | 1 | | |
| Nantucket | 16 | 57 | Hussey | Latham | 1 | | 1 | | | 1 | | | 1 | | | | 4 | | |
| Nantucket | 16 | 16 | Hussey | Nathl | 1 | | 1 | | | | | | 1 | 1 | | | 4 | | |
| Nantucket | 17 | 53 | Hussey | Paul | 2 | 1 | 1 | | | 1 | 1 | 1 | 1 | | | | 8 | | |
| Nantucket | 16 | 32 | Hussey | Peleg | | | 2 | | | 1 | | | 1 | 1 | | | 5 | | |
| Nantucket | 16 | 19 | Hussey | Peter | | 1 | 1 | | | 1 | | | 1 | 1 | | | 5 | | |
| Nantucket | 10 | 6 | Hussey | Reuben | | 1 | | 1 | | 1 | 1 | 2 | | 1 | | | 7 | Not Stated | |
| Nantucket | 18 | 16 | Hussey | Silvanus | | | 1 | | | 1 | 1 | | 1 | | | | 4 | | |
| Nantucket | 7 | 9 | Hussey | Simeon | 2 | 2 | | 1 | | | | 1 | | 1 | | | 7 | Not Stated | |
| Nantucket | 16 | 43 | Hussey | Stephen | | 2 | | 1 | | | | 2 | 1 | 1 | | | 7 | | |
| Nantucket | 15 | 21 | Hussey | Thomas | 2 | 1 | | 1 | | 1 | | | 1 | | | | 6 | | |
| Nantucket | 16 | 35 | Hussey | Tristram | | 1 | 3 | | 1 | | 2 | | 1 | | | | 9 | | |
| Nantucket | 18 | 51 | Hussey | Urial | 2 | 1 | | 1 | | 2 | | 1 | | 1 | 1 | | 9 | | |
| Nantucket | 17 | 50 | Hussey | William Junr | | 1 | | 1 | | | | | 1 | | | | 3 | | |
| Nantucket | 16 | 36 | Hussey | Wm | | | | 1 | | | | 1 | 1 | 1 | | | 4 | | |
| Nantucket | 18 | 62 | Hussey | Zaccheus | 2 | | 2 | 1 | | 3 | 2 | | | 1 | 1 | | 12 | | |
| Nantucket | 13 | 67 | Hutsey | Robert | 1 | | 1 | 1 | | 1 | | 1 | | | | | 5 | | |
| Nantucket | 9 | 36 | Irish | Thomas | 1 | | 1 | | | | | | 1 | | | | 3 | Not Stated | |
| Nantucket | 19 | 50 | Isop | Sarah | | | | | | | | | | | 1 | | 1 | | |
| Nantucket | 12 | 58 | Jackson | Timothy | | | | 1 | | | | | 1 | | | | 2 | | |
| Nantucket | 12 | 9 | James | Bejamin 2nd | | | 1 | | | 1 | | | 1 | | | | 3 | Not Stated | |
| Nantucket | 5 | 8 | James | Francis | 2 | 1 | 2 | 1 | | 2 | | | 1 | | | | 9 | Not Stated | |
| Nantucket | 5 | 13 | James | Hart | 2 | | 1 | | | | | 2 | 2 | 2 | | | 9 | Not Stated | |
| Nantucket | 17 | 36 | Jarwood | John | | | 1 | | | 1 | | | | | | | 2 | | |
| Nantucket | 16 | 61 | Jenkins | John | 1 | 1 | 1 | 1 | | 3 | | | 1 | | | | 8 | | |
| Nantucket | 17 | 64 | Jenkins | Jonathan | 1 | 1 | | | 1 | 1 | 2 | 1 | 1 | 1 | | | 9 | | |
| Nantucket | 11 | 3 | Jenkins | Lydia | | | | | | | | | 1 | | | | 1 | Not Stated | |
| Nantucket | 17 | 6 | Jenkins | Perus | 1 | 1 | | 1 | 1 | | | | 1 | | | | 5 | | |
| Nantucket | 15 | 27 | Jenkins | Tristram | 1 | 1 | 3 | | 1 | 1 | 1 | | 1 | | | | 10 | | |
| Nantucket | 10 | 13 | Johnson | Daniel | | | 1 | | | 1 | | | | | | | 1 | Not Stated | |
| Nantucket | 14 | 20 | Johnson | Polly | | | | | | 1 | | 3 | 1 | | | | 5 | | |
| Nantucket | 15 | 23 | Jones | Benjm | 3 | | | 3 | | 1 | 1 | 1 | 1 | | | | 11 | | |
| Nantucket | 16 | 73 | Jones | Danl | | | 1 | | | 1 | | 1 | 1 | | | | 4 | | |
| Nantucket | 18 | 75 | Jones | Ebenezer | 1 | | | 1 | | | | | 1 | 1 | | | 4 | | |
| Nantucket | 20 | 4 | Jones | Edmond | | | | | | | | | | | 2 | | 2 | | |
| Nantucket | 4 | 74 | Jones | Hezhibah | | | | | | | | 1 | 1 | | | | 2 | Not Stated | |
| Nantucket | 16 | 67 | Jones | Reuben | | | 1 | | | 1 | | | | | | | 2 | | |
| Nantucket | 13 | 76 | Jones | Silas | | 1 | 2 | | 1 | | 1 | 1 | | 1 | | | 7 | | |
| Nantucket | 19 | 57 | Jourden | Simon | | | | | | | | | | | 2 | | 2 | | |
| Nantucket | 16 | 4 | Joy | Anna | | | | | | | | | 1 | 1 | | | 2 | | |
| Nantucket | 15 | 70 | Joy | David | | 2 | 1 | | 1 | | 1 | 1 | 1 | | | | 7 | | |
| Nantucket | 15 | 42 | Joy | Francis | 1 | | | 1 | 1 | 2 | 1 | 1 | 1 | | | | 8 | | |
| Nantucket | 15 | 69 | Joy | Obed | 1 | | | 1 | | | | 2 | 1 | | | | 5 | | |
| Nantucket | 11 | 19 | Joy | Reuben | 3 | | | 1 | | 2 | | | 1 | 1 | | | 8 | Not Stated | |
| Nantucket | 15 | 67 | Joy | Thaddeus | 1 | | | 1 | 1 | | 1 | | | | | | 4 | | |
| Nantucket | 17 | 63 | Joy | William | 3 | | | 1 | | 2 | | | 1 | | | | 7 | | |
| Nantucket | 5 | 44 | Keen | Moses | 2 | | | 1 | | | 1 | | | | | | 4 | Not Stated | |
| Nantucket | 8 | 15 | Kellog | Seth | 1 | | | 1 | | | | | 1 | | | | 3 | Not Stated | |
| Nantucket | 18 | 26 | Kidder | Benjamin | | | | 1 | | | | | 1 | | | | 2 | | |
| Nantucket | 12 | 62 | Kimberlin | Jedida | | | | | | | | 1 | | 1 | | | 2 | | |
| Nantucket | 16 | 48 | Laurence | George | | 1 | | 1 | | | | 1 | | 1 | | | 4 | | |
| Nantucket | 7 | 11 | Lawrence | Jeremiah | 2 | | | 1 | | | | | 1 | | | | 4 | Not Stated | |
| Nantucket | 19 | 38 | Lee | Mike | | | | | | | | | | | 3 | | 3 | | |
| Nantucket | 19 | 41 | Limas | Prince | | | | | | | | | | | 3 | | 3 | | |
| Nantucket | 11 | 23 | Long | Jonathan | | | | 1 | | | | | | 1 | | | 2 | Not Stated | |
| Nantucket | 17 | 24 | Long | Nathan | | | 1 | | | 2 | 1 | 1 | | | | | 5 | | |
| Nantucket | 3 | 17 | Long | Peleg | | | 1 | | | | | | 2 | | | | 3 | Not Stated | |
| Nantucket | 6 | 55 | Long | Reuben | 1 | | | 1 | | | | | 1 | | | | 3 | Not Stated | |
| Nantucket | 7 | 1 | Long | Richard | 3 | | | 1 | | | | | 1 | | | | 5 | Not Stated | |
| Nantucket | 12 | 26 | Long | Samuel | | 1 | 1 | 1 | | | | | | 1 | | | 4 | Not Stated | |
| Nantucket | 12 | 54 | Long | Simeon | | 2 | | 1 | | 2 | 1 | 1 | 1 | | | | 8 | | |
| Nantucket | 19 | 21 | Luce | Elijah | 3 | 1 | 2 | | | 2 | 2 | | 1 | | | | 11 | | |
| Nantucket | 6 | 32 | Luce | Obed | 1 | | | 1 | 3 | | | | 1 | | | | 6 | Not Stated | |
| Nantucket | 10 | 7 | Macy | Abigail | | | | | | | | | 1 | | | | 1 | Not Stated | |
| Nantucket | 13 | 66 | Macy | Abigail | | | | | | | 1 | | 1 | 1 | | | 3 | | |
| Nantucket | 13 | 68 | Macy | Abishai | 1 | | 1 | | | | | | 1 | | | | 3 | | |
| Nantucket | 4 | 33 | Macy | Barnabas | 1 | 2 | | 1 | | | | 1 | 1 | 1 | | | 7 | Not Stated | |
| Nantucket | 10 | 49 | Macy | Elisha | | 1 | 1 | 1 | | | | | 1 | 1 | | | 5 | Not Stated | |
| Nantucket | 3 | 28 | Macy | Francis | 4 | 1 | | 1 | | | 1 | 1 | 1 | | | | 9 | Not Stated | |

| TOWN | PG# | LN# | LAST NAME | FIRST NAME | FREE WHITE MALES | | | | | FREE WHITE FEMALES | | | | | TOTAL ALL OTHER | TOTAL SLAVES | TOTALS | DISTRICT/ TOWNSHIP | NOTES |
|---|---|---|---|---|---|---|---|---|---|---|---|---|---|---|---|---|---|---|---|
| | | | | | under 10 | 10 to 16 | 16 to 26 | 26 to 45 | 45 and over | under 10 | 10 to 16 | 16 to 26 | 26 to 45 | 45 and over | | | | | |
| Nantucket | 10 | 19 | Macy | George | | | | 1 | | | | | | 1 | | | 2 | Not Stated | |
| Nantucket | 4 | 4 | Macy | Job | 2 | | 1 | | | 1 | | 1 | 1 | | | | 6 | Not Stated | |
| Nantucket | 11 | 6 | Macy | Job | 1 | | 1 | | | 2 | | | 1 | | | | 5 | Not Stated | |
| Nantucket | 11 | 4 | Macy | Job Junr | 2 | | 1 | | | 1 | | | 1 | | | | 5 | Not Stated | |
| Nantucket | 11 | 32 | Macy | Jonathan | 3 | 1 | | 1 | | | 1 | 1 | 1 | | 1 | | 9 | Not Stated | |
| Nantucket | 3 | 12 | Macy | Lois | 2 | 1 | 1 | 1 | | 2 | 1 | 1 | 1 | 1 | | | 10 | Not Stated | |
| Nantucket | 4 | 31 | Macy | Lydia | | | | | | | | 1 | 1 | | | | 2 | Not Stated | |
| Nantucket | 12 | 12 | Macy | Nathl | | | 3 | | 1 | 1 | | 1 | 1 | | | | 7 | Not Stated | |
| Nantucket | 3 | 23 | Macy | Obed | 1 | 2 | | 1 | | | | 2 | 1 | | | | 8 | Not Stated | |
| Nantucket | 6 | 9 | Macy | Peleg | 3 | 1 | 1 | 1 | | 2 | 2 | | 1 | | | | 11 | Not Stated | |
| Nantucket | 11 | 22 | Macy | Peter | 1 | 1 | | 1 | | 1 | 1 | | 1 | | | | 6 | Not Stated | |
| Nantucket | 14 | 17 | Macy | Richard | | 1 | 1 | | 1 | | | 1 | 1 | 1 | | | 6 | | |
| Nantucket | 11 | 8 | Macy | Shubael | | | | | | 1 | 2 | 2 | 1 | | | | 8 | Not Stated | |
| Nantucket | 4 | 7 | Macy | Silvanus Junr | 1 | 1 | 1 | 1 | | | | 1 | 1 | 1 | | | 7 | Not Stated | |
| Nantucket | 4 | 22 | Macy | Silvanus Juni | 2 | 2 | | 1 | | | | 2 | 1 | | | | 8 | Not Stated | |
| Nantucket | 4 | 30 | Macy | Simeon | | 1 | 1 | | | | | 1 | | | | | 3 | Not Stated | |
| Nantucket | 16 | 50 | Macy | Solomon | 2 | 1 | 1 | 1 | | | | 2 | | 2 | | | 9 | | |
| Nantucket | 11 | 5 | Macy | Stephen | 1 | | 1 | | 1 | | | | | 1 | | | 4 | Not Stated | |
| Nantucket | 13 | 29 | Macy | Stephen Junr | 1 | | | 1 | | 1 | | 1 | 1 | 1 | | | 6 | | |
| Nantucket | 18 | 45 | Macy | Uriah | 1 | | | 1 | | 3 | | 1 | | 1 | | | 7 | | |
| Nantucket | 3 | 9 | Macy | William | 2 | 1 | 1 | | 2 | | 1 | 6 | 1 | 1 | | | 15 | Not Stated | |
| Nantucket | 14 | 19 | Macy | Zaccheus | 1 | | | 1 | | 1 | | 1 | 1 | | | | 5 | | |
| Nantucket | 7 | 16 | Manter | Benjamin | 2 | | | 1 | | | 1 | | 1 | | | | 5 | Not Stated | |
| Nantucket | 7 | 26 | Manter | George | 1 | | 1 | | | | | | 1 | | | | 3 | Not Stated | |
| Nantucket | 7 | 5 | Manter | Joseph | | | 1 | 1 | | | 1 | 2 | 1 | | | | 6 | Not Stated | |
| Nantucket | 14 | 53 | Manter | William | 3 | | | 1 | | | | 2 | | | | | 6 | | |
| Nantucket | 7 | 14 | Marshall | Green | | 1 | 2 | | 1 | 1 | | | 1 | 1 | | | 7 | Not Stated | |
| Nantucket | 6 | 19 | Marshall | James | 1 | | | 1 | | 1 | | | 1 | | | | 4 | Not Stated | |
| Nantucket | 13 | 61 | Marshall | Joseph | | | | 1 | | | | | | 1 | | | 2 | | |
| Nantucket | 7 | 40 | Marshall | Josiah | | 1 | 2 | | 1 | | | | | 1 | | | 6 | Not Stated | |
| Nantucket | 3 | 25 | Marshall | Obed | | 1 | 1 | | 1 | 1 | | | | 1 | | | 5 | Not Stated | |
| Nantucket | 5 | 11 | Marshall | Samuel | | | | 1 | | 1 | 1 | | 1 | | | | 4 | Not Stated | |
| Nantucket | 13 | 16 | Marshall | Thomas | | | 1 | 1 | | 3 | | 1 | 1 | | | | 7 | | |
| Nantucket | 11 | 21 | Marshall | William | | | 1 | | | | | | 1 | | | | 2 | Not Stated | |
| Nantucket | 6 | 58 | Maxcy | Isaiah | 1 | 1 | | | 1 | | | 2 | | 1 | | | 6 | Not Stated | |
| Nantucket | 7 | 18 | Maxcy | Reuben | | | 1 | 1 | | | | | 1 | | | | 3 | Not Stated | |
| Nantucket | 10 | 56 | Mayo | Rachel | | 1 | | | | | | 1 | | 1 | | | 3 | Not Stated | |
| Nantucket | 15 | 29 | McCleave | Joseph | 1 | | 1 | | | 1 | | 1 | | | | | 4 | | |
| Nantucket | 6 | 27 | McCleve | Thos Varney | 2 | 1 | 3 | | | 4 | | | 2 | | | | 12 | Not Stated | |
| Nantucket | 14 | 14 | McMurphy | James | 1 | | 1 | | | 1 | | 1 | | | | | 4 | | |
| Nantucket | 18 | 32 | Meade | George | | 1 | | | | | | 1 | | | | | 2 | | |
| Nantucket | 6 | 46 | Meader | Nathl | 1 | 2 | 1 | | 1 | 1 | | 2 | 2 | 1 | | | 11 | Not Stated | |
| Nantucket | 9 | 2 | Meader | Nicholas | 3 | 1 | 2 | | 1 | | 2 | 1 | 1 | | | | 11 | Not Stated | |
| Nantucket | 5 | 2 | Merchant | Benjm | | | | 2 | 1 | | | 1 | 1 | | | | 5 | Not Stated | |
| Nantucket | 16 | 29 | Mirick | Coffin | | | | 1 | | 1 | | 1 | 1 | | | | 4 | | |
| Nantucket | 16 | 33 | Mirick | Jonathan Junr | 1 | 1 | 1 | 1 | | 2 | | 1 | 1 | | | | 8 | | |
| Nantucket | 18 | 33 | Mitchell | Aaron | 1 | | 1 | | | | | 2 | | | 1 | | 5 | | |
| Nantucket | 6 | 3 | Mitchell | Benjm | 1 | 1 | | 1 | | 3 | | 1 | | | | | 7 | Not Stated | |
| Nantucket | 6 | 4 | Mitchell | Christopher | | 1 | 1 | 1 | | 2 | 1 | | 1 | | | | 7 | Not Stated | |
| Nantucket | 17 | 65 | Mitchell | David | 1 | 1 | | 1 | | 2 | | 2 | 1 | | | | 8 | | |
| Nantucket | 10 | 42 | Mitchell | Elizabeth | | | | | | | | | 1 | | | | 1 | Not Stated | |
| Nantucket | 18 | 36 | Mitchell | Jethro | | 1 | 2 | | 1 | 1 | 1 | | | 1 | | | 7 | | |
| Nantucket | 18 | 11 | Mitchell | Laban | 2 | 1 | 1 | 1 | | 1 | 1 | | 1 | | | | 8 | | |
| Nantucket | 18 | 58 | Mitchell | Mary | | | | | | | | | | 1 | | | 1 | | |
| Nantucket | 18 | 37 | Mitchell | Moses | | 1 | | 1 | | | | | 1 | | | | 3 | | |
| Nantucket | 18 | 35 | Mitchell | Obed | 3 | 1 | | 1 | 1 | | 3 | | 1 | | 1 | | 11 | | |
| Nantucket | 18 | 12 | Mitchell | Paul | 3 | 2 | | 1 | | | 2 | 1 | 1 | | | | 10 | | |
| Nantucket | 13 | 51 | Mitchell | Peleg | 1 | 1 | 2 | 1 | | 2 | 3 | 1 | 1 | | | | 12 | | |
| Nantucket | 18 | 13 | Mitchell | Richard | | 1 | | 1 | | | | | 1 | 1 | | | 4 | | |
| Nantucket | 10 | 59 | Mooers | Abigail | | | | | | | | | | 1 | | | 1 | Not Stated | |
| Nantucket | 13 | 48 | Mooers | Jonathan | | 1 | 1 | 1 | 1 | 1 | | 1 | 1 | 2 | | | 9 | | |
| Nantucket | 13 | 17 | Mooers | Lucinda | 1 | | | | | | | 1 | | 1 | | | 3 | | |
| Nantucket | 11 | 17 | Morris | Jacob | 1 | | | 1 | | 1 | | | 1 | | | | 4 | Not Stated | |
| Nantucket | 16 | 56 | Morris | John | | 1 | | 1 | | 3 | | | 1 | | | | 6 | | |
| Nantucket | 11 | 16 | Morris | Jonathan | | 2 | | 1 | | 1 | | | 1 | | | | 5 | Not Stated | |
| Nantucket | 7 | 56 | Morslander | Cornelius | | 1 | | 1 | | | 1 | | | 1 | | | 4 | Not Stated | |
| Nantucket | 7 | 49 | Morslander | Cornelius Junr | 2 | | 1 | | | 1 | 2 | | 1 | | | | 7 | Not Stated | |
| Nantucket | 7 | 43 | Morslander | Linzey | 2 | | 1 | | | | | | 1 | | | | 4 | Not Stated | |
| Nantucket | 12 | 36 | Morton | Ruth | | | | | | | | | | 1 | | | 1 | | |
| Nantucket | 12 | 34 | Morton | William | 1 | | | 1 | | | | | 1 | | | | 3 | | |
| Nantucket | 17 | 25 | Murphy | David | | | 1 | | | 2 | 1 | 1 | | | | | 5 | | |
| Nantucket | 5 | 31 | Myrick | Abigail | | | | | | | | | | 1 | | | 1 | Not Stated | |
| Nantucket | 5 | 36 | Myrick | Andrew | | 1 | | 1 | | | 1 | | 1 | | | | 4 | Not Stated | |
| Nantucket | 13 | 24 | Myrick | Andrew | 1 | | 1 | 1 | | 2 | 1 | | 1 | | | | 7 | | |
| Nantucket | 5 | 34 | Myrick | George | 3 | 1 | 1 | 1 | | 2 | | 1 | 1 | | | | 10 | Not Stated | |
| Nantucket | 13 | 22 | Myrick | Hannah | | | | | | | | 1 | 1 | | | | 2 | | |
| Nantucket | 13 | 13 | Myrick | James | | 1 | | | | | | 1 | | | | | 2 | | |
| Nantucket | 13 | 56 | Myrick | Jemima | 1 | | | | | | | 2 | 1 | | | | 4 | | |
| Nantucket | 13 | 11 | Myrick | Jonathan Gorham | | | | 1 | | | | 1 | 1 | | | | 3 | | |
| Nantucket | 8 | 21 | Myrick | Sarah | | 1 | 3 | 1 | | 1 | | | | 1 | | | 7 | Not Stated | |
| Nantucket | 16 | 15 | Narbeth | John | 1 | 1 | 1 | | | | | 2 | | | | | 5 | | |
| Nantucket | 19 | 39 | Nation | London | | | | | | | | | | | 3 | | 3 | | |
| Nantucket | 12 | 27 | Newbegin | George | | | 1 | | | 3 | | | 1 | | | | 5 | Not Stated | |
| Nantucket | 4 | 70 | Newbegin | James | | | | 1 | | | | 3 | 1 | | | | 5 | Not Stated | |
| Nantucket | 17 | 10 | Nichols | Horatio | 2 | | 1 | | | 1 | | 1 | | | | | 5 | | |
| Nantucket | 16 | 13 | Nichols | Joseph | | | | 1 | | | | | 1 | | | | 2 | | |
| Nantucket | 18 | 3 | Nichols | William | 3 | | 2 | 1 | | | 1 | 1 | 1 | | | | 9 | | |
| Nantucket | 16 | 62 | Norris | Charles | | | 1 | 1 | | | 1 | | 1 | | | | 6 | | |
| Nantucket | 15 | 55 | Nye | Maltiah | 1 | | | | | | | | | | | | 4 | | |
| Nantucket | 11 | 36 | Nye | Nathan | | | 1 | 1 | | | | | 1 | | | | 3 | Not Stated | |

# 1800 Nantucket County, Massachusetts Index

| TOWN | PG# | LN# | LAST NAME | FIRST NAME | FREE WHITE MALES under 10 | 10 to 16 | 16 to 26 | 26 to 45 | 45 and over | FREE WHITE FEMALES under 10 | 10 to 16 | 16 to 26 | 26 to 45 | 45 and over | TOTAL ALL OTHER | TOTAL SLAVES | TOTALS | DISTRICT/ TOWNSHIP | NOTES |
|---|---|---|---|---|---|---|---|---|---|---|---|---|---|---|---|---|---|---|---|
| Nantucket | 17 | 73 | Osborn | Saml | 3 | | | 1 | | 1 | | 1 | | 1 | | | 7 | | |
| Nantucket | 4 | 37 | Paddack | Abishai | 3 | 1 | 3 | | 1 | | 2 | | 1 | | | | 11 | Not Stated | |
| Nantucket | 10 | 34 | Paddack | Barnabas | | 1 | | 1 | | | | | | 1 | | | 3 | Not Stated | |
| Nantucket | 4 | 35 | Paddack | Benjamin | | | 3 | 1 | | | | 1 | 1 | 1 | | | 7 | Not Stated | |
| Nantucket | 14 | 50 | Paddack | Eliphalet | 1 | | 2 | | 1 | 1 | | 3 | | 1 | | | 9 | | |
| Nantucket | 5 | 21 | Paddack | Francis | | | | 1 | | | | | 1 | | | | 2 | Not Stated | |
| Nantucket | 5 | 19 | Paddack | Hephzibah | | | 1 | 1 | | | | | 1 | 1 | | | 4 | Not Stated | |
| Nantucket | 11 | 44 | Paddack | Jonathan | 3 | | | 1 | | 3 | | | 1 | | | | 8 | Not Stated | |
| Nantucket | 14 | 47 | Paddack | Joseph | 2 | | | 1 | | 2 | 1 | 1 | 1 | | | | 8 | | |
| Nantucket | 15 | 8 | Paddack | Nathaniel | 2 | | | 1 | | 1 | | 2 | 1 | | | | 7 | | |
| Nantucket | 10 | 38 | Paddack | Peter | 1 | | | 1 | | 1 | | | 1 | | | | 4 | Not Stated | |
| Nantucket | 4 | 36 | Paddack | William | | 1 | | 1 | | | | | 1 | | | | 3 | Not Stated | |
| Nantucket | 17 | 27 | Paddock | Anna | | | | 1 | | | 1 | 1 | 2 | | | | 5 | | |
| Nantucket | 5 | 50 | Padduck | Benjm | 2 | 1 | | 1 | | 1 | | 1 | | 1 | | | 7 | Not Stated | |
| Nantucket | 19 | 28 | Painter | Joseph | | | | | | | | | | | 5 | | 5 | | |
| Nantucket | 10 | 25 | Parker | Elizabeth | 1 | | | | | 1 | | | 1 | | | | 3 | Not Stated | |
| Nantucket | 6 | 10 | Parker | Francis | 2 | 2 | | 1 | | | 2 | 1 | 1 | | 2 | | 11 | Not Stated | |
| Nantucket | 19 | 11 | Parker | Jonathan | 1 | | | 1 | | | | | 1 | | | | 3 | | |
| Nantucket | 3 | 6 | Parker | Josiah | | | | 1 | | | | | 1 | | 6 | | 8 | Not Stated | |
| Nantucket | 19 | 13 | Parker | Nathan | | 2 | 1 | 1 | | | | | 1 | 1 | | | 6 | | |
| Nantucket | 4 | 39 | Parker | Nathan Junr | | 1 | | | | | | | 1 | | | | 2 | Not Stated | |
| Nantucket | 11 | 41 | Parker | Silas | | 1 | | 1 | | | | | 1 | 1 | | | 4 | Not Stated | |
| Nantucket | 10 | 15 | Paul | Phebe | | | 1 | | | 2 | | 2 | 1 | | | | 6 | Not Stated | |
| Nantucket | 14 | 43 | Pease | David | 1 | | 1 | | | | | | 1 | | | | 3 | | |
| Nantucket | 17 | 42 | Pease | Elijah | | 2 | 1 | | 1 | | 1 | 1 | 1 | | | | 6 | | |
| Nantucket | 15 | 9 | Pease | Valentine | 2 | | | 1 | | 3 | | | 2 | | | | 8 | | |
| Nantucket | 7 | 37 | Perkins | Gilbert | 1 | | | 1 | | 2 | | | 1 | | | | 5 | Not Stated | |
| Nantucket | 7 | 38 | Perkins | John | | | 1 | 1 | | 1 | | 1 | 1 | | | | 5 | Not Stated | |
| Nantucket | 8 | 41 | Perkins | William | 1 | | | 1 | | 2 | | 1 | 1 | | | | 6 | Not Stated | |
| Nantucket | 14 | 38 | Perry | Jonath | 1 | 1 | | 1 | | 1 | 2 | 1 | | 1 | | | 9 | | |
| Nantucket | 17 | 13 | Perry | Jonathan Junr | 1 | | 1 | 1 | | 1 | | | 1 | | 1 | | 6 | | |
| Nantucket | 4 | 55 | Perry | Reuben | | 1 | | 1 | | | | | 1 | | 1 | | 4 | Not Stated | |
| Nantucket | 14 | 2 | Perry | Saml | | 1 | 2 | 1 | | 1 | 1 | 2 | 1 | | | | 9 | | |
| Nantucket | 8 | 16 | Perry | William | 1 | | | 1 | | | 1 | | 1 | | | | 4 | Not Stated | |
| Nantucket | 5 | 12 | Peters | John | 1 | | | 1 | | | | | 1 | | | | 3 | Not Stated | |
| Nantucket | 19 | 54 | Pheniz | George | | | | | | | | | | | 4 | | 4 | | |
| Nantucket | 5 | 18 | Pinkham | Andrew | 2 | | | 1 | | | | | 1 | | | | 4 | Not Stated | |
| Nantucket | 5 | 42 | Pinkham | Bethiah | | | | | | | | | 2 | | | | 2 | Not Stated | |
| Nantucket | 17 | 68 | Pinkham | Charles | 1 | | 1 | | 1 | | | 2 | 1 | | | | 6 | | |
| Nantucket | 17 | 12 | Pinkham | Henry | | 1 | | 1 | | 1 | 1 | | | | | | 4 | | |
| Nantucket | 18 | 69 | Pinkham | Hezekiah | | 1 | | | | 1 | 1 | | | | | | 3 | | |
| Nantucket | 12 | 29 | Pinkham | Jemima | | | | | | | | | | 1 | | | 1 | Not Stated | |
| Nantucket | 9 | 56 | Pinkham | Jethro | | 1 | 1 | 1 | | 1 | | 2 | 1 | | | | 7 | Not Stated | |
| Nantucket | 18 | 5 | Pinkham | John | | 1 | | | | | | 1 | 1 | | | | 3 | | |
| Nantucket | 14 | 40 | Pinkham | Matthew | 1 | 2 | 1 | 1 | | | | | 1 | | | | 6 | | |
| Nantucket | 17 | 69 | Pinkham | Obed | | 1 | | 1 | | | | 1 | 1 | | | | 4 | | |
| Nantucket | 11 | 56 | Pinkham | Peleg | | | 1 | | | | | | 1 | | | | 2 | Not Stated | |
| Nantucket | 17 | 17 | Pinkham | Peter | | | | 1 | | 1 | 1 | | 1 | | | | 4 | | |
| Nantucket | 15 | 52 | Pinkham | Shubael | 2 | | | 1 | | 2 | | | 1 | | | | 6 | | |
| Nantucket | 18 | 18 | Pinkham | Shubael | | 1 | | 1 | | 2 | | | 1 | | | | 5 | | |
| Nantucket | 15 | 16 | Pinkham | Tristram | 2 | 1 | 2 | 1 | | 1 | | 3 | | 1 | | | 11 | | |
| Nantucket | 11 | 55 | Pinkham | Uriah | | 1 | | 1 | | 2 | | 1 | | | | | 5 | Not Stated | |
| Nantucket | 17 | 23 | Pinkham | Wm | | | | 1 | | | 1 | | | | | | 2 | | |
| Nantucket | 15 | 75 | Pitman | Charles | | 1 | | | | | | 1 | 1 | | | | 3 | | |
| Nantucket | 15 | 74 | Pitman | Saml | 1 | | | 1 | | 1 | | | 1 | | | | 4 | | |
| Nantucket | 10 | 2 | Pitts | Obed | 3 | | | 1 | | 1 | | | 1 | | | | 6 | Not Stated | |
| Nantucket | 16 | 71 | Pitts | Silvanus | 1 | | | 1 | | 1 | | 1 | | | | | 4 | | |
| Nantucket | 14 | 7 | Pitts | William | | | | 1 | | | | | 1 | | | | 2 | | |
| Nantucket | 19 | 42 | Plato | James | | | | | | | | | | | 2 | | 2 | | |
| Nantucket | 18 | 8 | Plum | Urial | | | 1 | | | | | 1 | | | | | 2 | | |
| Nantucket | 19 | 26 | Pollard | George | 2 | 1 | | 1 | | 1 | 1 | 1 | | | | | 7 | | |
| Nantucket | 9 | 51 | Pollard | Peter | 2 | | | 1 | | 2 | 1 | 1 | | | | | 7 | Not Stated | |
| Nantucket | 20 | 10 | Pompey | Dinah | | | | | | | | | 6 | | | | 6 | | |
| Nantucket | 19 | 40 | Pompy | George | | | | | | | | | 3 | | | | 3 | | |
| Nantucket | 6 | 31 | Pruff | Jane | | 2 | | | | | | 1 | 1 | | | | 4 | Not Stated | |
| Nantucket | 19 | 49 | Quady | Abram | | | | | | | | | 3 | | | | 3 | | |
| Nantucket | 20 | 14 | Quam* | Nimrod | | | | | | | | | 3 | | | | 3 | | |
| Nantucket | 19 | 31 | Quary | Joseph | | | | | | | | | 4 | | | | 4 | | |
| Nantucket | 7 | 46 | Quin | Mary | 1 | | | | | 1 | | | 1 | 1 | | | 4 | Not Stated | |
| Nantucket | 3 | 31 | Ramsdell | James | 3 | 2 | | 1 | | | 1 | | 1 | | | | 8 | Not Stated | |
| Nantucket | 7 | 6 | Ramsdell | Priscilla | 1 | | 1 | 1 | | 1 | | 1 | 1 | 1 | | | 7 | Not Stated | |
| Nantucket | 3 | 32 | Ramsdell | Silvia | | | | 2 | | | | 1 | | | | | 3 | Not Stated | |
| Nantucket | 10 | 54 | Ramsdell | William | | 2 | 1 | | | | | | 1 | | | | 4 | Not Stated | |
| Nantucket | 17 | 57 | Rand | David | | 1 | | | | | 1 | | | | | | 2 | | |
| Nantucket | 16 | 60 | Rand | Ebenezer | | 1 | 2 | 1 | 1 | 1 | | 1 | 1 | 1 | | | 9 | | |
| Nantucket | 4 | 49 | Rand | Miriam | | 1 | | | | | | 1 | 1 | | | | 3 | Not Stated | |
| Nantucket | 5 | 16 | Randal | Constant | | 1 | 1 | | | | | | 1 | | | | 3 | Not Stated | |
| Nantucket | 5 | 15 | Randal | Gideon | 1 | | 1 | | 2 | | | | 1 | | | | 5 | Not Stated | |
| Nantucket | 17 | 70 | Rawson | Abel | 1 | | 1 | 1 | | 2 | 1 | 1 | | | | | 7 | | |
| Nantucket | 17 | 75 | Rawson | Deborah | | | | | | | | | 1 | 1 | | | 2 | | |
| Nantucket | 14 | 25 | Rawson | Stephen | 3 | | | 1 | | 1 | 1 | | 1 | | | | 7 | | |
| Nantucket | 17 | 72 | Rawson | Wilson | 1 | 2 | 3 | 1 | | | 1 | | 1 | | | | 9 | | |
| Nantucket | 5 | 49 | Ray | Alexander | 2 | 2 | 1 | | | | | 3 | 1 | | | | 9 | Not Stated | |
| Nantucket | 12 | 25 | Ray | David Junr | 1 | | | 1 | | | | 1 | | | | | 5 | Not Stated | |
| Nantucket | 9 | 13 | Ray | Enoch | | 2 | 1 | | | | | | 1 | | | | 4 | Not Stated | |
| Nantucket | 12 | 4 | Ray | George | | | 1 | | | | | | 1 | | | | 2 | Not Stated | |
| Nantucket | 5 | 37 | Ray | Isaiah | 1 | | 1 | | | | | | 1 | | | | 3 | Not Stated | |
| Nantucket | 12 | 6 | Ray | John | 2 | 2 | | 1 | | | | | 1 | | | | 6 | Not Stated | |
| Nantucket | 10 | 44 | Ray | Nathl | 2 | | | 1 | | | | 1 | | | | | 4 | Not Stated | |
| Nantucket | 14 | 21 | Ray | Paul | 1 | | 1 | 1 | | | | | 2 | | | | 6 | | |

144

# 1800 Nantucket County, Massachusetts Index

| Town | PG# | LN# | Last Name | First Name | FWM under 10 | FWM 10–16 | FWM 16–26 | FWM 26–45 | FWM 45+ | FWF under 10 | FWF 10–16 | FWF 16–26 | FWF 26–45 | FWF 45+ | Total All Other | Total Slaves | Totals | District/Township | Notes |
|---|---|---|---|---|---|---|---|---|---|---|---|---|---|---|---|---|---|---|---|
| Nantucket | 18 | 70 | Ray | Reuben | | 1 | 1 | 1 | | | | 1 | | 1 | | | 5 | | |
| Nantucket | 12 | 23 | Ray | William | | | | 1 | | | | 1 | | 1 | | | 3 | Not Stated | |
| Nantucket | 6 | 43 | Ray | William Junr | | | 1 | 1 | | | | 1 | | | | | 4 | Not Stated | |
| Nantucket | 19 | 3 | Raymond | Benjm | 2 | | | 1 | | 2 | | | 1 | | | | 6 | | |
| Nantucket | 12 | 52 | Raymond | Ebenezer | 1 | | | 1 | | 2 | | 2 | | | | | 6 | | |
| Nantucket | 12 | 24 | Raymond | Elisha | 2 | | 1 | 1 | | 1 | | | 1 | | | | 6 | Not Stated | |
| Nantucket | 6 | 6 | Raymond | William | | | 1 | | 1 | 1 | | 1 | 1 | 1 | | | 6 | Not Stated | |
| Nantucket | 15 | 53 | Raymond | Wm | 1 | | 1 | 1 | | 1 | | 1 | | | | | 5 | | |
| Nantucket | 15 | 30 | Reilley | Daniel | 2 | | 2 | | 1 | | | 1 | 3 | 1 | | | 10 | | |
| Nantucket | 18 | 50 | Remson | Arnold | 1 | | 1 | | | 1 | | | 1 | | | | 4 | | |
| Nantucket | 12 | 16 | Rice | Phebe | | | | | | | | | 1 | | | | 1 | Not Stated | |
| Nantucket | 17 | 44 | Rice | Randal | 2 | | 1 | 1 | | 1 | 2 | | 1 | | | | 8 | | |
| Nantucket | 13 | 45 | Riddell | Henry | | 2 | | 1 | | 2 | 1 | 1 | | | | | 7 | | |
| Nantucket | 18 | 68 | Riddell | Linzey | | 1 | | | | | | 1 | | | | | 2 | | |
| Nantucket | 11 | 54 | Riddell | Saml | 1 | | 1 | 1 | 1 | 2 | 1 | | 1 | | 1 | | 9 | Not Stated | |
| Nantucket | 18 | 10 | Riddell | William | 2 | | 1 | | | 1 | | | 1 | | | | 5 | | |
| Nantucket | 20 | 7 | Roberts | Benjm | | | | | | | | | | | 3 | | 3 | | |
| Nantucket | 19 | 5 | Robins | John | 2 | 1 | | 1 | | 1 | 1 | | 1 | | | | 7 | | |
| Nantucket | 19 | 8 | Robinson | Saml | 1 | 1 | | 1 | | 1 | 1 | 1 | 1 | | | | 6 | | |
| Nantucket | 18 | 2 | Ross | Isaac | | | | | 1 | 1 | 2 | | 1 | | | | 5 | | |
| Nantucket | 15 | 71 | Ross | L* | 1 | 1 | | | | 1 | 1 | | 1 | | | | 5 | | |
| Nantucket | 20 | 11 | Ross | Matthew | | | | | | | | | | | 2 | | 2 | | |
| Nantucket | 17 | 7 | Rothbon | Jonathan | | 1 | 1 | 1 | | | | | 1 | | | | 4 | | |
| Nantucket | 4 | 32 | Roy | Thomas | | 1 | | | 1 | | | | 1 | | | | 2 | Not Stated | |
| Nantucket | 8 | 52 | Russell | Charles | 3 | | | 1 | | | 1 | 1 | | | 1 | | 7 | Not Stated | |
| Nantucket | 6 | 20 | Russell | Elihu | 2 | | | 1 | | | 1 | | 1 | | | | 5 | Not Stated | |
| Nantucket | 11 | 25 | Russell | Fanna | 1 | | | | | 1 | | | 1 | | | | 3 | Not Stated | |
| Nantucket | 11 | 53 | Russell | George | 1 | 1 | | | 1 | | 1 | | | 1 | | | 5 | Not Stated | |
| Nantucket | 17 | 22 | Russell | George Junr | 1 | | 1 | | | 1 | | 1 | | | | | 4 | | |
| Nantucket | 9 | 28 | Russell | Hephzibah | | | | | | | | | | 1 | | | 1 | Not Stated | |
| Nantucket | 8 | 1 | Russell | Hezkiah | | 1 | 1 | | 1 | | | | 1 | | | | 4 | Not Stated | |
| Nantucket | 17 | 58 | Russell | John | 1 | | 1 | | 1 | 4 | 2 | 2 | 1 | | | | 12 | | |
| Nantucket | 10 | 41 | Russell | Joseph | | 1 | 2 | | 1 | 1 | | 2 | 1 | | | | 8 | Not Stated | |
| Nantucket | 11 | 24 | Russell | Nathaniel | | 1 | 1 | | 1 | | 1 | 1 | | 1 | 1 | | 7 | Not Stated | |
| Nantucket | 8 | 26 | Russell | Reuben | | | 2 | | 1 | | 1 | 2 | 1 | | | | 7 | Not Stated | |
| Nantucket | 13 | 23 | Russell | Reuben 2nd | 1 | | | 1 | | | 1 | | 1 | | | | 4 | | |
| Nantucket | 15 | 38 | Russell | Saml | | | | | 1 | | 1 | 1 | | | | | 3 | | |
| Nantucket | 15 | 56 | Russell | Saml | | | 1 | | 1 | | 1 | 1 | | | | | 4 | | |
| Nantucket | 9 | 22 | Russell | Seth | 1 | 1 | 1 | | | 2 | 1 | | 1 | 1 | | | 8 | Not Stated | |
| Nantucket | 8 | 23 | Russell | Silvanus | 1 | | | 1 | 1 | | | 1 | | 1 | | | 5 | Not Stated | |
| Nantucket | 11 | 10 | Russell | Silvanus Junr | | | 1 | | | 2 | | 1 | | | | | 4 | Not Stated | |
| Nantucket | 10 | 23 | Russell | Simeon | | 1 | | 1 | | 1 | | | 1 | | | | 4 | Not Stated | |
| Nantucket | 9 | 5 | Sandford | Samuel | 3 | | | 1 | | 3 | 1 | | 1 | | | | 9 | Not Stated | |
| Nantucket | 15 | 73 | Sanford | Giles | | 1 | | | | 1 | | 1 | | | | | 3 | | |
| Nantucket | 10 | 29 | Shaw | John | 1 | | | 1 | | 2 | | | 1 | | | | 5 | Not Stated | |
| Nantucket | 19 | 4 | Sheffield | Josiah | | 1 | | | | | | | 1 | | | | 2 | | |
| Nantucket | 6 | 17 | Sherman | John | 2 | | 4 | | 1 | 2 | | 1 | 1 | 1 | | | 12 | Not Stated | |
| Nantucket | 14 | 71 | Sherman | Nathaniel | 1 | 1 | | | | | | | 1 | | | | 3 | | |
| Nantucket | 9 | 24 | Silver | John | 1 | | 1 | | | 1 | | 1 | | | | | 4 | Not Stated | |
| Nantucket | 20 | 6 | Simmons | Toby | | | | | | | | | | | 2 | | 2 | | |
| Nantucket | 20 | 3 | Simons | Ephraim | | | | | | | | | | | 3 | | 3 | | |
| Nantucket | 19 | 45 | Simons | Jeffry | | | | | | | | | | | 6 | | 6 | | |
| Nantucket | 12 | 35 | Sinclair | Abigail | | | | | | | | 1 | 1 | | | | 2 | | |
| Nantucket | 15 | 58 | Sisson | Isaac | | | 1 | | | 3 | | | 1 | | | | 5 | | |
| Nantucket | 12 | 10 | Skinner | Mary | | 2 | | | | | | | | 1 | | | 3 | Not Stated | |
| Nantucket | 8 | 50 | Slade | Benjn | | 1 | 1 | | 1 | 1 | 1 | | 1 | | | | 6 | Not Stated | |
| Nantucket | 7 | 7 | Smith | Abigail | | 1 | 1 | | 1 | | 1 | 1 | 2 | 2 | | | 9 | Not Stated | |
| Nantucket | 9 | 3 | Smith | Armstrong | 3 | | 1 | | | | 1 | 1 | | | | | 6 | Not Stated | |
| Nantucket | 16 | 6 | Smith | Hepzibeh | | 1 | | | | | | | 2 | 1 | | | 4 | | |
| Nantucket | 6 | 44 | Smith | Job Junr | 2 | | 1 | | | | | | 1 | | | | 4 | Not Stated | |
| Nantucket | 9 | 29 | Smith | Job Junr | 2 | | 1 | 1 | | 1 | 1 | 1 | | | | | 7 | Not Stated | |
| Nantucket | 6 | 30 | Smith | Slvanus | | | 1 | | | 1 | | 1 | 1 | 1 | | | 5 | Not Stated | |
| Nantucket | 8 | 39 | Smith | Solomon | 2 | | 2 | 1 | 1 | 1 | | | 1 | | | | 8 | Not Stated | |
| Nantucket | 16 | 5 | Smith | Thos | | | | 1 | | | 1 | | | 1 | | | 3 | | |
| Nantucket | 8 | 12 | Snow | James | 1 | | | 1 | | 3 | | | 1 | | | | 6 | Not Stated | |
| Nantucket | 3 | 7 | Spencer | Judith | 2 | | | 1 | | 1 | | | 1 | 1 | | | 6 | Not Stated | |
| Nantucket | 13 | 36 | Spooner | Dinah | | | | | | | | | 1 | 1 | | | 2 | | |
| Nantucket | 13 | 64 | Stanbuck | David | 1 | 2 | | 1 | | 2 | | | 1 | | | | 7 | | |
| Nantucket | 13 | 65 | Stanbuck | Silvanus | | | | | 1 | | | | 2 | 1 | | | 4 | | |
| Nantucket | 5 | 27 | Starbuck | Benjamin | 2 | | 1 | | | | | | 1 | | | | 4 | Not Stated | |
| Nantucket | 4 | 27 | Starbuck | Christopher | | | | 1 | 1 | | | | | 2 | | | 4 | Not Stated | |
| Nantucket | 11 | 31 | Starbuck | Deborah | | | | | | | | | 1 | 1 | | | 2 | Not Stated | |
| Nantucket | 6 | 50 | Starbuck | Jethro | | | | | 1 | | | | 1 | 1 | | | 3 | Not Stated | |
| Nantucket | 5 | 45 | Starbuck | Joseph | | | 1 | | | 2 | | | 1 | | | | 4 | Not Stated | |
| Nantucket | 5 | 26 | Starbuck | Kimbal | | | 1 | | | 2 | | 1 | | | | | 4 | Not Stated | |
| Nantucket | 10 | 57 | Starbuck | Levi | 2 | | | 1 | | 1 | | | 1 | | | | 5 | Not Stated | |
| Nantucket | 17 | 56 | Starbuck | Nathl | 1 | | | | 1 | | | 1 | 1 | 1 | | | 5 | | |
| Nantucket | 5 | 28 | Starbuck | Reuben | 1 | 1 | 2 | 1 | | 3 | 1 | | 1 | | | | 10 | Not Stated | |
| Nantucket | 17 | 33 | Starbuck | Reuben | | | 1 | | | 1 | | 1 | | | | | 3 | | |
| Nantucket | 19 | 1 | Starbuck | Simeon | 1 | | | 1 | | | 1 | | 2 | | | | 5 | | |
| Nantucket | 5 | 29 | Starbuck | Thomas | 2 | 1 | 1 | 1 | 1 | 1 | | 1 | 1 | 1 | | | 10 | Not Stated | |
| Nantucket | 4 | 28 | Starbuck | Tristram | 2 | | | 1 | | 2 | | | 1 | | | | 6 | Not Stated | |
| Nantucket | 5 | 23 | Starbuck | William | | 1 | | 1 | | | | 1 | | 1 | | | 4 | Not Stated | |
| Nantucket | 5 | 57 | Stetson | Barzillai | | | | 1 | | 1 | | 1 | 1 | | | | 4 | Not Stated | |
| Nantucket | 5 | 63 | Stretton | Abigail | 1 | | | | | | | | | 1 | | | 2 | Not Stated | |
| Nantucket | 8 | 42 | Stretton | Naomi | | | | | | | | | | 1 | | | 1 | Not Stated | |
| Nantucket | 8 | 25 | Stretton | Obed | | | | 1 | | | | | 1 | | | | 2 | Not Stated | |
| Nantucket | 18 | 60 | Stubbs | James | 1 | | 2 | | 1 | 3 | 2 | | | 1 | | | 10 | | |
| Nantucket | 15 | 61 | Stubbs | Saml | 1 | 1 | | 1 | | 1 | 1 | | 1 | 1 | | | 7 | | |
| Nantucket | 16 | 25 | Stubs | Wm | | 1 | | 1 | | | | | 1 | | | | 3 | | |

| TOWN | PG# | LN# | LAST NAME | FIRST NAME | FWM <10 | FWM 10-16 | FWM 16-26 | FWM 26-45 | FWM 45+ | FWF <10 | FWF 10-16 | FWF 16-26 | FWF 26-45 | FWF 45+ | TOTAL ALL OTHER | TOTAL SLAVES | TOTALS | DISTRICT/TOWNSHIP |
|---|---|---|---|---|---|---|---|---|---|---|---|---|---|---|---|---|---|---|
| Nantucket | 19 | 61 | Summons | Cesar | | | | | | | | | | | 8 | | 8 | |
| Nantucket | 6 | 54 | Swain | Abigail | 1 | | | 1 | | 2 | | | 1 | 1 | | | 6 | Not Stated |
| Nantucket | 7 | 24 | Swain | Abishai | 2 | | 2 | 1 | 1 | 2 | 1 | | 2 | 1 | | | 12 | Not Stated |
| Nantucket | 16 | 52 | Swain | Barnabas | 1 | 1 | 1 | | 1 | 1 | 1 | | | 1 | | | 7 | |
| Nantucket | 19 | 15 | Swain | Batchelor | | | 1 | 1 | | | | 1 | | | | | 3 | |
| Nantucket | 19 | 6 | Swain | Benjm | 1 | 1 | | 1 | | 1 | | 2 | 1 | | | | 7 | |
| Nantucket | 19 | 7 | Swain | Benjm Junr | | | 1 | | | | | | 1 | | | | 2 | |
| Nantucket | 8 | 5 | Swain | Charles | 1 | | 1 | | 1 | | | | 1 | 1 | | | 5 | Not Stated |
| Nantucket | 10 | 3 | Swain | Christopher | | | | 1 | | | | 2 | | 1 | | | 4 | Not Stated |
| Nantucket | 6 | 47 | Swain | David | | 1 | 1 | 1 | | 2 | | | 1 | | | | 6 | Not Stated |
| Nantucket | 8 | 13 | Swain | Ebenezer | | | 3 | | 1 | | | 1 | | 1 | | | 6 | Not Stated |
| Nantucket | 9 | 40 | Swain | Elizabeth 3 | | | 2 | | | | | | | 1 | | | 3 | Not Stated |
| Nantucket | 16 | 30 | Swain | Eunice | 2 | | | | | | | | 1 | | | | 3 | |
| Nantucket | 17 | 19 | Swain | Francis | 1 | 1 | 2 | | 1 | 1 | 1 | | | 1 | | | 8 | |
| Nantucket | 8 | 35 | Swain | Franklin | | | 1 | | | 2 | | | 1 | | | | 4 | Not Stated |
| Nantucket | 18 | 64 | Swain | Gardner | | | 1 | | | | | 1 | | | | | 2 | |
| Nantucket | 13 | 37 | Swain | George | 1 | | 1 | | | 1 | | | 1 | | | | 4 | |
| Nantucket | 19 | 22 | Swain | George | | 1 | | 1 | | 2 | 1 | 1 | 1 | | | | 7 | |
| Nantucket | 16 | 66 | Swain | Gilbert | 1 | | | 1 | | 1 | | | 1 | | | | 4 | |
| Nantucket | 9 | 41 | Swain | Grafton | 3 | 1 | | 1 | | | | 1 | 1 | | | | 7 | Not Stated |
| Nantucket | 5 | 56 | Swain | Hannah | 1 | | 2 | 2 | | | | | 1 | 1 | | | 7 | Not Stated |
| Nantucket | 11 | 1 | Swain | Hannah | | | | | | | | | 1 | 2 | | | 3 | Not Stated |
| Nantucket | 18 | 56 | Swain | Hezekiah | 1 | | 1 | | | 1 | | 1 | | | | | 4 | |
| Nantucket | 16 | 55 | Swain | Howland | | 1 | 1 | | | 1 | | 2 | | | | | 5 | |
| Nantucket | 12 | 5 | Swain | Hows | | | 1 | | | 1 | | 1 | | | | | 3 | Not Stated |
| Nantucket | 9 | 43 | Swain | James | 2 | 1 | | 1 | | 1 | | | 1 | | | | 6 | Not Stated |
| Nantucket | 9 | 26 | Swain | Job | 1 | 1 | 1 | | 1 | | 2 | | 1 | | | | 7 | Not Stated |
| Nantucket | 16 | 53 | Swain | John | | 2 | | | 1 | 1 | | 1 | | 1 | | | 6 | |
| Nantucket | 3 | 20 | Swain | Jonathan | | | 2 | 1 | 1 | | | | | 2 | | | 6 | Not Stated |
| Nantucket | 8 | 49 | Swain | Jonathan 2nd | | 1 | | 1 | | | | 1 | | 2 | | | 5 | Not Stated |
| Nantucket | 18 | 59 | Swain | Jonathan Junr | 3 | | | 1 | | 2 | | | 1 | 1 | | | 8 | |
| Nantucket | 4 | 1 | Swain | Joseph | | 1 | 2 | | | | | | | | | | 3 | Not Stated |
| Nantucket | 17 | 35 | Swain | Lewis | | | 1 | 2 | | | | | 1 | | | | 4 | |
| Nantucket | 9 | 38 | Swain | Mercy | | | | | | 1 | | | | 1 | | | 2 | Not Stated |
| Nantucket | 11 | 40 | Swain | Moses | 3 | | | 1 | | 1 | | | 1 | | | | 6 | Not Stated |
| Nantucket | 12 | 65 | Swain | Myer | | 1 | | 1 | | 3 | | | 1 | | | | 6 | |
| Nantucket | 14 | 30 | Swain | Noah | 1 | | | 1 | | 2 | | | 1 | | | | 5 | |
| Nantucket | 7 | 51 | Swain | Paltiah | 2 | 1 | | 1 | | | | | 2 | | | | 6 | Not Stated |
| Nantucket | 19 | 14 | Swain | Paul | | 1 | | 1 | | | | | | 1 | | | 3 | |
| Nantucket | 14 | 33 | Swain | Peter | | | | 1 | | | | | | 2 | | | 3 | |
| Nantucket | 5 | 25 | Swain | Rebecca | | 1 | 3 | | | | | | 2 | 1 | | | 7 | Not Stated |
| Nantucket | 11 | 20 | Swain | Rebecca | | 1 | 1 | | | | | | 3 | 1 | | | 6 | Not Stated |
| Nantucket | 19 | 16 | Swain | Reuben | 1 | | | 1 | | 1 | | 1 | 2 | 1 | | | 8 | |
| Nantucket | 18 | 63 | Swain | Richard | | 1 | | 1 | 1 | | | | 1 | 1 | | | 5 | |
| Nantucket | 17 | 48 | Swain | Saml | 4 | | | 1 | | 2 | 1 | | 1 | | | | 9 | |
| Nantucket | 11 | 18 | Swain | Silas | | | 1 | | | 2 | | 1 | | | | | 4 | Not Stated |
| Nantucket | 7 | 29 | Swain | Simeon | | 1 | 1 | | 1 | 1 | 1 | 1 | 1 | | | | 8 | Not Stated |
| Nantucket | 14 | 10 | Swain | Solomon | 2 | | | 1 | | 1 | | | 1 | | | | 5 | |
| Nantucket | 10 | 32 | Swain | Susanna | | | | | | | | | 1 | 1 | | | 2 | Not Stated |
| Nantucket | 17 | 37 | Swain | Thaddeus | 3 | | 1 | | | 1 | 1 | | 1 | | | | 8 | |
| Nantucket | 19 | 18 | Swain | Thankful | | | 1 | | | 2 | 1 | | 1 | | | | 5 | |
| Nantucket | 17 | 39 | Swain | Thomas | 1 | | | 1 | | 3 | 1 | | 1 | 1 | | | 8 | |
| Nantucket | 8 | 29 | Swain | Timothy | | | 1 | | | | | | 1 | 1 | | | 4 | Not Stated |
| Nantucket | 8 | 27 | Swain | Timothy Junr | 1 | | | 1 | | 2 | | | 1 | | | | 5 | Not Stated |
| Nantucket | 11 | 15 | Swain | Tristram | 1 | 1 | 1 | | 1 | 1 | | 1 | 2 | 1 | | | 9 | Not Stated |
| Nantucket | 13 | 55 | Swain | Uriah | 2 | | 2 | 1 | 1 | 2 | | 1 | 1 | 1 | | 1 | 12 | |
| Nantucket | 4 | 21 | Swain | Valentine | 1 | | | 1 | | 1 | 2 | | 1 | | | | 6 | Not Stated |
| Nantucket | 13 | 47 | Swain | Valentine | 1 | | | 1 | | 1 | | | 1 | | | | 4 | |
| Nantucket | 16 | 64 | Swift | Benjm | 1 | | | 1 | | 1 | 1 | | 2 | | | | 6 | |
| Nantucket | 13 | 31 | Taber | Antipas | 1 | 2 | | 1 | | 2 | 1 | 1 | | | | | 8 | |
| Nantucket | 19 | 46 | Thomas | John | | | | | | | | | | 3 | | | 3 | |
| Nantucket | 20 | 13 | Thompson | George | | | | | | | | | | 2 | | | 2 | |
| Nantucket | 11 | 14 | Thurston | Job | | | 1 | | | | | | 1 | | | | 2 | Not Stated |
| Nantucket | 3 | 33 | Tillingham | Parson | | 1 | | | | 1 | 1 | | | | | | 3 | Not Stated |
| Nantucket | 19 | 29 | Toby | Jemima | | | | | | | | | | 4 | | | 4 | |
| Nantucket | 12 | 33 | Townsend | Thomas | | | 1 | 3 | | | | 1 | | | | | 5 | |
| Nantucket | 14 | 34 | Tuckerman | Stephen | 2 | | | 1 | | 1 | | | 1 | | | | 5 | |
| Nantucket | 15 | 15 | Turner | Baker | 2 | | | 1 | | 2 | | | 1 | | | | 6 | |
| Nantucket | 6 | 56 | Upham | Jonathan | | 1 | 2 | | 1 | 1 | 1 | 2 | 1 | 1 | | | 10 | Not Stated |
| Nantucket | 17 | 45 | Walcutt | Benjamin | 1 | 1 | | | 1 | 1 | | 1 | | 1 | | | 6 | |
| Nantucket | 8 | 3 | Waldron | Nathan | 1 | | 2 | 1 | 1 | | | 1 | 2 | 1 | | | 9 | Not Stated |
| Nantucket | 19 | 47 | Wamsley | Benjm | | | | | | | | | | 8 | | | 8 | |
| Nantucket | 19 | 32 | Warren | Paul | | | | | | | | | | 5 | | | 5 | |
| Nantucket | 13 | 14 | Waterman | Mary | | | | | | | | | 2 | | | | 2 | |
| Nantucket | 19 | 37 | Waterman | Prince | | | | | | | | | | 4 | | | 4 | |
| Nantucket | 13 | 15 | Waterman | Sarah | 1 | 1 | | | | | | | 1 | | | | 3 | |
| Nantucket | 5 | 60 | Waterman | Thaddeus | 2 | 1 | 1 | 2 | 1 | 2 | | 1 | 2 | 1 | | | 14 | Not Stated |
| Nantucket | 12 | 11 | Watson | Elizabeth | 1 | 1 | | | | | | | 1 | | | | 3 | Not Stated |
| Nantucket | 11 | 7 | Way | Lydia | | | | | | | | | 1 | | | | 1 | Not Stated |
| Nantucket | 20 | 2 | Weeden | Charles | | | | | | | | | | 4 | | | 4 | |
| Nantucket | 8 | 2 | Weeks | Joseph | 2 | | | 1 | | | | | 1 | | | | 4 | Not Stated |
| Nantucket | 17 | 26 | West | Charles | | | 2 | 1 | | | 1 | 1 | 1 | | | | 6 | |
| Nantucket | 4 | 50 | West | Joseph | | | 1 | | | | 2 | | | | | | 3 | Not Stated |
| Nantucket | 16 | 76 | West | Peleg | | | 1 | 1 | | 1 | 1 | | 1 | | | | 4 | |
| Nantucket | 8 | 14 | West | Stephen | | | 1 | | | | | | 1 | | | | 2 | Not Stated |
| Nantucket | 11 | 29 | Whippy | Benjamin | | 1 | 2 | 1 | 1 | 1 | 2 | | 1 | | | | 9 | Not Stated |
| Nantucket | 15 | 65 | Whippy | Benjm Junr | | 1 | | | | | | | 1 | | | | 2 | |
| Nantucket | 15 | 68 | Whippy | Coffin | 2 | | 1 | | 1 | 1 | | | 1 | | | | 6 | |
| Nantucket | 8 | 31 | Whippy | Davis | 1 | | 1 | | 2 | 2 | | | | | | | 6 | Not Stated |
| Nantucket | 17 | 62 | Whippy | George | | 1 | | | | | 1 | | | | | | 2 | |

# 1800 Nantucket County, Massachusetts Index

| TOWN | PG# | LN# | LAST NAME | FIRST NAME | FREE WHITE MALES under 10 | 10 to 16 | 16 to 26 | 26 to 45 | 45 and over | FREE WHITE FEMALES under 10 | 10 to 16 | 16 to 26 | 26 to 45 | 45 and over | TOTAL ALL OTHER | TOTAL SLAVES | TOTALS | DISTRICT/ TOWNSHIP | NOTES |
|---|---|---|---|---|---|---|---|---|---|---|---|---|---|---|---|---|---|---|---|
| Nantucket | 6 | 38 | Whippy | James | 1 | | 2 | | 1 | | | | | 2 | | | 6 | Not Stated | |
| Nantucket | 7 | 39 | Whippy | Nathaniel | | 1 | 1 | 1 | 1 | | | | 1 | 1 | 1 | | 7 | Not Stated | |
| Nantucket | 12 | 50 | Whippy | Reuben | 1 | | | 1 | | 2 | | | 1 | | | | 5 | | |
| Nantucket | 7 | 13 | Whitehouse | James | | 1 | | 1 | | | | | 1 | | | | 3 | Not Stated | |
| Nantucket | 9 | 37 | Whiters | James | | 3 | 1 | 1 | | | | 2 | 1 | | | | 8 | Not Stated | |
| Nantucket | 4 | 41 | Whitney | Daniel | 2 | | | 1 | | 1 | 1 | 1 | | | | | 6 | | |
| Nantucket | 13 | 57 | Wiederhold | John | 2 | | 1 | | | | | | 1 | | | | 4 | | |
| Nantucket | 15 | 2 | Wilber | John | 1 | | | | 1 | 3 | 1 | | 1 | | | | 7 | | |
| Nantucket | 14 | 64 | Wilcox | Hannah | | | | | | | | | 2 | 1 | | | 3 | | |
| Nantucket | 8 | 17 | Williams | Anna | | | | | | | | | | 1 | | | 1 | Not Stated | |
| Nantucket | 4 | 24 | Williams | Laban | | 1 | 1 | | | 2 | | 1 | 1 | | | | 6 | Not Stated | |
| Nantucket | 6 | 7 | Willis | Eliakim | 1 | | 1 | | | | | | 1 | | | | 3 | Not Stated | |
| Nantucket | 8 | 24 | Wilson | Abigail | | | | | | 2 | | | 1 | | | | 3 | Not Stated | |
| Nantucket | 14 | 3 | Wilson | Elihu | 1 | | 1 | | | 1 | | 1 | | | | | 4 | | |
| Nantucket | 16 | 65 | Winslow | Benjm | | 1 | | 1 | | 1 | | 2 | | | | | 5 | | |
| Nantucket | 20 | 1 | Winslow | Philip | | | | | | | | | | | 4 | | 4 | | |
| Nantucket | 15 | 54 | Wood | Amos | 2 | 2 | | 1 | | | | 1 | | | | | 6 | | |
| Nantucket | 15 | 34 | Worth | Benjm | 2 | 1 | | 1 | | 2 | | | 1 | | | | 7 | | |
| Nantucket | 18 | 42 | Worth | Christopher | | | | 1 | | | | | | 1 | | | 2 | | |
| Nantucket | 8 | 55 | Worth | David | 1 | | 1 | | | | | 2 | | | | | 4 | Not Stated | |
| Nantucket | 12 | 32 | Worth | Elihu | 1 | | 1 | | | | | | 1 | | | | 3 | | |
| Nantucket | 8 | 9 | Worth | Francis | | 2 | 1 | | | 1 | 1 | 1 | 1 | | | | 7 | Not Stated | |
| Nantucket | 8 | 38 | Worth | George | 2 | | 1 | | | 1 | | | 1 | | | | 5 | Not Stated | |
| Nantucket | 14 | 56 | Worth | Henry | | | 1 | | | 2 | | | 1 | | | | 4 | | |
| Nantucket | 14 | 67 | Worth | John | | | | 1 | | | | | | 2 | | | 3 | | |
| Nantucket | 14 | 72 | Worth | Jonah | | | | 1 | | | | | | | | | 1 | | |
| Nantucket | 3 | 29 | Worth | Judith | | 1 | | | | | | | 2 | 1 | | | 4 | Not Stated | |
| Nantucket | 14 | 70 | Worth | Matthew | | | 2 | 1 | | | | | 1 | | | | 4 | | |
| Nantucket | 10 | 9 | Worth | Miriam | | | | | | | | | | 1 | | | 1 | Not Stated | |
| Nantucket | 3 | 30 | Worth | Obed | 2 | | 1 | | | 2 | | | 1 | | | | 6 | Not Stated | |
| Nantucket | 13 | 62 | Worth | Paul | | | | 1 | | 1 | | 1 | 1 | | | | 4 | | |
| Nantucket | 8 | 33 | Worth | Richard | 2 | | 1 | | | 1 | | | 1 | | | | 5 | Not Stated | |
| Nantucket | 8 | 32 | Worth | Shubael | 1 | 1 | 1 | | | | | 1 | | | | | 4 | Not Stated | |
| Nantucket | 18 | 40 | Worth | Silvanus | | | | 1 | | | | | | 1 | | | 2 | | |
| Nantucket | 18 | 43 | Worth | Uriah | 4 | 1 | | 1 | | | | | | 1 | | | 7 | | |
| Nantucket | 9 | 55 | Wotton | William | | | | 1 | | | | | 1 | 1 | | | 3 | Not Stated | |
| Nantucket | 6 | 25 | Wright | Thomas Jackson | | | 1 | | | | | | 1 | | | | 2 | Not Stated | |
| Nantucket | 8 | 36 | Wyer | David | 1 | | 1 | | | 2 | | | 1 | | | | 5 | Not Stated | |
| Nantucket | 7 | 36 | Wyer | Edward | 2 | | 1 | 1 | | | 1 | | 2 | 1 | | | 8 | Not Stated | |
| Nantucket | 7 | 35 | Wyer | Hephzibah | 1 | | 2 | | | | 1 | 1 | 2 | 1 | | | 8 | Not Stated | |
| Nantucket | 18 | 47 | Wyer | Hugh | 1 | | 1 | | | 2 | 1 | | 1 | | | | 6 | | |
| Nantucket | 13 | 58 | Wyer | John | 1 | | 1 | | | 1 | | | 1 | | | | 4 | | |
| Nantucket | 17 | 71 | Wyer | Joseph | 1 | | 1 | | | | | | | | 1 | | 3 | | |
| Nantucket | 6 | 26 | Wyer | Nathaniel | | | 1 | | | | | 1 | | | | | 2 | Not Stated | |
| Nantucket | 8 | 57 | Wyer | Obed | 2 | | 1 | | | 1 | | | 1 | | | | 5 | Not Stated | |
| Nantucket | 13 | 18 | Wyer | Obed Junr | | | 1 | | | | | | 1 | | | | 2 | | |
| Nantucket | 12 | 67 | Wyer | Owen | 1 | | 1 | | | | | 1 | | | | | 3 | | |
| Nantucket | 12 | 66 | Wyer | Robert | | 1 | | 1 | | | | | 1 | | | | 6 | | |
| Nantucket | 13 | 1 | Wyer | Timothy | 1 | 1 | 1 | | | 1 | | 2 | | | | | 6 | | |
| Nantucket | 8 | 37 | Wyer | William | | | 1 | 1 | | | | | | 1 | | | 3 | Not Stated | |
| Nantucket | 8 | 18 | Wyer | Zaccariah | | | | 1 | | | | | 1 | 1 | | | 3 | Not Stated | |

# NOTES